T0244331

BYSTANDER SOCIETY

BYSTANDER SOCIETY

CONFORMITY AND COMPLICITY IN NAZI GERMANY AND THE HOLOCAUST

MARY FULBROOK

OXFORD
UNIVERSITY PRESS

OXFORD
UNIVERSITY PRESS

Oxford University Press is a department of the University of Oxford. It furthers
the University's objective of excellence in research, scholarship, and education
by publishing worldwide. Oxford is a registered trade mark of Oxford University
Press in the UK and certain other countries.

Published in the United States of America by Oxford University Press
198 Madison Avenue, New York, NY 10016, United States of America.

Library of Congress Cataloging-in-Publication Data
Names: Fulbrook, Mary, 1951- author.
Title: Bystander society : conformity and complicity in Nazi Germany and
the Holocaust / Mary Fulbrook.
Other titles: Conformity and complicity in Nazi Germany and the Holocaust
Description: New York, NY : Oxford University Press, 2023. | Includes index.
Identifiers: LCCN 2023022536 (print) | LCCN 2023022537 (ebook) |
ISBN 9780197691717 (hardback) | ISBN 9780197691724 (epub) |
Subjects: LCSH: Holocaust, Jewish (1939–1945)—Moral and ethical aspects. |
Holocaust, Jewish (1939–1945)—Social aspects. |
National socialism—Social aspects—Germany. |
World War, 1939–1945—Collaborationists. |
Antisemitism—Social aspects—Germany—History—20th century. |
Conformity—Germany x History—20th century. | Apathy—Germany.
Classification: LCC D804.3 .F848 2023 (print) | LCC D804.3 (ebook) |
DDC 940.53/180943—dc23/eng/20230520
LC record available at https://lccn.loc.gov/2023022536
LC ebook record available at https://lccn.loc.gov/2023022537

DOI: 10.1093/oso/9780197691717.001.0001

Printed by Sheridan Books, Inc., United States of America

Contents

CONCLUSION

Preface

I have long been puzzled about how the many millions of Germans who were neither enthusiastic supporters nor political opponents or direct victims of Nazism—what I have called the 'muddled middle'—accommodated themselves to living within the Nazi dictatorship; and how, in the face of escalating violence, so many could become complicit in systemic racism, some even actively facilitating mass murder, and yet later claim they had been merely innocent bystanders. The development of the Third Reich, and the unleashing of a genocidal war, in which millions of civilians were wilfully murdered with the active participation of collaborators and auxiliaries in other countries across Europe, cannot be understood solely in terms of a chronology of Nazi policies, or the actions and reactions of key individuals, groups, and institutions in Germany, important as these are. We also have to understand how far wider groups became involved—and why so many people stood passively by, either unable or unwilling to intervene on the side of victims.

To do this, we need in some way to put together the social history of prewar Nazi Germany with the explosions of violence that began with territorial expansion in 1938 and the invasion of Poland in 1939, and escalated massively in the 'war of annihilation' on the Eastern Front from 1941. We have to understand what social changes occurred that made the extraordinary radicalization of violence possible even in the renowned 'land of poets and thinkers', and even before murderous violence was exported to the Eastern European borderlands that had so often witnessed bloody pogroms in preceding decades. In short: we need to understand how, in their daily lives, vast numbers of Germans began to discriminate against 'non-Aryan' compatriots; and what were the longer-term implications for ignoring, condoning, or facilitating genocide beyond the borders of the Reich.

By exploring individual responses to common challenges, I have sought in this book to evaluate the processes through which people could variously

become, to widely differing degrees, complicit in the murderous consequences of Nazi rule. Viewed in this way, it becomes clear that significant
changes in German society through the Nazi period are more complex,
more messy, than some accounts of the Third Reich would suggest. The
long-standing view of 'German society' as some monolithic mass subjected to totalitarian rule is clearly inadequate; but so too are summary
notions of a 'perpetrator society' (*Tätergesellschaft*), or a 'consensual dictatorship' (*Konsensdiktatur*), or 'implicated subjects' that have variously gained in
popularity in recent decades. Similarly, appeals to notions such as endemic
antisemitism, or obedience to authority, risk drifting off into a disembodied
history of ideas, or typecasting 'the Germans' with some supposedly persisting characteristics.

I have tried in this book to understand, through personal accounts, the
gradual and at first seemingly minimal shifts in people's behaviours, perceptions, and social relationships within Germany during the peacetime years
of Hitler's rule; and then the rapid, radical reorientation of attitudes and actions as the Reich expanded, and during the genocidal war that Germany
unleashed on Europe and the world. Although focussing on individual experiences in selected locations, and exploring the development of complicity in the conflagration of crimes that we call the Holocaust, I have sought
to develop a more broadly applicable argument about the conditions for
widespread passivity in face of unspeakable violence.

These are huge topics, posing questions that people have grappled with
for decades; this horrific history of brutality and mass murder remains in
fundamental respects utterly incomprehensible. Yet we have to try to make
sense of it in whatever ways we can, in order to develop a fuller understanding of the multiple ways in which the reprehensible and unthinkable ultimately became possible. It seemed to me that the vexed issue of
bystanding—of standing passively by, failing to intervene and assist victims,
effectively condoning violence by not standing up to condemn it, even
sustaining the perpetrator side by appearing to support public demonstrations of violence—required far more systematic analysis than the various
loose uses of the term had so far suggested. It is in principle impossible to
try to remain neutral under conditions of persistent, state-sponsored violence. The question then becomes one of why so many people choose to
act in one way rather than another, and under what conditions people's

perceptions and behaviour shift, with what (often ultimately fatal) consequences for others.

The argument is developed in this book with respect to German society
and the Holocaust. But there are significant wider implications. Passivity,
indifference, choosing to ignore the fates of others are not historical givens;
they are actively produced and fostered under certain conditions and vary
with historical circumstances. In face of persisting discrimination and persecution, and repeated eruptions of collective violence, understanding the
production of what I have called a 'bystander society' is of continuing and
far wider relevance.

Acknowledgements

The research for this book was based in a collaborative research project sponsored by the UK Arts and Humanities Research Council (AHRC), with additional funding for impact activities very generously provided by the Pears Foundation. I would like to thank both the AHRC and Trevor Pears for their crucial financial support for the project. I would also particularly like to thank my close academic collaborators for their invaluable support and intellectual stimulation over the course of the research and writing of this book: Stephanie Bird, Stefanie Rauch, Christoph Thonfeld, and Bas Willems. Writing a book is always necessarily a somewhat isolated endeavour, but this was made infinitely more enjoyable by regular interactions with members of the research group, always appropriately both critical and constructive in their comments.

Impact activities relating to the wider collaborative project were greatly enhanced by working on the production of short films with Graham Riach, to whom I am extremely grateful for his seemingly unshakeable good humour—whether tramping around death sites in Lithuania, tracing Nazism through the streets of Berlin, or dealing with rambling academic discussions in my office and on Zoom. Bringing the project to the attention of wider audiences was ably facilitated by our Impact Fellow, Dan Edmonds, also generously funded by the Pears Foundation; and by co-operation with colleagues from the Centre for Holocaust Education in the UCL Institute of Education, particularly Helen McCord, Andy Pearce, and Corey Soper, who assisted in outreach to teachers and schools. Catherine Stokes of the UCL IAS provided invaluable administrative support to our group throughout. I would also like to take this opportunity to remember the late documentary filmmaker Luke Holland, whose recorded interviews with people who were involved in or close witnesses to the Holocaust played a significant role in our wider project, even though I have not drawn on his material in this book. His commitment and continuing engagement with key issues around those 'on the side of the perpetrators' was much appreciated, and his archival legacy will, I hope, encourage and facilitate far more research in this area.

The ideas in this book have been developed and presented in a number of versions over the years. Early stimulation for my own approach came from the 2015 conference on Bystanders organized by Christina Morina and Krijn Thijs in Amsterdam, and I am very glad now to be able to continue the discussion with Christina Morina in a new collaborative project funded by the AHRC and the German Research Foundation (DFG) with a broader pan-European focus. Further impetus for the project came from being asked to deliver a keynote at the Nottingham conference on Privacy and Private Lives in Nazi Germany, organized by Elizabeth Harvey, Johannes Hürter, Maiken Umbach, and Andreas Wirsching. I am also grateful to colleagues at Yad Vashem for their valuable comments on the occasion of my David Bankier Memorial Lecture in 2018. I received helpful input to my thinking specifically on Kristallnacht at the conference held at the University of Southern California to mark the anniversary of this event in November 2018. A further location where I was able to benefit in person from reactions to my evolving ideas was at the University of British Columbia in Vancouver in March 2020; I greatly enjoyed that occasion and was then fortunate to catch virtually the last plane out before airports closed for travel.

Much of my writing took place during the Covid pandemic from spring 2020, with repeated lockdowns. There were some unexpectedly beneficial aspects of this otherwise horrendous worldwide public health crisis. Interacting on screen with colleagues near and far, across the world, in workshops, seminars, and conferences, was a constant source of pleasure, made possible by the wonders of internet technology, even if somewhat constrained by circumstances. I would particularly like to thank members of the informal regular discussion group on History and Psychoanalysis, with whom I have had so many stimulating and invigorating discussions over the years, first in person and more recently on Zoom; they have sustained this project in many ways. I have also benefitted from the input of members of a seminar group wonderfully hosted by Irene Kacandes that arose from a cancelled Lessons and Legacies conference. The persistent travel restrictions affected the book in less beneficial ways too. Most obviously, the pandemic put a sudden end to further archival research and site visits, and for long stretches of time even access to secondary materials in local libraries was severely restricted. Not least, as for so many other people, family health issues were often severely distracting. Writing was therefore a far more disjointed process than it might otherwise have been.

I am immensely grateful to Jürgen Matthäus for his careful reading and perceptive comments on a full draft of the manuscript, as well as assistance with obtaining images from the United States Holocaust Memorial Museum (USHMM). Through coediting and coauthoring with him on another project, I had already come to appreciate his incredible expertise, as well as his sheer good humour, efficiency, and reliability. I would also like to extend particular thanks to David Silberklang for his expert and helpful comments on one of the later chapters, and his assistance with obtaining key photographs from the Yad Vashem archive. Needless to say, I take full responsibility for any remaining errors and infelicities.

My particular thanks go to my agent, Emma Parry, for her enduring encouragement; this means a lot to me. And I am extremely grateful to Tim Bent of Oxford University Press for what he nicely called his 'meddlesome' comments in the final stages of editing the manuscript; I really appreciate his close engagement with the text, even if I have neither accepted all his suggestions for stylistic changes nor satisfied his repeated quest for greater statistical quantification in an area that I see as intrinsically characterized by fluidity, ambiguity, and ambivalence.

As always, members of my family have variously sustained, supported, and distracted me throughout the writing of this book. Conrad, Erica, and Carl, and their respective partners, have continued to be wonderful companions in their very different ways, while particular mention should be made of the growing band of life-enhancing grandchildren on both sides of the Atlantic. Julian has, as ever, unfailingly accompanied me throughout the research and writing, helping me to explore disagreeable places and uncomfortable material, while abandoning any hope that I might one day turn to work on a more congenial subject.

Mary Fulbrook
London, 12 February 2023

Introduction

Bystanders and Collective Violence

In April 1933, just over two months after Hitler had been appointed chancellor of Germany, a prominent lawyer was forced to parade through the streets of Munich with his clothes in tatters, bearing a placard with the words 'This filthy Jew shall no longer stand in judgement over us!' A young businesswoman whom I shall call 'Klara' happened to be passing by when she witnessed this public humiliation. Hardly able to believe her eyes, she was overwhelmed by a combination of horror and compassion. She tried to push her way through the crowds in the hope of being able to help in some way—but to no effect. Nor was she able to gain assistance from other bystanders: neither 'Aryans' nor Jewish Germans were willing to intervene. Eventually the lawyer was taken to the public square by the railway station, where he was repeatedly kicked on the ground 'for the pleasure of the gaping masses,' before finally being allowed to go home. This incident shocked Klara so much that she wrote vividly about it in an essay penned some six years later, in 1939.[1]

Not only this lawyer, whose name we do not know, but other Jews too were subject to abuse and victimization following Hitler's rise to power; when Klara ran to get help from Jewish friends, she found that one of them, a rabbi, had himself been arrested. But why did non-Jewish Germans not raise their voices in protest? Why did so many of them watch, whether silently or even in apparent approval? And—the question so many of us ask ourselves in the aftermath of the Holocaust and in the face of violence to this day—what would we have done in these circumstances?

The passivity of bystanders deeply affected Klara, who saw herself as a patriotic German. Her brother had died in active service in the Great War, and she had herself nursed wounded soldiers. She was full of 'national pride', coming from a family that had lived in Germany for generations, able to trace ancestors back into the seventeenth century.[2] Yet this incident challenged all sense of what it meant to be German. 'What hurts is not the fact that I witnessed this, but rather that my compatriots, whom I love so much, for whom I joyously gave all that I am, that they allowed this, that is what hurts so unspeakably! I am ashamed for them.' The fact that her compatriots now supported a regime claiming that Jews were 'parasites' on the German people was for Klara 'far harder to struggle with than the humiliations and injuries that we had to take in our stride'.

It was the apparently enthusiastic and supportive reactions of bystanders, the crowds who gathered to watch the public degradation of the Jewish lawyer, and the fundamental redefinition of what it meant to be German, that caused Klara, a patriotic German Jew, so much distress.[3]

Taking action, whether by assisting victims or alerting authorities, is widely encouraged in liberal democratic societies. The 'bystander'—a term that does not translate well, with no direct German equivalent—is generally urged not to remain passive, but rather to 'stand up' for what is right—whether by speaking out against bullying; challenging sexist, racist, or homophobic language and behaviour; calling for outside assistance; or providing witness statements to help bring perpetrators to account.[4] 'Standing up' is often framed in terms of individual courage. Such an approach may be necessary; but the fundamental message of this book is that it is also insufficient. What might be morally laudable stance in a liberal, democratic regime may be, in other circumstances, both ineffective and potentially suicidal.

To understand bystanding under conditions of persisting violence sponsored by those in power, we have to understand more than elements of individual courage or small group psychology. We also, with respect specifically to Nazi Germany, have to go beyond simplistic assumptions about supposed 'national character' or long-lasting traditions of antisemitism of obedience to authority. Bystanding is socially constructed and can change over time.

This book argues that certain types of social relations and political conditions produce a greater likelihood of widespread passivity in face of collective violence. In what I call a 'bystander society', fewer people are likely to stand up and act on 'the courage of their convictions' in face of violence against those ousted from the community and vilified as 'others'.

In Nazi Germany, as this book reveals, these conditions were historically produced, rather than pre-existent, in a process that developed over several years. It was not intrinsically a 'perpetrator society', but over time it became a society in which widespread conformity produced growing complicity in establishing the preconditions for genocide. In wartime Eastern Europe, the more rapid and ever more radical dynamics of violence mean that active involvement in perpetration, as well as complicity, passivity, and resistance, need to be examined in a different way. By exploring the development in more detail through personal accounts, it becomes clear that experiences in the prewar years played a significant role both in the facilitation of ever more radical acts of perpetration during wartime and in wider responses to atrocities among both Germans and local populations.

To embark on this enquiry in historical detail, we need first to clarify some wider, theoretical issues around the concept of bystanders and then also consider some more specific questions about the nature of German society and varying degrees of responsibility for the persecution and murder of European Jews.

First, the more abstract theoretical issues. Inactivity in the face of violence is in itself a form of action, effectively condoning or even appearing to support the perpetrators, and certainly not halting or hindering the violence. Certainly some of the German terms used—*Zuschauer* (onlookers), even more so *Gaffer* or *Schaulustiger* (gawper, rubbernecker)—imply a degree of fascination or enjoyment in watching a spectacle involving violence. Perhaps equally frequent, though, is not so much *gazing at* but rather *looking away from* violence (*Wegschauer*): pretending not to have seen, not to have registered what is going on, in order to avoid becoming uncomfortable or involved. It is simply easier to have 'not known', thereby not having to face any questions of guilt about an outcome that might potentially have been averted.

Passivity therefore raises the question of whether 'bystanders' also bear some responsibility for the outcomes of violence, and whether indeed there can be such a thing as the proverbial 'innocent bystander'. It is perhaps easy enough to pose this question in circumstances where help—police or some kind of official authority—may be readily to hand.

People of course vary in their capacity for action, and distinctions have to be made. On one view, the notion of a 'moral bystander', to use the philosopher Ernesto Verdeja's term, allows us to distinguish between, on the one hand, those who do not fully comprehend what is happening or are powerless to act effectively and, on the other, those who are, as Verdeja put it, 'in a position to intercede and consequently alter the direction of events, and yet fail to act'.[5] This approach highlights two crucial features for the interpretation of bystander behaviours: appropriate awareness of what it is that is going on, and the degree to which a person is able to intervene effectively. A child, for example, is less likely to be able to assess the situation or exert effective power and authority than an adult; parents or caregivers may feel it too risky to intervene in a fight between others without putting their own children at risk; a passerby may witness a police officer holding down a man by kneeling on his windpipe, despite protestations that he could not breathe, and wonder whether, since this was an incident where police were already involved, it would really be right to intervene. People happening to witness such scenes of violence could readily be labelled 'innocent bystanders', who cannot be held personally responsible for physical injuries or fatal outcomes. Yet these examples also underline the fact that 'bystanders' cannot be considered purely at an individual level, without taking into account the wider context. As the last example indicates, wearing a uniform does not necessarily demonstrate that certain actions are acceptable; and a bystander's video evidence of the incident in Minneapolis on 25 May 2020 in which a police officer, Derek Chauvin, held his knee on the neck of the dying George Floyd, proved crucial in the trial and murder conviction of Chauvin.[6] Circumstances matter.

Accounts of bystanders generally focus on the immediate participants and dynamics of specific incidents of violence, assuming that chance witnesses can at least potentially come to the assistance of victims, whether directly or indirectly. The external environment of the conflict is taken as in some sense neutral, a regime or system committed to upholding 'law and order'. Even when it is a police officer exerting unwarranted violence, as in the Chauvin case, it is assumed that he can be brought to account. In principle, then, the bystander should be able to intervene in some way.

But bystander support for victims is a very different matter when it is the regime itself that is at the root of the violence: when it is the authorities who have instigated or are actively involved in violence, or wilfully refrain from intervening on behalf of victims. The conundrum people faced in in Nazi Germany arose from the combination of violence actively instigated or sanctioned by the regime and wider, systemic and structural violence that seeped through society in both policy-related and informal ways.

The context is not neutral and needs to be taken into account more explicitly. This is particularly the case when a regime based on violence itself persists over a lengthy period of time. The dynamics of the system change, and people themselves are changed by accommodating themselves to living within such a state. Perceptions change, too, affecting how situations of violence are interpreted and acted upon (or not).

Awareness and capacity for effective action are therefore not just questions of what individuals 'see' or their capacity for effective action, as in the somewhat abstract formulations of philosophers, but also of the wider cultural frameworks within which witnesses interpret what they think they are seeing, and the social and political conditions in which they assess what action they think might be appropriate or effective—or too risky. Some of this may be a matter of prevalent norms, as in unwillingness to speak out in circles where racist, sexist, or homophobic comments are seen as acceptable, or made light of when criticized (as in the dismissive notion of 'just banter' or 'locker room talk').[7] Similarly, the view of victims as in some way to be feared as well as vilified may be more widely shared. Given unequal power relations and a sense that speaking up is futile, critics may be unwilling to share their disquiet, and this is particularly the case if these norms are officially propagated and publicly enforced. So the wider context of both perception and choice of action matters enormously. We have therefore to explore the conditions under which people believe that violent action against particular groups may be justifiable, proportionate, even desirable; or feel that there is little point in speaking up. We also have to understand, by contrast, the circumstances in which individuals feel it necessary or even possible to dispute dominant interpretations. Challenging violence under dictatorial and repressive conditions is a quite different matter from reporting a fight on the street or confronting playground bullying in a democracy, however terrifying the violence may be for unwilling victims in such cases.

The meaning of 'bystanding' depends on context—and this context can almost by definition be only temporary. People may be 'neutral' bystanders when they first witness an event: but within moments, neutrality will no

longer be possible, as onlookers variously move in the directly opposite directions of either condoning or condemning the violence, and with differing degrees of activity in each case: indicating sympathy for one side or the
other, more actively engaging in support for one side or the other, calling
for help, or participating in and benefitting from perpetration. Building in
the time dimension, it can even extend to the ambiguous double meaning
suggested by former US president Donald Trump in the first presidential election debate of September 2020. When challenged on his refusal to
condemn the violent actions of white supremacists and racists, including a
right-wing, anti-immigrant group called the Proud Boys, Trump exhorted
the Proud Boys to 'stand back and stand by', since 'somebody's got to do
something about antifa and the left'. 'Standing by' was clearly here intended
as an injunction to remain quiet for the time being, but to be prepared for
future action when conditions were right.[8] And, indeed, Trump then unleashed anti-democratic violence by inciting supporters to march on the
Capitol on 6 January 2021 to disrupt the formal adoption as president of
Joe Biden, the legitimate winner of the election that Trump falsely claimed
was 'stolen'. In the United States, ultimately, democratic institutions and
authorities prevailed in 2021, and despite all Trump's prevarications Biden
duly became president. Even so, election 'denialism' continued to be a
strong force in American politics.

   Conditions were of course quite different in Germany under Nazi rule.
We know a great deal about Hitler, the Nazi party and movement, and
official policies in the Third Reich; victims and survivors have left painful
traces and searing accounts with agonizing details about their persecution.
But what about members of the wider population? We have a far less precise view of the ways in which those who were not themselves directly
perpetrators or victims accommodated themselves and participated in an
evolving system of collective violence, or the extent to which members of
mainstream society were themselves in part responsible for, or complicit
in, the ultimately murderous outcomes of Nazi persecution. After German
defeat in 1945, the myth of the 'innocent bystander' was born. Refusing to
accept the accusation of indifference to the fate of Jewish fellow citizens,
people claimed they had been either ignorant or impotent; they would
bear no responsibility for what they had allowed to happen in their midst,
let alone concede that they had themselves played a significant part in unfolding processes of discrimination and exclusion, the essential precursors

to genocide. Was the notion of having been 'an innocent bystander' merely a convenient postwar myth?

It is abundantly clear that violence against Jews—as Klara Rosenthal and many others witnessed in the very first months of Nazi rule—was both instigated and sanctioned by the Nazi regime. But it was the reactions of the wider population—whether enthusiastic or passive—that shocked Klara most of all. It was the response of bystanders—or rather their non-response, their failure to act—that allowed the public humiliation of the prominent Munich lawyer to take place. Although Jews and socialists, often combined in the catch-all pejorative concept of 'Judeo-Bolshevism', had been vilified as the 'enemy within' at least since defeat in the Great War, Jewish Germans were an integral part of German society—as indeed the social status of the Munich lawyer illustrated.

To cast Germans of Jewish descent as 'other' required first of all, during the period up to 1938, an active process of social segregation. It should be emphasized, however, that the ultimate goal of Nazi ideology was not to return to any kind of pre-emancipation status for Jews, nor to bring about a form of segregation along the lines practised in the United States, but rather something far more radical: to achieve an ill-defined, unprecedented, and irreversible aim, the complete removal of 'the Jewish race' and all that 'the Jew' supposedly stood for; not merely to imagine, but actually to achieve, what has been called a 'world without Jews'.[9] This Nazi ambition took a variety of practical forms on the tangled route to the policy of extermination that the Nazis conceived of as a 'final solution' for the 'greater good', driven by what Saul Friedländer terms an ideology of 'redemptive antisemitism'—something on a wholly different and infinitely more murderous scale than the segregation and subordination of an allegedly 'inferior' race.[10] In the meantime, however, as far as the wider population in Germany was concerned, this first entailed a process of classifying, stigmatizing, and separating out those who were to be targeted—essential in a society where people of Jewish descent were often indistinguishable from compatriots of other backgrounds. The process of segregation transformed the character of social relations and conceptions of identity within Germany in ways that would subsequently facilitate growing complicity, widespread involvement in perpetration, and a capacity to turn a blind eye to mass murder during the war.

This period raises questions about the ways in which conformity can, over time, effectively turn into complicity. Social segregation and the racialization of identities were, crucially, not only a matter of official policies and practices but also involved the everyday actions and attitudes of the wider population. Following decades of increasing assimilation and integration, Germans of Jewish descent, whether or not they were of the Jewish faith, were from 1933 singled out as in some way 'racially' different—and now there was no possibility of seeing conversion to Christianity as a 'solution'. Over the course of just a few years, the social dynamics of exclusion consisted in not only the imposition of official policies but also the informal actions of ordinary people in everyday life. Jewish Germans were cast out, losing social contacts and personal friendships as well as citizenship rights, livelihoods, and property; during the peacetime years, even those who escaped direct physical violence suffered what Marion Kaplan, following Orlando Patterson, has called a form of 'social death'.[11] These processes not only created the preconditions for the isolation of victims but also for growing complicity among 'Aryans', paving the way for involvement in the ever more radical persecution and perpetration that followed. Once Nazi Germany had unleashed an expansionist and ultimately genocidal war, mass deportations and organized extermination unfolded across Europe; around 6 million Jews, and many millions of other civilians, lost their lives as a consequence of the fatal combination of Nazi initiatives and differing forms of local complicity and collaboration.

Within Germany, the story may readily be—and has already often been—recounted in terms of Nazi policies and Jewish experiences; it is far less easy to understand the significance of changes in the wider society out of which people of Jewish descent were being ripped. Yet in this process, non-Jewish Germans too were changing, shifting their perceptions of themselves and others, and adapting their behaviours and expressed attitudes. Later, the vast majority of those who had been caught up in the violence, willingly or otherwise, would try to distance themselves, claiming variously that they had 'known nothing about it' or had been powerless to act differently.

The role of so-called ordinary Germans was and remains highly controversial. Some commentators and scholars have fallen prey to the temptation to homogenize 'society', as though all Germans were in some way similar, even that some persisting underlying 'mentality' could be identified. The role of supposedly persisting traditions of antisemitism has been highlighted as a key causal factor. Others, however, have tried to present a more differ-entiated picture, using the adjective 'ordinary' only in relation to specific groups and exploring the reasons for their behaviours within particular his-torical contexts, which may have had more to do with peer group pressure than ideological motivations.[12] Similarly, the radical changes in outlooks and behaviours that were brought about by socialization under Nazism and exposure to brutality in wartime conditions have been emphasized as more important than any supposedly longer-term features of 'German society' or mentalities. Even so, there has been a widespread tendency to use terms such as German 'majority society' (*Mehrheitsgesellschaft*) or to talk about Germany as a 'perpetrator society' (*Tätergesellschaft*).

The pre-eminent Holocaust scholar Raul Hilberg explicitly brought to attention the now familiar triad of 'perpetrators, victims and bystanders'.[13] But this somehow suggests discrete actors, leaving out the wider environ-ment within which violent incidents occur, and which crucially shapes the actors' perceptions, capacity for action, and likely outcomes in any given situation. And classically, Hilberg claimed that in Germany 'the difference between perpetrators and bystanders was least pronounced; in fact it was not supposed to exist'.[14] He was certainly right about the latter point; but, as explored in this book, I am not so sure about the former. Other scholars, in critiquing blanket notions of a 'perpetrator society', want to distinguish between 'acts of murder (or supportive actions directly leading to murder) and social behaviour that goes no further than contributing to social exclusion'.[15] This distinction raises serious questions, however, about the longer-term implications of behavioural conformity 'contributing to social exclusion', which may indeed at first be seen by those engaging in it (although less so by their victims) as in some sense sufficiently harmless to warrant the phrase 'goes no further than'. Ultimately, we have to find some means of making distinctions that allow us to explore the complexity of varieties and degrees of involvement and responsibility, if not outright culpability.

So this remains a highly contentious field, in which not only the con-cepts but also the sources require intensive and sensitive evaluation.

Klara's recollections, at the start of this chapter, are taken from a rich archive of personal accounts that provide fascinating insights into the emotional and psychological landscapes of the 1930s, with details of social interactions that would later often be forgotten or overwhelmed by the horrors of war and genocide. In 1939, three Harvard professors were keen to explore what was going on in Nazi Germany—not at the level of political events and policy developments, but rather in terms of everyday life. The three—Gordon Allport, Sydney B. Fay, and Edward Y. Hartshorne—announced a competition for essays to be written under the title 'My life in Germany before and after January 30, 1933' (the date Hitler was appointed chancellor), and advertised this competition widely in German-speaking and exile newspapers. They offered a first prize of $500—an attractive sum at that time for anyone, and particularly for penniless refugees or impecunious exiles, although not all essay writers fell into these categories. Even the smallest prizes of just a few dollars could make an enormous difference to someone on the run from Nazi persecution. But the aim of the competition, to understand the massive social and psychological transformations occurring in Nazi Germany, was important in principle even for those not in need of any prize money—including those relatively few respondents who recounted their experiences in order to praise aspects of Nazism.

The three professors came from different disciplines: Allport was a psychologist interested in personality traits; Fay was a historian who had written a significant book on the causes of the First World War, as well as a classic work on the rise of Brandenburg-Prussia; Hartshorne, who was married to Fay's daughter, was a young sociologist who had in the mid-1930s spent a year in Germany undertaking research for his doctoral dissertation on German universities under National Socialism. They were united in their determination to understand more deeply what was going on in Nazi Germany and felt that lengthy accounts of personal experiences would give them a better understanding of the impact on people living under Nazi rule than could any observations by diplomats, journalists, or foreign travellers, fascinating though these too might be as external perceptions of changes in Germany under Nazi rule.[16]

More than 250 essays were submitted to the Harvard competition, written from the late summer of 1939, through the first wartime winter, to the spring of 1940. Nearly two-thirds were written by exiles and refugees living in the United States (155, of whom 96 lived in New York City); roughly one in eight (31) came from the UK; another twenty from Palestine; thirteen from Switzerland; essays also came in from Shanghai, South America, Australia, South Africa, Japan, and a few more from European countries including France, Belgium, Holland, and Sweden.[17] Most of the essays were written in German, but a few were penned in the somewhat awkward phrasing of non-native English, producing a slightly more stilted style on occasion.[18]

A predominance of educated professionals among the authors was to be expected. But the urgency of a desire to communicate experiences and the hope of winning a prize led more people from humble backgrounds to write than might have been predicted. Moreover, although the essays mainly reflected the experiences of Jewish men and women, the collection also includes accounts by non-Jewish individuals who were variously supportive or critical of the regime, as well as individuals whom Nazis defined as of 'mixed' descent, and 'Aryans' in 'mixed' relationships, whose experiences have to date been generally less well explored.[19] They were not among the directly persecuted, the primary victims and targets of Nazi policies; nor were they necessarily active resisters, dissidents, or opponents of Nazism. They were in many ways astute observers of what had been going on in their name, and some had become increasingly uncomfortable with their forcible incorporation into the Nazi 'national community' (Volksgemeinschaft). Some émigrés had chosen to leave Germany because of their personal relationships with Jewish loved ones; others left out of a more general sense of discomfort, unwilling to expose themselves or their children to the complicity that they felt living under Nazism entailed. Some were fortunate in having the resources and necessary connections to get out; most were reliant on a combination of luck, determination, and the goodwill of others.

But of course the overwhelming majority of Germans, critical or otherwise, Jewish or gentile, did not leave the Reich—and while German gentiles were mobilized for war, Germans of Jewish descent who had not got out in time were eventually faced with deportation, most of them to their deaths. So the accounts of these predominantly critical essay writers, written at a pivotal moment before Europe was plunged into war and mass murder, have to be supplemented by other sources. Even so, their perceptions of the prewar years are invaluable in trying to understand changing aspects of life under Nazism before the outbreak of war and genocide.

The essays in the Harvard collection provide insights into a diversity of experiences from a range of perspectives, and from different areas across the Reich or territories it later annexed or occupied. Many of them are particularly perceptive about the ways in which the racialization of identity was effected in everyday life. They record how people with whom they had previously interacted socially started to look away, to distance themselves. Those not excluded from the 'national community' were increasingly drawn into playing roles that made them complicit in Nazism, effectively sustaining and assisting the escalation of persecution. The essay writers were only too well aware of how others were treating them—including the many who would later claim they had 'known nothing about it' and were merely innocent bystanders.

There is a further advantage offered by such material. Opinion reports and surveys, whether by the regime's own organizations or by opposition groups such as the Social Democratic Party in exile, are of course invaluable sources. But such sources only provide snapshots, with evidence of specific attitudes on particular issues at certain moments; and the individuals whose views are recorded generally remain anonymous, simply seen as representatives of their class, gender, religion, or region.[20] This mapping of wider patterns is important.[21] But to grasp the transformation of society in Nazi Germany, we need also to explore emotional connections, social relations, and sense of identity and community. For this, personal accounts of experiences over time are invaluable in giving some access to subjectivities and changing relationships with others.

The life stories collected by the Harvard researchers reveal in greater depth the conflicting attitudes and degrees of ambivalence, as well as contradictions between views and behaviours, speech, and actions of individuals, over a period of time. They offer a more rounded picture of the ways in which people led lives marked by conflicting priorities and emotions, and engaged in compromises. They bring together wider analyses of social and political structures with the inner feelings and actions of individuals.

Of course, personal accounts do not tell the whole story, and a worm's-eye view can provide only a limited perspective from a specific location. But there is more than this affecting the account. Autobiographical memory is always characterized by selective recollection, amnesia, or silencing. Some moments are recalled vividly; long periods are glossed over or sink into obscurity; key incidents are omitted, and others overemphasized. The slant given to the past varies with the context of later telling. Experiences when young—aspiring towards a still-open future—are often cast in a nostalgic light. Each individual has not only specific events to relate but also a wider 'story' to tell. In portraying how they dealt with particular challenges, people construct an image of their own selves (resilient, heroic, victimized, and so on). Self-representations are shaped by wider environments and the vocabulary of different communities, as well as the specific context in which they are produced. In the case of the Harvard essay prize collection, at least some of the essay writers may, in desiring to be a winner, have sought to enhance the literary merits of their narratives—an effort more evident in some essays than others. Yet they were all clearly impelled to convey some sense of their intrinsically dramatic and indeed life-changing experiences. No collection of auto-biographical accounts will tell us 'how it really was', and they always have to be read as texts produced in a particular place for a particular purpose. They are nevertheless invaluable in illuminating significant subjective experiences and the quality of social relationships—and this before knowledge of the 'catastrophe', the Shoah or Holocaust, that was about to engulf European Jews and countless others.

The overwhelming majority of these essay writers were victims or critics of Nazism, while a handful of essays praise what they see as the good points about Nazi Germany. They stand in some contrast, then, to the essays collected by Theodore Abel in 1934, whose appeal for personal accounts was specifically targeted at people who had become Nazi enthusiasts relatively early on.[22] The writers of the Harvard essays in 1939–1940 are predominantly either marginalized or self-marginalizing figures. But if read appropriately, this perspective from the margins of mainstream society constitutes a distinctive strength of the material: the authors are all the more acutely aware of the responses of other Germans who were going along with the tide. Their experiences and perceptions illuminate the social processes through which, in the micro-negotiations of everyday life, other people—those often seen simply as 'neutral bystanders'—in fact played an active role in progressively redefining what it meant to be 'German' and stigmatizing those who were to be outcast. The marginalized are, in a sense, the best barometer of the historical significance of bystander passivity, conformity, and growing complicity.

Composing their accounts just as the war was starting, these writers did not yet know the horrific events that would follow. They had some intimations of what was brewing already in the winter of 1939–1940, but most had little inkling of the 'euthanasia' programme that had already started and would continue informally even after its official termination in 1941, or the savage 'resettlement' policies, mass terror, and murders that had begun to take place following the invasion of Poland in September 1939. It is highly unlikely that they would even be able to imagine the sheer magnitude of the genocide that would erupt from 1941: the 'Holocaust by bullets', following the German invasion of the Soviet Union, would kill around 2 million Jews, as well as Roma ('gypsies'), the mentally ill and disabled, and those designated as 'partisans', across the Eastern Front; perhaps 2.5 million Jews would be killed in the dedicated extermination camps that started to come into operation from December 1941, reaching a murderous peak in 1942–1943 and continuing in Auschwitz through 1944; another million would die in the extensive system of ghettos, concentration camps and forced labour camps, and the death marches of 1944–1945; these essay writers, in short, did not yet know what would be the horrendous character and scale of the Nazi 'Final Solution'.[23] Any personal account written after these events would inevitably be overwhelmed by their shadow, casting a quite different light on their prehistory. This was not the case for the Harvard essay writers.

For the writers of the Harvard competition essays in 1939–1940, the most significant and worst imaginable changes in their lives had already taken place before 1939: the dropping of friendships; the loss of occupations and livelihoods; the violence and terror of Kristallnacht in November 1938 and incarceration in concentration camps; the suicides, departures, separations from family and friends; the loss of any chance of a civilized life in Germany or Austria, previously such renowned centres of civilization. Precisely because of their limited time horizon, the essay writers have no benefit of hindsight; they do not know how these momentous developments in their lives within Germany were paving the way for organized mass murder across Europe; they paint an all the more detailed picture of social changes in the six prewar years of Nazi rule, from 1933 to 1939, without framing their stories in light of postwar interpretations, or feeling that everyday experiences before the war were in some way less significant or overshadowed by the mass death and destruction that followed. Their autobiographical accounts are therefore an extraordinary resource for gaining a deeper understanding of how German conceptions of themselves and their relationships with others were changing under Nazi rule during the prewar years. They can help us understand the multiple—and at the time seemingly trivial—ways in which conformity with the Nazi regime could, over time, shift into complicity with racism, paving the way for mass murder.

Curiously, the Harvard professors barely used the essays. There is one significant piece by Hartshorne, essentially more of a pamphlet than a book, in which he selects a few accounts to illustrate the experiences of 'Aryans' of different generations, genders, and classes. This essay is more typological than explanatory, but Hartshorne's concern to explore the experiences of non-Jewish Germans reveals how far they were prepared to compromise.[24] Hartshorne was never able to follow up at greater length on these preliminary observations. During the war, he first worked in the US Office of Strategic Services (OSS) and the Psychological Warfare Branch and then returned to Germany during the last months of the war, working in the Psychological Warfare Division. Following German defeat, he took over tasks relating to denazification and the refounding of German universities, building on his academic expertise in this area. In late August 1946, while he was engaged in investigating reports of former Nazis still active in German universities, he was fatally shot in the head by an individual in an overtaking jeep on the autobahn from Munich to Nuremberg. There has been speculation that Hartshorne's assassination was related to his work in uncovering the tracks of former Nazis, or American attempts to suppress exposure of the 'ratline' through which former Nazis were being assisted in escaping via Italy to South America, as part of the American fight against communism; but the evidence remains inconclusive.[25]

I have used selected essays from the Harvard collection extensively, following individuals' reflections on their own lives before and after 1933 to explore the challenges of life under Nazi rule in the peacetime years. But the Harvard materials need to be complemented by sources from other perspectives and woven into a wider picture covering the years of war and extermination. This book therefore also focuses on individuals whose life stories intersect with, run alongside, or can be contrasted with those of the essay writers. Using contemporary letters and diaries as well as later recollections, the book goes on to explore the experiences of individuals during the war years in parts of occupied Eastern Europe, particularly Poland, Lithuania, and Latvia, as well as people who remained within the Reich.

Taken together, these accounts help us to understand different patterns of involvement during the war, in face of the escalation from persecution to extermination. In a situation of extreme, all-pervasive violence, it became ever less possible to remain an 'innocent bystander'—indeed the question arises of what can be meant by bystander at all when violence is all-encompassing. In a rapidly changing context, those who were neither the initiators and executors of violence, nor the direct and immediate targets, almost immediately had to face extreme choices. For some, complicity could readily turn into perpetration; the repertoire of justifications in terms of the supposed threat of 'Judeo-Bolshevism', the ideological arsenal of variants of antisemitism that had been battered into Germans and others over preceding years, could potentially be resorted to in an attempt to silence any sense of unease. But among a few, by contrast, passive bystanding could tip into more active attempts at assisting the victims of persecution, even as such actions became ever riskier. Any discussion of 'bystander' responses at this point might be better framed in terms of 'surrounding societies'.

This is neither a history of Nazi Germany nor a history of the Holocaust. While I have been selective in the examples chosen, there are many more that could have been included, and no account can ever hope to render the full complexity and diversity of personal experiences. But this book will help to illuminate how, at a personal level, the Holocaust became possible: how the organized mass murder of fellow human beings of Jewish descent could be initiated by a country in which the integration and assimilation of Jews had been among the most advanced in Europe; and how it could be carried out beyond Germany's borders in areas of radical persecution and highly visible mass killings with the assistance of numerous local people.[26] The widespread conformity that propelled the racialization of identity within the Reich before the war could readily shift into complicity in wartime perpetration, partially devolved and disguised in ways that meant involvement could later be buried under the myths of innocence and ignorance.

In what follows, I have chosen to foreground the stories of individuals, and paint in the wider developments as a form of historical backdrop. This approach is almost exactly the opposite way around from conventional ways of writing history, where—apart from in biographies—'ordinary' individuals often only enter historical accounts as illustrative snapshots, representatives of a particular social group or gender, and often anonymously. Here, however, I am writing history, in a sense, from the inside out: prioritizing selected accounts of personal experiences, while wider events form the context, of which people were sometimes only partially aware—much as we generally experience and live our own lives, especially when outside events do not intrude unduly on what we take to be our 'private lives'.

There is a difficult balance to be considered here. Unlike major historical figures who made their mark on politics, society, or culture, the individuals whose life stories are explored here are not, in themselves, either exceptional or exceptionally significant. They are largely figures on the margins—generally disaffected by wider developments, mostly either victims of persecution themselves or close to people who were being persecuted. They reflect not only on their own experiences but also on the attitudes and behaviours of those with whom they came into contact in everyday life, contemporaries who stayed in Germany, and who were persuaded or constrained to conform to the Nazi regime. The complex interplay between the marginalized and the conformers illuminate how wider developments were experienced and enacted in everyday life.

These individuals came from a range of areas and backgrounds, but they have not been selected as supposedly representative of wider groups. Personal experiences can vividly reveal aspects of life within a dictatorship but also highlight the diversity of individual responses to common challenges. People's values, families, emotional attachments, and access to resources all influenced diverging reactions to Nazi rule. How each person navigated the challenges had implications not only for their own life but also for the lives of others—both for those they knew and for those they did not. By exploring personal accounts in more depth, as circumstances changed, we can begin to understand, particularly from the acutely perceptive vantage points of those who were being marginalized, how large numbers of people—probably a social majority—entered into compromises and altered their beliefs and behaviours over time. Sometimes they clearly felt constrained and awkward in their shifting social interactions with the marginalized; but we can also see ways in which, under Nazi rule, people began to internalize new views, and how conformist behaviours became more or less unthinking habits. We can also start to evaluate the wider consequences of the choices they made, as conformity increasingly slid into complicity with the radicalization of Nazi racism.

This raises, of course, the crucial question of degrees of guilt and responsibility for the Holocaust. Unlike approaches that seek for an all-encompassing term to indicate how, in effect, more or less everyone who was not a victim was in some sense 'implicated' in violence, both past and present, I suggest we need a more differentiated picture, distinguishing between passive or active conformity, compliance, and complicity, as well as downright culpability.[27] People living under Nazi rule were involved and responsible to quite different degrees; everyone was in some way affected, but not everyone was equally implicated; some were more responsible than others, even if, as I explored in a previous work, *Reckonings*, only a tiny minority were ever actually found guilty of specific crimes in a court of law.[28]

I do not focus here on the actual perpetrators, those in positions of significant power and authority—the elites who facilitated Hitler's rule—nor on those few who were involved in organized resistance. I am concerned with what might be called the 'muddled middle'—arguably the majority of the population—in short, those who are often termed bystanders. But I shall argue that that we need to think in broader terms about changes in society.

Historians have highlighted the significance of class, politics, religion, and generation; the radical violence unleashed against political opponents, social outcasts, and those considered racially inferior; the impact of Nazi propaganda, enthusiasm, and support as well as mass terror and coercion; and the significance of the Volksgemeinschaft.[29] Many were active in roles sustaining a regime based ultimately on repression, and many others felt constrained to such a degree that one could hardly talk of freely given consent. Such overviews of structures and events are essential. But they do not provide insights into the more subtle and gradual ways Germans changed their behaviours and attitudes, the varying degrees of willingness and discomfort. Many benefitted in a whole variety of ways from Nazi policies, some eagerly and proactively, others more uncomfortably aware of ethical issues; and some became ever more complicit in the Nazi project, justifying previously unthinkable actions both to themselves and to others. The road to conformity was not even. Probably a significant number of people who were in a position to do so opted for some form of retreat, or at least inner self-distancing, trying to minimize the degree to which, simply by living within such a system, they were inevitably having to engage in some form of moral compromise. A very few—a tiny minority—engaged in more active resistance or rescue efforts, however ultimately ineffective. It was the conformity or passive acquiescence of the vast majority that ultimately allowed the violence to expand across wartime Europe.

The greater problem then lies in how we explain and evaluate conformity. Some historians argue that the Third Reich was a 'consensual dictatorship', based on evidence such as willingness to denounce others to the
Gestapo, as well as mass participation in rallies, membership of Nazi organizations, and the evidence of visual imagery of cheering crowds. Other historians suggest, however, that apparent conformity was more widely rooted
in fear, in a regime based on terror and repression. Postwar accounts by
contemporaries, self-defensively trying to account for their former involvement in Nazism to different audiences under quite different political conditions, play on and variously develop both these lines of argument: some
highlight having being supposedly blinded by ideology or Hitler's charisma,
while others emphasize the role of fear or of having had to obey orders.[30]

There are clearly difficulties in assessing these issues at a distance, and
evaluating degrees of ambivalence and hypocrisy at different times. Outward
performances could cover a wide range of inner feelings, ranging from enthusiasm to ambivalence to disgust. Raising an arm in the 'Heil Hitler'
salute looks much the same in a photograph, whether done out of conviction, habit, or pressure; smiling or laughing can reflect support or derision;
a disaffected expression can reflect anything from principled disapproval to
something as mundane as registering blisters, hunger, or thirst, following a
long morning of marching or waiting and then being forced to display energetic enthusiasm. And it was all too easy, after 1945, for Germans to claim
that they had acted out of fear rather than enthusiasm, and to emphasize
their own suffering. It was also relatively easy for those who had been quite
young during the Nazi period later to claim that they had not in fact been
aware of the darker sides of the Nazi regime.[31]

When we explore in greater depth how individuals behaved and explained their actions to others at the time, a more complex and multifaceted picture emerges. Outward conformity and even apparent enthusiasm
could actually have been rooted in a sense of constraint—fear of social
opprobrium, public humiliation, loss of privileges; or it could have variously arisen from ideological convictions, a desire for enhanced opportunities, increased power over others, professional advancement, or material
acquisitions.

There were many twists to be observed here—twists that may simultaneously reinforce and undermine postwar accounts about trepidation,
terror, or supposed inner resistance. Many people were indeed enthusiastic

supporters of Nazism and later tried to downplay or deny this. But among those who appeared to support the regime were also those who were not initially enthusiastic, and we can observe a process of change over time.

Put very simply, for the muddled middle, this process ran roughly as follows: early evidence of Nazi brutality and widespread social pressures led initially to constrained consent and public conformity; over time, repeated rehearsals of behaviours and attitudes could become second nature; and eventually, as the apparatus of repression grew and millions were mobilized in service of a genocidal war of aggression, compliance would lead into more active complicity with the criminal acts of the Nazi regime. While some may have been motivated by Nazi prejudices, others now drew on antisemitic discourses to justify actions in which they had become involved for all sorts of other reasons.

By building up a composite picture of personal stories—essentially a pattern built out of individual mosaic stones—we may gain a deeper understanding of the differing roles, perceptions, and experiences of this muddled middle, as large numbers of people went from apparently trivial acts of discrimination in everyday life, through compliance with persecutory measures, to active participation in genocide. Some managed to retreat into passive backwaters, which might salve their own conscience; but inaction did little to alter the direction in which the regime was heading. In Nazi Germany, choices were limited. Very few individuals had the material circumstances or inner resources to refuse to comply. There were extremely high risks involved in trying either to put hurdles in the way of the Nazi project or to assist the persecuted along the way. But the actions of the muddled middle who stayed and conformed had a significant impact on the lives of those who were ousted.

Most of the Harvard essay writers tended to have rosy memories of the years before Hitler came to power, and even Jews who experienced social exclusion or rising antisemitism before 1933 felt that they had alternative bases of support. Most of all, autobiographical accounts highlight the sheer variation in personal experiences before 1933—varying with social class, gender, and region as well as individual circumstances—that would start to disappear once supposedly racial criteria became overwhelmingly significant under Nazi rule. The immense significance of this becomes clear, as ever larger numbers of people behaved according to Nazi precepts in everyday life. People began to 'perform' Nazism in public, not only raising

their arms in the Heil Hitler salute but also expressing the kinds of utterances expected of them; even in their private lives, they readjusted their
self-perceptions and conceptions of others along racial lines, and adapted
their behaviours accordingly.[32] As a sense of identity shifted, so too did
social relations, constructing invisible borders between diverging communities with which people identified. Once racial discrimination was enshrined in law in 1935, compliance became normalized and increasingly
internalized; acting appropriately according to newly introduced distinctions between 'Aryans' and 'non-Aryans' began to become second nature.
Within less than three years of Nazi rule, identity had become racialized
and German society was deeply divided on racial lines.

The radicalization of Nazism from the later 1930s onwards meant that
conformity entailed ever more difficult choices: either go along with
Nazism, effectively becoming complicit by both facilitating and benefitting from the system, or attempt to refuse to condone what was going on,
with all the risks this might entail. Often people engaged in both kinds of
behaviour, shifting according to circumstances. Once war broke out, the
stakes became infinitely higher, the choices ever starker—often literally life
or death. Many more people were involved in one way or another. While
a few risked everything in attempts at rescue or resistance, most simply
tried to survive. Individuals reacted differently according to circumstances,
but everyone was living within a dictatorship at war. To highlight the radical challenges in wartime, I have traced selected experiences during the
occupation of Poland after the outbreak of war, and in the Baltic states of
Lithuania and Latvia following the German invasion of the Soviet Union
in 1941. The situation in these areas was so very different, and the escalation
of face-to-face killings so dramatic, that these cases reveal key features of
what it takes for discrimination to turn into full-blown genocide—and for
bystanders to become either abettors or rescuers.

Ultimately, people faced dilemmas and choices: most starkly, between the
risks of engaging in some form of protest or resistance, or the complicity
that was inevitably entailed by continuing conformity. Through exploring
people's experiences through this turbulent period, we can begin to understand the conditions under which 'bystanders' move towards or away from
complicity in collective violence. Perhaps the most common configuration,
however, is also the most complex and least clear-cut in terms of where
it fits on this spectrum: people who manage both to convey sympathy for

individual victims yet also continue to facilitate the system that is victim-
izing them; and those who move from one position to another in the complex swirl of history.

One challenge facing this history is that of terminology. To use obviously
racist Nazi concepts without scare quotes may seem to lend credence to
them, as though we too believe that society was made up of 'Aryans' and
'non-Aryans', including Jews and varying degrees of '*Mischlinge*' (mongrels,
mixed-breeds), as well as other supposedly 'inferior beings' ('sub-humans',
Untermenschen). Using such terms can unintentionally reinforce racist ways
of categorizing people. Yet the repeated use of scare quotes does not help
readability. And, for a while, these categories, however absurdly unscientific,
did indeed attain a deadly social reality.

There are other, less frequently noted problems of terminology. Even
when using apparently far less pejorative categories by simply referring to
'Germans' and 'Jews' is in effect to enshrine and perpetuate distinctions
that the Nazis forced upon people: all Germans of Jewish descent had their
identity as 'Germans' taken from them, whether or not they also identified
themselves in terms of religion, culture, or ethnicity as Jews. Yet after Hitler
it has remained all too easy to speak of Germans and Jews as though these
were distinctly separate categories at a time when in fact most Germans
of Jewish descent considered themselves to be Germans (whether or not
they also considered themselves Jewish by either religion or 'race'). Yet to
re-include 'Jews' among other Germans in phrases such as 'Germans of
Jewish descent' (as I have just done and will do repeatedly in what follows)
may again seem to emphasize the importance of 'racial' distinctions, even
without the infinitely more evident flagging up of 'non-Aryan' status by
using the Nazis' own category. Moreover, such qualifications are cumber-
some, contrasting with the simplicity of just saying 'Germans' for members
of what is now often called the 'majority society'—a supposedly more neutral reiteration of what is still, effectively, the ethnically defined and somewhat narrower Nazi Volksgemeinschaft.

All these attempts at using less pejorative terms, however qualified, inevitably end up underlining Nazi distinctions, given their overwhelming
historical importance. After all, we hardly feel the need to use 'hyphenated
identities' for other groups of Germans—'Catholic Germans', 'Lutheran
Germans', rather than just Catholics or Lutherans, for example—except for

those resident beyond German borders, who might be known as 'ethnic Germans' to distinguish them as a cultural or linguistic minority within a wider population of non-Germans.

It is moreover difficult to shake off an invidious minority status, once deeply embedded, however much attitudes towards minority groups change. Even today—and understandably—many Germans in public positions have a habit of garnishing mentions of marginalized groups with a little extra flourish to emphasize acceptance, as in phrases such as 'our Jewish fellow citizens'. The notion of 'our fellow citizens' subtly signals that not everyone might automatically think of them as such: 'we' are the obvious 'citizens'; 'they' are 'fellow citizens' towards whom 'we' have to be particularly sensitive. Such perceptions of difference die hard, even when a positive spin is put on them, and persist with reference to other minority groups, as in the notion of 'Germans with a migration background' (*Migrationshintergrund*) applied to second- or third-generation descendants of Turkish immigrant workers (euphemistically initially termed *Gastarbeiter*, 'guest workers', to indicate that while they were welcome, they were not expected to outstay their welcome).

However unfounded, Nazi terminology and 'racial' categorization did, within the space of a few years, have ever more ghastly effects; racist social constructs became increasingly toxic, eventually fatal. We need therefore both to deploy and yet also distance ourselves from Nazi terminology while exploring the processes through which such terms can be adopted, internalized, and acted upon. This may help to reveal just how quickly large numbers of people can be persuaded to buy into a distorted view of the world and to behave accordingly, with ultimately fatal consequences.

What is the wider significance of this analysis of individual experiences and changing social relations under Nazi rule? How can changes in German society under Nazism help us to understand both the conflagration of violence in the Holocaust and more generally passivity in relation to other instances of violence?

Bystander responses have long been a topic of interest in liberal democracies, where intervention may indeed be both possible and beneficial. But such discussion of bystander responses presupposes a wider context in which personal actions, including calling for help or providing evidence, are effective. This was not the case in the Third Reich. Nor, indeed, is it the case in any society where it is the dominant group that is initiating

violence—where those in authority themselves sustain the system of violence, promoting and justifying it, whether at the level of the state or some
much smaller group or institution. Bystanders in places where violence in
word or deed is legitimated or encouraged by those in positions of power
and authority are in a difficult situation. It is far easier to turn away, fail to
react, pretend not to have witnessed a difficult situation, or even to find
ways of agreeing with the dominant view.

Under such circumstances, we need to develop other ways of understanding bystander responses and how to read them. In any situation,
bystander choices are shaped not only by personality, individual characteristics, and small group dynamics, but also by a wide variety of social and
contextual factors. These include a sense of both individual and collective
identity, empathy with one community or another, perceptions of potential risks and benefits of different courses of action, both in the immediate
situation and with a view to longer-term horizons. We need then to focus
not merely at the level of individual or social psychology, but also on wider
patterns of interpersonal relations, economic and political configurations,
cultural understandings, and emotional connections over time.

In short: this book seeks to bring together an awareness of elements of
individual psychology with the broader patterns that foster what I call a
'bystander society'. This is a society in which a majority of people are indifferent to the suffering of others, or feel powerless to intervene on their
behalf, or claim ignorance of their fates. The reasons for varying degrees of
indifference, impotence, and ignorance are complex and changing; the following chapters will explore elements of each in turn, across the different
stages of Nazi persecution from conformity within a racist regime, through
compliance with discriminatory measures, to complicity in persecution and
facilitation of mass murder. The notion of a bystander society allows us, in
this way, a more complex set of routes into trying to answer the fundamental question of 'how could this happen'.

Understanding bystander society is far more than an academic or historical exercise. This is not simply past history. Millions were mobilized in
support of Nazism and later claimed they had 'known nothing' about its
consequences. That so many people, across Nazi-dominated Europe, were
involved in making murder possible on such a massive scale is an unavoidable legacy of life under Nazi rule.

PART I

The Slippery Slope

Social Segregation in Nazi Germany

I

Lives in Germany before 1933

Memories of a golden age of childhood are not always merely the result of looking back through rose-tinted spectacles. Even if memory is always selective, and particularly when writing at a time of dramatic change, as in the case of the Harvard essay writers fleeing Nazi Germany in the winter of 1939–1940, it is precisely the selective emphases that highlight the most significant differences between one period and another.

Memories of life before Hitler came to power reveal the difference Nazi rule made to the relations between German Jews and German gentiles. Social relations among Germans of different faiths and backgrounds were changing before the Nazis came to power, but having a Jewish family background was not, for most, the determining factor it would become under Hitler. While antisemitism is a refrain in some accounts, the essay writers generally emphasized how, before 1933, social class, gender, regional, family, or individual issues had been far more significant than religious affiliation or Jewish ancestry. Some recalled childhood incidents in which they were teased or taunted for being Jewish—rarely anything serious, but stigmatizing. The essay writers also register how awareness of difference became more problematic as antisemitism become more prevalent during and after the First World War. Some Jews encountered antisemitism during the war, including men who found military promotion was blocked; others, particularly women from well-to-do backgrounds, barely encountered antisemitism at all before the rise of right-wing movements after the war. A few individuals of mixed descent did not even register that they had any Jewish ancestry until much later.

There were some 600,000 Jews in the German Empire counted in a census before the First World War, amounting to less than 1 percent of the total population—a tiny minority. Yet they were a disproportionately visible minority. Since the early nineteenth century, German Jews had gone from being mostly impoverished paupers to well-to-do professionals, even while they still experienced legal restrictions and widespread prejudice. Excluded from many areas of endeavour, they were highly active in the arts and politics, and stood out in professions such as banking, medicine, science, the law, and publishing.[1] Jews were also particularly concentrated in urban locations. In 1910, around one-quarter of all Germany's Jews lived in the capital city, Berlin; by 1933, the figure was nearly one-third. There were also large Jewish populations in other cities, such as Frankfurt, Hamburg, and Breslau (now Wrocław in Poland). However, unlike Austrian Jews in the 1920s, most of whom lived in the capital city of Vienna, German Jews lived not only in major cities but also in provincial towns, villages, and hamlets, with significant differences between, for example, cattle-dealers and traders in rural areas and bourgeois Jews in urban areas. The most marked differences were between recent immigrants from Eastern Europe—the so-called *Ostjuden*—and long-established German Jewish families. There were also stark contrasts between Jews of different religious persuasions—orthodox, liberal, and increasingly assimilated or converted Jews, as well as Jews in mixed marriages and their offspring—and between Jews of different political views. From the 1890s, Zionists, 'Emperor's Jews' (*Kaiserjuden*), and German patriots clashed over the best ways forwards to a secure future, while political opinions ranged across the full spectrum from conservative nationalism through liberalism and socialism.

Germans of Jewish descent therefore did not themselves agree on what it meant to be 'Jewish', whether in terms of religious beliefs, ethnicity, cultural practices, or politics.[2] But before 1933, most non-Jewish Germans—with notable exceptions—did not view Jewish Germans as an alien community that should be excluded from German citizenship. Antisemitic parties and movements had been growing since the later nineteenth century, rooted in more generally shared views about 'race', on which the Nazi movement would build; and longer-term intellectual traditions included notions of 'racial purity' and policies based on eugenics, also long predating Hitler. But the direction of travel as far as social practices were concerned had for decades been in the opposite direction: towards growing integration of Jews as part of the notable 'German-Jewish symbiosis'.[3] Indeed, orthodox Jews often feared, and not without reason, that assimilation through conversion and intermarriage, in combination with a low birth rate, was proceeding

so fast that within a couple of generations Jews would be effectively disappearing. Assimilation could be seen, from this perspective, as essentially a
form of cultural suicide. The situation of integrated and assimilated German
Jews was, then, very different from that of the 'shtetl' Jews in many areas of
Eastern Europe.[4] 'Racial' segregation in Nazi Germany was not in any way
akin to the notion of 'caste'. In Germany, while there were clearly longer-
term roots to Nazi ideas, social segregation between Jewish and gentile
Germans under Nazi rule would have to be actively co-produced from
both above and below.[5]

Paradoxically, the First World War—in which many German Jews gave
their lives in service of their country—proved a turning point. Many non-
Jewish Germans believed the widely circulated myths about Jews sabota-
ging the war effort or prolonging hostilities in order to make a profit—the
so-called Jewish enemy within that was allegedly responsible, along with
communists, for the 'stab in the back' that brought down an otherwise supposedly invincible army. The myth of 'Judeo-Bolshevism' that would later
prove so potent in Hitler's 'war of annihilation' was launched.

And paradoxically too, the liberal and democratic Weimar Republic that
emerged from the chaos of military defeat, revolutionary upheavals, and the
Emperor's abdication, and that gave Jews full and equal rights as German
citizens, also provided the conditions in which right-wing parties and antisemitic movements would flourish. The definitions of what it meant to be
'German' and who was to be construed as 'Jewish' were increasingly challenged and reconfigured, even before Hitler was appointed chancellor.

Integration and assimilation before the Great War

There were significant regional, class, and gender variations in Jewish life in
Imperial Germany, reflected in individual life stories. Eugen Altmann was
born in 1876 in Gumbinnen, East Prussia, and grew up in the Prussian town
of Memel (Klaipėda), at that time on the Russian border and later bitterly
contested between Germany and the postwar state of Lithuania. Altmann
had as a child played happily with Christian schoolfriends, who had on
occasion teasingly called him 'Jew boy'. This changed, however, when
Altmann entered high school in 1882. Antisemitism was spreading, legitimized by influential figures such as the composer Richard Wagner, Emperor

Wilhelm I's court chaplain Adolf Stöcker, and the (British-born) German racial theorist Houston Stewart Chamberlain. But at a local level in Memel, social tensions were far higher, as Jews subjected to pogroms in Russia fled across the border. An influx of impoverished and traumatized refugees exacerbated relations between Jews and gentiles, with a major impact on Altmann's life. He was now taunted by schoolmates, who jeered that Jews were 'weaklings'. Determined to prove them wrong, Altmann opted for a physically demanding apprenticeship instead of university. Yet however much he proved his physical strength or acted tough, he found he could never be, as he put it, 'one of them'; to his fellow workers he was always the outsider, 'the Jew', while former friends now also avoided him. Altmann moved from one job to another, frequently being let go, supposedly for the sake of workplace harmony. In 1894 he entered military service and did well but, being Jewish, was blocked from promotion.

Altmann later felt that, despite years trying to disprove the slurs about Jews being weaklings, by the time he was in his late twenties he had only succeeded in isolating himself, alienated both from his community of origin and from wider society. In his 1939 essay, written from the safety of the United States where he had by then immigrated, he bitterly reflected on his experiences as a young man: 'Who was it that was not yet mature—the times, society, or I myself?'

Yet, particularly in large cities in Imperial Germany, attitudes were already changing, as Altmann realized when in 1906 the family moved to Breslau (Wrocław) in Lower Silesia. Breslau was rapidly expanding, from around 400,000 inhabitants at the end of the nineteenth century to some 650,000 by the 1930s, and was noted for business, university-based science, and religious diversity. Jews formed an important part of the growing middle classes and helped to shape associational life. This was arguably not a question of a minority seeking assimilation into a 'majority society', but rather a co-creation—or negotiation and reinterpretation—of emergent forms of bourgeois culture. Yet the development was far from uniform: antisemitism remained rife in some quarters, particularly in circles close to the state, the military, and the nobility. And in their private lives, Jews tended to remain among themselves; even if close friendships between Jews and gentiles were sometimes formed, these might remain fragile.[6] Jewish-gentile relations were often a matter of registering difference, with perhaps a lack of complete trust rather than any hostility, as Altmann observed. In his thirties when they moved to Breslau, Altmann took over the family firm and found he was suddenly an attractive marriage proposition even in non-Jewish circles. He noted that there were a number of mixed marriages: generally a Christian woman marrying a wealthy Jewish man, since the Jewish partner had to compensate in wealth for what he lacked in status. But there were still hesitations about mixed marriages, if not always easy to articulate. Even one of Altmann's best customers confessed to reservations about Jews being in powerful positions and would never allow his daughter to marry a Jew. This was, he told Altmann, just a matter of 'feeling'.[7]

Altmann's experiences registered significant wider changes at this time. There were growing rates of conversion to Christianity among Jews in Imperial Germany: in the last decades of the nineteenth century, around 11,500 Jews converted, and in the forty years from 1880 to the end of the First World War, some 20,000 German Jews were baptized. Intermarriage also became increasingly frequent, eased by legislation in 1874–1875 designed to facilitate marriages between Catholics and Protestants, but applying also to marriages between Jews and Christians. Orthodox Jews feared the consequences for the future of the Jewish community, but liberal Jews held different views, and markers of social, cultural, and religious identity began to shift. By 1914 there were on average thirty-eight intermarriages for every hundred purely Jewish marriages in Germany, with regional variations. In pre–World War One Berlin, one in five Jewish men and roughly one in eight Jewish women married Christians. In Düsseldorf and Breslau by the early war years, approximately one-third of all married Jews had Christian spouses. In Hamburg the figure was as high as seventy-three intermarriages for every hundred purely Jewish marriages. By 1933, almost 40 percent of all marriages entered into by Jews in Germany were mixed. And by this time, around 300,000 Germans were descendants of mixed marriages. Under Nazi rule they would be called *Mischlinge*, with pejorative connotations as 'mixed-breeds' or 'mongrels'.[8]

In the sixty years between the 1875 legislation allowing intermarriage and the ban on such marriages by the 1935 Nuremberg Laws, the German Jewish community became more porous, with many Germans having relatives on both sides of what would be construed by the Nazis as a 'racial' divide. Even so, there remained an asymmetry of perceptions: while most Germans of Jewish descent saw themselves as Germans, many gentile

Germans still saw Jews as in some way different.[9] The question was then whether, in any given context, this difference really mattered.

Autobiographical accounts offer windows into subjective perceptions and personal experiences. For Else Behrend-Rosenfeld (the last part of her name added following her marriage), who was born in Berlin in 1891, Jewish descent on her father's side at first barely mattered. Her mother was a Christian from a well-to-do family, and her Jewish father was a doctor specializing in social welfare and patients in poverty.[10] The oldest of eight children, Behrend-Rosenfeld was baptized and confirmed in church and greatly influenced by Christian teaching at school. An intelligent girl, she was somewhat hampered by a birth defect rendering her left arm partially paralysed, but her father encouraged her independence. Behrend-Rosenfeld gained experience helping in her father's surgery and caring for her seven younger siblings and trained to be a kindergarten teacher. Deciding at the age of twenty-four to follow her intellectual interests, she completed high school examinations through an adult education course and entered university, an opportunity open to women only since 1908; she eventually earned a doctorate in history. In 1920, she married Siegfried Rosenfeld, a nonreligious Jew whose first wife had died giving birth to their daughter, Gustel. Else now cared for Gustel as her own, as well as having two more children with Siegfried. This couple in many ways typifies a particular milieu in early twentieth-century Germany, and particularly cosmopolitan Berlin, moving with ease between the Jewish, the mixed, the ex-Jewish, and the non-Jewish worlds.

Conversion and assimilation were not always this easy at a personal level. Considerable tensions were evident, for example, in the Haller-Munk family. Hans and Erich Haller-Munk were raised in comfortable circumstances in the north German town of Kiel; their father, Dr Heinrich Haller-Munk, was a pharmacist from West Prussia; their mother, Paula, came from Berlin.[11] The family was nonreligious, and in 1906, hoping to improve his children's future prospects, Heinrich converted to Christianity and had his two sons, then aged six and four, baptized. He hoped that his elder son, Hans, would take up the prestigious profession of state prosecutor (*Staatsanwalt*). But Hans realized he could break off his studies sooner if he settled for the lesser status of *Rechtsanwalt*—legal counsellor, or company lawyer, depending on function—and opted for the fastest route to earning money. He entered a legal practice in Magdeburg, married a Christian, and sought to submerge himself in provincial bourgeois society by revealing no trace of his Jewish origins. Erich, the younger son, was very different in interests and inclinations. Repeatedly taunted as a 'fantasist', Erich embarked on a career on the fringes of theatre production and cultural journalism. Writing his 1939 essay for the Harvard competition in the third person (using the pseudonym 'Peter'), Erich also hinted that he was gay—a further cause for friction with his father and brother, although he enjoyed a close relationship with his mother.

The two sons treated their Jewish family heritage quite differently. Erich saw Hans as a social climber with few moral scruples. One of their uncles, a professing Jew, also lived in Magdeburg, in somewhat straitened circumstances. According to Erich, Hans refused to acknowledge the relationship and went out of his way to avoid contact. He was furious when Erich visited and insisted on associating openly with their Jewish uncle. This threatened to reveal their Jewish family background and risked destabilizing the enhanced social status, as Hans saw it, that he was gaining in his new surroundings.[12]

On the western borders of the German Empire, class and nationalism were often far more important than religious heritage. Alfred Oppler was born in 1893 in the disputed territory of Alsace-Lorraine.[13] His parents had converted to Christianity shortly after their marriage, and he was baptized and brought up a Protestant. Oppler only realized that he had Jewish ancestry when, at the age of twelve, he was taken to visit his grandfather's grave. His grandfather had been a military doctor in all three wars of unification, including against France in 1870, and had been buried with full military honours in a Jewish cemetery, accompanied by both his rabbi and the officer corps led by the regiment commander. Apart from the passing impression made by this graveyard visit, Oppler recalled that he had no interest in the religious beliefs of his grandparents. His father was a judge, and he grew up in comfortable bourgeois surroundings, attending an academic high school along with the offspring of local elites; he went on to study law and political science and married a fellow Protestant who, unlike him, had no Jewish ancestry. Prior to 1933, Oppler seems to have experienced no antisemitism whatsoever.

Fritz Goldberg similarly grew up in Germany's western borderlands, in a garrison town in Alsace. His hometown was, he recalled, torn by rivalries— between 'patriots' or 'traitors', 'French' and 'Germans'. Goldberg's father, the

local theatre director, had to ensure that coveted front-row seats were re-
served for the German military and aristocracy, while French locals were
given seats further back. When his family moved to Berlin in 1910, Goldberg
found that his political attitudes and social status were far more important
to his schoolmates than the fact that he was Jewish. The 1912 election, in
which the Social Democrats emerged as the largest party in the Reichstag,
was particularly bitter, and it was fought out also in the school playground.
His best friend came from an aristocratic military family; children of professional people shunned those from poor or lower-middle-class backgrounds.
Although Goldberg occasionally heard antisemitic remarks, these were not
directed at him personally.[14]

In the recollections of many women too, class and gender seemed more
significant than Jewish heritage in shaping their lives. Klara Rosenthal,
whose shocked responses to the persecution of Jews in 1933 we have already noted, was born in the mid-1890s (as well as anonymizing her name,
she never gave her date of birth in the essay) to a well-respected business
family in Munich. She grew up mingling with children from aristocratic or
professional backgrounds, in a highly patriotic, nationalistic, authoritarian
atmosphere: as she put it, 'even laughing was dictated'.[15] Alice Baerwald,
born in 1883, painted a similar picture for Berlin, having no recollection of
antisemitism as a child. Her father ran a store specializing in woollens and
hosiery in Friedrichstraße, a major commercial street cross-cutting the central thoroughfare, Unter den Linden; her mother came from a rich provincial merchant's family. Baerwald's childhood was filled with leisure activities:
music, gymnastics, country walks, and socializing with friends, Jewish and
Christian alike. In 1906, she married a man from a wealthy Jewish family,
celebrating the ceremony in the large Oranienburger Straße synagogue;
they soon bought a car, symbolizing affluence and modernity; and by 1910
they had two sons and a daughter. Her husband's business and estate were
located in Nakel, around 380 kilometers northeast of Berlin; after moving
there, Alice enjoyed a life filled with socializing and celebrations, as well as
visits to family and friends in Berlin.[16]

In Baerwald's memories of her Berlin youth, social status was more
important than Jewish identity. But this did not apply to Jews who were
more visibly 'different'. Nearly three quarters of Berlin's Jews lived in
affluent western areas of the city and the leafy and lakeside suburbs.[17]
By contrast, many Ostjuden ('eastern Jews') lived in a run-down area

of decrepit buildings, overcrowded alleyways, and dark back courtyards known as the Scheunenviertel ('Barn Quarter'), on the fringes of the city centre. The Jewish community here was very unlike their West Berlin co-religionists in appearance, social profile, and language—a distinction that was eventually played on in Nazi propaganda, which highlighted Jews at both ends of the social spectrum: the 'dangerously' assimilated and affluent Jews as well as the poverty-stricken 'vermin' who were allegedly carriers of disease.

Similarly, the essay of Lotte Popper, a dentist's wife in Hamburg, emphasizes social standing. Born in 1898 in Preussisch Stargard, south of Danzig (Gdańsk), Popper studied mathematics and natural sciences in the universities of Königsberg and Breslau—unusual for a woman at that time—and became a high school teacher. Popper often helped in her husband's dental practice in an impoverished district of Hamburg, where she was shocked by seeing 'women aged thirty already looking fifty', girls decked out 'in cheap elegance', and 'narrow-chested boys', as well as 'pale-faced children'.[18] She wrote that her husband helped unemployed patients with a meal or a coin tucked into a pocket and dispensed kindly words alongside dental treatment, often without full payment. Since Popper was a teacher, people valued her advice on their children's upbringing. The Poppers felt well respected as social benefactors, model parents, and good neighbours. Being Jewish was also noticed, but in what can be described as 'philosemitic' terms—still stereotyping Jews, but with a positive rather than negative spin. One patient, for example, describing how a Jewish neighbour had helped her, added, 'I always say, the Jews, they have a heart'.[19]

Many Jewish Germans were aware of being made to feel subtly different at a relatively early age, not always in positive terms but also generally not in ways that could be considered actively hostile. It was often a matter of registering differences in conceptions of the wider community of which they were a part. This would become far more significant later on, but in pre-1933 Germany was not a cause for major conflicts. Later recollection of the years before Hitler are of course coloured by comparison with what was to come. But some memories, like those of Altmann and Popper, also inadvertently highlight a degree of marginalization by recording a common experience of out-groups: those who are stigmatized often find they have to be 'better than the best' in order to be appreciated, recognized, and accepted, with varying degrees of success.[20]

This was not easy. And even being 'better' could in and of itself be construed as a problem. Martin Andermann, born in 1904, was the son of a prominent lawyer and politician in the East Prussian garrison town of Königsberg (Kaliningrad). He characterized the atmosphere in which he grew up as 'a German-Jewish synthesis' and saw no contradiction between his Jewish heritage and the German culture that he loved. Once, another schoolchild asked if he was a 'Jewish boy' and then scoffed, 'Well, you look like one too'. Only later did Andermann realize that the distinction between Jews and non-Jews might have seemed clearer to his classmates than to him. Gradually, Andermann realized that Jews were seen as 'outsiders'. He realized, too, that his own patriotism differed from that of his classmates: while he drew his heroes from literature, music, and art, theirs came from the Prussian bureaucracy, monarchy, and military traditions. They saw it as an arrogant form of cultural appropriation that he knew far more about German literature and history than they did; and they held it against him that no one in his family had held high military office, been a large estate owner, 'or even a pastor', and that he himself displayed little by way of 'military bearing' or aptitude for physical sports. Somehow his easy intellectual superiority seemed suspect. Yet Andermann's schoolmates remained basically 'decent', he wrote, restricting themselves to teasing. He felt that antisemitism would not have posed a problem had it not been for war, revolution, 'and the whole economic and moral collapse that affected Germany in the following years'.[21]

Much depended on the character of local communities and social and economic environments. In the little village of Gailingen, on the southernmost border of Germany with Switzerland at Lake Constance (Bodensee), the Jewish and Christian communities lived together relatively harmoniously in the decades prior to the First World War.[22] Jews had obtained full citizenship rights with emancipation in the state of Baden in 1852. With emancipation, many left for new lives in towns and cities, and the proportion of Jews in the local village population declined: in 1852 the village consisted of roughly equal groups of 910 Christians and 913 Jews; by 1875, five years after the foundation of the German Empire, the proportions had shifted significantly, with now 1,024 Christians and only 704 Jews.[23] While Christians were generally peasants or day labourers, often suffering extreme poverty, Jews engaged in trading, particularly over the border with Switzerland. The fact that they could not be seen actively at work within the village, as well as the Jewish prohibition on working on the Sabbath, provided the basis for accusations of Jews being 'lazy'. Moreover, many earned a great deal more than the local Christians and lived in better houses, further fuelling social envy. The building of a large synagogue, along with superior institutions for education, welfare, and poor relief, further underlined social distinctions.

There was therefore a degree of symbiosis punctured by tensions. Significant Jewish tax contributions to community funds helped to support essential public services such as the local fire brigade, and public health and sanitation measures. Yet the fact that fires tended to break out more frequently and with more devastating consequences in the poorer quarters inhabited by Christians, and not in the better-constructed houses of Jews, led to widespread resentment about the unwillingness of Jewish men to play a role in the fire brigade. And social and cultural practices also deterred intermingling. Jewish women played no role in the local women's organizations, while Jewish girls were withheld from school cookery classes to learn kosher cooking at home. There was therefore always a sense of quite distinct communities in Gailingen; and issues of class, culture, gender, and religion were clearly aligned. Even so, and despite the frictions that surfaced in detailed reports on particular issues, such as shared use of school buildings and the distribution of teachers, cooperation between Jews and Christians was sufficient to ensure a prominent status for Jews in public life. From 1870 to 1884, the mayor of Gailingen was Leopold Guggenheim, a well-respected local Jew whose grandson would, after Kristallnacht in 1938, be interned in Dachau concentration camp.

The impact of World War One

Nazism did not come from nowhere. Antisemitic attitudes and behaviours, in various forms, could be found across Europe for centuries, while supposedly scientific theories about 'race' and eugenics were widespread in the later nineteenth century, well before Hitler picked up on more easily digestible versions. But in understanding the social and political origins of twentieth-century mass murder, the Great War—supposedly the 'war to end all wars'—was transformative; and postwar conditions fostered the growth of ethno-nationalist and right-wing populist movements in many areas. Again, this was not distinctive to Germany. If the Holocaust could have been predicted anywhere, it would have seemed far more likely that the mass genocide of Jews would break out not in Germany but in the areas of Eastern Europe that saw horrific pogroms in the first three years after the First World War, causing the deaths of more than 100,000 Jews—pogroms that arguably paved the way for the 'Holocaust by bullets' some two decades later.[24] Yet also in Germany, the war itself, and its wider consequences, began to shape the experiences of German Jews.

In 1914, the vast majority of Germans of Jewish descent were just as nationalistic as other Germans. This was not only true among Jewish intellectuals, politicians, opinion formers, bankers, and other professionals, as so easily documented in their public speeches and published writings, but is also evident in the memories of ordinary people.[25] During the war, and in the years thereafter, their patriotism was increasingly challenged.

When war broke out in 1914, Klara Rosenthal's brother volunteered for the army, while she trained as a nurse to care for the wounded. She would have liked to study medicine but faced the dual obstacles of parental disapproval and being a woman. Rosenthal was an ardent supporter of the war, despite being acutely aware of the human impact. She registered the grief on people's faces, the ways in which mothers took the place of their menfolk, children had to look after the household, and old people stood for hours in line for the necessities of life. And the war brought personal tragedies. Rosenthal's brother was fatally wounded and posthumously awarded an Iron Cross; her father, already suffering from heart problems, took his son's death very badly; and in the end Rosenthal gave up her aspirations for a career in nursing in order to help run the family business. Even so, she continued to justify Germany's role, and disagreed with her fiancé, whose letters from the Western Front were deeply critical of the war.[26] In these experiences and differences of opinion, Rosenthal and her fiancé were typical of many other Germans. In her 1939 essay, she does not even mention the fact that she was Jewish until this became salient in the course of the 1920s.

Nor was being Jewish particularly significant in the choice of marriage partners, as we have seen. Born in 1897, Verena Hellwig was a Christian who was already engaged to a somewhat older man, Hans, when he was called up to serve in the war.[27] As a student in Berlin, Verena became an active feminist and pacifist, and sought to rouse other women to the antiwar cause. Her anxiety and anger about war were compounded when both her brothers were killed, and she worried desperately about the fate of her fiancé, taken captive in Russia. In her 1939 account, she did not even mention that Hans Hellwig came from a Jewish family background until her narrative reached the 1920s. It was simply not worthy of note before that point, when their lives began to be affected by this. He was as staunch a nationalist as so many other Germans and had been just as involved in the war effort.

Like many other schoolboys, Martin Andermann joined in the patriotic fervour of August 1914. Conditions in his hometown of Königsberg soon deteriorated, but the Battle of Tannenberg, a decisive German victory over the Russians, brought some relief after a month of warfare. Andermann recalled that his 'gratitude and adulation' for Field Marshal Paul von Hindenburg 'knew no bounds'. In the longer term, the legends constructed around this battle would endow Hindenburg, who took credit for the military success, with a halo of prestige that helped him in the election as German president in 1925 and re-election in 1932, and in 1933, Hindenburg, by now senile, would serve as handmaiden in the appointment of Hitler as chancellor. Even after Tannenberg, for Andermann and others in Königsberg hunger and suffering prevailed; schools were transformed into field hospitals; boys, many barefoot, were co-opted to help in auxiliary war work, making collections on behalf of the wounded and needy. The Prussian spirit of 'just keep going' (*durchhalten*) was imbued in them; differences in class and politics were supposedly dissolved in a common cause, buoyed by patriotism and certainty of Germany's eventual victory. Being Jewish did not make Andermann stand out in any way.

As a schoolboy in Berlin, Fritz Goldberg was initially also swept up by the spirit of 'heroism and patriotism' of August 1914. By the time he was himself called up, however, he was already harbouring doubts. Even so, looking back in his 1939 essay, Goldberg felt he learned something from his war experiences. He met people from quite different social backgrounds; he discovered that once soldiers were promoted, they soon refused to recognize former comrades; and, not least, he witnessed the transformation from enthusiasm to disaffection, as well as growing social unrest on the home front. In 1918 Goldberg had his first real experience of antisemitism: despite performing brilliantly in examinations, he was refused officer status, and only now realized that simply being Jewish was sufficient to block military promotion.[28]

Edmund Heilpern, too, only came to a realization of the significance of antisemitism at the end of the war. Heilpern had been brought up in Vienna as a Protestant, and he was proud of his Austrian identity as a citizen in a multinational empire. Serving during the war in Austria, Heilpern was in charge of a company. He recalled the comradeship and spirit of together-ness as some of the 'nicest experiences' of his life. He had, however, to keep quiet about three uncomfortable aspects of his identity: that his mother was Russian; that he was in principle a pacifist; and that he was a member of the Social Democratic Party. Being Jewish was, however, simply not an issue. Most Austrians he knew felt more at ease with people from Prague or Budapest than Berlin; they saw Prussians as very different from themselves, despite also speaking German—in an accent they did not like. Heilpern's Jewish ancestry had meant little to him. In 1906, a schoolmate had asked if he was 'Aryan'. Neither he nor his friends had any idea what this meant and went away to look it up; the curious racial theories outlined in the book they consulted seemed both questionable and unimportant, and they soon forgot about it. A few years later, at university in Vienna, Heilpern en-countered the right-wing antisemitism fostered by politicians such as Karl Lueger, leader of the populist Christian Social Party and former mayor of Vienna. Heilpern was of the view that Hitler's virulent antisemitism was shaped by his Austrian background, which he imported into Germany: while in Berlin antisemitism had been a matter of 'theory and business', he felt, in Vienna it was 'really instinct and hatred'.[29] Nonetheless, throughout the war years, in Heilpern's experience a sense of comradeship prevailed.

At the end of 1918, however, Heilpern was exposed to antisemitism in Salzburg, where he was in hospital recovering from war wounds. A senior doctor was prevented from holding an elected office in a Revolutionary Soldiers' Council simply because he was Jewish, and a plenipotentiary rep-resenting the Soldiers' Councils was dispatched to Salzburg from Vienna to enforce the decision. Heilpern described this man as a former sergeant, 'small, stocky, with the nose of a drunkard and a voice to go with it', who spoke in a strong Tirolean dialect. Despite the doctor's professions of pat-riotic commitment to his Austrian fatherland, emphasizing that he was 'Israelite' by religion only, the prevailing view was that 'German blood' was the most important issue. As the plenipotentiary put it: 'we want to emphasize our nationality, just like everyone else is doing, the Czechs, the Hungarians, the Serbs, the Poles, etc. We believe therefore that the leader-ship . . . must be in purely German hands'. The senior doctor, publicly hu-miliated, left the room; after the meeting, many people expressed sympathy, but none dared stand up for him in public. In Heilpern's view, they were all essentially good-natured but lacking in civil courage.[30]

Contradictions were evident on all sides. Respect for former military service to the fatherland persisted, even trumping antisemitism in sometimes unlikely quarters. Heilpern moved to Germany after the war. When working as a research chemist in 1924 in Fürstenwalde, he had a young assistant, Albert, who at the age of nineteen was an early supporter of the National Socialist German Workers Party (NSDAP, or Nazi party, which grew out of what was originally just the DAP). Yet Albert chose to ignore the fact that Heilpern was Jewish; instead, keen to experience the war vicariously—like so many others of the 'war youth generation' who had been too young to fight—Albert was far more interested in hearing about Heilpern's war experiences.[31] Heilpern got along well with Albert, understood his enthusiasm for military comradeship, and did not take his NSDAP membership too seriously. By the time he penned his essay, however, Heilpern could barely believe that being in such agreement with a young Nazi could ever have been possible.[32]

There would even remain traces of respect for military service in the first couple of years of Hitler's rule, when war medals could still provide a degree of protection against antisemitism. Alfred Oppler had volunteered for military service and was awarded the Iron Cross. When Alsace-Lorraine was ceded to France in the territorial resettlement after the war, the Opplers were forcibly expelled from their home and moved to Berlin. In the 1920s, Oppler qualified as a lawyer and embarked on a promising career: aged thirty-eight, he was at that time the youngest person ever to be appointed associate justice of the Supreme Administrative Court (Oberverwaltungsgericht); a year later, he became vice president of the Supreme Disciplinary Court. In 1927 he married a Christian, Charlotte Preuss, and they had a daughter, Ellen. Until Hitler came to power, Alfred was not in any way disadvantaged by his grandparents' Judaism. For this bourgeois Protestant family, all seemed set for a glittering life; and even in 1933, Oppler hoped he could weather what might only be a temporary political storm by wearing his war decorations.[33]

But conditions were changing in postwar Germany. Antisemitism had been actively fostered during the war. With food shortages and military stalemate, rumours were spread about Jews not pulling their weight, allegedly even prolonging the war in order to profit from it. A 1916 census proved that Jews were actually playing an entirely proportionate role in military service; but the results were not published, and the fact that they had been singled out, that there was even a question about their participation, sharpened perceptions of Jews as unpatriotic 'shirkers'.[34] The 'stab-in-the-back' myth, propagated by the German military leadership before the end of the war and endlessly repeated following defeat, portrayed Jews, alongside socialists and communists, as an 'enemy within'. And across Europe, the postwar settlement would foster further nationalist movements fomenting antisemitism.

US president Woodrow Wilson's 'Fourteen Points' of January 1918 enunciated the principle of 'national self-determination' in determining new state boundaries after the cessation of hostilities. This was widely hailed as progressive, but it enshrined the idea of ethnically homogeneous 'nations', with often horrendous consequences for minorities who found themselves marginalized, displaced, or stateless. The Austro-Hungarian Empire was broken up, and any future union between Germany and the rump Austrian First Republic was explicitly forbidden. The area covered by the former Russian Empire was also reconfigured, with significant changes following the 1917 Revolution, through a period of civil war, until 1922, when the USSR was established within redefined borders. In the newly created states of Central and Eastern Europe, nationalist movements sought to define borders along supposedly mono-ethnic lines. Jews were no longer part of a multinational tapestry of social and cultural diversity; rather, they were frequently an unwanted minority, yet one (like 'Gypsies') with no state of their own to which they could be expelled. In conditions of massive social and economic distress, Jews were victims of violent pogroms and forced to flee. The influx of poverty-stricken, stateless Jews from Eastern Europe contributed significantly to rising antisemitism not just in Germany but also in many other areas of Europe, such as France, where recent immigrants contrasted markedly with fully integrated Jewish citizens.[35]

Experiences of antisemitism in the Weimar Republic

The declaration of a Republic on 9 November 1918 following the abdication of the German Emperor was rapidly followed by a series of unstable compromises between revolutionary forces, the more moderate social democratic left, and old elites. In a situation of continued paramilitary violence, nationalistic '*völkisch*' movements spread scare stories about supposed international Jewish conspiracies or portrayed Jews as dangerous agents of 'Judeo-Bolshevism'—a terrifying spectre following the 1917 Russian Revolution. References to the Jewish origins of prominent communists was accompanied by pointing to powerful Jews in high places in Western societies—bankers, politicians, media moguls—supposedly revealing international conspiracies dominated by 'cosmopolitan Jewry'. Hitler's role in the nascent NSDAP grew out of this situation, and right-wingers capitalized on the humiliating terms of the Versailles Peace Treaty of June 1919 as well as the social, economic, and political turmoil of succeeding years. The early years after the war were a time of widespread poverty and disorientation; while many demobilized German soldiers managed to reintegrate into civilian life, a minority were readily mobilized into the service of right-wing and paramilitary causes.

In Berlin, Verena Hellwig was shocked by the sight of exhausted, dishevelled, half-starved returning soldiers; even officers had torn epaulettes. All the years of sacrifice and self-discipline had apparently been for nothing; they seemed without hope and lacking in prospects. Her cousin, badly wounded, told her of men continuing to fight in the paramilitary Free Corps movements, glorifying comradeship in violence, and unwilling to accept national defeat. The streets of Hellwig's neighbourhood were filled with barricades; the sounds of gunfire echoed across courtyards, traffic came to a standstill, people hurried about their business keeping their heads down. Beggars, agitators, people out to make quick money from stolen goods, and innumerable activists of one party or another dominated the district. Hellwig noted, too, the rise in antisemitic slogans and incidents, even in the university. A sign was posted outside a bookshop, forbidding Jews entry. Flyers were distributed accusing Jews of responsibility for the national defeat, allegedly having shirked their war duty, having made massive profits at home or sent their money abroad. Hostility against Jews was being whipped up everywhere.[36]

Already politicized, Hellwig became increasingly incensed that women— who had kept homes and businesses running while menfolk had been away waging this senseless war—were largely excluded from serious political discussions; and that even her own female friends felt it was now alright, indeed even welcome, to restrict themselves to the domestic sphere. She campaigned actively for women's rights and applauded the new right to vote in the Weimar Republic.

Hellwig eventually heard from a hospital that her fiancé, Hans, had returned—physically ill, mentally exhausted, a shadow of the person she had known. As he began to recuperate, they visited art exhibitions and bookshops, discussed recent events, and in August 1920 finally celebrated their wedding. The following years were marked by contradictions between private happiness and concern about the wider situation. Hellwig felt blessed by the births of her son and daughter; and her husband, who had returned to his former employment, rose to a position of authority. But she also noted that the times were marked by the catastrophic consequences of inflation. The poor were becoming poorer, with people on fixed incomes or pensions—including war widows and orphans—suffering the most, while speculators and gamblers made fortunes. Hans left early for work and came home late, barely seeing his family and still suffering from the long-term consequences of war—frequent illnesses, insomnia, and anxiety. He was furious that right-wing assassins were allowed to roam freely simply because the army and many lawyers and politicians sympathized with their cause. Even as the national situation began to stabilize in the mid-1920s, Hans worried about massive state debts and political uncertainties. Yet at the same time, Verena was enjoying the company of her growing children. She liked to take them swimming—in a municipal swimming pool financed by American loans and local initiatives to get the unemployed off the streets— as well as giving herself time to read, attend talks, and visit galleries and art exhibitions. She felt that it was important, despite all, to recognize that life was good. As yet, although she registered rising antisemitism, her husband's Jewish family background seems barely to have impinged on her own life. Private lives could still run alongside and be relatively unaffected by wider developments in this respect.

Klara Rosenthal, too, was reunited with her fiancé after the war, and the couple married in December 1918. Rosenthal's new life was also dramatically affected by the revolutionary upheavals, with battles on the streets of Munich and the end of Bavaria's monarchy. The Rosenthal home and factory were stormed by left-wing radicals, savaged, and torn apart, and the family briefly had to flee for safety. Even on returning, things did not entirely settle down. In the following years, Rosenthal noted the impact of rapid industrialization, technological advances, urban growth, and the ways in which, as she wrote in her Harvard competition essay, 'people were being turned into machines'.[37] Inflation meant that while some became rich overnight, others rapidly became poorer than ever. Rosenthal knew of innumerable suicides, as people gave up hope for the future. For men who had given their all for Germany during the war, this was a bitter situation. In Rosenthal's experience as a businesswoman, workers increasingly viewed their employers and capitalists generally as the enemy, and she was discomfited by the rise of the so-called nouveau riche or newly rich, people lacking in education and social etiquette with whom she felt she had very little in common. Her 1939 essay looks back nostalgically at the society and culture of prewar times. She often sought to escape social events by taking refuge in the company of her growing family, with three children. Yet like Verena Hellwig, in her essay Rosenthal regards this period as 'the most peaceful and happiest' of her life.[38]

While there was antisemitism in high places—notably within the army leadership, the judiciary, and conservative political elites—it was not official policy in the new Weimar Republic (so named after the Thuringian city where the constituent National Assembly met in 1919, given the dangerous situation in revolutionary Berlin). The paradox of the Weimar Republic was that, just as it represented the most complete integration Jews had yet attained in Germany, it simultaneously embodied the political and socioeconomic conditions in which antisemitic movements could grow. Widespread resentment at the 'war guilt' clause of the Versailles settlement, acute social distress, impoverishment, and uncertainty, together provided fertile soil for propaganda targeted against those allegedly responsible for the 'stab in the back' causing Germany's defeat. For a while, however, Germans of Jewish descent could move easily between different social and cultural environments, some choosing to 'pass' by concealing their Jewishness or only offering clues to their Jewish identity when doing so seemed appropriate or advantageous. There was a lively literature on this topic at the time, with contested views among Jews on the merits of 'passing' or 'coming out', and different strategies for achieving a degree of 'invisibility'. In principle, these discussions resonated with the experiences of other minorities suffering from other forms of discrimination, such as racism or homophobia. Yet the very fact that many German Jews were able to play with different cultural codes, and could choose whether or not to perform one or another aspect of their (always multifaceted) identities according to circumstances, exemplifies both the relatively liberal context of Weimar Germany and the fluidity of Jewish identities at this time.[39]

Many Jews, particularly active Zionists, of course fully and openly embraced their Jewish identity. Some Germans, however, only became aware of having Jewish roots as antisemitism grew. For many children or grandchildren of mixed marriages, Jewish ancestry was of no concern whatsoever—until it suddenly was. The discovery of a Jewish ancestor could come as something of a shock, even before Hitler's rise to power. This was, however, a matter of specific circumstances, as illustrated in the case of Friedrich Reuss.[40] Born in 1905, Reuss was, like Alfred Oppler, the son of a judge. The family could afford lengthy holidays and held formal dinner parties. During the war, like other schoolboys, Reuss had initially been swept up by his teachers' nationalist enthusiasm; then his enthusiasm waned, as he was affected by the deaths of three former pupils in the war and by increasing awareness of hunger and social unrest. His uncle also returned from the front deeply embittered. In his essay, Reuss remembered that he had also noted the antisemitism of the 'stab-in-the-back' legend. But none of this seemed to affect him personally until 1923, when as a student in Munich he applied to join a coveted club, the 'Korps Makaria'. The club's many attractions included a sailing boat on the Starnbergersee, a lake south of Munich with spectacular views of the Alps. The application process included a lengthy questionnaire that Reuss's father insisted on reading through before submission. Then, 'with a strangely serious expression on his face', as Reuss recollected, he called Reuss into his study and revealed to him that his maternal grandfather, who had died when he was four, had been born Jewish but converted to Christianity. Reuss's parents had hoped to spare their son this 'dreadful revelation', but recently they had received threatening letters. So, his father concluded, 'we must draw the consequences'.[41] Reuss was completely taken aback. His anxious parents barely let him out of their sight for three days. Reuss, however, found it easier than they had anticipated: 'It definitely threw me, but no way would I want to commit suicide just because of this.' When he told the Korps Makaria club that he could not, after all, supply three generations of pure 'Aryan' ancestry, one friend jovially wondered why 'the old fool of a grandfather' could not 'simply have been a decent thief and murderer or some such'. Accepting the inevitable, Reuss joined a less prestigious club where no questions were asked about ancestry.[42]

In face of similar challenges in the early postwar years, non-Jewish Germans could choose whether or not to go along with antisemitic practices at this time. Not all students who could show an impeccably 'Aryan' ancestral tree were, for example, willing to condone the exclusionary practices to which Reuss had been subjected. Bruno Gebhard, a convinced Protestant and social democrat, had like so many been carried along by patriotic fervour while at school during the war and was shocked at defeat. He was, however, increasingly influenced by the work of English and American Quakers in welfare relief and reconciliation, and his attitudes began to change during the inflation crisis of 1923, as he witnessed the consequences of poverty and destitution for millions. Pursuing medical studies in Munich, Gebhard became ever more aware of political unrest on the streets, and observed with concern the rise of Hitler and political violence. Like Reuss, he would have liked to join a prestigious student organization; but unlike Reuss, he would not have been rejected on grounds of family background. However, he was in principle repelled by the demand for proof of 'Aryan' ancestry and had no desire to be associated with people for whom it was important.[43]

If antisemitism had always been prevalent to some degree, including in the army and universities, there was now also rising violence on the streets. Clashes between left and right did not end with the early postwar upheavals but continued through the 1920s and into the 1930s. Economic and social distress were widespread, contributing to continuing political instability. Involvement in paramilitary formations gave some individuals a sense of belonging to a wider national community in service of a common patriotic cause.

Intimations of Nazism

In 1934, some 683 Nazis who already supported Hitler and his party before 1933 and styled themselves 'old fighters' responded to an appeal by an American academic of Polish origin, Theodore Abel, to write about their personal experiences in the 'times of battle' (*Kampfzeit*). The vast majority of respondents were male; only thirty-six essays were written by women.[44]

These essays reveal how the experience of the war and military defeat in 1918 and the turmoil of the 1920s made them long for a saviour figure. Many searched for a scapegoat for their discontents; and the answer for some essay writers was simply 'the Jews'. These early Nazis often became involved in paramilitary units or engaged in spontaneous fights and armed confrontations between rival groups, particularly during political rallies. Speakers would be shouted down, and scuffles taken out onto the streets, where gang members lay in wait; many returned home beaten, bruised, and bloodied; a few were killed, and subsequently portrayed as heroes and martyrs who had died for the cause. Political violence was glorified in terms of self-sacrifice on behalf of the German fatherland.

The growing violence on the streets, between the radical left- and right-wing groups inevitably had an impact on experiences of German Jews who had up until now felt relatively secure in their own homeland. Yet it took them a while to register what was going on and to judge whether or not there was any real personal danger in the longer term. Most felt it easy enough to avoid specific situations of risk. They could readily retreat into their own sphere, observing the new political violence with varying degrees of apprehension but remaining personally untouched by it.

Some nevertheless soon found they had to deal with the new situation more directly. As we have seen, Klara Rosenthal's experiences as a young woman had been shaped more by gender and class than by religion. The first mention of her Jewish heritage did not occur until the 1920s, when a person her acquaintances referred to as 'Adolf Schicklgruber'—although he had always used the surname 'Hitler' that his father Alois Hitler (or Hiedler), had adopted—began to make waves on the Munich scene. Everyone in Rosenthal's circle was both horrified by Hitler and yet also dismissive, commenting that he was 'not really a German', as she later wrote, and that his followers consisted entirely of rabble, the 'workshy and unemployed'.[45] But Rosenthal's husband attended one of Hitler's rallies to see for himself and came home extremely disturbed. He felt that Hitler 'was not only a special danger for us Jews, but also for Germany itself'.[46] Hitler was having a significant influence on other Germans—and for increasing numbers, the impact was entirely positive, with rising support for Nazism. One enthusiastic woman who also attended a rally in Munich in the 1920s had lost her fiancé to what she called a 'hero's death' in the First World War. When Hitler started to speak, she recalled, at first the room became 'stiller and stiller' and then there were 'ever more cries of enthusiasm', and, as he announced his vision for Germany, there was 'huge cheering'. 'Since that day', she felt, 'Germany had its leader and saviour'.[47] Even if not many yet shared this sense of ecstasy, things were changing. And now for the first time, antisemitism began to play an explicit role in Rosenthal's perceptions of her own identity and future.

Friedrich Reuss, who had only just been made aware of his Jewish grandparent, also became increasingly disturbed by Hitler's existence. One day, probably in late 1922 or early 1923, Reuss and some friends were engaged in a heated discussion of politics over sausages and beer in the Café Victoria in Munich. Suddenly, a person whom Reuss described as 'a dishevelled-looking, darkly scowling fellow' ('*ein ungepflegt aussehender, finster blickender Geselle*') at the neighbouring table introduced himself and proceeded to yell at them for the best part of an hour, emitting a tirade about how social democrats, Jewish capitalists, and the international churches were guilty of everything, 'and that we should hate all of them and "destroy them without mercy"'.[48] This man was Adolf Hitler. He left the café without paying his bill.

On 9 November 1923—exactly fifteen years before Kristallnacht—Reuss witnessed a couple of Jews being beaten nearly to death in the University Hall (Aula). He was himself beaten by soldiers with batons as he and other students tried to get out of the building. They ran as fast as they could to what they thought would be safety at the Feldherrnhalle end of the street. But here they found 'wild shooting' taking place; at this precise moment, Hitler's attempted march on Berlin—in imitation of Italian fascist leader Benito Mussolini's march on Rome the previous year—was being halted in its tracks, and some of his co-conspirators were gunned down. Hitler would later stylize the men killed at the Feldherrnhalle as martyrs to the Nazi cause, occasioning annual commemorations during the Third Reich. In the immediate aftermath however, as Reuss noted, Hitler derived the maximum possible benefit from his trial, with his speech being widely praised and publicized. Hitler's subsequent imprisonment of less than a year in relatively comfortable quarters in the Landsberg prison gave him the opportunity to commit to paper the diatribe published as *Mein Kampf* ('My Struggle'), a work intimating what he had in mind for the future.

Although the general thrust of Hitler's hate-filled rhetoric clearly found popular resonance in some circles, few people at this time would have interpreted this rambling tract as a serious political programme likely to have any practical consequences. Indeed, it seemed to Reuss and many others that it was unlikely that Hitler would ever gain a sufficient following to put his ideas into effect. His little party had been only one of many *völkisch* groups and was now clearly in some disarray—at least temporarily. In 1924, Reuss settled back into his law studies, spending some time in the north German university town of Kiel. He visited Finland and then Italy, where in 1925 he met Mussolini through personal connections. Returning to Munich in the winter of 1925–1926, Reuss found the Nazi movement recovering after Hitler's premature release from prison in late 1924. Reuss's parents had also been subjected to threats and financial maltreatment accompanied by antisemitic insults about his dead grandfather. Although the NSDAP still remained on the fringes of politics, Nazism and with it racially based antisemitism had not gone away.

Willy Bornstein, born in 1883, experienced brushes with Nazism in Nuremberg that were more directly violent.[49] His family could trace back their residence in Germany for around four centuries, and the family was deeply patriotic. Like Reuss's grandfather, Bornstein's father had been distinguished for his military service in the wars of 1866 and 1870–1871 and had been buried with full military honours in 1909, and Bornstein was himself awarded honours for service in the Great War. Situated in the Franconian area of northern Bavaria, Nuremberg was at that time rapidly expanding outwards from its medieval town centre, its business facilitated by the introduction of railways. A population of under 100,000 in the 1870s quadrupled within a matter of decades, with rapid industrialization following German unification. Bornstein inherited from his father a fruit store that sold, among other exotic items, coconuts imported from the German colonies, and the family business flourished. He was well settled and comfortably off.

The majority of the Nuremberg population at this time were Protestant, but a substantial minority were Catholic, and around 1 percent were Jewish. Bornstein's friendship circles almost exactly reflected these proportions. Ninety-nine percent of his friends were Christians, including his wife; together, they had two children, who would eventually be categorized as '*Mischlinge*'. But for now, 'race' seemed unimportant. Bornstein was well connected and belonged to a variety of sporting associations, an athletics club, and the Apollo Theatre Society. The Apollo Theatre, founded in 1896, with seating for 2,000, staged not only plays and musical events but also acrobatics and special acts, including an appearance by the escape artist Harry Houdini. For Bornstein, life was varied and good.

But, as for so many others, in the early 1920s things began to change. The extreme racist Julius Streicher gained increasing influence over public opinion through his weekly tabloid, *Der Stürmer*, founded as a propaganda weapon of poisonous antisemitism. The first edition was published on Hitler's birthday, 20 April 1923, in the run-up to the putsch attempt later that year. The paper lambasted the supposed financial greed and murderous lust of Jews, highlighting lascivious stories of 'interracial' sex, and appealing to people wanting sensationalist stories and easy scapegoats. Every front page bore the strapline 'The Jews are our misfortune'. Antisemitic stereotypes were subtly conveyed in striking illustrations featuring crude images of thick-lipped, hook-nosed villainous faces and quasi-pornographic images, subconsciously affecting even those who did not read the text. Streicher's income was based only in part on the growing circulation figures of this vicious broadsheet. He also gained substantial sums through blackmail and hush money from people who wanted their names kept out of *Der Stürmer*. While this may have marginally eased the strain for individuals, at a price, it did little to diminish the impact of the murderous racism propagated by the paper. To ensure as wide a readership as possible, copies were eventually displayed in glass cabinets known as *Stürmerkasten* ('Stormer boxes'), although the paper remained controversial even in Nazi circles.

Streicher was agitating in fertile soil, and Willy Bornstein registered rapidly just how radically Nuremberg society was changing. More and more cafés and shops now excluded Jews from their premises. Young people started sporting swastika armbands and getting organized in activist groups. Streicher provided financial support, but there was also income from Nazi party subscriptions and donations at meetings attracting audiences of thousands. Bornstein noted how Streicher 'preached' to the desperate members of the crowd before him, urging them to beat up the 'cowardly' Jews without being caught by the police; the rabble chanted back, in chorus, 'The Jews are our misfortune', 'Don't buy from Jews', 'Death to the Jew!' (*Jude verrecke*), and other slogans. This rabble-rousing went on day after day, night after night, and street fights inevitably ensued.[50]

Bornstein adopted a gendered response of seeking to combat antisemitism through demonstration of physical strength. Although in his forties by

the late 1920s, Bornstein prided himself on being fit, well-built, and ath-
letic; fighting in self-defence, he felt he was able to give as good as he got.
In scuffles with Nazis on the streets, he was generally able to emerge relatively unscathed, if shaken. But eventually he became embroiled in a legal
case, which was potentially far more damaging. Streicher chose to feature
this case prominently both in the headlines of *Der Stürmer* and on placards
around the town, adversely affecting Bornstein's reputation and business
interests. Infuriated, Bornstein went to Streicher's office to confront him
in person about the issue—and here too fisticuffs ensued. Streicher, taken
aback after Bornstein had vigorously punched him in the face, sought to
shift the blame for the adverse publicity to his assistant. Bornstein went off
to find the assistant, who had in the meantime made himself scarce.[51]

This did not put an end to Bornstein's troubles, however. He had increasing difficulty going to public events; even where there were no placards
announcing that entry was forbidden to Jews, he was recognized as Jewish
and often turned back at the door. On one occasion this rebuff was softened
by the friendly comment that 'if only all Jews were like him, then everything would be alright'—the kind of back-handed compliment, suggesting
an individual was an exception while reinforcing the prejudiced stereotype,
that would be heard repeatedly across Germany as people extended sympathy to individuals even while excluding them. Previously intimate friends
and acquaintances also began to avoid Bornstein. Christian work colleagues
with whom he had always been on good terms, and with whom he had
celebrated holidays—whether Jewish or Christian—refused to be seen with
him outside work. Married as he was to a Christian, Bornstein became
aware that if non-Jewish women were seen with Jews in cafés, they would
frequently receive threatening notes urging them as 'German women' to
stop consorting with Jews. Daily he heard chants of 'Germany awake', 'Jews
out'. Nazi songs were loudly sung in public places, and even café musicians,
concerned to make a living, played along in accompaniment. On days when
there were large Nazi rallies, Jews who could afford to do so stayed home
from work or even went away for a few days until the ensuing antisemitic
fervour had died down.

Bornstein noted bitterly that though the Nazis complained that Jews
always kept themselves to themselves, they were in fact the ones exacerbat-
ing this progressive social isolation. As a leader of the Central Association
of German Citizens of Jewish Faith explicitly told him, Jews increasingly

felt that the best they could do was to retreat and attract as little attention as possible. A widespread response, well-practised by the stigmatized and excluded at all times, was that of attempting a degree of invisibility through self-effacement—'*nur nicht auffallen*', 'just don't attract attention'.

A degree of anonymity might help. Bornstein sadly concluded that, if he were to continue in business, he would have to get out of Nuremberg—the city where his family was rooted, and where he had grown up and lived happily for decades. He decided his family would have to move to what he hoped would be the anonymity of a large city. In 1925 the family relocated to Bavaria's capital, Munich, where Bornstein was not well known personally. Munich was roughly double the size of Nuremberg, its population having grown exponentially in preceding decades, from 170,000 in 1871 to 640,000 in 1914; Bornstein had good reason to hope that he could simply melt anonymously into the crowds.[52]

In Munich, Bornstein observed, Nazi activists were generally young people with criminal records, disturbed and pitiful figures who sought power on the streets. He no longer felt he had to prove at every turn that he was not a coward, the jeering taunt so frequently made to male Jews. Every so often there was a provocation, but he was now able to escape down sidestreets without fearing he would be recognized. It took considerable courage for Bornstein to adopt this strategy; he had to bite his tongue, clench his fists in his pockets, and keep himself under control. It clearly challenged his sense of masculinity. Still, he had persuaded himself that this would be best for his family in making a new start. And life in Munich did in fact at first prove a little better for the Bornstein family.

Growing tensions

There were varying responses to antisemitism; and decisions made before Hitler came to power often affected subsequent reactions to Nazi rule. Yet in the closing years of the Weimar Republic there was still no reason to expect that things would take such a turn for the worse. It was still possible to lead individual lives in the expectation of a relatively secure future.

Hans Haller-Munk and his brother Erich, as we have seen, had already had sharp disagreements about Hans's denial of his Jewish family background and refusal to recognize his uncle. Family tensions rose again when Hans got married without first letting his parents know. His wife, Beate, was four years older, divorced, and not Jewish. Hans was aware that his parents might not consider this a suitable match, but it would help his social advancement in provincial bourgeois circles. When Hans's mother, Paula, heard about the marriage, she went to visit the couple, but stayed only briefly, then left hastily to meet Erich in Berlin. Erich was by now well established in the theatre world, and he took her to one of the first performances in 1928 of the *Threepenny Opera* (*Die Dreigroschenoper*) by Bertolt Brecht with music by Kurt Weill. Mother and son would both later, under different circumstances, look back on this evening with nostalgia.

The Haller-Munk brothers went their separate ways. Erich became ever more immersed in theatrical life, while Hans seemed all set up in his legal practice in Magdeburg. Beate's first pregnancy ended in a stillbirth, but by late 1932 she was pregnant again. Now well established in bourgeois society, Hans had high hopes for the future. He had actively cast off his Jewish origins, at the price of estrangement from his family. The different strategies of these brothers would radically affect the paths their lives would take under Nazi rule.

Adaptation varied according to location—and the loss of German territories following the Versailles Treaty massively affected the lives of many people, including some of the Harvard essay writers. Alice Baerwald, who had happily left Berlin and settled in Nakel following her marriage, found that even without moving an inch the family's surroundings and home had radically changed. With the postwar creation of the Second Polish Republic and the so-called Polish corridor of land stretching up to the Baltic Sea, many areas that had formerly been part of Imperial Germany suddenly became Polish, including Nakel. The Baerwald family, well established and wanting to stay on their Nakel estate, initially opted for Polish citizenship. But despite early hopes, the family business experienced difficulties. The Baerwalds took the decision to move to the predominantly German city of Danzig, a seaport on the Baltic coast that was considered 'free'. Here, things went well at first. But when the Depression hit, political and social unrest began to rise, and in 1931 the Baerwalds' eldest son decided to emigrate to America. This was an emotional blow for Baerwald at the time; later, her son's emigration at this early date would prove to be their path to escape from Nazi persecution.[53]

Those who held significant positions within Weimar Germany also faced unexpected challenges. Reuss had easily taken in his stride the revelation of his own partially Jewish ancestry—the existence of one Jewish grandparent had, after all, merely meant that he had to join a less prestigious student club than he had envisaged, which really meant little in the wider scheme of things. But in the later 1920s, he began to be confronted by problematic issues in his professional life. By 1928, Reuss had qualified as a junior lawyer (*Gerichtsreferendar*) and found that politics was increasingly interfering with legal decisions. He became aware of just how much Nazis were beginning to control areas of the press and public opinion, doing as they wanted with little risk of being penalized. In 1930, Reuss was compelled to compromise in a case involving a Nazi in a senior position, resolving a legal tangle by having the Nazi effectively promoted out of trouble. He was particularly horrified when he heard about another case, where a doctor refused to treat a Jewish boy who was bleeding to death, saying there were enough Jewish doctors who could treat him; the boy, however, died before any help could arrive. The doctor was accused of failing to fulfil his medical duty of assistance—but the court found him not guilty on the grounds that, even if he had treated the patient, the boy might have died anyway, and he would not want to face the charge that 'a Jewish boy had died while under the treatment of a Nazi doctor'. Such considerations had become sufficient to justify death by refusal to treat. Little over a decade later, the deaths of Jews would be actively caused, rather than merely permitted, by Nazism.

Unhappy in this job, Reuss decided to accept the offer of working as a senior civil servant in Berlin. Here, for the first time, he came into contact with Jews in higher social circles, something he had not experienced in Munich. Despite their professional and social status, however, his Jewish acquaintances were nervous and tended to avoid political discussions. Everywhere, the question of whether one was Jewish was becoming more salient. Even in political cabarets, Reuss noted, on some evenings there seemed to be more jokes about Jews than there were Jews in Berlin.

Despite his somewhat disconcerting experience with the Korps Makaria student club a few years earlier, Reuss was not at all worried about his own situation. He was after all a Protestant from a good family, with only a single Jewish grandparent who had converted long ago. And in any event, most people in his circle were of the opinion that while Germany was a powder keg, Nazism would be a short-lived political explosion: were Hitler actually brought to power, he would be blamed for everything and not last very long. The government led by the Centre Party's chancellor Heinrich Brüning from March 1930 to May 1932 was sustained through use of emergency decrees by President Hindenburg, who was no fan of democracy in principle. But before then cabinets in the Weimar Republic had lasted on average barely eight months. There were indeed two further very short-lived cabinets in late 1932, led by Franz von Papen and Kurt von Schleicher. Hitler might well be appointed chancellor, but most of Reuss's acquaintances felt he would soon prove his utter unsuitability. They were of the view that he would be out within a year. It was not a pleasant situation, but it would be over soon. Despite continuing signs of the ways in which Nazi views were increasingly dominating the media and public discourses in the Depression of the early 1930s, Reuss settled into his new job and started to make a new life in Berlin.

Contemporaries were well aware that the world was rapidly changing. The Wall Street Crash of 1929 sent the German economy into the fastest and deepest depression of all the affected countries. Rapidly rising unemployment was accompanied by increasing political violence and clashes on the streets between Nazis and communists. The old political leaders—from chancellors such as Heinrich Brüning, Franz von Papen, Kurt von Schleicher, to the ageing former war hero President Hindenburg—seemed incapable of finding any solution. The outlook seemed hopeless, and—with many Germans casting admiring glances at full employment and peace on the streets in Mussolini's Italy, if at the expense of individual freedom—more and more people were seeking someone who could pull them out of national bankruptcy and political chaos. The man making the most promises and acquiring a growing following, particularly in small towns and rural areas in Protestant regions, was Adolf Hitler.

The presence of Nazis and associated antisemitism was increasingly impossible to ignore, but this did not yet pervade life in the ways that it would once the Nazis were in power. Regime change would make an absolutely crucial difference in terms of the wider context of particular incidents of violence, as numerous stories illustrate. Walter Jessel had been born into a relatively well-to-do Frankfurt family of assimilated, patriotic, and non-religious German Jews; his father was an entrepreneur in the new field of electronics, working for a recently founded machine production and welding company, Idealwerke. In the 1990s, Jessel wrote a memoir primarily intended for his grandchildren, using letters and diary entries from the time to try to convey to them some understanding of how his life had been shaped by the Nazi period. He recounted what would, after 1933, become a fairly typical story; but when it occurred, in 1929, non-Jewish fellow citizens reacted quite differently from how they would after the Nazis had come to power. The story ran as follows: Jessel, along with his blonde blue-eyed sister, and her dark-haired, dark-eyed Catholic friend, were all riding on a very full train. Then 'in came a brown-shirted storm trooper, looked at my girls and harangued the burghers [sic]. "Look at these two: isn't it obvious? The dark-haired Jewess and the blonde Aryan!"'. He got off at the next stop.' Jessel went on: 'The three of us laughed and told our fellow travellers that he'd gotten it wrong. All laughed. The Aryan race idiocy hadn't yet taken hold.' Moreover, Jessel recalled in his memoir, social class still mattered far more than so-called race at this time. As economies deteriorated, and with the rise of more virulent antisemitism in Poland and Russia, Eastern European Jews migrated to Germany. Even among the Jewish community in Jessel's circle, as elsewhere, they were not always welcomed; Jessel recalled dinner table conversations in which they had been quite critical. Similarly at school: 'Two immigrant youngsters, one speaking better Yiddish than German, had joined our class. They had little social contact with any of us. To the assimilated Frankfurt Jewish families they appeared to be a threat. To them we were anti-Semites like the rest of the Germans.' But, among mainstream society, perceptions were heading in a quite different direction: 'Unemployment rose, and Jewish enterprise was perceived to prosper by comparison. The culture of envy flourished among the unemployed.'[54]

There remained however a crucial difference regarding the responses of citizens and the upholders of law and order before and after January 1933. Before 1933, some bystanders were willing to call for and expect police assistance when witnessing attacks on Jews. After 1933, the police were harnessed to the other side of the dynamics of violence. This is vividly illuminated by the experiences of Fritz Goldberg. He had already encountered some antisemitism among student circles while he was at university; following receipt of his doctorate in 1924, however, he found life in Berlin exhilarating. He threw himself into the life of the theatre, also working as a journalist, in adult education, and in a publishing house. He was a keen observer of Berlin life at all levels, enjoying the little corner bars (*Kneipen*) and beer gardens. While witnessing the rise of political violence on the streets, he felt he personally had little to fear. One evening, however, Goldberg was chatting on the street with a Jewish friend just outside the latter's apartment block. A rowdy group came around the corner, took one look at Goldberg and his friend, and yelled, 'They're Jews! Kill them!' The pair were badly beaten up but managed to escape into the friend's apartment.

This might be taken simply as evidence of rising antisemitism. But from the perspective of understanding bystander responses to violence, there is one further crucial element of this disturbing incident in the late Weimar years. On witnessing the punch-up, bystanders called the police to come to the victims' assistance—something that would after 30 January 1933 become first rare and then unthinkable. On this occasion, the police did indeed show up shortly after they were called, but too late to catch the group responsible for the violence. In his essay, Goldberg recalled that he was later very relieved he had decided not to make a formal report on the attack: anyone who had entered such a complaint against Nazi thugs would subsequently be among their first victims.[55]

Before 30 January 1933, in the retrospective views of the Harvard essay writers, everything still seemed possible. Even allowing for the vicissitudes of selective memory, many German Jewish women—Lotte Popper, Klara Rosenthal, Alice Baerwald, among others—seem to have been barely exposed to antisemitism before Hitler came on the scene.[56] Like all Germans, their lives were deeply affected by the impact of war, revolution, inflation, political instability, economic depression—but violent racism on the streets largely passed them by. Some German Jewish men—Eugen Altmann in the northeastern borderlands, Willy Bornstein in the early heartlands of Nazi radicalism in Bavaria, even Fritz Goldberg in Berlin—had experienced antisemitic taunts and physical attacks, while others, such as Edmund Heilpern or Martin Andermann, saw it mainly in terms of social exclusion or promotion blockages. People who had converted, or were of mixed descent, experienced occasional difficulties—Friedrich Reuss's unsuccessful attempt to join an exclusive student fraternity, Hans Haller-Munk's family tensions—but these had not seemed insurmountable, determining the whole shape of their lives. Indeed, before 1933 Alfred Oppler's life seemed barely affected at all.

Before Hitler, few would have thought it possible that a European-wide slaughter of Jews could originate in Germany. While Jewish communities in Eastern Europe were periodically devastated by violent pogroms, and

France was still reeling from the Dreyfus affair of the 1890s, German Jews and Germans of Jewish descent were highly integrated.

The change came when the violent racism of thugs on the streets turned into the official programme of the government in power—backed by the organs of state, upheld by the forces of law and order, implemented by the civil service, effected through the economy, pervading society and leisure time, and enacted in every aspect of everyday life, even in the privacy of people's own homes.

2

Falling into Line

Spring 1933

On the evening of 30 January 1933, the day on which President Hindenburg appointed Hitler chancellor, jubilant Nazis marched through the streets of Berlin in a torch-lit parade. Crowds lined the streets to cheer the procession, hoping for a new dawn: an end to the time of rising unemployment, political instability, and violent clashes between formations of right and left. Everywhere, Friedrich Reuss noted with distaste, the streets were bedecked with flags and slogans: 'Germany greets its Führer!'; 'Germany has regained its honour!'; 'Germany is throwing off its chains!'[1] Franz Albrecht Schall, at that time not yet quite twenty years of age and an enthusiastic Hitler supporter, was overwhelmed with joy. On 30 January he recorded in his diary how he could not manage to get hold of a newspaper, and he could barely believe it yet, but that everywhere swastika flags were flying. On the following day, he recorded that work was now beginning in earnest, and although it would likely take a while to establish 'a completely purely national socialist cabinet, Hitler's dictatorship', the motto now was 'full steam ahead!'[2]

Across the country, around one-third of the electorate had cast their votes for the NSDAP in the elections of November 1932—somewhat down from the high of 37 percent in July 1932, but still more than had voted for any other party. Hitler's supporters were now filled with hope that he would be able to fulfil his promises to heal the divisions and unite the nation.[3] But the nation was deeply divided, and people opposed to Nazism were filled with horror. One of the Harvard essay writers, Carl Paeschke, felt he was 'living through times like people in the Middle Ages, when the plague raged', and 'those still living were dancing on the dead'; it seemed to him that 'Germany consisted only of swastika flags, brown and black uniforms, and distorted, murderous faces'.[4]

A society marked by violent clashes between left and right now had a regime in power that held a monopoly on violence. While large crowds hailed the new regime, the few who tried to stand out against it soon learned the brutal limits of effective opposition. Among those who had been active supporters of Nazism prior to 1933, there was, naturally, massive enthusiasm. In essays written in 1934 under the title 'why I became a Nazi', some recalled 'hours of the greatest inner happiness' and remembered proudly how they went from the margins to suddenly gaining new positions of power and respect.[5] Many more who had previously supported other parties, or had been waverers, now jumped on the bandwagon.

But across society more generally, the picture was mixed. Public enthusiasm, private apprehension, and widespread conformity became key characteristics of life in Germany in 1933. And in the first months of Hitler's rule, there was little sense that this Reich could or would last very long. Among those who initially felt they were merely bystanders to these momentous changes, passive conformity appeared the best option. This effectively not only condoned but also in part contributed to the remarkably rapid shift from parliamentary democracy into populist dictatorship.

The Nazi appropriation of power

Opponents of Nazism tried to reassure themselves that Hitler's government, like its Weimar predecessors, would soon falter. After all, Hitler was head of a mixed cabinet, with only two other Nazis. Conservative nationalists had gambled that they and the moderate Catholics would hold him in check while capitalizing on his popular support. And it was widely thought that Hitler—who had never held a serious position of responsibility and had no experience of government—would soon discover that it was easier to storm around the country, making fiery political speeches and promising all things to all groups, than to run a coherent programme.

Hitler's first weeks in office, however, proved that this was going to be no ordinary administration along the lines of its relatively short-lived Weimar predecessors. He rapidly engaged in discussions about rearmament, forbidden in the Versailles Treaty, making quite clear to army leaders where he intended German foreign policy to go. Hitler and other Nazis dominated the radio waves, with a barrage of speeches that were boomed out through loudspeakers in public places. Coordinated press reports presented news in terms of stark choices between the left-wing demons of 1918 and the forces of glorious renewal of 30 January 1933. Communists and socialists were portrayed as a national threat; brutal beatings and murderous reprisals by Nazis against left-wingers were justified as legitimate defence of the nation and national wellbeing.[6]

The Nazis also took advantage of events—or created circumstances of which they could take advantage. On the evening of 27 February 1933, the Reichstag—the seat of the German parliament—was set on fire, with evidence suggesting that a number of people must have been involved. A Dutch communist found in the building, Marinus Van der Lubbe, was arrested and the communists blamed for the arson. Many people thought that the blaze had been started by the Nazis and Van der Lubbe used as a convenient scapegoat to blame communists. Although Van der Lubbe and five other communists were put on trial later that year, Nazi claims about a wider communist conspiracy were unconvincing in court, with senior Nazi Hermann Göring's tirade effectively backfiring, and eventually only Van der Lubbe was found guilty. As Hermann Stresau, a librarian, noted in his diary on 30 September 1933, in discussions among the wider public 'a note of extreme scepticism' prevailed. Although the 'feeble-minded Dutchman' may have ignited the fire, it seemed 'quite miraculous that he could have burned down half the Reichstag inside twenty minutes, all on his own, with just a couple of napkins, an old shirt, and similar paraphernalia' unless someone else had thoroughly prepared the ground for him in advance— which seemed most obviously to point to Nazi involvement. Even those mounting the trial seemed to have lost any hope of demonstrating communist guilt.[7] At the time, however, the implications of the fire became clear. Within minutes of the Reichstag's going up in smoke, Hitler and Göring blamed the communists. The fire was used to declare a national state of emergency. The Communist Party (KPD) was outlawed, political opponents on the left were intimidated, with hundreds arrested and incarcerated in makeshift prisons, camps, and cellars. In the course of 1933, the paramilitary SA (Sturmabteilung) held somewhere between 60,000 and 75,000 political opponents of Nazism in 'wild' (provisional or make-shift) concentration camps, where they were beaten up and many were murdered.[8] And on 22 March 1933, the first official concentration camp, Dachau, was opened to much public fanfare.

Despite intimidation both on the streets and at the polling booths, and despite massive Nazi propaganda, in the general election of 5 March the NSDAP still did not pull off the desired majority designed to secure Hitler's mandate. The Nazi party increased its electoral support only to 44 percent—short of the two-thirds majority required to put through legis-lation to change the constitution and put an end to democracy. This pro-cess was managed in other ways. Since the Reichstag building had been rendered unusable by the fire, the ceremonial opening of the new parlia-ment on 21 March took place in the historic Garrison Church in Potsdam. In images designed to impress the public, Hitler was portrayed standing beside President Hindenburg, symbolically claiming a mantle of respect-ability in the hallowed footsteps of Prussia's eighteenth-century king, Frederick the Great; the unification chancellor, Bismarck; and President Hindenburg himself, the revered hero of the Battle of Tannenberg. Two days later, on 23 March 1933, the newly elected representatives met in the Kroll Opera House, close to the burned-out Reichstag at the edge of the Tiergarten—Berlin's major public park—to engage in an act of collective suicide for parliamentary democracy. With KPD deputies banned, and in face of the opposition of only some brave individuals in the German Social Democratic Party (SPD), Hitler managed to gain the two-thirds majority required to pass the Enabling Act, giving him dictatorial powers. Hitler was able to count on the support not only of the swollen ranks of NSDAP deputies but also of conservative nationalists and the Catholic Centre Party, marking the capitulation of those in positions of power and influence who could still have stood up to Nazism.

The path was now set for dismantling any legal opposition to Nazi rule. By July 1933, the NSDAP was the only permitted political party, asserting sole control over Germany. Other institutional bases of opposition, includ-ing the trade unions, were either abolished or brought into line. By then, some 100,000 opponents had been imprisoned; countless numbers had been murdered or had fled into exile. In the course of 1933, a total of around 200,000 political prisoners were held for varying lengths of time, including 50,000 communists just in the two months of March and April alone.[9]

It would in the event take a further year for Hitler to secure his own position. In late June 1934, he sacrificed the leaders of the SA, including his longtime loyal political associate Ernst Röhm, in a bloodbath dubbed the 'Night of the Long Knives' or 'Röhm putsch'. This organized murder of the leaders of a major paramilitary force assured Hitler of the support of the supposedly honourable army. And with Hindenburg's death in August 1934, Hitler combined the offices of Reich president and chancellor, making himself the self-proclaimed supreme leader or 'Führer' of Germany. The army swore a personal oath of obedience to him and subsequently made this a touchstone of honour, whatever the criminality of Hitler's regime.

Yet even if it took Hitler a full eighteen months after his appointment as chancellor to secure the structures of power in this way, people's experiences in everyday life were changing rapidly from the outset, as measures were introduced to establish the Nazi Volksgemeinschaft. The progressive capitulation of elites who could potentially have stood up to Hitler made things very much more difficult for the vast majority of the population who were not in positions of power and influence. The destruction of independent institutions and democratic processes, and the concentration of control over the use of force, narrowed the options for ordinary people in the 'muddled middle'. These processes also made it increasingly difficult to separate private lives from public pressures for conformity.[10]

To understand the development of a bystander society, in which people remained passive in face of violence, we have to explore in more detail what was going on behind the façade of these by now familiar external events. Why did so many Germans 'fall into line' early on, and how did they justify this to themselves and others? Those who were being marginalized began to see how compatriots, by their very conformity—for whatever reasons, whether a result of external pressures or genuine enthusiasm— were in effect now sustaining the new regime. And changed behaviours began to have implications for social relations and emotional connections among Germans, newly separated by the 'racial' and political gulfs effected by Nazism, who variously jostled for a place in the sun or escape into the shadows, even as a vanishingly small minority still tried hopelessly to change the situation.

Joining in: Enthusiasm, expedience, and ambivalence

Many Germans, across and beyond the borders of the Reich, were enthusiasts for what seemed the dawn of a new and better era; others joined
in with an eye to the advantages to be gained from merging with the
crowds. Reasons for expressing support for Hitler fell into several patterns.
Notably, despite all the obvious motivations rooted in a sense of national
humiliation, social and economic distress, and desire for a strong saviour
figure—all the issues that have been highlighted in analyses of support for
Nazism—there were also probably just as many who in 1933 were following the herd, hedging their bets and trying to find a degree of cover or
even power by joining in.

The active support first. What was seen as a humiliating defeat in the
Great War, as well as social and economic distress in the Weimar years, was
clearly significant for many early enthusiasts. Ernst Hemicker's biography
exemplifies some of the ways in which the Weimar Republic played a significant role in the rise of support for Nazism.[11] Hemicker was born in the
small town of Kierspe in Westphalia in 1896 as the third of nine children.
The Great War, which started when he was eighteen, was a formative experience. In the course of his military service, he travelled across Europe: he
was stationed in France, Poland, and the Carpathians; he fought in Serbia,
Bulgaria, Galicia, and the Baltic provinces; and in 1916, in Latvia, he got to
know Riga—a place to which he would return, some twenty-five years
later, as a technical facilitator of mass murder.[12]

After the war, unwilling to accept the postwar settlement, Hemicker
joined a Free Corps unit defending the German borderlands. Then for
Hemicker as many others, things began to stabilize in the mid-1920s.
Following the death of his father in 1923, Hemicker took over the family
building firm, and in 1926 he got married; all seemed set for a secure
future. With the onset of the Depression in the late 1920s, however, the
family business ran into economic difficulties. Hemicker blamed this not
only on the economic downturn but also on loss of contracts from the
local authority, allegedly because of his nationalist political attitudes and
criticism of Weimar democracy. Nazism seemed to offer a better future;
and on 1 January 1931 Hemicker applied for membership of the NSDAP.

Within three weeks of Hitler's coming to power, he had also applied to join the SS.

Many others too saw Hitler and the Nazi movement as signalling the dawn of a new era when Germany might become great again. This was not only true for Nazi supporters within the Reich (while remembering that fewer than half the electorate voted for the NSDAP even in the March 1933 election) but also, crucially, among so-called ethnic Germans (*Volksdeutsche*) abroad. Germany's international standing, both within and beyond the borders of the Reich, was particularly important for Jürgen Ernst Kroeger, a Baltic German living on his family's estate in the hamlet of Wiexten (Vecumnieki), around fifty kilometres (thirty miles) southeast of Riga. Kroeger had bitter personal experiences of the consequences of war and revolution. His father had been murdered by Bolsheviks in 1919, and the rest of the family, following rescue by a German Free Corps unit, had to flee to safety with relatives in Mecklenburg. They returned to the newly founded state of Latvia in the early 1920s to continue to work the family farm, although in much reduced circumstances. At the time of Hitler's appointment in 1933, Kroeger had just married another ethnic German from Riga, Gerda, and the young couple, like millions of others, were swept up by the spirit of the times. They had suffered the consequences of war and revolution and were now excited by Hitler's vision of a strong, united Greater German Reich.[13]

Even those who had no direct experience of the war were influenced by its aftermath. Joseph Aust, not yet twenty years old in 1933, was a young Nazi by conviction—and was one of the few convinced Nazis who submitted an essay to the 1939 Harvard competition, outlining his experiences before and after 1933.[14] Aust had been born into a Catholic family of nine children in a small village in Lower Silesia. The railway workers' children with whom he went to school were poor and always hungry; and their fathers were generally communist or socialist, colloquially known as 'Sozies'. With the Depression, Nazis became increasingly active in the area, and at first, people were suspicious. But soon, Aust felt, the young Nazis had earned their respect. Having completed an apprenticeship, he moved to live with his uncle in Berlin. Here, Aust's fellow factory workers were all 'Sozies', but his uncle was a Nazi. Under his uncle's influence, Aust became critical of what he denigrated as 'Jewish' and 'nigger' erotic music—jazz, in other words—and Berlin theatre culture. He was at first shocked by the

violence on Berlin's streets in late 1932, with frequent fights between Nazis
and communists; but following the Nazi assumption of power at the end
of January 1933, Aust felt relieved that the streets seemed more peaceful.
He also noted that there was more and more talk of the 'fatherland', which
began to seem important to him too.[15]

The next few months went by in a whirl of new insights. It seemed
perfectly acceptable to Aust that, once communists had been dealt with,
Jews should be cleared out of leading positions in economy and society.
Yet he also noted that not everyone who had joined the Nazi bandwagon
was genuine in their enthusiasm. People who had previously wavered were
now leaning over backwards to demonstrate what committed Nazis they
were, denouncing others in order to cast themselves in a better light; and
even former communists were converting to Nazism. A woman of his acquaintance, Irene, told him that her brother, a former KPD functionary,
had disappeared without a trace, presumably into a concentration camp.
Far from concern about her brother's fate hardening her against the Nazi
movement, she too joined the bandwagon, mouthing Nazi sentiments. She
told him enthusiastically that, although the company for which she worked
still technically belonged to a Jew, a new 'Aryan' management had been
imposed. There were many, Aust reckoned, who were determined to cover
their former tracks by being overly enthusiastic Nazi party members, even
denouncing former comrades in order to curry favour in their new circles.[16] This awareness of a distinction between early enthusiasts and recent
converts was widespread.

Early enthusiasts were not the only ones to support Nazism in 1933.
Indeed, in October 1933 a new term was introduced, 'Alte Kämpfer', to distinguish those who had already joined the NSDAP in what they called the
'times of struggle' before 1933, and those who held particularly low membership numbers, having been among the first 300,000 to join up to 1930.
The 'Old Guard' were a particularly distinguished subgroup who had been
active from the earliest days The flood of new applications in the months
after Hitler's accession to power in January 1933 led to Nazi suspicions
about opportunists: a temporary ban on accepting any new party members
was imposed at the beginning of May 1933 (with a few exceptions, such as
for young people from the Hitler Youth, and members of the SA). People
who had joined in their masses in spring 1933 were often mocked as those
who had 'fallen in March' (Märzgefallene), playing on the term given to

casualties of the revolution in March 1848. The party only opened up to new applications again in 1937 and was once again closed in February 1942. By the time Nazism was defeated in May 1945, well over 10 million people had joined the party: 10 percent of the overall population, and around 15 percent of the electorate.[17]

If the statistical breakdown of party membership and overall figures are becoming increasingly clear, the motivations are more complex. Autobiographical accounts reveal some of the internal considerations and personal compromises that were entailed in the course of outward realignment with the now-triumphant hardcore Nazis. Sometimes this was, as indicated, a matter of real hope, imbued with a sense of working towards a new and brighter future; but very often it was more a matter of nervously shuffling for position, fearful of committing oneself too far in any direction, indecisive about whether or not to join the party. Remaining uncertain about which way the wind might shift in the future could readily cause mutual suspicion among colleagues even in otherwise quite genteel professional conditions, such as the literary, cultural, and librarianship circles in which Hermann Stresau moved.[18] Sometimes fear precipitated a decisive plunge into Nazism and a sudden reversal of political polarities. Gerta Pfeffer noted that in the factory where she worked, former socialists had become the most visibly committed Nazis. One new enthusiast had been just a 'bundle of nerves' since the Nazi takeover, and he was typical of many: 'When Hitler's speeches were played in the factory, the ones who were the most over-zealous in singing the Horst Wessel song'—the Nazi party anthem since 1930, officially declared a national symbol in May 1933—and who were most energetically 'raising their arms, calling out Heil', were, she noted, 'those who had previously belonged to a party on the left'.[19] One of Alfred Oppler's colleagues was a distressed former social democrat who, terrified of the implications for his family of his past political activities, felt impelled to join the Nazi party. Hating the idea, he had to gulp down three cognacs before he could bring himself to take this step. He urged Oppler to join too and was surprised to hear of Oppler's 'racial' background (of Jewish origin, although brought up a Christian) which had so recently taken on real significance. Oppler commented that this man was 'just one example of hundreds of thousands'.[20]

Former socialists and communists could sometimes find themselves on opposing sides in quite surprising ways. The distinguished communist

lawyer James Broh was thrown into a makeshift SA prison for having engaged his legal expertise on behalf of a political case. In the SA cellar, Broh
was told he was about to be killed—first that he would be shot, then that
he would be hanged. He was then beaten up by a boxer practising on hand-
cuffed bodies. Finally, though he was feverish and had been left to lie on the
floor, Broh noted that some SA men were themselves former communists;
one, apparently suffering pangs of conscience, even asked Broh if he now
thought badly of him. When Broh's coat kept sliding off as he tried to sleep,
another SA man kindly pulled it back over him as though concerned for
the elderly prisoner's wellbeing. When Broh was finally taken to the regular
police station, officials expressed outrage at the rough treatment by the SA.

There were clearly tensions between the old and the new forces of 'law
and order'. Broh, though Jewish, was still well connected and, following
interventions in high places by his wife, he was transferred to Spandau jail,
where many prison officials were still socialist by inclination and not fully
acclimatized to Nazism. Here he found himself in the company of political comrades. They tried to keep their spirits up through singing, playing
cards and chess, and sharing newspapers and food parcels. Broh was released
and left Germany for Czechoslovakia in April 1933. He eventually moved
to France where, shortly after the German invasion in 1940, his trail ends.[21]
Broh's story of finding former communists among his new oppressors is
typical of many. It was easier just to switch sides and surf with the Nazi tide.

The opportunistic side-switching and the violence of some older Nazi
adherents as well as of more recent enthusiasts is vividly evoked by Martin
Andermann, who had grown up in Königsberg and was now working as
a doctor in Berlin. After the March elections the SA went wild, breaking
into the hospital where he worked and, with the help of some nurses, seeking out easy prey among bed-ridden patients. These nurses now seemed
completely transformed: 'Their eyes were glazed over, their voices cracked,
they were beside themselves, sometimes one had the impression they
did not recognize you anymore.' One nurse cut all contacts with former
Jewish friends, without even taking the time to explain and disregarding
how deeply this hurt them. Many doctors, too, as Andermann wrote, 'now
openly revealed themselves as having long been Nazis, and no longer hesi-
tated to turn up in storm trooper uniforms'. He and others who did not
share Nazi views 'were all shaking with fear'. Soon the former cordial and
professional atmosphere had entirely disappeared. A few individuals tried

to compensate for a stigmatized identity. One colleague trying to join the NSDAP was 'unmasked' as a Jew; he was so ashamed of his ancestry that he had tried to disguise it by exaggerated commitment to Nazism. A committed social democrat soon turned up wearing a Nazi brown shirt, explaining to Andermann that he had converted in order to survive; he had been repeatedly harassed by Nazis and could not bear to risk the wellbeing of his wife and children.[22]

Former socialists of Edmund Heilpern's acquaintance similarly switched allegiances, with varying degrees of conviction or reservation. Even before 1933, some people had taken out what they saw as 'insurance policies' in case of a Nazi victory. Heilpern, a research chemist, knew paid-up socialists who also carried a 'green card' marking them as a Nazi 'sympathizer'. He was critical of their lack of 'civil courage' and 'lack of character'. And he could never be sure who among his acquaintances might betray his confidences, trying to confirm their political credentials in different directions. This growing atmosphere of mutual distrust was exacerbated once Hitler was in power. One former friend immediately became active in the SA. A colleague, Geo Wagner, with whom Heilpern was coauthoring a book, at first gave Heilpern financial assistance when his job became insecure; but subsequently, Wagner took Heilpern's first draft of the book and published it, without revisions, under his own name, refusing to answer Heilpern's letters and dropping all contact. Another friend, Paul, stayed on good terms despite becoming a minor Nazi functionary as NSKK-Führer (NSDAP motorized corps leader). Paul was an idealist who still sought to help Jews and socialists—and Heilpern was both—even after switching sides. But Paul was highly unusual. More typical of ambivalent friends whose personal sympathies conflicted with new political commitments was someone Heilpern names only as 'S.B.' This man intervened when Heilpern was arrested by the Gestapo and subjected to lengthy interrogations, and continued to send him work after he had been exiled in 1934. Yet despite persisting reservations about brutality and racism, S.B. became ever more committed to the Nazi cause. He claimed that Hitler was doing a good job for the economy, and that the 'Führer principle'—as he reported to Heilpern—was better than the 'endless speechifying' of democracies.[23]

There was inevitably some ambivalence on both sides when previously close social relationships were disentangled or severed. Andermann noted that even among Nazis radical antisemites were in a minority, and that

brownshirts were still perfectly willing to visit Jewish doctors.[24] Many patients reassured Andermann that they had nothing against him personally,
or his family, which had lived in Germany for generations, but only against
the *Ostjuden*. He reported that people made comments to the effect that
it was 'terrible that those who are innocent now also have to suffer for the
crimes of others'. They felt that 'something had to be done about the Jews',
but what the Nazis were doing was too 'radical'. Some even 'consciously
took the side of the Jews, or rather were explicitly opposed to Nazism', but
were aware that they 'had to be careful, in order not to put themselves in
danger'.[25]

'Beef-steak Nazis': Uneasy compromises and cautious conformity

Some Germans after Hitler's seizure of power felt demoralized by having
to engage in compromises. One aristocratic friend told Andermann that
his family and others expected him to join the SS; professionally, he was
hoping to become a teacher, and this too required engaging in endless pretence. In his view, Jews were the only people who could remain morally
uncompromised, since they did not have to engage in constant lying. He
was, Andermann recalled, 'resigned and dead tired'; eventually, the Third
Reich led him to collapse with a nervous breakdown.[26]

Even if millions were now jumping on the Nazi bandwagon, a minority
were still unwilling to compromise. This was much easier for those in secure
circumstances who had little to fear at a personal level. Bruno Gebhard, a
committed social democrat, had been seconded from the Dresden Hygiene
Museum to work as research director for the Exhibition and Trade Fair
Office of the city of Berlin. While his colleagues seemed to be falling over
themselves to join the NSDAP, Gebhard stood out by refusing. Even so,
he recognized that those who were switching to support Nazism, whatever their previous allegiances, were just trying to do the best for themselves and their families. The party badge was colloquially referred to as the
'*Rettungsring*' ('life-buoy'), invaluable in these troubled waters. Yet Gebhard
too had to engage in small compromises, tailoring his exhibitions to Nazi
ideals, and behaving in ways that might be at odds with his convictions. On
18 March 1933, for example, he had the dubious honour of having to show

Reich Propaganda Minister Joseph Goebbels around a new exhibition on
'Women' (*Die Frau*) and, while uncomfortable, did his best to maintain a
suitably conformist public face. On this occasion he was also friendly towards the Hitler Youth leader Baldur von Schirach, whom he had known
from his schooldays; von Schirach's brother Karl had been one of Gebhard's
schoolmates, who at the age of nineteen had committed suicide in despair
at German defeat in the First World War.[27]

Cautious conformists, as we might call them, bowing to social and professional pressures, often tried to justify their compromises in light of other
shared values. Georg Abraham was a well-connected Jewish wholesale
agent, born in 1905, who had worked his way up through a series of jobs
and as a travelling salesman for a large tobacco goods company, until he was
able to set up his own business in Neustettin (now Szczecinek, Poland).
Friends who had joined the NSDAP told him that by doing so they were
able to secure the workplaces for their employees. They remained friendly,
despite simultaneously behaving in ways that furthered the policies of the
regime. But in the company where Abraham still worked in 1933, which
had a Jewish director, 'Aryan' employees involved in Nazi activities wanted
to have nothing more to do with their Jewish colleagues and boss. Before
Hitler's appointment, none of these workers had wanted to join the NSDAP,
and Abraham had got along well with them; but now, they felt under pressure. They worried about losing their jobs; and the more they were exposed
to Nazi propaganda and activities, the more they shifted their allegiances.
Moreover, the company's future was uncertain. Because the director was
Jewish, supplies were cut by 20 percent compared to 'Aryan' companies, affecting the company's capacity to manufacture wares—including specialist
tobacco products and especially cigars—and satisfy customers, who were
being urged to cease dealing with a Jewish company anyway. Yet many partners continued to trade, asserting that they knew best where to order the
goods they needed for their own businesses.[28] People jostled to work out
the best strategies and compromises while protecting and pursuing their
own interests.

Those in in academic circles also hedged their bets. The philosopher Karl
Löwith, at that time a junior academic at Marburg University, summarized
what he saw as the pusillanimity of his colleagues: 'The general mood was
to wait and see how things would develop, and to avoid any personal exposure. . . . Coordination, therefore, came about of its own accord'. Some

sought to gain advantages by visible support of the new order: 'No less lam-
entable was the general currying favour with the political "world-view".'[29]
Generally, by 1933, across schools and universities the ground had already
been well prepared by antisemitic and right-wing circles during the preceding years.[30]

Wider changes were soon evident in the ways in which people looked,
talked, and related to each other. As an actor, journalist, and dramaturg,
Fritz Goldberg travelled to theatre productions across Germany. In the early
days of the Nazi regime, he felt, one needed only to glance at a person's
newspaper or appearance to know their politics, without even listening to
what they were saying. 'A staid-looking worker, no longer quite so young,
passably dressed, with a moustache and a slightly careworn expression—
that was the social-democratic type.' By contrast, 'a bourgeois person of
slightly arrogant appearance, with his hair cut short and with a parting in
Prussian fashion, with an embittered look and lips pressed tightly together,
always angry and aggressive—that's what the National Socialist looked like;
at least in those days'. But with growing conformity from 1933, public faces
changed. As Goldberg commented, 'later, they all wore the same uniform
and the distinctive characteristics disappeared'.[31] Society had become 'coordinated'—*gleichgeschaltet*. And this happened not only in terms of political
repression and institutional co-ordination but also at the level of interpersonal relations.

Victor Paschkis, a Viennese Christian of Jewish descent who lived in
Berlin, vividly recalled the delights of Sunday outings before 1933; around
half the city's population, it seemed to him, went hiking and swimming in
the surrounding woods and lakes, and overcrowded trains in the evening
were crammed full of people chatting as they returned home. Paschkis
had already noted changes in atmosphere with the worsening economic
situation and rising political violence on the streets before 1933. In the
Depression, people 'gradually avoided public utterances of their opinion'
and the character of conversations changed. 'Intolerance grew, and increasingly it became a habit of "discussion" to knock down your adversary, if you
could do so, and were sure of success.'[32] But after Hitler came to power, 'the
gaiety in the trains, and the nearly universal chatting was dropped: people
mostly spoke only at low voice, mistrusting the neighbor'.[33]

Things also became more difficult for Paschkis himself in his work as a
consulting engineer. Making exploratory trips that summer to investigate

possible new job opportunities in Italy or Switzerland, he observed a dramatic difference in the behaviour of Germans once abroad. He was struck that the moment the train had crossed the border, 'people in the trains started to talk and criticize Germany immediately'; and they 'bought liberal papers and papers of the emigrant press and made no attempt to hide it'. But on returning towards the Reich, 'Germans and other nationals became more and more silent'. People 'carefully hid the name of the paper or the book'. And if there happened to be a liberal or anti-Nazi paper lying around in the compartment, people were 'anxious to throw it out of the window, because it was not deemed advisable to be found with such a paper by the German officers' even if it had not belonged to them. The desire to get 'rid of it showed the general fear of the police officers'.[34]

In spring 1933, Hermann Stresau lost his job in Berlin's Spandau library because one of his superiors accused him of having uttered some anti-Hitler comments. Stresau, who unsuccessfully sought to get reinstated, and despite not being Jewish was unable to find other secure employment, managed to eke out a precarious existence as a writer and translator, as well as, at first, occasional adult education teaching stints. On 10 June 1933, Stresau noted in his diary what a pleasure it was occasionally to be able to relax in the company of like-minded people, 'while outside a plague poisoning people's souls and characters was driving people into the ground'. It was 'a rare feeling today' not to have to 'regard your neighbour with suspicion'.[35]

Those who were critical were not sure how long the new regime would last and what was the best course of action: outward shows of apparent enthusiasm, or passive silence. In her essay penned for the Harvard competition, the teacher and dentist's wife Lotte Popper recalled an early conversation over dinner with non-Jewish friends in Hamburg. They told her that their children's classmates were eager members of the Hitler Youth, but they thought this enthusiasm would soon pass. Besides, they thought, the government was unlikely to put its programme into practice. One reassured Popper: 'It would in any case be impossible here. People in the highest places, officers and officials, are all related to Jews in some way.'[36] But Popper also noticed that most of her husband's working-class dental patients were less willing to chatter as they used to, back and forth in local dialect, but rather looked around anxiously before whispering their news. She described how one or another patient would recount how he had suffered a house search; thank God, he would say, 'nothing had been found', but 'his neighbour, in possession of old social democratic newspapers, had been arrested and taken away'. The fathers, brothers, and friends of her husband's patients seemed all to be among the first victims of the regime. Few wanted to become what they called 'Beef-steak Nazis'—'red inside, brown on the outside'—which seemed to be the only way of surviving the crackdown on left-wingers.[37]

Even Germans of Jewish descent thought cautious conformity might be a viable option. Others discussed emigration very early on, as Popper noted.[38] A few acted immediately, while others at this stage thought they should just keep their heads down and wait it out. Hans Haller-Munk's partner in his legal firm was Jewish; he left for Amsterdam the day after Hitler became chancellor. But Haller-Munk, a converted Christian with an 'Aryan' wife, felt more secure. He now took sole control of the firm. His clients trusted him and were unaware of his Jewish family background. Just to be on the safe side, as he thought, Haller-Munk wrote to his parents requesting copies of their baptism certificates. He was furious to discover that only his father had converted when they had their sons baptized as children. Mortified and filled with anxiety about her son, his mother wrote back: 'It's all my fault, if you have any difficulties just because of me, I am just a stupid old woman and could not tear myself away from the faith of my childhood. I beg you to forgive me, I will gladly do everything I can to cover this up.'[39] She hastened to a pastor who knew her well, and sought to get baptized quickly. Her son waited impatiently for the proof of baptism to arrive and continued to keep his clients in the dark about his background.

But cautious conformity—while it worked for millions of other Germans—was not, in the longer term, a viable option for anyone of 'non-Aryan' background, whatever their own sense of identity or religious beliefs.

Fight or flight

A vanishingly small minority engaged in active resistance. As noted, in the course of the political crackdowns of 1933 around 200,000 people were imprisoned for their oppositional activities. Viewed from one perspective, this is a truly significant figure of courageous individuals who had been sufficiently active to land up under arrest; viewed from another angle, the numbers amounted to less than one-third of 1 percent of the total population of around 67 million. But the numbers arrested do not tell the whole story and are arguably merely the tip of a far larger iceberg of clandestine opposition, which slowly morphed into resigned but largely passive disapproval of the regime. The essays for the Harvard competition by two young socialists, Erica Stein and Lore Taut, illustrate some of the challenges facing those opposing Nazism at the grass roots.

Stein was born on 4 February 1914 to a nonreligious family living in a typical tenement block—a '*Mietskaserne*', with the pejorative implication of 'rental barracks'—in northern Berlin.[40] These dwellings, with their sunless back courtyards where latchkey children played among the rubbish bins, housed the growing multitudes of workers who had come to the metropolis during rapid industrialization around the turn of the century. Stein grew up in a working-class neighbourhood dominated by communists and social democrats, where, as she recalled, faces were pinched by poverty and political disagreements were fought out on the streets.

Stein's childhood was hard. Her father was away in the First World War when she was a baby; she first remembered meeting him when he came home on leave towards the end of the war, and she did not like this unwelcome intruder in the cramped apartment where she lived with her mother, her grandmother, and her baby brother. Moreover, after the war, Stein's father, like many other demobilized soldiers, found reintegration into civilian life challenging. In the early 1920s, he became a heavy drinker and had difficulty holding down any job. Stein's mother worked hard to support the family on a pittance. As a child, Stein suffered severe malnutrition, resulting in rickets and spinal deformity. But she was bright and won a scholarship to the Aufbauschule Friedrichshain, a good high school.

Stein's was, so far, a fairly typical working-class childhood in northern Berlin. There was, however, an added twist: Stein's father came from what she described as a 'fully assimilated Jewish family in Silesia', and her parents had apparently married against their families' wishes. But Stein's life was shaped more by class and political convictions than by her Jewish family background. Her impoverished childhood was very different from that of the wealthier Jewish children living in the Berlin districts of Tiergarten, Schöneberg, and Wilmersdorf, or in the leafy southwestern suburbs of Dahlem, Zehlendorf, the Grunewald, all the way out to the lakeside villas of the Wannsee. No grand pianos or violin lessons in Erica Stein's home; no

Sabbath observance or aspirations to a professional future. Class and politics mattered far more to Stein than being of Jewish descent.

Stein developed an interest in writing and journalism, and in 1929, at the age of fifteen, wrote an article for a Berlin newspaper. She did not have the penny needed for the stamp to send it in, and her mother would not give her the money; but she finally managed to acquire a stamp and mail the article. Remarkably, it was published in the *Berliner Tageblatt* and, extraordinarily, Erica received the then-magnificent sum of 50 marks for it. For three years she became a regular contributor to newspapers and magazines. But her headteacher disapproved, and eventually she had to leave this school. She transferred to the Karl-Marx-School in the working-class Neukölln district of Berlin. Headed by Fritz Karsen, the school was renowned in the Weimar Republic for its progressive pedagogy, its commitment to comprehensive education—as the first genuinely integrated school complex in Germany—and to continuing education to give working people opportunities generally barred to them in an educational system highly divided on class lines. Here, Stein became ever more involved with socialists. But in the surrounding neighbourhood there were frequent fights, and Nazis often lay in wait to beat up older students as they left school.

By the time Hitler came to power, Erica Stein was already well known locally for her anti-Nazi articles.[41] One day, hearing that trouble was brewing at the school gates, the headmaster called in police officers for additional protection—but far from providing the support requested, these policemen actually intervened to help the Nazi thugs who were beating up left-wing students as they left school. This shift in the position of those tasked to uphold law and order marked, of course, the key change for all subjected to Nazi rule.

This also proved to be Stein's own last day at school. A friend intercepted her on her way home and warned her that the SA was watching her house. Rather than going directly home, Stein sought shelter with friends; meanwhile, her mother and brother were arrested and held hostage. Clearly more terrified than she would later admit, Stein somehow made the lengthy journey across Germany and escaped to England via Holland, arriving 'as one of the first refugees in 1933', as she put it. Her mother and brother were released after a few weeks.

Despite being abroad and on her own, Stein did not give up her fight against the Nazis. In the late 1930s, she worked for the 'Germany Emergency

Committee' of the Society of Friends (Quakers) in Bloomsbury. By 1940, she had obtained a scholarship to study journalism at Kings College London and subsequently became a journalist for British newspapers, including the *News Chronicle* and the *Evening Standard*. Stein was determined to work in any way she could, even from abroad, against the Nazi government. As she noted in her 1940 essay, England 'is a difficult country to settle in' despite 'the generosity and hospitality of a great part of its population'.[42]

Lore Taut's entry into politics took a different route, coming as she did from a bourgeois family background. She was born in 1909, in a town she does not name, of around 350,000 inhabitants.[43] Taut's father, a highly regarded surgeon of Jewish descent, was sympathetic to social democratic views; her mother was a Protestant from a well-to-do family with a more conservative outlook. Neither parent was religious, and, growing up, Taut was aware of neither religion nor 'race' as an issue. At school, Taut was excused from Christian religious education, along with classmates categorized as *freireligiös*—those not belonging to any church. They enjoyed the free time together; the reasons why they could skip lessons in Christianity were of little significance. Things became more difficult for Taut after Hitler came to power, by which time she was a politically active and newly married young adult. With the Nazi crackdown in early 1933, the left-wing circles in which she and her husband moved were tearing themselves apart over the best way forwards. Even in the highly constrained conditions of the March 1933 elections, the two left-wing parties had between them garnered nearly one-third of the vote, with just under one in five Germans voting for the SPD (18.25 percent) and more than one-tenth casting their vote for the KPD (12.32 percent); but the two parties would not work together. None of Taut's social democratic comrades believed the Nazi line that communists were responsible for the burning of the Reichstag; but only around one-third of the local social democrats were willing to make common cause, while most social democrats of her acquaintance did not fully trust communists. Many on the left were however also critical of the leadership of the SPD, which was at that time still legal, unlike the KPD; by contrast, they wanted immediate action. Lore Taut and her husband, Richard, decided to go with the social democrats prepared to work with communists. They learned valuable tactics from communist friends, who tended to be far more vigilant and suspicious.

It was not long before many comrades were in trouble. In the 'red settlement' where they lived there was a wave of arrests, and many were advised to flee. Richard was among those told to get out quickly and to continue political work from abroad, which he did. Now on her own, Taut threw herself into undercover political activities. In the run-up to the March 1933 elections, her group printed illegal flyers on a copier machine secreted in one of the houses and spread these around a wide area. They painted equally illegal election slogans at night, including on the newspaper display cabinets for Julius Streicher's *Der Stürmer*. Two people kept a lookout, while the two daubing the slogans were always a male and a female: if alerted that someone was approaching, they would hastily wrap themselves together in amorous embrace, concealing the relevant part of the glass case. On one occasion, Taut got spots of white paint on an expensive coat that had been a present from her husband, but it all seemed adventurous and worthwhile at the time. By 1939, she thought it laughable that they had really believed this frenetic activity could make any difference whatsoever.

It was not only in the red settlement where Taut lived but also in the law office where she worked that the consequences of Hitler's rule rapidly became clear. One of the Jewish directors had already fled; other colleagues were engaged in destroying, burning, or hiding files that could potentially endanger their clients, many of whom were socialists, Jewish, or both. Nine SA members raided her office, and she tried to keep outwardly calm as they searched the files. They asked where her husband was. Taut lied and said that they had separated; she had no idea of his whereabouts. They asked who her father was. When she gave his name, one said: 'What, Dr Simon, that old quack is your father? We'll go do a thorough clean-out of his abortion clinic.' And another added: 'So, you're Jewish. Well then it makes sense that you're shacked up with these Jewish dogs here.' Taut countered politely: 'Excuse me, but my mother is a Protestant.' The retort: 'Bastard, even worse.'[44]

Taut knew that she probably should warn her father of an impending raid. But she had not told her parents of Richard's flight and did not want to unsettle them, particularly since her mother was ill with kidney trouble. Moreover, workplace difficulties continued. On 4 March 1933, the two remaining Jewish directors decided to quit. One commented, with weary resignation: 'It's all senseless now. After all, this state no longer operates under the rule of law. No laws any more. Everything is pointless.'[45] They handed over the firm to a colleague, a blond and blue-eyed lawyer named Bremer, whom they trusted.

Bremer, however, now revealed himself to be a member of the NSDAP. He immediately sacked many colleagues and installed another Nazi in a prominent position. Taut felt cowardly in not resigning in protest, but she needed the income to support not only herself but also Richard, now living underground in Paris. It was hard enough to find ways of sending him money hidden in objects while living primarily on her garden produce. As a 'half-Jew', she had little chance of gaining employment in an 'Aryan' legal practice, and other prospects seemed equally dim. So for the time being, she stayed put. Taut was subsequently incensed to discover that Bremer had not joined the NSDAP opportunistically in 1933, like so many others, but had secretly been a member for many years. He was an 'old fighter' (*Alte Kämpfer*) who had in the early 1920s fought in illegal right-wing paramilitary forces commanded by the 'black army' (*Schwarzer Reichswehr*), and had masqueraded as a leftist to fit in with this Jewish legal practice, and to spy on its activities. Colleagues' attempts to destroy incriminating evidence had been of little use.

It was not only at work that Taut faced a Nazi intrusion: she was soon subjected to a house search. Asked again about Richard, she gave a by-now carefully rehearsed answer: following marital difficulties, they had separated; if she knew where he lived, she would have served him with divorce papers; but she had lost all trace.

This story served well enough for the moment. One of the investigating officers showed her some sympathy and then, when the others were not looking, as she remembered, winked and shrugged his shoulders, intimating understanding. Taut ensured that while the others rifled through the house it was only that investigating officer who might come across the one genuinely incriminating piece of paper—an address list of people in their political network. The house was searched for four and a half hours, after which the group left. Taut was not sure whether the sympathetic officer had in fact found the address list, or indeed, if he had, whether he had actually realized its significance and simply replaced it quietly in its hiding place. Ten days later, there was another house search, this time for weapons. Again Taut and her neighbours managed to get through it relatively unscathed.

Constrained passivity: Intimidation and discrimination

On 1 April 1933, the surgery run by Taut's father was subjected to a 'thorough search'—an exercise in destruction and intimidation. Half of Dr Simon's medical instruments were smashed, while 'Aryan' patients were prevented from attending his clinic. An 'Aryan' assistant was banned from working with him, nurses were sworn at for taking 'Jewish money', and Taut's father was forbidden to treat his largest group of patients, workers in the local metal industry. Dr Simon professed his German patriotism and showed his Iron Cross from the First World War, to no avail. The premises were left in disarray, the practice half destroyed. Taut's parents were totally shattered.

Taut's father was not alone in this experience. Nazi-organized attacks on Jewish premises and boycott of Jewish stores took place all across Germany on 1 April 1933. The reactions of witnesses to this national boycott action provide intimations of the first stages of the spectrum leading towards a bystander society. People were beginning to explore the limits of what was possible and in their own interests without too much personal risk. Among the muddled middle, 1 April marks the start of widespread retreat in the face of intimidation, right across Germany.

Willy Bornstein, as we have seen, had already fought Julius Streicher in Nuremberg, before moving to Munich to start afresh. Here, he had set up his daughter—a 'half-Jew', the product of a 'mixed marriage', like Taut—with her own confectionery shop near Munich's central station. On the day of the April boycott, this store was surrounded by youths bearing armbands and weapons, seeking to prevent customers from entering. But people took little notice and simply pushed past them, intent on making their purchases. All around Munich, Willy noted, people tried to disregard the Nazi boycott—until intimidation was augmented by public humiliation. At first, when the word 'Jew'—*Jude*—was daubed on shop windows or office nameplates, people continued with their business. But once they were photographed and their names published with prominent captions accusing them of consorting with Jews, and once gangs of teenagers jeered and taunted them when approaching Jewish shops and businesses, people had second thoughts. It was simplest just to stay well clear.[46]

In Berlin, the 'Aryan' journalist and playwright Ernst Schwartzert, then in his late twenties, was struck by the 'withdrawn, sickened faces of passers-by'. He noted that there was an 'invisible wall dividing the rampaging hordes of young people and the perplexed bourgeoisie'. The police, meanwhile, 'dumbly' ignored it all. Schwartzert wrote in his essay that he 'waited in vain for any German who would have the courage to express his disapproval, loud and clear'.[47]

In Frankfurt, Erna Albersheim, a widowed businesswoman with a Jewish mother and Christian father, commented on how people there were similarly frightened into passivity. Jewish merchants had been called to attend a meeting where they were taken by surprise: 'Suddenly they were surrounded by storm troopers' who forced them to march along Frankfurt's central business street, 'with arms uplifted, bayonets pointed at them'. This had dramatic effects on onlookers. 'The crowd stared horrified', wrote Albersheim in her essay. 'Some exclaimed aloud. These were immediately arrested and forced to march with the Jews.'[48]

In Neustettin, a small town in northeastern Germany, the company for which Georg Abraham worked was subjected to the boycott, with SA men posted at the doors. The reason officially given was that this was 'retaliation'—a typical Nazi ploy, blaming the victim for the aggression—for the alleged 'fact' that the Jews of America were boycotting German wares. Abraham's elderly boss was forced to send a telegram to the United States (he does not clarify to whom this was addressed), asking that American Jews should desist. Eventually help for the company came from unlikely quarters: the town's Nazi mayor produced an affidavit, suitably adorned with a swastika. 'This firm, which was established in 1812, is not to be boycotted', it read, 'since it employs a large number of German workers and is economically valuable to the town'. This affidavit continued to make an impression on otherwise doubting customers after the boycott had officially been called off.[49]

If people tended to remain uninvolved in public, they often continued to support or express sympathy with victims in private—another response that would become magnified later on. Lotte Popper noted that many of her husband's 'Aryan' patients continued to come to his dental practice. A Jewish doctor of their acquaintance whose practice covered a more affluent area was overwhelmed by bouquets of flowers; the Poppers too received flowers, but were more touched by the continued loyalty of patients who

were too poor to afford material signs of sympathy. Those who had joined
the SA took care not to wear their uniforms, while NSDAP members removed their party badges before entering.[50]

Despite the intimidating effect of the April boycott, the Nazi leadership
saw that it was not popular and called it off. In early April 1933, lessons
were learned on both sides. Anyone who openly intervened on the side of
the victims might also be victimized: bystanders betraying sympathy for the
persecuted might be forced to join those on whose behalf they had raised
their voices. The position of a supposedly neutral bystander was ceasing to
be an option.

And persecution continued. On 5 April, armed police arrived at Willy
Bornstein's door. They stayed until well past midnight, turning everything
inside out. As he wrote in his essay, 'no piece of paper remained unread,
[they looked] in the oven, under the beds, behind the pictures, nothing was
left undisturbed, no cupboard, no chest, no pot went untouched, and to
begin with all very roughly'. When they came across Bornstein's war medals as well as those of his father, they became a little more respectful—and
by this time anyway they had decided there was really nothing to find. On
leaving, they even commented sympathetically that 'decent' individuals had
to pay for those who were not.

The building's housekeeper later told Bornstein that the police had said
that he had been 'denounced'—but he never discovered who might have
denounced him and for what. It was increasingly clear that Jews did not
need to be 'denounced' for anything in particular; simply being Jewish was
enough. Over the following nights, Bornstein was unable to sleep. Yet he
felt he could not talk to his Christian wife and their 'mixed-race' children.
All of them were silently afraid that he would simply be taken away, but
they had no idea how to deal with the situation.[51]

Intimidation was soon followed by legalized discrimination. On 7 April
1933 the 'Law for the Restoration of a Professional Civil Service' was introduced. Under this legislation, anyone with 'non-Aryan' ancestry—even a
single Jewish grandparent—was excluded from state employment. So too
were communists and others considered politically unreliable. The scope
of the 'Aryan paragraph' was extended in the 25 April 'Law against the
Overcrowding of German Schools and Universities', which restricted the
percentages of 'non-Aryans' attending schools, colleges, and universities. On
30 June 1933, the category was expanded to include 'Aryans' married to a

'non-Aryan'. People with lengthy records of professional service, veterans of the First World War, or people whose fathers had fought at the front, were exempted as a concession to the elderly but clearly failing President Hindenburg. Hitler had however no intention of allowing such exceptions to persist; as he cynically remarked, Hindenburg would not last long, and there would be plenty of time to amend the law later. In the meantime, however, some 'non-Aryan' Germans could still demonstrate their patriotism through their record of military service to the fatherland.

The first day of May was a traditional day for the celebration of labour. In 1933, Hitler turned this into a Nazi 'National Labour Day' with compulsory demonstrations orchestrated by the regime. Across Germany there were rallies, parades, and speeches, with much cheering, waving of swastikas, and raising arms in the Nazi salute. This official adulation of labour was merely a cynical ploy. The following day, in a preplanned raid, members of the SA, the SS, and the National Socialist Factory Cell Organization (NSBO) stormed trade union offices across the country, arresting union leaders and seizing assets. With unions now under Nazi control, there were new restrictions on workers' rights, and on 10 May 1933 the official Nazi German Labour Front (DAF) was established under the directorship of Robert Ley (a long-standing and committed Nazi, also noted for drinking and womanizing, who eventually committed suicide in his cell during the Nuremberg International Military Tribunal after the war).

Not everyone joined in the May Day celebrations. Bruno Gebhard and his family lived near the Tempelhof Field in Berlin where the big official event was held. They had no desire even to be silent witnesses to this adulatory festival. Gebhard took a short holiday from his science museum job, going with his wife to the somewhat remote Frisian island of Sylt in the North Sea.[52] Hermann Stresau's view was that outward appearances disguised inner realities: 'Germans are not really a people given to enthusiasm.' Even from his village quite a way outside Berlin, he could see the display of fireworks at the organized festivities in Berlin's Tempelhof field. But the ceremonies in his village were far quieter.[53]

Despite growing intimidation, a handful continued to prioritize active political resistance over passivity. Attending the May Day parade in order to subvert it, Taut and her comrades organized a chant of 'Down with the Nazi demagogues!' then melted into the crowd. During this event Taut met an old acquaintance, the wife of a teacher who had been fired because of his social democratic politics. Coincidentally, during a house search this acquaintance had met the same policemen who had apparently overlooked the incriminating address list in Taut's home. This policeman had also helped the schoolteacher's wife to hide anti-Nazi newspapers behind the cellar door while his colleagues were searching the premises, and had whispered to her, 'look, you have to burn that sort of thing nowadays'.[54] Taut later often thought of this kindly policeman, who tried to remain true to the former principles of the police force, and whose surreptitious assistance probably saved some of her comrades.

In the late spring and early summer of 1933, Taut registered a change in tactics: anti-Nazi political work was being carried out ever more carefully, and the main objective was to influence opinion and keep channels of non-Nazi communication open. Taut's group was involved in printing and distributing an illegal KPD-dominated newspaper, the *Red Spark* (*Rote Funken*). Intended as an antidote to the Nazi-controlled press, it included translations from English, French, Dutch, and Swiss newspapers, giving readers an outside view on Nazi Germany. Group members were only to know personally two or three others in the network. Even living conditions in the left-wing colony were becoming increasingly difficult, as a Nazi residential management took over, and many were given notice to quit their homes.

On 10 May 1933, in the Opera Square opposite the university in central Berlin, and in thirty-four university towns across the Reich, students gathered with members of the SA and SS, watched by curious and often cheering crowds, as they symbolically burned what they held to be representatives of an 'un-German spirit'. Books thrown into the bonfires included not only works by German-Jewish writers and scholars, from Heinrich Heine and Karl Marx to Sigmund Freud, but also by non-Jewish Germans supposedly embodying an 'un-German spirit', such as Heinrich Mann and Erich Maria Remarque, author of the antiwar novel *All Quiet on the Western Front*. In Berlin, the children's author Erich Kästner, noted for *Emil and the Detectives*, watched from the crowd as his own books went up in flames, alongside works by authors ranging from Ernest Hemingway and Jack London to the more predictably included Stefan Zweig. The pyre was augmented by a substantial truckload of books taken from the library of Magnus Hirschfeld's Institute of Sexology, which had been raided and closed down four days earlier, marking the Nazi attack on homosexuality and the rights of gay and transgender people. More generally, the book burning dramatically symbolized not only the rejection of the 'Jewish spirit' but also the Nazi transformation of what it meant to be 'German'. Racialized identities would henceforth override evidence of German patriotism, including military service for the fatherland.

As the Berlin journalist and actor Fritz Goldberg noted in his essay, people were still making a distinction between individuals whom they knew personally and a more general notion of 'the Jew' as a legitimate target for hostility. Goldberg had been shocked by the violence of spring 1933, wondering if these could really be the same people among whom he had grown up, whose language he spoke, whose culture he loved, who had been his friends since his youth, and for (and with) whom he had gone to war. Some apparently committed antisemites now waving swastika flags still expressed sympathy with him personally. A group of former students from when he had taught at an institute of further education even sent a delegate with a collective letter of support. While this boosted his morale, it did little to save his current job; he was soon squeezed out of his profession. And he noticed, too, how policemen on whose authority he had formerly been able to rely, upholding traditional conceptions of law and order, no longer patrolled the streets alone: every policeman seemed to have a member of the SA at his side, and they patrolled in pairs to ensure the police kept in line with Nazi conceptions of legitimate violence.[55]

Attacks on politically active individuals went on through the summer of 1933. Knowing the risks he faced, Edmund Heilpern disposed of incriminating political literature accumulated over years of activism. He burned so much that, one warm day, a neighbour alarmed by the unexpected smoke came over to warn him that something must have caught fire. He nearly clogged the toilet by sustained attempts over twenty-four hours to flush away torn-up sheets. Despite his frantic efforts, however, Heilpern had not yet destroyed all the debris when he was subjected to a house search and was, accordingly, arrested as an 'enemy of the state'. In his essay he reflected that he was 'thankful' for this arrest, which led to his emigration first back to his native Vienna and, in 1938, to the United States (he settled in Topeka, Kansas): 'Had I stayed longer in Germany, I would probably today have been in the Jewish reservation in Lublin.' As far as away as Topeka, and at this relatively early date in the war, Heilpern was aware of what he explicitly termed a 'Jewish reservation in Lublin' and knew that this was not a place anyone would wish to be.

At the time of his arrest, however, Heilpern was lucky enough to en-counter sympathetic German policemen. Held for a few days at the Gestapo headquarters in Berlin's Alexanderplatz, Heilpern noted that the young SA men dealing with him seemed unsure of what they were doing and almost surprised to find themselves in positions of power. Bantering with one of them, Heilpern found ways of mitigating some of the discomforts of im-prisonment. Meanwhile, a more senior Gestapo officer treated him with respect and seemed to enjoy their exchanges, commenting, 'Well, at one time we were all old soldiers at the front together, after all'.

Following Heilpern's early release through the intervention of the Austrian consulate, the same senior Gestapo official was assigned to keep an eye on him, and they soon developed a friendship of sorts. The offi-cial revealed that a neighbour had brought Heilpern's political activities to the Gestapo's attention; this neighbour had long been a secret Nazi and had been observing him for some time. The well-disposed Gestapo offi-cial wrote up good reports on Heilpern and gave him advance warnings of further house searches so that he could tidy up and stay well clear. In the course of their conversations, the Gestapo official expressed his out-rage about 'the boundless capriciousness of the Nazis, the thrashing and torturing of prisoners'. Heilpern was initially concerned that he might be setting a trap, and was wary of believing criticisms of Nazi violence voiced by someone holding a senior position in the Gestapo. But over the course of eighteen months of regular encounters, Heilpern came to the view that the officer was simply, as he put it, 'an official of the old school, a servant of the law' and that this Nazi 'lawlessness was totally against his nature'. Then, suddenly, this official was no longer there; his replacement told Heilpern that he had been 'removed'. Heilpern could only hope that nothing too bad had befallen his unlikely Gestapo friend; he never found out.[56]

Even as late as 1938, as we shall see, there were still occasional instances when people in official positions would turn a blind eye or show sympathy to persecuted individuals. They were in a tiny minority. It had been clear from 1933 onwards that the supposed authorities and upholders of law and order were there purely for the purposes of furthering Nazi rule.

By the summer of 1933, Hitler's regime was becoming ever more en-trenched, backed up by both a monopoly of violence and celebratory dis-plays of populist nationalism. Society was divided, and the 'seizure of power' still far from complete; elites were still in a position to have made a stand, and it took until the summer of 1934 for Hitler to feel his position was more secure; but as far as the wider population was concerned, the balance was clearly tipping. Nazi enthusiasts were delighted by what they saw as a justified crackdown on communists and other 'enemies of the people', and a belligerent determination to return to national greatness; opponents, victims, and waverers had no idea how long the Nazi regime would last, or what might be the best step to take next. For most, conformity or retreat seemed safer options than resistance.

In May 1933 the NSDAP temporarily closed new applications for membership, overwhelmed by the tidal wave of recent converts. Among the growing ranks of supporters were genuine enthusiasts, careerists, and opportunists, as well as those who joined out of fright or determination to prove new credentials. Some hoped to evade notice by merging into the new society; others resisted, in whatever ways still seemed possible; and a few got out. For, those who did not have the resources to leave, or prioritized family, friends, jobs, and homes in Germany, the best strategy seemed to keep a low profile. People in the muddled middle learned how to perform Nazism in everyday life and gradually became accustomed to it, seeing also the potential benefits of conformity. As others fell into line, it became less and less easy to risk standing out.

In a snowball effect, increasing numbers behaved according to the new norms in public, whatever they may have privately thought. For some, Nazi norms also invaded private lives, as individuals strove to transform themselves in light of what they thought the Third Reich demanded of them, and what they felt they should try to become.[57] Strategies varied and frameworks shifted, as people made compromises between previous aspirations, personal preferences, and potential future prospects, and then tried to justify their choices.

The outward conformity of the muddled middle—those who were neither enthusiastic supporters nor immediate targets of the regime—ultimately served to further the Nazi project. This became evident in a growing racialization of identity in everyday life, well before the Nuremberg Laws of 1935. But the option of behaving in accordance with Nazi norms was not open to everyone. For those defined as 'non-Aryan', it was impossible. And for those on the borders, situated at the social seam where ties of love and family spread in both directions, it required constant vigilance and negotiation.

3

Ripping Apart at the Seams

The Racialization of Identity, 1933–1934

In 1933, Edmund Heilpern's daughter Gertrud was fourteen years old. She attended the same progressive comprehensive school to which the schoolgirl journalist Erica Stein had previously transferred—the Karl-Marx-School in Berlin's Neukölln district—and from which Stein had been forced to make a hasty exit in early 1933. After the Nazi takeover, the Karl-Marx-School rapidly changed in character. Within three weeks of taking office, the new Prussian minister of culture Bernhard Rust (who from 1934 was in charge of the Reich Education Ministry) sacked the school director and nazified the teaching body.

The students retained an independent outlook, for a while at least. 'Muz', as Heilpern affectionately called his daughter, told her father how the old teachers were being removed and replaced by committed Nazis. But, she assured him, their teaching made little difference to her or her classmates. When forced to spend a whole lesson practising the Hitler salute with their right arms extended, they all put their left arms behind their back and crossed their fingers, symbolically nullifying its meaning. This kind of secret gesture is a classic means of staying true to oneself while seeming to comply. Such gestures were long practised by marginalized or forbidden groups. Catholics in post-Reformation England, and Protestants in Catholic countries in sixteenth- and seventeenth-century Europe, had intensively discussed the merits of different ways of deceiving others about their beliefs and identities while not actually lying, such as by muttering something inaudibly that nullified an apparent affirmation or admission of guilt.[1] Deceit through maintaining a conformist public face while retaining a sense of inner authenticity and honesty would become ever more common in Nazi Germany. Ultimately, even unwilling compliance would make little difference to the fate of victims.

This little gesture of defiance may have made Muz and her schoolfriends feel better about what they were doing, and it seems to have escaped the teacher's notice. But it was less easy to ignore more obvious protests. The class had to practise the now official Nazi anthem, the Horst Wessel song. Muz and her classmates amended the words to sing 'Hitler verrecke!'— 'Death to Hitler!' or 'Let Hitler perish!' playing on Juda verrecke, 'Death to Jews', a horrific and common refrain at Nazi rallies (along with 'When Jewish blood spurts on the knife, things go twice as well'). The teacher was apparently aware that something was not quite right.[2] Possibly, of course, the teacher might also have chosen to pretend not to register this act of defiance. Either way, the dynamics of dissimulation and apparent conformity were becoming widespread from 1933 onwards—and in many respects essential to survival, particularly as the Nazi glorification of violence and hideously explicit threats to Jews left little space for hope that reason might prevail.

Gertrud Heilpern and her schoolmates remained cheekily defiant. But not for long. Unwilling to compromise on their socialist principles, and of Jewish descent, the Heilpern family eventually had to get out of Germany in late 1934; we do not know what became of her 'Aryan' schoolmates, as pressures on young people increased. Meanwhile, more Germans were learning the racist language of the new regime and enacting racism in everyday life. The process of assimilation to Nazi views and practices was never straightforward, as both official definitions and popular perceptions shifted.

In pre-Nazi Germany, antisemitism had not been a universal principle of discrimination. But under Hitler, 'race' became a structuring feature of all social life. As early as 1933, German gentiles were already discriminating against 'non-Aryan' compatriots in even the most fleeting encounters. Informal discrimination could initially appear relatively minor, but these were the first small steps on a slippery slope. Demotion, stigmatization, and loss of status followed, as Germans—both 'Aryan' and 'non-Aryan'—learned and acted on the new criteria of distinction and exclusion. These criteria were internalized over succeeding years, amended further, as we shall see, by the 1935 Nuremberg Laws, which imposed distinct categories prescribing degrees of exclusion. The process was uneven: already in 1933, people were proactively implementing racist distinctions in everyday life; in 1935, citizens were constrained to comply with new legal requirements; yet as late as 1938, some German Jews were still appealing to medals won for bravery in the Great War as evidence of their patriotism, and some non-Jewish Germans were still trying to sustain connections, however tenuous, with the excluded. But these were increasingly rare.

So what happened in the first period, between 1933 and 1935? It is crucial to understand that, in the first two and half years of Hitler's rule—before the promulgation of the Nuremberg Laws that formalized the definitions and rules of discrimination—Germans were already learning and practising distinctions between 'Aryans' and 'non-Aryans' in everyday life, and with far-reaching effects. First, the extraordinarily widespread voluntary severance of social ties with the persecuted would contribute not only to the progressive isolation of the victims, aptly termed 'social death', but also, on the part of 'Aryans', to accommodation and passivity in face of ever more radical violence against their 'non-Aryan' compatriots. Persecution was effectively condoned not only by inaction but also by varying degrees of active compliance with the informal creation of a hostile environment. As radicalization proceeded, people would become more active participants in one direction or another: either hastening the downward path of the persecuted, or partially easing their plight, whether through small acts of kindness or continuing contact, if often based as much in self-interest as in sympathy. Emotional and economic ties were not always easily severed; and personal motivations as well as moral frameworks affected the choices people made. In the process, many Germans found it possible to maintain a sense of their own moral integrity while at the same time furthering the Nazi cause by public conformity. This ultimately proved to be a fatal compromise.

Individual experiences provide insights not only into personal survival strategies but also the changing character of everyday interactions and social relationships, illuminating the conflicting pressures that, over time, informed the social dynamics of persecution.

Demotion

Well before the 1935 Nuremberg Laws, people were learning to think and act in terms of 'racial' distinctions. Starting in 1933, the so-called Aryan paragraph (an exclusionary clause known as the *Arierparagraph*) proliferated across organizations, institutions, and associations, permeating all areas of social life. Those deemed 'non-Aryan' by descent, whether or not they identified themselves as Jewish, were increasingly excluded from areas of professional employment, organizations, clubs, leisure associations, and social networks. Although this had already been the practice in some quarters during the Weimar Republic, as in selective student fraternities or leisure clubs, it had been far from universal. In some relatively exclusive social circles, 'class' still mattered more than 'race'; in the 1920s, the elite Wannsee Golf Club, for example, had members of prominent Berlin Jewish families among its members and executive committee, including the founding president, the leading banker and art collector Herbert Gutman, as well as the vice-president and honorary secretary. And indeed the Nazis continually sought to highlight the prominence of Jewish names in elite circles—among professionals, financiers, and big business owners—as well as in left-wing politics; the claim that the 'nation' was under threat from the Jewish 'enemy within'—in all sectors—as well as internationally was central to the Nazi worldview.

In 1933, new 'racial' categories remained inflected by class, status, and family connections. Professional and personal situations affected how people now designated as 'non-Aryans' could maintain a sense of self-respect in face of growing discrimination. Some individuals sought to cling on to social status by maintaining outward appearances, even if this meant entering into compromises over the means. Others drew on reserves of inner security or supportive personal relationships. It was in every case difficult to withstand the challenges. How people treated them made a great deal of difference.

Alfred Oppler, a Christian by conviction but of Jewish descent, as we have seen, and married to an 'Aryan', was by 1933 associate justice of the Supreme Administrative Court in Berlin. Oppler did not identify in any way as Jewish and had never previously thought much about his distant Jewish heritage. Even when witnessing the violence on 1 April 1933, as he wrote in his 1939 essay, he had been somewhat reassured, in an odd sort of way, by popular reactions. He had seen how the Nazi party first unleashed 'wild actions' by mobs, and then distanced themselves by claiming the violence was an expression of the 'outraged soul of the *Volk*'; and he had noted how the boycott of Jewish shops was generally not well received by the supposedly 'outraged' populace. He had been surprised when a Jewish friend, a physician, decided to flee; both Oppler and his wife Charlotte thought their friend must be crazy to take it so seriously rather than waiting for things to blow over.[3]

Yet with the 7 April 1933 passage of the Law for the Restoration of a Professional Civil Service, Oppler realized he, too, might be affected. Initially relieved to hear he was protected by his Iron Cross, he and his wife took a holiday near her former family home in the Silesian hills. Here, they were disconcerted by the open antisemitism of the now Nazi-infested local society. Oppler then received a letter from his employer, the Ministry of the Interior, offering him the choice between being pensioned off entirely—despite having only just turned forty—or demoted to the post of state councillor (*Regierungsrat*) in Cologne. Cutting short their holiday, the Opplers returned to Berlin. Oppler found that other 'non-Aryan' colleagues were being forced to retire, including the 'half-Jewish' fifty-four-year-old senate president of the Supreme Administrative Court, Viktor von Leyden. Oppler was so angry with the 'choice' being offered that he refused to hand over his red judge's robe. He accepted demotion and transfer.

In Cologne, Oppler was struck by the pusillanimity of his new colleagues. Even in a predominantly Catholic region—generally less receptive to Nazism than Protestant areas—civil service colleagues were bending with the wind, demonstrating loyalty to the Nazi regime.[4] Everyday pressures to conform seemed impossible to evade. One of the more mundane and apparently harmless techniques was that of extracting 'voluntary' donations to the National Socialist People's Welfare organization (Nationalsozialistische Volkswohlfahrt, NSV). Nazis would go around collecting donations, accosting people on the streets and badgering others in their homes. Civil servants such as Oppler were to commit a regular percentage of their salary; it was implied—and Oppler did not want to risk finding out whether or not this was true—that refusal would land the offender in a concentration camp.

A decree then proclaimed that it was 'expected' that civil servants would become members of the NSV, on confirmation of Aryan ancestry. Since the 'expectation' was not an order, Oppler tried to let this pass. One day, however, as he later recalled, a representative of the NSV came to Oppler's home to ask why he had not yet joined. On being told by Oppler that he was not eligible, the functionary asked if he was a Freemason, a category that was explicitly excluded. Oppler confessed his 'non-Aryan' ancestry. 'My God!' exclaimed the functionary. 'But you are blonder than I am! Well, society has gone crazy.' Oppler was momentarily taken aback by this remark and feared a trap. He responded quickly: 'You say that as a Party functionary! Well, I'm surprised!' The functionary was also taken aback but equally quick to reply: 'Surely you won't denounce me right away!' 'You can be sure of that', Oppler answered, 'since for me there is nothing lower in the world than a denouncer'. The functionary quickly agreed and confided that he was not really a Nazi; he had only taken this position for the sake of his son, not wanting to damage the schoolboy's chances in life.[5] Oppler felt uneasy but later took soundings and confirmed that the NSV functionary's story was true.

The appearance of conformity among uncomfortable 'Aryans' as well as 'non-Aryans' was produced through uneasy negotiations, repeated attempts at mounting an acceptable performance, and mutual reassurance when cracks appeared. This form of public 'passing' combined with private signalling of dissent when in secure company was and remains a familiar practice for many living in dictatorships, not just Nazi Germany. It is practised even in far less fraught situations in liberal democracies, where in the workplace or social settings people seek to 'place' others and in this way avoid potentially embarrassing revelations or unintended insults, with varying degrees of success and a much lower risk of severe penalties for failure. In Nazi Germany the stakes were far higher; but Oppler and his 'Aryan' acquaintances became adept at reading the signs and mutually adjusting their reactions in the micro-negotiations of everyday life.

Despite some unsettling incidents, Oppler generally got on well with his conformist colleagues. Most seemed fundamentally decent, anti-Nazi at heart, and had 'fallen into line' for reasons other than conviction. Even when told of Oppler's 'racial' background, they remained friendly. Very few senior colleagues were what he called '150 percent Nazis', convinced and fanatical supporters of Hitler. Most were simply hoping the Nazi regime would soon blow over and were trying to uphold the old rules and regulations as best they could in the meantime. They put on a performance when required, took out subscriptions to the local Nazi newspaper, the *Westdeutsche Beobachter*, and continued to read their old Catholic periodicals. There was however, in Oppler's view, a marked contrast between senior professionals and lower-level employees, many of whom he saw as 'fanatical Nazis' and Gestapo informers. Avoiding trouble with the latter was made easier by Oppler's blond, blue-eyed appearance; as he sardonically noted in his essay, 'their much vaunted racial instinct seemed to have failed them entirely' since 'they apparently had no idea of the mistake I had made at my birth'.[6] The Oppler family benefitted from his still-elevated professional status, even after partial demotion, and willingly put on public performances to avoid difficulties. While Oppler noted with relief that the so-called German greeting of 'Heil Hitler' had not become widely accepted in this Catholic region, the Opplers themselves used it when they felt under observation.[7] Inadvertently, in this way they—like millions of other Germans—contributed to the external picture of a nation united behind Hitler.

Even individuals with only one Jewish grandparent were, under the new regulations of April 1933, now considered 'Jews'. For people of mixed descent, this early discrimination could have long-term consequences for their subsequent lives, as Friedrich Reuss's experiences made clear. The renegotiation of identity and sympathy also placed them uneasily between different camps, sensing they did not belong to either side. Already well established in his professional career as a civil servant in Berlin, Reuss was initially confident about his own situation; but he was growing increasingly uncomfortable. One day, he was tasked with giving notice to two Jewish doctors employed by the German national railway (Reichsbahn), one of whom turned up in full military uniform, bearing war medals and honours. Reuss sought to console the two as best he could, saying they should consider themselves as simply being on leave until things got better, and talking—as Reuss put it in his essay—'every bit of nonsense that occurs to one in such a situation'. Despite all his efforts to dress it up, indicate sympathy, and exhort them to make the best of it, Reuss was utterly ashamed of himself. Registering a newly awakened awareness of a common 'racial' identity, he recounts that he would have liked to surprise them with a sentence in Hebrew, but this was not a language he knew—and, although he does not himself seem to have considered this, probably neither did the two highly educated German Jews in front of him, whose first and possibly only language was also German. Suppressing any self-revelation, he recalled that he ended the meeting by rising in as dignified a manner as he could manage and bringing himself to say 'Heil Hitler, gentlemen' as he ushered them out.[8]

A couple of minutes later he heard a shot fired in the antechamber. Startled, he ran out and saw the older man in his soldier's uniform, with all his medals, lying dead on the floor. His open eyes seemed to reproach Reuss with the refrain 'and you too, my son'.[9]

Appalled at the sight, Reuss described needing a moment to recover himself. Then he became aware of a kindly, well-meaning, moustachioed colleague leaning over him and saying in a gentle voice: 'But Herr Councillor, how can you take this as such a tragedy. After all, it's only an old Jew there who shot himself.'[10] This colleague was a member of the Association for the Protection of Animals and bred canaries, Reuss thought bitterly; he would hardly kill a fly without anaesthetizing it first. This new callousness towards Jews, Reuss reflected, was the result of Nazi propaganda.

This particular incident would likely have ended no differently had Reuss 'revealed' both his aversion to Nazism and his recently discovered partial Jewish heritage, and had he not merely expressed his sympathy but openly challenged the new regulations, even while carrying out his duty in dismissing the two doctors. Perhaps Reuss himself would have felt less ashamed about playing the part of a functionary faithfully serving the Nazi regime, but the doctor he dismissed might well nevertheless have chosen to take the same way out. Although it is impossible to attain exact figures, there were hundreds of Jewish suicides at this time. German Jews were responding not merely to the loss of their professional occupations but also to the existential humiliation of no longer being considered 'German'—particularly devastating for those Jewish Germans who had served their nation in the war, as well as those who did not consider themselves to be Jews.[11] But would the future course of developments have been any different if Reuss had acted differently? Was the colleague mouthing Nazi propaganda perhaps only doing so because he thought this would comfort the horrified Reuss? We cannot know. There must have been many such incidents, perhaps not ending quite as tragically as on this occasion, but where the interactions could potentially still have swung things in a different direction, at least in a small way for a few individuals. Even so, the wider conditions have to be taken into account. Psychological research on bystanders in liberal democracies emphasizes the ways in which people are hesitant to stand up against injustice if they feel others do not share their views; but if just one person is prepared to speak out, others who had also been privately discomfited may also stand up in support of a victim, potentially tipping the balance and turning the situation around. The problem with applying these theories to situations where the regime itself is involved—where there is no neutral or supportive external environment—is that the pressures for outward conformity are infinitely greater, the penalties for noncompliance far more severe. It is a difficult conundrum, particularly for individuals at lower levels with little by way of resources. At this very early stage of the Nazi regime, things might have developed differently if significant institutions and people in positions of power and influence had been more willing and able to speak up and stand out against Hitler, rather than falling into line so rapidly. But people at the level of Reuss's colleague need not have contributed proactively, whether through fear or more willing conformity, to the furtherance of the wider environment of hostility.

Reuss himself was deeply upset by this incident. He recounted how he succumbed to a heavy cold and took to bed for a while, where he lay trying to work out what to do. But soon any decision was taken out of his hands: as a 'non-Aryan', he too was forcibly ousted from his position with no pension. He had no idea where to turn for employment. As a Christian with one Jewish grandparent, he fell between stools. Colleagues who had never previously suspected any Jewish ancestry about him were generally solicitous and well-meaning but had little by way of useful suggestions for a 'non-Aryan'. Yet Jewish organizations were unwilling or unable to offer assistance, since he was not Jewish by any of the relevant criteria: self-identification, religious conviction, maternal line of descent. Excluded from both sides of the new racially defined divide, Reuss felt that everywhere people were treating him more coldly than before. While he had been an up-and-coming civil servant in a government ministry, 'from a good family, and known for his scholarly publications', he had enjoyed many friends; but now, he discovered sadly, 'no one could remember the poor descendant of Jews'. Former friends melted away; only a couple of people unexpectedly offered help and sympathy in his new plight.

In 1934, Reuss married his 'Aryan' fiancée, fearing a change in the law that might make this more difficult. The wedding was attended by their parents and a few close friends, but none of Reuss's former colleagues accepted the invitation. Desperate now to find employment, Reuss and his wife were able to stay with an anti-Nazi landowner during the summer. Reuss eventually managed to find work as a travelling insurance salesman, but others whom he met were not so lucky.[12]

Experiences varied with location and profession. Hertha Nathorff, who had, unusually for a woman at that time, qualified to practise medicine, was shocked at developments in the medical profession in Berlin. On 14 April 1933 she recorded in her diary how Jewish surgeons were being pulled out of hospitals, even in the middle of performing an operation, and forbidden to re-enter the premises. Others had been thrown onto trucks and 'driven through the city accompanied by jeering crowds'. The hospital at which she had previously worked had lost some of its 'most competent and best' physicians, and patients were thrown into despair. Yet, Nathorff sadly reflected, people listened in silence as Goebbels delivered rabble-rousing speeches; most concerning of all was the fact that leading doctors and prominent professors were doing nothing on behalf of their 'betrayed' Jewish colleagues.[13] Silence and outward conformity were already prevalent in the medical profession, even among those who were not themselves active Nazis.

Also working as a doctor in Berlin, Martin Andermann had been similarly shocked by the sudden influx of Nazis into medical circles. Yet he initially thought that this, and silence in face of developments such as those described by Nathorff, would be merely a temporary phenomenon: few thought the political situation would stay the same for long. No one was sure who could eventually topple the Nazis; some thought Catholic politicians, others thought the army, a few thought the communists. But as the months went by and Hitler consolidated his power bases, a change of regime seemed ever less likely. At the end of August 1933, Jewish doctors were forbidden to treat patients registered through insurance policies, making Andermann's own medical practice unviable. In early 1934 he took the decision to return to his native Königsberg, thinking that people there would at least still know him personally. But he was immediately struck by how different the atmosphere was from Berlin. Jews in Königsberg were, as he later wrote, 'vegetating away'; they felt they were now 'only allowed to live as pariahs'. Almost all places to eat or drink, with the exception of a Swiss café, bore signs saying that Jews were 'unwelcome' or 'not wanted here'. Theatre and musical events were virtually all now run by the Nazi 'Strength through Joy' (*Kraft durch Freude*, or KdF) movement and closed to Jews, with new audiences apparently attending operas and concerts as a duty rather than pleasure. Andermann remembered that he felt that Jews were 'having to live in a virtual ghetto'. He began, like others with Jewish heritage, to try to accustom himself to this restricted existence; he and his wife tried to focus on enjoying walks, nature, and reading.[14]

Jews employed in business and trading were initially less affected by the April 1933 regulations. Georg Abraham was not at immediate risk of losing his job in Neustettin as a sales representative for tobacco goods. Even in this predominantly Protestant small town, with barely more than 15,500 inhabitants, including fewer than 150 Jews, Abraham still maintained a vigorous trading network. 'Aryan' customers were under pressure not to trade with Jews; but good customer relations and mutually beneficial business interests generally overrode political pressures. Abraham wrote that one his clients was the manager of a sizeable inn and frequently put in orders for cigars for his customers; he also became a member of the NSDAP in order to protect and enhance his business. On one occasion, an especially large order from Abraham was delivered just as the innkeeper was hosting a Nazi party meeting; on entering, the courier announced loudly, 'Hey Walter, here's a big case of cigars from the Jew'. This announcement 'dropped like a thunderbolt' into the party meeting. Walter, the innkeeper, quickly turned the situation around, saying it must be a mistake: the letter referencing this order had in fact said that, as a good Nazi, he would never accept goods from a Jew; it must now all be sent back. This went down very well with Walter's Nazi comrades in the pub. A few days later, Walter arranged for the goods to be redelivered, a little less ostentatiously this time around. Another longtime customer also arranged for deliveries to be made surreptitiously. Abraham noted that it was easier for larger firms to organize appropriate cover to continue trading without loss of face or political credibility than it was for smaller ones.[15] In Abraham's experience of the 'Aryans' with whom he traded, self-interest seemed always to trump any potential difficulties occasioned by continuing social relations with Jews.

Not everyone managed to hang on as long as Abraham. Klara Rosenthal, based as we have seen in the Bavarian capital city of Munich, did not initially worry about the future of her business. She was more upset about the impact of the Nazi regime on others, such as the humiliated lawyer being dragged through the streets, watched by a variously passive or applauding crowd.[16] Yet things were starting to change for Rosenthal too. Even after the April 1933 boycott was officially over, her business continued to suffer from SA attempts to prevent people from entering the store: stormtroopers threatened customers, sometimes physically preventing them from crossing the threshold. Rosenthal often witnessed these so-called cleansing operations; but she also noticed how her customers disliked Nazi interference in their freedom to conduct their affairs as they wanted. In light of their reactions, she still thought her own business was safe, and was more concerned about the fates of people who had been ousted from their professions, and the constant attacks on Jews on the radio and in newspapers. She felt that her own clients, employees, and friends would remain loyal. She could not believe that those she knew personally could turn against the family.[17]

But one day, she recalled, the general manager came to talk to her. He had been with the business for many years, was loyal and well-respected, and was imbued with the same love of the German fatherland as were Rosenthal and her family. He now explained, however, 'with great conviction, that Hitler was the up-and-coming man' for their country. He dressed up his new enthusiasm for Nazism with supposed concern for her personal wellbeing, warning Rosenthal that there would be further violence, and she should take precautions. In a manner that became increasingly widespread in Germany after 1933, behaviour furthering the Nazi cause was combined with expressions of solicitude for its victims.

Rosenthal suddenly realized that the manager, whom she had known and trusted for so long, was speaking on behalf of many 'genuine and good Germans'—and in this moment she realized, too, that she and her family would have to find some way out. This became even more clear when a thirty-year-old employee, a former communist, became an ardent Nazi, active in the Nazi Labour Front (DAF) and the shop floor works council representing employees, and started to make trouble. Before long, Rosenthal was indeed forced to sell up, although it would still be a few years before her flight from the Reich after Kristallnacht.[18]

Individual character traits affected choices of action, informed by circumstances, including the social dynamics of relations between the newly excluded and 'Aryans'. Members of the Haller-Munk family, for example— Jewish by descent, Christians by conversion, as noted—followed quite different survival strategies following Hitler's accession to power. The elder son, Hans, the lawyer intent on rapid social climbing, had been waiting with growing impatience for his mother's baptism certificate, thinking this would protect him from disagreeable revelations about his Jewish origins. On 1 April his legal firm had already been subjected to the SA boycott, while his mother's baptism certificate only reached him two days later. Hans was furious about the slight delay, not realizing the ultimate worthlessness of this piece of paper at a time when 'race', not religious belonging, was paramount. Within days of its passage Hans learned he would be affected by the Law for the Restoration of a Professional Civil Service. In anticipation of difficult times ahead, Hans and his 'Aryan' wife Beate moved from their luxurious villa into more modest accommodation—although still compatible with the lifestyle of a respectable lawyer. Here, in August, Beate gave birth to a daughter; but short-lived joy subsided with the confirmation, at the beginning of October, that Hans had indeed been disbarred and could no longer pursue a career in the law. A monthly allowance from his parents helped the couple keep up appearances in provincial bourgeois circles. They did not stint on expenditure on Beate's clothes, Hans's cigars, or the needs of their baby. But simply keeping up appearances was not enough. Once his Jewish ancestry was revealed, Hans rapidly became socially isolated. Acquaintances avoided him; and he would have found it embarrassing—he, a previously respected 'well-known lawyer'—to approach people for assistance. Beate urged him to consider emigration, not realizing he had no funds of his own. Hans began to use family money to engage in increasingly dubious financial deals, with ever less regard for the law.

While Hans thought all might be well if he could somehow 'pass' among the 'Aryan' bourgeoisie, his younger brother Erich made different choices, leaving Berlin to make a new life in Vienna. Erich intended to emigrate permanently and wanted a share of family money to assist him; but his father, Heinrich, a pharmacist with a doctorate, insisted that one had to abide by the law of the land, even under Nazi rule, and accused Erich of being a 'fantasist'. Even without his parents' help, however, Erich managed to make a living. Meanwhile his father believed that things would be alright if he simply cut down on business and tried to sit it out. These three strategies typified different generational and personal responses to the new challenges. None, in the early years of Nazi rule, could know how long the situation would last.

Even people engaged in voluntary work were affected by the 'Aryan para-graph' or exclusionary clause. Else Behrend-Rosenfeld had been baptized and brought up in Berlin as an active Christian, with an 'Aryan' mother and a nonreligious Jewish father. Following her university studies, she had in 1920 married a prominent lawyer and social democratic politician, Siegfried Rosenfeld—nonreligious, but of Jewish descent. When Behrend-Rosenfeld felt that their three children—Gustel from her widowed husband's pre-vious marriage, followed by their own children Peter and Hanna—were old enough, she had taken up voluntary work in the Barnim Straße Women's Prison in Berlin, volunteering on behalf of the Workers' Social Welfare Charity. She enjoyed this work with female offenders, who were mostly working class and drawn into petty crime through poverty; and she eagerly discussed political and social issues with her socialist husband in the even-ings. Family life and work in the 1920s were fulfilling.

But in April 1933, two months after Hitler was appointed chancellor, the blow came: just as Behrend-Rosenfeld was about to leave for her regular stint volunteering at the women's prison she received a phone call. The rep-resentative of the prison politely told her that she should not come in, and asked if she could recommend an 'Aryan' to take her place. Flabbergasted, Behrend-Rosenfeld refused. She also noted the discomfort felt by the woman at the other end of the line: her voice 'clearly betrayed her embar-rassment about this duty that she had to fulfil'.[19] Here again, there was the increasingly widespread combination of conformity combined with a de-gree of concern for the victim.

To lose a voluntary position helping out at a women's prison because of her father's 'non-Aryan' family background was both depressing and sur-prising. Less surprising was the fact that Siegfried Rosenfeld was neither able to continue his work as a lawyer in the Prussian Ministry of Justice nor to serve as a representative of the SPD in the Prussian legislative assembly (*Landtag*). They were also deeply distressed by the experiences of many of their close friends, who were being arrested and tormented in the early months of the Nazi regime. In July 1933, the Behrend-Rosenfeld family sought to find respite by taking a holiday in the Bavarian resort of Schönau am Königssee, in the picturesque Alpine border region not far from Hitler's mountain retreat at Berchtesgaden. Deciding to stay for a while, they took lodgings with a seemingly friendly landlady. It soon turned out, however, that the façade of friendliness was deceptive; enticing them with sympathy and encouraging confidences, while observing their every movement, the landlady turned out to be an informer, out to denounce them for personal gain. Her unfounded accusations led to the arrest and incarceration of Siegfried Rosenfeld. The couple were fortunate still to have high-level support among principled individuals prepared to make a stand in Siegfried's defence, and he was eventually released after several agonizing months.[20]

The couple decided to relocate close to Munich, at Icking in the Isar valley, close to the Starnberger lake, where they settled among supportive neighbours and friends. Despite growing antisemitism, family life was for a while even happy; like so many others—particularly 'non-Aryans'—they hoped the bad times would sooner or later blow over if they could just, for the moment, keep their heads down. They were fortunate in having both the material means and social networks to sustain them.

The negotiation of status

Nazi racial policies were introduced from above and often violently implemented by activists on the ground. There are key moments that punctuate the outward and by-now familiar narrative of the development of Nazi rule. But widespread acceptance and more or less willing enactment—which went beyond mere conformity, more than 'falling in line'—was key to the broader impact of Nazi racism over time. Germans were starting to apply racist principles in their everyday lives. In this way they transformed social relations and assisted the drift towards a society in which the unthinkable eventually became plausible.

As someone who was fully 'Aryan'—although as noted her husband Hans was from a Jewish family—Verena Hellwig had previously given little thought to how much her own family, bourgeois and Christian, would soon also be affected by the new times. She had barely even kept abreast of the news, since her daughter Irene had been struck down by polio and spent months in hospital. Slowly, however, Irene regained the use of her limbs, and, much weakened, returned to school in the late spring of 1933. Emerging from a long dark period in which her world had revolved only around her daughter's health, Verena was now shocked to witness how a close friend, a local social democratic politician, was arrested and driven through the town on a truck accompanied by a jeering crowd. The fact that her husband Hans was considered 'non-Aryan' had never really crossed her mind. But now this too became relevant, if at first only in a small way—and even trivial challenges to status could be humiliating.

Hans Hellwig had worked for the same company for many years and held a senior position. Every year—as was customary in Germany—employees had celebrated his birthday; but in 1933, they decided against it. Hearing about this in advance, Hans announced that he would unfortunately have to be elsewhere that day, avoiding the embarrassment. Even so, Verena noted, he was hurt by 'the crumbling away of his authority'. He was now marked as different, to be shunned. She was concerned about her husband's distress but was more keenly affected by the impact of his family background on her children. Irene was bright and easily able to catch up with the schoolwork she had missed while in hospital; she again came top of her class. This year, however, a well-disposed teacher explained that 'mixed race' children, just like full Jews, were no longer allowed to receive school prizes. Her daughter Irene had, as Verena Hellwig wrote in her essay, her 'first bitter experience' of discrimination. Worse, many of her friends no longer visited her, with their families whispering that the Hellwigs were 'connected to Jews' (*jüdisch versippt*), and 'one should not maintain relationships with them'. These may each seem very trivial slights in retrospect, but Verena registered the cumulative impact on her family: 'loneliness grew on an almost daily basis'.[21]

It was not only loneliness but also the children's future prospects that began to worry her. Their son Douglas, now fifteen, had to fill out a form at school detailing his ancestry. Soon, he was being taunted as 'Jewish spawn' (*Judenbrut*), and classroom bullying began to overwhelm him. Verena, as a concerned 'Aryan' mother, took it up with the director—but he was himself just then facing dismissal for his anti-Nazi attitude and, beyond suggesting it would be worse if Douglas were a 'full Jew' and that he should just stick it out, was of little help. When Douglas left school and tried to find an apprenticeship, no company would take him on. One friend explained that 'racially pure companies' were given priority in government contracts and large orders, so it was not in their interest to train 'non-Aryans'. An official provided an additional gloss, as Verena described it: 'Mixed-breeds pose the biggest danger for us. Either they should revert to the Judaism of their grandparents and suffer the fate of Jews, or, like imbeciles, they should be operated on to prevent reproduction.' Eventually, with all avenues in

Germany apparently closed, Verena organized an apprenticeship for Douglas abroad. She felt she would have to accompany him—he was too young to relocate on his own—leaving her increasingly frightened husband to look after their daughter. This decision would prove to be the beginning of an unfolding family tragedy.[22]

At that time, however, their main concern was to avoid whatever difficulties they could. Verena Hellwig had heard enough stories to feel she must take action. One that affected her particularly concerned a Jewish woman married to an 'Aryan' lawyer. His practice had been severely affected because, as a lawyer now 'racially contaminated' by marriage to a Jew, he was no longer allowed to represent clients in court; and people were increasingly unwilling to come to him for those legal services that he could still offer. Feeling she was simply a burden to her beloved family, the lawyer's wife committed suicide. She left a letter saying that she was doing this out of love, to help her husband and son to have a better life without her. This act of desperation was far from uncommon.[23]

Turning away from Jews was the new norm. As Verena made her rounds to bid farewell to friends, relatives, and acquaintances before leaving the country with her son, she became aware of how rapidly people had been prepared to alter their outlook and character in public. One acquaintance, a theatre director, was doing very well out of the new times. His budget had massively expanded, as he explained, 'because whoever is working for the [Nazi] Cause can spend money, and that is a wonderful experience'. And he added, 'with a little wink', this was easy enough for anyone involved in theatre: 'we people of the stage are used to altering our character, we do it every night, it is second nature to us'. Verena Hellwig wrote that she left reflecting bitterly on this 'fish who will always swim with the tide'.[24]

Many 'Aryans' found it convenient to change course. One acquaintance confided in Verena that his brother, a hospital director, was now forced to attend Nazi lectures, which he 'hated like the plague'. But, the brother told Verena, 'he has to stand to attention in any case, and he finds it easier if you pretend to yourself that you are doing it of your own free will'. In her experience, the only people now capable of standing up against the rising tide of Nazism were those with a strong alternative faith, 'like those with religious convictions, or Freemasons, and Quakers'; everyone else, she wrote, 'accepted the injustices that were taking place simply as facts that are regrettable but cannot be changed'.[25]

The process of absorbing racial distinctions was gradual, and context made a difference to how people acted. Between 1933 and 1935, social class and status still seem to have partly compensated for 'race'. Watching her own children playing in the garden, the Jewish dentist's wife Lotte Popper noted how a neighbour's child was looking on wistfully; when Popper's daughter called out to him to join them, he replied that his mother had forbidden him 'to play with Jews any more'. But this prohibition seems to have been only with respect to places where they could potentially be seen by others, as in outdoor play. When it was pouring with rain a few days later, the neighbour's child was allowed to play indoors with Popper's children.

In this case, the key factor seems to have been fear of social opprobrium. Other neighbours of the Poppers, including even known Nazis, were somewhat less concerned about this. Herr and Frau Jantzen were both committed Nazis. But Frau Jantzen was fond of Popper's three children and often invited them over to play in her garden, as well as sending her Brown Shirt friends to buy them ice creams, and letting them pick cherries from her tree. These neighbours seem at this time to have been sufficiently secure and confident to retain social ties with people whom they liked without fearing the consequences of being seen to be friendly. In Popper's account, her social status—despite the stigma of being Jewish—still played a significant role: socially, Popper's neighbours could still see her as similar to themselves. Or perhaps it simply helped Popper to portray herself in this way, to maintain her own sense of self-respect.[26]

'Aryans' who were of lower social status, however, used 'race' to challenge class hierarchies. Popper was shocked when her maidservant Hedwig, who had reportedly served the family loyally for six years, now changed her behaviour. Without asking permission, she invited her boyfriend to stay overnight; she fed him richly from the family food stocks and they raided the cupboards and cellar to take goods and provisions in preparation for their wedding, on the assumption that the Popper family would have to leave sooner or later anyway. Popper reflected sadly on how the 'good Hedwig', as she described her, whose 'modesty and honesty had made her the envy of all the local housewives' had done her Führer the ultimate honour of foreseeing 'how all the worldly goods of Jews were now free prey' for anyone to take as they wished.[27]

Class differences and supposedly racial awareness could intersect in unpredictable ways. Friedrich Reuss lived in an apartment block where another tenant, a post office employee, clearly wanted to be friendly. Reuss, a Christian with a single Jewish grandparent, was not obviously 'Jewish' in appearance; neighbours could not be aware at first glance that he was a 'non-Aryan' and that it would be unwise to foster social relations with him. Fearful of making difficulties, Reuss remained cool and distant. The neighbours, who were far more sensitized to the obvious class differences, misinterpreted his reticence.

One day, as Reuss remembered, the neighbour's wife confided in Reuss's wife that she assumed that Reuss, 'with his higher education', presumably saw himself as 'far too good to want to consort with a simple postal worker'. On hearing this, Reuss went to tell the neighbour he had only 'held back in order to protect him'. The postal worker was staggered to hear that Reuss had some Jewish ancestry. He also revealed that he had indeed previously been in trouble for vicariously consorting with Jews: he had been threatened with dismissal because his wife, while carrying a heavy laundry basket down the stairs, had accepted help from a kindly Jewish neighbour, Frau Rosenberg. The matter had only been resolved by Frau Rosenberg's going in person to his manager to swear that she had imposed her help against her neighbour's wishes. The postal worker confessed to Reuss that he was 'really ashamed' by this incident. His effective complicity in enforcing isolation on 'racial' grounds was forced upon him by circumstances; a low-level employee, he could not risk losing his job, but he felt bad about it. Reuss and the postman now became friends, but visited each other only secretly in the evenings.[28]

Racial distinctions in everyday encounters

While it was relatively straightforward to apply 'racial' principles in formal settings where providing an 'Aryan certificate' or 'ancestor passport' was required, different challenges were posed in the informal encounters of everyday life. And, given that there were few readily visible physical markers of difference between 'Aryans' and 'non-Aryans', knowing how to put racism into everyday practice was not always easy.

At least in the early stages of the Nazi regime, attempts could sometimes be experienced as almost comic. Fritz Goldberg recalled walking in the woods one day with his blond, blue-eyed, wife; in terms of racial stereotypes, he looked far more obviously 'Jewish' than she did. A group of three well-dressed women walking towards them suddenly stopped and accosted them. One, 'with an outraged expression,' challenged Goldberg's wife: 'Are you not ashamed of yourself, you, as a German woman, going out with a Jew! This will turn out badly for both of you. We'll see you are arrested by the nearest policeman we can find.' At first, the Goldberg couple were speechless; then they burst out laughing. 'Do what you like!' countered Goldberg's wife. 'I'm looking forward to your humiliation. First of all, we have been married for ten years. But secondly, you don't seem to have studied your Racial Science properly: I am actually Jewish myself.' At this spirited rejoinder, 'the women stammered the usual apologies and withdrew in some embarrassment'. A few years later these women would have been less embarrassed and, far from apologizing, would likely have reported the 'Jewess' for 'cheekiness'; but this was still early days.

Although Goldberg and his wife managed to laugh at the time, Goldberg commented that 'such incidents were frequent' and demonstrated how the Nazi project of racializing German identity was taking root. As this and similar incidents illustrate—there are many stories of mis-recognition in the classroom, on a tram, in public spaces—racial distinctions were being spontaneously acted upon even when there was apparently no need for any sort of intervention. Not even a walk in the woods could be free of it.[29]

Given the high level of integration, assimilation, conversions, and inter-marriages among Germans of Jewish descent, racial awareness and invidious distinctions had to be explicitly taught. Distinctions between 'Aryan' and 'non-Aryan' were conveyed to children at an early age, even when they had little idea what it was all about. Oskar (Otto) Scherzer's family moved to Elbing, in East Prussia, when he was of school age. He was the only Jewish boy in class, and while some pupils were antisemitic before 1933, many were close friends. But one day in spring 1933, a girl who had been a good friend suddenly called to him from across the street: 'My father has forbidden me to talk to you because you are not Aryan. Do you know what that means?'[30] She had apparently no idea of what being 'not Aryan' meant, though she intended to follow the rules.

Parents informally policed what was now held to be appropriate behaviour for their children. Alfred Oppler noted how their six-year-old daughter, Ellen, first began to be aware of antisemitic sentiments while out playing with a friend in a park; when Ellen cooed over a baby lying in her pram, the friend told Ellen she should not do that because the baby was Jewish. The two mothers, witnessing this from a park bench, then conducted a disagreement about race via their little daughters. As committed Christians, the Opplers chose to put Ellen into a Catholic school. But there they had to reveal Oppler's Jewish ancestry, marking her out for discrimination as a '*Mischling*' or 'mixed breed'.[31]

Racialization often led to tensions and splits within families. Revelations about Jewish ancestry when applying to join the Hitler Youth (HJ) could further heighten awareness of 'race'. Being unable to participate in the activities of the Nazi youth organizations, some of which looked like fun, Jewish children lost touch with former friends, while 'mixed-race' children who were excluded sometimes blamed the parent who was Jewish.

Young people often became far more convinced Nazis than their parents. A former schoolfriend in Königsberg poured her heart out to Martin Andermann's sister about the fact that her only son was an 'enthusiastic Nazi'. The family 'was at risk of breaking apart, father and son could not understand each other anymore', and the mother just 'stood helplessly between them'. Complaining that her husband, a vehement anti-Nazi, could 'never just hold his tongue', this friend 'was terrified about their future'. A widow who, with difficulty, had brought up her children alone told Andermann that 'her two boys were now virtually never at home'. She complained that 'they spent the whole day in the Hitler Youth, where they were constantly being stirred up, against their own mother, against religion, and against everything'.[32] In Hamburg, a friend spoke to Lotte Popper about how his son was in the Hitler Youth, strutting around in his uniform and swearing about Jews. Fritz Goldberg described how the son of a neighbour in Berlin was increasingly involved in the Hitler Youth and ever more enthusiastic about the 'new times'; his father, however, had previously belonged to the Social Democratic Party and was vocal about his sympathies. Eventually, the father barely dared open his mouth at home when his son was present. Both Goldberg and his neighbour knew many families where a father had been arrested as a result of denunciations by one of their children; people were becoming increasingly wary.[33] Alfred Oppler witnessed family tensions among some of his 'Aryan' colleagues in Cologne. One was terrified of being denounced by his son, who held a significant position in the Hitler Youth, and felt he could no longer talk openly at home. Yet this colleague still socialized with Oppler, perhaps because his social standing compensated for the 'racial' taint, or because his wife was an 'Aryan', and their daughter Ellen also had blond hair and a 'totally German' appearance.[34]

Children were affected by being together in organized groups. They often spent more time in Hitler Youth activities than on family outings.[35] Some unwittingly betrayed what their parents had said in unguarded moments at home. Gerta Pfeffer frequently visited a family with whom she got on very well; but they had stopped talking politics whenever their fourteen-year-old daughter entered the room, because 'they were afraid that the girl might quite innocently talk in school about what she had heard'.[36]

Hans Kaufmann, a Jew in his twenties who worked in a shoe store in Essen and observed many people passing through every day, summarized in his essay the generational divisions that started widening in 1933 as follows: 'the German family is slowly but surely being torn up by the roots. It is the old generation against the new, and in a more realistic sense, the sons and daughters against the parents—who cannot become reconciled to Nazism'. He went on: 'the Nazi young are being taught to venerate Aryanism and armed might above all else', while 'the older generation has been driven back to a kind of lip service, repugnant to them but necessary if they are to live'.[37]

There was a gradual but discernible jostling and shifting of perceptions and practices, as people learned new norms and adjusted their behaviours and relationships accordingly. The impact on families was almost inexorable, and home life could be fractured in a myriad of ways, as private lives and public developments intersected, reshaping its very nature.

Friendship and the fiction of the 'normal community'

It is nearly impossible to provide a legal definition of 'friendship'. It was therefore not easy initially to draft legislation to ban it, although the Nazis eventually got about as close to this as conceivable. What is all the more startling, then, is that right from the outset in 1933, innumerable 'Aryans'— probably a majority of those who had personal contacts with Jews— spontaneously broke off friendships with 'non-Aryans' and were wary of being seen consorting with them, even when this was not yet technically against any law. Proactive severing of informal social contacts and dropping

former friendships both constructed and reinforced the still relatively invisible 'racial' boundaries. This furthered the development of what Erving
Goffman has called the 'fiction' of the 'normal community'.[38] It certainly
both hurt the victims and actively assisted in the process of separating out
communities along lines desired by the Nazi regime. Nor can it be brushed
away in terms of 'only obeying orders'. The process was both insidious and
subtle.

A main impetus among 'Aryans' was the desire not to be seen to be different. A somewhat generalized fear of standing out seems to have been more
important than direct social pressure or genuine penalties. Communities
redefined themselves, shifting apart, excluding those who did not fit the
new constructions of identity. Walter Gottheil, with a Jewish father and
Protestant mother, found he was no longer able to socialize in the area in
which he had happily lived for half a century; everywhere, he was now
made to feel unwanted, ousted, 'superfluous'; there 'was no place any more'
for himself and his family.[39]

Fear of denunciation played a role. The non-Jewish friends of Albert
Dreyfuss, for example, for a while continued to be friendly with him if
they met in private, but if they chanced to meet on the street they would
become, as he later wrote, 'cautious, short-sighted, and awkward'. In a
relatively small town everyone knew one another, and they all believed
that they were 'being observed, spied upon, and there was nothing one
feared more than denunciation'; one would rapidly be 'stigmatized in
public as a "Jewish lackey" [*Judenknecht*], an "enemy of the people" and
similar'.[40]

Social opprobrium also played a part. Those who felt at risk of being
labelled 'oppositional' were particularly concerned about being seen with
Jews.[41] Former left-wing friends who now had reason to fear being disadvantaged at work might find it particularly hard. As Gerhard Miedzwinski
put it in his essay, such friends 'did not dare to meet us openly and when
one of them came up to us we had to take the strongest possible precautions
so that nobody saw him'. Everyone was becoming aware that Nazi racism
could be manipulated for personal advantage: 'Younger colleagues, out for
their jobs, tried to get them out of the way.'[42] In Gottheil's experience, previous acquaintances were profiting from the new situation: they or their
children were finding jobs, and 'every tie to the regime caused yet another
to no longer greet us on the street'.

Desire for career advancement caused many 'Aryans' to drop friendships with 'non-Aryans'. Lotte Popper recalled how excited she had been when she ran into a formerly close friend, Eva G., with whom she had shared all the highs and lows of student life together in Königsberg. Popper was delighted to hear that Eva G. had become a high school teacher in Hamburg and, hoping that they could pick up where they had left off, invited her home for coffee and cake. Eva G. did not show up. In the evening, she telephoned to say she had suddenly developed a cold. That was the last Popper heard from her. Popper subsequently discovered that her former friend was now an ardent Nazi and instigator of a campaign to oust the anti-Nazi director of the school where she worked. For Eva G., pursuit of professional advancement was more important than friendship.

Whatever else it is, friendship is based on a degree of mutual trust.[43] Once that is gone, so are its bonds. Elisabeth Bartels was a Protestant who had been brought up by adoptive parents; her biological family included three Jewish grandparents. Growing up in Berlin in the early 1930s, her general impression was that criticism of the Nazis was common; but this was, in her experience, accompanied by fear of being heard saying anything untoward, and associated mistrust now even of one's closest friends.[44] This alone could render the ties of friendship inherently tenuous—while at the same time making those friends with whom one remained close all the more precious.

Having moved back in late 1933, Martin Andermann felt increasingly socially isolated in his native Königsberg. He was initially delighted when he met a formerly left-wing school friend on a tram in Königsberg. As youngsters they had spent many happy days together in the *Wandervogel* youth movement, going on long rambles through the countryside. Moreover, this friend's father had died when he was very young, and he had been brought up by a Jewish couple. Now, he utterly renounced all of that; he had become an active Hitler Youth leader, saw the future under Nazism in rosy terms, and was not at all happy to be seen talking to his former friend, even in a brief and accidental encounter on a tram.[45]

Among former friends, there were, Andermann wrote, 'so many who only too hastily let it be known that they would rather not see you any more'. It was clear that 'a non-Jew who visited ran a considerable risk'. Given this situation, he was all the more delighted by visits from former friends, and even made some new friends. Since, as he noted, 'purely conventional social visits' were infrequent, when they did happen they were all the more precious and genuine. A friend who was determined to visit 'wanted to show you that, in taking this risk, he was confirming his respect and loyalty'. But even despite loyal friends, Andermann's relationships with non-Jews 'became ever rarer'.[46]

Dropping friendships could be instigated by 'Aryans' and 'non-Aryans' alike. Anna Bernheim, a Jewish housewife in southwestern Germany, had for most of her life considered class to be more significant than 'race'. But seeing how former friends were adapting to the new conditions in 1933, she made an effort not to see people whom it would be awkward to greet. There was a subtle interplay here, with an interactive process of both being shut out and shutting oneself out in order to avoid trouble either for oneself or for others.[47]

When reading personal accounts, it rapidly becomes clear that most 'Aryan' Germans dropped friendships with Jews before they had to. Why did they do this? It could not be rooted in any pre-existing antisemitism, since this would have prevented such friendships from developing in the first place. Appealing to notions of supposedly long-standing German antisemitism neither explains the high degree of social intermingling (and intermarriage) up to 1933, nor the very sudden dropping of social contacts once Hitler came to power. Nor can it be explained by any supposed German tendency for obedience to authority, at least in the sense of obeying specific orders, since the full panoply of Nazi legislation on this front was yet to come. Rather, these radical changes in people's private lives, which were so hurtful to those affected by exclusion, have to be understood in terms of a changing wider social environment, in which people were variously either jostling for position and seeking advantages or apprehensively attempting to avoid unnecessary risks, or simply trying to keep their heads down and fit in. Whatever their reasons, the impact was, as we shall see, ultimately massive.

Resisting this overwhelming and even spontaneous pressure was very hard. Some 'inter-racial' friendships persisted for quite a while before other considerations affected the equation. Even amongst committed Nazis, friendships might be sustained until quite late, and only then broken off for reasons that had nothing to do with 'race' or politics. Money was a component. As Borge Nielsen, a young Danish man who worked in Germany, observed about his landlady and her family: 'During the time I lived with Mrs.

S. and her son Albert they changed quite a bit and became quite Nazified. They had several Jewish friends, with whom they broke in 1937 for no other reason than Nazi propaganda.' But, he went on to observe, it was also rather useful for them to break off the friendship at this point: 'From one of these friends Albert had borrowed several hundred Marks, and a break came, therefore, rather handy, I believe.'⁴⁸ Financial interests sometimes supported ideological underpinnings and precipitated a break.

It took a combination of personal determination, favourable conditions, and professional security for 'Aryans' to resist the pressure to drop Jewish friends. It helped when sustaining a friendship in private was perfectly compatible with conformity in public. When Georg Abraham got married, he and his wife had many non-Jewish friends. They initially shared a large apartment with a non-Jewish couple, eating dinner together, and listening to the news on foreign radio stations rather than the Nazi-dominated German radio broadcasts. Despite the fact that the non-Jewish husband 'had to join the Party', they remained in contact. Another close friend from before 1933 soon 'held a leading position in the Party'. He nevertheless continued to visit Abraham, and invited him to his own house, grumbling about the time taken up by his NSDAP functions. He criticized the Nazi treatment of Jews, suggesting it will 'one day take its revenge, and we who did not want it will have to live with the consequences'. He felt that in light of 'the injustice in the way they are treating you, you just want to chuck everything in. But', he went on, 'what can I do, if I don't go along with it I and my family will be run into the ground'. He told Abraham, whom he always greeted on the street, that he continued to buy from Jewish merchants despite official disapproval. When Abraham suggested he should be more careful, for his own wellbeing, he responded, 'if the Party members don't like it, they can chuck me out'.⁴⁹

But, as I have suggested, these examples were rare. More generally, Abraham thought, 'most people felt a certain anxiety and restraint with respect to their Jewish fellow citizens'. Only one official who had dealings with Abraham's company while it was still in Jewish hands tried to keep up private social contacts with the company director. As a result, 'he was very soon penalized by being moved to a different job by the office which employed him'. Another of Abraham's friends, who worked independently and resisted pressure to join the NSDAP, remained close and warned him whenever danger was in the offing. He was called in by the local district leader of the Nazi party and told to stop visiting Abraham, to which he replied that these were essential business visits as a company representative. Abraham reported in his essay that this friend remained in close contact, even supplying Abraham with some equipment prior to his emigration in 1939.[50]

Professional security—with confidence in position and status—was clearly helpful in being able to keep up friendships between 'Aryans' and 'non-Aryans'. The fully 'Aryan' Bruno Gebhard was research director of the Berlin Office for Exhibitions and Trade Fairs (Ausstellungs- und Messeamt der Stadt Berlin). With the introduction of questionnaires about ancestry, Gebhard and his wife had, as he later wrote, been 'surprised to find among our friends more people with Jewish ancestors than we had realized before'. However, they were determined to retain their friendships, 'and with some of them we even came closer together'.[51] Maintaining their circle of friends was dependent on favourable social circumstances, but it was far from easy. He and his wife had previously been keen adherents of the *Wandervogel* movement, with its 'back to nature' emphasis on rambling, health, and alternative lifestyles; life under Nazism ran counter to all their principles and convictions. Gebhard admitted that first they 'did not know how to deal with brutal force turned against the own members [*sic*] of our nation'. Yet despite hoping for change, 'we accustomed ourselves to these daily half-lies and only tried to save some of our ideals and hopes for our personal lives'. Even here, things changed. When they met up with friends, they found it hard to talk about 'all the sad things that were going on'. Despite having never previously indulged in alcohol, they started to drink when meeting up with Jewish friends. Gebhard's view was that it helped that they lived in an area where people did not like to 'bother their neighbors', and also because they 'were fortunate enough to have a devoted and very decent maid' who 'had such a strong feeling for justice and decency' that she would never dream of reporting visits by supposed 'enemies of the people' (*Volksfeinde*). Nonetheless, Gebhard noted, their household 'was very exceptional'. Most families lived in fear of those who worked for them. As he put it: '"You never know".'[52]

Gebhard sought to retain personal integrity in his private life. It was a question of what could be done without attracting adverse attention, as distinct from behaviour required in public. Like many others, he and his wife were unhappy about raising their arm in the 'Heil Hitler' greeting;

like others, they avoided doing this wherever possible. However, like the vast majority of 'Aryan' Germans, they raised their arms when there was no alternative. In Gebhard's view, 'most Germans have such a respect for given orders that they carry them out even if they don't approve of them'. This salute—even if given reluctantly—served to lend an aura of mass support for the Nazi regime, creating a spurious sense of widely shared norms that it would be unwise to try to stand out against, influencing the behaviour of others.[53]

In the end, it did not matter what Gebhard felt internally about what he was doing, but rather what were the practical outcomes of his behaviour during the early years of the Nazi regime. No doubt in the private sphere, among friends, he helped to sustain the morale of people excluded from other circles. But in his professional capacity, Gebhard contributed to the ideological construction of the Nazi national community. He felt fortunate that he could discuss any qualms he had with the director, Dr Albert Wischek, and after 1933 initially determined that it was worth compromising in order to achieve at least something in his work: 'It would even be worthwhile to go so far as to pretend that we were on the side of the government.' But by the time of writing his essay in 1939, he thought rather differently: 'This wishful thinking that by sticking to one's job and by compromising one could moderate the politics of the Nazis was a mistake made by quite a number of sincere and well-meaning people.' And while he himself had pangs of conscience, others, he recognized, 'were pretty much indifferent'.

Gebhard and Germans like him effectively furthered the Nazi cause, whether or not they approved of it. He and Wischek, mounting ideologically laden exhibitions in Berlin's trade fair centre, were increasingly constrained by Berlin's Gauleiter and Reich Propaganda Minister Joseph Goebbels. Just three days after being awarded the newly created propaganda post, on 18 March 1933, Goebbels gave a major speech at the opening of the exhibition on 'Women' (*Die Frau*), which Wischek and Gebhard had already planned prior to the Nazi takeover but had rapidly repurposed for the new regime. A further major exhibition under the title 'German *Volk*— German Work' ran from 21 April to 3 June 1934. Visitors entered through a 'hall of honour' highlighting the 'racial question' and 'the nurturing of hereditary health'. Questions of 'racial hygiene' were featured throughout, informing visitors about Nazi racial policies, and offering practical advice about matters such as whom they should marry, and how to 'prevent the reproduction of inferior people', among topics extolling the virtues of Nazi racial practices.

Gebhard was clearly affected by his proximity to power, despite inner principles and growing misgivings. He gleaned from his work with the Propaganda Ministry that 'Goebbels had no conscience at all', but felt that Hitler was 'honest'. Commenting on a photograph showing himself standing next to Hitler, admiring a Bronze Age burial coffin with precious items, Gebhard recalled that Hitler's 'eyes were bright and sincere' and he 'could not help the feeling: this man believes in what he thinks and says'. After being shown a small blade with which the ancient Germanic tribes had shaved their beards, Hitler 'suddenly burst into a long and excited speech clenching his fists'. Gebhard felt uneasy that he was actively involved in all this, despite his inner misgivings; but for the time being he still offered his professional expertise in service of a deeply racist cause.[54]

Gebhard's principled opposition to racism in the private sphere was therefore heavily dependent on both favourable domestic circumstances and professional security. And it was bought at the price of conforming in public and in professional work. The experiences of Gebhard and many others highlight the ease with which life within a racist regime could compromise even those who were consciously trying to withstand its pressures— and yet allow them to continue feeling they were in some way against it.

The wider effect not only of exhibitions, such as those mounted by Gebhard and Wischek, but also of ubiquitous antisemitic propaganda across the Reich was to make it abundantly clear to every German that social relations across racial divides were to be avoided at all costs. Again, many Germans were already prepared to redirect their personal connections into racially approved directions.

By 1934, insidious changes had taken place in everyday social relations. As 'Aryan' Germans were energized by a sense of national regeneration, and as they dropped social contacts with Jews and snubbed any they met on the street, so they increasingly lost touch with the lives of the outcast. The growing social and spatial difference made it easier, too, no longer to care about those with whom they were no longer in contact: indifference grew more easily if one simply did not know, or chose to ignore, the fates of the excluded.

There were regional variations, and local economic and social considerations affected the course of developments. Big cities such as Berlin,

Hamburg, and Munich were not typical of the rest of the Reich. Protestant towns in northern Germany, such as Marburg or Northeim, not only had different social, economic, and cultural profiles from the southern states of Württemberg or predominantly Catholic Bavaria; they also were more easily penetrated by Nazi organizations.[55] In small village communities in southern Germany, such as Gailingen, located close to the border with Switzerland, where everyone knew everyone else, economic considerations tempered the speed of the onward march of Nazi politics. As we have seen, the mayor of Gailingen in the later nineteenth century had been Jewish, and despite periodic frictions and tensions over, for example, the use of school buildings, Jews and Christians had lived together fairly harmoniously, or at least symbiotically: members of the Jewish community had been particularly prosperous, providing employment for many in the surrounding Christian population. In 1934, the Jews of Gailingen were still, even in the view of local Nazi party leaders, the 'best taxpayers' and remained significant employers in the area; and even the convinced Nazi 'old fighter' (*Alte Kämpfer*) who was now mayor had, 'for economic reasons', to adopt 'an accommodating attitude' towards the Jewish community, for which he had the explicit support of the NSDAP district leadership.[56]

This situation would not, however, last for much longer. By late 1934, the vast majority of non-Jewish Germans, now privileged as 'Aryans', had gradually shifted their allegiances. The 'bystanders' to Nazi policies had become in effect key actors in a society based on outward conformity, whether constrained or enthusiastic. 'You just can't understand it', 'Aryan' friends explained to Martin Andermann. 'We are Germans, our place is here, the only way forwards for us is to join the Party, join the Movement, only in that way can we prepare for whatever will eventually replace the current regime'.[57]

Yet even while actively supporting the Nazi movement, many non-Jewish Germans still sought to signal some form of inner disquiet; a classic instance of the metaphor of eating one's cake and yet still having it, enjoying both the benefits of public conformity and the moral glow of private dissidence. However good they may have felt about themselves, or however ambivalent they felt about the wider situation, it nevertheless also has to be pointed out: in the process, this pre-emptively conformist behaviour only served further to define and deepen the rifts that Nazi ideology introduced. It not only redefined the status and affected the morale of individuals but also irrevocably shifted the borders of wider communities of identity and empathy.

4
Shifting Communities
Dissembling and the Cost of Conformity

In the first couple of years after Hitler came to power, Gerta Pfeffer often spent evenings with friends in an inn. One evening, when they were all in an unusually good mood, as Pfeffer recalled in her essay, she had been laughing again for the first time in quite a while. But the next day the inn-keepers, who were a generally friendly and well-disposed couple, treated her coldly. On asking why, she was told that guests at a neighbouring table had 'used many crude expressions' to the effect that 'if they saw the Jewess laughing again, they would throw her out onto the street'.[1] That was when it became absolutely clear to Pfeffer that she was no longer part of the German national community in which she had grown up and to which she felt she belonged. Her presence as a Jew was not welcome. Non-Jewish Germans were acting out new conceptions of being 'among ourselves' (in German, *unter uns*) and ousting the unwanted. Gatherings at an inn could be as significant as political rallies.

Nazism was not just about power, repression, and persecution. It was also about mobilizing people in the Volksgemeinschaft, infusing those who were included with a powerful sense of belonging and aspiration. The Nazi vision of a 'people's community' made a fundamental difference to people's lives—and this not only in terms of particular incidents that have caught the historical headlines but also in broader and less immediately evident ways.

For decades, historians have pointed out that the Nazi rhetoric of a social revolution was never fully realized in practice, at least in terms of transformations of the class structure, even if perpetually claimed in ideology. More recently, however, historians have begun to focus on practices of 'self-empowerment', interpreting violent incidents in the provinces—such as the public humiliation of Jews—as effectively enacting the Nazi aspiration for a Volksgemeinschaft. Other scholars have dismissed the notion of Volksgemeinschaft as Nazi rhetoric, or seen it as a term so specific to Nazi Germany that it is of little value for understanding dictatorial rule more generally. These historical debates have stimulated significant contributions to the development of a more complex picture of Nazi society and the exercise of power and agency at the grass roots.[2] Yet such debates do not go far enough if we want to understand wider questions of conformity and the implications of living within a dictatorial regime for growing complicity.

Across the board, in subtle ways, emotional connections and social relations were changing in Nazi Germany—among everyone, including not only the radicals and Nazi enthusiasts, those actively engaged in overt self-empowerment, but also the politically passive majority. Those who were uncomfortable about quiet conformity explored what limited avenues of activity were open to them; but most began to accommodate themselves to new ways of living and relating, laying the groundwork for the formation of a bystander society. What may be called communities of identification and empathy were shifting, often almost imperceptibly, but nevertheless significantly, in ways that would become immensely important once Germany was at war.

Some people were of course genuinely enthusiastic, having fought for Hitler and the Nazis well before they came into power.[3] Once Hitler had been appointed chancellor, as we have seen, hundreds of thousands of others immediately jumped on the bandwagon, with more than 10 million eventually joining the NSDAP for a whole variety of reasons across the lifetime of the Reich. The rhetoric of Volksgemeinschaft became significant in a range of ways. Some used it to seek personal advantages, to acquire positions of power and influence, and to dominate others; others internalized it and adapted their social behaviour more broadly. Those who were excluded felt its impact far more acutely in the face of growing discrimination. Despite the forceful new rhetoric and associated mentalities and practices, previous social and political distinctions were never entirely overcome. As Bruno Gebhard observed in his 1939 essay: 'in this state where the word "Volksgemeinschaft" was used every day', people nevertheless retained a strong sense of 'the old class distinction'.[4] However, despite qualifications, something fundamental had shifted in Nazi Germany, and it had to do with more than specific incidents of exclusions and 'self-empowerment': it affected also the quality of social relations across society and the character of everyday interactions between people.

'Aryan' Germans were from the beginning exposed to multiple pressures to conform; they learned to act the part, as well as to distrust other people for fear of the potentially adverse consequences of speaking openly. Depending on the situation, individuals had various options: conform sufficiently to 'pass'; refuse to conform, even if at a personal cost; openly conform but resist in undercover ways; or retreat into circles where they felt potentially more secure. What no one could avoid was the imperative to perform. From 1933 onwards, there were significant shifts in a sense of connection with others, and these shifts initiated a process of redefining oneself. There were many little steps along the way, at first imperceptible; but over time, and by 1935, encompassing a transformation not only in social behaviour but also in the sense of personal and collective identity.

German society was, in effect, being ripped apart in new ways. Continuing distinctions of class and status were now being complemented by Nazi criteria. Even if conforming only outwardly to new norms and expectations, those 'Aryans' who were initially bystanders were increasingly engaged in a variety of compromises—which had consequences, both immediate, in terms of furthering processes of social exclusion, and longer term, in practices of 'looking away', learning to ignore, 'not knowing about', or not registering violence against outcasts. Not all of this was a question of so-called self-empowerment (*Selbstermächtigung*): some compromises were painful even for those doing the excluding. But simple conformity made a crucial difference—both to the development of new patterns of identification and indifference in peacetime and, eventually, fatally, in the ways in which, in wartime, so many either facilitated or turned a blind eye to mass murder.

Conformity forced Germans to put everything in question—and, in effect to become complicit with systemic racism in steps that were so small at first that they hardly seemed worthy of notice. Initially, starting in 1933 and continuing over the following years, the vast majority learned to negotiate ways of going along with the demands of Nazism in order to achieve their own aims, whether political, personal, or professional, and whether in pursuit of long-term or immediate goals that, for people in subordinate positions and limited resources, could be simply a matter of trying to survive and even prosper again after the depths of the Depression. Conformity inevitably meant making compromises, large and small: weighing the cost of belonging against the price of standing apart.

Already before the promulgation of the Nuremberg Laws in 1935 there was a seemingly unstoppable process of renegotiation of collective identities, a process that is vital to understanding growing accommodation among 'Aryan' Germans to systemic racism. If conformity was felt necessary to survival, dissembling was essential; but fear of betraying one's own inner feelings might in effect necessitate betraying others—even if not individually, then collectively, by helping to sustain the fiction of the national community and the associated exclusion of the marginalized. In this process, the character of society changed significantly—and in ways that would facilitate later complicity in mass murder. The leap seems almost unthinkable, when put like that; but in a society like 1930s Germany, these early gradual steps laid the essential groundwork for the challenges to come.

Individual experiences offer an intimate understanding of the pressures on people to fall into line, to perform Nazism, to enact conformity—ultimately easing the path to remaining silent, looking away as violence escalated against those now designated outsiders. Redrawing the borders between communities was a crucial step in creating both the alleged ignorance and the capacity for indifference, that would ultimately allow so many to ignore the path to genocide, even when it was evident all around.

We need to remember the risks and immense difficulties—the near-impossibility—of active opposition in Nazi Germany, before moving to explore the varieties of dissembling and mutual distrust that came to permeate life even in the early peacetime years of the Third Reich.

Opposition and retreat

In the spring of 1933, Nazi enthusiasts were jubilant. Franz Albrecht Schall, who turned twenty that year, filled his diary with outbursts of praise for Hitler, the 'Führer of the German people' who has 'sown the seed from which a free Germany will grow'. Having just heard a speech by Hitler in the Berlin Sportpalast, he vowed that the 'battle' against those he held responsible for the miseries of the past fourteen years would be 'unrelenting', until Marxism and all its proponents had been totally 'eradicated'. Like millions of other Germans he started to devote all his energies to this fight, now with the full backing of the new regime.[5]

For those against whom the 'battle' was to be fought—socialists, Marxists, Jews—attempts to engage in political opposition were increasingly fraught. The experiences of the left-wing activist and '*Mischling*' Lore Taut, and of those with whom she interacted and whose responses she observed, illustrate very clearly how so many committed opponents of Nazism among 'Aryan' Germans found it easier simply to withdraw, to retreat into quiescence; for some, this was the only way to survive and sustain family life in Nazi Germany.[6]

In the early summer of 1933, Taut was struggling on in her activist colony, distributing oppositional leaflets and the underground newspaper, *Der rote Funken*. But she was also worrying about her husband, Richard, who had been forced to flee and hide abroad, and about her own situation, and the growing unwillingness of others to continue the fight. In June 1933, Taut went for what she hoped would be a restorative weekend camping with friends. There she found former social democratic comrades talking, singing songs, and waiting for better times. They showed her what the SPD leadership in exile—now known as the Sopade—was producing, including the new version of the SPD newspaper, *Vorwärts*, which had been banned in Germany at the end of February. Taut was shocked that it was still bad-mouthing communists rather than fighting Nazis and tried to persuade the others to engage in more active resistance. Taut also visited old friends living further away. One couple had given up political work entirely. They told her just how difficult family life now was, with their daughter under the sway of both school and the League of German Maidens (Bund deutscher Mädel, BDM, the Hitler Youth organization for girls).[7]

Later in the summer Taut spent a week with friends in a small village in the Vogtland area in Saxony. She took with her illegal pamphlets and newsletters, hoping they would distribute them among the rural populace. But two of these friends had been arrested earlier in the year; one had been held for two weeks, the other for three months. They now barely dared even to greet each other on the street or to recognize other former comrades, in case of being accused of conspiring; and both used the 'Heil Hitler' greeting in public. The village, previously alive with workers' organizations, singing clubs, and sporting associations, had totally changed.

Everyone knew everybody, and former left-wingers were completely at the mercy of the Nazis. Taut realized that town and country were entirely different universes, and what might seem possible in a city was unthinkable in a small rural community. Here, people across the political spectrum were adapting as best they could. Taut noted that even the children in the highly political families with whom she was friends were learning survival tactics at an early age. When they went swimming in the local stream on hot summer afternoons, they kept their distance from other children. At school, one friend's thirteen-year-old son was careful in what he said; but the eight-year-old daughter found it even harder. Their father told Taut that he had come to the view it would be prudent not to talk openly in front of his children at all, just to make things easier for them.[8]

In her 1939 essay, Taut recalled clearly how she came to realize the potentially horrendous consequences of political activism when she visited a comrade in hospital who had been beaten up by the Nazis over the course of four days. He was barely recognizable, and his wife, in an advanced stage of pregnancy, was nearly beside herself. Desperate to help, Taut suggested she should contact the Quakers, whose humanitarian work, particularly on behalf of children, was widely respected.[9]

At the same time, Taut was missing her husband, wondering how he was doing, and how she could carry on herself. She was able to visit Richard in Paris on one occasion, as part of a political mission. Under the pretext of the death of a (mythical) French aunt, she was to deliver an empty suitcase to a Monsieur Boulanger in a flower shop and exchange it for an identical suitcase to bring back to Germany; what illegal material this might have been filled with she was either not told or chose not to reveal in her 1939 essay, for fear of incriminating anyone involved. In this mission she succeeded. On another occasion, Taut smuggled foreign newspapers stuffed under her clothes, pretending to be pregnant. She also made a point of shopping in stores owned by Jews, but again realized how different things were in rural communities. There, everyone knew each other, and anyone who supported Jewish stores was derided as a 'Jewish lackey' (*Judenknecht*). Even in her own urban community, things were becoming tense and personal animosities more acute.[10]

One day, a former comrade named Gerhart called Taut and told her how he had been arrested and had managed to escape from a Gestapo prison by jumping from a window. He was now desperate to link up again with

Richard. She told him that this would be difficult, as she was not sure where he was. On revealing this incident to her political leader, a man by the name of Henning, Taut suddenly realized how naïve she had been to fall into what was very likely a trap. She knew that she immediately had to give up her illegal work and avoid seeing anyone until they could be sure any danger might have passed. Her life seemed suddenly very empty and pointless. A couple of weeks later, she met up with Henning again in a coffee shop. He handed her a newspaper from the café newspaper stand, into which he had slid a piece of paper indicating that Gerhart was indeed now spying for the Gestapo. Fortunately, although she had revealed that Richard was 'abroad', she had not been more precise about his whereabouts, nor had she told Gerhart anything else that might be of use to the Gestapo. Henning taught her how to check if anyone might be following or watching her. And after about ten weeks, in spring 1934, she took up her political work again.[11]

But the strain was taking its toll. A skiing trip with friends near the Czech border reminded Taut, on returning, just how awful it was to go 'back into the prison that was Germany, the greyness of the everyday, the isolation, the permanent danger'. Working now with a Jewish company specializing in emigration counselling, she often felt 'more like a nurse than a secretary'. She noted that people 'seeking advice were generally in a to-tally distraught state of nerves, agitated and always in a hurry'. This was en-tirely understandable. Many of them had, she found, already 'spent months in concentration camps and prisons'. She realized that 'every day that they still had to wait in Germany for the completion and handover of the nu-merous documents that were necessary for their emigration was a torture for them, every SA-man on the street, every early morning ringing of the doorbell, made them tremble'. Political opposition seemed fruitless, work was stressful, private life nonexistent. Like so many others who came up against the brutality of the Nazi regime, Taut recalled that by late 1934 she had realized that there was little she and her small band of political asso-ciates could accomplish. For Taut, too, there was an added problem: her 'mixed race' status, as a '*Mischling*', which brought further disadvantages. She determined to get out. In the winter of 1934–1935, she skied over the Czech border with the help of a man who often assisted emigrants finding their way across the mountainous terrain.[12]

Despite all her experiences, Taut missed her homeland and did not lose her faith in what she described as the 'good nature of the Germans'. But, as she wrote in 1939, she would also 'never forget how impossible it is for most people to stand up against this terror and to get organized'. She had confidence that thousands were resisting and believed that hundreds of thousands more would join them, but was by now convinced that internal resistance would never be enough to bring down the Hitler regime.[13] In this, she was sadly all too right, even if she maintained an optimistic view of most Germans.

Some saw it far more pessimistically, and from an earlier date. In the summer of 1934, Friedrich Reuss—whose maternal grandfather had been Jewish—was approached by an old acquaintance sounding out the possibility of engaging in opposition. As we have seen, Reuss's promising civil service career had already been shattered by the April 1933 law, and he knew that the odds against success were stacked too high. As he summarized it in his own mind:

> It was too late. All parties had been disbanded. Their leaders were dead, in concentration camps, or abroad. Every telephone was under surveillance, in every apartment block there was a Nazi supervisor, Gestapo, no possibility of keeping secrets in letters, every maidservant a paid spy, all higher state offices replaced with Nazis, and a death sentence for everything. Attempt at high treason: sentence of death. Preparation for such an attempt: sentence of death. Founding a new party: sentence of death. Meeting for purposes of founding a new party: sentence of death. (Is what we are currently doing actually preparation for an attempt or something like it??) Sentence of death retroactively for crimes that still have to be invented. The ancient German principle of clan responsibility is to be reactivated, in other words, if I manage to get away with it my young wife and my elderly mother will be murdered in a barbarous manner.[14]

In view of all this, Reuss chose to decline the invitation.

The muddled middle and the price of compromise

Those on the margins of German society feared for their lives. Those caught up in the enthusiasm for Hitler and what they saw as national regeneration under the swastika were variously energized by mass rallies, political speeches, and community activism. Significant institutions and people in prominent positions had fallen into line, making adjustments and sustaining the regime in one way or another. But what of those 'ordinary Germans'—the muddled middle—who were neither fired by a sense of political mission nor automatically excluded on grounds of 'race'? They were, numerically, probably a majority of the population. They had a far greater range of options about possible ways forwards in the early years after 1933, and yet most played a role, with varying degrees of conviction or unease, in conforming and thereby contributing to the discourses and practices of the Nazi Volksgemeinschaft. Pressures could be subtle, and potential hazards of nonconformity might in retrospect seem almost trivial. At the time, even early on, it was far from easy to avoid the general slide towards compliance with the Nazi project. Personal commitments often had to be weighed against the potential benefits of compliance or engaging in moral compromises. Difficult choices had to be made, with associated emotional costs. Unless there were strong pre-existing commitments, conformity was clearly the easiest option.

In 1933, as he noted in his diary entries at the time, Robert Breusch was enjoying teaching in the small Birklehof boarding school in Hinterzarten, a picturesque village in the Black Forest. Founded as an offshoot of Kurt Hahn's progressive school in Salem, the Birklehof started with only ten pupils, rising to twenty soon after Breusch's arrival. The children would sit around one big table for lessons. As the school grew to around thirty pupils, slightly fewer than a quarter were 'non-Aryan'. All were respected as members of the residential community, which, unlike the generally authoritarian, hierarchical German school system, involved a degree of self-government by pupils. Alongside the lessons, there were sporting activities, hiking, and skiing expeditions in the surrounding countryside, and longer residential excursions to a cabin in the forest. Breusch felt secure in a school where the progressive outlook was compatible with his own.

Yet by the summer of 1933 there were warning signs he could not ignore. For one thing, his Jewish fiancée, Käte Dreyfuß, increasingly aroused critical comments; even having a drink with her in a nearby inn at weekends, after an afternoon walking in the hills, occasioned disapproving gossip among locals, just as it had for Gerta Pfeffer. For another, pressures to join the NSDAP or an affiliated organization grew. One by one, Breusch's friends— even those who had previously been members of quite different political parties—took on Nazi uniforms and swastika pin badges. Some tried to persuade Breusch to join at least the SA, if not the NSDAP, but he steadfastly refused. Yet all around, people were falling into line 'like withered trees in the wind', as he wrote.[15] Even the great philosopher Martin Heidegger, he noted, had converted to Nazism and become rector of Freiburg University. The few exceptions seemed to be from an older generation, not so easily swayed; but Breusch could not understand how so many even among them were now keen to demonstrate support for the new regime.

The leadership and atmosphere of the Birklehof school also began to change. On 25 February 1933, not even four weeks after Hitler's appointment, the charismatic director of the main Salem school, Kurt Hahn, was arrested simply on grounds of being Jewish. The Birklehof school was subjected to a police search, but Breusch noted that since the local gendarme had three children enjoying free places at the school, this search was not carried out very thoroughly. It seemed more a tactic of intimidation, emphasizing superior force. Hahn, however, was refused permission to re-enter his Salem school and subjected to further intimidation. Later that year he left for Great Britain, and in 1934 founded what would become a well-known school for 'outward-bound' activities in Scotland, Gordonstoun (attended by members of the British royal family, including the Duke of Edinburgh and Prince Charles). In Birklehof, a new director was appointed, along with another teacher. Both were Nazis. Breusch thought them quite sympathetic, on a personal level.

By June 1933, the school had been forced to found a Hitler Youth group. It was agreed that the new Nazi teacher, Herr Fluck, should direct the group, and that all 'Aryan' children would receive uniforms. This meant, however, excluding six 'non-Aryan' children. The teachers tried to ensure these children did not feel excluded, but it was not easy to avoid the new sense of difference. The school was also told that every lesson was to start with the 'Heil Hitler' greeting. In such a small community this seemed absurd. It was therefore agreed that the whole day constituted, in effect, a single 'lesson', and that the greeting therefore needed only to be made once, at the morning sports session. Breusch had always enjoyed this early morning exercise session but decided no longer to attend.

Eventually, Breusch could not evade growing pressure to fall into line. On 25 February 1934 he was called to a meeting in Freiburg, along with thirty other teachers. They were instructed to extend their arms in the Hitler greeting and to repeat an oath of obedience to the Nazi regime. Everyone around Breusch mumbled along, but he kept his own mouth firmly shut.

He wanted to drop his arm—but he could not quite bring himself to take the risk. Writing about this in his diary, he fretted about his response. Was it cowardice? But what would he have achieved by refusing the Hitler salute? He did not inwardly feel at all bound by the oath. But he was troubled by the feeling that he had compromised his own values.

During the following weeks Breusch was incessantly urged to join the Nazi party, the SS, the SA, or the National Socialist Teachers' League; he was now the only teacher who had not yet joined any affiliated organization. By May 1934, he was beginning to waver. Perhaps it would be a good idea to join at least the SA. He and his Jewish fiancée, Käte Dreyfuß, were, after all, objects of attention. And one of his colleagues, Dr Max, was a persuasive advocate of the view that 'one could work from within' the Nazi party. This meant joining up, going along, carving out a position for oneself—and then trying to influence the direction in which things were going.

Yet despite his respect for his colleagues, Breusch came to the view that anyone justifying their Nazi affiliations had capitulated. He decided, for the time being at least, to maintain his distance—even if only to keep his evenings free from too many meetings, and so as not to have to wear what he saw as a 'laughable' uniform.[16]

The main reason Breusch could not bring himself to fall into line was his fiancée. Despite pressure from family, friends, colleagues, and acquaintances, he and Käte Dreyfuß continued with their plans to stay together, and eventually to get married. In June 1933, Käte's mother had received an anonymous threatening letter with a newspaper article reporting how an 'Aryan' had been publicly humiliated and severely punished for committing 'racial treason' by having intimate relations with a Jew. The letter, understandably, had upset her terribly. But it had little effect on Breusch and Dreyfuß. That summer, the couple went on holiday in Switzerland, to escape the increasingly oppressive atmosphere in Germany; Breusch realized that it was not only the clear mountain air that let them breathe more freely. Yet even here, among vistas of ice-capped peaks, fir trees, and lush green valleys, the echoes of Nazism reverberated. Two tourists from Berlin turned up at the mountain hut where they were staying, and when these tourists saw the name "Dreyfuß" in the visitors' book they proceeded to attempt to persuade the surprised chalet owner of the virtues of Nazism. Later on, in November, Breusch and Dreyfuß went on a walking tour in the Black Forest, planning to meet up with Breusch's closest friend, Wolfgang von Blittersdorf. The latter insisted Dreyfuß use the name of 'Dreher' rather than her own.

On 30 December 1933, Breusch and von Blittersdorf met up again at a ceremony commemorating local Scouts who had died in the Great War. Afterwards, they hiked up the Feldberg mountain, where they had spent many happy times together on trips and camps when younger. As they walked through the familiar countryside, beautiful even in the bareness of winter, they chatted as in the old days about anything and everything. But they also talked about Käte. Von Blittersdorf again warned Breusch to break up with her. Breusch knew that his friend meant well; but he refused to listen.

Within three months, in late March 1934, von Blittersdorf celebrated his own wedding. And he did not invite Breusch, as that would have meant inviting Dreyfuß, too. Breusch, remarkably, was still close to von Blittersdorf: the old ties of friendship were not so easily severed. But this marked a distinct separation of ways. Although Breusch did not share his friend's pro-Nazi views, he could understand von Blittersdorf's reasoning: in Nazism, his friend saw a return to national greatness and a social programme offering a return to full employment. But Breusch could not share von Blittersdorf's views on fellow Germans of Jewish descent. Not inviting someone to your wedding was symbolic of the emergent gulf between communities, a gulf that was growing ever wider—not just as a result of Nazi policies, or violent incidents on the part of activists, but even in these apparently almost trivial, informal decisions and differences between friends.

Unwilling conformity and small refusals

The Nazis strove to construct a sense of national community not only through propaganda and ideology but also through regular group activities, including parades, rallies, Hitler Youth meetings, or Reich Labour Service and other camps. There were also endlessly repeated symbolic acts of belonging in daily life, as in the 'Heil Hitler' salute. The outward appearance of a nation united did not entirely correspond, however, to a more complex range of inner feelings, even among those who 'belonged'.

Barbara Sevin's experiences of Reich Labour Service provide insights into the balance of rewards, pressures, and tensions. A Lutheran 'Aryan', born in Berlin in 1912, Sevin wrote in her 1939 essay that she had studied in both Heidelberg and Munich universities. As a doctoral student she had to 'volunteer' for a Labour Service camp in Neckarbischofsheim, southeast of Heidelberg, in the winter of 1933–1934, and felt that this was in fact far from voluntary.[17]

At the camp, Sevin soon discovered that there was neither time nor space for individual thought or activity: 'The intention was to reduce us to a "mass", a "porridge", devoid of individual traits and thus all the more easily managed.' Sevin, like many others at the camp, was not enamoured. The young women found the 'endless marching . . . thoroughly detestable'. They had to parade through villages singing, ceasing only as soon as they were out of earshot. They had to attend talks by visiting lecturers and follow compulsory courses of instruction: 'Even when the girls were interested, they didn't enjoy being ordered around.' Some, she recalled, 'yawned audibly and made every possible disturbance'. On occasion, they explicitly made fun of Nazi ideology. When, for example, an angry leader asked who was guilty of turning on the dormitory lights after curfew, they responded in chorus, 'the Jews, of course!' In this first winter of the Nazi regime, they expressed political dissent by singing socialist songs, although they felt they had to watch out for the presence of known Nazis. But even the true believers at this time seemed relatively harmless to them: the enthusiasts 'had espoused the Nazi cause, for the most part, as a result of boredom'. Sevin and her group organized evening discussions to foment anti-Nazi sentiments and felt lucky that they were not betrayed by a woman who seemed, Sevin recalled, 'the only one who was intelligent enough to perceive what was going on'. This woman 'had certain pro-Nazi leanings, though not to a fanatical extent'. Sevin thought that she was 'too well-bred to do anything to injure us'.[18]

Sevin noted that many others were play-acting to achieve personal ends. The woman in charge of registration was outwardly a Nazi, although Sevin doubted whether this was 'really from the bottom of her heart'. Quite presciently, in view of the widespread changes of heart professed by Germans after 1945, Sevin thought her behaviour was pragmatic: 'She was a Nazi now without any doubt, but there was also no doubt that under a democratic regime she would have been a democrat and under a communistic regime a communist.' The woman was in Sevin's view simply an opportunist: 'Since the regime and the whole chaotic state of affairs offered undreamed of possibilities, she recognized with a natural instinct on which side her bread was buttered, took circumstances as they were and felt very, very happy about it.'[19]

Even rural farmers and labourers were now being opportunistic. According to Sevin, they thought 'that the National Socialists were a bit cracked'. But they also were willing to play their parts in the national script—again providing visual fodder for propaganda images. They dressed up in traditional costume at 'gatherings such as those on the Bückeberg, where the Führer once a year addressed "his peasants" at harvest time'. They knew that these 'costume assemblies' were purely for show. Sevin said they mocked the practice—until they realized the material benefits of playing along: once 'they found that they received much better treatment when they appeared before the authorities (for the payment of taxes, etc.) in costume—well, they did so'.[20]

In late 1934, thinking that she had now fully served her time in service of the Nazi cause, Sevin was engaged in writing her doctoral thesis in an idyllic retreat on the Neckar River near Heidelberg, when she received a letter informing her that participation in yet another labour camp was a precondition for receiving further financial aid. Though furious, Sevin tried to make the best of it, reflecting philosophically on life's 'vexations and contretemps'. By this time—following the murder of SA leaders including Ernst Röhm, and the death of President Hindenburg—Hitler's power was more firmly entrenched and Sevin was unnerved: 'A mood of uncanniness and anxiety pervaded everything in Germany', she wrote. 'Danger might be lurking behind the most innocent appearances'. She was not sanguine. While she thought people did not believe the Gestapo was all-powerful, they pretended, but no one was sure. Ultimately, she concluded: 'in Nazi Germany one has no choice but to obey; otherwise one shows that one is afraid or actually suspicious.'[21]

So Sevin temporarily dropped work on her dissertation and attended the second 'voluntary' labour service camp as ordered, this time in northeastern Germany. Another year of Hitler in power had already had an effect, and she immediately noted that the atmosphere was very different from that in the first camp. Gone were the dissenting opinions and boundary testing, where her previous group had engaged in subversive discussions and sung socialist songs, and where even a known Nazi had not denounced them. Now, authority, obedience, and mutual distrust prevailed. The 'word of the

leader was everything' while 'a human being was a mere speck of dust, a ci-
pher'. The other young women were 'like automatons or puppets, all more
or less alike in what they said, did, or wished'. Rather than using their own
initiative, everyone 'sought to divine in advance the wishes and thoughts
of the leader, so as to make a good impression'. Sevin found the degree of
uniformity 'astounding'.[22]

In an atmosphere of mutual suspicion, Sevin found it impossible to connect with any potentially sympathetic souls, as they were practising the
art of survival through performance and dissimulation: 'What these girls
actually thought—they who cooperated so obediently, peacefully, and attentively in heeding every expressed or unexpressed wish and command of
their leaders, just like little dachshunds—what they actually thought, say, no
one knew.' She went on, 'all that was to be seen, however, was a competition
in the practice of servility'.[23] The Nazis were training people to be 'hypo-
critical puppets'. Even without a leader present, the young women 'showed
the utmost distrust and preserved the maximum of silence'. Fear of betrayal
played a significant role within the group, for denunciation had become 'a
recognized method of government and was no longer branded as dishon-
orable'. Sevin now felt 'it was a question, during this period, of keeping my
nerves steady and not letting myself become provoked'.[24]

The atmosphere in camp contrasted sharply with the outer displays of
the Nazi community, underlining the difference between public image and
personal experience. The camp leader's style was characterized by a 'men-
acing and boastful tone'. But in public there were only displays of community harmony. One of the final gatherings was held in the open, along
with other organizations, including the Men's Labour Service, the National
Socialist Women's League, the Hitler Youth, and the League of German
Girls (BDM), as well as the SA and SS. Sevin recounted that the 'extraordinarily large field was black with their figures' but the 'customary loudspeakers had not been installed out here in the country'. The outcome was
predictable: 'As in connection with all Nazi festivities, it meant, for those
who did not belong to the inner circle, interminable standing and waiting.
Then we were suddenly aroused from our state of torpor or musing by an
ear-piercing outburst of "Sieg Heil, Sieg Heil!"' This did not make it any
more intelligible: 'Judging from the little that could be understood, it was
evident that the formations were once more being praised for their pledges,
their work, their loyalty, and so forth, which, together with the unerring

spirit of the leaders, would achieve the glory of Germany.' This, however, bore little or no relation to Sevin's experiences in camp.[25]

On completing labour service, Sevin took up her studies again, now in Munich rather than in Heidelberg. Combining scepticism with enforced conformity, she thought it might be easier in a larger city to find like-minded people without attracting too much attention. Munich was known by the Nazis as the 'Capital of the Movement' (*Hauptstadt der Bewegung*), given Hitler's pre-1933 base and Brown House headquarters, and therefore, Sevin thought, did not need to prove itself loyal to Nazism as the previously more liberal Heidelberg was now doing. In common parlance, people called Munich the 'Capital of the Anti-Movement' (*Hauptstadt der Gegenbewegung*). As in Berlin, there were many foreigners in Munich, including diplomatic representatives, further contributing to a slightly more open atmosphere. Sevin managed to find lodgings with a landlady who turned a blind eye to the meetings she held with dissident friends. Sevin had a high opinion of this woman and others like her: 'They are perhaps not well-suited to going out on the streets to make speeches or organize acts of violence'; but, importantly, they 'have never let themselves be conquered by the regime, have never given themselves up'.[26]

Sevin's landlady and others like her were not prepared to play a supporting role in the drama of orchestrated mass enthusiasm designed to create public images of a homogeneous national community united behind its Führer. Their refusal to perform according to the national script was, however tiny, in a sense a minor act of principled resistance: they refused to be among the visible onlookers whose very presence appeared to condone the regime, but who would later claim to have been merely innocent by-standers. Yet such refusals, as we shall see, were ultimately insufficient.

Reorientations: Communities of identity and empathy

Almost immediately, living under Nazism began to affect social and emotional connections between people. Even if largely ill-defined, often barely consciously registered (particularly among those who were doing the excluding), informal communities emerged in everyday life, based on those with whom people identified, and viewpoints with which they could readily empathize. This would become increasingly significant for a society in which previously a sense of German patriotism and national belonging had been extremely high among Jewish and non-Jewish Germans alike. After 1933 those who were excluded from the narrower Volksgemeinschaft definition of what it meant to be 'German' by virtue of 'non-Aryan' descent were made to feel the rejection all the more.

New identities were being imposed. As Gerhard Miedzwinski put it: 'My personal outlook is that of a Jew who is not religious and felt more German than—well, I cannot say: Jewish, because I do not believe in a Jewish people or race, but, perhaps, better—who felt German only.'[27] Martin Freudenheim, a Jewish lawyer who in April 1933 had managed to retain his position because of his war service, had similar feelings: 'Germany was my fatherland. German was what was dominant in me. It was my language, my culture, my love.' The Nazis were 'robbing' him of his fatherland, as well as his human rights; he 'belonged inwardly' more to Germany, he felt, than did many of the screaming nationalist socialists.[28] But for Miedzwinski, Freudenheim, and many others, it was clear that 'feeling German' was no longer an option under Nazi rule; and indeed, what it meant to be 'German' was in the process of being radically redefined on 'racial' lines.

German Jews, whether or not they were religious, started to gravitate towards others. Martin Andermann, having found that many former friends in his native Königsberg now shunned him, and that most social, cultural, and culinary outlets were effectively closed to Jews, thought that 'it was quite obvious that the Jewish families who had been turned to their own resources would get together more frequently than they had done previously'. The 'sense of common need' produced a bond; the 'constant state of anxiety' was mitigated a little by 'a certain warmth and cordiality' among those dwindling numbers who had not emigrated, and who 'came ever closer together'. Moreover, he recalled in his essay: 'we began to value more highly the things that were still possible, that were not yet prohibited, and we were thankful for many things which would previously just have been taken for granted.'[29]

In the southern village of Gailingen, close to the Swiss border, the schoolboy Heinz Heilbronn, whose grandfather had been mayor of Gailingen from 1870 to 1884, kept a diary of his experiences from before the Nazi takeover through the years of Nazi rule.[30] Heilbronn's father, a doctor who had distinguished himself in the First World War, was gradually squeezed out of his practice. Heilbronn was able to remain in school and, remarkably, was the only (and last) Jew to be able to take the final examinations, the *Abitur*, in the academic high school in Singen in 1938; but he was prevented from going on to university.

During these years, Heilbronn's diary illustrates how a boy who was well-liked and respected among his peers, and an active participant in school activities, was progressively socially isolated. He noted days on which the SA marched, singing 'the Jew must be got out'; days such as the 1933 April boycott when the SA terrorized and pressured local people not to enter Jewish premises; days such as 1 May 1933, on which a number of Jews from Gailingen took a day trip over the border to Switzerland in order to escape the Nazi festivities and likely consequences.[31] Heilbronn noted repeated incidents of violence and intimidation, and recorded the legislation that progressively reduced the status and living conditions of Jews. At the same time, he records how those who sought to raise their voices in protest were also intimidated. In early March 1934, for example, members of the Hitler Youth were marching through the streets singing anti-Jewish songs. A local woman, Frau Zivi, looked out of her window as they went by and said 'Pfui'—an expression of disgust, roughly meaning 'Shame on you!' On hearing this, the teacher stopped, accosted her, and asked her what she had said. She repeated 'Pfui' to his face. He then denounced her, and she was arrested that evening. She spent a night in an unheated cell in Gailingen and the next day was sent to the neighbouring town of Radolfzell, where she spent a further four days in prison. Following her return, she had to pay a significant 'voluntary' donation to the Gailingen branch of the Nazi Winter Help charity.[32]

Even as he was increasingly excluded from activities, Heilbronn was still treated with some personal respect in school, with individual teachers occasionally intimating sympathy. When he was officially forbidden to take part in the shooting lessons, for example, that were introduced in February 1935, a teacher sought to arrange for his participation.[33] But for all the individual goodwill he experienced, the chasm between the Jewish and 'Aryan' communities was growing. In April 1935, Heilbronn spent two days in a Jewish Youth Hostel in Wangen on Lake Constance, in the company of fifteen Jewish boys from Frankfurt and roughly the same number of girls from Karlsruhe (about whom he somewhat cryptically noted, in parentheses, that they were 'inhibited' or 'uptight'). He summarized his experiences of this night away: 'It was wonderful, just to be among Jewish people.'

His impressions were 'amazing', particularly the sense of 'comradeship'. He added: 'It is hard, to be a Jew, and yet nevertheless good.'[34]

As he had been brought up in a practising Jewish community in a small village, it was relatively easy for Heilbronn to find a sense of community with other Jews, increasingly thrown together through their common plight. For people who had not been practising Jews and were now excluded from their previous social circles, however, getting together with other Jews entailed a larger cultural shift. Some found that to have a social life, they would have to engage with people who were far more orthodox.

This was the case with Margot Spiegel. Born in a well-to-do family in Konstanz, 'just two blocks away from the frontier with Switzerland', as she put it in her 1939 Harvard essay, Spiegel had barely registered her Jewish family background; wealth, social status, and culture were far more important. Her father had earned an Iron Cross in the war and was a nonreligious and well-respected lawyer, and her mother had inherited property. Spiegel was one of only three Jewish girls in her school class, and her best friend was a Catholic. Like her schoolmates, Spiegel loved not only Goethe and German culture but also hiking, skating, and playing tennis. She and her friends identified themselves as 'Swabians' (*Schwaben*), feeling they had more in common with others from Württemberg and Bavaria than with north Germans; they were critical of the acerbic Berliners with their renowned 'Berliner *Schnauze*' (sharp tongue). In spring 1933, however, things changed dramatically. On graduating from high school, Spiegel was not awarded a prize she had expected for her outstanding academic achievements. The girl who did receive the prize tore off the haphazardly affixed label and discovered Spiegel's name beneath hers; the school director had already preemptively followed the new Nazi line, which was officially only announced the following day, that Jewish pupils were no longer to receive prizes.[35]

Spiegel had wanted to go on to university but now knew that her prospects were radically constrained. She took a short-term job as a governess to acquire language skills in Italy. Here, she was surprised at how little Italian Jews felt exposed to persecution. It was even more of a shock, on returning to Germany in 1934, to see how things had changed at home. Many former friends and acquaintances had become Nazis, although 'the general opinion was still strongly against those people as goldseekers and weak characters'. Even Spiegel's remaining friends made her feel different by emphasizing that she was being explicitly included. They went together on a hiking trip around Lake Konstanz, singing and chatting; but it was no longer the easy friendship of earlier days. When newcomers joined the group, one of her friends told her not to worry, reassuring her that 'they won't know, because you don't look Jewish'. As she put it, 'this very saying "they won't know" made me decide not to join them' again once the group had expanded.[36]

Spiegel began to explore what it might mean to be Jewish. She had long been aware of the social gulf between her own family and the 'Russian or Polish Jews' who 'talked with their hands', spoke with a Yiddish accent, and were, in her opinion, 'less particular about manners and clothes', but had, as she added, 'a heart of gold'. She had never wanted to be seen associating with these Jews in the street and felt ashamed if she was seen with them by any of her gentile friends. But it was becoming increasingly clear to her that she could no longer be a member of the community to which she felt she really belonged.[37]

Turning to the company of others who had also been excluded from the Nazi national community was not without its tensions. She noted that Jewish boys and girls in her town remained close 'because there was no other place for them to go'. They met up informally in discussion groups, and studied Judaism, the Bible, and history, to try to find out why all this was happening. Spiegel had to force herself to attend this group, which also discussed Zionism; she did not feel at all at home there, despite having the sense that here she was 'a little more sheltered'. She found 'the completely Jewish atmosphere' very strange, and could not get used to the sound of Yiddish or the 'language and mannerisms' of some members.

Going to these meetings also led to conflicts with her father, who did not like the conspicuous Zionism of the group; at one point he refused to talk to her for weeks. He felt he was a German and, as Spiegel put it, 'belonged to the "*Frontkämpfer*" [front-line soldiers] who fought for Germany and are and remain in Germany till they die'. He was proud of the fact that 'our ancestors had been in Germany since before the 30 years war in 1600 [sic]' and simply could not contemplate the way in which his daughter was now being forced into the company of Jews with whom she had so little in common. Spiegel noted they had lived in same town for years but that it was only the recent process of 'persecution, recognition of our fate, and suffering' that 'brought us all together'. With a growing desire to emigrate, Spiegel again left Germany, this time to learn English. On her return, she widened her circle of contacts among Jews of all ages and saw 'how much this common period of stress had united them'.[38]

By 1934, Spiegel felt there was little alternative, as gentiles no longer dared to talk to Jews in the street, though a few still visited them at home. The proximity of Switzerland, and Swiss distancing from Nazism (even while continuing to do business with Nazis), seemed to have some impact on the atmosphere in Konstanz. But crossing the border was becoming ever more difficult, and people could no longer simply go across to read foreign newspapers or shop.[39]

The process Spiegel was experiencing was difficult in other ways for those who were in mixed marriages and for their offspring, who often felt doubly excluded, being neither fully Jewish nor 'Aryan'. Christians of Jewish descent, particularly those in mixed marriages like Christian Oppler, were far less likely to gravitate towards Jewish communities. Their 'Aryan' partners and children of mixed descent were emotionally closer to them, and they interacted frequently with friends and relatives who were not of Jewish descent—although this could easily give rise to family tensions, es-pecially once there was pressure on people in mixed marriages to divorce. Similarly, those 'Mischlinge' who were considered neither 'Aryan' nor Jewish had no other obvious community of identity to turn to. Friedrich Reuss, for example, was rebuffed by even well-meaning Jewish aid organizations, and felt ousted from both worlds. Eventually, he came into contact with a 'society for non-Aryan Christians'. Members of this society jokingly called it the Diabetics' Club because, they explained, the higher the percentage of the offending substance in your blood, the more dangerous the condition for your health. Attendance at the weekly meetings declined sharply after 1935, and individuals were registered as missing: stories circulated that some were in concentration camp and others had committed suicide.[40]

For many people, then, the Nazi distinction between 'Aryan' and 'non-Aryan' did not easily map onto previous conceptions of cultural or social identity. People were in effect now forming communities brought together by sharing a similar fate.

Apprehension: Dissimulation and mutual distrust

Even as identities were being reshaped during the early Nazi years, there was a marked growth of mutual distrust between individuals. Denunciation could be deadly, encouraging dissimulation.[41] And how people perceived

the situation—whether accurately or otherwise—had significant consequences for their behaviour or inaction in face of systemic violence. In this
area, Jews and non-Jews interacted in a variety of revealing ways.

Perspective is everything. The accounts of adults writing in 1939, with
the mid-1930s fresh in their minds, offer a rather different story from the
kinds of story offered in oral history interviews much later, some more than
half a century later, and predominantly involving people who had been
young at the time of the Third Reich. Many of those later interviewees,
looking back on the years of their childhood and youth from the perspective of old age, emphasize how they did not feel afraid of the Nazi regime;
but even if these respondents came from a cross-section of social classes and
political viewpoints, they remain a quite narrow generational cohort.[42] The
1939 essays also paint a somewhat different picture from what we can construct from other sources at the time. The hard statistical evidence for the
mid-1930s is not reflected in perceptions based on a time-lag of memory,
hearsay, and apprehension: following the massive wave of arrests and imprisonment of around 200,000 political opponents in makeshift camps and
prisons in the first year of Hitler's rule, the numbers of people held in concentration camps declined significantly in the mid-1930s. By this time, the
inmates of the newly established permanent camps run by the SS in Dachau
(1933), Sachsenhausen (1936), and Buchenwald (1937) were primarily those
labelled 'workshy' or 'asocial'; in October 1934, there were 2,400 prisoners;
in summer 1935, the average daily prisoner count was 3,800, rising slightly
to 4,761 on 1 November 1936 and to 7,746 at the end of December 1937.
This figure would more than triple, to 24,000 in June 1938, with a campaign against people deemed to be engaging in deviant behaviours, and
then more than double again to around 50,000 in November of that year,
following the wave of arrests of Jews after Kristallnacht—more than seven
times as many as a year earlier—dropping slightly to 31,000 with the release
of prisoners and the encouragement of Jewish emigration towards the end
of the year.[43] Yet despite the evidence to the contrary in the mid-1930s,
and before the expansion of 1938, growing public knowledge of conditions in camps seems to have dampened any desire for activism against the
Nazi regime; and, among those who were wavering, further encouraged the
shift towards ever greater conformity, both in public and in private. Partial
knowledge of the possibility of appalling treatment seems by the mid-1930s
to have played a disproportionately large role in affecting the behaviour of

millions of people in the muddled middle. Historical realities and subjective perceptions were not perfectly aligned, while people remained caught between awareness of the potential benefits of conformity and continuing unease about the compromises this entailed.

Identities, as I have noted, were continually shifting, as people repositioned themselves and sought to calibrate their self-image. Growing suspicion and unwillingness to talk openly outpaced the actual number of denunciations, and mutual distrust was widespread. This atmosphere was not easily captured in sources such as the records of denunciations, but appears to have been all-pervasive in the experience of many of the essay-writers. As Gebhard recalled, 'one of the worst things at that time was the increasing suspicion of each other'. When his family saw some of their friends return from concentration camps they were deeply shaken. They looked, he said, 'terrible', and they refused to talk about their experiences. He noted that this was when 'the first people started to emigrate'—or worse. One of their friends, a Jew who was dismissed from his position in the Dresden Social Welfare Department of Saxony, 'was so depressed that he committed suicide'.[44]

Lotte Popper noticed when shopping in Hamburg that customers in her local grocery store no longer chatted about politics as they had done previously but instead now 'bought their cabbages and potatoes in silence', while the shop assistant also served them in silence. Popper remembered how one woman 'looked around anxiously, fearful that one of the customers might perhaps remember her big tirades against the Hitler-hype before the elections, and she hurried to get out of the store with her basket'. Some 'Aryans', she thought, only talked openly with Jewish friends whom they knew were not in any position to betray them. As her husband's dental practice declined in the mid-1930s, Popper and her family had to rent a smaller home. Here, they were visited by an 'Aryan' friend, a concert singer from Vienna. She almost envied the Poppers for their capacity to talk freely, while in her circles 'everyone was afraid of everybody'. If she was invited for a social gathering, no one dared speak, which she found 'deadly boring'. But of course these were people who were sufficiently critical of the Hitler regime to be fearful of expressing their sentiments openly.[45]

In Munich, Klara Rosenthal heard of the experiences of a friend who had been imprisoned in Oranienburg, a concentration camp founded in 1933 north of Berlin. It was run by the SA until July 1934, when the SS took control; in 1936 it was replaced by the better-known Sachsenhausen camp. Rosenthal wrote that she would not have believed such horror to be possible had she not heard directly from someone she trusted to tell the truth. By the mid-1930s, she thought, denunciations were 'flourishing', and nobody 'dared' to 'behave in ways they wanted to within their own homes'. The Gestapo would come to arrest Jews in the early hours of the morning, between three and five o'clock, in order to avoid attracting any attention. Rosenthal reflected, 'sleep was a matter of listening out for the doorbell, and our nerves were in a constant state of high tension'.[46]

It is not easy to establish the extent to which fear of denunciation was present among people who supported Hitler and were basically happy about wider developments. Joseph Aust, the young Nazi from Silesia who had been impressed by his uncle's commitment and the ways in which Nazis had cleared the streets of Berlin in early 1933, was in his mid-twenties when he penned his essay in 1939. He was at this time writing from a British internment camp, Warner's Internment Camp G in Devon, where he was challenged by new views and experiences from different perspectives. He was repeatedly surprised by being confronted with the allegation that people in Nazi Germany were 'unfree' and 'could not do or say' what they wanted. This was not, he claimed, his own experience of living in Nazi Germany: he felt he had always been able speak freely and say anything he wanted, even if friends had often warned him to hold his tongue. He did not pause to consider what the friendly warnings might have implied for restraints on full freedom of expression even in Nazi circles. But, he went on, now that he had been exposed in the internment camp to 'Jews and political émigrés', he had actually changed his views on this question. The talk of Gestapo and unfreedom 'might well be true for those people who absolutely do not want to feel national or social, and who are so little really German that they absolutely cannot grasp German manners and customs but by contrast always just want to do precisely those things that National Socialism does not want them to do'. Here, despite conceding that some people might indeed have been constrained from openly expressing their views, he simply reiterated the Nazi worldview: to suppress the freedom of those who thought differently was perfectly justifiable in light of Nazi aims; and 'Jews and political émigrés' were not really 'German', so their repression and exclusion was also justifiable. He did add, however, a small qualification about methods in relation to some of them: 'But I do feel real sympathy for those few who, because of the really guilty, were often affected particularly harshly by the necessary measures taken by National Socialism.' This too echoed the sentiment offered by other Nazis that it was a shame that their one 'good Jew' had to suffer because of all the others. Ultimately, even with his supposedly evolving transformation of political perceptions, Aust continued to support the Nazi exclusion and repression of what he too criticized as 'un-German'; and he did not in any way seem to understand that this did indeed constitute a restriction on freedom.[47]

This essay was written for the Harvard competition before the wartime atrocities that would later make the expression of any such Nazi sympathies utterly taboo. It is remarkably revealing in its combination of naïvety and confusion in face of new perspectives. One has to wonder, then, about how best to interpret conflicting postwar claims about the extent to which fear had played a role in outward obedience and apparent support. Clearly for some individuals who had been genuinely committed to the Nazi cause at the time, fear might be simply a useful postwar excuse to cover up conformity rooted in implicit agreement with the Nazi worldview. For others, who had been young during the Third Reich and were only interviewed in old age at the turn of the century, the contrary claim that they had not actually been afraid might accurately reflect a degree of former belief in Nazi views; but given their lack of real responsibility during the Nazi period, they felt less need more than half a century later to provide as much by way of self-exculpatory narratives as did the more culpable adults in the immediate postwar years.

On balance, the essays written in 1939 provide insights into widespread ways of thinking and feeling that are not so easily captured in other contemporary sources such as the cases that made it into the Gestapo records.[48] These essays, written largely but (as in the case of Aust) not always from the political margins, suggest that there was indeed an all-pervading atmosphere of mutual suspicion even among those supportive of much of what Nazism was doing, or at least a sense that people widely felt they had to be more careful about what they said to whom and when. Notable examples are given by, for example, Friedrich Reuss, who in the course of his work as a travelling salesman selling insurance policies engaged in many discussions with engineers and skilled workers in the Leipzig area, including those working in the Leuna plant, one of the largest in Germany. He noted strong support for the Führer and the belief that he would create a

better future for Germans. He also noted widespread underlying antisemitism. Nonetheless a few of these workers grumbled about how society had
changed. Reuss recorded a representative litany from one worker: 'There is
no family life any more, and whenever there is a Mass in Church it clashes
with a Party meeting, after all you have your own faith but all that is supposed to be taken away from you, and the sort of ideas the children bring
home with them, well I could tell you a thing or two about that. . . . Not
even in your own home can you talk freely.' Reuss remembered that the
man stopped suddenly in his outburst and asked him, 'Oh my God, you
are not an informant are you? I haven't said a single word. Who are you, in
fact?' Reuss remembered trying to reassure such individuals and, he noted,
'sometimes the man would then sign the insurance policy contract'.[49]

Reuss was surprised to find himself a particularly valued conversation
partner. Even as he was feeling increasingly socially isolated, as a 'non-
Aryan', retreating into his family circle and socializing only with fellow
members of the 'non-Aryan association', he found that a few people still
came to visit him and talk to him in the relative safety of his home. The explanation, he thought, was quite simple: 'I was hardly likely to be a Gestapo
spy. They would not have believed anything I said anyway. I was therefore a
good garbage dump for people's mental debris.'[50]

One visitor unintentionally revealed the degree of antisemitism among
even those who remained well-disposed to Reuss. He told the story of a
Catholic woman who had registered a complaint because the death of her
husband, who had been murdered by the SS, was being recorded as 'suicide',
a cause of great distress for a Catholic. The lawyer acting on the Catholic
woman's behalf was arrested and 'disappeared' for two weeks. The friend
recounting this tale was full of righteous indignation, and wanted advice
from Reuss. 'If only it had been a Jew', Reuss reported his friend telling
him, 'then I would not have said anything, but he was demonstrably Aryan,
and that is after all an injustice.'[51]

Another story Reuss recounted—whether he had been told it directly or
simply heard it at second hand is not clear—involved a German priest who
had been approached in a confessional by a man who wanted him to write
an article for a Dutch newspaper about the position of the Catholic Church
in the new Germany. The priest had refused because he wanted neither to
lie nor to write anything that might be construed as being in some way
critical of Nazi Germany. The next day the man came back and tried again

to persuade the priest, emphasizing the need to let the outside world know what was going on. The priest again refused and this time threw him out of the confessional. The man pleaded with the priest not to tell anyone about this incident. He had a wife and children to support and did not want to get in any trouble. The priest promised not to say anything and to treat the conversation as an entirely confidential matter. The following day, however, the priest was himself arrested and sentenced to ten years in prison for 'high treason'. It turned out that the 'family man' was in fact a Gestapo agent. Whatever its truth, this particular story illustrates the level of fear prevalent in many circles in mid-1930s Germany.[52]

In this climate, it was impossible to tell who was dissembling and who was not. Social psychologists have identified 'pluralistic ignorance' and conformity with 'false norms' among people in democracies. People who do not know what others in a group actually think often decide that it is safer to go along with what appear to be the dominant norms in order not to stand out.[53] In the Third Reich, however, there could be horrific consequences for not going along. The concept of pluralistic ignorance is far less well suited to understanding behaviour in conditions where stepping out of line might easily lead to denunciation and potentially severe penalties.

Those 'Aryans' who stuck by their Jewish friends were aware of the risks they were running but ran them nonetheless. Yet mainstream Germany was shifting in the mid-1930s. Ernst Rathgeber summarized the situation as he saw it: 'the proportion of supposed supporters of this regime rose in direct proportion to the rising pressure on people.'[54] In the view of Ernst Schwartzert, those who were outraged by the way things were going would only grumble in private because of 'people's mutual distrust of each other'.[55] Whether or not the extent of denunciations in Nazi Germany in the mid-1930s can be interpreted as an index of popular support for the regime, as argued by some historians, the experiences recounted by these contemporaries highlight the significance of unspoken fears and perceptions for self-censorship and the outward appearance of conformity.

These accounts also reveal, if indirectly, the degree to which some aspects of Nazi racism had already become internalized by this point: how it seemed obvious to Reuss's friend, for example, that righteous indignation at a miscarriage of justice would not be applicable in the case of a Jew; or how Gebhard, who remained loyal to his Jewish friends, did not simultaneously recognize how mounting a major public exhibition, approved and opened by Goebbels, was reinforcing the Nazi racist view of the world. Notions of identity were gradually being reshaped in ways that were both blindingly obvious—as in regime propaganda and ideology—and more subtly, as communities of empathy increasingly drifted further apart.

The photographs of enthusiastic crowds waving swastika flags, cheering and smiling, give no sense of how many non-Jewish Germans were, like Barbara Sevin, unwilling participants in collective performances. It is equally hard to peel away layers of unjustified self-exculpation, either in the Harvard essays written in 1939 or in interviews conducted decades later. Some Germans did indeed later admit to having been genuinely enthusiastic about Nazism but claimed they were young and taken in by Hitler's charisma; in their recollections, they highlight the 'good times', portrayed as having been at nobody else's expense, and very few recall being involved in acts of humiliation or exclusionary behaviour. But accounts written closer to the time indicate some of the conflicting pressures felt by the muddled middle. Strong moral and political views or emotional ties with excluded individuals could provide a countervailing force, on the one hand, while on the other hand ambition or sheer desire for a quiet life or outright fear could make conformity seem the only option. Location and context could provide a very different gloss on how the idea of Volksgemeinschaft was interpreted.

No one in Germany could escape the all-pervasive atmosphere of Nazism. Nonetheless, most 'Aryans' still had choices about how to respond, in light of their own priorities and purposes. Many did of course enthusiastically comply and enjoyed the new sense of national community. Others felt uneasy about the ways in which outward conformity entailed compromises with previously held views and suffered pangs of conscience. Many 'Aryan' Germans chose to go along with it all; others felt the price to be paid was too high; while those who were less willing to conform soon realized the futility of opposition in face of overwhelming repression. Meanwhile, the excluded 'non-Aryans' had little choice but to come together, whether or not there was much else, aside from exclusion, that they had in common.

Many Germans could value the sunny side of the Volksgemeinschaft while yet retaining a sense of traditional class and status distinctions. To discount the notion of a 'national community' as unhelpful in describing the continuing structural inequalities in the Third Reich is to repeat the mistake of so many contemporaries: to ignore, in effect, the dramatic implications this notion had for those who were inexorably being excluded. But it also, less obviously and in the long term perhaps even more importantly, risks overlooking the subtle changes in the ways in which 'Aryan' Germans perceived themselves, redefined their own sense of identity, and altered their behaviour towards others.

The construction and normalization of systemic racism became institutionalized with the enactment of the Nuremberg Laws in 1935, requiring not merely conformity but also legally enforceable compliance. Ironically, this compliance would make it all the easier for 'Aryans' to ignore the consequences of conformity and take them to the next stage of engagement: growing complicity in systemic racism, whether or not they agreed with the aims of the Nazi regime.

5

A Nation of 'Aryans'?

The Normalization of Racial Discrimination

By the mid-1930s, most Germans had a sense of a return to national greatness and palpable improvements in living standards. Hitler's reputation was boosted by his overturning aspects of the hated Treaty of Versailles: following a plebiscite in January 1935, the Saar region was returned to Germany, and in March 1936 the demilitarized Rhineland was occupied by German troops in direct contravention of the Treaty. In 1936, Hermann Göring was appointed head of a newly established 'Four Year Plan' (*Vierjahresplan*) office, tasked with preparing Germany for war, while ensuring that military production was compatible with consumer satisfaction. Meanwhile, the 1936 Summer Olympic Games showcased Nazi Germany to the eyes of the world and strengthened international confirmation of the regime. This also raised morale within the Reich. Among Martin Andermann's 'Aryan' friends, as he put it, there was 'no longer that earlier, tired, pessimistic air of resignation, but rather an—artificially stoked up, but powerful—faith in the future, which one can only call a kind of secular religion'.[1]

Social changes contributed to stabilization. Younger Germans were brought under the spell of Nazi education and youth organizations, while members of older generations, generally likely to be more sceptical, sought ways of accommodating themselves to a regime that now seemed firmly established. With accommodation came, for some people, a degree of re-thinking: persuading themselves that the support they demonstrated in public reflected inner conviction. This was not hard. Participation in swastika flag-waving ceremonies and events, and a sense of a national upturn, could be infectious, while a return to full employment and growing material wellbeing also gave an impression of 'good times' returning after the political turmoil of the Weimar years and the economic privations of the Depression. Even so, many Germans—more at some times, and in some circumstances—still had a sense of leading a double life, with public conformity combined with private disquiet. Surprisingly too, some diaries from the time indicate that it was possible to move in the opposite direction: to switch from early enthusiasm to increasing scepticism and self-distancing. What virtually no one could do, however, was to separate issues about personal identity from issues to do with the Nazi project for the nation.[2]

As we have seen, shifts in social relations in the mid-1930s were profoundly affected by the legalization of discrimination. While the process had begun in 1933, it was accelerated and exacerbated in significant ways by compliance with the Nuremberg Laws. The implications were very clear from the perspective of those subjected to them. And again, though they were a tiny percentage of the overall German population, their experiences help to clarify also what it meant for the dominant community who were, by their actions and inactions, helping to propel the Nazi project towards genocide.

The redefinition of identity in the Nuremberg Laws

Feeling that the promised Nazi revolution had not yet been fully delivered, party radicals were constantly searching for further measures to deal with the 'Jewish question'. In September 1935, members of the Reichstag were called down to the Nazi party conference in Nuremberg at relatively short notice, for the announcement of the new legislation.[3] Although far longer in the planning, these laws were rather suddenly introduced in public against a background of violence on the part of youthful activists over the summer months of 1935; indeed the Social Democratic Party in Exile (Sopade) saw the laws as in some sense a capitulation by Hitler to party radicals, and social

democrats abroad continued to hope that the Nazi party's position was precarious.[4] But, as with the switch in April 1933 from the short-lived boycott
of Jewish stores to the legislation excluding Jews from state employment,
this 'legal' discrimination followed physical violence that had not met with
popular approval. There had been, for example, vicious attacks on Jews in
Berlin's shopping streets in summer 1935, which occasioned critical remarks
on the part of observers—but no intervention by bystanders. Moreover,
while vandals on the streets could do immense harm to particular victims,
legislation had far broader and highly significant long-term consequences.
No longer was this a question of isolated activism by radicals; rather the
entire population had to adapt behaviours to accord with the new legal
requirements.

The Nuremburg Laws covered both interpersonal relations and relations
between individuals and the state. On the personal front, the Law for the
Protection of German Blood and German Honour prohibited Jews from
marrying or having sexual relations with non-Jews, and—implying that Jews
would take sexual advantage if they had the opportunity—forbade them to
employ non-Jewish women under the age of forty-five—the childbearing
years—in their household. It was evident to contemporaries that this law
was deliberately framed in line with Julius Streicher's quasi-pornographic
portrayals of the supposedly lustful Jew who could not be trusted if German
maidens were to remain safe and the 'Aryan race' kept pure.[5] Cases of 'racial defilement' inevitably had more serious consequences for the Jewish
partner than for the 'Aryan' involved. In terms of relationships with the
state, the Reich Citizenship Law deprived Jews of citizenship, classifying
them as state subjects without citizenship rights. Jewish veterans who had
been exempted from the 1933 Law for the Restoration of a Professional
Civil Service by virtue of their military service—Hitler's temporary concession to the wishes of President Hindenburg—now also lost their jobs.
A supplementary decree of 21 December 1935 also led to the sacking of
Jews in many other previously exempted professional roles. Alongside these
measures, Jewish economic activities were further squeezed, contributing to
a continuing decline in material wellbeing as well as social status.

The intended consequences of these laws were clear. But it was less clear
whom precisely they applied to. There were conflicting opinions among
party radicals and moderates in the Reich Ministry of the Interior as
to who should actually be designated as a 'Jew', which was an imposed

category combining 'racial' and religious criteria rather than a matter of self-identification. Following weeks of wrangling, a compromise set of definitions was passed in a supplementary decree on 14 November 1935. German people of colour and Roma and Sinti—'Gypsies, Negroes, and their bastards', as the Nazis put it—were also included two weeks later, although policies towards these groups were inconsistent and differed somewhat from the treatment of Jews.[6] 'Mixed-race gypsies', for example, often had a harder time of it under Nazi persecution than did those of supposedly 'pure' descent, the reverse of the Nazi treatment of 'half-Jews' and Jews.[7]

Despite the Nazi emphasis on 'race' and 'blood', the definition of 'Jew' in the Nuremberg Laws combined 'racial' descent with religious practice and behavioural attributes. The religious status of grandparents was the primary determining factor, with three or four grandparents who were adherents of Judaism sufficient to deem a person to be Jewish by 'race'. In some cases—it is impossible to tell how many—individuals managed to evade persecution under Nazism if a couple of immigrant grandparents, despite Jewish origins, had been marked as Christians on immigration papers. A Jewish woman in Berlin, for example, only discovered as an adult that she was Jewish by descent, although she had always been dimly aware that there was some mysterious secret in the family that must never be spoken of. After the war her grandfather had revealed to her mother, who was only a child during the war, that he had succeeded in passing as a gentile due to his converted parents' documentation as Christians on their immigration papers and their missing birth certificates. He had apparently been agonized about what he felt to be his own lack of solidarity with other Jews; he had refused to go into air raid shelters and insisted on standing outside on the roof when there was bombing, tempting death. He had physically survived the war but sustained considerable psychological damage.[8] This was of course an extreme example, but obtaining proof of descent could take some time, and there were many potential avenues for dispute and challenge.

Marital status and the religious upbringing of children could also affect who was designated Jewish after Nuremberg. Those who had only two Jewish grandparents were considered to be 'mixed-breeds' or *Mischlinge* of the first degree' and subjected to fewer restrictions and less discrimination than full Jews, but there were qualifications. They were to be 'counted as Jews' (*Geltungsjuden*) if they were of the Jewish faith, or were married to a Jew, or were bringing up their children in the Jewish faith; even, on occasion, if they fell afoul of the authorities in some way and their appearance or behaviour corresponded to antisemitic stereotypes, tipping the balance of evaluation. Those with one Jewish grandparent were termed '*Mischlinge* of the second degree'. These categories—applied since 1933—did not correspond to any pre-existing collective identities, let alone cultural or social communities. Although many individuals with mixed ancestry emigrated during the 1930s, being generally of a younger generation, according to the census of 17 May 1939 there were still some 72,000 'half-Jews' in the Reich. They posed, in the Nazi view, a continuing threat to the supposed purity of the 'Aryan race'. Even Nazi policymakers could never fully resolve the question of how 'half-Jews' could be prevented from contaminating German 'racial stock'. At the Wannsee Conference of January 1942, convened by Reinhard Heydrich to discuss with representatives of Reich ministries and authorities the implementation of the 'Final Solution of the Jewish Question', the issue was still not resolved. Considerable time was devoted to discussing whether '*Mischlinge*' should be given the unpalatable choice between being forcibly sterilized or simply slaughtered alongside those deemed to be full Jews and those 'counting as Jews'.[9]

The Nuremberg Laws should in principle have meant some alleviation of the situation for the children of mixed marriages. But in practice, by September 1935 so many 'non-Aryans' of mixed descent had already lost their jobs and status, or had career opportunities blocked to them, that this made little difference; moreover, employers were still entitled to include an 'Aryan clause' excluding them from employment. Their private lives were also affected. With only a handful of exemptions granted on the basis of personal requests, '*Mischlinge*' suffered prohibitions on whom they were allowed to marry: 'half-Jews' could only marry other '*Mischlinge*' or Jews, in which case they would themselves be considered Jews, but they could not marry non-Jewish Germans; 'quarter Jews' were not allowed to marry Jews, 'half-Jews' or even other 'quarter-Jews', the idea being to 'breed out' what was seen as 'Jewish blood'.[10] '*Mischling*' status could also cause significant family tensions. Alfred Oppler recalled a case where a family broke up because the daughter tried to prove that her Jewish father was not her biological father, preferring to smear her mother's reputation by accusing her of an extramarital affair than be classified as a '*Mischling*' herself.[11]

With a view to not unduly antagonizing 'Aryan' relatives, in 1938 additional considerations were introduced concerning whether Jews were deemed to be in what was called a 'privileged mixed marriage' (*privilegierte Mischehe*), where a Jewish woman was married to an 'Aryan' man. In these cases, the couple's surname would not immediately suggest any taint of Jewish connections; this might also make it easier for the children, if their maternal Jewish background was not immediately evident. Marriages were only held to be 'privileged' when the wife was Jewish and the husband 'Aryan', and there was either no children or any offspring being brought up as Jewish. But if the husband was Jewish, while the wife was 'Aryan', and there were either no children or the children were being brought up as Jewish, then the marriage was 'nonprivileged'. Mixed marriages provided a degree of protection for a while for those whose 'Aryan' partners stuck by them, despite growing pressures to divorce, and could eventually make all the difference—as in the case, for example, of Victor Klemperer, whose extensive diaries recording his life before, during, and after the Nazi period remains an important ego-document. But being in one of these 'mixed' categories would not, ultimately, have made much difference had Germany eventually won the war, or indeed even had it gone for much longer: policies towards people in mixed marriages or of mixed descent were already changing from 1943 onwards, and in the closing months of the war such individuals were slated for deportation (Klemperer was ultimately saved by the bombing of Dresden, allowing him to escape before a planned deportation). It was simply a pragmatic question of prioritizing a hierarchy of places in the line for eventual extermination and not wanting to unsettle 'Aryan' relatives until the last possible moment.

Nazi lawyers and bureaucrats had taken an interest in American laws restricting citizenship rights and banning 'racial miscegenation' when formulating their own policies, as well as sharing a wider Western interest in sterilization measures. In some ways, the racial distinctions embodied in the Nuremberg Laws were marginally less harsh than those in the United States enshrining notions of white supremacy, where just 'one drop' of the wrong sort of ancestral blood was sufficient to stigmatize a person as 'black'. But Nazi state-imposed racism was subsequently implemented with more central direction and ultimately far more deadly effect than was ever the case in the more liberal, democratic, and federal United States where, despite entrenched racism and persisting, deep-rooted structural inequalities, murderous violence continued to take the form of lynching individuals rather than state-sanctioned genocide. At this stage, of course, Nazis were most interested in developing policies of racial segregation, where they felt they could draw on or learn from experiences elsewhere, including the United States.[12]

The racialized categories of the Nuremberg Laws also did not easily map onto visible markers of difference, though crude Nazi caricatures tried to impose them. This made antisemitic distinctions in Nazi Germany potentially more difficult to act on without further proof of a person's identity, in contrast to racism against people of colour in the United States. This would give some space, subsequently, for the use of subterfuge and deception in order to evade persecution.

Yet however artificially constructed, the Nazi categories of the Nuremberg Laws soon turned into horrific social realities for nearly all 'non-Aryans'.

'Violence had established itself as law': National compliance with a hostile environment

The Nuremberg Laws, in the view of Ernst Schwartzert, effectively 'tore a gash' through German society. Many were surprised by what the legislation revealed: 'not only was the degree of interconnection through the marriages of relatives far higher than had ever been believed, it also turned out that people about whose germanness there had never been the slightest doubt were suddenly burdened with non-Aryan grandmothers and grandfathers, who now effectively tore them out of the fabric of German life. There were legions of such people, and further legions were added who, through their intellectual, spiritual or economic connections, were intimately tied to Jews.'[13] Schwartzert, an 'Aryan' living in Berlin, wrote that he was himself one of those affected by intimate ties: his girlfriend was Jewish.

The legislation had an obvious, immediate impact on Jewish Germans who lost their rights of citizenship and freedom to form close personal relationships with others irrespective of 'race'. But the Nuremberg Laws had implications for all Germans. Racial discrimination was now enshrined in law. It was not merely okay to discriminate: it was legally no longer permissible not to discriminate. It was also now right to benefit from the progressive exclusion of Jews from economic and social life. The circle of beneficiaries from Nazi racial policies widened with the 'aryanization' of property and the growth of professional opportunities, as Jewish educationalists, medical practitioners, and business people were forced out of their former positions. Whether or not 'Aryan' Germans seized such opportunities, virtually everyone who still came into contact with German Jews was now under increased pressure to reconsider. Accepting the new legal situation meant, in effect, growing complicity in nationally prescribed racism.

From late 1935 onwards, it was impossible to reject or ignore the new terminology and sub-classifications, however absurd and scientifically unfounded they may have at first appeared. This was especially the case among those adversely affected by them. As Fritz Goldberg put it in 1939: 'Cleverly promoted, this "Aryan" concept, doubted by all scientists, had within a few years entered into the everyday language of Germans.' But, he went on, 'the legal definitions contributed more to confusion than clarification' with the proliferation of distinctions between full-, half-, and quarter-Aryans 'and all other fractions', and specifications regarding what such people could or could not do. And however crazy the new system seemed, Goldberg commented, 'even we "Non-Aryans", who of course inwardly rejected these concepts soon had to recognize, to our horror, that we too could no longer do without them in conversations and discussions'.[14] With startling speed, a fake scientific theory became a social reality that was internalized and acted upon in everyday life.

Some non-Jewish Germans were deeply troubled by this implication. Ernst Rathgeber, a committed Christian with strong moral convictions, felt that, despite being fully 'Aryan' himself, he was personally affected. 'For the first time this Nazi madness attacked my private life!' he wrote in his 1939 essay. The laws would have 'ghastly and inhumane consequences', and this growing realization 'lay like a nightmare on my soul'. He felt caught in an impossible situation: if he remained friends with a Jewish brother and sister to whom he was very close, he would be guilty of 'treason to my Volk and race'; but to break off the friendship would not only be emotionally painful but also went against all his Christian precepts. The sister with whom he was friendly 'increasingly sank into a deep depression and despair', he recalled, and eventually her mother arranged for her to stay with relatives in England, while mother and son left for Switzerland. Three members of this Jewish family were now safely out. But for Rathgeber, a fully 'Aryan' member of the Volksgemeinschaft, the passage of the Nuremberg Laws was the beginning of the end of his being able to identify as German.[15]

In Schwartzert's view too, what had previously been a 'latent question of conscience' now became 'an acute conflict'. But arguably the vast majority of Germans could not quite face up fully to what this all meant—and possibly did not even register that it had implications not only for those who were now excluded but also for their own identities. As Schwartzert went on to reflect, conflicted as a minority of people might be, this was not sufficient to provoke action against the regime. More than two years under Nazi rule, an all-pervading sense of apathy, of underlying impotence, had set in among the German mainstream. While they continued to see each other every day, Schwartzert and his Jewish girlfriend now took separate apartments, not daring to live together openly any more. They began to lead a double life that was at times 'worthy of a crime novel'. Determined to get out of this situation, Schwartzert concentrated on making enough money for them to emigrate. This meant, in effect, also engaging in the compromises necessary to benefit from new opportunities now being offered: Schwartzert not only made an increasingly good living from his plays but also branched into the film industry where there were numerous openings due to the exclusion of so many Jewish colleagues. From 1936 onwards he threw himself into writing one film after another in preparation for his intended flight from Nazi Germany. Even as he raged against the regime, and flouted its racist prohibitions by remaining faithful to his Jewish girlfriend in private, Schwartzert found himself taking advantage of wider benefits offered by the antisemitic measures.[16]

Among the artistic circles in which Schwartzert moved, every social event inevitably turned into a political discussion. Friends and trusted acquaintances tried to reassure themselves and each other that things could not go on like this for much longer. They had argued this in the early months of 1933 with more conviction; now, by 1935, they were merely mouthing the thought, with a growing sense of resignation and fear. These professionals were afraid less of penalties or imprisonment than of something less readily definable: conforming with the laws of the land, they feared rather, as Schwartzert saw it, for the state of their own souls. Everyone Schwartzert knew was unhappy—although the film industry was booming, having readily fallen into line in the Third Reich. There was, among those who talked openly, a 'sense of personal disintegration', a feeling verging on despair. They engaged in endless discussions about 'their position on the problems of the times and the eternal questions of law, freedom, honour and conscience'. They questioned whether one could still look in the mirror 'without having to throw up, because one had become such a swine'. The term 'national socialist' no longer had a political meaning but was rather 'an expression for mental and spiritual death'.[17]

Many of these were the very people who after 1945 would profess that they had 'always been against it' (*immer dagegen*); but at a time when they could have acted, their primary concern was their own spiritual wellbeing and not the fates of the persecuted. Unless they had personal reasons to make emigration a priority, like Schwartzert, the vast majority of those Germans who felt conflicted did not consider abandoning their homeland; and they did not take advantage of their professional positions to combat the influence of Goebbels's propaganda machinery. The agony of the soul remained a purely private affair.

As Schwartzert himself recognized, musing in 1939 on his own mixed feelings: 'Violence had established itself as law. One was far too weak to stand up to it.' All he could do was develop a 'bad conscience'.[18]

However uncomfortable at least some non-Jewish Germans may have felt after Nuremburg, the vast majority of the 'Aryan' population seemed outwardly to be suffering few pangs of conscience. As they had in 1933, most people simply fell into line with the new developments, accommodating themselves where necessary and benefitting when possible. Their compliant behaviour exacerbated trends that had already been evident.

From late 1935 onwards, even sympathetic 'Aryan' Germans avoided 'non-Aryans'. Hans Kosterlitz recalled how former friends and acquaintances no longer visited him, and they ostentatiously turned away if they happened to pass by in the street. A newspaper vendor told Kosterlitz that the NSDAP had issued 'strong directives' that 'forbade any interaction and any personal contact with Jews in the strongest possible terms'. Kosterlitz and other Jews were now slinking around trying to attract as little attention as possible. He just sought to keep his head down, since under current circumstances any attention could rapidly turn dangerous for a Jew.[19]

Friedrich Reuss, similarly, summarized the basic precept of life as a 'non-Aryan' in terms of the risks of simply being noticed: 'Just don't attract attention.' In his essay he recalled how the wife of a Jewish doctor received a parcel for which she had had to pay extra postage. It came from the concentration camp where her husband had been interned and supposedly contained his ashes. She was not sure whether to believe this, thinking 'perhaps he is still alive and it was just a joke. But', she concluded, 'the best thing for us to do is stay nicely at home, so that no one sees us'.[20]

In Konstanz, Margot Spiegel had previously felt that proximity to the Swiss border fostered a more open atmosphere. But in late 1935, people stopped saying hello to her, or other Jews, on the street. She gave up visiting her former friends, and they made no attempt to visit her. Signs went up outside restaurants, cafés, swimming pools, and other public places, announcing Jews were 'not wanted'. Social status had previously given some protection against antisemitic discrimination. But now, Spiegel registered how the behaviour of those she called 'the masses' changed, as they became openly more insolent towards Jews who had been their social superiors. The son of the local cobbler who had repaired their shoes, for example, had formerly been full of 'nice courtesies' towards Spiegel and her family, but he 'now became arrogant'. Meanwhile, she noted, there was a rise in open fanaticism and expressions of faith in the Führer. Hitler increasingly appeared an almost god-like saviour figure; many seemed to worship the ground on which he stood and treated his mountain retreat in Berchtesgaden as a sacred spot.[21]

Klara Rosenthal, in Munich, was eternally grateful for the support and assistance of the few Christian friends who remained loyal to her family. But so many others were fickle, and she found it 'astonishing how the narcotic worked that the Nazis were spreading among people'. Many long-standing friends simply 'turned their backs', whatever private doubts they may have harboured: 'We actually felt that they were not absolutely convinced that what they were doing was right, but they were learning to do things differently. They were learning the Party's recipes as being right for the Volk and the Fatherland.' Rosenthal found this painful. One of the few exceptions was their family maid, who she noted was 'an outspoken opponent of Hitler, and also a fervent Catholic as well as utterly bound by love for our children'. Already over the age of forty-five and not automatically banned from employment in a Jewish household under the Nuremberg Laws, this loyal servant simply refused to leave. She insisted on staying even after it was made increasingly difficult for her: a close friend of hers was a committed Nazi; she received weekly visits from various Nazi associations; and the Nazi block warden (colloquially known as the *Blockwart*, charged with keeping an eye on people) openly spied 'in order to do her some harm'. Even in face of all this, the maid stuck with Rosenthal and her family, and over time 'became a good friend, honest and genuine', unlike so many other acquaintances who simply melted away at this time.[22] By 1935 this woman was a notable exception.

Fritz Goldberg registered that the Nuremberg Laws had an 'ever deeper impact' on his social relationships. 'Most Aryan acquaintances understandably withdrew more and more, there was nothing else they could do.' Even the Goldberg family's 'most intimate friends', who refused to give up any social contact with them, 'began to take precautionary measures'. While not wanting to break off entirely, these friends were fearful of being seen with Jews and preferred to enter their home only 'after darkness had fallen'. They also 'tactfully suggested' that the Goldbergs should no longer come to visit them: 'they were terribly ashamed, and kept beating about the bush' but, as Goldberg recalled, he and his wife were only too well aware what their friends were driving at well before they had finished trying to express their embarrassed request. Shame may have meant that some Germans resisted complete compliance with Nazi norms, but they were not prepared to flout them in any way that might be visible to others. This was going for risk-free noncompliance, rather than any real form of resistance.[23]

Lotte Popper, who had up until then managed to maintain a degree of standing through her educational and social status, now experienced the Nuremberg Laws as a 'direct punch in the face'. There could, she thought, be 'no game of hiding any more'. Fewer and fewer friends came to visit them. A rare exception was a student in Hamburg, a pastor's daughter who felt she could speak freely in the Popper household. This young woman complained about how she had to 'put on a face' (*heucheln*) at university and was forced to engage in shooting practice for her fatherland, which she hated. Another elderly pair of close friends were a mixed couple who recently met and had been looking forward to a new life together; but they were now accused of 'racial defilement,' and the Jewish partner was briefly imprisoned. On his release he was given three days to get out of the country and return to his native Holland where, in part because of the maltreatment he had endured in Germany, he died of a stroke. Meanwhile the Poppers were receiving more and more letters from Jews who had emigrated.[24]

Most German Jews found that their 'Aryan' friends had melted away by late 1935. Whatever their responses, the best that could be achieved was a risky compromise. By seeking to survive in a state characterized by systemic racism, most Germans were inevitably constrained to comply with

Nazi regulations, with varying degrees of willingness or unease. Whether constrained compliance should be distinguished from more willing acceptance or even enthusiastic embrace of systemic racism is open to discussion. Certainly we may want to make a moral distinction between those who felt forced to comply, or saw no viable alternative, and those who acquiesced in or actively supported the new developments. Either way, compliance inevitably meant that the ground was shifting, in directions that would make eventual passivity in face of deportations to the east more possible.

'Weakening feelings of common humanity': The social conditions for ignorance and indifference

As we have seen, Alfred Oppler had managed in 1933 to hold on to a lower-level position due to his war veteran status. But in 1935, with the abolition of this exemption in the Nuremberg Laws, Oppler lost his job entirely. In 1936 he and his family took an enforced holiday while considering what to do next. During their travels Oppler noted, on visiting a small Bavarian village close to the Austrian border, how 'politically careful' the population were: 'each observed the other, so that most people offered the Hitler greeting out of fear.' In October, having returned to Berlin, he was struck by the extent to which the atmosphere of the capital city had changed. Not many people seemed carefree or laughing: 'Anyone who had not given up the habit of thinking was now greatly concerned about the future.'

Living conditions too had changed as a result of the Nuremberg Laws, and the Opplers faced considerable difficulty in finding lodgings. 'Aryans' with rooms to rent out generally also employed 'Aryan' maidservants, often young women; now stigmatized as a Jew, Oppler could be accused of breaking the law if residing in such a household and therefore had to look for rooms elsewhere. As Oppler noted: 'in this way, racial separation of Jews and Aryans was beginning to take place in spatial terms as well.' The Opplers thought one option might be to buy a plot of land where they could build their own home; but even Oppler's 'Aryan' wife could not gain permission to purchase land, merely because she was married to a Jew. However hard they tried, each official referred their case to a higher level; eventually, they recognized that permission would never be forthcoming and gave up.[25]

Eventually, the Opplers managed to find a place to live on the edge of the Grunewald forest in western Berlin. Fellow residents, including the Nazi block warden, were initially pleasant and welcoming towards this good-looking couple of relatively high professional status, with their delightful blond and blue-eyed daughter Ellen. But then the day came when, marking some national celebration, all households were required to hang swastika flags from their windows; Jews alone were now expressly forbidden from displaying the flag. The lack of any flag from the Opplers' windows was a marker in space just as wearing the yellow star would be on clothing from September 1941. From this point on, neighbours became distinctly cooler, with a single exception: a committed Catholic and 'German patriot in the good old sense'—as Oppler described him—had a daughter of roughly the same age as Ellen, and allowed his daughter to continue playing with the 'mixed-breed' daughter of his Jewish neighbour. This Catholic confided in Oppler that the block warden had warned him against having any contact, but this had merely strengthened his resolve to remain friendly.[26]

The Opplers were relatively lucky that they experienced no direct aggression at this point. Many Jews were terrified of national holidays: they were expressly forbidden from raising a flag and yet did not wish to appear 'unpatriotic', which could provide 'a pretext for the anger of the people [*Volkswut*]' to be expressed in violence, as one Jewish lawyer, Max Moses Polke, observed. But Polke observed too that many non-Jews were also a little bit jealous of Jews for no longer having to pretend to support Nazism by flying the swastika or having to vote for the regime in rigged elections.[27]

The Nuremberg Laws affected everyone. Friedrich Reuss, a Christian and a 'quarter Jew', was now designated a '*Mischling* of the second degree' under the new categories. This should have meant some improvement in his position but came far too late to set his previously promising career back on track. He had already been reduced to the role of travelling salesman of insurance policies—and had even been lucky to get this job, unlike some acquaintances who had fallen further and faster down the social scale. Reuss increasingly retreated into his own small family circle and socialized only with a dwindling group of fellow '*Mischlinge*' in the 'non-Aryan' association.

Reuss's growing sense of social isolation was compounded by being exposed through his work to the views of an apparently thoroughly nazified population in the provinces. On his travels, Reuss found himself engaged in house-to-house sales pitches in a very poor area of Thuringia. Families here could barely afford a couple of potatoes or a herring for dinner, let alone buy an insurance policy. But he was also flabbergasted at the adulation of Hitler that he came across among these poverty-stricken people in small communities. 'They were virtually all thoroughly enthusiastic about the new times. Did the Kaiser ever shake hands with a child of the working classes? Did [former social democratic President] Ebert ever serve as a simple soldier at the front? No, but our People's Chancellor [Hitler] did.' There was much more of the same by way of Hitler worship among these impoverished people, who lapped up Nazi propaganda, including the lie that rich Jews were at the root of all their misery and suffering. Reuss muddled through for a while, even managing to relocate from Berlin to Leipzig, where his wife could join him. But his position worsened as people began to cancel their insurance policies, disturbed by rumours that the insurance company was employing 'people descended from Jews'.[28]

By late 1935, among the wider population, as Ernst Schwartzert noted, people were becoming used to life under Nazism. Germany's loudly proclaimed achievements—from autobahn building to 'Strength through Joy' cruises—prevailed over discussion of the darker sides of Nazism. Even if they feared that economic recovery was unlikely to last, many people felt there was at last a certain stability. And few had cause to note the disappearance of Jews from their neighbourhoods and therefore their consciousness. For many Germans, what had previously seemed to be blatant lies increasingly became 'half-truths'; with incessant repetition, some even began to believe in what they had formerly been constrained into saying. In Schwartzert's view, it was not so much that antisemitism was rising but rather that 'feelings of common humanity' were becoming weaker. In Nazi Germany, he thought, 'human relationships died away, slowly and hesitantly, but inexorably'.[29]

'Good persons' in difficult times: Personal interests and continuing connections

Unless there were strong personal reasons—whether emotional or economic interests—'Aryan' Germans generally did not feel it worth the risk of sustaining relationships with 'non-Aryans'. When they did, it was with some risks, but also occasional benefits, both material and psychological.

Georg Abraham experienced a common disjuncture between behaviour and attitude. Many 'Aryans' maintained good relations with individual Jews while consenting to official stereotypes of 'the Jew'. Abraham's work as a sales representative and trader required him to do business with a large number of companies, travelling and staying overnight in different places. In the course of his travels, Abraham met a number of people who acted against the injunctions of the regime in dealing with him. Many hotels where he had regularly stayed now bore 'Jews not welcome' (*Juden uner-wünscht*) signs. But these hotels were also his business customers and knew him well; some managers would write to him to say they that he should continue to stay there. One reported that, in response to objections by the Nazi party, he had pointed out that the state railway service (Reichsbahn) was still carrying Jewish passengers and letting them use sleeping compart-ments, so why could not hotels act in the same way. Other hotelkeepers joked to Abraham that although Nazi party members would go from one hotel to another to hang up the signs themselves, unfortunately the signs seemed to keep falling down.

In his hometown of Neustettin (now Szczecinek, Poland), a community of some 20,000, there were many who, Abraham recalled, 'remained loyal' to him 'until the very end'—which in Abraham's case came with his emi-gration in 1939. Every day, Abraham noted, there were signs of goodwill on the part of customers. One large entrepreneur always conveyed his purchase order to Abraham on the street, or by telephone, to avoid doing it in person on the shopfloor. He had been so pestered by the party, he explained, that this was the only way to keep the peace. On one occasion a 'notorious Jew-hater' had made a scene about the fact that he was still engaging in trade with a Jew. The proprietor had replied that 'up to now he [the proprietor] was the one who always made the decisions in his own business'. These at-titudes among clients and innkeepers helped to keep Abraham's spirits up, as well as allowing him to keep his business going far longer than might otherwise have been possible.[30]

Local business people were engaging in a mental balancing act, as they weighed the potential risks of continuing to exchange goods and services with a Jew against the likely material gains to be accrued from these trans-actions. In Abraham's case, too, it seems to have been important that he was known personally and had maintained good relations at an individual level over many years. This personal aspect helped to counter the grotesque caricatures and stereotypes about 'the Jew' that were being propagated by the Nazi regime.

Despite all the difficulties that the regime was making for Jewish entrepreneurs, Abraham managed for a time to keep going. Unlike Klara Rosenthal, whose business in Munich had already been taken over by Nazis and who nearly lost faith in her fellow Germans, Abraham insisted on retaining his belief in the fundamental goodness of his compatriots. He made a sharp distinction between the Nazi party and his business associates, customers, and acquaintances. 'Every day', he recalled after he had emigrated, 'there were renewed good wishes' from those with whom he was in contact.[31]

Between the 1935 Nuremburg Laws and 1938, when he was forced to sell his business, Abraham had managed to cling on with considerable success in unfavourable circumstances, in a small town in Protestant, northeastern Germany where Nazism flourished. The man who took over his business was a long-standing NSDAP member, a so-called old fighter who had joined before 1930; even so, in Abraham's view, he 'had not forgotten the good manners he acquired as a child, and during the months we got to know each other we became such good friends that the final parting was difficult for both of us'. This Nazi repeatedly assured Abraham that because of having known him 'he would have to revise radically all the teaching he had received in Party training courses on the Jewish Question'. Until he emigrated, Abraham still visited the inn run by this man's parents: 'his father told me that he had never believed the lies that the National Socialists were spreading about the Jews' and 'until the end of his days, he would never be a Jew-hater'. Both father and Nazi son often visited Abraham and his wife and went on to bring foodstuffs and small presents to his wife after Abraham's arrest following the violence of November 1938, as we shall see.[32]

By the later 1930s the vast majority of Germans—even if not active Nazi supporters or members of the NSDAP—were in effect sustaining the regime, whether by benefitting from aryanization or simply by complying with the discriminatory legal framework of the state. Yet at the same time some conformists and beneficiaries were also partially undermining or at least mitigating the regime's exclusionary policies by continuing to maintain some limited social contacts with Jews. This could be seen as largely instrumental, as in Abraham's trading transactions, or in the case of cattle traders in rural areas of Württemberg or Bavaria who prioritized personal business interests over party injunctions. It could also be seen as psychologically beneficial for the 'Aryan' conformists, in maintaining self-respect and bolstering an image of oneself as remaining a 'good person' in difficult times. This was, in effect, complicity tempered by kindness.

And even after the Nuremburg Laws had made clear the distinctions, there were still small acts of kindness among the general population toward Jews. They cost little but helped to alleviate the potential pangs of an uneasy conscience. They were, in some cases, moral wrapping for continued participation in systemic racism: normalizing difference and reinforcing racial distinctions while at the same time feeling a moral glow about an apparent generosity of spirit towards the victims. It may indeed, as with Abraham, have made the targets of persecution feel somewhat better in the course of their exclusion from the circle of those deemed to be equal human beings. And it was certainly infinitely better than being assaulted.

Nevertheless, after the Nuremburg Laws there was a disconcerting degree of compliance with racism in Nazi Germany. To some, after the war, these uncomfortable compromises and conflicting experiences would be transformed into feelings of ambivalence among those who asserted they had been 'always against it' and yet had continued to go along with it.

Professional conformity, political impotence, and personal integrity

Germany in August 1936 was dominated by the Olympic Games. Everywhere, in the interests of securing international approval of the new Germany, antisemitic propaganda was downplayed and overt signs of racism removed from the streets. Hordes of people were carried along by a new spirit of national enthusiasm; particularly among those who were young at the time, there was an invigorating sense of belonging to a great national mission, and a desire to be part of the nation's glorious future. Some had clearly internalized both the words and the spirit of the Nazi regime. Friedrich Reck noted in his diary on 11 August his shock at seeing a boy in the Hitler Youth tear down a crucifix from a schoolroom wall, his 'young and still soft face contorted in fury', and throw it 'out of the window into the street' while crying out, 'Lie there, you dirty Jew!' (reflecting the Nazi twist on the Christian version of antisemitism that accuses Jews of killing Christ). Generational tensions that had been simmering, with growing splits within families, now became even more pointed. Reck reflected that 'Among people I know, I have heard of more than one case of children denouncing their parents politically, and thereby delivering them to the axe.'[33]

Those who did not go along with the wave of enthusiasm for the Nazi project retreated ever more into the private sphere. But it was not always easy to combine public conformity with morality in the private sphere. Conformity was a balancing act, with the practical consequences often simply tipping into complicity.

In his professional life, Bruno Gebhard continued to conform: in the spring of 1935, as we have seen, he had prepared the huge exhibition on 'Wonders of Life', which included sections on 'degenerate art' and 'the chosen people'. But, as noted, Gebhard was ever less happy with the way things were going: 'In the winter of 1935/36 we felt more vividly than any time before that the big Nazi machine had crushed all public life—so we sort of retired to our private life and cultivated our friendships.' Gebhard and his friends 'had chamber music together' or sustained each other's morale by telling the latest jokes. Increasingly, he and like-minded friends began to feel that there was nothing much else they could do. Even among previously politically active circles there was a growing sense of weariness and impotence.

In the course of his public health work in a 'social settlement' in a poor quarter in eastern Berlin, Gebhard met many former social democrats and trade union activists who were now unemployed. Virtually all of them could relate some personal experience—whether their own or those of close friends and family—of the horrors of concentration camps. Now they were resigned to inactivity. Among these people, Gebhard reflected, 'the growing feeling was "Ist ja doch alles egal" (nothing really matters)—life did not seem to have any real sense for those people who had lived and worked for a Republican Germany on a Trade Union basis. They were all so terribly tired—tired of struggle, of thinking, of starting again.' The repetition of phrases such as 'nothing really matters' 'it's all the same to me' or 'I couldn't care less' reflected growing recognition of sheer impotence in the face of Nazism.[34]

Yet among a younger generation there was increased energy and a sense of enthusiasm for a very different kind of future. And in his professional work, whatever he may privately have felt, Gebhard continued to contribute to building the picture of a new Germany along Nazi lines. In this combination of inner disagreement and outward quiescence, Gebhard was arguably typical of many educated Germans. But professional conformity in his case amounted to outright complicity: his work entailed making a significant contribution to building the Nazi image of the Reich in a highly public forum.

The Olympic Games encouraged this surrender. From 18 July to 16 August 1936 Gebhard and his boss, Dr Albert Wischek, the director of the Berlin Office for Exhibitions, Trade Shows and Tourism, mounted the huge Olympia exhibition, 'Deutschland', portraying Germany in a self-congratulatory and flattering light for the world's visitors. Goebbels, with whom the draft design had been discussed in April 1935, officially opened the exhibition with a speech picking up on words and phrases previously suggested in discussions with Wischek, proclaiming that the exhibition was 'a testament to the nation's newly awakened will to life' and a 'display of national achievements'. Though fully engaged with mounting the exhibition at the time, Gebhard subsequently remembered it with some ambivalence: 'This exhibition was a Farewell to the Germany we had lived and worked for.' He felt that Hitler had stolen their '*Heimatland*' (homeland) from them: 'We felt like strangers in a country where people talked the same language but did not understand each other.'

Gebhard was nonetheless on his best behaviour during the opening ceremony, disguising his personal feelings: 'I had to guide Dr. Goebbels again but I could only do it with a kind of armour around my heart.' Gebhard was convinced that his colleague Wischek was also not really convinced, yet he too put on a compelling performance: 'Outwardly my director acted as a 105% Nazi'. When Wischek made speeches, 'he delivered them exactly as the Government wanted them'. Perhaps Gebhard did not feel he had made compromises in terms of the exhibition's contents; but he failed to acknowledge the significance of the deliberate omissions. The exhibition played up Germany's achievements and productivity, presenting the best picture possible to the world, while hiding and downplaying the dark sides: antisemitism, brutality, repression. Sinti and Roma had been cleared out of sight and forcibly moved to the newly established 'Gypsy camp' in the Berlin suburb of Marzahn, and antisemitic posters had been removed from the streets and advertising pillars (*Litfaßsäulen*); persecuted minorities did not feature in the display. Even more, they should not attend in person:

Wischek ensured that Jews and Jewish businesses would find it hard to enter the exhibit halls or display their wares in the trade fair. The exclusion of Jews was secured with greater subtlety and less obvious force than elsewhere, but it was nevertheless integral to both the design and functioning of the exhibition.[35]

Gebhard and others may not have seen their actions as active support for Nazism; but it seems impossible in hindsight not to see that it directly furthered Nazi policies. It conveyed a particular picture of what was now considered to be 'German'. This was not perpetration—a step beyond complicity—as it would later be widely understood, during and after the war, in the sense of shooting someone into a ditch, or shoving people onto a train headed for the gas chambers; but it aided in constructing the kind of society that normalized discrimination, persecution, and exclusion—and in which violent acts of perpetration would become possible, however horrified people like Wischek and Gebhard might have been by these later developments.

Others already saw these developments more clearly. Feeling that he was 'the prisoner of a horde of vicious apes', in August 1936 Reck agonized in his diary 'over the perpetual riddle of how this same people which so jealously watched over its rights a few years ago . . . *is incapable any longer of perceiving its shame for the shame that it is*' (italics in original).[36] People no longer had to think: they simply conformed. And this conformity led inevitably to complicity.

This realization began to dawn on Gebhard too at this time, even if not in quite such stark terms. While Wischek remained in post through the Third Reich—and was still active in design in postwar West Berlin—Gebhard felt increasingly uncomfortable. In 1935 he had a small and relatively insignificant brush with the Gestapo; but it served to unsettle him. He agreed with his wife that they had, as they phrased it, to live under 'the law of caution': closing their windows 'even in the hottest summer time' for fear of being overheard, and worrying about the impact of the situation on their children. The Gebhards had taken a couple of summer holidays in Switzerland, and the contrast in atmosphere sharply highlighted the moral deterioration in Germany. In the course of his work on public health, moreover, Gebhard also made a couple of professional trips to the UK and the United States, offering him other perspectives. He was surprised at the strength of anti-German feeling in New York; but even more surprised to register how even he, with his private misgivings, had increasingly come under the subtle influence of propaganda and now took aspects of life in Nazi Germany for granted. He was 'ashamed' when he read in New York about 'the atrocities in the concentration camps'—and this referring just to brutality in 1933–1934, well before any hint of the extermination camps that were to come. He was also amazed at the way in which Americans made jokes about 'crazy Adolf': it 'seemed nearly unbelievable' to him that he could 'hear people express their opinion in such a natural, teasing way'.[37]

After the Olympic Games were over, things seemed to be getting ever worse in Germany. Gebhard, entangled in the political machinations of cultural production in the nation's capital, observed key shifts: 'In the earlier years it was possible—and we did it deliberately—to play one group of the Nazis against another one or to play the Party against members of the Government. But around winter 1936/37 this was out of the question. The Nazification of Germany was more or less completed, and even in the Army as a whole the Nazi influence was increasing rapidly.'[38]

With the normalization of racial discrimination, people faced in every direction, both conforming with Nazi rule and also continuing to pursue their own interests in relation to victims of persecution, with some variations in how they managed to juggle growing complicity and humanity. Eugen Altmann, who had struggled so hard to try to become like his rougher contemporaries as a young person in Memel, and who had eventually established himself as a businessman in Breslau, observed the transformations of his non-Jewish compatriots in the later 1930s with a critical eye. In his 1939 essay he divided them into different categories. The first consisted of the 'careful ones, the somewhat lukewarm', who 'did not want to queer their books with anyone'. If they belonged to the NSDAP, 'then they would, when not in Party meetings, wear their Party badge on the inside of their lapel' so that it could not be seen by others. And, to establish their credentials among those who were more sceptical or even opponents of Nazism, 'they would make it clear at every possible opportunity that they had been forced to join to the Party for one reason or another: generally, it was a matter of business that had necessitated their joining the NSDAP.'

The second category, somewhat more honest in Altmann's opinion, were the 'waverers'; they might change their opinions if Hitler pulled off the project of making Germany great again.

The third group remained 'faithful to the Kaiser', as Altmann saw it, and found it hard to accept having to be ordered around by 'a man with the background and appearance of Hitler'. They also 'felt uneasy about having to belong to a party that called itself "socialist" and even demanded an identification with "workers"'. Yet they capitulated, moving from conformity to complicity, even while registering their sense of social distance. Furthermore, while disagreeing about means there was some agreement regarding Hitler's overall aims: they were 'critical of his methods in relation to Jews, without wanting to deny that there was a certain justification for trying to roll back the amalgamation of Jews with the Germanic tribes of feudal times'.

Then, fourthly, there were the socialists, who remained principled opponents of Nazism and formed a very clearly defined group.

Finally, Altmann defined all the others as those who were 'running around entirely without any opinions of their own'. These, Altmann thought, were 'colourless, they say yes to everything and no to everything, entirely according to what seems opportune'. He thought they could potentially 'even be won for a genuine democracy'.[39]

In the willingness of so many to change their political colours according to circumstances and self-interest, Altmann was highly prescient, as events after 1945 would show. In the meantime, however, the combination of opportunism, riding the bandwagon, or passively bending with the prevailing wind, furthered the Nazi project. Events in Germany were, moreover, being closely followed elsewhere and also had an impact on the meaning of being an 'ethnic German' abroad. After 1936, the Nazi empire of violence—and the 'Nation of Aryans'—began to expand.

1. Adolf Hitler being cheered by crowds on the way to the Kroll Opera House
for the first working day of the parliament at the Reichstag in central Berlin,
23 March 1933, following the ceremonial opening with President Hindenburg
in Potsdam two days earlier. This is a typical image seeking to portray Hitler as
charismatic Führer adored by the population, with no sign of any opponents or
critics of the regime, whose views have to be gleaned from other sources.
*United States Holocaust Memorial Museum, courtesy of National Archives and Records
Administration, College Park, 78604.*

2. A Jewish-owned department store in Berlin during the boycott of Jewish shops and businesses, 1 April 1933. It is difficult to tell from the facial expressions captured in the photograph what people might have been thinking, but many would certainly have been intimidated by the guards at the entrance, while a few were still cheekily defiant and openly critical of Nazi policies at this time.
United States Holocaust Memorial Museum, courtesy of National Archives and Records Administration, College Park, 78589.

BVG

BERLINER VERKEHRS-AKTIENGESELLSCHAFT

BERLIN W 9, LEIPZIGER PLATZ 14

FERNRUF:
A 2 FLORA 0036

BERLINER STADTBANK GIRO-K. 2, BERLIN W 9
POSTSCHECKAMT: BERLIN NW 7, KONTO 696

An den Bsch

Herrn Viktor S t e r n ,

Bi.U/N
- - - - - - -

Personalabteilung
Berlin SW 11
Stresemannstr. 111
Telef.: Sammel-Nr.
B 2 Lützow 7771

IHRE ZEICHEN	IHRE NACHRICHT VOM	UNSERE ZEICHEN	TAG
BETREFF		Pers.Arb. B./S.	15. Sept. 1933.

Mit Bezug auf § 3 des Gesetzes zur Wiederher-
stellung des Berufsbeamtentums vom 7. 4. 1933 und die
dazu ergangenen Ausführungsverordnungen und -bestim-
mungen kündigen wir Ihnen das Dienstverhältnis zum

30. September 1933
- - - - - - - - - -

mit der Massgabe, dass Sie mit Ablauf des Tages der
Zustellung dieses Schreibens aus unseren Diensten aus-
scheiden.

Gegen diese Kündigung ist unter Ausschluss des
Rechtsweges nur das Rechtsmittel der Beschwerde bei
dem Herrn Oberpräsidenten der Provinz Brandenburg und
von Berlin, Berlin-Charlottenburg 5, Kaiserdamm 1, zu-
lässig. Die Frist für die Anbringung der Beschwerde
beträgt 2 Wochen nach Zustellung dieses Schreibens.

BERLINER VERKEHRS-AKTIENGESELLSCHAFT

Personalchef

A 28 (A 4 DIN 676). 15 000. 11. 32.

3. A letter dated 15 September 1933 giving an employee notice under the terms of the 7 April 1933 'Law for the Restoration of a Professional Civil Service'. In this case, Viktor Stern, an employee of the Berlin transit authority (*Berliner Verkehrs Aktiengesellschaft*) was dismissed with effect from 20 September 1933. 'Non-Aryans' were defined under this law as anyone with even a single Jewish grandparent, whether or not they identified themselves as Jewish by either religion or descent, as in the case of Friedrich Reuss, who only discovered he had one Jewish grandparent when he tried to join an exclusive student club in the 1920s, and now also lost his promising professional career. This paved the way for exclusion from society more broadly, whether through the so-called Aryan paragraph or Aryan clause introduced by many institutions, businesses, clubs, and associations, or through informal dropping of contacts and friendships in everyday life.
United States Holocaust Memorial Museum, courtesy of Henry Stern, 27393.

Die Juden sind unser glück

4. A display box for Julius Streicher's viciously antisemitic *Der Stürmer* newspaper, defaced to read 'The Jews are our fortune' instead of 'The Jews are our misfortune' (by erasing the 'Un' in 'Ungluck', turning 'misfortune' into 'fortune'). Date circa 1933. Location: Saint Peter, Baden, Baden-Württemberg. This seems to have been an act of politically motivated vandalism similar to the undercover resistance activities in which Lore Taut was engaged at this time.
United States Holocaust Memorial Museum, courtesy of Miriamne Fields, 18523.

5. A chart illustrating how 'racial' categories were to be defined in order to implement the 1935 Nuremberg Laws, including regulations to 'protect German blood' by prohibiting 'intermarriages'. The chart portrays distinctions between individuals categorized as: 'German-blooded'; 'second-degree *Mischling*' ('half-breed' or 'mongrel' with one Jewish grandparent); 'first-degree *Mischling*' (with two Jewish grandparents); and 'Jew', with either three or four Jewish grandparents. Jewish grandparents were defined by religion rather than 'race'. Further qualifications were introduced for 'first-degree *Mischlinge*' if they were married to a Jew or were of the Jewish faith, in which case they would be 'counted as Jews' (*Geltungsjuden*), as in the case of Else Behrend-Rosenfeld. Supplementary decrees legalized discrimination not only against Jews but also against black Germans and 'Gypsies' (Roma and Sinti). From 1935, compliance was mandatory in law, furthering the process of social segregation and fostering growing indifference to the fate of those who were outcast. Some citizens, such as the fully 'Aryan' Ernst Rathgeber, realized this also meant a redefinition of what it meant to be German, precipitating his decision to emigrate rather than be complicit with systemic racism.

United States Holocaust Memorial Museum, courtesy of Hillel at Kent State, n13862.J.

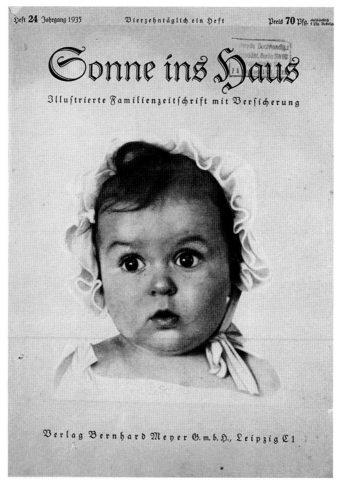

Heft **24** Jahrgang 1935   Vierzehntäglich ein Heft   Preis **70** Pfg.

Sonne ins Haus

Illustrierte Familienzeitschrift mit Versicherung

Verlag Bernhard Meyer G.m.b.H., Leipzig C1

6. Photograph portraying the six-month-old winner of the 'most beautiful Aryan baby contest', reprinted on a 1935 cover of the 'Illustrated Family Magazine' entitled 'Bringing Sunshine into the House' (*Sonne ins Haus: Illustrierte Familienzeitschrift mit Versicherung*). Unknown to the Nazis who had run the competition, as well as the publishers of the magazine, the photograph actually portrayed a little Jewish baby, Hessy Levinsons. The photographer who had taken her portrait photograph for the family was an anti-Nazi who secretly submitted it to the competition as a small act of defiance against Nazi racism.
United States Holocaust Memorial Museum, courtesy of Hessy Levinsons Taft, 66659.

7. German citizens salute Adolf Hitler at the opening of the 11th Olympiad in Berlin, August 1936. Images such as this convey an impression of a Volk united behind its Führer. The International Olympic Committee (IOC) had awarded Berlin the Games in 1931, having little idea of what Nazism would mean for the Olympic ideals of equality and cooperation. In order to make a better impression on international visitors, the Nazi regime ensured that antisemitic propaganda was cleared away from the streets of Berlin, while 'Gypsies' (Roma and Sinti) were moved out of sight to a 'Gypsy camp' in the Marzahn suburb in northeastern Berlin.
United States Holocaust Memorial Museum, courtesy of National Archives and Records Administration, College Park, 14495.

8. During the 11th Summer Olympic Games, held in Berlin in 1936, enthusiastic Germans wave swastika flags in support of German athletes. Photographer Heinrich Hoffmann/Studio of H. Hoffmann, August 1936.
United States Holocaust Memorial Museum, courtesy of National Archives and Records Administration, College Park, 21764.

9. Bruno Gebhard, research director of the Berlin Office for Exhibitions and Trade Fairs (background centre left), with Joseph Goebbels, Reich Minister of Propaganda (background centre right), during the opening of a public exhibition in Berlin on 'The Woman at Home, at Work', March 1933. A committed social democrat, the fully 'Aryan' Gebhard was increasingly uncomfortable with the compromises he had to make in the course of his duties, such as adapting the contents of exhibitions to serve Nazi ideology, as well as the strain of living under Nazism and the effects on his children. He was fortunate enough to be in a position, financially and professionally, to be able to emigrate to the United States in 1937.
Dittrick Medical History Center, Case Western Reserve University, 1976-023-gf03.

10. Local people, including children, stare at Jews who are being expelled from the picturesque medieval small town of Uffenheim, in Franconia, Bavaria, under police guard. The exact date of this photograph is not known, but it serves to illustrate the ways in which Jews were 'not wanted', as towns and villages across the Reich put up signs to exclude Jews, or proclaimed that they had become 'Jew-free'—with the apparent consent or quiescence of local people who passively watched expulsions, as in this case, in full public view.
United States Holocaust Memorial Museum, courtesy of Henry Landman, 51996.

11. Onlookers watch as three Jewish businessmen are publicly humiliated by being forced to march down Brühl Straße, in central Leipzig, carrying placards bearing the message: 'Don't buy from Jews; Shop at German stores!' This photograph, taken in 1937, was reproduced and sold as a postcard, effectively replicating both the message and the public humiliation.
United States Holocaust Memorial Museum, courtesy of William Blye, 20210.

12. Group photograph of members of the 'Non-Aryan War Veterans Society' (*Nichtarischer Kriegerbund*) in 1937. Many patriotic Germans of 'non-Aryan descent' mistakenly continued to believe that their military service to their fatherland in the Great War would protect them, and left it too late to emigrate.
United States Holocaust Memorial Museum, courtesy of George Fogelson, 08943.

13. A decorated beer wagon, functioning as a float in a parade in the small town of Hochheim am Main (with just over 4,000 inhabitants at the time) passes a *Der Stürmer* display box proclaiming that 'Without a solution to the Jewish question, there is no salvation for the German people'. This sort of slogan became ubiquitous in the mid-1930s, creating a repertoire of prejudices among people who had accommodated themselves to the Nazi regime.

United States Holocaust Memorial Museum, courtesy of Hochheim am Main, 97958.

14. On 13 March 1938, the Vienna Boys' Choir and other young people gather to welcome Adolf Hitler on the occasion of his first official visit to Austria following annexation (*Anschluss*) to the Reich, under a banner proclaiming 'We sing for Adolf Hitler!' Many Austrians turned out to welcome Hitler's 'return home' with apparent enthusiasm, giving little impression of Austria being 'Hitler's first victim', as it was later portrayed. At the time, official photographs sought to convey the image of a united Volk cheering their Führer.
United States Holocaust Memorial Museum, courtesy of National Archives and Records Administration, College Park, 00410.

15. In Vienna immediately after the Anschluss in March 1938, people gather
to watch as Jews are forced to scrub the pavement on their hands and knees.
Onlookers appear to approve of this act of public humiliation. The introduction
of violent antisemitism was extremely rapid in Austria, while political opponents
were dealt with brutally.
*United States Holocaust Memorial Museum, courtesy of National Archives and Records
Administration, College Park, 03741.*

16. In the early weeks after the Anschluss, Viennese pedestrians pass a Nazi sign on a restaurant window informing them that Jews are not welcome. The social segregation that had taken months or even years in Germany took a matter of weeks in Austria.

United States Holocaust Memorial Museum, courtesy of National Archives and Records Administration, College Park, 73943.

17. In March 1938, a dog lies on a park bench in Vienna which is marked 'Only for Aryans' (*Nur für Arier!*). Presumably no local Nazi was sufficiently concerned about whether the dog might be a mixed breed, or whether this might imply that 'Aryans' were akin to dogs, to try to shift the pet from a comfortable perch. The situation would have been quite different for a human being of 'non-Aryan' descent.
United States Holocaust Memorial Museum, Unknown Provenance, 63705.

18. View of the Loos Haus in Vienna in April 1938, with a banner bearing a quote from Hitler, 'Those of the same blood belong in the same Reich!' Banners with this kind of extreme ethno-nationalist slogan were hung all over Austria in the run-up to the plebiscite mounted on 10 April 1938, to confirm apparent near-universal support for the incorporation of Austria into an expanded German Reich.
United States Holocaust Memorial Museum, courtesy of Library of Congress, 64403.

19. On 10 November 1938, local people look at the ruins of a synagogue that had been set on fire during Kristallnacht in Ober Ramstadt, a small town near to Darmstadt in Hessen. An anti-Nazi, Georg Schmidt, took a series of photographs of onlookers by the smoking remnants of the synagogue, capturing degrees of concern and uncertainty about how to react to this act of violence. The film reel of Schmidt's photographs was confiscated by police but later recovered from the city hall by a policeman in the service of the American occupation forces at the end of the war.
United States Holocaust Memorial Museum, courtesy of Trudy Isenberg, 23608.

20. People looking at Ober Ramstadt Synagogue burning, 10 November 1938; another photograph in the series taken by Georg Schmidt (see also figure 19, photo 23608). It was now clear to the Nazi regime that even if there was an outcry internationally, there would be little by way of public protest within Germany; people who were shocked remained largely silent.
United States Holocaust Memorial Museum, courtesy of Hessisches Staatsarchiv Darmstadt, 36339.

21. On 10 November 1938, passers-by look at the smashed-in windows of a business owned by the Lichtenstein family in Berlin. Many people took the opportunity to loot goods from stores where the windows had been smashed. Others were shocked by the destruction of property, or muttered quietly that they were 'ashamed to be German'. While some people helped individuals in private, very few dared to utter criticisms of the violence in public.

United States Holocaust Memorial Museum, courtesy of National Archives and Records Administration, College Park, 86838.

22. On 10 November 1938, onlookers line the streets to watch as around sixty Jews, who had been arrested before the Baden-Baden synagogue was set alight in Kristallnacht, are marched through town. They were forced to watch the burning of the synagogue, followed by a series of public humiliations, after which around forty male Jews were deported to the Dachau concentration camp.
United States Holocaust Memorial Museum, courtesy of Lydia Chagoll, 27224a.

23. Bystanders in Oldenburg watch as members of the SA march Jewish men through the streets for deportation to a concentration camp following Kristallnacht in November 1938. In total around 30,000 male Jews were arrested and sent to concentration camps after Kristallnacht.
United States Holocaust Memorial Museum, courtesy of Abraham Levi, 62167.

24. On 23 March 1939, Hitler arrived in the Lithuanian port city of Memel (Klaipėda), following its annexation and incorporation into the expanded German Reich the previous day. While local Nazis and 'ethnic Germans' were jubilant, many Jews and Lithuanians fled over the border rather than remain under Nazi rule. This would be of little help some two and a half years later, when Germans crossed the border into Lithuania in the 'war of annihilation' against the Soviet Union and started to commit mass killings of Jewish civilians. *United States Holocaust Memorial Museum, courtesy of National Archives and Records Administration, College Park, 20351.*

PART II

The Expansion of Violence at Home and Abroad

6

Changing Horizons
Views from Within and Without

From the beginning of his chancellorship in 1933, Hitler always had an eye to ensuring popular support. His charisma was constructed through projections of personality, image, and leadership style; but it also depended on keeping people content with their lot. And for this, Hitler was sensitive to the barometer of opinion, particularly relating to economic wellbeing, social satisfaction, and a sense of national greatness. Over time, even those who had retained a sense of inner distance increasingly followed the growing majority. By the time applications for membership of the NSDAP were opened up again in 1937, following earlier closure in May 1933, the futility of opposition had become more than apparent, underscored by periodic crackdowns on dissent and campaigns against people deemed to be 'a-socials' or breaking behavioural and sexual norms. By the late 1930s, simply by virtue of compliance, and whether or not they were happy with this, the majority of the German population had become effectively complicit in the structural racism of Nazi Germany. There were nevertheless still differences in the degree to which, in everyday life, individuals continued to express sympathy towards the victims of persecution.

There were also less immediately obvious but highly significant developments elsewhere, as Nazi conceptions of the Volksgemeinschaft had an influence far beyond the borders of the Reich, even before the territorial expansion that began in 1938. While some individuals within the Reich increasingly felt they had to get out, many people living outside the

Reich's then borders were in different ways caught up in the Nazi project. Experiences from both these sides shed light on the dramatic changes
taking place in German society within less than five years of Nazi rule.

Compromised choices: Conformity or departure

For people who were personally disquieted or intimately affected by developments in Nazi Germany, life within the borders of the Reich felt
increasingly untenable. Yet for most people—unlike those in high places,
in elite circles, who had a greater degree of leeway to act differently—the
range of choices was more restricted: conformity, complicity, persecution,
or, depending on personal situation, emigration.

Relatively pain-free exits were only possible from a position of privilege.
Bruno Gebhard, for one—former social democrat and official in public
health education—was not only becoming more and more uneasy about
the compromises he was making as an 'Aryan'. As we saw in the previous
chapter, he was also acutely aware that things were changing in Germany
following the propaganda success of the Olympic Games. When, in early
1937, the NSDAP reopened for new members, increasing pressure was ex-
erted on people to join; and Gebhard noted that while most of his friends
managed to resist, those living in small towns where their 'every step ... was
controlled' felt they had little choice. Gebhard had considerable sympathy
for them. In his view, 'nobody in Germany had the right to look down on
those who—against their inner will—had joined the Party and behaved as
100% Nazis'. He reasoned that anyone who had a family to care for and
saw no change forthcoming simply did what they had to do. They coped.
People felt 'desperately sick of everything' but consoled themselves with
little jokes, repeating the witticism that it was simply impossible to 'eat
enough to make yourself as sick as you feel'.

When their eldest daughter started school in 1937, the Gebhards worried about indoctrination by Nazi teachers and the impossibility of being
honest with her, given the chance that she might betray the anti-Nazi attitudes expressed at home. As a high-profile professional in the public health
education world, however, Gebhard was fortunate in having other options.
He organized an initial six-month trip to the United States on a visitor's
visa and sought an offer of employment; and in 1938 the Gebhard family

was able to start, as he put it in his Harvard essay, 'a new life in a new World'.[1] Despite upheavals and discomforts, relocation was relatively easy in Gebhard's case, privileged as he was by professional standing, material means, and personal connections. Having left Germany, he was able to preserve a degree of self-respect and personal integrity, though it could do little to help those with far fewer options, let alone 'non-Aryans'.

For those in mixed relationships, the tensions became ever more acute. Robert Breusch remained steadfastly committed to his Jewish fiancée, Käte Dreyfuß. But it was becoming absolutely clear that they could have no future together in Germany. At the same time, things were not going well for Breusch's own family. His brother, recovering from a life-threatening illness, had been arrested for making anti-Nazi comments and sent to Oranienburg concentration camp (the precursor of Sachsenhausen). Additionally, although both his parents were anti-Nazis and not antisemitic, Breusch was aware that his mother was distressed that by refusing to give up Dreyfuß, her son was compromising his career. One evening she poured out her heart to him: she had devoted thirty years of her life to doing the best for her sons, and now, while one was in genuine danger, the other was threatening to throw it all away 'just to be able to marry some girl'. Breusch could understand her feelings; moreover, he was increasingly subjected to pressures at work. One teacher, who 'passionately hated the Nazis', he wrote, had joined the SA to protect his job, saying he had a wife and child to support. Other colleagues were discussing openly how long his relationship with Dreyfuß could go on. Breusch felt things were getting 'far too hot for comfort'. He and Dreyfuß sought again to have a restorative holiday in Switzerland but had difficulty finding a room even in a previously quite hospitable environment. With the passage of the Nuremberg Laws, Breusch realized with finality that the struggle to remain together in Germany could not go on.[2]

Breusch and Dreyfuß managed to keep their relationship going during the closing months of 1935, meeting only under cover of darkness in locations where they would not be recognized, and relying on others not to denounce them. Breusch felt they were living in an increasingly dangerous situation, one in which 'it was hard to breathe'. In December 1935, all Jews in Freiburg had their passports withdrawn, which made further planning extremely difficult. Despite being an 'Aryan', Breusch was not an entirely free agent: while exploring options he found that, being of conscription age, it was almost impossible to get a visa to travel.[3]

Even so, Breusch did not give up. In case his passport was confiscated in light of what officials called 'suspicion of intention to flee' (*Fluchtverdacht*), he told a story about having lost it, and managed to obtain a replacement. In his spare time, he studied Spanish and English. And he continued to resist growing pressures to conform. Looking out of the window of his lodgings at the beautiful Black Forest valley beyond the Birklehof school, where he had previously felt so happy, he reflected in his diary on 16 January 1936: 'The area looks just the same as it did three years ago. Just the people are totally transformed.'[4]

Breusch and Dreyfuß finally made it out, separately: he leaving for Chile, she a few months later, managing to get to relatives in the United States. In mid-July 1936 they were reunited, and on 25 July they celebrated their marriage in Valparaíso, Chile. The exit, while making possible what would become a lifelong partnership, was not without immense personal cost on both sides. When he said farewell to his mother on 1 April 1936, and aware that she was suffering from heart disease, Breusch knew he would never see her again. His brother was still languishing in a concentration camp, his fate still in the balance. Most of his friends disapproved of his decision to leave. He loved his *Heimat*, the hills and valleys of the Black Forest, and the town of Freiburg. He faced an entirely unknown future among people with whom he had previously had no contact whatsoever, and had no idea how he could pick up the pieces of a career or make a family life. He had every sympathy for those of his former friends and 'Aryan' colleagues who felt it was easier to make the compromises necessary to remain in Germany, even under Nazism, than engage in the pain of emigration and abandonment of all one had previously held dear.[5]

'No-one', Breusch wrote after his emigration, 'who has only observed developments in Germany from abroad, should talk of lack of character if someone in Germany against his own will converts to National Socialism. Since for anyone who wants to continue in a career there are only two alternatives: either go along with it, or get out. And to leave, voluntarily, for ever, is hard.'[6]

Agonized exits

For 'non-Aryans' there was far less leeway for choice. Acquiescence and compromise was not an option in the way it was for 'Aryans'. Older 'non-Aryans' often trusted their German fatherland and thought they should just sit out the bad times, because things would surely change for the better, or simply lacked the means and energy to explore emigration. Younger people who could more readily make the plunge sought to embark on new lives abroad.

While Erich Haller-Munk had early on left his theatre life in Berlin to settle in Vienna, his brother Hans, ousted from the legal profession in 1933, had tried to keep going with his 'Aryan' wife Beate, and their baby, maintaining the appearance of a bourgeois lifestyle on money sent by his parents. As a Christian of Jewish descent, he could not disguise his 'racial' origins for long, however. He was rattled by two days' imprisonment in 1934, but released following an intervention by Beate's brother, who was in the SS. He was also quite unnerved by 'a couple of immature lads' who had paraded under his windows chanting 'hang the Jewish swine'. By 1935 a sense of growing danger was dawning on him; showing signs of increasing strain, he attempted to prepare for departure by getting money out of the country illegally. His brother Erich, in Vienna, voiced opposition to his plans and methods, but to little avail. Hans and family eventually made it to Italy, taking all the furniture they could transport, but the money they had sought to smuggle out never turned up. Even so, Hans took on a large apartment, acquired an expensive car, and he and his wife separately squeezed more money from his parents. Hans returned from one trip home with a large sum of cash, some of which was due to Erich but never handed over; Erich discovered this much later, as he wrote in his essay.[7]

Hans now went into a downward spiral. In July 1937, as debts mounted and creditors caught up, and unable to hold out in Italy any longer, he left for France, claiming he would take soundings about setting up a business in Paris. That was, for a while, the last his family heard of him.[8]

In August 1937, Beate wrote to his parents in desperation: she had received no word of Hans; the rent on their apartment had never been paid; possessions were confiscated; and she was penniless. But the Haller-Munks refused to send further financial help, since it became clear that Beate had been well aware of the impending financial ruin and had been trying to squeeze as much money out of them as she could before his disappearance. Beate herself, an 'Aryan', returned to live with her own mother in Germany.[9] The marriage, like so many mixed marriages in Nazi Germany, was now clearly under terrible strain.

Then Hans sent a suicidal note, timed to arrive on his mother's birthday, stating that he was destitute and sleeping on a park bench in a French border town. This card, in Erich's view, was 'terrifying, without any sign of human dignity, and betrayed his total inner collapse'. Their parents, utterly shocked, engaged in mutual recriminations about where they might have gone wrong. In a frenzy of parental concern, they wrote to the local police, sending money to fund a search and rescue operation.[10] Hans was found.

The previously well-respected lawyer, now a shadow of his former self, was finally returned to his parents' home. He was given some nominal work to do in his father's pharmacy, which was still managing to keep going, and his parents tried to help him recover. Hans was half-destroyed, physically and psychologically. He would not talk about his experiences, although he did eventually contact Beate through letters.[11]

Beate, however, had other ideas. She had no intention of remaining married to a Jew, let alone one who had so dramatically broken down. Beate 'pronounced herself outraged', wrote Erich, and filed for divorce. She was at first rebuffed. A Nazi official informed her that 'if she had managed to endure living with "the Jew" for so long, despite the fact that the Reich service for enlightenment had made so clear to her the extent to which she was debasing herself, then she did not suddenly now have the right to talk about "being Aryan"'. Later, however, Beate was successful in her quest for divorce. Meanwhile, she and their baby were fully ensconced again with her 'Aryan' family and friends, and she paid little further attention to the fate of her husband.[12]

Not everyone ousted from the Volksgemeinschaft experienced such personal disintegration, and some were far better supported by their non-Jewish compatriots in their efforts to get out, even if they remained critical of the compromises many 'Aryans' were now making. Lotte Popper had been wanting for some time to emigrate to Palestine; her husband was finally persuaded there could be no future for them in Germany, despite the fact that his dental patients had remained faithful to him. He obtained a position in Palestine that he had to take immediately, leaving Lotte to dismantle the family home and sell their possessions. Lotte was scathing about the people who now came to scavenge: 'Yes, the Aryans had it good. They could now enhance their own apartments on the cheap, with the well-cared-for furniture of the Jews who were leaving'; they bragged about how they had 'picked it up for a song, so to speak'. And yet, nearly everyone who came to pick up a bargain expressed sympathy, whether genuine or assumed for the occasion. They assured her of their 'outrage about this "driving out of innocent people"', even as they were benefitting from the situation and exploiting her plight. Meanwhile, and more importantly, it also proved impossible to sell her husband's dental practice at a fair price.[13]

And yet, Lotte still retained her faith in ordinary Germans in Hamburg, where she felt, with some basis, that people had not capitulated to Nazism quite as comprehensively as elsewhere. She took a brief trip to Rathenow in Brandenburg to make a last visit to her sister, who had to remind her, 'this is not Hamburg, and you cannot trust your neighbours'. Back in Hamburg, on 20 April 1936 she met a friend for lunch in town. Crossing the marketplace—now Adolf-Hitler-Platz—they were brought to a standstill. It was Hitler's birthday, and when the clock-bells rang at 2 P.M. everyone was supposed to stand for two minutes with their arm raised in the Heil Hitler salute. There were barely a hundred people in the marketplace. As the swastika flag was raised, a few people raised their arms 'after first carefully looking around, slightly ashamed'. Popper and her friend 'were definitely among the majority who did not raise their arms'. This sustained her faith in the fundamental goodness of many fellow Germans—whether or not her optimistic view of her compatriots was really justified. There is no trace in her essay of any doubts about the efficacy of simply refusing to raise an arm in the Heil Hitler salute.[14]

When the last of the things they were allowed to take with them to their new life were packed, Popper had an unlikely exchange with the customs officer who was formally tasked with overseeing the legalities of her departure. As he checked the contents of her packing cases, the elderly officer kept shaking his head and muttering, 'Terrible, that I have to go along with this! Every day having to see how decent citizens are being driven out like this.' It turned out that the customs officer also originally came from Popper's native West Prussia; they soon started talking about the good old days, rehashing fond memories of an area they both loved. Eventually, the man approved the boxes Popper had carefully packed according to the regulations. But he then saw to it that an additional box was packed with all the children's toys, including items that were expressly forbidden. He sealed the boxes, signed the necessary documents, and gave instructions to his team to send the packages on their way. Only later, Popper reflected, did the irony of the situation dawn on her: while the Third Reich was officially denying her citizenship or any right to belong to her homeland, one of its senior officials was calling her a 'fellow countryman', and their mutual love for the soil of their common *Heimat* seemed simply taken for granted.[15]

Like many others who left before the war, Popper recalled that some envied her being able to get out and wished they could leave too. One friend said quite openly that she would 'also not go along with this racket [*Schwindel*] much longer'. As the boat pulled away from the Hamburg quay side, Popper watched another friend's pale face fading in the distance, 'condemned to death' by the Nazis. This middle-aged 'Aryan' woman had committed the ultimate sin of falling in love, late in life, with a Jewish man, and they had hoped for a happy few years together; but this would no longer be possible. In 1939, when Popper wrote her essay, despite all she had herself experienced and all the news that reached her following emigration, she sustained a belief in the majority of Germans as essentially decent but forced by an awful regime into a conformity with which they internally did not agree.[16] Again, she did not seem to pursue the logic of the situation: she did not query whether, ultimately, compliance with state-ordained racism would not eventually lead to more active complicity in its radical consequences.

Others too had similar experiences on departure. For Friedrich Reuss, even though only tainted by 'non-Aryan blood' from one grandparent, emigrating was clearly more attractive than trying to remain in Germany. He had been forced to give up his job with the insurance company as customers were cancelling their policies, supposedly incensed that the company was still employing someone of Jewish descent. Coming to the view that he must get out, Reuss found a distant relative in New York willing to supply an affidavit and help organize a visa. Based now with his in-laws in Berlin, Reuss spent hours queuing alongside innumerable applicants caught in the torment of waiting lists and financial demands, trying to pack up their entire lives and rescue what they could. When Reuss finally made it onto a train to Holland, he recorded one last encounter with a German border official. The would-be emigrants had been forced to disembark at the border station and watch as the train puffed on without them while they were subjected to intensive checks. Reuss himself was passed up the chain of command until he was finally faced with the man in overall charge. Seated at his desk, this senior official offered Reuss a cigar. 'In 1918 we were despised by a few foreigners—perhaps', Reuss recalled him saying. 'And certainly wrongly. Now we despise ourselves. And rightly so.' The official went on: 'I wish I could exchange places with you. Pass on greetings to America from the old Germany that has died. And forget the new Germany as quickly as you can.' They shook hands, unseen by anyone else, Reuss noted. Once outside, the official raised his arm in the Hitler salute, while Reuss thought he could detect the hint of a smile at the corners of his mouth.[17]

While Reuss felt that darkness had fallen over Germany, he nevertheless—like Lotte Popper and others who encountered well-disposed officials even as they left their homeland—retained some faith in the goodwill of at least some of his fellow countrymen. Even while conforming, these officials clothed their actions in a garb of kindness towards individual victims of the systemic racism.

But conformity alone, however tinged with cordial expressions, was sufficient to allow the regime to continue unchecked, creating the conditions for the actions of radical activists. And in the later 1930s things were taking a turn for the worse, not only within but also well beyond the borders of what would, following territorial expansion from 1938, soon be called the 'old Reich' (*Altreich*). Germans living abroad played a role both in fostering nationalism and racism, and, eventually, in welcoming and assisting the invading German armed forces.

Germans abroad

The ties between German-speaking communities in other states and the Reich were manifold, as was evident in Austria but also widespread across other areas of Europe where there were significant German minorities. An organization for 'German-ness abroad' or 'Germandom abroad' (this works better in German: *Deutschtum im Ausland*) had existed in different forms well before Hitler came to power and readily accommodated itself to racial views and aspirations for 'living space' (*Lebensraum*). Germans abroad often shared a sense of common ethnic and cultural identity as what some have called an 'imagined community', in clear distinction to the Eastern European ethnic and linguistic groups among whom they lived.[18] In some areas, Germans considered that the land on which they lived had been snatched following defeat in 1918 and the redrawing of Europe's borders that followed. The newly reconstituted state of Poland had been given a broad swathe of land, the 'Polish corridor', cutting through West Prussia to provide access to the Baltic Sea. The predominantly German-speaking port of Danzig (Gdańsk), along with surrounding towns and villages, was pronounced a Free City under the protection of the League of Nations and tied in a customs union with Poland. And to the northeast, beyond the now geographically marooned German province of East Prussia, lay Memel (Klaipėda), initially under the administration of the League of Nations as exercised by the French but taken over by the new state of Lithuania in 1923.

In other places, isolated German-speaking communities represented historic remnants, living traces of migration and colonization long before the nineteenth-century formation of a 'small German' nation-state. This in itself, of course, had excluded the large German-speaking population of Austria, the western part of the Austro-Hungarian Empire. Language, culture, and sense of ethnic belonging did not straightforwardly map onto the borders of the Reich in 1937. And wherever they lived, 'ethnic Germans,' (*Volksdeutsche,*) often had relatives within the Reich, reinforcing a feeling of belonging to a wider national community. With their emphasis on 'race' and the need for *Lebensraum*—literally, 'living space'—the Nazis could readily build on these sentiments.

In Latvia, the 'Baltic German'—as he described himself in his 1989 memoir—Jürgen Ernst Kroeger had a strong sense of German cultural and social superiority. Living on a substantial landed estate in the small hamlet of Wiexten (now Vecumnieki), in the countryside southeast of Riga, Kroeger's family had long been employers of Latvian farmhands. Kroeger felt thoroughly at home there and had happy childhood memories of his parents entertaining guests in their large house. All this had changed with the First World War, the Russian Revolution in 1917, and the murder of his father by Bolsheviks in 1919. Freed, as Kroeger saw it, by German paramilitary Freikorps activists, surviving family members fled to safety with relatives in Mecklenburg, and as a teenager Kroeger attended high school in the small north German town of Neubrandenburg. In 1921 the family decided it was safe to return to what they still saw as their *Heimat*, but then the newly founded state of Latvia expropriated land belonging to Baltic Germans. Kroeger's family managed to retain a modest portion of their former estate, including the house, surrounding buildings, and fifty hectares of land. Previously, Germans had enjoyed superior social status and quasi-colonial relationships with the Latvians who had for centuries tilled their land, and most reacted angrily to the new situation. But the Kroeger family came to terms with their reduced status and even conceded that Latvia was treating its minorities relatively 'decently'. Kroeger now attended school in Mitau (Jelgava) and Libau (Liepāja), where there were substantial German-speaking communities. On completing his schooling, he returned to his uncle's estate in Mecklenburg to receive training in agriculture. Following his marriage in 1931 to Gerda, another Baltic German whose family lived in Riga, Kroeger returned to farm in his native Wiexten.[19]

When Hitler was appointed chancellor in 1933, Kroeger and other Baltic Germans were enthusiastic about the fact that 'a former front soldier had appeared, who held up before our eyes a vision of a strong, Greater German Reich, and above all said to all Germans, across the world, things that they wanted to hear'. Many young Baltic Germans joined what they called the 'Movement' (*die Bewegung*), infused with a national socialist spirit, and marched through the streets of Riga wearing clothes symbolizing unity with Germany. Some youth groups were invited to visit Germany and came back brimming with enthusiasm; a few were arrested by the Latvians, who were becoming increasingly concerned about what was going on. In the hamlet of Wiexten, Kroeger and his wife sat listening to the radio, enthralled by speeches given by Hitler and others. But, he later claimed, they were shocked when in May 1934 the Latvian prime minister, Karlis Ulmanis, effected a coup with army support, proclaiming himself Latvian Führer, abolishing parliamentary democracy, and radically constraining the voices of Germans. Kroeger and other Germans resented the slogan 'Latvia for the Latvians', and now many Baltic Germans decided to move to the Reich. Kroeger himself, however, felt bound by love for the soil and landscapes of his family home, and he and Gerda, with her family roots in Riga, decided to stay and support the German cause in Latvia. Kroeger also tried to foster good relations with his Latvian neighbours. But his support for Nazism would eventually bring him into ever closer contact with Nazi crimes in wartime.[20]

In Danzig, too, the new era in Germany was greeted with enthusiasm in right-wing nationalist circles. As a Free City under the protection of the League of Nations, Danzig had in the 1920s attracted newcomers seeking a better life; in particular, the population, overwhelmingly German, was rapidly augmented by an influx of Polish and Eastern European Jews. The number of Jews rose from 2,717 in 1910—less than 1 percent of the population—to 9,239 in 1924 (2.4 percent), rising again to 10,488 in 1929. In Danzig, as in Berlin, there were significant differences between the better-off German-speaking Jews and the predominantly Yiddish-speaking *Ostjuden*, among whom there were many Zionists and Orthodox Jews, as well as socialists.[21]

The Berlin-born Alice Baerwald, who had moved with her assimilated Jewish family to Danzig, had at first been well integrated in wider German social and cultural life: bourgeois German-speaking circles in 1920s Danzig had been reminiscent of those in her native Berlin. But things had begun to change with the economic downturn in the late 1920s; and as the Depression worsened, the previously insignificant Nazi party began to make rapid political gains in Danzig as in Germany. Baerwald was devastated when her eldest son, seeing the writing on the wall, chose to emigrate to the United States in 1931. But the real change came with Hitler's accession to power, giving local Nazis a huge boost. Taking control of the Danzig Senate in June 1933, the Danzig Nazi party, influenced by events in Germany, would dominate politics over the following years. Antisemitism rapidly rose.

Baerwald's accounts of her encounters at this time vividly portray both how society was changing around her and the ways in which she sought to maintain her own sense of self-respect, asserting herself in whatever way possible. One of the Baerwalds' non-Jewish friends was a well-respected lawyer whose son became an important Nazi; this friend now also felt he would have to join the party. Baerwald met him by chance one day on a tram, and started to chat to him, not having seen him for a while. As they got off the tram they met an acquaintance in SS uniform, who was astonished that the now-Nazi lawyer was talking in such a friendly manner to someone he knew to be Jewish. Baerwald 'could see how embarrassing it was for him to be seen with a Jew', but she retained her cheeky self-assurance. 'I said goodbye, but teasingly added "oh yes of course, you are not allowed to talk to me", to which he responded, well, it wasn't that bad. I replied "then apparently I am better acquainted with your laws than you are". The whole situation was clearly very disagreeable for him', Baerwald wrote in her essay, 'but it is hard to imagine the cowardice of this educated class'.[22]

Baerwald's husband was badly affected by an antisemitic incident on the tram so, despite her attempts at self-assertion, the couple began to avoid using public transport. Like others, too—here as in Germany—the Baerwalds increasingly withdrew from non-Jewish social circles. Jews now began to discuss in earnest where they might emigrate, summarizing the relevant search criteria in a defusing joke: 'I would like to live in a country where if the doorbell rings at seven in the morning it really is the milkman.'[23] Meanwhile, tensions were mounting between Poland and Danzig, alleviated only temporarily by the 1934 German–Polish Nonaggression Pact. Polish agreement not to help any opposition to Danzig's Nazi government only strengthened Nazi propaganda and German nationalism among Danzig Germans.

Events in Germany also had a significant impact in Austria. The economic depression and financial crises, with the near collapse of the Austrian banking system and rapidly rising unemployment, provided fuel to both right-wing and left-wing parties, with the Nazi party appearing increasingly attractive in some quarters. But the predominantly rural and Catholic character of Austria outside the socialist stronghold of 'Red Vienna' set limits to the lures of Nazism, and political allegiances were further divided between Catholic conservative support for the Christian Social Party and working-class support for the social democrats. The Austrian chancellor from 1932, Engelbert Dollfuss, unsuccessfully sought to balance competing political interests. In 1933, dispensing entirely with parliamentary democracy, he introduced an Austrian variant of authoritarian rule, 'Austro-fascism', influenced by Mussolini's Italy. The Communist Party and the Austrian Nazi party were now banned.

Nonetheless, political unrest continued in Austria. There was violence verging on civil war during two weeks in February 1934, as workers in Linz protested the suppression of the labour movement; this rapidly spread to other industrial centres, including Vienna. Following brutal crackdowns, in which around 200 people lost their lives, there was vicious retribution, with ten leaders of the riots put to death and hundreds given prison sentences. The social democrats were also banned. A new constitution was approved in April 1934, effectively destroying the last vestiges of the previously democratic First Republic. The new Fatherland Front (*Vaterländische* Front), created by amalgamating the former Christian Social Party and other conservative nationalists, now sought to impose order; but things were not so simple. On 25 July 1934 a group of (now illegal) Austrian Nazis attempted a coup, succeeding only in assassinating Chancellor Dollfuss. Much to Hitler's surprise, Mussolini sprang to the defence of Austrian neutrality; the assassins were executed, and Kurt

Schuschnigg, previously education minister, took over as chancellor. Yet despite this setback, and the fact that the Nazi party was illegal, neither the Austrian Nazis nor Hitler gave up on the ultimate aim of bringing Austria into the fold of an expanded Reich.

Austria was a deeply divided country. The bouts of violence in 1934 not only revealed how bitterly contested were alternative visions of the future but also exacerbated tensions. These fissures even extended deep into individual lives and had to be negotiated at an emotional and personal level, as their stories reveal.

Gertrud Lederer (née Wickerhauser) was a Catholic born in 1895 in the hamlet of Gresten Scheibbs, south of the Danube between Linz and Vienna. A clever young woman, she was educated at a Catholic girls' boarding school, the Sacré Coeur in Vienna, that specialized in foreign languages, and later became a professional translator and writer. At the age of eighteen, she married a physician with whom she had a son and a daughter. But in 1920 her husband died from the lingering consequences of war wounds. In 1922 she remarried, again to a medical doctor: a young Viennese Catholic by the name of Dr Kurt Lederer. They too had a son, born in January 1932. Although Catholic, Lederer was of Jewish descent; and from the moment Hitler was appointed chancellor in neighbouring Germany, the question of whether one was 'Aryan' or 'non-Aryan' became massively significant in Austria too. While the children from her first marriage were unequivocally 'Aryan', her husband, under the 'racial' definition, was Jewish, and their son, Tony, was a '*Mischling*'.[24]

The Lederer family was deeply split, and not only between the Jewish and 'Aryan' sides; there were also deep political rifts among non-Jewish family members. One of Gertrud Lederer's two brothers lived in the Austrian city of Graz; he eventually became a Nazi and cultivated political contacts in high places. The other had moved to Germany, which he felt had now 'fallen back into sheer barbarity' and was 'hell for Jews and everyone who opposes Nazism'; in 1934 he chose to leave Germany for the UK. Meanwhile, the backwash of events in the Reich was evident to Lederer in Austria. One evening in January 1934, she and her husband were visiting friends when an ashen-faced friend of their host suddenly turned up. He explained that the Gestapo had arrested him for telling jokes about Hitler in a café in Bavaria; he had been thrown into Dachau concentration camp and later released on condition that he leave Germany immediately;

he was now seeking refuge with these Austrian friends. The Lederers began to hear of more and more such experiences in Germany. But this did not unsettle them personally as yet: Gertrud reflected in her essay that they were somehow getting used to the situation, however painful, just as one gets used to a nagging toothache.[25]

Nevertheless, developments closer to home, in Austria, soon caused more immediate concern. The street battles in Linz in February 1934 spread to the suburbs of Vienna near the Lederers' home. Left-wing violence on the streets was, Gertrud Lederer thought, politically counterproductive: the Austrian middle classes had developed a vitriolic hatred of anything that smacked of socialism, while conservative nationalists and Nazis decided just 'to watch and stir up hated', creating even greater rifts. Lederer recalled that when Chancellor Dollfuss was murdered that summer, she too began to feel hatred—but on her part it was hatred for the Nazis. She had little faith in Schuschnigg's competence as the new chancellor, agreeing with a friend who knew him personally from schooldays that he was simply not up to dealing with the Nazis.[26]

Meanwhile Lederer's teenage daughter from her first marriage, Christl, was choosing to hang out with Nazi boys in their suburb. Christl explained that these boys were better at swimming and skiing than the others; her mother thought they were simply lazy and could not be bothered with school, clearly preferring the excitement of secretly singing the Horst Wessel song—although the Nazi anthem was still strictly forbidden in Austria—to attending boring Catholic processions. Lederer tried to quell her own anxiety by seeing their Nazi activities as a harmless game, Cowboys and Indians for teenagers. But there were also heated family arguments about more significant matters. She and her daughter quarrelled about the murder of Dollfuss. Christl, influenced by her Nazi friends, felt that killing for idealistic motives was not actually murder; her mother maintained that murder was murder. These family conflicts and political differences would develop new configurations following the Anschluss—the 'union' with Germany—in 1938.[27]

Responses among Austrians to the rise of Nazism in Germany were initially mixed. But open antisemitism was rising. Edmund Heilpern, having been forced to leave Germany in September 1934, was advised on his return to Austria to report to the Fatherland Front, who would find work for him because of his distinguished war service. He duly turned

up, and all seemed to be going well—until he revealed his Jewish ancestry, at which point he was instantly dropped. Heilpern turned instead
to the Jewish community. He was shocked to find how terrified its members were. Battered by rising antisemitism, many felt it was only a matter
of time before Hitler and the Nazis would take over and urged him to
emigrate to Palestine. Heilpern, who was both a Christian and an active
socialist, angrily refused. Despite these initially vehement disagreements,
however, Heilpern did at least get help with contacts and was able to find
work; four months later his wife and daughter were able to leave Berlin
and join him in Vienna.[28]

Over the next couple of years, Heilpern found like-minded souls. Some
were former reserve officers of the Austrian army, 'Aryan' comrades who
had shared experiences at the front and were not antisemitic; many of
them, Heilpern noted, were arrested following the Nazi takeover in 1938.
Heilpern also enjoyed the company of members of the League of Jewish
Front Soldiers (Bund Jüdischer Frontsoldaten); most were later arrested.
And among his students in the adult education college (Volkshochschule)
where he taught, Heilpern found many old socialists, few of whom took
the Nazis seriously. If Hitler tried to take over, they thought, people
would soon see what Nazis were like and would oppose them. Many
of these anti-Nazi students later turned into what were jokingly called
'beefsteaks'—brown on the outside but still red inside—and fell into line
under Nazism. By contrast, Heilpern was particularly impressed by Irene
Harand, a Christian working on behalf of Jews. Her organization was
strapped for funds, but she sought to expose Hitler by writing a book
entitled Sein Kampf, playing on the title of Hitler's own tract.[29] But there
were very few people like Harand. Even so, Heilpern tried to console
himself with the thought that Hitler had too many problems in Germany
to divert his attention to Austria.[30]

Almost until the Anschluss, Heilpern felt reasonably secure. He, like
Gertrud Lederer's husband Kurt and many others, felt that patriotism and
commitment to his Austrian homeland would surely protect him. But
when, in March 1938, Hitler's troops marched into Austria—which after
the war readily adopted the Allies' convenient designation of Austria as
'Hitler's first victim'—the ground for Nazi violence had already been well
prepared from within.

Annexation and expansion: The explosion of Nazism in Austria, spring 1938

The Anschluss came as no surprise. In November 1937, Hitler announced radical plans for territorial expansion and colonization of new Lebensraum; his ultimate aim of world mastery was increasingly displacing the more limited revisionist goals of military leaders and conservative nationalists. The coalition of elites that had brought Hitler to power and coexisted in something of an uneasy compromise, based on a congruence of aims, was now openly challenged; it was clear that Hitler harboured far grander visions, and anyone standing in his way was dispensable. Scandals were created around the private lives of War Minister Field Marshal Werner von Blomberg and the Army Commander General Werner von Fritzsch: threats were made to reveal the criminal record of Blomberg's wife, who had allegedly not only engaged in prostitution but also pornography, while Fritzsch was falsely accused of homosexuality, at that time an offence. Blomberg duly resigned on 27 January 1938, and Fritsch a week later, on 4 February. This effective purge provided the occasion for reorganization of the German armed forces. Hitler now created the High Command of the Armed Forces (Oberkommando der Wehrmacht, or OKW) under his own overall military control as supreme commander. Disputes among military leaders continued—often more about tactics and timing than about overall strategic aims and values—but Hitler ensured that policies developed in ever more radical directions.

By spring 1938, Austrian Chancellor Kurt Schuschnigg presided over an authoritarian government ruling by decree rather than parliamentary democracy. While widely regarded as ineffectual, he was fiercely committed to Austrian independence. Despite initial backing from Italy's fascist leader Mussolini, Schuschnigg's government faced mounting difficulties, including the rise of paramilitary forces and an increasingly strident—if still illegal—Austrian Nazi party. In February 1938, Hitler staged a showdown. Schuschnigg, invited on 12 February to Hitler's Alpine Berghof headquarters in Berchtesgaden, was faced with an ultimatum: release Nazis imprisoned for previously illegal political activities, and give Nazis a voice in Austrian government. This included appointing Arthur Seyss-Inquart as minister of public security, controlling the police forces.

Returning to Austria, Schuschnigg sought to reaffirm independence by calling a national plebiscite for Sunday, 13 March. Schuschnigg secured the support of social democrats by legalization of the party and its trade unions. People under twenty-four years of age who were not members of Schuschnigg's Fatherland Party would not be entitled to vote, effectively diminishing the likely number of Nazi votes. Hitler, unsurprisingly, demanded that the plebiscite be cancelled; he forced Schuschnigg's resignation and his replacement as chancellor by Seyss-Inquart. During dramatic hours through the afternoon and evening of 11 March 1938, the transformation was effected; Seyss-Inquart took over shortly after midnight. Meanwhile, Hitler had issued the order for the mobilization of German troops, which, he claimed (with a forged telegram), had been 'requested' by the not-as-yet-officially-in-post new Austrian chancellor to assist in restoring order.

In the early hours of 12 March, German troops crossed the border to Austria, welcomed in many places by adoring crowds with flowers, flags, and Heil Hitler greetings. A few hours later, Hitler, too, entered Austria via his birthplace, Braunau, and was received with tumultuous greetings in his former hometown of Linz. On 15 March, Hitler triumphantly entered Vienna, welcomed by huge crowds, and was demonstrably overwhelmed by the emotional support manifested in his native country. While Schuschnigg's proposed plebiscite in support of Austrian independence had been called off, legislation incorporating Austria as the 'Ostmark' region of the enlarged Greater German Reich was to be subjected to a referendum. This was held on 11 April 1938, with an officially declared outcome of more than 99 percent support.

Nazi control brought about an immediate transformation in the situation of Austrian Jews and political opponents of Nazism. Unlike the slower, piecemeal process in Germany over the preceding five years, radicalization in Austria was far-reaching and rapid. Jews were immediately set to work scrubbing off the pro-independence slogans that had been chalked on the streets in the runup to Schuschnigg's cancelled plebiscite. Kneeling on the sidewalks, often forced to use toothbrushes, Jews were jeered at by crowds clearly enjoying the spectacle of public humiliation. Gertrud Lederer, who had, as we have seen, been disturbed by her daughter Christl's enthusiasm for the local Nazi boys but had been prepared to put it down to the follies of youth, was now horrified by her compatriots: 'that the SA who were supervising this were sneering, I could understand. That was what they

were there for. But that the Viennese had sunk so low, to stand there laughing and cheering, that was the first blow of the axe into the roots of my love
for my *Heimat*.' Meanwhile her husband, a medical doctor, was desperately
trying to save the life of a Jewish patient who tried to commit suicide. His
efforts were unsuccessful; after the patient's death, the 'Aryan' widow went
mad and had to be committed to an institution.[31]

The situation in Austria was complex and Austrian responses were mixed;
but enthusiasm was the only safe reaction in public. The changes were evident to contemporaries, who noted strong support for the Nazis among
young people. Arthur Goldstein, born in the late nineteenth century in
Czernowitz, at that time part of the Austro-Hungarian Empire, had lived in
Vienna since 1914. At high school, in university, and as a young adult employed in his father's business, Goldstein had experienced no antisemitism.
His first realization that his Jewish ancestry might cause problems had come
when, in 1926, he fell in love with a Christian, occasioning much 'talk', as
he recalled. They had stayed together for five years, reassuring each other
of their everlasting love, but had held back from getting married in face of
the tacit disapproval of friends. Their happiest times came when travelling
abroad, in places where differences of religion—they did yet not think in
terms of 'race'—seemed to matter less. But in the end, sadly, they parted;
Goldstein's girlfriend married a non-Jew and later revealed she was deeply
unhappy she had not stayed with her first love.

Goldstein, meanwhile, was ever more aware of social unrest following
the Depression, precipitating revolutionary violence and regime repression,
and the growing support for Nazism, particularly among the young. Now,
following the Anschluss, he watched trucks driving through the streets of
Vienna, packed with young men screaming 'Heil Hitler!' at the top of their
voices, while older people were visibly cast down by 'the end of their cosy
Vienna'. He saw, too, government officials, with tears in their eyes, taking off
their lapel badges signalling previous affiliation to the Austrian Fatherland
Party.[32]

Jews and political opponents immediately registered the change. Stephen
Jaray was the son of a Jewish artist and a Christian mother from a family of
the lower Austrian nobility studded with army officers and government of
ficials. Jaray had, like many other schoolchildren during the First World War,
been infused with patriotism and impressed by all things military. Defeat
in 1918, along with hunger and the end of the Austrian monarchy, came to

the then-twelve-year-old Jaray as a shock. The product of a mixed marriage, he experienced little antisemitism while growing up. With the Anschluss, he suddenly realized that his very life was under threat. 'Overnight', he recounted, 'the whole country had wrapped itself in swastika flags'. Over the following days he witnessed not only how Jews were made to scrub the streets, but also the effective licence to violence that was issued to the young: 'Bands of young SA men simply went into shops and stole the gold from the till', while 'the Nazi bands, drunk with victory and thirsty for robbery, took the law into their own hands and went to steal wherever they could'.[33]

Jaray was soon arrested and thrown into jail. His cellmates included 'an outstanding former socialist member of parliament, and a significant number of intellectuals'. It was not long before they were taken by train to Dachau concentration camp, from where, in September 1938, those who were still alive were transferred to Buchenwald, where prisoners 'looked pale, with sunken cheeks, like ghosts'. Buchenwald struck Jaray as 'an insane asylum where normal people were being guarded by the insane'.[34]

In light of the likely penalties for nonconformity, most Austrians were circumspect. Edmund Heilpern, who could make the comparison based on his own experiences, noted that in Vienna the Nazis 'rampaged far worse than they had in Berlin in 1933'. But, just as in Germany, many Austrians had taken out what he described as 'insurance policies', holding three different party membership cards in their pockets to be ready for any eventuality. Some former socialists now emphasized that the part of National Socialism with which they identified was still socialist. There was a lively black-market trade in old Nazi party membership books and badges, with cards backdated to show membership at the time of illegality. Three or four days after the Anschluss, Heilpern recalled witnessing an old woman come into a butcher's shop with a basket full of old party badges; she said quite loudly to the housewives queuing up for meat that they should snap up a Nazi party badge while they were still going at bargain rates—two schillings today, fifty schillings tomorrow, then they would run out. Officially, applications for party membership were now closed, but this did not prevent people from desperately trying to jump on the new bandwagon, particularly if they could acquire backdated credentials to cover up more compromising past affiliations.[35]

Heilpern also noted how shopping could be used as a covert means of indicating opposition. In the street where he lived there were two shops selling fruit and vegetables. One was efficiently run by a young couple, who ensured a constant supply of fresh produce with a wide selection; this shop was doing very well. The other was run by two elderly sisters; with its more restricted range and lower quality of produce, it was not doing so well. Following the Anschluss, the first store, run by the young couple, was rapidly bedecked with swastikas and transactions were accompanied by enthusiastic Heil Hitlers, while the elderly sisters in the other shop refrained from any ostentatious displays of support. Suddenly, people were staying away from the Nazi store and choosing rather to make their purchases from the elderly sisters, whose business suddenly and unexpectedly flourished to such an extent that they had to call in a younger brother to assist.[36] Whether or not this and similar incidents recounted by contemporaries were true— it is impossible to verify at this distance—such observations about everyday life are indicative of widespread perceptions of a divided society at the time.

Some Austrians demonstrated, in however small a way, a distaste for the Nazi takeover. Some intervened more actively, choosing not to remain passive bystanders to incidents that were part of the evolving violence. Arthur Goldstein's company was taken over by a commissary director who, despite having effectively 'aryanized' his firm, acted decently towards Goldstein and 'protected him from every humiliation'. Neighbours, too, were helpful. On one occasion some 'immature youths' had smeared anti-Jewish slogans in oil paint on the fences around his storage yard. When a Christian living nearby saw from his windows what was going on, he came over, spoke to the director, rebuked the youngsters, and praised Goldstein and his Jewish colleagues as good people. A Nazi helped Goldstein's brother to escape to England. But in Goldstein's experience, such express support became increasingly rare after the Anschluss. Every day, by contrast, there were further examples of profiteering from the Jews' distress, with frequent cases of blackmail, extortion, unlawful transactions, raids on cafés, baseless arrests, and incarceration of Jews.[37]

Whatever they may have felt in private, most Austrians, just like Germans before them, now performed Nazism in public and, through their everyday behaviours, contributed to the rapidly increasing social isolation of Jews. Yet in Austria the progression from conformity through compliance to complicity was massively accelerated. Gertrude Schneider, a Viennese Jew born in 1928, was one of a large family with relatives across the city. She and her family witnessed the frightful treatment meted out to Jews within hours of the Nazi invasion, and soon began to experience the impact themselves. For Schneider, as a child of ten at the time, one of the most painful moments came when Ilse Jank, her best friend through the four years since they had started school together, came over to tell her 'in a kind of gloating manner' that she could no longer be her friend. Jank's father, now a 'high-ranking' Nazi, had instructed her 'never to speak or play with Jewish children'. Schneider at first felt 'more hurt than surprised'; but it soon became an omen of the worse that was to come.[38]

Gertrud Lederer, too, witnessed, through the experiences of her husband and his Jewish relatives, as well as the experiences of her six-year-old 'mixed-race' son Tony, the many ways in which rifts grew between newly racialized communities. Tony wore Lederhosen to school; these characteristic alpine leather shorts with decorative braces now bore a swastika that he wanted his mother to remove; but they felt this absence would mean 'being, so to speak, naked among the Aryan children'. At school, while the half-Jewish Tony was forced to draw swastikas and sing the Horst Wessel anthem, his best friend Natascha, fully Jewish, was relegated to the back benches of the class. On one of their last walks to a favourite hillside spot overlooking Vienna, Lederer and her son found it crawling with members of the SA; one came over and talked amicably to the little boy, ignorant of his family background. This friendly SA man showed Tony how to use his revolver and promised that when he was older 'he could have one too and would be allowed to shoot as many Jews as he wanted to'. Tony, to his mother's shock and consternation, 'clearly regretted the fact that he would not be able to experience this wonderful time in Austria'; she, for her part, knew that she 'had to get the child out of this crazy country as quickly as possible!'[39] If such little incidents were ominous, they were indicative of ways in which the minds of young Austrians were being guided towards the previously unthinkable.

Other incidents were even more frightening. One day, Lederer's Jewish mother-in-law and two sisters were out for a walk when they were stopped by members of the SA and forced to join a group of Jews being paraded past the 'big wheel', the Prater, in a Vienna amusement park. As they walked they were whipped and hit by the SA, 'accompanied by the laughter and jeering of the crowd' while 'Aryan children spat at them, encouraged by their parents'. Lederer's mother-in-law suddenly saw a familiar face in the crowd: the daughter of the caretaker of her apartment block, whom she had known since her birth, and whose family she had helped for years. Desperately, she called out, appealing for help. But this seventeen-year-old simply turned away and said loudly to her friend, 'and now the Jewess even dares to use the familiar form of "you" [*Du*] when talking to me!'[40]

Yet in Austria as in Germany, assistance to Jews could sometimes come from unlikely quarters. Lederer and her husband, actively planning to emigrate, had their passports confiscated during a Gestapo raid on their house. Lederer's Nazi brother in Graz had initially been infuriated by her refusal to divorce her Jewish husband. But following the Gestapo raid he relented and pulled strings among Nazi contacts in high places; Lederer and her husband managed to regain their passports and make arrangements to get out of Austria. But there was little that could be done for Lederer's mother-in-law, who steadfastly refused to sell her home (for a pittance) and clung on desperately to her possessions, wanting to protect the family inheritance for her little grandson, Tony. Increasingly it all became too much for the elderly lady. One day she simply put her head in the oven and turned on the gas, choosing to take her own way out.[41]

She was far from the only Jew to feel this was the last choice left to them. It has been estimated that in the first two months alone after the Anschluss, some 218 Jews took their own lives rather than face further violence—on average between three and four Jews killing themselves every day because they could see no other way to escape.[42] Others had the material resources and contacts to get out: around 192,000 Jews had lived in Austria at the beginning of 1938, concentrated mostly in Vienna, where 9 percent of the population was Jewish; by the end of the year there remained only 57,000 Jews in the country.

Those Germans who had chosen to ignore the fates of Jews—the majority of the population—were oblivious to all this, untouched by the suffering and agony. Breusch's former best friend, Wolfgang von Blittersdorf, who had unsuccessfully urged him to abandon his Jewish fiancée, Dreyfuß, remained an enthusiast for what he continued to see as the Nazi new dawn. But he also remained friends with Breusch, even after his emigration. In a letter to Breusch written on 22 March 1938, shortly after the Anschluss, von Blittersdorf was gushing about it. He had driven through Austria in the wake of the advancing German troops, staying briefly in Salzburg, 'and

it was fabulous, how everything was decorated with flags and pictures';
even the 'most isolated farmhouses' along the way 'had raised flags'. Another
friend of Breusch's wrote in October 1938, perhaps with a touch of irony,
that in Germany 'naturally everything here is constantly on the up and up,
it is a joy to live, in short, indescribably wonderful'. A former colleague,
who had written on 7 April 1938 that 'we are heading for wonderful times'
(also with a touch of irony, perhaps) and that he could 'hardly control [his]
excitement', added a more sombre note in a letter a year later. On 15 April
1939, writing from Milan, where he was engaged in scientific research, this
friend discussed his plans to embark on a second doctorate (the German
Habilitation). But, he added, 'no one knows whether it will really come to
that, perhaps—or almost certainly—I shall die as a hero before then. Right
now the prospects for that seem pretty favourable again'.[43]

Indeed, across Europe ethno-nationalism was on the rise, and not only
within the Reich but also in a wide variety of places abroad German nationalists were agitating ever more energetically. Some developments
seemed like a speeded-up echo of political and social processes that had
taken place more slowly in the heart of Germany over the preceding years.

Radicalization beyond the Reich

By 1938, Danzig, though nominally still a Free City, had been under increasingly radical Nazi rule for several years, if marked by a power struggle
between Albert Forster and Arthur Greiser. Both these committed Nazis
would go on to become significant figures following the outbreak of war and
annexation of Polish territories, with Forster presiding over the Reichsgau
of Danzig–West Prussia and Greiser over the Reichsgau Wartheland.[44] In a
city dominated by Nazi politics, Jews experienced growing discrimination
in everyday life.

Alice Baerwald recounted how, in Danzig as in Germany, there were
increasing restrictions on what Jews were permitted to do, from sitting
on park benches, or bathing in the same swimming areas as non-Jews, to
shopping in certain stores. And as in Germany, there were individual expressions of sympathy. One shopkeeper refused to serve Baerwald's cook
because she worked for Jews; but he added that in future, if she did not turn
up in person but rather phoned in the order, he would be pleased to make

a delivery. He told her that if he refused to put up a sign forbidding entry to Jews, he would have his shop windows smashed in. The baker delivered a similar message. As Baerwald summarized the situation: 'everyone cursed, swore, and was too cowardly to do anything against it.' It was also made increasingly difficult for Jews to run a business without extortionate tax charges and pressures to sell up at ludicrously low prices. Those who refused to sell were often exposed to trumped-up charges, at risk of arrest and confiscation of their property, until they capitulated, to their own financial ruin. Jewish doctors were attacked, forced to give up their practices, and leave.[45]

Racial distinctions were often policed by bystanders. One of Alice Baerwald's sons was out on a picnic with friends on a hot summer's day in 1938. They ran out of drink and on the way home, feeling thirsty, they stopped at an inn by a little lake. There, they deliberately chose a table at the far end of the beer garden, well away from other guests. One of the group of friends was a blond, blue-eyed girl who did not look obviously 'Jewish'. Suddenly, people at a distant table stood up and came over to the group with 'threatening expressions'. They stationed themselves in front of the blond girl and shouted: 'Aren't you ashamed of yourself, a German girl going with Jews', adding that a girl like her 'should be chucked into the water'. They did indeed then try to grab her and throw her into the lake, but the young people managed to escape. Following this and similar incidents, Baerwald's son and his friends felt it was barely possibly to breathe in Danzig. On free weekends they either stayed at home or drove along the coast to the nearby Polish port of Gdynia.[46]

Baerwald was remarkably resilient, retaining a sense of self-respect and, like some of her friends, prepared to be impertinent in encounters that could have been humiliating. She engaged a man wearing a swastika and spouting antisemitic stereotypes in a long conversation about literature; at the end he shook her hand, thanked her for the interesting discussion, and whispered that, despite his Nazi party badge, 'he was really also not in agreement with everything'. One of Baerwald's friends, a Jewish woman with blond hair who liked to wear a lot of make-up, was accosted by an SA man who bawled at her: 'A German woman does not wear make-up'. Baerwald's friend replied cheekily, 'Fortunately I'm Jewish and I can do whatever I like with my face'.[47]

As in Germany over preceding years, it was increasingly rare for Jewish and non-Jewish communities in Danzig to intermingle, and Jews were excluded from many areas of social life. Baerwald tried, however, to retain a sense of control over her social environment. Most mixed social gatherings had ceased entirely, but the Cuban consul in Danzig still included Jews in his invitations, and the Baerwalds were often guests at his sumptuous dinners. On one occasion they heard that among the guests who had accepted the invitation were two German officials—the German consul general and the highest tax official—and Baerwald had no intention of socializing with people 'whose programme it was to exterminate my people', as she put it presciently, well before mass murder had become official policy. She maintained her self-respect and turned down the next invitation. In general there was little that Jews could do, other than ensuring that they could continue to gather among themselves. As public places were increasingly closed to them, Jews in Danzig founded a club for social events, lectures, art exhibitions, and a little library; Baerwald's husband became director of this club, which was attended by between 200 and 300 people at a time.[48]

If they could maintain some relatively protected spaces for a while, it was becoming far more difficult. There were ever-more violent attacks on Jews in the streets, and Baerwald recounted how unpleasant it was becoming to go for a walk, since the 'brown columns were marching from early until late' and loudly singing their favourite song, 'When Jewish blood spurts from the knife, then it's all going twice as well'. They carried swastika flags, which everyone apart from Jews was obliged to greet. When one elderly Polish man refused to hail the flag, he was 'beaten frightfully around the face' and lost his hearing as a result.[49]

In Danzig, as in the Reich, the wild actions of the SA went far beyond ordinary policing; and even when ordinary police officers clearly felt distaste for the brutality, they chose to turn a blind eye to the violence of the SA. A sports club for Jewish children had for a while made it possible for around 1,500 youngsters to enjoy sporting activities. But more and more frequently, on their way home they were attacked by 'brown hordes'; even when older siblings or parents came to collect them, stones were thrown and attacks took place, until eventually no one dared to go down the alley to attend the club and it had to close. So, too, did the Jewish school that had been run informally for a while and the Jewish club that Baerwald's husband had directed.

There was simply no protection against violence on the streets, whether for children or for adults, even when bystanders were willing to offer assistance and police were present at the scene. One evening, friends were on their way home from a visit to the Baerwalds when they were attacked by a group of young people. A policeman standing nearby simply looked in the opposite direction. When a bystander came up and asked him to intervene to help the Jews, the policemen turned around and responded: 'Don't get me into trouble, I have a family to feed, and I will lose my job if I intervene.' On another occasion, an old man was picked up by two SA men and used as a tool with which to smash in windows; when a woman came running out of her house, trying to intervene on the victim's behalf, and offering to act as a witness to the police, she was brusquely told to go home, since the man was dead now anyway. The next day the incident was reported in the local newspaper as merely a 'street accident'.[50] Again, whatever the truth of any individual incident—which can so readily be dismissed as anecdotal—the subjective perception among victims of racial violence of complete abandonment by even sympathetic authorities and impotent bystanders was very real.

The extraordinary inhumanity was shocking, and not only to Jews. One of the Baerwalds' non-Jewish friends was a Polish diplomat who had happened to be in Vienna at the time of the Anschluss. He told Alice Baerwald on his return to Danzig how a good friend of his, an Austrian Jew, along with his wife and child, had committed suicide in face of the violence; they could bear it no longer and saw no other way out. Already devastated by this loss of his friends, the diplomat was further distressed by what followed. As their coffins were carried down into the street, an SS officer had appeared and put placards on the coffins bearing the words: 'Following their example is to be recommended.' At this, the diplomat had totally broken down. He had to spend time recovering in a sanatorium before he was able to return to Poland and resume his duties.[51]

As conditions worsened throughout 1937–1938, more and more Jews sought to leave the Nazi Third Reich. Aware of the growing plight of Jews, in July 1938 representatives of a number of states met in the French Alpine town of Évian, picturesquely situated on the banks of Lake Geneva, to discuss how best to organize quotas for the numbers of refugees each was prepared to receive. The discussion was revealing and depressing; implicitly blaming the victims, other countries were unwilling, as they saw it, to import the 'problem of antisemitism'; quotas were massively restricted, as the doors of the world were largely closed to the increasing numbers now desperate to get out.

A few individuals only belatedly discovered their 'non-Aryan' ancestry. Karl Sorkin had been born in Basel, Switzerland, in 1908; the family lived first in Baden and then moved to Freiburg in the late 1920s. Both Sorkin's parents were originally from Russia. While his mother greatly missed her Russian homeland, his father had taken on German citizenship in 1914 and fought in the First World War. Sorkin considered himself German, and was a stalwart member of local Freiburg society. An avid chess player, he served in an honorary capacity both nationally, as a chess coach for the Greater German Chess League, and locally, in adult education and in the chess association of the Nazi Strength through Joy (Kraft durch Freude, KdF) organization. Sorkin married in 1934, and the couple had a child; he also took over the store owned by his wife's parents and ran a successful grocery business there in the 1930s.[52]

Despite being committed German citizens, by the summer of 1938 there was growing discomfort and disquiet in Sorkin's family. Sorkin felt it safer to transfer the grocery shop into his 'Aryan' wife's name and to think about selling up, should the need arise. On 4 September 1938 the news finally broke: his parents informed him that he was indisputably of Jewish descent. They had received a letter from Berlin to the effect that his father's Jewish ancestry was confirmed in a passport dating from 1904, while his mother's birth certificate from Vilna (Vilnius) showed that her parents were of the Judaic faith. Sorkin's world fell apart in a moment.[53]

Karl Sorkin's parents did not want him to show the letter to his wife, Thilde, but he insisted. Her face 'went as white as chalk, but she did not say a word. The truth hit her very badly.' Sorkin continued: 'The fact that my parents had kept the truth about their Jewish ancestry a secret even at the time of our marriage hit us both badly.' Thilde went to bed early, and when Sorkin followed her, he found her 'close to a total nervous breakdown'; he could 'hardly calm her down'. He immediately offered her a divorce, which 'would have the advantage that she and their child would be spared any potential difficulties that might be coming up', although he felt that they both would be deeply unhappy.[54]

Now it was his mother's turn to have a nervous breakdown. She kept imploring them not to divorce. His wife's family, by contrast, took the opposite view and thought their daughter should get a divorce as soon as possible. Thilde herself was distraught. Meanwhile, Sorkin's father adopted a more ebullient tone, saying he would fight the finding and claim that only his wife was of Jewish descent; but none of them thought this strategy had much hope of success. They had to radically rethink their lives and future.[55]

The Sorkins discovered that they had American relatives; and, because of the accident of Karl Sorkin's place of birth, Switzerland, the consulate was prepared to put them on the Swiss quota, which entailed a far shorter waiting time than on the German quota. Meanwhile the situation had changed. Following the Sudeten crisis, precipitated by Hitler's demand for the incorporation into the Reich of Czech border regions with signifi-cant ethnic German populations, when war had appeared imminent, there was a general sense of relief at the Munich agreement—but there was also a palpable shift in attitudes. Sorkin 'suddenly hardly saw anyone who was prepared to greet with Heil Hitler'. He did not as yet dare to tell his wider circle of acquaintances in Freiburg about his Jewish background, and it was only the authorities in his parents' place of residence who knew about it. He rapidly switched his registration to their address and applied for a pass-port from their regional office.[56]

On 9 November 1938, Karl Sorkin's father had a serious motorcycle ac-cident and suffered a fractured skull. He was taken to hospital in a critical condition and was treated for the life-threatening injuries he had sustained. The hospital knew nothing of his Jewish ancestry; it is unlikely that he would have received the medical treatment he needed had they known; but in the event, after two weeks where his life hung in the balance, Sorkin's father made a full recovery.[57]

Ironically, by virtue of his accident and hospitalization just a few hours earlier, Sorkin's father missed being caught up in the events of the night of 9–10 November. Kristallnacht marked a radical shift in Germany's trajec-tory towards genocide.

7

Shock Waves

Polarization in Peacetime Society, November 1938

On the evening of 9 November 1938, Jenny Bohrer, the wife of Rabbi Dr Mordechai Bohrer in the south German village of Gailingen, close to Lake Constance, was putting her seven children to bed in their home above the Jewish prayer room and directly opposite the synagogue. She was disturbed by the raucous noises and 'hate-filled' speeches of local Nazis at the nearby war memorial, celebrating the by now-traditional anniversary of Hitler's 1923 Beer Hall putsch. Within hours, the gathering was transformed into frenzied but clearly coordinated action.

In the early hours of 10 November, a Nazi mob stormed into the rabbi's house, throwing Mordechai Bohrer down the stairs and taking him away; that evening he would be put on the back of a truck and taken to Dachau concentration camp. In the course of the morning Jenny had to gather her small children—the older ones she had already sent to school as usual—and they were marched down the street along with the other Jews of Gailingen to the local gym hall. Jenny's terrified older children had already been taken directly from school but managed to find her in the throng. Her mind raced with fears, from what might have befallen her husband to whether her younger children might wet themselves, adding further to the chill of a November day where they had not had time to dress warmly enough before being hustled away. Soon they were marched to the synagogue, which was surrounded by a huge group of SA men. There was then a 'colossal detonation'; and they were forced to watch as a side wall of their 'beloved old synagogue crashed down, pulling down with it a part of the front, and completely destroying the inside of the synagogue'. Outside, the frightened Jews 'were shaking like leaves'. A man in a leather jacket, who had already been in charge of the violent arrest of the rabbi, stood in front of the crowd and delivered an inflammatory and abusive speech commanding the Jews to get out of Germany within weeks, and forbidding their children to go to school with 'our Aryan children'.

With this, the Jewish women and children were allowed to leave. Jenny Bohrer found a scene of devastation at home but tried as best she could to feed and calm her children and clear up what she could of the breakages and mess. Barely able to sleep that night, plagued with worries about her missing husband, she heard noises below in the courtyard and screamed out to ask what was going on. She received an unexpected response: a local man whom she knew by name called up to her, letting her know that it was just the fire brigade and that they would ensure she was protected. At this reassurance—which she felt must have 'bought him eternal life'—she was finally able to doze off.[1]

Bohrer's account provides insights into her own responses to these events. It also illuminates who was involved, and gives us some sense of the responses of local people. Bohrer had initially asked herself what she had to fear from these people 'whose language we spoke, whose faces we knew'. But she did not in fact know all of them. Those who broke into her apartment were a mixed bunch: perhaps ten SA men, probably shipped in from elsewhere, whom she did not recognize; a few unknown men in civilian clothing; but also the 'well-known vicious faces [*Hundegesichter*] of the Gestapo men' as well as the 'red-haired mayor'. The mayor was the Nazi and 'old fighter' (*Alter Kämpfer*) who had just a few years earlier faced challenges in nazifying Gailingen, given the relative wealth of the Jewish community and their significant contribution to the community's tax base. Now, however, he had no qualms.

Later, a local gendarme, also well known to Bohrer, was more well-disposed; in the course of the march through town he secretly let her know that her husband was still alive. (Rabbi Bohrer, however, survived less than a month in Dachau, where he and other prominent Jewish men were taken.) Local people seem to have stayed away and did not line the streets to watch this march to the gym hall. The streets were still 'empty of people' a couple of hours later, when the group of men, women, children, the ill, and the 'fragile elderly whom they had dragged out of their houses and beds' were marched along to witness the destruction of the synagogue. But they must have been watching through their windows, since Bohrer was later told by local Christians that it had been terrifying to see the 'stoic quietness' of the Jews—'no one crying, screaming, or pleading for mercy'. At the synagogue, however, many people had gathered; according to Bohrer, it was the 'rabble' who had come to watch the 'spectacle', while 'all the decent citizens had kept their distance'.[2]

Whether they came to stare, watched from behind their curtains, or simply kept away, non-Jewish Germans in November 1938 could no longer claim ignorance. The events in Gailingen were repeated right across the now expanded Reich. On the night of 9 November and through the following morning, synagogues went up in flames, set on fire by organized groups of SA, SS, and other Nazis. In towns and villages across Germany and the newly annexed territories of Austria and the Sudetenland, Nazi activists broke into the homes of Jews, beat up those who tried to prevent entry, and destroyed their possessions or threw property out onto the street. Mobs smashed the windows of Jewish shops, in an orgy of collective violence; individuals were arrested, and everywhere processions of Jews were marched through streets and public squares, often accompanied by the jeering of onlookers, while others observed in shocked silence. Over the following days some 30,000 adult males were taken off to concentration camps, watched by crowds lining the sidewalks or waiting at railway stations. Hundreds of Jews died as a result of Nazi violence, either during or in the aftermath of these events.[3]

Very few people in the Reich could now remain unaware of the violence that Goebbels sought to portray as a 'spontaneous' seething of public outrage. 'Knowing nothing about it' could be no excuse, no explanation for the passivity. And 1938 proved to be a turning point, as the majority of Germans were engaged in moral compromises, caught between willing complicity, constrained conformity, and frustrated impotence.

Kristallnacht

The violence and mass arrests of Jews in November 1938 had been long in the planning. But the immediate pretext was given by the fatal shooting of

Ernst vom Rath, an official in the German Embassy in Paris, by Herschel Grynszpan. Grynszpan was a young Jew of Polish descent who had been born and brought up in Germany. Lacking appropriate identity papers, he was now living illegally in Paris. Grynszpan wanted to protest against the recent violent expulsion of his parents, along with innumerable other Jews in Germany who were of Polish extraction. Forcibly deported over the German-Polish border, they had been refused entry in Poland and were effectively stateless, barred from returning to Germany. In a highly emotional state, Grynszpan entered the German Embassy in Paris on 7 November, where he shot vom Rath; two days later, on 9 November, vom Rath died of his wounds. This incident provided Goebbels, quietly sanctioned by Hitler (who maintained a public distance from the ensuing events), with a useful pretext for unleashing a wave of violence that he had in fact been planning for some time.

Hitler and Nazi leaders were gathered in Munich on 9 November, for the annual commemoration of the Beer Hall putsch, when the news came in of vom Rath's death. Goebbels's desire to use this as an excuse for giving directions for coordinated attacks on Jews, their places of worship and sacred objects, and their property, was soon approved. Late in the evening, Goebbels conveyed an order through Nazi party officials across the newly expanded Reich. Synagogues everywhere were to be set alight; fire brigades were to stand by, acting only where there was potential danger to neighbouring 'Aryan' properties; and the regular police forces were not to intervene, while thugs from the SS, the SA, and the Hitler Youth were beating up Jews and smashing their property. The multiple, coordinated explosions of terror were to be represented as expressions of the 'people's rage', a supposedly spontaneous and justified reaction to what 'the Jews' had done to the representative of the German nation, personified in Grynszpan's assassination of vom Rath. In the style that had become typical and was to be repeated throughout the war, violence was portrayed as a supposedly proportionate 'response' warranted by some prior 'provocation', a form in effect of 'defensive retaliation'. During the night of 9–10 November, hundreds of synagogues were set on fire, and 7,500 Jewish business and homes were attacked. The violence was more extreme in some regions than others: in Vienna alone, so recently incorporated into the Reich, forty-two of the city's forty-three synagogues were set alight and more than 4,000 Jewish stores were looted, while in the course of the arrests, beatings, and murders several hundred Viennese Jews committed suicide.[4]

Colloquially, the events of this night soon became known as 'Kristallnacht', the 'night of broken glass'. The extension of this term, 'Reichskristallnacht' or 'Reich night of broken glass', also used, played on the Nazi propensity to add the word 'Reich' to all its official doings. The word 'pogrom', with its implication of spontaneous popular violence, is clearly a misnomer: this was state-organized terror.[5] The SA and SS were at the forefront of organized violence; many members of these organizations had been instructed not to turn up in uniform, in order to give a more plausible impression of this being a spontaneous outburst of the 'people's rage', but even this was in itself evidence of organization and direction from above. The Hitler Youth were officially mobilized and actively engaged, and schoolchildren were brought along in busloads to witness the violence and participate in humiliation of the Jews.[6] Even so, there was far more widespread popular participation than many people would later like to admit. Significant numbers of ordinary Germans and Austrians now rapidly became involved on the side of the perpetrators, joining crowds to jeer at Jews, or taking the opportunity to loot goods from shops and homes. Continuing, apparently spontaneous violence against Jews was evident particularly in Vienna, where radical anti-semitism had been so rapidly unleashed, encouraged, and fomented in the preceding months.

Early postwar trials in the western zones of occupied Germany reveal that a wide cross-section of the population was involved in acts of perpetration, whether in violent attacks or by applauding the humiliation of Jews in rituals of public degradation, desecrating Jewish graves, and larceny. Offences relating to self-enrichment included engaging in blackmail, extorting money, confiscating accounts, and forcing Jews to cancel debts. People who were brought to court included both locals who knew the victims and non-locals who had travelled in ready-armed, to set fire to synagogues and participate in events. Unlike the social profile of offenders of other crimes—generally young and male—many women were involved in offences relating to Kristallnacht. So there was a significant cross-section of society, males and females of all age groups, who were active on the side of the perpetrators.[7]

Yet the populace was deeply—and perhaps more or less evenly—divided in November 1938. We can never be sure of precise proportions on either

side, but it is clear from other sources that many Germans were shocked by
the destruction of property and aghast at the broken windows and shards
of glass on the streets. Individuals were sometimes prepared to show sympathy, expressing a sense of shame, and offering assistance in private.[8] But
in public, the vast majority of Germans and Austrians sought to appear indifferent or tried to affect an air of non-involvement.[9] They rehearsed the
combination of shame and incapacity to act against the violence that was
to become so widespread. The one thing that was common to them all was
awareness of what was happening.

Contemporary opinion reports provide details about reactions and attitudes towards specific aspects of the violence—including widespread
expressions of shame, as well as disapproval of the damage to property,
and concerns about the impact on Germany's international reputation.
Mutterings about being 'ashamed to be German'—frequently heard, for
the first time since 1933—register a diffuse sense of moral outrage. Yet such
comments are not easy to evaluate. Disapproval of destruction of property and reputation might be linked to suppressed feelings of shame, but
comments about these matters were nevertheless in a sense 'safe' to utter
in public, since they could be interpreted as being perfectly in line with
Nazi priorities for the economy and Germany's standing in the world; even
Göring was furious about what he saw as the wanton destruction of property on an unwarranted scale. Criticism of these aspects was not necessarily linked to any more fundamental disapproval of violence against Jews,
however. Reports of opinions in Vienna suggest a considerable degree of
popular approval of the treatment of the Jews, but similar rejection of the
destruction of property.[10]

Despite the wealth of sources on popular opinion, they yield only illustrative snapshots. In some ways, they buttress a perception of 'bystanders' as
people who are quite distinct from the persecutors and the victims, people who simply look on and occasionally betray their attitudes towards
what they were witnessing, rather than people who are themselves inte-
grally involved in an unfolding process within a more all-encompassing
system of violence. Autobiographical accounts and diaries written close to
the time of Kristallnacht, by contrast, reveal a rather more complex picture.
There are surprising webs of continuing interconnections between 'Aryans'
and their 'non-Aryan' compatriots, as even now personal ties and empathy
proved difficult to disentangle from the national antisemitic script and the

behaviours required in specific roles. Despite growing distance, there remained a sense of common humanity and personal bonds that were not
easily severed. Or, looked at another way: when 'Aryans' knew they were
engaged in potentially compromising behaviours in their official roles, they
could at least feel better about themselves on a personal level if they were
sympathetic towards those who were suffering as a consequence.

So a somewhat paradoxical situation developed: even as people conformed to the requirements of their roles and supported the regime by
their actions, they often continued, even now, in this heightened context of
violence and clear parting of the ways, to extend sympathy to those whom
they were in the process of ousting. The experiences portrayed in personal
accounts provide insights into both how the events were perceived by contemporaries, and how they experienced the reactions of others.

Divided society, divided selves: Participation and aversion

Despite official propaganda, it was clear to contemporaries that the violence
of 9–10 November was no spontaneous pogrom but had rather been initiated and coordinated from on high. The networks of knowledge and intimations of suspicion were various, but it was abundantly clear to the majority
of Germans that the simultaneity of attacks was rooted in careful direction
and orchestration from on high.

Yet some people thought—mistakenly, in fact—that there had been more
precise planning many months earlier than was actually the case. Rumours
about preparations for mass incarceration of Jews had been rife for several
months. Eugen Altmann, for example, had an 'Aryan' friend whose brother
was a high-up Nazi. The latter had told his wife already in March 1938 that
a big action against Jews was being planned for later that year, probably for
October; she then passed this on to her brother-in-law, Altmann's friend,
who warned Altmann to get out before anything big exploded. Altmann
saw this as 'a service of friendship in a difficult time, dangerous on both
sides'.[11]

Martha Lewinsohn, a working-class 'Aryan' whose husband was both
politically active and of half-Jewish descent, had been made aware by
her brother-in-law of preparations for mass arrests and incarceration in

concentration camps. This brother-in-law had been in and out of concentration camps since he was first arrested in March 1933; Lewinsohn's husband had met him at one point in Dachau, at that time an almost unrecognizable skeleton and very ill. In the summer of 1938, the still politically active brother-in-law let Lewinsohn know that for some weeks there had been rapid building works to expand the concentration camps 'at a furious tempo' in preparation for mass arrests.[12] Similar reports came to others from a variety of quarters.

The people discussing these rumours were unaware that Heinrich Himmler had in fact been expanding the concentration camp system earlier that summer to accommodate an increase in the incarceration of 'a-socials' and those seen as repeat criminals, rather than in preparation for mass arrests of Jews.[13] Yet their perceptions, if mistaken, are indicative of a growing sense of being increasingly endangered. Just as important is also something quite different: these rumours reflect a lingering sense among some 'non-Aryans' of being able to rely on the support of individuals in the dominant 'Aryan' community, people who were better placed to alert them to imminent danger and to assist them if need be. This sense of embeddedness in a wider community might have been a misperception on the part of many victims, given the marginalization and exclusion of the preceding years; their appeals would be spurned. Yet it would indeed be a source of help for at least some of the persecuted—those individuals for whom assistance of 'Aryans' played a role in their physical and psychological survival—during the days and weeks after Kristallnacht.

Himmler's prior expansion of the concentration camps might have been the outcome of other priorities earlier in the year; but the simultaneity and similarity of the 'actions' across the Reich on the night of 9–10 November made it quite clear that the events of Kristallnacht amounted to regime-sponsored violence coordinated from above. As Erna Albersheim, a forty-eight-year-old 'half Jewish' owner of a store in southwestern Germany, put it in her 1939 essay: 'it was marvellously organized and carried out with an expediency we had grown accustomed to when the party gave an order; carried out with exactly the same methods and at the same time in every part of Germany, in large cities, in towns, in the smallest villages. No mob could have done that—no unorganized mob without the cunning and the brains of Goebbels behind it.'[14] Her confident summary of the details probably outran what she could actually know with any degree of certitude at the time; but her perception was well founded, indicating widespread awareness that this went way beyond anything that could be portrayed as a spontaneous 'pogrom'.

Meanwhile, Hitler's strategy of distancing himself was paying off, as far as popular perceptions were concerned. In Albersheim's view: 'After all this had happened many people said that they considered Hitler honest in his ideals of bringing peace and good to the German people; that all this treatment of a minority was not wished by him, but had been done by his too revolutionary followers.' She went on: 'There was one unanimous opinion—the hatred for Goebbels!'[15] Goebbels had, in the view of people to whom Albersheim talked, 'done more than anyone else to discredit Germany'.[16] Hitler, however, had succeeded in staying above it all.

Albersheim recalled how her store had been shattered: 'They had come to smash the place and smash it they would. They ordered me to turn on the lights. This I refused to do. I stayed long enough to get a good look at them. They were all very well dressed in civilian clothes, between twenty-five and thirty-five years old—not riffraff off the streets. I looked at them steadily, hoping that some day I would be able to identify them.'[17] She never had the chance. In the course of the attack, Albersheim was injured and her store was destroyed. So, too, was the neighbouring shoe store, owned by 'a very nice old Jewish gentleman'. Albersheim added: 'Three days later he was dead. The excitement had been too much for him.'[18] Another casualty of the violence, somewhat later, was her seventy-five-year-old uncle; following the attack on his home and his own arrest, he became ill and died within three months.

While organized and directed by party stalwarts, the violence was fuelled and sustained by the energy and enthusiasm of youth. Contemporaries across the Reich noted the predominance of young people among active participants. Jochen Klepper, a Protestant writer in Berlin whose wife was a converted Jew, recorded in his diary a morning walk on 10 November through the highly Jewish 'Bavarian quarter' (Bayerischer Viertel) of Berlin, when he was struck by the disapproving reactions of older people. Startled, he observed that 'the antisemitism which had been widely prevalent since 1933 had very largely disappeared since the Nuremberg Laws of 1935 had been so excessive'. Whether antisemitism had genuinely decreased, as Klepper thought, or whether, as seems more likely, people had simply turned their attention to other matters, feeling that the self-imposed 'Jewish question' had now been more than dealt with, is disputable. But now it could certainly no longer be ignored. And while older Germans both in this district and across Berlin rejected what they saw as 'excesses', whether effected through legal measures, as in 1935, or in violent attacks, as now, 'things were quite different among young Germans who were socialized by the all-encompassing Hitler Youth organizations'. Klepper seriously doubted 'whether parental homes can still act as any kind of counterweight' to the influence of Nazism on this younger generation. Klepper and his wife, Hanni, however, took some consolation from the supportive responses of even 'totally Nazi' fellow residents in the Steglitz area of Berlin where they lived, 'from the wife of the naval officer to the women in the bakery, from the men at the newspaper kiosks to the little neighbours of what is probably the very last Jewish shop here, now totally destroyed'. Their reactions confirmed, in Klepper's view, that 'now as before, there could be no need to doubt the German Volk'. But, he added, while 'the Volk is reassuring, its moral weakness is terribly concerning'.[19] Remaining passive and only quietly critical was, however, arguably less a sign of 'moral weakness' than a consequence of weighing up the risks of public protest under Nazi rule: the cause lay more in the repressive system than in personal character. This was a notable element in the active production of a bystander society.

Among the young, there was not only the impact of Nazi organizations but also of five years of education and socialization, resulting in what might be called innocent belief without the benefit of countervailing viewpoints. Young people, and particularly children, were clearly strongly influenced by Nazi propaganda. As a contemporary report for the Social Democratic Party in Exile (Sopade) put it: 'Insofar as one can talk at all about excitement or enthusiasm in this whole action, it was only present among children and young people.'[20] Young people spontaneously joined in and even went beyond what was required of them, seeing the occasion as a licence for the enjoyment of collective cruelty, or at least a bit of excitement and sense of empowerment. A report from the Saarpfalz region of the Saarland, in western Germany, for example, commented on the 'sad fate' of the 'few Jews who still live in the towns' and who 'could no longer walk the streets in the daytime. As soon as one of them shows himself in the open, hordes of children run after him, spit at him, throw dirt and stones, or use crooked sticks to "hook in" his legs and make him fall down.' Such experiences were further exacerbated by the impossibility of any kind of redress. Neither the victim nor the miscreants' parents dared tell the children not to behave like this: 'The Jew who is persecuted in this way cannot say anything, because that would count as threatening the children. Parents don't have the courage to hold their children back, because they are afraid of difficulties.'[21]

Children also took the opportunity to benefit from the destruction of Jewish property and premises; as one report commented, 'a particularly sad sight was the participation of children in plundering'. But their participation was again in some sense innocent: lacking 'any independent life experiences' of their own, children believed what they had been taught and viewed 'the Jews as really being criminals and evil beings (Bösewichter)'. They therefore saw it as 'an important and necessary task to participate in the destruction of Jewish property. And because they had been told that this had all been stolen, or acquired illegally, they saw nothing wrong in taking home a few bits and pieces to make their parents happy.'[22]

While some children clearly enjoyed engaging in spontaneous persecution, not all young people were equally willing to assist in organized activities. Erna Albersheim commented that while the 'Hitler youth was forced to help in this work', she knew of 'boys who pretended to be sick so that they did not have to join the mob'.[23] A distaste for violence was also sometimes evident among young adults. A contemporary report recounted how two students in SS uniform were clearly uncomfortable at the task they had been given of destroying Jewish property. On entering an apartment, each of them carefully broke only one vase. They then reported back to their superior that they had carried out their orders to destroy Jewish property.[24] Erna Albersheim, too, noted such attitudes: 'One S.S. man was foolish enough to openly voice his disgust. On the following day his parents were informed that he had accidently shot himself while cleaning his rifle.' It seems unlikely that this was purely an 'accident'. But, as Erna sadly concluded, these were exceptions: there were other Nazis 'who were such fanatics that they rejoiced at the misery they had caused'.[25]

'Making a face as if asking forgiveness': Contexts of engagement and impotence

The German population was now not merely deeply divided but moving to quite different ends of the spectrum, with active engagement on the perpetrator side, in contrast to resigned passivity among those who dis-approved. There was no longer the possibility of inhabiting any 'neutral' middle ground; and the dynamism was all heading in the direction de-termined by the Nazis. On the one side, there were many who joined in with the jeering, the insults, and humiliation, and willingly participated in the plundering and self-enrichment made possible by the devastation un-leashed by the violence. On the other side were those who were shocked and ashamed yet unable to act effectively. A sense of impotence was height-ened by the all too evident use of force and mass arrests.

It is easy enough to sketch a schematic typology; but it is vital also to understand that how people actually behaved varied significantly with con-text. It is certainly the case that younger people were more likely to be engaged on the side of the perpetrators, older Germans more likely to ex-press disapproval or shame. But there were also significant contrasts between people's reactions in larger cities, small provincial towns, villages, and rural areas, as well as broader regional variations.

The range—and often self-contradictory nature—of popular responses is well captured in the diary of the middle-aged Jewish historian and teacher Willy Cohn, penned from the perspective of a fearful victim alert to the dangers outside his home in Breslau. On 11 November 1938 he observed that 'the mood on the street is probably thoroughly antisemitic, and people are pleased that this has happened to the Jews'.[26] Cohn decided it was safest to stay quietly indoors for several days, to avoid arrest and being taken away like other adult males; in his diary, he called this a 'self-imposed house ar-rest'. During this time, he gained a more differentiated picture of responses from the few 'Aryan' visitors who continued to drop by. These visitors in-cluded his barber, Herr Duscha, who was a long-standing member of the Nazi party. Despite Duscha's party membership, he was very unhappy about what was going on. During his visit on 13 November, Duscha apologized for the unwillingness of fellow Germans to act on their disquiet. He argued that 'even Aryans had to be very careful with every word, if they did not want to suffer highly disagreeable consequences', since 'people had already been arrested' for uttering any kind of criticism. Other acquaintances told Cohn that 'civilian officials everywhere seem to have behaved with de-cency; they are after all quite different from the others'; Cohn consoled himself with the thought that 'the Volk cannot all be bad!'[27]

Duscha visited Cohn again the following day and now brought news from his own children who lived in Trebnitz (Trzebnica), a small spa town around twelve kilometres north of Breslau. The Jewish population of Trebnitz had fluctuated in size, generally somewhat under one hundred in total but numbering around 120 at the time of Kristallnacht (in a population of about 8,500). As was rather typical in small towns, Nazi violence against this handful of people who were well known among the local community seems to have gone unopposed, facing only silent or passive disapproval. Duscha's children in Trebnitz had described to their father 'how terribly people had gone on the rampage there', so that 'even Aryans were appalled'. Duscha's conclusion was that 'the people do not want this'.[28] A couple of days later, Duscha's son dropped by and reaffirmed this view, also being 'of the opinion that the people are not in agreement with these events'.[29] But in Trebnitz as elsewhere, it seems, they felt there was little they could or should do in the circumstances.

Cohn continued for a while to grasp at any signs he could that there was broad sympathy for the victims. He had heard rumours that Catholics were apprehensive that the Church would be next in line for attack.[30] A former pupil of his, who was now a Protestant pastor, came by to give him words of comfort and to reassure him that there 'were also decent human beings'.[31] But sympathy for victims did not amount to action on their behalf.

Sympathy could, however, be helpful on an individual level in the days and weeks that followed. Karl Sorkin, who had so recently been made aware of his Jewish ancestry, had escaped over the border to his native Switzerland to escape arrest on 10 November. As we have seen, his father, somewhat ironically, was safe in hospital being treated for the life-threatening injuries he had sustained in a motorbike accident the previous day, the medical staff being unaware of his Jewish descent. After the immediate violence of Kristallnacht and the threat of arrest had died down, Sorkin returned to Germany, to organize the passports for which he had recently applied, and to pick up his 'Aryan' wife Thilde and their child. He was relieved to find that his father was recovering, and that his mother had remained safely at home. His 'Aryan' father-in-law now gave him a vivid account about the course of events in Freiburg, having been one of the many onlookers during this time. He said that the procession of Jews to board the train had looked like one big funeral; the silence of the bystanders had, he thought, implied widespread disapproval. Sorkin heard too from the regular customers in his grocery store. Those who were willing to talk to him were deeply disturbed by the events. But no one, it seemed, had been prepared to intervene in any way; this would have been far too risky.[32]

In small- and medium-sized provincial towns, it was hard to defy the pressure of the dominant political forces, to stand out against the Nazi activists. In rural areas and villages, people seem to have been more actively caught up in the rush of excitement, feeling part of a wider movement, and displaying more enthusiasm as they lined the streets to watch Jews being marched away. There were fewer opportunities to consider different views or counter prevailing discourses; it was perhaps easier to blame the victims for the troubles, to accept the propaganda about Jews being 'our misfortune', or simply to agree that it would be better all round if the village or town were rendered 'Jew-free'. Even so, in some places, such as the small provincial town of Geilenkirchen close to the Dutch border, activists seem to have preferred to be bussed to neighbouring communities where they could more anonymously wreak havoc rather than engage in violence against their own long-term neighbours whom they knew personally.[33]

Considerations were rather different in large, metropolitan cities. Here, when people did not know Jews personally, they had often been relatively unaware of how their situation had been deteriorating in recent years. Erna Albersheim noted that in Frankfurt am Main, before November 1938 many people 'had no contact with Jews', and many therefore 'thought that they were being treated well; they saw them on the streets, in their stores. Some even thought that they were being treated with too much consideration. Now, their eyes were opened.' Witnessing the violence, many felt caught between revulsion and a sense of powerlessness: 'For the first time I heard open criticism. The people were shocked and disgusted.' Kristallnacht had clearly shaken many people, yet they were also afraid: 'If they made a remark, in public, they were arrested. You could hear more whispering than formerly.'[34] Indifference and ignorance were being challenged and displaced by awareness of impotence—for some, deeply frustrating; but among others, increasingly accepted. All of these aspects led, in effect, to passivity—and hence potentially also to complicity in condoning and permitting the radicalization of persecution. Yet complicity rooted in a sense of impotence may be evaluated rather differently from complicity resulting from wilfully ignoring or not caring about the fate of the victims.

Active support for the perpetrators could also easily be whipped up. Carl Hecht, who was arrested and marched along the streets of Frankfurt on the afternoon of Saturday, 12 November, felt that most of the crowds were watching the sorry procession 'with sympathy and not hatred'. But on arrival at the large hall where they were held prior to deportation, Hecht found a mob had been mustered to receive them with catcalls and jeering.[35] One victim was assaulted and suffered a heart attack on the spot. Later that night, the thousand or so Jews who had been arrested were taken to the station for transportation to Buchenwald. Even at around one o'clock in the morning, they were exposed to a mob gathered specially to hurl abuse as they were forced to walk through the crowd, with their hands held up in the air, to board the train. A similar distinction between sympathetic people and organized mobs at places of departure was noted by Klara Rosenthal in Munich. But it was the mobs who were active in support of the regime's violence, while others held their silence.

The situation was somewhat different in Berlin, where around one-third of Germany's Jews lived. While the more recent immigrants living in the Scheunenviertel quarter were visibly distinct, many Berliners of Jewish descent were entirely assimilated, well-nigh indistinguishable from fellow Berliners of the same social class. Of course in the preceding six years in-dividuals had suffered loss of status, increasing social isolation, progressive segregation, and degradation. But the metropolis had a sizeable population, and many non-Jewish Berliners felt sympathy for the victims of such radical violence. Again, it was not so much indifference as a quite realistic sense of impotence that determined reactions in public, while help was extended to some individuals in private.

Having sought refuge overnight with non-Jewish friends, on 10 November Alfred Oppler wandered the streets of Berlin, not wanting to return home for fear of being arrested. He noted 'shame and anger' on people's faces, the atmosphere being somewhat like a funeral.[36] Everywhere he went that day, Oppler registered a 'wave of sympathy' for the Jewish vic-tims. But, he continued, this was generally expressed quietly, with a degree of secrecy; and, 'quaking with anxiety', most people dared not express their feelings out loud.

Not everyone remained passive at this time. In one place, Oppler saw a man shouting at the vandals and actively trying to stop them from plun-dering a Jewish shop. This did not end well. The man was dealt a hefty blow

on the head with a hammer by one of the 'jackals', as Oppler put it, and 'had
to pay for his courage by death'.[37]

For all the expressions of sympathy, everywhere fear of the potential consequences of public opposition far outweighed any desire to help victims.
Eugen Altmann, in Breslau, reported that 'anyone who uttered a word, even
made an expression of regret, was lost'. He was certain that 'many Aryan
people had been arrested on the spot' and 'their relatives had heard no
more of them'. He also recounted a story that was doing the rounds: twelve
workers in a factory who had organized a demonstration of solidarity with
the Jews had been shot dead on the spot, and four hundred others had been
taken to a concentration camp. That was, Altmann concluded, in the 'spirit
of the SS and SA'.[38] Whatever the accuracy or otherwise of this particular
and quite dramatic account of popular protest (for which there appears to
be no surviving archival evidence), such stories clearly acted as a potent
deterrent to anyone else minded to stand up in public to support Jewish
victims; and they possibly also helped some of the persecuted to feel that
compatriots continued to care about their fate. Either way, rumours helped
to fill the gaps in secure knowledge, as people sought to make sense of the
unprecedented violence that had so openly erupted all around.

Those who had no personal contact with Jews might remain more or
less unaware of the extent of their subsequent plight, since the press remained silent on what happened to them after being arrested. In Oppler's
view, however, among those who did know what was going on, it was not
only fear of immediate consequences—the sudden blow on the head with
a hammer—that deterred them from taking action. Another element was
also at play: a 'dull apathy of the soul; one gradually got used to the fact that
the Jews were being persecuted and that they had to suffer.'[39]

This apathy was in part a self-protective reaction: unable to change things,
it was easier to accept the way things were, numbing oneself to any sense
of frustration or outrage by simply assuming this was now the way things
had to be. Rationalizations could justify passivity, if need be; this was what
had to happen, in service of a greater cause, the future of the German Volk.
Indifference towards the fate of Jews, or attempted legitimation in terms
of a wider collective good, could assist in assuaging any possible feelings of
personal discomfort.

Non-Jewish Berliners had similar impressions. The 'Aryan' playwright
Ernst Schwartzert was told by 'an old newspaper woman, in a tone that

was less agitated than resigned, that in the city windows had been smashed and the synagogues were burning'. Her husband, who was with her, 'just dumbly shrugged his shoulders'. Going to look for himself, Schwartzert 'saw about twenty people standing in front of one burning synagogue, not in groups, but all standing alone as though keeping their distance, ashamed.' They were, he said, 'looking dumbly up at the smoking cupola. If two of them did speak to each other, then only very quietly.' He was struck by the fact that 'if another person came past, they would immediately fall silent.' People 'only stood there for a short time, then went on their way. They also went very quickly past the shops that had been destroyed in the business streets.'

Schwartzert was struck, too, by their appearance: they had 'neither concerned, nor agitated faces, but rather faces without any trace of arousal, as though they would prefer not to see this unwelcome sight'. The same, oddly, was true even of the officials stationed at the scene, as Schwartzert observed: 'The police officers who were set to guard the heaps of rubble were just staring into the air. No-one dared to ask them anything.' When he got back to his apartment block, Schwartzert encountered the cleaning lady, who 'was generally not well-disposed to National Socialism and was easily aroused' but who now 'just grimly and silently wiped my room clean and refused to express her opinion'. In the following days, Schwartzert heard only one man, who worked in insurance, loudly expressing his outrage that the state was making insurance companies pay up to the state for the damage but not to the victims, the Jews whose property had been destroyed; in this man's view, the state consisted of 'robbers, murderous arsonists, bandits!' When warned that he should keep his voice down, he said that at least if he ended up in a concentration camp, he would know he would be in there 'together with decent people'. But the vast majority of the people Schwartzert encountered preferred to keep their mouths shut.[40]

The Berlin-based 'Aryan' journalist Ruth Andreas-Friedrich—who managed to maintain a fine balance between critical opposition to the regime and keeping her job—recorded a similar range of responses in her diary entries. Even on 9 November, before vom Rath had died from his wounds and the wave of radical violence was unleashed, she noted how the Jewish shops in Berlin's central shopping district—the Kurfürstendamm, the Leipziger Straße, and the Tauentzienstraße—had been marked as such and were 'notably empty'.[41] People were 'afraid' and 'dared not' be seen shopping in Jewish stores. The following day, the devastation that had been wrought during the night was there for all to see; but once again fear dampened any expressions of shame and rejection of what was being done in their name. She travelled to work on a bus that ran down the Kurfürstendamm, but was held up at the corner of a side street, Fasanenstraße. Here, among an 'ocean of shards of glass', there was a 'silent crowd' of people looking shamefacedly at the Fasanenstraße synagogue, with its cupola shrouded in smoke. The crowd, she felt, seemed united in unspoken shame. Similar feelings of suppressed shame were, she thought, shared by those travelling on the bus: 'The conductor looks at me as if he wants to say something important. But then he just shakes his head and looks away guiltily.' Other passengers 'don't look up at all' but 'everyone is making a face as if asking forgiveness'. One man, sitting close to her, whispered 'damned scandal!' Andreas-Friedrich, though touched by a common sense of humanity, did not dare to respond—and later felt deeply ashamed of her own cowardice. Even so, she noted, 'we all feel a sense of brotherhood. We, who are sitting here in the bus and nearly expiring for shame. Brothers in shame. Comrades in the same remorse.' But, she pondered, 'if everyone is so ashamed, who then broke the windows? It wasn't you, it wasn't me. Who is X, the great unknown?'[42]

The feeling of shame accompanied Andreas-Friedrich into work. On arrival at her office, she went into the room of an equally 'Aryan' colleague, Karla, who greeted her by saying: 'My eyes are virtually popping out of my head with shame.'[43] Going out during a break, they watched crowds looking at the windows being broken in, and Andreas-Friedrich noted how people were standing, silently: 'Hypnotically attracted, hypnotically repelled, they stand at an anxious distance, framing the scene of the activity.'[44]

Andreas-Friedrich and her colleague debated what could be done. Karla, 'shaking with anger', said she felt sick at the thought that they were simply standing there, not daring to open their mouths. Andreas-Friedrich countered: 'Who would it help if you spoke up, only to be grabbed by the collar the next moment and in all secrecy made shorter by a head? Martyrs need a public. Anonymous sacrificial deaths have so far not helped anyone.' But, she added to herself in her diary, 'however clever I appear to myself . . . something does not seem to be quite right in this line of reasoning'.[45] Andreas-Friedrich was perhaps unusual in her self-awareness and recognition that post hoc justifications served mainly to make herself feel better about the compromises she had already made; her excuses to herself did not fully hold water or quiet her pangs of moral discomfort.

The following day, Friday, 11 November, Andreas-Friedrich commented on widespread reactions of like-minded people in her circle: 'While the SS was raging, innumerable fellow Germans were ready to die of pity and shame'. Even so, they were attempting to take action in private: 'Almost all our friends have people quartered on them.'[46] While people were unwilling to step up and be martyred in public at the immediate sites of violence, their sense of shame turned into practical expressions of help and assistance at an individual level over the following days. The court records in Berlin show on a broader scale just how little indifference there actually was, as people were prepared to provide small gestures of assistance even to individuals whom they did not know.[47] Across the Reich, victims reported both horrific experiences and occasional expressions of sympathy; they also, on occasion, found refuge with 'Aryan' friends, managing to evade arrest.[48]

Austria, which later gladly accepted the label of 'Hitler's first victim', was distinctive in many respects.[49] Since the Anschluss in March, Nazi mobs had run riot, stealing from Jews and assaulting them. At the same time a nazified administration under the newly appointed Reich Commissioner Josef Bürckel had seen to more organized measures for expropriating Jewish property and funds while forcing them into emigration. Developments included the appointment of a young SS officer named Adolf Eichmann, who oversaw the establishment of a Central Office for Jewish Emigration. During the months from March to November 1938, a whole series of measures had rapidly heightened discrimination against Jews, including, on 20 May, the extension of the Nuremberg Laws to apply in Austria. In face of the rapidly rising tide of persecution, around one-quarter of Austria's Jews—roughly 50,000—fled the country in the summer of 1938 (followed by a similar number by May 1939), while many hundreds, possibly more than 3,000, saw suicide as the only viable way out of an increasingly intolerable situation.

The speed of developments in Austria was breathtaking, in comparison to the slower progress of exclusion and persecution in Germany over the preceding five years. Popular antisemitism in Austria was partly rooted in the fact that the Viennese Jews were distinctively different from the predominantly Catholic rural population of most of the rest of the country. Although Jews in Germany were concentrated in large cities, they also lived in towns and villages across the Reich; in some respects, they were more integrated into the wider fabric of German society. In Austria, by contrast, more than 90 percent of Jews lived in Vienna, making up nearly one in ten of the capital city's population; there was also a high proportion of Jews in the professions, given them a prominent public profile and high visibility. The Jewish population was in fact highly heterogeneous, both socially and in terms of religious convictions and political opinions; there were deep internal divisions, reflected in a diversity of mutually competing organizations. But in the popular imagination, bolstered by Nazi stereotypes, Jews could readily be framed as easy scapegoats or objects of social envy.

Once unleashed, the violence of activists in Austria was widespread and had predated the organized violence in Kristallnacht. When this erupted, it was indeed radical; and contemporary opinion reports suggest greater popular approval of anti-Jewish actions, even if combined with criticisms of the destruction of property. But in Austria, as in Germany, closer examination of individual experiences recounted in the months following Kristallnacht (rather than years or even decades later) reveals that non-Jewish compatriots were similarly polarized in their responses on an interpersonal level. Non-Nazi bystanders in Austria, as in Germany, arguably remained passive more out of fear than indifference; and despite the prevailing climate of antisemitism, there are many instances in which victims of persecution received gestures of sympathy and attempts at assistance in private.

Henry Albert, a patriotic Austrian Catholic whose father was Jewish and whose mother was Christian, had increasingly identified with the Jewish community because of the rising antisemitism. Now, in November 1938, he was acutely aware of developments in his hometown, Vienna, as he wrote in somewhat faltering English in his 1939 essay, following his rapid emigration. Albert recounted the familiar scenes in the centre of Vienna: there 'were thousands of people. Reflectors illuminated enormous red swastika-banners. Pictures of Hitler were to be seen in many windows. Nazis in Uniforms or similar dresses marched around and cheered police and army.' The atmosphere was extraordinary: 'Women sobbed hysterically. Children cried and yelled. Youths climbed the monuments and columns around the place and waved swastika-banners, the air rung with roar.'

All this is evident in photographs and other observations of the time. What is particularly interesting in Albert's account, however, are the insights into the state of mind of the small minority who were not out in public screaming and roaring but were rather, like himself, huddled away seeking security in attempted isolation: 'I met hundreds of people showing these symptoms. Fright and terrified nervousness were the first two reactions of the indifferent or anti-Nazi circles of the public.' Soon, however, people crept back out into the open, as 'everybody tried to change and to adapt to the situation'. Albert commented on how a 'muddy flood of hypocrisy, lies, deceit and falsehood drowned every decent feeling and behind all this was pale fright'. There were conflicts within families, as people differed in their reactions; but everywhere, there was a sense that existential choices had to be made, necessitating moral compromises whichever way one turned: 'It was no more a question of honest or dishonest, of morally allowed or forbidden, of right or wrong; it was the very "to be or not to be" that was at stake.' Albert noted that 'the average citizen, the indifferent, the less persecuted non-Aryans and similar large groups suffered more psychically than in any other respect. It was a nervous shock the nation had to undergo.'

By the time Albert left Austria later that month 'this nervous strain had not abated'. He would never forget 'the nervous shock of a terrified public' or 'the general sad expressions the pale faces showed. Everybody seemed concerned. Strange how brutality causes cast-down feelings even in those not directly concerned.'[50] This is a view of Austrians deeply divided, apparently as polarized as their neighbours in the German core of the Old Reich.

Violence even affected those living beyond the borders of the Reich. Alice Baerwald, whose hopes of finding an easier life had been dashed in an increasingly nazified Danzig, nevertheless initially felt a little distant from the events of Kristallnacht within the Reich. This changed when she was called to help members of her family in Königsberg, where two of her nephews had been arrested and held in makeshift prisons; their young wives had asked for her support. While the firemen had been, they told her, quite well-disposed and 'correct' in their behaviour, the people who had dealt with the men in the makeshift camps where they were held were brutal. Baerwald also heard from her niece and her mother-in-law about their horrific experiences in a smaller East Prussian border town. Both women had been arrested, held in the police prison, and then made to parade through the town chanting in chorus 'we have betrayed Germany'. They recounted how 'the crowd ran alongside them and shouted to the police "Just beat them dead, why are you still feeding them"'. Released after two days, the two women fled for what they hoped would be greater safety in Berlin.[51]

Complicity and the cloak of humanity

Perhaps the oddest feature of this period, following the violence of November 1938, was the way in which a sense of common humanity was sustained between those who were persecuted and those on the side of the perpetrators, sometimes even in an official capacity. While enacting Nazi roles and practices, some individuals also expressed sympathy and assisted the persecuted.

There are surprisingly numerous examples of friendly officials and people in positions of authority who were critical of the violence and sought to help the victims in their efforts to emigrate or gave expressions of support and sympathy at crucial moments. Their numbers should clearly not be exaggerated; the majority were very likely as brutal as so many accounts by those on the receiving end of Nazi violence suggest. But there is nevertheless a curious phenomenon here that is worth exploring in a little more detail—the phenomenon of those who, while performing their official roles, still behaved in ways that in some sense counteracted the impact of Nazi persecution or at least mitigated its effects on some.

Jochen Klepper, engaged in a property contract connected with moving house, was faced with detailed questioning, as he noted in his diary entry of 17 November, just a week after Kristallnacht. The officials 'had been instructed by the police to confirm whether either of us was Jewish and they would have to include that explicitly in the contract'. But, he went on, playing on the Nazi representation of the alleged anger of the Volk, 'that is the key thing about the "people's rage" in Berlin: the moment they have confirmed [that someone is Jewish], people become more polite, full of interest, warmly engaged'. The fact that Klepper's wife was Jewish clearly seems to have elicited sympathy on the part of the officials in the office dealing with his contract. Meanwhile, however, sympathy could not extend to very much by way of action in public: a couple of days later, Klepper noted that 'people who had expressed criticism of the plundering of Jewish shops had simply been arrested straight off the streets'.[52]

What is somewhat more striking, and as yet little written about, is that even among those specifically tasked with policing the violence, official responses could be quite unpredictable. Alfred Oppler observed that ordinary police officials on occasion seemed to dislike the task of arresting people and treated those they did arrest relatively decently, in contrast to members of the Gestapo and the SS.[53] And even some of the latter seem to have adapted their behaviour to the immediate context, at least as far as their treatment of non-Jewish bystanders was concerned. When officials were on their own and felt no one was checking on their actions, they seem to have been more prepared to be lenient, at least towards 'Aryans' protesting against the violence. Ernst Rathgeber recounted the experiences of a Protestant community worker whom he knew. She had openly voiced her 'regrets about the destruction of Jewish apartments' and was immediately arrested by a member of the SS, who started marching her off in the direction of the police station. But on the way there, and presumably once safely out of sight of his colleagues, he said to her: 'You can think what you like! Just don't say anything!', and let her go free.[54]

Eugen Altmann, caught up in the violence in Breslau, was struck by how people who had joined the SA and SS were now engaged in acts of violence they would never previously have dreamed of committing. But a few still retained a sense of decency. One young man in SS uniform even saved him from being sent to concentration camp, helping him to formulate answers that would provide valid reasons why he should not be arrested. And he was not the only one to offer help. When subsequently organizing his emigration, Altmann was grateful for the assistance of decent police officers, 'particularly those of the old school', who were even 'friendlier than one was used to on the part of German officials in normal times'. He had the 'impression that through their polite and accommodating behaviour these police officers wanted to express their distaste for their opposite numbers, the Gestapo'. Altmann heard many similar stories from others.[55]

The widowed businesswoman Erna Albersheim too repeatedly 'heard of Aryans helping their former Jewish friends during this terrible time'. The stories told among her acquaintances included that of a Nazi party member helping his Jewish brother-in-law whom his sister had married.[56] In Düsseldorf, some Jews were only able to flee in time because members of the population, local police officials, and even some committed Nazis had warned them in advance and managed to help them escape.[57] Willy Cohn in Breslau noted in his diary that older officials were behaving in a civilized or more 'decent' manner, but 'these were after all quite different sorts of people'. He again consoled himself with the thought that 'the whole Volk cannot be bad!'[58] But, he felt, 'Germans also are very afraid'.[59] Klara Rosenthal fondly remembered an ever decent and friendly official in Munich who sat down to eat and drink with her family and helped them get the final paperwork together for the emigration. For Klara, this man reinforced her 'faith in her compatriots'.[60]

In Austria, as in Germany, there were helping hands and 'decent' officials. Arthur Goldstein, for example, who had experienced the assistance of a helpful Christian neighbour when young Nazis had daubed antisemitic slogans on his workplace, was determined to get out of Austria. He recalled how 'elderly Viennese officials expressed their sympathy and shook their heads when they heard what was going on and how, by incarcerating us, we were being forced into emigration'. In the days of violence around Kristallnacht, Goldstein managed to stay with a friend to avoid arrest. During the remaining few weeks he spent in Austria, Goldstein was touched by friendliness in practice: 'all my acquaintances, both Christians and Jews, tried to help me with emigration.' He received offers of help and good wishes both from friendly officials and Christian acquaintances, and managed to depart for Shanghai (for which no visa was required) on an Italian ship at the end of December 1938. These experiences sustained Goldstein's morale and faith in fellow Austrians: he felt that 'a majority of the population was against the brutal methods of systematic persecution and cowardly torment of a small minority, and despite the strongest pressure had expressed its opposition to the terror'. Despite the fact that a 'brutalized minority with weapons in its hands had for a short time imposed a change in the system', Goldstein did not want to 'doubt the essential goodness of humanity'.[61]

One of the most insistent on retaining his faith in fellow citizens as essentially humane at heart was the tobacco goods trader from Neustettin, Georg Abraham.[62] He distinguished most of those he knew personally from the 'Nazis' and had considerable understanding even for those who were members of the party, often showing some sympathy with their professed reasons for joining. He saw them as being in some sense forced into conformity—even though the outcome was for him still appalling. But their continued expressions of friendliness made the enactment of repression more humane, delivered with a coating of regret and sympathy, unlike the sadism and brutality of most members of the Gestapo and SS. Abraham's stories of his suffering in the winter of 1938–1939, just prior to his emigration, are repeatedly studded with illustrations of continuing humanity even on the part of those actively sustaining the Nazi regime.

In the summer of 1938, in preparation for emigration, Abraham decided he needed to gain experience in agriculture.[63] He found himself a job helping a Jewish farmer who lived with his family in a little village of around 500 inhabitants. The work there was agreeable, and the local inhabitants, including the country policeman and the mayor, were well-disposed towards the Jewish farmer and his family who enjoyed a good reputation in the area. The only serious difficulty the farmer himself had encountered was with his store, which sold mixed wares and farm produce: local Nazi party members had been spying on customers, and people no longer dared to be seen making purchases there. While also wanting to emigrate, the farmer had found it impossible to sell up and receive money for his farm, so for the time being any plans to start afresh elsewhere seemed impracticable. But otherwise things in this rural community were relatively peaceful.

Until November 1938, Abraham and the farmer's two sons were working in the fields as usual. Then, at around ten o'clock on the morning of Thursday, 10 November, they were suddenly arrested and told to report to the gendarme; the three of them were put behind bars in the village prison. Here, the three received what in Nazi Germany was extraordinarily gentle treatment. The local gendarme, who doubled up as the jail keeper, was a good friend of the farmer's family. His wife, moreover, had served as a maid for the farmer during better times, and had known the two sons when they were still schoolchildren. The gendarme assured the three prisoners that he would do his very best to make things as easy as possible for them; and his wife sent them her warm regards. Clearly somewhat uncomfortable with his current role, he explained to them that he had only joined the Nazi party because he had lost his previous job and had to join the NSDAP in order to gain employment. Unfortunately, however, he now had to do his duty by keeping them behind bars. But he would try to ensure they could stay in this village jail rather than being carted off to concentration camp.

The gendarme did indeed try to fulfil his promises. He allowed his prisoners to have personal visits every evening, once darkness had fallen, with the farmer and his wife bringing in fresh food for their sons and Georg Abraham. Abraham's wife also came to stay nearby so she could visit frequently. She arrived in the evening of 10 November with the news that, starting at six in the morning, all the Jews in Abraham's hometown had been arrested, with the sole exception of one old sick man. In addition to allowing these visits, with the physical and psychological comforts they afforded, the gendarme provided additional protection for the farmer's home and for Abraham's wife. Even so, members of the local population—or perhaps rowdies from another area—did not share his benevolence. One night a stone was thrown through the bedroom window of the farmhouse. Fortunately, it did not hurt the elderly couple who might otherwise have been sleeping there because they were, at precisely this time, visiting their sons and Georg in the prison cell.

For more than a week Abraham and the farmer's sons hoped their confinement could continue this way, with both the gendarme and the local mayor trying to make the case that they were essential for Germany's agricultural productivity and should be released back into production. But after eight days the Gestapo arrived and informed them of their impending deportation to a concentration camp.

Even now, the gendarme strove to assist his prisoners as best he could. Rather than risking their exposure to the predicted public 'gaping and jeering' if they were taken on the local light railway by the Gestapo, he drove them in his own car to the main railhead station and delivered them in person onto the Berlin train with other deportees. This, and all his previous acts of personal kindness—even while performing his official duties—meant a lot to Abraham, who felt that the gendarme and mayor had given him a measure of succour and hope.

Experiences on arrival in the concentration camp of Sachsenhausen, half an hour's train ride north of Berlin, were very different. The train doors were 'suddenly ripped open' with 'loud cries and swearing'; once out on the platform, 'the first blows fell on us, and a wild horde gave us to understand that we were now in the hands of the SS'.[64] Life—and death—in the camp proved dreadful. Every day the prisoners faced a long walk to the construction site where they were put to heavy manual labour; anyone who could not manage the march or the work was either kicked to death or beaten to death; anyone who attempted to escape was shot. Every day, Abraham reckoned, an additional eighty or so sick or elderly Jews died. His block elder was a political prisoner, a former member of the SPD who had already been there for two years. He told the new inmates that the concentration camp now had some 13,000 prisoners, of whom around 6,000 were Jews. The new barracks to house the influx of Jewish prisoners had, he said, been built during the summer, but up until now the Nazis had not found a suitable pretext for the long-planned mass arrests. But, he thought, had the assassination of Ernst vom Rath in Paris not happened, sooner or later another reason would have been thought up.

Sachsenhausen was nightmarish. Most of the SS were, in Abraham's view, sadistic brutes. But even here, Abraham came into contact with a member of the SS who still displayed some evidence of humanity. One day a camp guard in SS uniform came to sit down with the prisoners and sought to reassure them in various ways. He advised them that they could hope to get out quickly if their relatives could sort out emigration papers for them. He told them that Sachsenhausen was not now, in the winter, as bad as it had been in the heat of the summer, when inmates had been dying simply from thirst and dehydration. Nor were conditions here, in his view, as terrible as in Buchenwald, where he had previously served. There, men had been hanged from the trees, and the sound of their screams as well as their recitation of prayers while dying was still ringing in his ears. The barracks had been even more overcrowded, and even more people had been beaten to death. This young SS man continued to confide in Abraham, telling him that he was himself the son of a police officer, and he had not actually wanted to join the party; but he had been unable to find work, and then proved unable to do the farm work with which he had been tasked. He was subsequently given the choice: either join the NSDAP and work for the Nazis, or be designated as 'workshy' and incarcerated in a concentration camp. He chose the former and ended up in the SS. It pained him terribly to see all the misery and suffering here, and he was disillusioned with the Nazi party, which he had previously thought had higher ideals.[65] Again, Abraham seems to have found some solace in being able to have this kind of conversation, even under the most adverse circumstances.

Meanwhile Abraham's wife was doing everything she could to obtain the necessary papers confirming the possibility of his emigration to England. When all this finally came through, Abraham and other prisoners who were released at the same time were fearful about how they might be received by the wider populace. But again, Abraham was pleasantly surprised: 'Already at the railway station friendly people greeted us, everyone could see where we had come from, and there were many sympathetic glances. People pressed money and refreshments into our hands. No one asked us how it had been, they all knew well enough.' Once he got home, Abraham was pleased to find that 'all our friends had remained the same. Everyone was critical of the injustice that had been done to us.'[66]

Georg Abraham's account suggests neither wider indifference among the population, because there was much evidence of empathy and sympathy, nor ignorance, because those he encountered certainly knew what was happening at every stage. The question of impotence is more complex to evaluate (let alone to measure). On the one hand, they found themselves on the other side of the newly imposed divide between members of the Volksgemeinschaft and the outcasts; and they were complicit in the sense of conforming to what was required of them, playing their allotted roles, acting to sustain the regime. But at the same time, in so far as this was possible, they were trying their best to reassure and provide some sort of psychological and on occasion physical comfort to the victims of persecution. They were, in a sense, waving and extending best wishes even while playing their allotted roles in the drama that was causing his distress and that of countless others.

Principled refusals

What else could ordinary 'Aryans' who were opposed to Nazism really hope to do at this time? The signs were clear from November 1938 onwards. It was becoming increasingly difficult, even impossible, to remain in the Reich and claim to be an innocent bystander.

For some, individual exits seemed the only way to salvage self-respect and indicate refusal to become ever more complicit. In the last peacetime months, it was not only people of Jewish descent who felt they had to get out. Ernst Schwartzert had—unlike many other 'Aryans'—remained in close contact with Jewish friends and acquaintances. Many Jews told him how courageous individuals had hidden them during the initial wave of violence and arrests; how others had contributed significant sums of money for them to be able to bribe their way out of concentration camps; these Jews, who had managed to survive the days and weeks of terror after Kristallnacht, had personal evidence to confirm that there were still some decent Germans, despite all.

But in Schwartzert's view, the wider picture was more complex. No one in Germany could have 'not known' what was going on this time; indeed,

Goebbels's talk about how the 'people' (*Volk*) had supposedly spontaneously risen up against the Jews was a way of making everyone guilty, taking a share of the blame. Yet many people did not want to bear this burden of guilt: they tried, Schwartzert said, to 'repress any consciousness of Jews, to avoid the burden on their soul'. Many Germans, he thought, were trying to 'wash themselves clean' of guilt by claiming to be jealous of Jews for being able to emigrate, saying they wished they could leave too but were not allowed to.

Here, in Schwartzert's observations, we see what would become a typical pattern: expressing sympathy with the victims, even in some sense casting oneself as a victim of the situation, while remaining in practice on the side of the perpetrators and conforming to what was required. Some—perhaps most—of Schwartzert's acquaintances had, moreover, gradually become convinced Nazis. They claimed that they had come to support Nazi views of their own free will, rather than simply parroting Nazi propaganda as a public performance. Perhaps this pretence of conversion was a form of denial, refusing to recognize the ignominy of capitulation to superior power; or perhaps, in face of the barrage of ideology and the lack of alternative viewpoints or free debate, they had genuinely shifted ground. A feeling of group identification in any event made people feel safer in uncertain times. This was not a time in which it was wise to stand out against the crowd, to think, speak, or act differently; the penalties were far too high. For the previously independent-minded, it was face-saving to pretend to oneself as much as to others that one had come to Nazi viewpoints of one's own accord and was not simply going along with the crowd.

More generally, Schwartzert observed, Germans were no longer even trying to form their own opinions, but rather, even if they had resisted this in the early years of Hitler's rule, had now decided 'finally to fall into line'. Jokes had become softer, more harmless, less frequent. People no longer joked about essentials, about real questions, but skated around on superficial issues or joked only about personalities and not policies. There was also what Schwartzert called a tendency to deify Hitler ('*Vergöttlichungstendenz*'), calling him an 'idealist', somehow placing him above everyday considerations. It is clear from a range of sources that this idealization of Hitler had been both actively fostered and widespread since the very earliest days of Hitler's rule; by the later 1930s it was simply becoming more evident, even among the formerly more sceptical intellectual circles among which Schwartzert moved.[67]

Deeply troubled and scarcely able to bear the atmosphere in Germany any more, Schwartzert finally reached the decision to emigrate. He felt the stirrings of an uneasy conscience and could no longer identify with most of his compatriots. The community of empathy that had been constructed in the Volksgemeinschaft was not one he wanted to have any part in. But it was not only the distaste for the way German society was going; love too played a role, as, like Robert Breusch a couple of years earlier, Schwartzert was totally unwilling to abandon his Jewish girlfriend. They left for the United States, hoping to embark on a new life in an environment where it would be possible to live together as human beings.[68]

Ernst Rathgeber, too, was troubled by evidence of widespread 'falling into line', making him feel ever less at home in his own native country. As he travelled through Germany, he noticed that growing numbers of people were wearing party badges or uniforms of one sort or another. He recognized that some might well have become party members under pressure, forced to show evidence of commitment to the Nazi cause or join the party in order to keep their jobs. Even so, for Rathgeber this was problematic. Their inner sense of distance from the outward insignia might have allowed them to maintain a sense of self-respect, but it made little difference to the practical impact of their behaviour: they were serving a party 'whose goal it was to destroy spiritual Germany'. He was exceptional in registering just what living within the Nazi regime was doing not only to those who were persecuted but also to those who were becoming complicit in persecution.

For Rathgeber, such behavioural conformity was inexcusable, even when accompanied by claims about enforced conformity. He saw even unwilling compliance as a compromise that had gone too far: for him it was morally unacceptable. At a personal level, he had a growing sense that there was 'no place' for him any longer in Germany, living 'in an indescribably homeless and godforsaken state'.

Rathgeber was without romantic ties to anyone of Jewish descent; unlike Breusch and Schwartzert, he had no immediate need to get out to preserve a close personal relationship. It was, rather, the unacceptable clash between an increasingly deformed construction of German collective identity and his own personal morality that swayed him; and shock at the events of November 1938 finally precipitated the decision to leave. For Rathgeber, it was now 'unbearable to remain any longer in a country in which there was no right to life' for people of Jewish descent, including his former friends who had already left; he was filled with a growing desire to turn his back 'on this inhumane Nazi-Reich as soon as possible'.

Rathgeber managed to leave for England in January 1939; a few months later, he was deported from Britain and interned as an 'enemy alien' in Australia. Here, he reflected on the reasons for having abandoned his home-land. For Rathgeber, the sense of being part of a national community with which he could no longer identify was decisive: 'As long as such vandalism is carried out against no resistance, by a regime that styles itself the "moral barometer of the German race", then my own *humanity* forbids me to feel a member of this state any more. And should the German people, as their current masters claim, genuinely assent to and support this barbarism, then *I* am no longer a German!'[69] The redefinition of what it meant to be German was, in his view, complete.

What more general conclusions can be drawn about the behaviour of non-Jewish Germans at this time of heightened violence? In November 1938, it was neither ignorance nor indifference that shaped the polarization of popular responses, but perceptions of the relative risks versus potential benefits of different forms of action, which varied widely. Some clearly wanted to be part of a moment of national historical greatness, shaping the glorious Nazi future. Where people were antisemitic or simply indifferent to the fate of Jews, where they saw easy opportunities for material gain, or wanted to demonstrate public commitment to the 'national community', they actively participated in plundering goods or humiliating victims. Fear and a desire to be seen to conform could potentially even play a role in prompting some to participate on the side of the dominant Nazi forces. Fear of adverse consequences for themselves certainly deterred many peo-ple from helping victims in public or speaking up on their behalf.

Where they were ashamed or outraged by the violence, however, and particularly when it mattered for personal or moral reasons, even the most unlikely people were prepared to offer help privately, at an individual level—and this across different areas of Germany, and across different com-munities, with even on occasion cases of Nazis helping their 'non-Aryan' compatriots. Some individuals managed to face in both directions at once, in what might seem to us to be mutually incompatible ways and acting in self-contradictory directions, but which made emotional sense in view of different pressures at the time.

The mental worlds that people inhabited, or their broader frameworks of interpretation, were important. Ways of perceiving the situation could to some extent be adjusted, or muddied, by regime propaganda and racialized ways of thinking. This might work in principle for broader categories— generalizations about 'the Jew'—but less well with respect to individuals who were known or even only fleetingly encountered at a personal level. This helped to sustain the distinction between public role-playing in service of the Nazi cause and private acts of humanity towards individual victims of persecution.

These events had a long-term impact, even on those who were not themselves victims. As late as July 1939, people were still discussing the violence of the previous November. A politically critical observer for the Social Democratic Party in Exile (Sopade) overheard the following conversations between people walking past remnants of the damage wrought in Kristallnacht in North-Rhine Westphalia: 'Two petty bourgeois individuals who came by said loudly enough for others to hear: "Heavens; even the communists couldn't have managed to do worse than this." Another day I observed a mother with her eight-year-old little girl. The child said to her mother: "Look Mummy, is that what the Jews have done again?" The mother however was of the view that "Come away from here, that wasn't the communists that did it, it was the National Socialists." At this she [the mother] started to cry.'[70]

In this last exchange there seems, on the part of the child, to have been complete internalization of Nazi ideology, while the mother's response, despite an apparently critical stance towards Nazism, also indicated an un-thinking equation between 'Jews' and 'communists'—an association summarized under the image of the 'Judeo-Bolshevik enemy' that would soon turn infinitely more deadly following the outbreak of war.

8

Divided Fates

Empathy, Exit, and Death, 1939–1941

Many Jews who emigrated later saw the extreme violence of Kristallnacht as paradoxically having been the turning point that ultimately saved their lives, precipitating their exit despite all difficulties; had it not been so violent, had they remained under the illusion that they could still cling on in Germany, they would not eventually have made it through.

The official death toll was put at just under one hundred, but in fact many hundreds died, whether as a direct result of the violence, subsequent incarceration, or because they took their own lives. In the wake of Kristallnacht, the regime introduced new measures to tighten the noose around the necks of Jews. Nazi policies were precisely designed to make life ever more difficult for them: they were forced to give up businesses, professions, and possessions, losing the right to make a living; and they were subjected to numerous restrictions on movement, attendance at cultural events, theatres, concerts, cinemas, lectures, exhibitions, losing the right to lead a human life. In January 1939, Reinhard Heydrich opened the Reich Central Office for Jewish Emigration (Reichszentralstelle für Jüdische Auswanderung) in Berlin, based on the model trialled since the previous summer by Adolf Eichmann in Vienna. There was now ever greater pressure to emigrate, despite tight immigration quotas in other countries, and bureaucratic nightmares around visa, currency, and affidavit requirements. More than 50,000 German Jews had emigrated in 1933, and an average of 30,000 every year up to 1937; in 1938 more than 47,000 emigrated; and in

1939, despite apparently almost insurmountable hurdles, 68,000 Jews emigrated from the now-expanded Reich.[1]

Germans and Austrians of Jewish descent faced impossible choices. Attempts to argue that it would be best just to sit it out and wait for things to pass, as in previous bouts of persecution, now seemed far less persuasive. But, as numerous accounts attest, the decision to leave one's homeland for the uncertainties of an impoverished life in an unknown country and a foreign language was far from easy; nor were the practical hurdles around finances, taxes, affidavits, and permits simple to navigate, even for those with energy, resources, and connections abroad; and the tight immigration quotas imposed by other countries made it even harder. Desperate since Hitler's ascension in 1933, the situation was increasingly dire. Those who failed to get out before the outbreak of war in September 1939 would find that even worse awaited them.

Kristallnacht was also a turning point for those 'Aryans' who wished to remain passively on the sidelines. They could no longer claim ignorance about the fate of Jews—radical violence had been all too visible in cities, towns, and villages across the Reich. People often expressed sympathy with Jews at a personal level. But with the shifts in national policies there was widespread and growing complicity among Reich citizens, as non-Jewish Germans and Austrians benefitted from the 'aryanization' of property and the opening up of professional opportunities. Later, some would profess a sense of shame about the events of Kristallnacht while overlooking the ways in which they had themselves been both enablers and beneficiaries of the violence.

Once the nation was at war, Nazi priorities and policies for creating 'Jew-free' realms shifted. Pressures on Reich Jews to emigrate to anywhere willing to accept them were displaced, and ultimately replaced, by enforced deportation to places where they would find it difficult, or impossible, to survive. The German invasion, occupation, and annexation of parts of Poland meant massively increased numbers of Jews in areas under Nazi control. Now, Jews were variously subjugated, ghettoized, or terrorized into flight to the Soviet-dominated east, created as a consequence of the Molotov-Ribbentrop Pact of August 1939. 'Germanization' policies, entailing forced population movements, further shifted the parameters. As Nazi plans for Jewish 'reservations' foundered, and as ghetto administrators struggled with the challenges of overcrowding, disease, and malnutrition, alongside exploitation of labour, so, too, secretly planning for a 'war of an-nihilation' against the Soviet Union provoked new thinking about potential 'solutions' to the self-imposed 'Jewish question'. And, as Nazi policies be-came ever more radical, it became all but impossible to remain an 'innocent bystander'. The outbreak of the war in September 1939 marked the final division between the distinctive communities of fate.

The ways in which members of the Volksgemeinschaft interacted with victims of Nazi persecution reveal the futility of any attempt at maintaining 'neutrality' in the transitional period, between Kristallnacht and the out-break of war in September 1939, and in the first two wartime years before the invasion of the Soviet Union in June 1941. Personal accounts again re-veal the ways in which individuals could combine continuing conformity, and indeed often unexamined complicity, with a sense of their own essen-tial goodness and morality. People's situations gave them various degrees of choice in how to react. But for all, social negotiations, redefinitions of the situation, and unstable compromises were now inevitable.

Unwilling exits and ambivalent farewells

Many refugees derived some brief comfort from small acts of practical sup-port, expressions of sympathy and good wishes, or confessions of a sense of frustration and beleaguered impotence on the part of Germans. In February 1939, Gerta Pfeffer, the former factory worker, finally received a permit to go to England. Leaving her temporary refuge with relatives in the Galician capital, Lemberg (Ukrainian Lviv, Polish Lwów), she was able to travel back through Germany and visit her old home one last time.[2] The last 'Aryan' she talked to before leaving her homeland was a man who told her how terrible it now was to live in Germany. He impressed on her the import-ance, once she was out, of telling the world how things really were in the Reich. As he put it: 'Don't you believe that we Aryans have it any better, we have to fear speaking the truth even in front of our own children. The devil in person, lies, and brute force now rule in this once so highly regarded Germany.'[3]

Less than a week after Kristallnacht, on 16 November 1938, Hertha Nathorff had expostulated in her diary that she would try to write up what had happened so that her child would one day be able to read about what 'had been done to his mother, and why she would say to him: Never again back to this land, if we first manage to leave it alive!'[4] Despite encounters with humane and kindly individuals who tried to help her or expressed sympathy, Nathorff was appalled at the general failure to oppose Nazi brutality. It was not that all Germans were bad; it was rather that so many had failed to stand up to the few who were at the forefront of violence. There seemed to be no sense of the 'civil courage' that would later be seen as so important. The passivity of bystanders had allowed violence to escalate and then dominate; and this Nathorff could not ignore. Passivity was complicity.

Popular responses to the new situation of Jews were varied; but some unusual cases highlight more general issues. Karl Sorkin had, as we have seen, only discovered remarkably late that he was of Jewish descent. He was also extremely fortunate that, due to the accident of his birth in Switzerland, he quickly gained an emigration visa on the Swiss quota. He let his regular customers in his Freiburg store know that he would soon be closing down, and was relieved that, despite the sudden revelation of his Jewish ancestry, all but two continued to make purchases from him. This occasionally required a little negotiation, and long personal acquaintance could clearly compensate for the sudden stigma of 'race'. On hearing that Sorkin was Jewish, one 'arch-Nazi' exclaimed that 'she should be ashamed of herself, having gone shopping all these years in a Jewish store'. Sorkin pointed out that 'a person who for thirty years had been considered alright could not suddenly take on a different character through a change of race', and he reassured her that 'it would be scandalous if she felt she should be ashamed of herself'. The next day she came back to tell Sorkin that, after all, 'she was not so totally in agreement with the Nazis', and that it was actually a 'scandal' how Jews 'were being messed around'.[5]

Sorkin was fortunate that his 'racial' heritage was revealed so remarkably late—September 1938—and he had remained on good terms with customers and friends through nearly six years of Nazi rule. The separation of communities of empathy had not taken place; Sorkin was still, in effect, one of their own rather than an outcast about whom they no longer cared. His regular customers not only remained loyal, but some also bought more than usual, so he was left with relatively little stock to dispose of at the end. And even his Nazi friends made comments to the effect that there were indeed some 'good Jews' and they were very sorry that he had to go through with this.[6] This was a repeated pattern, addressed explicitly by Himmler in his infamous Posen speech of 4 October 1943, in which he referred 'to the evacuation of the Jews, the extermination of the Jewish people' and complained that 'then they all come along, the 80 million worthy Germans, and each one has his one decent Jew. Of course, they say the others are swine, but this one, he is a first-rate Jew'.[7] Himmler, alas, was grossly overstating this; had there really been '80 million worthy Germans' prepared to stand up openly for their 'one decent Jew', the story of the Holocaust would have developed very differently. As it was, expressions of sympathy with individuals took place in private, in quiet places where there could be no real consequences—and frequently even as the sympathizer continued to be complicit in the process of persecution.

Context made a considerable difference to experiences of exit. Under Nazi rule in the still nominally Free City of Danzig, Alice Baerwald was shocked by the deterioration of the situation for Jews when, as she put it, 'a new era of terror began'.[8] The imposition of exorbitant taxes was followed by confiscation of the property of Jews unable to pay, as well as automatic arrests on the spot. Many of the Baerwalds' friends left the country, simply abandoning homes and property, while she and her husband worked in Zionist organizations assisting young people to emigrate to Palestine. Soon, the Baerwalds came to the view that they too would have to get out, and they put their house on the market.

Maintaining her own self-respect, Baerwald generally refused to accept any Nazi definition of the situation, and often got through difficult moments by effective banter. When Baerwald was showing her house to a potential buyer eager to acquire it at a knock-down price, the purchaser commented what a nice house it was, and how terrible it must be to have to give it up and leave. Baerwald cheekily countered that no, in fact, she 'had it a great deal better' than the German woman because she could go 'out into the world' while the German woman would have to remain under Nazi rule; at which, according to Baerwald, the buyer 'turned bright red, took off her gigantic swastika badge, and said quietly' that she had 'to bear these things and hated them from the depths of her heart'.[9] Expressing sympathy while also profiting from compliance could do little to assist victims of persecution; but such encounters provide insights into the ambivalence that many Germans would later feel about the compromises they had made in the past, as well as the strategies of self-assertion among those cast in the role of victims.

In early March 1939, Alice Baerwald moved to modest rented accommodation. Here, she registered just how much everyone felt under the surveillance of the local Nazi 'block warden' (*Blockwart*) keeping an eye on what was going on in the building. Wanting to be able to eat out occasionally, she found the only place still open to Jews was the railway station restaurant, which remained in Polish hands. Here, there was lively company: it became a 'real gathering place for emigrants', as she wrote in her essay.[10] Baerwald also made a trip to her native Berlin to bid farewell to relatives and friends. She was amazed at the shortage of suitcases in shops: mountains of leather bags and cases were marked as already sold, and the waiting time for new orders was two or three months. People were also trying to muster what resources they could to prepare for new lives, despite Nazi confiscation of their personal wealth and severe restrictions on what they could take with them on emigration. With some trepidation, Baerwald smuggled pieces of jewellery from Berlin to Danzig on behalf of relatives who wanted her to send valuables from there to contacts in faraway destinations.

Back in Danzig, following brushes with the law and fear of discovery of her own emigration plans, Baerwald designed a way of leaving with as much of her own baggage as possible. Ostensibly taking the Berlin train and buying a through ticket all the way to the Reich capital, she in fact got off at the Polish port of Gdynia, about thirty-five kilometres from Danzig, at which point the long-distance train made a halt. Unlike those living within the Reich, Jewish passport holders in Danzig did not yet have to use the imposed middle names of 'Sara' or 'Israel' as a sign of their 'racial' heritage; and Baerwald was fortunate to have a Danzig passport that was not stamped with a J.[11] But she was stopped by the German Gestapo at the border controls and spent some uneasy minutes as the official mustered her passport photo and her baggage. He then asked her directly: 'Do you want to emigrate?' Quick-witted as ever, she replied, sounding as sincere as possible, 'Why should I? It is, after all, so lovely here in our country.' At that 'he clicked his heels together and, laughing too, replied "I think so too, Heil Hitler".' It took her a while to recover from this final encounter with a Nazi official. Once on the boat, steaming out of Gdynia to London on 17 August 1939, Baerwald collapsed in tears.[12]

Not all were so lucky or had so much by way of personal resourcefulness and organizational talent; and many had simply been ground down by their experiences over the years, culminating in Kristallnacht. As we have seen, the rabbi of the south German village of Gailingen, Mordechai Bohrer, like many other Jews who had been incarcerated following Kristallnacht, did not survive more than a month in Dachau. His family had already made arrangements to emigrate together to Palestine, but in the event his widow and seven young children had to make the difficult journey and try to start a new life on their own.[13] Erich Haller-Munk had managed to leave Vienna for Switzerland at the time of the Austrian Anschluss. His brother Hans, meanwhile, had been vegetating with their parents in Kiel following his rescue from near suicidal despair in France. Erich held out little hope for their parents who were, he thought, too elderly to want to emigrate; but he 'could not believe the apathy, the indolence, the breakdown' of his brother. Despite Erich's best efforts, Hans refused to follow his brother out of the Reich. Hans was picked up, one of the 30,000 or so Jews arrested in November 1938, and was taken to Sachsenhausen concentration camp. A few weeks later, Erich heard from mutual friends about his brother's fate. Already in a poor physical and mental state, Hans had rapidly declined further in camp. At the end of December 1938, deathly ill, Hans was released from Sachsenhausen, penniless and feverish, to wander the streets of Berlin on a cold winter night. Despite seeking shelter with friends, he died within twenty-four hours of his release, at the age of thirty-eight.

Writing in the winter of 1939–1940, a year later, Erich was trying to reassure himself that he had done all he could to persuade Hans to act differently; instead, he blamed his brother's death on character weaknesses evident from his youth and on Hans's failure to choose the right course of action at decisive moments. In these awful circumstances, and perhaps trying to assuage his own feelings of guilt, Erich seemed almost incapable of blaming the Nazi system or the compliance of the German people and perhaps found it easier to frame the story as tragedy rooted in the victim's own character.

Erich now feared for the safety of his elderly parents, still in Germany, which is why he changed the family's names in his written account. At the time of writing—during the first wartime winter, 1939–1940—Erich still held out some hope that his parents would get out.[14] The Haller-Munks did in fact manage to organize tickets to Shanghai; but, perhaps devastated by the death of their son Hans, Erich's parents did not leave their native country. In April 1942, having being forced into a 'Jew house' (*Judenhaus*) for deportation to Theresienstadt, Dr Heinrich Haller-Munk and Paula chose, along with seven other Jews in Kiel awaiting the same fate, to take their own lives.[15]

This was a far more typical fate than those of the émigrés who wrote their accounts in the winter of 1939; and no amount of human kindness experienced by a few individuals as they departed the Reich could override the fact that most of their former 'Aryan' compatriots had—by their silence, their passivity, or their more active compliance with Nazi racism— effectively betrayed and abandoned them.

Fractured experiences

The situation for people in mixed marriages or of mixed descent was of course never secure, despite the elaborate categorization of degrees of *Mischlinge*, and despite the degree of protection afforded the 'non-Aryan' partner in a 'privileged mixed marriage' (*priviligierte Mischehe*). Pressure to divorce, as well as growing personal tensions, put an end to many mixed marriages—including, for example, the marriage between Hans Haller-Munk and his socialite wife Beate. The laws about 'racial defilement' and the consequences of transgressing 'racial' boundaries were enough to persuade others not to contemplate such relationships or, if firmly committed, to emigrate, like Robert Breusch and his long-suffering fiancée Käte Dreyfuß. Yet despite all, many couples stuck together, as in the case of the Dresden philologist Viktor Klemperer, whose 'Aryan' wife Eva remained with him throughout.[16]

The experiences of those in mixed marriages and their children often receive inadequate attention in accounts that, in effect, reproduce the distinction between 'Germans' and 'Jews' that was introduced under the Nazi regime. The numbers are relatively small, but the experiences of people in families straddling the 'racial' divide help to illuminate the transformation of German society within just a few years. In 1933 there were some 35,000 so-called mixed marriages in Germany; in 1939, there were still some 20,454 mixed marriages across the Reich. In December 1942, 16,760 Jews in mixed marriages were still alive; by September 1944 the figure had gone down to 12,487.

In 1933 there had been perhaps as many as 300,000 people who were *Mischlinge* or 'non-Aryan' descendants of mixed marriages. A higher proportion of them emigrated than was the case with their parents or grand-parents, generally being of an age when starting afresh in a foreign country still seemed possible. By 1939 only 72,738 remained in Germany, of whom about 8,000 were 'counted as Jews' (*Geltungsjuden*) under the Nuremberg Laws, and therefore persecuted as full Jews. Other 'mixed breeds of the first degree' (*Mischlinge ersten Grades*) would face an ever worsening situation with the outbreak of war; by the later war years, despite failure to reach an agreed policy in the 1942 Wannsee Conference where the question was dis-cussed extensively, they too would in practice be caught up in forced labour or slated for deportation and murder.[17]

The relationships with wider society in these mixed cases are significant despite their relatively small numbers. Some accounts suggest that, even if Germany had undoubtedly changed, not all Germans had fallen entirely si-lent. The Protestant Jochen Klepper and his wife Johanna, a widow of Jewish descent who had converted to Protestantism, had, as we have seen, become aware that fellow Berliners after Kristallnacht were increasingly 'tired and despairing'. In his diary, Jochen Klepper commented on a growing sense of 'nihilism and apathy' among Berliners, as people were ever more casual with their money, did not put themselves out in their work, and 'hopelessly' let themselves be pushed around. A friend visiting Klepper from Munich confirmed that 'everywhere there was the same sense of weariness and bit-terness'. Individual reactions varied and were sometimes surprising: 'while many people that one thought one was close to are now silent, some, from whom you would never have expected it, now write in the most intense way.'[18]

The Kleppers had two daughters, both Jewish by descent from Johanna's previous marriage. One daughter had emigrated to Sweden while this was still possible. Their main fear now was for their other daughter, who re-mained in Germany. Klepper's wife had the relative protection of being in a mixed marriage, while her daughter, being 'racially' Jewish even if Protestant by both conviction and conversion, had no protection at all. At this point, surrounded by supportive voices, they remained in Berlin; Klepper hoped for the best.

Else Behrend-Rosenfeld, the Christian daughter of a mixed marriage, had seven siblings, all technically 'first-degree *Mischlinge*'. But as a re-sult of her marriage to the 'racially' Jewish Siegfried Rosenfeld, she was herself to 'count as a Jew' (*Geltungsjüdin*). Following Kristallnacht, the

Behrend-Rosenfelds were determined to get out of Germany. Their three children, by now teenagers or young adults, were the first for whom arrangements could be made. At the end of August 1939, Siegfried's visa also came through and he too was able to leave just a few days before the outbreak of war. But despite their best efforts, Else Behrend-Rosenfeld's papers did not arrive, and she could not follow her husband. Now stranded in Munich, she took up work as a carer for the Jewish community whose fate—despite her own mixed background and Christian upbringing—she increasingly shared. It was not religious conviction but current identification with a community of fate that counted most at this time.[19]

Families with mixed backgrounds could be deeply divided; the post-1945 distinction that is so easily made between 'Germans' and 'Jews' entirely misses the complex social realities of the period. Erna Albersheim's mother was Jewish, and her father was gentile; she was brought up as a Protestant, with American citizenship. She married a German Jew and took on German citizenship; her husband died, however, in 1932, and she subsequently regained her American citizenship. Her 'Aryan' relatives on her father's side, living in Hamelin, were supporters of Nazism: one aunt had written her a letter saying, 'she had to vote for Hitler because God had sent him to save Germany'.[20] While she was herself counted as a 'first-degree *Mischling*', her daughter was counted as fully Jewish; when they made what she saw as a 'crazy' day trip to Stuttgart to get her American visa in order to emigrate, they found they were unable to eat anywhere or stay anywhere because her daughter was Jewish and not allowed in anywhere except one Jewish restaurant that had a 'sign that the proprietor was only allowed to cater to Jews' and therefore she could not also enter with her daughter.[21]

Verena Hellwig, the 'Aryan' wife of Hans Hellwig, had already emigrated—to protect her family at the time of writing, she does not tell us where—in order to give their 'mixed-breed' son a better chance in life, while her husband and daughter had remained in Germany. In the wake of the Nuremberg Laws, however, Verena and Hans had decided that it would, after all, be better if their daughter Irene could join her mother and brother abroad; as Hans put it in a letter to his wife, 'no child can over time withstand all these humiliations without being psychologically damaged'. A bright child, Irene settled well in her new environment and flourished at school. Now alone in Germany, however, Hans was increasingly isolated, compounded by the fact that he had been given notice and lost his job.

He was further depressed by bad news from friends who had emigrated and moved from one place to another—first Spain, where in 1936 the civil war broke out; then Italy, where they were caught by antisemitic legislation in 1938 as Mussolini belatedly followed in Hitler's footsteps; and finally Havana in the hope of gaining a visa to the United States, which was highly uncertain. Their efforts seemed only to confirm Hans's view that it required more courage to seek a new existence abroad, in a strange environment, than it did to sit things out in Germany. Worse still, though, was the fate of another Jewish friend: although he had been offered a post abroad following release from a concentration camp, his 'strength to live was broken', and he could not summon the will and energy to emigrate.

Over time, Verena Hellwig grew increasingly worried about her husband and felt he should not remain alone. But it was not easy to reconcile their views on what to do. Hans warned Verena against coming back to Germany and told her stories about other mixed marriages confirming his view that their own 'mixed-breed' children 'would have had no future in Germany' and should remain abroad. Yet Verena could not persuade Hans to join them and embark on a new life. From the sparse details she gives in her essay, we cannot be clear about where she was living or the languages that would be needed by her husband if he were to join his family; she only recounts how she was working from dawn to dusk running a small hotel, fearing that Hans would have few prospects if and when he joined her. This fear was confirmed when he came on a brief exploratory visit and found that his language skills were inadequate to find suitable employment. Not only this: their own relationship was strained, their former marital harmony severely challenged by the changes in their roles and circumstances. Hans found Verena 'had aged a lot' and was 'stressed well beyond her capacity to cope' with all the demands of her work. He presumably also felt diminished in his own status. He decided at some point—the dates are left vague—to return to Germany for the time being.[22]

Hans, despite having non-Jewish family connections, appears to have received little help or even solace from his in-laws, and his return did not go well. Verena's 'Aryan' siblings were deeply integrated into the Reich. One brother had now become an army officer, working long hours that left little time for independent thought. In Verena's opinion, he was doing what every German soldier did: 'carrying out orders, without taking a view on them. Obedient, uncritical, brash, the ideal educational product of the new regime.' Her sisters' main complaints seemed to focus on the frequent absences of their respective husbands, 'who were all subjected to systematic training' courses.[23]

Kristallnacht was the shock that finally precipitated Hans Hellwig's departure from Germany to join Verena abroad. As soon as he arrived, she could see that he was not in a good state. He was 'not only physically weakened, but also suffering a total psychological breakdown'. Not long after their reunion, Hans took an overdose. He died after an agonizing week in hospital.[24]

In the winter of 1939, Verena sadly reflected on all she had lost; all her efforts on behalf of her family had been in vain. For years she had lived in a state of acute anxiety, plagued by fear and terror. Yet even now, and despite her husband's suicide, life had to go on. She still wanted to give her children a secure future and new home. But she felt that she herself no longer had any home. Her own '*Heimat* was lost' as 'Germany had fallen silent'.[25]

War and flight

War had only narrowly been averted with the Munich Agreement of September 1938, when the Sudetenland was ceded to the Reich. Yet Hitler was far from satisfied with this territorial gain by peaceful means; he was still intent on expanding German 'living space' and actively pursued his goals through the spring of 1939. Stripped of its former defences, what remained of Czechoslovakia was invaded by German forces in mid-March 1939; the western Czech territories were taken under Nazi rule as the 'Protectorate of Bohemia and Moravia', and a Slovak Republic was established to the east. On 22 March 1939, following a German ultimatum, Lithuania ceded the disputed Baltic territory of Memel (Klaipėda) to Germany. Disputes continued over the Free City of Danzig, in which Nazis held political power, as well as the so-called Polish corridor of formerly German territories. On 31 March 1939, Britain and France guaranteed support for Poland; but Hitler assumed that, given their unwillingness to intercede by force in previous months, they might not act on this guarantee. Even so, this was scarcely an issue for him. The signing of the Molotov-Ribbentrop Pact on 23 August 1939, with its secret protocol agreeing the future division of Polish territory between the Soviet Union and Germany, made it all the easier for Hitler to ignite the war for which he had so long been planning. Britain failed to achieve a diplomatic solution during last-minute negotiations, while Polish hopes for a settlement left its forces relatively unprepared. On the night of 31 August 1939 the Germans staged an incident in the Upper Silesian border city of Gleiwitz (Gliwice), in order to portray their military invasion in the early hours of the morning of 1 September as 'defensive', unleashing what would become the Second World War. Two days after the German invasion of Poland, on 3 September, Britain and France declared war on Germany; two weeks later, on 17 September, the Soviet Union invaded Poland from the east.

Most Germans were initially apprehensive about the prospect of another war but elated by the rapid defeat of Poland in a 'lightning war' (*Blitzkrieg*).[26] The young in particular were heavily swayed by Nazi propaganda. The diary of a teenage girl, Wolfhilde von König, an enthusiastic member of the League of German Maidens (BDM) in Munich, is revealing; she wrote continuously from her early teenage age years through to 1946, when she turned twenty-one and felt she had 'come of age'.[27] The diary entries gain in length and sophistication of expression as she matured, but the almost un-filtered reflection of Nazi ideology barely changes, providing a barometer of how a totally convinced young Nazi could see the world so very differently from the ways in which marginalized others saw developments—from the undecided, through independent-minded and critical spirits, to the perse-cuted. Von König gushed in her diary on 1 September 1939 that the Führer had 'called his people to arms, to protect the German lands and *Heimat* and to defend itself against its enemies'. She joyously recorded Hitler's reference to the new tasks of German youth, so that she and her friends were 'proud and confident about the times that were coming'. In the following days, she recorded the detailed advance of the German troops, as well as violence against 'ethnic Germans' in Poland, with the exaggerated figures in Nazi propaganda about a bloodbath in Bromberg (now Bydgoszcz) giving fur-ther fodder to the myth of a defensive war.[28]

The German invasion and occupation of Poland was marked by violence against civilians going well beyond the accepted rules of warfare. Already in June 1939, before the outbreak of war, the German leadership had drawn up lists of members of the Polish intelligentsia, clergy, political leaders, and others deemed to be a danger; and in early July, Reinhard Heydrich had laid plans for four groups of special squads, or *Einsatzgruppen*, initially made

up of around 2,000 men from the Security Police and Security Service
(SD) of the SS, and authorized by Hitler. Immediately following the invasion, the *Einsatzgruppen* set to work, targeting Polish Jews in an early wave
of organized terror. They set fire to synagogues filled with Jews, who were
burned alive or shot as they tried to escape; they collected Jews in town
squares and subjected them to public humiliation, cutting off men's beards,
forcing them to lie on the ground, and then treading on them; individual
Jews were arrested, injured, shot, or killed in other ways.[29]

In the early and confused days of fighting, many Jews fled in search of
safety further east. Herman Kruk, a librarian steeped in Yiddish culture and
an active member of the Bund socialist party in Warsaw, was among them.
His diary entries describe in horrific detail the chaos, fear, and violence of
the early days of the war, as thousands sought to get out through roads and
forests clogged with people, cars, wagons, and horses; the bodies or limbs of
those who had been hit by snipers or bombs; the sight of villages burning;
the difficulties in finding food and shelter; the exhaustion and chaos of people not knowing which way to turn; whether to return; what route or place
might offer safety. Kruk himself decided to leave Warsaw on 5 September.
He was on the road until finally arriving in Vilna (Vilnius) on 10 October;
there were around 20,000 other Jewish refugees pouring into the city at
this time, hoping to find shelter with the 60,000 Jews already resident there.
Along the way, Kruk heard on 17 September of the Soviet takeover of the
eastern parts of Poland. The choice for fleeing Jews was now between the
Germans and the Bolsheviks.[30]

The division of Poland between the Soviet and German forces took place
along the lines secretly agreed between Molotov and von Ribbentrop in
August. The western areas of Poland were incorporated into the expanded
Greater German Reich, while a rump Polish state, termed the General
Government, was placed under German administration. The Soviet Union
not only occupied the eastern parts of defeated Poland but also established military bases in the independent Baltic states of Estonia, Latvia, and
Lithuania. In a bid to gain acceptance of its military presence, the USSR returned to Lithuania its former capital, Vilnius, by moving the Polish border
and incorporating Vilnius and surrounding territory into Lithuania. This
region had been a bitterly contested part of the recreated state of Poland
since 1922, and Kovno (Kaunas) had been the temporary Lithuanian capital. Building on its new military strength in the area, in 1940 the Soviet

Union annexed the Baltic states and asserted Soviet rule. The destruction of independence and the introduction of communist policies exacerbated social tensions. Jews were now able to take up positions in government and administration previously denied to them; only a few were actually willing to do so, but their presence was highly visible.

The expropriation and confiscation of property in these formerly independent states affected both Jews and non-Jews alike, as did the expulsion of significant numbers to inhospitable camps in the inner reaches of the Soviet Union; in fact, disproportionately more Jews were forcibly deported than non-Jews.[31] Yet, ignoring the fact that the vast majority of Jews were suffering from communist social and economic policies in just the same way as gentiles, nationalist Lithuanians and Latvians highlighted the involvement of some Jews in Soviet rule to spread the antisemitic myth of a supposed 'Judeo-Bolshevist' threat. These experiences in eastern Poland and the Baltic states during the brief period of Soviet rule would play a significant role in antisemitic violence following the German invasion in June 1941.[32]

The early wave of German violence against Jews in Poland was intended less as the start of any policy of extermination—that was yet to come—but rather as a means of instilling terror and precipitating flight. The *Einsatzgruppen* were officially instructed on 21 September 1939 that Jews were to be disposed of by 'concentration, expulsion, and prevention of return'.[33] The policy was intended, in effect, to render German-occupied territory 'Jew-free', and was in this sense a continuation of earlier policies to drive Jews out of the Reich.[34] Those Jews who fled eastwards ultimately had slightly higher survival chances, despite subjection to extremely harsh conditions and often imprisonment in the Soviet Union. These early acts of terror can be seen as a violent continuation of previous policies—now effectively precipitating rapid flight, rather than enforced emigration via bureaucratic hurdles. But they also prefigured and prepared the way for later escalation. The threshold of the unthinkable was being crossed.

Jews were not the only victims, nor were the *Einsatzgruppen* the only perpetrators. Polish priests, intellectuals, and politicians were systematically arrested and murdered; indeed, Polish elites were the primary targets for murder in this early phase of the war. And the cooperation between *Einsatzgruppen* and army, although still marked by occasional friction, was developing. The army was already involved in killing civilians in conjunction with the *Einsatzgruppen* within days of the invasion, sometimes put down, as one official report had it, to 'the marked nervosity everywhere and the desire to shoot (*Schießlust*)'.[35] Early and muted protests by a few army officers about 'partially illegal measures', and disquiet among some soldiers that young SS men were 'proving their courage against defenceless civilians', had little effect.[36] Among soldiers, violence against civilians was not only ideologically inculcated but also exercised in practice. There was an official policy of 'reprisals' against whole communities, including civilians. Inexperienced army recruits were trained to suspect *franc-tireurs* (civilian snipers) everywhere; and they set fire to houses, barns, and whole villages, as spurious acts of 'retaliation' or pre-emptive strikes against supposed partisans.[37] Additionally, members of 'ethnic German self-protection' units (*Volksdeutscher Selbstschutz*) were actively involved in perpetration.

Following the rapid military defeat of Poland, 'racial' principles determined brutal policies at every level. Civilian administrators organized reductions in rations, requisitioned buildings, and instituted curfews and other regulations with serious penalties for any infringement. Ordinary Polish citizens were subjugated and exploited as labourers for the allegedly superior German 'master race'. In this way, the occupiers were putting into practice their perception of 'inferior races' as people to be used or disposed of solely in light of the priorities of the 'master race'. The German community of empathy was, in effect, being narrowed to members of their own national community. Others were seen either as inferior beings to be rendered subservient, or as dangerous enemies, an existential threat to the German national community to be dealt with by any means deemed necessary, including death.

Race and space: Resettlement

Race and space were closely related issues. The German agreement with the Soviet Union entailed the 'repatriation' of ethnic Germans from the expanded Soviet area of domination, including the Baltic states. Heinrich Himmler, Reichsführer of the SS, now took on an additional role as Reich Commissar for the Strengthening of German Ethnic Stock (Reichskommissar für die Festigung deutschen Volkstums, RKFDV) and effectively controlled the distribution of land and people as well as the means of terror. He was supported by his deputy Reinhard Heydrich, who headed the Reich Security Head Office (Reichssicherheitshauptamt, RSHA), established on 27 September 1939 to control and coordinate the work of Nazi Germany's security and police forces.

Policies of 'germanization' and 'the Strengthening of German Ethnic Stock' entailed categorization on 'racial' lines and significant population transfers: moving out the unwanted groups, while retaining and augmenting supposedly 'racially' valuable stock by settling 'ethnic Germans' in place of the forcibly ousted. Arthur Greiser, Gauleiter and Reichsstatthalter of the Wartheland (as the newly incorporated territories of western Poland were now called), put it clearly in a lecture of 1942: if in this war 'a Volk must and wants to survive, then the soil on which the Volk must and wants to live must also belong to the Volk, and it is impossible that another Volk also has space there'.[38] This meant classifying people in 'racial' categories, and massive population transfers. 'Ethnic Germans' from Galicia, Volhynia (an area now straddling Poland and western Ukraine), the Baltic states, and elsewhere were moved into areas to be 'germanized'. Already resident 'ethnic Germans'—frequently including Poles who claimed some German descent and passable acquaintance with German language or culture—were privileged. Individuals who looked as if they were from sufficiently 'Aryan stock' to be worth adding to the collective gene pool were also the subject of special attention, even if this meant taking particularly 'Aryan-looking' children away from their Polish parents, sending them into the 'old Reich', and placing them with Nazi families to develop new identities. Crucially, in addition 'germanization' meant excluding those who did not belong to the Volk, either by expelling them entirely without much thought for their future or subjugating and exploiting them to serve the needs of the 'master race' (variously, *Herrenrasse, Herrenmenschen, Herrenvolk*).

Space was reconfigured in an ambitious and hasty programme marked by repeatedly revised short-range and intermediate plans in light of continually contested long-term strategies. There were the typical rivalries between different Nazi organizations and individuals, including not only Himmler and Heydrich but also other senior Nazis: Hermann Göring, whose economic remit was undermined by Himmler's newly won control of the land; Hans Frank, in charge of the General Government, which had to cope with the influx of the unwanted; the bickering Gauleiters of the newly acquired territories; and Adolf Eichmann, promoted in December 1939 to head the

RSHA section IV B4 dealing with Jewish affairs, despite the failure of his earlier plan to deport Jews from Ostrava and the Katowice district to Nisko at the start of the war. Rapid germanization of annexed areas of Poland was further hampered by practical considerations around how to balance the conflicting needs for labour power, appropriate housing for German incomers, the limited capacity of Reich rail transport, and the needs of the army, in the context of different views in principle on the relative priority of antisemitic goals, economic productivity, and ethnic German resettlement.[39]

Despite being improvised, haphazard, often self-contradictory, the enforced population transfers that now took place had a massive impact. Around 1 million people were removed from their homes, farmsteads, and livelihoods. In the process, the civilian administration worked hand in hand with the SS and police forces, just as the army and the *Einsatzgruppen* cooperated in terror. Ghettoization of Jews began, with the major ghettos of Warsaw and Litzmannstadt (Łódź) established in 1940. Numerous other, smaller, and often unfenced ghettos were established, concentrating Jews in cramped and unhygienic conditions, living on minimal rations, and subjected to draconian punishments for infringement of new regulations. Members of the civilian administration of annexed and occupied territories would later, like the army, paint their own compromised pasts as entirely clean, laying all the blame on the organizations charged with responsibility for 'excessive' physical violence and choosing to ignore the crucial role that their own administration of Jewish housing, employment, and food provisions had played in restriction of human rights, heightened mortality from disease and malnutrition, and eventually ease of deportation and death.[40]

What of those who had, years before, been bystanders to Nazi policies, observing and variously criticizing or applauding from a distance? Faraway from the events, the young teenager in Munich, Wolfhilde von König, was sufficiently enthused or interested to note the resettlement of Baltic Germans in her diary: on 16 November 1939 she recorded the arrival in Danzig of ships carrying Baltic Germans, coming to 'resettle in their real homeland', and on 2 December she noted that the 'return home' of the Baltic Germans had been completed and would now be followed by the settlement in the won-back territories of the 'German east'.[41] She made no mention whatsoever of the impact of this resettlement on those who had been forcibly expelled from their homes. Those who were more directly involved could less easily overlook this—but even here, it was possible to practise 'looking away', not seeing the victims of Nazi policies but registering only the positive aspects for their own community. Complicity could in this way be combined with a sense of personal innocence.

Some ethnic Germans who were now involved in resettlement policies insisted on seeing this as a question of patriotic duty to their fatherland and obedience to the wishes of their Führer, rather than motivated by personal interests, as illustrated in the case of Jürgen Ernst Kroeger.[42] At the outbreak of war, Kroeger, a Baltic German farming what remained of his family's estate in Wiexten (Vecumnieki) in Latvia, enthusiastically discussed the new situation with his wife Gerda. Returning from a brief visit to relatives in Riga, Gerda reported that 'everyone was ecstatic about the great German victory in Poland'. Along with others in their rural area, the Kroegers sat listening to the radio every day, marvelling at rapid German victories, certain that the war would soon be over, and making plans for an extension to their house. But they were more ambivalent about subsequent developments. They were deeply concerned to hear that the Russians had obtained agreement to establishing military bases on the Baltic coast in Estonia and then also in Latvia.

One day their 'Apple Jew' (*Apfeljude*)—a Jewish boy who came to help with sorting and packing the fruit from their orchard—suddenly asked them whether, since the Bolsheviks would soon be coming to Latvia, they would consider relocating to Germany. Kroeger 'of course indignantly replied that he would not'.[43] But soon after, Kroeger went on, 'something totally unexpected occurred', something he could not ignore: 'The Führer held a speech and announced the resettlement into the Reich of all ethnic German groups living in the East'. In a flurry of activity, racing from discussions with one acquaintance to another, Kroeger and his wife agonized over what they should do. A neighbouring landowner and leading personality, one 'Baron H. in Linden', advised him to sell up and heed the call to resettlement. Following resettlement, Baron H. continued, everyone capable of bearing arms should join the army or the SS as a sign of their gratitude to the Führer.[44]

Kroeger and his wife discussed the pros and cons intensively. 'It is difficult', Kroeger ruminated, 'to come to the right decision, particularly since for years we Baltic Germans have had it hammered into us that we should stick it out in our *Heimat*. Now, from one day to the next, there should be a one hundred and eighty degree turn. We are enthusiastic supporters of the Führer and love Germany as our Fatherland. But this is our *Heimat*, and we are firmly bound to the soil.' They went back and forth in their discussions, weighing up conflicting considerations and emotions: 'We farmers have always made huge sacrifices to be able to stick it out in the *Heimat* on the soil we have inherited. Townspeople did not always understand us, and sometimes they even laughed at us a little pityingly. Not long ago I still thought that no one could drag us away from our soil, and now it is precisely the Führer who is ordering us to go away, although not into nothing, but rather into the arms of the powerful Fatherland.' Turning it over and over, the Kroegers finally came to the view that, as good Germans committed to the national community, it was their duty to respond to the Führer's call to come 'home into the Reich' (*heim ins Reich*).[45]

The Kroegers' journey, arrival, and resettlement in the Warthegau were eventful, but Jürgen Ernst Kroeger was ultimately, he felt, one of the luckier ones. They were first put up in a provisional camp in a former Polish school in Posen (Poznań). The town, which had been German before the loss of territory in the Versailles Treaty, had well-stocked shops and made a good impression on Kroeger. As a Baltic German and former landowner, he found he was entitled to choose any property he liked from those now available in the new Gau districts of Danzig–West Prussia and the Wartheland; and in the meantime, he and his wife were given an apartment in Posen. This home, he noted, must have been vacated very suddenly by its previous inhabitants: 'There were plates laid out on the dining table, and in the kitchen there was a dish of potatoes that had been peeled.' He was later told that the former occupants had been deported in large transports into the General Government, and 'no one knows what will become of them'. Beyond this, he did not seem to feel any need to comment; his passing hint of sympathy with their unknown fate seems not to have led to any deeper reflection.[46]

Within the next couple of days, Kroeger met up with Gunter, an old friend who was now in a nearby resettlement camp, and they set out to search for suitable properties together. Despite snowy conditions, they lost little time, hoping to snap up a good estate before others could get there. Not everything they witnessed was as it should be, but, typically for so many Germans at this time, Kroeger made a clear distinction between Hitler himself and any injustices or improprieties taking place on the ground. He was highly critical of Nazis who were, in his view, going too far, although 'every revolution brings to the surface a range of adventurers without a conscience, and unscrupulous careerists'. He saw himself and his friend Gunter as people who had pangs of conscience and could distinguish between good and bad. Summarizing an early discussion with Gunter, Kroeger commented: 'He believes in the Führer, just as I do. He resettled because his conscience bade him to, just as I did. Why do things have to happen here in the Warthegau that we as decent people can't understand? What can we do against this?'

Nonetheless, the latter question was clearly not of immediate concern to them—and may indeed only have been added in Kroeger's postwar publication, supposedly reproducing diary entries from the time but clearly influenced by the need to present himself in the light of a later moral framework.[47] Leaving their philosophical discussions about what they could potentially 'do against this' hanging in the air, Kroeger and his friend continued their search for desirable properties. Critique of the unacceptable behaviour of individual Nazis was a way of reinforcing their own sense of themselves, by contrast, as 'decent' people. This (very typical) individualization of morality was perfectly compatible with blindness to the fundamental immorality of the system as a whole—a system which they supported in principle and from which they were perfectly happy to benefit.

Kroeger's descriptions of his subsequent travails in finding and settling on a landed estate, his relations with his new neighbours, his farmworkers, and the local Nazi officials, reveal a characteristically bounded moral universe. He encountered those towards whom he warmed personally, and others whom he disliked; he evaluated individual personality attributes without querying the wider system in which they were all playing their respective roles. Nor did he spare much thought for those at whose expense they were claiming their new homes and possessions. Although his somewhat idiosyncratic germanized spellings of Polish place names do not allow complete certainty about his location, it is highly likely from his description that what he calls 'Podbice' refers to what is now Poddębice. A ghetto was created here in November 1940 for the 1,400 Jews of the town, as well as a further 600 Jews displaced from their homes in the surrounding area; conditions in the ghetto were sufficiently disgusting—overcrowding, stench, disease— as to trouble even the Nazi civilian administrator, Franz Bock, who was eventually stripped of his NSDAP membership and lost his job because of refusal to demonstrate sufficient conformity.[48] When the ghetto was finally cleared in 1942, the Jews were sent to the nearby extermination camp of Chełmno—currently a half hour's drive from Poddębice—where they were gassed. Yet we get no mention of the ghettoized Jews in Kroeger's account. His little world is entirely made up of 'decent' Germans, as contrasted with unpleasant and less moral Germans, and subjugated Poles. Anecdotes either serve to set himself in a good light, or naïvely record the world as he saw it through ideological blinkers that he suggests were perfectly justified at the time. His imagined community of empathy did not extend beyond those with whom he could identify. Kroeger's capacity to ignore the impact on Jewish victims of expulsions would prove even more useful when, on his return to Latvia nearly two years later, it came to ignoring also the victims of extermination.

Ignoring the victims entirely was less feasible when this was the direct subject of an interview, as was the case with Martha Michelsohn, interviewed by the French documentary filmmaker Claude Lanzmann in the summer of 1979 in Laage—a town near Rostock in what was, at the time of the interview, still the communist GDR.[49] Being interviewed leaves far less leeway for easy selective omission, and though Michelsohn displays some similar attitudes to Kroeger, she cannot avoid paying more explicit attention to the plight of the Jews—not least because they had been herded into gas vans in sight of her own house. During the Third Reich, Michelsohn had been a young woman enthusiastic about the adventure of going east and had volunteered to help resettlers in the Chełmno area, where she arrived in December 1939. Michelsohn's husband was, like Kroeger, a Baltic German from Latvia. Born in Riga, he too had answered the call to come 'home into the Reich' and took up a post as a schoolteacher in Chełmno; he was also head of the National Socialist People's Welfare organization (NSV) in the area. He apparently did not feel any guilt about his role in building up the Reich, even at the expense of those who were at this time being 'resettled'.

From December 1941 onwards, organized gassing of Jews by exhaust pipes redirected into vans started at Chełmno, the first static extermination camp to come into operation. From their house, the Michelsohns could see members of the Sonderkommando working, hear the terrible screams and cries, and smell the fumes. Martha Michelsohn claimed they had been outraged and upset that they had to witness all this but were impotent against the SS; furthermore, people back in the *Altreich*—the 'old

Reich'—dismissed what they thought were just atrocity tales. She also recalled that the Poles were pleased about the removal of Jews, claiming (in line with the Nazi slogan) that the Jews had brought them 'misfortune', and benefitting from their abandoned clothing. The Michelsohns did not question their own roles and mission in service of Nazi policies and the Volksgemeinschaft.

The situation looked very different from the perspective of those being moved out of their homes, and also to some within the 'old Reich' who cared about the fates of fellow human beings in distress.

Conflicting communities of empathy

Ghettoization and flight enforced by terror were soon supplemented by organized deportations—including the first expulsion of German Jews from the Reich itself. In this context, passive bystanding was no longer an option: people had to make decisions between more active complicity, wilful benefitting, or various forms of refusal, including small acts of resistance, rescue, or retreat.

As elsewhere, Jews living in the southwest German state of Baden were subjected to ever worsening living conditions. In the village of Gailingen, Jews were moved out of their houses and squeezed into inadequate and overcrowded accommodation with other Jews, who were understandably often resentful towards the newcomers taking over parts of their houses; whole families squeezed into single rooms, some only finding space in the Jewish old people's home and the hospital.

Betty Frieslander-Bloch later provided a detailed account of her experiences at this time.[50] The hours in which they were permitted to go shopping were severely restricted, and the areas in which they were allowed to take a walk were reduced to a minimum, just around the Jewish cemetery. Meanwhile, 'Aryans', who in previous decades had lived together relatively harmoniously with their Jewish neighbours, began to take over Jewish property: Nazis 'requisitioned' their houses, and furniture or possessions that Jews had been unable to squeeze into their new accommodations were auctioned off at knock-down prices to other locals. Jews had also been forced to hand over bicycles, cars, radios, and other possessions. Gangs of Nazi youths had free rein to terrorize them. Even when Jews were seeking security walking in the grounds of the Jewish hospital and old people's home, young people bombarded them with stones and rotten fruit. On Sundays, when there was little else to occupy them, Hitler Youth gangs roamed around, spitting at Jews, cursing them, singing antisemitic Nazi songs, and, if they were on bicycles, making as if to run Jews over. All the efforts of Frieslünder-Bloch to obtain emigration papers, along with her husband and their small son, were in vain. They simply tried to sit it out and await their fate.

On 22 October 1940 the Frieslünder-Bloch family, along with other Jews in Baden and the Palatinate (the Pfalz, a region in the west of Germany), were forced to sign documents 'voluntarily' giving up all claim to their possessions and were deported to the camp of Gurs, in southern France. Photographs of the village of Gailingen show this deportation taking place in full view of other local people, who stood and watched as their former neighbours, friends, colleagues, employers, and schoolmates were bundled into the awaiting vehicles. The whole village, Frieslünder-Bloch recalled, was 'already full of trucks and gaping spectators'. The SS men who were masterminding the deportation had mostly been sent in from the nearby town of Radolfzell. On the steps of the town hall—where in the late nineteenth century a Jewish mayor had been in charge—stood the current acting mayor, dressed in 'the style of Mussolini', and accompanied by an official photographer. He addressed a cynical farewell to Frieslünder-Bloch's husband: 'So Frieslünder, now you're off to the Promised Land!' With this departing shot, amidst the passive silence or tacit approval of most bystanders, as well as the occasional stone thrown by the more enthusiastic Nazi supporters, the Frieslünder-Blochs and their small son were squeezed into a 'cage-like' truck headed for the trains to the camp.

Frieslünder-Bloch's husband did not survive the dreadful conditions in Gurs. The vast majority of those who did make it through the first couple of years there were then put on trains to the east, many of them dying eventually in the gas chambers of Auschwitz. Very few managed, liked Frieslünder-Bloch and her son, to survive. In 1970, when she gave her testimony, Frieslünder-Bloch was particularly bitter about the total failure of her former neighbours to intervene on their behalf or even to show any sympathy or support. Indeed, she recalled, the worst Nazis among the 'Aryans' had been not the Hitler Youth, but members of the women's organizations, people whom she knew by name; and 'today', she added, 'they all claim they were not there'. None of them 'showed any shame or regret' for their abominable actions.[51]

These were probably the most typical responses of the German majority who later claimed to have been merely bystanders, echoing the refrain that they had 'known nothing about it'. Not all actively joined in the humiliation of Jews or showed hostility; most simply looked on passively, whether with approval or perhaps a sense of powerlessness and shock. Yet whatever their feelings towards the deported Jews, significant numbers of 'Aryans' actively and knowingly benefitted from their forcibly abandoned possessions; the number of beneficiaries is immense.

A tiny minority of people refused to remain passive bystanders or to become beneficiaries but rather now attempted, in a variety of ways, to assist those of their compatriots who were being persecuted.

In the winter of 1939–1940, Else Behrend-Rosenfeld and other Jews in Munich started to receive news of Jews being expelled from Posen—the 'German' town that had so impressed Jürgen Ernst Kroeger—to 'resettlement' in terrible conditions in the General Government. They then heard, through the Munich rabbi Bruno Finkelscherer, whose brother Herbert was a rabbi in Stettin, that German Jews from Stettin had been deported as a group on 12 February 1940 to Lublin and the surrounding villages of Piaski, Belzyce, and Glusk. A non-Jewish wife who was deported with her Jewish husband wrote an account of their experiences in this deportation and resettlement action, which she sent to contacts in Munich. She and her husband had already managed to send their five 'mixed-race' children abroad, in order 'to protect them from the brutality in school'; what she and her husband now faced was infinitely worse.[52]

The switch to enforced 'resettlement' was, in effect, another crucial turning point in Nazi policies towards Jews within the Reich. Up until now, by creating a hostile environment in which it was barely possible to live, Nazis had been forcing Jews into emigration. But now, unwilling emigration was replaced by enforced expulsion. Moreover, deportation was into inhospitable circumstances where the likely outcome would be starvation, disease, and ultimately, for many, death. This prefigured the shift, over the following year and a half, to contemplating more 'efficient' ways of speeding up the fatal outcome.

Hearing of this development, it was clear to Else Behrend-Rosenfeld and others in Munich that, despite their own difficulties, they must stay in contact with the deported Jews and send not only letters but also packages that might help in small practical ways. Subterfuge as well as the assistance of non-Jews was urgently needed. Else Behrend-Rosenfeld contacted Quaker friends who had a reputation for helping people in need. But the operation of sending packages depended on the involvement of many more individuals. Sending essential clothing, equipment, and medical supplies was not easy, and they were far from certain that desired scarce goods would actually arrive intact at the intended destination. People packing up the parcels therefore tried to make things look old and unusable, knowing that otherwise they would likely be confiscated or stolen along the way. They often cut apart good winter coats and other valuable clothing, and sent the different sections—sleeves, collars, front, back—in separate parcels, while letters conveyed instructions about how to sew them together again. Similarly, they decanted urgently needed medical supplies into anonymous containers, marked only by numbers, and separately sent codes to explain what numbers corresponded with which medications.

Innumerable volunteers were engaged in surreptitious support networks. They were mainly not themselves Jewish; and indeed only non-Jews were actually allowed to send money to the East, under the pretext of sending contributions to 'Aryan' relatives in support of the germanization effort. In Munich alone, anonymous volunteers managed to send around one hundred packages every week, through different post offices and using different 'Aryan' names for the senders—a significant effort, and one that made a real difference to the recipients in terms of both practical and moral support.[53]

Not only immediate practical assistance but also moral support was offered. Signs of friendship and concern were vitally important to the beleaguered Jews. A Quaker, Margarethe Lachmund, had been working for the Church Aid Office for Protestant Non-Aryans in Pomerania, in the wake of the violence of November 1938. She now engaged in sending parcels, keeping up personal correspondence over many months with individuals she had never met personally, and intervening wherever she could on their behalf.[54] This work went way beyond the remit of her job: Lachmund tried to help all those in distress, whether or not they were 'Protestant Non-Aryans'. Erich and Cläre Silbermann, for example, were Jewish by both religious commitment and descent. They had earlier moved from Anklam to Stettin, and were among those first deported to Bełżyce near Lublin, and subsequently to the Trawniki work camp. They exchanged letters with Lachmund from 3 April 1940 right through to 25 June 1943, when Lachmund lost all trace of them. It is not hard to imagine what fate befell them at this time, when the extermination camps in Poland had been in full swing for well over a year—and apart from providing a degree of solace, there was little more at this point that Lachmund could have done for them.[55]

Despite its exceptional nature, one of Lachmund's cases illuminates both the complexities of the situation and the need to compromise and appear to conform in order to subvert Nazi policies. Lachmund intervened actively with the authorities on behalf of a 'Frau A.G.' She was born and bred a Christian, but had converted to Judaism before getting married in 1913, out of respect for her future mother-in-law; she was, in a sense, an 'Aryan Jew' rather than a 'Protestant non-Aryan'. The children of this mixed marriage were, as they grew up, drawn more to Christianity than Judaism; but they had not completed the process of conversion before the promulgation of the Nuremberg Laws, so they were categorized as 'counting as Jewish' (*Geltungsjuden*). The daughter's engagement to an 'Aryan' had been seen by the Nazi authorities as a case of 'racial defilement' (*Rassenschande*), for which she was incarcerated in Ravensbrück, but she was lucky enough to have been released and was able to emigrate in May 1939.

Frau A.G. herself, her husband, and their son, Adolf—born at a time when this name did not yet have the connotations it would soon acquire—were far less fortunate. They were arrested during the night of 11–12 February 1940 and deported from Stettin along with other Jews, eventually arriving in Piaski, near Lublin. Here they lived in terrible conditions; Frau A.G. did her best to keep their spirits up, although this was difficult. Adolf was put to forced labour and there was a rapid decline in her husband's health, despite the packages they received from both Lachmund and their daughter. Frau A.G.'s letters are full of attempts to take pleasure in little things: she had work mending shoes; she was able to celebrate her birthday by buying some bread rolls and was given a present of beans; she repeatedly professed her faith in God. But her husband was weakening and suffered a series of heart attacks; in early February 1941, just under a year after their arrest and deportation, he died. At the same time, living conditions were worsening: the ghetto was becoming ever more overcrowded; she was forbidden from walking out of the ghetto area to visit her husband's grave; and her son was ill from the conditions in which he was forced to work, on inadequate food rations, standing knee-deep in freezing water all day.

The letters between Frau A.G. and Margarethe Lachmund would, remarkably, continue for more than another year, effectively telling people within the Reich just how terrible conditions had become. In her letters of March 1942, Frau A.G. was becoming increasingly desperate, noting that people were being taken from the ghetto and not returning, and registering that she herself was losing strength, both physically and mentally, and felt unable to keep going much longer.[56] By the summer of 1942, she was desperately seeking some way to return to the Reich. She argued that, since she was herself of purely 'Aryan' descent and now a widow, no longer married to a Jew, she should no longer 'count as Jewish'. But all their property had previously been confiscated as 'Jewish', so she was entirely lacking in means, and she was also insistent that her son, a 'first-degree *Mischling*' (*jüdischer Mischling ersten Grades*), should be released with her. Frau A.G.'s letters through the summer betrayed occasional glimmers of hope, but on 25 September 1942 she noted difficulties. Her last letter was dated 2 October, saying she and her son would go to Lublin in pursuit of their efforts to sort out documentation. After this, all traces of Frau A.G. and her son Adolf were lost. On 9 October 1942, Himmler ordered all remaining Jews to be collected in concentration camps for the Final Solution; in mid-October 1942, Lublin was officially declared 'Jew-free'.[57]

Frau A.G. had a blind sister, Frau S., who was increasingly desperate about her whereabouts, and whom Lachmund also sought to help. Their letters trying to contact Frau A.G. were however returned, stamped with the phrase '*Unbekannt wohin gezogen*' ('moved to unknown destination'). Lachmund continued her efforts, approaching relevant authorities in Germany on behalf of Frau S., who was further concerned by the fact that her own two sons were both soldiers, away fighting at the front. Knowing Lachmund, it is unlikely that she entirely agreed with her own tactical phrasing, but she deployed all her rhetorical skills to appeal to official representatives of the fatherland at war: 'if only the authorities knew how the life of a mother of soldiers is being destroyed, they would do everything in their power, as fast as possible, to rectify the terrible fate of Frau G. and her son.'[58] Needless to say, this appeal was fruitless.

These cases illustrate the ways in which by 1942 German society had, by the development of extreme racism, been completely torn apart at the seams, completing a process begun almost a decade earlier. The fact that the brother of the Munich rabbi was a rabbi in Stettin, one of the first communities to be affected by deportation from the Reich and ghettoization in the General Government, was clearly important in stimulating the initial attempts at help. A wider sense of a common collective identity, or concern for fellow Jews subjected to persecution, was also important. But even without specifically personal or Jewish connections, strong religious and moral beliefs could help a person to quell fears of the consequences of stepping out of line, as in the case of Margarethe Lachmund. A sense of obligation to the weak and dispossessed could arise from explicit political or religious convictions, or from a far wider sense of common humanity and empathy with those who were suffering.

Some cases of individuals who engaged in active attempts to challenge the Nazi regime are well known: Hans and Sophie Scholl and the 'White Rose' group in Munich; or Georg Elser, the lone carpenter who in 1939 single-handedly hollowed out a pillar in the Munich Beer Hall where Hitler always spoke on the anniversary of the 1923 putsch, and whose attempt failed solely because on this occasion Hitler left the premises early, before the bomb exploded. All three of these, and many others engaged in active resistance, paid with their lives. But there were many more who felt uneasy about the way things were developing at this time, and who, like the Scholls or Elser, certainly 'knew' more than enough to want to act in some way.

We do not know exactly who the hundred or so additional volunteers in Munich and others elsewhere might have been, those individuals who were prepared to take the risk of sending parcels of clothing, medical supplies, and money to beleaguered deportees huddled in misery in the General Government. Some volunteers may have been discomfited at the disjuncture between their own relative privilege and the sufferings of others, and—as with donors to good causes today—may have felt better if they were able to act in some way, however small, to help people, even those faraway whom they did not know personally. Unlike people who were paid to assist Jews in hiding or trying to escape (and some of whom also betrayed the very same Jews when rewarded more handsomely by the Gestapo), these hidden helpers in Munich and elsewhere had no personal reward—not even that of 'virtue signalling', or the recognition provided by public acknowledgement of major donors and charitable benefactors today. Giving was risky, clandestine, yet possibly far more widespread than we realize.

Most of those who felt inner opposition to Nazism were, however, far more cautious. Many felt they were in such a small minority that they could barely dare to express their thoughts, let alone act on them. Friedrich Kellner, for example, who kept a detailed diary of his thoughts and feelings alongside a record of daily events during the war, commented on 6 October 1939 that people who, like himself, 'did not for a moment agree with such politics' were, in his view, 'such small handfuls within the abyss they had to live like hermits'. After expressing his thoughts in his diary, he would often add words to the effect that 'for precaution, I only thought that'; and he repeatedly reminded himself, as he wrote about policies and opinions with which he disagreed, that 'to be safe I have to restrain myself' and 'I have to let all this go for now'. Clearly his diary was an outlet for opinions that he dared not voice.[59]

A quite different sense of collective identity and community was significant for Jürgen Ernst Kroeger and other ethnic German resettlers who streamed 'home into the Reich' on Hitler's bidding. They seem to have experienced no ethical qualms about asserting their domination over the land and possessions wrenched from others. The supposed interests of the German Volk took priority. They still lived within a moral universe in which it was possible to distinguish between 'decent' people and other individuals at a personal level, but this universe was relevant only within their strictly bounded community of empathy. Many hundreds of thousands of people actively supported germanization efforts across Europe in wartime. Their numbers massively outweigh the few brave souls who felt their moral obligations should lead them in a quite different direction. It is not easy to develop precise estimates of the tiny numbers who may have assisted Jews once deportations from the Reich started in earnest from October 1941. By this time, the division of German society and the segregation of German Jews had become ever more visible.

The yellow star

In September 1941, all Jews over the age of six in the Greater German Reich were forced to wear a yellow star on their clothing, bearing the word

'Jew' in mock Hebraic lettering—'so that no one could fall into the mistake of thinking these might be Aryans who had been designated as quite exceptional', as the former librarian, Hermann Stresau, sitting quietly in 'inner emigration' Göttingen, commented somewhat sarcastically into his diary.[60]

Else Behrend-Rosenfeld had also noted these developments, from a far more involved situation. Not having written her diary for over a month, she started her diary entry of Sunday, 21 September 1941, by saying she barely knew where to begin. She recounted her own experiences and those of fellow inmates of the 'Jewish house' (*Judenhaus*) in Berg am Laim, Munich, where they were now forced to live. It had been like a 'slap in the face' for them to be told to wear the Jewish star. But, she went on, most people they met in the streets tried to pretend they did not see the star. Occasionally someone on a tram would express satisfaction that the 'Jewish pack' were finally being recognized in this way; but more often there were expressions of sympathy and disgust about the new measure. Some of Behrend-Rosenfeld's fellow residents were given little presents by sympathetic Germans, including a soldier on leave who handed over his own bread ration card for the week. The butcher and dairy supplier to the home, both 'cursing mightily about this humiliation' of Jews, said they would now deliver additional food and milk. Jewish reactions were mixed, as they tried to maintain their self-respect even while wearing the stigmatizing badge. Many could be seen walking the streets 'with stony faces' or 'hanging their heads', but some, including Behrend-Rosenfeld herself, 'proudly kept their heads held high'. Behrend-Rosenfeld thought it was worse for children who were just old enough to have to wear the star, and frequently observed fights. On one occasion two boys, around seven years old, were being beaten up by an 'Aryan' of roughly the same age. On another occasion, an elderly gentleman intervened, swearing and tearing two boys apart; he then accompanied the tearful victim back to his home.

Behrend-Rosenfeld still felt the Nazis would not achieve the desired effect in Munich, where she thought people would be unwilling to go along with the degradation of the Jews. Nevertheless, she added sadly, it was still far too early to be sure. A month later, on Sunday, 26 October 1941, she confided hopefully in her diary that many 'Aryans' were still acting as though they did not see the yellow star; some showed friendly gestures in public, and even more did so in private. Expressions of contempt and hatred were, in her experience, rare.[61]

The Nazi regime also kept a close eye on public reactions—and their official reports had a tendency to overemphasize what they saw as positive developments. On 9 October 1941 the Security Service (SD) of the SS claimed that 'the overwhelming majority of the population greeted the proclamation about the marking of the Jews, and were all the more gratified since for many this had been long awaited'. It was, in their view, only among 'Catholic and bourgeois circles' that 'lone voices had been raised in sympathy'. Nazis typically projected their own suppressed sense of guilt onto others by claiming that they were acting in pre-emptive self-defence and fearing 'that Germans living in enemy territories abroad would be branded with a swastika and subjected to repressive measures'. More widely, the SD reported, 'people were surprised to register just how many Jews there still are in Germany'.[62]

Other sources suggest that, across the Reich, reactions were mixed. Survivors remember—often with gratitude, but also ambivalence—specific occasions when individuals showed solidarity and sympathy, offering their seats to Jews in crowded buses and trams, or surreptitiously making little gifts of food.[63] But numerous Germans used the introduction of the yellow star as an opportunity to express hostility towards the now clearly marked targets of officially legitimized discrimination. In accounts written in the Soviet zone of occupied Germany after the war, victims of Nazi persecution vividly recalled how some people had watched carefully to see whether Germans of Jewish descent were partially covering their stars by holding an arm or a briefcase across their chest. One person knew of five Jews who had been caught and sent to Auschwitz as a result of denunciations made in this way. Another, a Christian of Jewish descent, recounted that when wearing the star he was frequently subjected to ridicule and humiliation. On one occasion, he was attacked by a young man who screamed at him: 'you accursed Jews are the guilty ones, that there is a war and that we have nothing to eat'. He was 'thrown backwards onto the ground, and grabbed tightly around his neck' so that he nearly died by strangulation, and was then punched in the face, leaving him with a swollen black eye and the loss of two teeth. On this account, it would seem that the young aggressor was taking out more general pent-up frustration on a now visibly designated and officially legitimated scapegoat. The incident also demonstrates a depth of feeling that was not simple or one-dimensional: it was possible to be angry about the war and accompanying food shortages, and at the same time to have deeply internalized the Nazi worldview and ideological message that this was all the fault of the 'accursed Jews'.[64]

The majority of Germans, however, observed the introduction of the yellow star impassively. Perhaps they were fearful of being seen to express reactions of sympathy; or perhaps they felt merely passing curiosity, soon tempered by indifference to the victims.[65] The teenage BDM enthusiast in Munich, Wolfhilde von König, did not even consider it sufficiently important to mention in her diary during these months, while she noted the fates of all manner of significant Nazis and the pleasure she took in her Nazi-related activities, including singing and marching through Munich, which strengthened her sense of community belonging.[66] No doubt she would have approved in principle, had she even noticed the development.

Contemporaries did not find it easy to gauge the reactions of the wider population. In Berlin the journalist Ruth Andreas-Friedrich noted hopefully in her diary that 'the greater part of the people are not pleased with the new decree. Almost everyone we meet is as much ashamed as we'. She went on to suggest that 'even the children's jeering has little to do with serious anti-Semitism'. But the immediate significance of the measure was self-evident: it served to separate German Jews ever more sharply from the rest of German society; it was, in short, a form of individual ghettoization. As Andreas-Friedrich commented: 'The yellow star makes segregation easier. It lights the way into the darkness—the darkness called the ghetto.'[67] The Dresden philologist Victor Klemperer even thought that the yellow star actually 'completed' the ghettoization of Jews: whereas previously the word ghetto had referred only to places where Jews were made to live together, segregated from non-Jews—as in the Litzmannstadt ghetto—now 'every starred Jew carried his or her own ghetto around like a snail carries its house'.[68] As soon became clear, it was not merely to ghettos that Jews were being deported. It was to their deaths.

Whatever people felt, this marked a new stage in the relations between Jewish and non-Jewish Germans. As the Nazi-controlled press emphasized, the marking of Jews in this way would now make it impossible for Jews to secretly infiltrate 'German' society or to 'live in the German Volksgemeinschaft disguised in the mask of an honest, upright citizen'.[69] To ensure that the separation between Jewish and non-Jewish Germans was complete, on 24 October 1941, the RSHA announced that any 'German-blooded person' who continued to maintain friendly relationships with

Jews would be subjected to strong measures, including arrest and potential imprisonment.[70] Germans had themselves spontaneously been dropping their informal friendships with fellow citizens of Jewish descent ever since 1933; now, there was an explicit legal ban even on the nebulous and ill-defined area of friendship, accompanied by designated punishment. The separation of communities of empathy was sealed in law.

Once the country was at war, there was a stark and ever more radical choice between commitment to the national cause and continued concern for the ousted and persecuted. What determined whether individuals went one way or the other? A sense of identification with a particular community, particularly if there were personal connections, was important. So, too, was a degree of individual certainty about right and wrong, and unwillingness simply to go along with the opinions that prevailed among the majority. But people's views could take many forms and lead in different directions.

In the peacetime years, many 'Aryan' members of the 'national community' had managed to combine growing complicity in systemic racism with continuing gestures of humanity towards individuals who were marginalized and excluded. It had already been difficult to try to remain, in effect, a neutral bystander: it was increasingly only possible to be a compromised participant, acting in one way, waving in another. But in wartime, citizens were faced with far more difficult choices: between mobilization in service of the national cause, with its increasingly radical policies; conformity that could easily become more active complicity; or ever more risky attempts to support those who were being persecuted, including people who were, already from the winter of 1939–1940, being deported and ghettoized in the first steps on the road to mass murder. Attempts to balance conflicting interests and values—self-preservation, integration in a national community, a continuing sense of oneself as a decent person—and justifying morally difficult choices were far from easy, as people took very different directions. The vast majority of people included in the Nazi Volksgemeinschaft were effectively now drawn into some form of complicity, and from there it was a small step towards more active involvement in perpetration.

9

Over the Precipice

From Persecution to Genocide
in the Baltics

The extermination camps in Poland—especially Auschwitz-Birkenau, but also Chełmno, Majdanek, and the 'Reinhard camps' of Bełżec, Sobibór, and Treblinka—have been in the spotlight as far as public perception of the Holocaust is concerned. These camps were concentrated factories of death: places for the most 'efficient' killing of the largest number of people with minimal numbers of staff, separating killers from victims by gassing rather than shooting, and in various ways camouflaged from wider view. It was particularly to Auschwitz-Birkenau that Jews from across Europe were brought; and because it was linked to an extensive complex of slave labour camps, prisoners from many countries managed to survive to tell of their experiences, eventually turning 'Auschwitz' into a metonym for the Holocaust across the world. Yet more deaths were caused in the face-to-face killings from the summer of 1941 across the Eastern Front than in the gas chambers of Birkenau. And Eastern Europe was where incidents of terrorization and isolated massacres turned into organized genocide. In the months following the German invasion of the Soviet Union, around 2 million Jews, Roma, communist functionaries, and people with mental and physical disabilities were murdered here.[1] The overwhelming majority were shot, often quite close to the places where they lived and worked, and often by people who knew them, while small numbers were killed using mobile gas vans. Tens of thousands of Jews from other places were also shot in selected locations here, once deportations from the Reich began in October 1941 and before the opening of the dedicated death camps in Poland.[2]

Massacres across Eastern Europe took place in the open—in fields, forests, ravines, villages, and some larger killing sites in or near towns. Mass shootings involved significant numbers of perpetrators, and the Germans frequently 'requisitioned' local people to assist with the logistics, by providing materials for fencing in ghetto areas, construction assistance for death pits, trucks for transport to and from killing sites, meals and refreshments for the killers, and cleaning up after the event. Local people not merely knew and often watched what was going on: some helped to identify and round up local Jews, or even assisted in the shootings; and many benefitted materially by appropriating some of the property of victims.[3]

These killings in the East also marked a crucial step in the process through which Germans sought to distance themselves from personal responsibility: to make themselves 'innocent bystanders'. People made distinctions between those doing the killing—portrayed as the truly guilty—and their own roles. Practices of both 'knowing'—indeed 'doing'—yet simultaneously refusing to register the significance of what they were seeing and doing, could sustain the fiction of 'ignorance'. 'Ignoring' required effort. This willed and conscious self-distancing, practised by some even on the very edge of the pits into which Jews were shot, was a crucial element in the formation of a bystander society on the brink of the abyss.

Self-conscious self-deception was accompanied by the attempt to deceive others. In fact, deception came in several forms. The victims were deceived at every turn to ensure maximum cooperation on the path to their deaths. Stories of 'resettlement' or being taken to a 'work camp' were intended to ensure docility and prevent unrest that could sabotage the orderly pursuit of mass murder. This was not always possible, as people became aware of the fate that awaited them and struggled or resisted. Deception was also used to reframe—often literally, through the camera lens—the images and perceptions of those responsible for murder. And then there was the self-aware self-deception, central to the formation of a bystander society, which made it easier for all Germans not to feel too bad about what was being done in their name—or what they themselves were actively doing—to fellow human beings. Emotional detachment and the pretence of ignorance made it easier for those involved on the per-petrator side.

These processes operated slightly differently depending on prior rela-tionships between persecuted and perpetrators, and on distance from the sites of killing. Individual experiences in the Baltic states of Lithuania and Latvia illuminate some of the complexities of the process on the ground. And while locals were co-opted into a spree of murderous violence insti-gated by the *Einsatzgruppen*, killing hundreds of thousands in a matter of a few months, some of the German facilitators—such as the Baltic German Jürgen Ernst Kroeger, who hastened back to his native Latvia after helping to 'germanize' the Wartheland—managed to persuade himself that he knew nothing about it. The fictions of innocence and ignorance could be main-tained even in midst of a conflagration of violence.

Fatal combinations

In the early hours of 22 June 1941, in defiance of the Molotov-Ribbentrop Non-Aggression Pact, Germany invaded the Soviet Union. Catching the Soviet forces unawares, 3 million Wehrmacht soldiers and half a million sol-diers from Germany's allies advanced across the border that stretched from the Baltic to the Black Sea, while 1,200 aircraft bombed Red Army air bases and stationary planes. This invasion was not just the opening up of another front in the war. It was also the start of quite another kind of war.

Operation Barbarossa, as the German leadership called it, was explicitly designed as a 'war of annihilation': an ideologically driven battle to the death. Vast areas of land were to be colonized for German 'living space', and millions of people subordinated to German needs for labour or food—either subjugated and exploited or left to starve to death. And this was also a war against Jews, who were ultimately to be annihilated entirely.[4]

Military planning was in itself explicitly murderous. German needs were prioritized above all else, and the Nazis' callous approach to the lives of those they considered 'sub-human' was clearly documented before the in-vasion. The 'Hunger Plan', confirmed in a meeting of high-level state bur-eaucrats and army leaders on 2 May 1941, envisaged the deaths of 'umpteen millions' ('*zig Millionen*') of Soviet citizens through starvation as a direct and deliberate consequence of German prioritization of their own food supplies. The 'Barbarossa Decree' of 13 May, along with the subsequent 'Guidelines for the Conduct of the Troops in Russia', gave German soldiers the leeway to act without any fear of penalties. The Guidelines enjoined 'ruthless and energetic action against Bolshevik agitators, guerrillas, saboteurs, and Jews, and the total elimination of all active or passive resistance'. These 'criminal orders' were in direct contravention of Article 50 of the 1907 Hague Convention. Soviet prisoners of war were to be summarily shot or held in makeshift camps, where, by the spring of 1942, more than 2 million had already died from disease and starvation. Operation Barbarossa was, as one expert puts it, 'an invasion plan characterized by colossal hubris and immorality'.[5]

Local conditions affected the implementation of German initiatives, including their 'war against the Jews'. In the Baltic states, there was a lethal combination of nationalism, antisemitism, and willingness to cooperate with German forces. Many Latvians and Lithuanians had felt oppressed by a year of Soviet rule and believed the propaganda about 'Judeo-Bolshevism'. Some, including members of the Lithuanian Activist Front (LAF, established in Berlin in November 1940 with Nazi support), were spurred on by the mistaken belief that by cooperating with the German occupiers they could facilitate a return to national independence. Others simply indulged in venting their rage against Jews, often energized by reference to recent experiences of Soviet rule but also coloured by recourse to older forms of antisemitism.

In Eastern Europe, Jews were more easily identifiable as a distinctive group than German Jews had been within the Reich, whether because they were Orthodox Jews who dressed distinctively or because Christian neighbours knew them to be Jews; no slow process of 'resegregation' was necessary here, as there had been in prewar Germany. Moreover, whether or not they were antisemitic, members of the newly subjugated populations were in a far weaker position to intervene on behalf of Jewish victims of violence even if they had wanted to. There was, too, an element of surprise: those Jews who did not have time to flee ahead of the advancing Germans were less likely to survive than those where invasion came slightly later, and where knowledge of prior massacres precipitated flight or other survival strategies while there was still the opportunity. So in the Baltic states the conditions for mass murder were, from a Nazi perspective, highly favourable.

Within a couple of days of the invasion, both Germans and locals were murdering Jewish civilians in Lithuania. On 24 June, Germans crossed the border from Memel (Klaipėda) and shot a group of 201 Jewish civilians in nearby Garsden (Gargzdai). The group included old men, at least one woman, and a child—clearly not significant military targets. When in March 1939 the Memel area had been reincorporated into the Reich, many Jews, fearful of Nazi rule, had fled to Lithuania, and others had been expelled; the local killers therefore knew some of their victims personally.[6] This murderous violence was a far cry from Eugen Altmann's experiences of local antisemitism as a child in Memel decades earlier, when antisemitic taunts had provoked him into trying to prove he was not a 'weakling' by taking up a tough apprenticeship. What had then been a matter of mockery and social exclusion had now turned deadly.[7]

Within hours of the German attack on Kaunas (Kovno), which had been the temporary capital of Lithuania during the interwar period before the return of Vilnius, violence broke out against Jews. As Germans were bombing the city, thousands of civilians tried to flee, heading for an overcrowded railway station or by cart, bicycle, or foot on clogged-up roads out of the city, hoping to find safety in villages in the surrounding countryside or further afield. Others stayed put, continuing with their daily work, hoping that as the German army advanced the acute danger would pass. It was impossible to be sure of the best strategy. But beyond the general fear of the bombing, which affected all civilians, Jews rapidly became aware of a further danger: attacks by fellow residents.

Spurred on by advance *Einsatzgruppen* forces, Lithuanian nationalist activists unleashed an early reign of terror. Avraham Tory, a Jewish resident of Kaunas, wrote in his diary around midnight on Sunday, 22 June—the very day of the invasion—that 'toward evening, suspicious Lithuanian characters appeared in the midst of the nervous crowds filling the streets, serving blows to Jewish passers-by'. The activities of these 'Lithuanian thugs' were well organized, taking place 'simultaneously in different parts of town', and it soon 'became clear that the attackers were members of Lithuanian "partisan" gangs, acting on the instructions of the fifth column of the indigenous local Nazis'.[8] Tory first sought to flee Kaunas by bicycle and on foot, but found he was no safer outside the city than within it. Over the following days, 'the Germans were joined by gangs of Lithuanians, which had sprung up in every forest and village'; most were armed, and Jews

'were easy prey for them'.[9] Returning to Kaunas, Tory felt no safer: 'Like a
pack of bloodthirsty dogs the Lithuanian partisans prowled the streets and
courtyards, seizing panic-stricken Jews who had managed to find various
hiding places.'[10] Robberies took place in ransacked apartments, often accompanied by rapes and beatings; Jews were arrested and taken away to
prisons, Gestapo buildings, camps, or one of the ring of forts surrounding
Kaunas, a legacy of tsarist fortifications.

What happened in Kaunas has become infamous, not least due to the
photographs and eyewitness reports on the massacre that took place on
the forecourt of Lietukis garage on Friday, 27 June 1941. One German
army officer, Colonel Lothar Bischoffshausen, recorded the event in detail. He saw how 'a blond man of medium height, aged about twenty-five,
stood leaning on a wooden club', taking a brief rest. 'At his feet lay about
fifteen to twenty dead or dying people. Water flowed continuously from a
hose washing blood away into the drainage gully.' The young man was not
carrying out his murderous task alone; he had both willing assistants and
apparently supportive onlookers: 'In response to a cursory wave the next
man stepped forward silently and was beaten to death with the wooden
club in the most bestial manner, each blow accompanied by enthusiastic
shouts from the audience.'[11]

Not all locals were enthusiastic; some were horrified. On returning from
work that day, Laimonas Noreika had been surprised to see that 'a large
crowd had gathered alongside the perimeter fence of the garage yard'. So
he and his brother 'also went over to see what was happening'. What he saw
shocked him deeply. He did not accept the sharp distinction between Jews
and other Kaunas residents, and his account explicitly stresses their common
humanity and similarity: 'In the middle of the yard, in broad daylight and
in full view of the assembled crowd, a group of well dressed, spruce intelligent looking people held iron bars which they used to viciously beat
another group of similarly well dressed, spruce, intelligent people.' Again
and again, 'they relentlessly battered the Jews until they fell to the ground.'
He noted details: 'They kept hitting them until finally they lay inert. Then,
using a hosepipe for washing cars, they doused them with water until they
came round following which the abuse would start all over again. And so it
went on and on until the hapless victims lay dead. Bodies began to pile up
everywhere.' Eventually Laimonas Noreika and his brother could bear it no

longer and left the scene. 'Those horrific events have been burned onto my memory and will remain there until my dying day.'[12]

Whatever their individual feelings, none of the observers made any attempt to intervene on behalf of the victims of this brutal violence. They stayed on the sidelines, some cheering and applauding, others shocked into passivity and disbelief, as innocent Jewish civilians were battered to death before their eyes.

The Lietukis garage massacre was not an isolated incident, not simply the work of one crazed killer. The image of the blond man wielding his massive club has been etched into our imagination; photographs also depicted the crowd of onlookers, including German soldiers as well as local civilians. This one particularly brutal, visible killing in broad daylight a mere 200 metres or so from the military headquarters was part of a far wider wave of violence, instigated by the Germans and made to look like one of a series of pogroms initiated by Lithuanians the moment the Soviets had left.

At the time of the invasion, a small advance group of *Einsatzgruppe A*, the *Sonderkommando 1b (Sk 1b)* led by Erich Ehrlinger, had been tasked with organizing apparently 'spontaneous' attacks.[13] And, as the head of *Einsatzgruppe A*, SS–Brigadier General Walter Stahlecker, later reported, the Germans had been successful in 'activating the partisans in Kovno'. The first to be recruited was the leader of a Lithuanian nationalist group, Algirdas Klimatis, who 'succeeded in starting a pogrom with the aid of instructions given him by a small advance detachment operating in Kovno'; most important in this context, the violence was carried out 'in such a way that no German orders or instructions could be observed by outsiders'. Stahlecker summarized the results: 'during the night of June 25/26, the Lithuanian partisans eliminated more than 1,500 Jews, set fire to several synagogues or destroyed them by other means, and burned down an area consisting of about sixty houses inhabited by Jews. During the nights that followed, 2,300 Jews were eliminated in the same way.'[14]

Crucially, this early violence against Jews relied on the acquiescence of the army. Some initial doubts, hesitations, and what Stahlecker called 'misunderstandings' had to be smoothed out through 'personal discussions'. Stahlecker had particular praise for General Erich Hoepner, commander of Panzer Group 4, who—despite his later association with the July 1944 plot to assassinate Hitler—had encouraged his officers to see the war against Russia as part of the 'battle for existence of the German people', a key element in the 'fight of Germans against Slavs, the defence of European culture against the Muscovite-Asiatic deluge, resistance against Jewish Bolshevism'. The battle must accordingly result in the total 'destruction' of Russia and be fought with 'unprecedented hardness'.[15] Those among the army leadership who had felt disquiet were soon brought into line. On hearing of the events, the commander of the Army Group North Rear Area, General Franz von Roques, came to see for himself what was going on, and voiced his concerns to his superior, Commander in Chief of Army Group North, Field Marshal Wilhelm Ritter von Leeb. Von Leeb, however, replied that he had 'no influence over these measures' and it was better just to keep one's distance. Both he and Roques agreed that the 'Jewish question' would need to be 'solved' in one way or another. In von Leeb's view, 'sterilization of all male Jews' might be preferable as a means of putting an end to the Jewish 'race'; but in the meantime, he and others were content to allow the murderous violence, instigated by the Germans and carried out by local activists, to continue unchecked.[16] The army agreed in principle on the ultimate goal—the removal of Jewry from German-dominated Europe—and had doubts only about the methods and timing. At this time, intervention could still have been publicly presented as bringing the supposedly spontaneous Lithuanian 'self-cleansing' under control; failure to step in made a profound difference to the future course of events.[17]

Inciting locals to violence did not take place in quite the same way in the capital city, Vilnius, only recently returned by the Soviets to Lithuania from Poland. Here, intergroup tensions in a more ethnically diverse city affected initial responses to antisemitic initiatives. Lithuanians felt threatened by Poles, and Poles disliked Lithuanians who were now asserting dominance. Population statistics are subjects of contention, but probably more than three-quarters of Vilnius residents did not consider themselves to be ethnic Lithuanians, even when the figures were massaged to register Lithuanian-speaking Poles as 'Lithuanians'. Conflicts between Poles and Lithuanians rendered matters more complex for the German occupiers—and Polish distrust and dislike of both Lithuanians and Germans could on occasion provide a limited degree of solidarity with and sympathy for individual Jews seeking to escape persecution, particularly if they had a fluent command of Polish.[18] Nevertheless, whatever the dynamics of Polish-Lithuanian tensions, with the German advance the situation for Jews was dire. On hearing news of the invasion, 3,000 Jews fled Vilnius on 22 and 23 June 1941; many failed to reach their destinations, were killed en route, or returned thinking they might after all be safer among family and friends in the city.

For the first ten days after the invasion, the city was under joint German–Lithuanian administration. Lithuanians sought to ensure their own domination over the Poles, whom they saw as a greater threat to their position than Jews. They wanted to show that they could maintain order, and there were no early 'spontaneous' pogroms along the lines of those evident in Kaunas or in the Šiauliai region of Lithuania.

Mass killings of adult males began in Vilnius with the arrival on 2 July 1941 of *Einsatzkommando 9*, led by Colonel Alfred Filbert, part of *Einsatzgruppe B* under the command of Arthur Nebe. Like members of Karl Jäger's *Einsatzkommando 3* which operated across the rest of Lithuania, members of Filbert's commando had been given explicit instructions before they left Germany by Reinhard Heydrich, and Heydrich's orders were verbally transmitted to lower ranks.[19] Now intent on rounding up and shooting anyone who could plausibly be considered a security threat, they found a convenient site just outside Vilnius. A series of pits had been built by the Soviets in Ponary for oil storage tanks but never actually used by them. Ponary lay in a wooded area around ten kilometres southwest of the city, easily reached by road and rail, and the pits and ditches were now repurposed as a mass execution site. In the early weeks of German occupation, young males as well as members of the intelligentsia were seized off the streets of Vilnius and told they were to be taken away to labour camps. At the beginning, this fiction was bolstered by asking them to bring suitable possessions for an overnight stay. Some were held for a couple of days in Lukiszki Prison in Vilnius before being taken to Ponary; relatives and friends often came and pleaded for their release or brought clothes and provisions for their journey to the fictional work camps.[20] Around 150 Lithuanians helped the *Einsatzkommando*, doubling its strength. Locals also functioned as 'abductors' or 'snatchers', kidnapping people on the streets or dragging them out of their homes at night; they were paid a sum of money for each Jew they handed over. Lithuanians also carried out most of the actual shootings at Ponary.

Those who were persecuted tried to puzzle out what was going on. The deception was clearly intentional, and it was almost impossible to understand these totally unprecedented developments: the organized mass murder now underway was quite different from the pogroms of earlier years. Herman

Kruk thought it through in his diary on 10 July 1941: 'The whole city is depressed about the men who have disappeared. Groups of Snatchers wander around the streets and courtyards, snatch men wherever they can, and drag them off. The excuse is that they are taken "for work", but seldom does anybody come back.' As 'snatching' increasingly took place by night, and in people's homes, many started to create hiding places, which they called 'malinas' or 'malines' (a word of Slavic origin implausibly meaning 'raspberry' in Yiddish and used, in effect, as a secret ghetto term that would be unintelligible to the German invaders).[21] Kruk himself hid in a mezzanine 'with old baskets, machinery, and an old broken cupboard' where he, his brother-in-law, the landlady's son, and 'somebody else we dragged along' would stay 'until the danger is past'. He concluded his diary entry by asking, 'Can we hold out like this for long?'[22]

Outside the larger urban centres, there were fewer places to hide. Violence against Jews and 'communists' spread rapidly across Lithuania. As survivor and historian Yitzhak Arad put it: 'In spite of the fact that, even in the past, the Jews had suffered enmity and much suffering at the hands of the local population, the eruption of savage, unrestrained hatred during the Nazi period came as a shock.'[23] Across the Lithuanian countryside, local inhabitants turned on their Jewish neighbours and workmates—in ways that are only recently beginning to be confronted directly by members of subsequent generations, undermining a more comfortable official memory of double victimhood at the hands of both Hitler and Stalin.[24]

The involvement of Lithuanian activists in violent antisemitic incidents in small towns and villages at the time of the invasion were described by more than 150 survivors and eyewitnesses interviewed shortly after the war by Leyb Koniuchovsky, who was himself a survivor of the Kaunas ghetto. This collection records in detail how people experienced the destruction of Jewish communities across the country. As soon as Lithuanian activists—known as 'partisans' for their opposition to the previous communist regime—took on local positions of power, 'there was a flood of new decrees, whose goal was to insult, degrade, and mock every Jewish and human sensibility'. Rituals of public humiliation were staged, some as symbolic attacks on Judaism as a religion, others to denigrate Jews and demonstrate their exile from the community of common humanity. Jews were, for example, dunked in water as a form of mock baptism, while symbols of religious faith were violated. In Eišiškės, one eyewitness recalled: 'As the Jews jumped into the cold water the Lithuanian gangsters forced them to shout, "Long live Hitler".' In Turmantas, 'the partisans ordered all the Jews to shave their beards and those who didn't were threatened with having their beards pulled out from the roots'.[25] 'Performances' became organized 'events' with assembled audiences. In a number of places, Jews were 'forced to sing Soviet and religious songs' or 'had to meow in chorus like cats, walk on all fours and sing various Hebrew and Yiddish songs'. Mockery was accompanied by violence and pillaging. In Gelvonai, as 'one group of partisans was busy tormenting the Jews in the field, a second group was robbing their goods and property in the townlet'. Work was designed 'to demoralize the Jews of the townlet who had to clean all the toilets, serve in the homes of the Lithuanian bandits and their leaders, etc.'[26]

Many testimonies record how suddenly Lithuanians dropped former friends and acquaintances—far faster than had happened in prewar Germany. In Vilkaviškis, Jews 'all complained that their Lithuanian acquaintances, friends, and even neighbours had driven them away as if they had lice. Some of the Jews cried when they said this.' Moreover, many interviewees emphasize that at the time there were no Germans in the area. In Žasliai, Jews were set to do work that was 'spiritually demeaning', while there 'were no Germans at all in the town'. In Viekšniai, Lithuanians 'drove all the Jewish men out of their homes to the market square', where they 'had to rip out the grass from between the stones in the marketplace, clean the toilets of the Lithuanians from town, etc. As they worked, the Lithuanian murderers mocked and beat them.' Moreover, 'during this period there were no Germans in the town; they would ride through it, barely stopping.'[27]

These testimonies from across Lithuania are profoundly disturbing. Even if the antisemitic activists were a minority, they clearly held sufficient power to impose their will. They were not merely willing helpers of the Germans but seemed eager to seize the opportunity to vent their own hatred towards Jewish fellow residents, to the shock and horror of Jews who had known them for years.[28]

But this situation could not last long. There were shifts in the balance of forces in the ensuing weeks. Once the activist furies had been whipped up, local initiatives had to be brought under control. Lithuanian hopes of regaining national independence were soon dashed; but unlike in Poland, the lower levels of the Lithuanian administrative and political structures were left intact, allowing Germans to organize and enact rapid radical violence with minimal input of their own forces. Meanwhile, the reliability of Lithuanian extremists was proven, and the process of mass murder began to be systematized and routinized. Organized units not only assisted in arrests, detentions, and killings across Lithuania, but were deployed beyond its borders; a roving commando of Lithuanians under the leadership of Joachim Hamann, known as the Rollkommando Hamann, was soon active in neighbouring Belorussia, killing tens of thousands.[29]

The combination of German initiatives and Lithuanian activists was lethal. In Kaunas, around 1,100 Jews were killed in early pogroms, while Stahlecker reported 3,800 by the end of June; and by the first week in July a further 5,000 had been killed in mass shootings. In Vilnius, 5,000 Jews and Poles had been killed by the end of July. In the whole of Lithuania, by the end of July, 20,000 Jews had been killed: more than 18,000 shot, and more than 1,100 killed in pogroms.[30] In Vilnius, from early July 1941, when military rule displaced the joint German-Lithuanian administration, the army and *Einsatzkommando 9* worked together; and, strengthened by Lithuanian forces, mass executions of Jewish males began.[31] During the first three weeks of July, *Einsatzkommando 9* and its Lithuanian assistants murdered some 5,000 people at Ponary. On 23 July they left for Minsk to engage in killing in Belorussia, leaving only a small group in Vilnius until *Einsatzkommando 3* of *Einsatzgruppe A* took over on 9 August.

By this point, Lithuania was under German civilian administration and the Lithuanian provisional government had been disbanded. The German army, the SS and police forces, and the civilian administration worked together, though there were conflicting areas and lines of responsibility that resulted in a degree of friction over specific policies. The general direction was, however, clear: increasingly, distinctions were made between those who could be useful for work and those to be killed. There was also a degree of latitude for district commissioners (*Gebietskommissare*) to determine specific policies within their own regions. Over the course of the following weeks, Franz Murer, the 'right-hand man' of Hans Hingst, the district commissioner for the city of Vilnius, extracted a vast amount of money and valuables from the Jews as a 'contribution' or 'tribute'; Jews desperately hoped this might help their survival.[32]

In Latvia too, despite General Stahlecker's later complaint that it had initially been less easy to find willing collaborators, locals were crucial to early killings.[33] The ultra-nationalist Pērkonkrusts (Thunder Cross) movement had laid the ideological groundwork for violent antisemitism in the 1930s; and here as in Lithuania the Soviet occupation in 1940–1941 provided the pretext for heightened propaganda about the alleged evils of 'Judeo-Bolshevism'. The first weeks of warfare in Latvia were a period of sheer terror for Jews, who were subjected to a wave of violence in which locals played a significant role.

As the Red Army retreated, a period of 'unbelievable chaos' ensued, as described by one survivor, Bernhard Press, a trained physician. The streets of the Latvian capital, Riga, were filled with people trying to flee—not only Russian soldiers but also Soviet citizens who had settled in Latvia, and Latvians who had worked with the Soviet regime and now feared for their safety. It took some Latvian Jews a couple of days to realize that their own fate was about to take an infinitely greater turn for the worse. Press's account provides horrific details of the ways in which Latvians now turned on their Jewish former colleagues, friends, and neighbours, in what he terms a period of 'unchecked, unchained slaughter'. Nationalist Latvians, celebrating what they mistakenly thought was going to be the restoration of independence, now turned on the Jews, whom they blamed for the period of communist rule. An early period of terror, punctuated by numerous murders, rapes, robberies, rituals of humiliation, random arrests, and detention under conditions of utmost brutality, made Jews fear for their lives. Some individuals fled eastwards, while others hoped to be able to sit it out. Families were separated, often never to meet again; very few who remained on Latvian soil ultimately survived the war.[34]

It was not only the violence unleashed by the activists; what was striking was the fact that so many others either applauded the violence and participated in the public humiliation of Jews, or remained silent. In his account, written in 1947, Max Kaufmann, one of the Jews who survived, recalled how 'Latvian youths forced their way into my apartment, plundered whatever they could find, and took me and my son, who was still sick, away with them'. As they and other Jews were marched along the streets to the police headquarters, 'we were joined by more and more Latvians who walked alongside us and beat us mercilessly', shouting 'Jews, Bolsheviks!' In the following weeks Kaufmann observed how the Pērkonkrusts movement 'attracted a considerable portion of the student fraternities to their side' and organized gangs who 'moved from city to city, from town to town, in order to kill the Jewish population there in the most bestial way'.[35] Press, too, reflected that 'the murderers raged with particular fury in rural areas and in the small Latvian towns where everyone knew everyone else and everyone knew where the neighbouring Jewish families lived'. Because of this detailed local knowledge, 'in some places it took the gangs of murderers only days to exterminate the entire Jewish population'.[36]

The more active complicity of locals also played a crucial role in the escalation of murder. Press reflected: 'As the corpses of our Jewish fellow citizens, friends and relatives piled up around us, as the blood of innocent people was spilled in streams, we looked for help to our Latvian fellow citizens, friends, and acquaintances, convinced that surely here or there a hand would be lifted to help us, surely a mouth would open to speak to us a word of comfort—but in vain. A bloody frenzy had overcome the country'. Locals were not merely passive, of course, nor did they even seem aghast at what was going on: many were enthusiastic about the turn of events. People threw Jews off public transport before Jews were officially banned; they prevented Jews from buying food; and they engaged in verbal abuse. Other simply turned their backs: 'Our Latvian friends, with whom we had only yesterday caroused and celebrated, acted as if they no longer knew us. Nobody sought us out, nobody comforted us, nobody did anything on our behalf. Suddenly we were alone; we had become strangers in our own homeland.'[37]

Press produced a damning evaluation of the responses of Latvian citizens: 'It was not only a sea of hatred that surrounded us; it was also a sea of silence. Tens of thousands and hundreds of thousands were witnesses of the most horrible crime in human history and remained silent about it. Nowhere was the faintest voice raised to protest the universal bloodshed.'[38] This was an almost total separation of utterly distinct communities, with those who were not persecuted having apparently little or no empathy with the victims of racist violence.

On the organizational front, in Latvia, too, the Germans rapidly harnessed the energies of extremists to carry out acts of genocide. In the Latvian provinces, where there were relatively small communities of Jews, individuals were collected together, often held for a while, and then taken out to nearby forests and shot. Many accounts of these killings in individual locations across the country mention groups of Germans, alongside 'Self-Defence' (*Selbstschutz*) forces.[39] And more than 1,200 activists volunteered for a notorious commando led by Viktors Arājs. Arājs, the son of a

Latvian father and a Baltic German mother, had in the 1930s been a low-ranking police officer who maintained an appropriate official distance from the Pērkonkrusts political movement.[40] Following the German invasion, Arājs was introduced by a mutual schoolfriend to General Stahlecker of *Einsatzgruppe A*, who saw how useful he could be in inciting and executing 'spontaneous' pogroms. The Germans and the Arājs commando appealed not only to Pērkonkrusts supporters but also to nationalist and antisemitic members of student fraternities, quickly garnering the commitment of extremists. One of the first acts in which the Arājs commando was involved was the burning of the Great Choral Synagogue in Gogol Street, Riga, on the night of 4 July 1941, trapping people inside in the flames. Although the total number of victims remains in dispute, the horror of what happened does not. As Press wrote, 'screams of the burning victims could be heard over a great distance and filled the souls of the people in neighbouring houses with horror'.[41] Most other synagogues in Riga were also burned down, as in the Reich in November 1938 being preserved only where fire might have posed a threat to neighbouring buildings.

Over the course of the first few months of occupation, the Arājs group murdered at least 30,000 Jews, accounting for roughly half of all Jews killed in Latvia in 1941. Having demonstrated their reliability, the Arājs commando, like the Lithuanian Rollkommando Hamann, was subsequently also responsible for tens of thousands of murders beyond the borders of its own country.[42]

Constructing innocence: The naïve and ignorant facilitator

As a Baltic German who had previously resettled 'home in the Reich' in the Wartheland area of conquered Poland, Jürgen Ernst Kroeger was only too glad to have the opportunity to return to his native Latvia in the summer of 1941.[43] Barely a week after the invasion of the Soviet Union, he responded eagerly to a call for Russian-speaking translators to serve with the invading troops. As well as Russian, he could of course speak Latvian, and was directed to work in Riga. Filled with joy at seeing his beloved *Heimat* again, Kroeger spent his first evening back in Riga wandering through the familiar streets of the old town. His initial impressions were of 'happy people—often arm in arm with German soldiers', as well as the sweet scent of blossoms in the summer air. Taken aback somewhat by seeing the ruins of a recently destroyed church in the old town centre, he spoke to an elderly Latvian living nearby. She assured him that they were 'all happy that the Bolsheviks had gone' and the Germans were now there, implicitly suggesting that the destruction of the church had been caused by the Russians rather than the invading Germans.[44]

Kroeger's account of Latvia in the summer of 1941 portrays his delight at returning to his Baltic homeland and his growing awareness, if only through apparently fleeting and carefully filtered intimations, of the tragedy being inflicted on Latvian Jews. At some point during the summer he delighted in spending a couple of days on an official trip, with car and chauffeur, to pick up butter, honey, and other delicacies from the countryside for the enjoyment of the German occupying forces in Riga. On this trip, he took the opportunity to visit his former home in Wiexten (Vecumnieki), some fifty kilometres to the south; and picking up with old acquaintances, he heard about the ways in which Latvian 'extremists' had apparently maltreated and dragged away local Jews. Kroeger does not seem to have inquired into these accounts too closely, or he might have been more discomfited by the killings that took place not too far from his former home, including the murder of several hundred Jews in the Likverteni Forest near Bauska. These killings were carried out by members of the Arājs commando, and by German soldiers and the local Self-Defence forces.[45] Being able to dismiss reports of organized violence against Jews across the Latvian provinces as merely passing acts by Latvian 'extremists' must have been easier for Kroeger; he was clearly unwilling to acknowledge that the deaths of so many Jews were part of a systematic killing operation organized and orchestrated by the German forces for whom he was himself working.[46]

Back in Riga, Kroeger tells us, he noticed that Jews in the streets were wearing the yellow star. Discussion of what was going on was, however, supposedly muzzled. In the office, his work colleagues engaged in debates about the treatment of Jews, terminated abruptly when their boss said they could leave such questions safely in the hands of their Führer. In this way, Kroeger suggests that he was very much at the margins of developments: dimly aware of violence perpetrated by others—Latvian extremists—but officially enjoined to leave all this to a higher authority, Adolf Hitler.[47] 'Looking away' was not merely condoned but actually encouraged, even ordered, by a person in a role with authority over him. This was, in effect, officially sanctioned ignorance.

Even so, Kroeger suggests it was not always easy to ignore what was going on. Moreover, he sought to demonstrate in his memoirs that his own sympathies had been with the victims. On one occasion, he tells us, he recognized one of his former schoolmates, whom he names as Rebekkah Davidson, in a Jewish women's work group tasked with cleaning his office building under the supervision of Latvian guards. Kroeger recounts how he tried to offer support, and how she responded, hopelessly, that the Jews were beyond help: her husband had already been taken away, and she had 'no other wish than to follow him soon', out of this 'barbarian, terrible world'. Her last words to him were, Kroeger says, a plea that he should not speak further with her because it could cause him trouble. Following this end to the encounter—which seems possible, if implausible, and cannot be in any way substantiated—Kroeger tells us that he never saw his former school-mate again, 'and also never heard anything more about her fate'. Again, Kroeger emphasized his own powerlessness combined with an injunction that he should not be involved or concerned. He was ignorant and he was following orders—the two classic postwar excuses. Moreover, in this case it was someone with the ultimate authority of victimhood who had absolved him of any personal responsibility, by not only condoning but indeed also pleading for him to remain passive; and the fact that he heard nothing fur-ther of her individual fate might buttress his claim to ignorance.[48]

Kroeger stresses that he cannot be accused of indifference, both in this and other anecdotes. By making distinctions between other people's re-sponses to the growing violence, and giving contrasting examples of 'de-cent' Germans with whom he eventually agrees (although he admits it took him some time to come around to their views), Kroeger highlights his own shock at murderous antisemitism. The fact that in the Warthegau he had personally benefitted from the forcible removal of Poles and Jews from their homes, which had been taken over in the 'germanization' programme, did not seem to bother him at all.

Kroeger seems aware this moral self-distancing from perpetrators is, on its own, not quite sufficient. So again and again he suggests that he was only obliquely aware of the violence against Jews, hearing only by hints and in-timations, often wrapped in a veil of secrecy or confidentiality by others whom he respected. Utterly implausibly, given the wider developments,

Kroeger conveys the impression that he never directly knew about the escalating violence against Jews. Kroeger's fiction of ignorance in his memoirs can really only be sustained for a later readership that knew nothing about what was going on in Latvia in the latter half of 1941. And it soon became clear that such techniques of self-distancing extended to the very brink of the death pits.

The Vilnius ghetto and the pits of Ponary

The summer of 1941 was a turning point for both the escalation of genocide and the groups who were targeted. Increasingly aware that this would not be a short war as envisaged, German policymakers became concerned about both pressure of time and scarcity of resources. Previous plans to postpone a 'solution' to the 'Jewish question' until after a hoped-for early victory were amended, and food rationing was introduced. Germans were the highest priority; locals who could assist the war effort came next; and Jews were last of all. Further distinctions were made between Jews who could work for the Germans and those seen as an expendable burden on scarce resources. Policy priorities shifted from 'securing the area' to getting rid of 'useless eaters'. This meant murdering people who were clearly not security risks: women and children, the elderly, sick and disabled.

Across the Eastern Front there were discussions between centre and periphery as the emphasis shifted. On occasion, commanders might refer back to the Nazi leadership for confirmation before issuing specific orders according to local circumstances. Spurious pretexts—such as 'retaliation actions'—were often used to justify the massacre of whole communities. This meant a degree of variation, with some localities seeing far greater and earlier bouts of violence than others, while individuals like Viktors Arājs could spearhead the development of more 'efficient' methods of mass murder. There were inevitably continuing tensions around conflicting priorities, including the balance to be struck between considerations around military security, food supplies, and the need for skilled labour. These considerations informed decisions as to who should die and who remain alive for the time being in service of German interests. The process was characterized by improvisation in the light of local circumstances as well as conflicting views on appropriate strategies at different times.

Two phases can be distinguished in the Baltic states.[49] First, the shooting of 'Bolshevik commissars' and other 'security risks', understood to include Jews, was portrayed as an essential security measure. In the early weeks, therefore, mostly adult Jewish males had been targeted for killing, while women and children were segregated in ghettos or held in barns, synagogues, or isolated camps on the periphery of towns and villages. At the same time, local people were, as we have seen, essentially given free rein to kill Jews and steal their property. Lithuanian and Latvian nationalists were, moreover, at first encouraged in the illusion that cooperation with the Germans was a step on the path to independence.

In the second phase, from around the middle of August 1941, the balance of Nazi priorities began to shift: the main question became that of who could more usefully be exploited for their labour, and who should be killed outright. The task of separating 'useful labour' from 'useless eaters' was made easier by selective ghettoization. In the context of raging local violence, some Jews had initially been persuaded that they might be safer in designated secure areas; later, they were compelled to move. Non-Jewish inhabitants were moved out of poorer areas, while Jews were forced into increasingly overcrowded, unhygienic, and cramped conditions, with multiple people sharing rooms and spaces. Food was utterly inadequate, and people soon succumbed to malnutrition and disease. Some of the larger ghettos were sealed off, with only the labour gangs allowed to leave under strict supervision. In Vilnius and Riga, the respective capitals of Lithuania and Latvia, the ghettos were temporarily divided, distinguishing between those deemed capable of work and those to be separated off, making it easier for subsequent deportation to killing sites and ghetto clearance.

Civilian administration had been established under the aegis of the Reich Commissariat of the Eastern Lands (Reichskommissariat Ostland, RKO), led by Alfred Rosenberg, a Nazi ideologist who was appointed Reich Minister for the Occupied Eastern Territories on 17 July 1941, and Reich Commissar Hinrich Lohse, who was in charge of the practical administration of the territories.[50] At the same time, the SS and the army continued to exert influence and kept control of military and security considerations, rendering disputes almost inevitable. Debates continued between those committed to the preservation of a labour supply useful to the Germans and those prioritizing the immediate killing of as many Jews as possible. These differences were never fully resolved, but in the course of the last six months of 1941, the mass murder of Jews continued, totalling more than 200,000 by the end of the year in the Baltic states.

Meanwhile, people who came to watch and often also benefit from the persecution and murder of the Jews seem to have responded with a combination of curiosity, self-interest, and moral indifference. Selective killings became routinized, as those around sought to make sense of what it was they were witnessing. Victims too tried to puzzle out the developments.

The early killings in the pits of Ponary, near to Vilnius, had been disguised under the pretence that men were being sent away to work camps. Even at the start, Jews doubted the truth of this, as word never came back from those who had gone. News of mass shootings spread quickly, but the reality was just too overwhelming to believe. The Jewish Council (Judenrat) in Vilnius, which had been established on 4 July, was initially sceptical. 'On the tenth of this month a rumor came to the Judenrat that people were shot in Ponar', Herman Kruk noted in his diary. But at first the Judenrat 'didn't want to hear anything and considered it an unfounded rumor'. Five days later, further reports came through from 'people who secretly repeated the rumor' about what was happening. One witness was a maid who saw a group of Jews being taken off, including her boss; she followed them all the way to Ponary. She returned and reported that 'all the Jews were shot'. Kruk noted that the 'Judenrat didn't believe it this time either'.[51] However, the following morning further information came to the Judenrat. Now it did begin to take notice.

So too did members of the wider population, as news of the killings rapidly spread. One local resident was Kazimierz Sakowicz, a Polish journalist who had moved out of Vilnius when the Germans invaded and now lived in a modest house in the village—situated on the road leading directly from the railway station to the death pits. He could hear the shooting in the woods, and could see close up from his windows or garden the victims being brought by rail, by foot, or in trucks along the road right by his house. Realizing that a crime of historic significance was unfolding before his eyes, Sakowicz watched carefully from his attic window and took detailed notes, hiding them in lemonade bottles that he buried in the garden. Sakowicz was himself killed late in the war, in circumstances that are not entirely clear; but an incomplete set of his diary entries were dug up after the war and held for decades in inaccessible archives, until finally they were painstakingly pieced together by a survivor and former partisan, Rachel

Margolis. These diary entries provide a detailed record of the perpetrators of violence and their methods, and of the reactions of local people.

As news of the killings spread, Ponary began to attract what might be called 'execution tourism', and not all observers were as shocked as Sakowicz by what they saw; some even seemed to take a pleasure in what they were witnessing. Sakowicz observed, for example, on 11 August: 'The passenger car NV-370 had two amused Lithuanian "ladies" (dames) in the company of a certain "gentleman" who were on a day excursion to see the executions. After the shootings they returned; I did not see sadness on their faces.'[52] Others were simply powerless to assist. Sakowicz recounted one such incident: 'One escaped in his underwear as far as Deginie. He was hunted down and shot. Children were herding cows, and he ran to them, but they ran away.'[53] Presumably the children were terrified by the sight, and there was little they could have done anyway.

In Vilnius, as the killings over the summer included increasing numbers of women and children, the fiction of being sent to work camps could barely be sustained. And now German policies entered a new phase. At the very end of August and beginning of September, they organized a 'provocation', staging the firing of shots by Lithuanians for which Jews were blamed, resulting in the murder not only of the supposed Jewish culprits but also of some 3,700 more Jews taken to Ponary as 'retaliation'. This incident was a pretext for clearing the streets in central Vilnius that had been designated as the ghetto area to accommodate Jews from outlying areas of the city. Shortly thereafter, on 6 September 1941, ghettoization began. As Jews proceeded from their former homes in the suburbs into the city centre, bearing what belongings they could carry, local Lithuanians and Poles looked on— some apparently showing compassion, others gloating with joy, most remaining silent, affecting indifference.[54] A few days later there were further mass killings in Ponary: *Einsatzkommando 3* gave a figure of 3,334, of whom the majority were now women (1,670) and children (771), with the lower figure of 'only' 993 men reflecting the extent to which men had already been killed in previous weeks.[55]

By now, Jews were having to face the truth. On Thursday, 4 September 1941, Kruk agonized into his diary, writing that if 'anyone anywhere comes upon [these lines], I want him to know this is my last wish: let the words someday reach the living world and let people know about it from eyewitness accounts.' He asked, 'Can the world not scream? Can history never take revenge?' and went on: 'The dreadful thing is hard to describe. The hand trembles, and the ink is bloody.' Escapees had given precise descriptions: 'They all tell: they shot us with machine guns. In the ditch lay thousands of dead bodies. Before being shot they took off their clothes, their shoes.' The whole area bore witness to the killings: 'The fields reek with the stench of the dead bodies. . . . A few crawl out of there, and a few drag themselves to villages. Six of these few are now in the Jewish hospital. As I write these lines, a 12-year-old child is lying on the operating table, and they are taking a bullet out of her arm. The child mentions names of those she saw shot.'[56] The following day, Kruk noted that four women who had escaped recounted how 'a group of Lithuanians, commanded by Germans, started shooting them with rifles. They were shot from behind as they walked. Some of them were told to sit on the edges of a ravine and were shot from behind. All the women and children were killed. When asked how many people might have been there, one of them replied several thousand. Others a few hundred.'[57]

These events were impossible for non-Jewish residents of Ponary to ignore; and many local people were actively involved. Sakowicz noted that the Lithuanian killers—whom he termed 'Shaulists' after an anti-Bolshevik paramilitary nationalist organization, many former members of which had volunteered to assist the Germans—were generally 'striplings of seventeen to twenty-five years'.[58] He recorded the exact number of victims brought on each occasion to the killing site; he registered the shift over the summer of 1941 from shooting only men to murdering groups with women and children; and he kept a running tally of the rising total of people killed. Sakowicz also recorded the ways in which both the Lithuanian killers and local residents profited from the murders. People took away what clothing, shoes, and valuables from the dead bodies as they could, keeping some items for themselves while bartering or selling the rest. And Sakowicz named the individuals who were involved in particular shootings or who hovered around the site and repeatedly engaged in self-enrichment.

Sakowicz captures the sheer brutality of the face-to-face killings, the excessive indulgence in alcohol, and the apparent indifference of the perpetrators to the fates of their anguished victims, some of whom fell to the ground pleading for mercy for themselves or their children or sought desperately to hide infants in piles of discarded clothing in the hope that at least their offspring might survive. Jews who attempted to escape rarely got very far before being gunned down, or were turned in by locals; there seems to have been remarkably little support among residents of the surrounding villages and countryside for fleeing Jews seeking to evade death.

The killings required coordination among many different groups of facilitators and executioners, and long hours of shooting and clearing up after the operations. Yet the Germans could see that their system was working. The division between those deemed still useful as productive labour and those designated for the death pits was further systematized by issuing 'certificates', or work permits, to a select number of people. Dividing the Vilnius ghetto allowed an easier method of rounding up people for killing: those with work permits were moved to Ghetto no. 1, while those without certificates were concentrated in Ghetto no. 2. On Yom Kippur, 1 October 1941, a major 'Aktion' was carried out: large numbers of Jews were easily located and arrested in the synagogues where they were praying, and temporarily imprisoned or taken directly to be shot in Ponary. Three more 'Aktions' followed, until three weeks later Ghetto no. 2 was fully liquidated and only Ghetto no. 1 remained.

With changes in the work permit system, workers were allowed to nominate a partner and no more than two children as their 'family' to be protected with a yellow certificate; unattached adults, orphans, or additional children from families with more than the permitted two hastened to team up to be registered as 'families' to protect the maximum number of people. Even for those entitled to rations, food was too scarce to sustain life; everyone depended on smuggling additional supplies, exchanging valuables and clothing for extra food that could be secreted and brought in through the ghetto gates when returning from a day at work.

The Germans had set the number to be preserved as a useful labour supply at 12,000. In July 1941, there had been 57,000 Jews in Vilnius. By December 1941, around 33,500 of them had been murdered. Perhaps as many as 3,500 had managed to flee to Belorussia or to hide elsewhere. Within the ghetto, 12,000 people were living legally, with work permits and ration cards; and several thousand more were crammed into the ghetto as 'illegals', not registered as resident, neither able to work nor eligible for food rations. Their presence made conditions even more difficult to sustain.[59]

Power struggles developed, particularly between the Jewish chief of police and effective head of the ghetto, Jacob Gens, and a variety of resistance organizations. Gens supported the strategy of 'work to survive': trying to keep in with the Germans and emphasizing Jewish productivity to miti-gate the extent of the catastrophe. Others proposed more active resistance. But they could not agree on whether to remain within the ghetto and prepare for an uprising, or to escape and try either to survive in the forests or in hiding, or to fight and die as partisans. There were not only the ob-vious dangers facing those involved in resistance, but also potentially fatal implications for the other ghetto inhabitants. A heavy moral responsibility came with any choice, and those in the resistance groups were conflicted, burdened by the thought of endangering the lives of those they loved and would leave behind.

But the German slaughter of the Jews was clearly comprehensive, brutal, and without obvious end; something had to be done. Shortly after mid-night, at a meeting disguised as a New Year's Eve party on 31 December 1941, and in the early moments of New Year's Day 1942, the young poet and resistance leader Abba Kovner read aloud a manifesto entitled 'Let us not go like lambs to the slaughter!'[60] Even if Kovner and other partisans were able to engage in the dangers of escape, resistance, and for a few ultimately survival, this was not an option for the vast majority of Jews at this time.

East meets West: The Ninth Fort at Kaunas

In Kaunas, the series of forts around the town provided the Germans and their auxiliaries with ideal settings for both imprisonment and mass murder. The Seventh Fort was used in the early summer for killing male Jews. Over the following months, the Ninth Fort became the preferred site for mass killings, as a similar pattern of killing those who were not considered to be essential workers was put into effect. Jews were contained in two ghettos on 15 August 1941: a smaller one with around 3,000 people, and a larger with more than 26,000. Here too, a Jewish Council was established, under the leadership of Dr Elkhanan Elkes, which, as everywhere under Nazi rule, faced impossible challenges and choices. And over the succeeding weeks, Jews increasingly came to realize that selections meant not only selections of the stronger for work duties, but also the weak, sick, and elderly for death. In many smaller and some larger 'Aktions', Jews were taken out and shot, increasingly in the Ninth Fort.[61]

Here, too, locals watched what was going on. On 30 October 1941 a Lithuanian woman doctor, Elena Kutorgiene, wrote in her diary, '10,000 people have been taken out of the ghetto to die. They selected the old people, mothers with their children, those not capable of working.' People had to wait for hours. 'The square was surrounded by guards with machine guns. It was freezing. The people stood on their feet all through that long day, hungry and with empty hands. Small children cried in their mothers' arms.' They had been unwilling to believe the rumours, but many knew 'that at the Ninth Fort (the death Fort) prisoners had been digging deep ditches'. Moreover, 'when the people were taken there, it was already clear to everybody that this was death. They broke out crying, wailed, screamed. Some tried to escape on the way there but they were shot dead. Many bodies remained in the fields.' For the rest, there was little hope: 'At the Fort the condemned were stripped of their clothes, and in groups of 300 they were forced into the ditches. First they threw in the children. The women were shot at the edge of the ditch, after that it was the turn of the men.' Those doing the shooting were drunk. Kutorgiene ends with a reflection on the reactions of a German onlooker, as told to her by an acquaintance: this 'German soldier, an eye-witness' had, she was told, written to his Catholic wife: 'Yesterday I became convinced that there is no God. If there were, He would not allow such things to happen'.[62]

Yet as far as earthly responsibility was concerned, Germans not only allowed 'such things to happen'; they actively made these things happen. Numerous local people were willing to assist—whether through identifying Jews and indicating where they lived, helping to round them up and take them to death sites, or even in shooting—and many more profited from their deaths after the event. Only around 600 to 900 Germans were involved—fewer than 1,000—alongside many thousands of Lithuanians.

Yet another major turning point in Nazi antisemitic policies came with the beginning of deportations of Jews from the Reich itself in mid-October 1941. Now the murder of local Jews close to their homes was augmented by a new phenomenon: the organized transport of Jews from further away. While many of the early deportations of Reich Jews—a total of forty-two trains between October and the end of December 1941—were transported to the ghettos of Łódź (renamed Litzmannstadt) and Minsk, five trainloads were killed immediately on arrival in Kaunas, and a further trainload was shot in Riga. Two strands of Nazi policy merged, even if at this early stage of the Nazis 'Final Solution' it is far from clear who took the decision to murder rather than provide space in the ghetto for the incoming Reich Jews on these particular trains; later deportees from the Reich were accommodated in the Riga ghetto.[63] Whatever the explanation, with the immediate shooting of some 5,000 Reich Jews in the Ninth Fort, and further 1,000 in Riga, in late November 1941 the persecution of Jews from Germany and Austria became intrinsically entwined with the murder of Eastern European Jews.

People within the Reich became increasingly aware that far more was going on in 'the East' than 'resettlement' of Reich Jews or considerations of 'military security' and killing local 'partisans'.[64] Else Behrend-Rosenfeld, as one of the managers of the Jewish home in Berg am Laim, was informed well in advance of the first deportation of people from Munich to the East.[65] In her diary entry of Sunday, 16 November, she hardly knew where to begin when trying to recount the events of previous days. Rumours about an impending deportation had begun to circulate on 5 November; she tried to quell these rumours so as not to unsettle the residents of the home. But on 8 November she was called in, along with other Jewish leaders, to the office of the Jewish community, and informed that around 1,000 Jews from Munich were to be deported in the following week. The Gestapo had not yet determined exactly who would be on the list for deportation, but would let them know precise names on the lists as soon as these had been collated. Moreover, Jews below the age of sixty were no longer allowed to emigrate. Behrend-Rosenfeld was at this time still desperately awaiting her papers. Just three days earlier she had received a telegram letting her know that a visa for emigration to Cuba was on its way. But her hopes of getting out to her family abroad were now entirely dashed.[66]

Even so, Behrend-Rosenfeld continued to do her best to calm the residents of her home, and to prepare those slated for deportation for what everyone still hoped would really be just 'resettlement'. The Catholic nuns in the Berg am Laim convent where the Jews were housed showed sympathy and even offered them luxuries they had not seen in a long time, including cocoa and sugar. Behrend-Rosenfeld recorded her deep gratitude for their solidarity; this helped not only those being deported but also those left behind, who would feel their absence keenly. Supported and nourished in spirit as well as body, on 20 November 1941 the group from Berg am Laim joined the rest of the transport from Munich, totalling some

999 Jews. Their train was initially bound for Riga but diverted to Kaunas before reaching its original goal. Here, the Munich Jews were kept in the cells of the Ninth Fort before being taken out to be shot by a group under the command of Karl Jäger's *Einsatzkommando 3*, five days after they had departed from Munich.[67]

Seeing is deceiving: The visual record

Everywhere, Germans observed, filmed, and photographed local people engaged in violence, often using these images to try to distance them-selves from their own roles or share of responsibility. They were no longer bystanders but constructing a role as supposedly uninvolved witnesses. A German policeman, for example, shortly after being involved in killing Munich Jews at the Ninth Fort at Kaunas on 25 November 1941, reported on his experiences to the Breslau Cardinal, Adolf Bertram. This policeman confirmed not only that the execution squads had been made up of mem-bers of the SS, the Security Police, and local Lithuanians, but also that the shootings had been filmed specifically 'in order to show that it was not the Germans, but rather the Lithuanians, who had shot the Jews'.[68]

There were key distinctions between German production of images as visual propaganda, and private photography and filming as a record of his-toric experiences. Staged photographs were used to perpetuate and spread stereotypes of Jews as 'vermin', in order to whip up antisemitic feelings and make the war on Jews appear justified back home in Germany. An extreme example is given by a German Jewish survivor of the Riga ghetto, Jeanette Wolff. She witnessed frequent executions of Jews in Riga for minor in-fringements, such as smuggling food into the ghetto when returning from a work detail. Sometimes executions had to be carried out by Jews—a ghastly task. The Germans in charge would choose a Jew with a large family and, if he refused to carry out the execution, not only he but also his whole family would be shot. Wolff was shocked to discover, on her return to Germany after the war, that photographs of these gruesome staged incidents had been published in German illustrated magazines under the deliberately mislead-ing title 'This is how Jews execute Jews' ('*So richten Juden Juden*').[69]

In the early months, using Lithuanian and Latvian auxiliaries in the killing process could be used both to test public reactions and as a pre-emptive alibi. Diary reports from small towns and villages across Lithuania emphasize how, while locals engaged in shooting Jews under German supervision, Germans took photographs of the Lithuanians doing the shooting. On 13 August 1941, Zenonas Blynas, general secretary of the Lithuanian Nationalist Party, wrote in his diary: 'it is difficult for the rural people to get used to the massacres of the Jews' and 'it is creating a discouraging and difficult atmosphere in the countryside'. He went on to consider the longer-term implications: 'It is a bad thing we have shot so many, and that Lithuanians have done the shooting. Especially if it is true that the Germans are filming those shootings.' On 6 November 1941, Blynas wrote in his dairy about the return of the 'Lithuanian battalion' from the Minsk region where they had 'shot more than 46,000 Jews (from Byelorussia and transported from Poland)'. He added: 'Hundreds of Germans filmed it.' Although Blynas, like other Lithuanians, had been hoping that their aspirations to an independent state would be realized by cooperation with the Germans, by mid-December he was deeply shaken by the process. On 13 December 1941 he wrote: 'I can't stand the fact that Lithuania is being turned into a cemetery-morgue' and 'that we Lithuanians are doing the shooting, that we have become nothing more than paid executioners, that we are being filmed while the Germans are not filming themselves.' He concluded this entry: 'I cannot stand this evil.'[70]

Some of the onlookers and even the killers never quite got over their experiences. A Lithuanian diarist wrote on 24 August 1941, not long after killings had expanded to include women and children: 'Brains and blood spattered. . . . The women screamed and yelled. People from the surrounding area gathered. At first they were laughing and smiling but later became horrified, and the Aryan women also began to scream. A massacre. Shameful.'[71] Killers too were often shaken. Accounts emphasize the role of alcohol before, during, and after killings—and even after the war was over, when some killers still seemed to be traumatized by what they had done. As another witness recalled, decades later: 'The people in Šeduva talked about the Jew-shooters. In Šeduva they all died shortly after the war. They simply drank themselves to an early death. They kept visualizing the mass murders again and again, and were driven to drink.'[72]

Killings where Lithuanians or Latvians were at the front line, carrying out the physical act of shooting or beating the victims, were often made into public spectacles that members of the German armed forces (sailors as well as soldiers) even appear, on occasion, to have been 'ordered' to attend. This was the case in the early weeks of occupation, in July and August 1941, in the Baltic coastal port of Liepāja (Libau), part of the Courland area in Latvia. Liepāja was home to around 7,400 Jews, many of them German speaking, and also had a significant population of Baltic Germans. The Jews in Liepāja were well integrated in the wider community, and many Jewish children attended the German high school. It was also, at the time, a port that was open to the wider world, and with a politically self-confident working class. Unlike elsewhere in Latvia, the local population in Liepāja did not welcome the invading German troops.[73]

The Nazi approach here was from the outset exterminatory; a ghetto for the few hundred remaining Jews whose labour was considered essential for the German war effort was only created in July 1942. In the meantime, Jews were targeted for shooting—at first sporadically, in small groups both in the town centre and at the harbour, and then in a major killing operation on the beach of Škēde, a few kilometres north of the town, from 15 to 17 December 1941. During the summer, a site close to the Liepāja lighthouse and harbour was identified for killing groups of people brought in on trucks from the town centre; it was also suitable for mounting something akin to a spectator sport, with onlookers coming to watch killings that were also photographed and filmed. (Today this site is a sports pitch, close to the sand dunes and beach, bearing little trace of its past.)[74] Surrounded by old bunkers, this wide flat area provided an enclosed location from which prisoners could not easily escape, while spectators could climb up high on the surrounding walls to get a better view of the shootings. Unauthorized amateur film footage by the German marine soldier and photographer Reinhard Wiener shows Jews being roughly pulled off the backs of trucks and beaten and chased to the place where they had to stand in order to be shot into a mass grave.[75]

Large numbers of people watched what was taking place, and some were even ordered to be present. One man working for the harbourmaster later recalled that he and a workmate 'once received orders to attend an execution of Jews as spectators'. He went on: 'we both had to be at the execution area at 20.00 hrs on the appointed day. We walked there and back. When we arrived at the appointed place a number of German soldiers were already there. There may have been over a hundred men, I still remember that they were not SS men but soldiers from the Wehrmacht, I think I would be correct in saying that men from all the units stationed in Liepāja were ordered to report to this execution area.'[76] Others simply heard that something out of the ordinary was going on and made their way to the execution site of their own accord. A boatswain's mate from harbour surveillance, for example, recalled that in August 1941 he 'had been hearing continuous rifle salvoes for some time in the harbour area', so he and others 'decided to see what was happening there' after finishing work. When they reached the site, they 'stayed there a while and climbed on to a bunker' to 'see better'.[77]

The head of the 2nd Company Reserve Police Battalion 13, police commander Georg Rosenstock, came from the centre of town, following the tracks of the condemned Jews 'as far as the area around the naval port'. On arrival at the site by the beach, he saw SS-*Untersturmführer* Wolfgang Kügler 'with some SD men and a number of Jews. The Jews were crouching down on the ground. They had to walk in groups of about ten to the edge of a pit. Here they were shot by Latvian civilians. The execution area was visited by scores of German spectators from the Navy and the Reichsbahn [railway].' Rosenstock recounted that he 'turned to Kügler and said in no uncertain terms that it was intolerable that shootings were being carried out in front of spectators'.[78] This police commander seemed more concerned by the public character of the killings than by the fact that Jews were being murdered.

One war correspondent who 'was stationed as a naval correspondent on board a minesweeper in Liepāja harbour' also made an effort to go and see what was going on, because he was particularly interested in people's reactions to the killings. He noted that the 'way these executions were conducted is well known, so there is no need for me to go into that'. What interested him more was 'the people who had to carry out such an action'. He noted very different personal responses to involvement in mass murder: 'I saw SD personnel weeping because they could not cope mentally with what was going on. Then again I encountered others who kept a scoresheet of how many people they had sent to their death.' He went on to wonder: 'Who today can determine which were those who wept as they carried out their duties and which the ones who kept a score-sheet?'[79]

It is almost impossible to determine, in retrospect, what proportions of killers were sickened by the task in which they were engaged, how many kept going only through the effects of alcohol or the desire for booty, and how many were enthusiastic, their hatred of Jews unleashed by legitimation and stimulation from above.[80] But however they may have varied in their inner reactions, it is clear that all had become not merely complicit, but now actively involved in perpetration—and this had a personal impact. Himmler was indeed increasingly concerned about the levels of mental illness among Germans involved in killing—one of the reasons why other methods of murder were being explored, including gassing, which would allow a greater distance between killers and victims. Yet even after more 'efficient' methods of killing had been developed, mass shootings continued.

The murder of women and children, and particularly of pregnant women, aroused widespread disquiet—not only among locals, their former neighbours, but even on the part of the German civilian administration. The regional commissary (*Gebietskommissar*) for the Liepāja area, Dr Walter Alnor, reported on heightened concerns when 470 women and children were murdered in Liepāja, as well as elsewhere in his region. A former *Landrat* in Holstein, Alnor knew personally the Reich Commissary for the Eastern Territories, Hinrich Lohse, who had formerly been the Oberpräsident in Schleswig-Holstein. On 14 October 1941 Alnor wrote to Lohse: 'The shooting of women and small children in particular, many of whom are screaming as they are taken to places of execution, is occasioning general horror.' The 'generally compliant' mayor of Liepāja had come to Alnor to protest about the unrest caused by the killings. And even German army officers had asked him 'whether this gruesome manner of execution was necessary even for children'. They had pointed out that 'in every cultural nation and even in the Middle Ages it was not permissible to execute pregnant women'. Alnor's view was that 'one day this will prove to have been a grave error. Unless all those who have been involved in carrying this out are also liquidated.'[81] This demonstrates an extraordinary combination: recognition of the horrific nature of what was being done, yet concern primarily about local reactions and possible future consequences—which might be mitigated, in Alnor's view, by yet further killings in order to eliminate those who had actually carried out the crimes.

One of the most infamous killing sites near Liepāja was the Šķēde beach, located in an area of pine woods and sand dunes to the north of the town. Here, from 15 to 17 December 1941, some 2,731 Jews as well as a couple of dozen other victims were ordered to undress and line up to be shot into the graves that had been dug for them. Even though the killing site was in a relatively isolated spot some way up the coast, the event was not kept out of sight. Germans took photographs of some young women, either in their underwear or totally naked as, shivering and terrified, they tried to cover themselves with their arms, seeking still to retain some privacy in face of the camera.

The spectacle over three days at Šķēde inevitably drew audiences from further afield. An adjutant from Naval Anti-Aircraft Detachment 707, for example, later recounted how he watched as 'about 300 to 500 people' were marched for 'about one to two kilometres north of our quarters to a little wood where a fairly large wide ditch had already been dug'. He described how the 'execution area was overgrown with pines. The trench was situated in this woody hilly area. The trench was about two to three metres wide, about three metres deep and about fifty to seventy-five metres long.' The weather that day was freezing: 'there was black ice on the roads and people were falling all over the road on the ice.' He returned the following day with some others from his unit 'to the execution area on horseback'. Here they 'could see the arms and legs of the executed Jews sticking out of the inadequately filled-in grave'. He and his colleagues felt they had to do something: 'After seeing this we officers sent a written communication to our headquarters in Liepāja. As a result of our communication the dead Jews were covered properly with sand.'[82] Again, it is remarkable that this officer was more concerned about the wider public impact—the remains of the corpses still being visible to any passer-by—than the actual fact of a mass killing of innocent civilians.

Germans stationed in the area seem to have been relatively impervious to any moral qualms, and were apparently driven more by curiosity than sympathy with the victims. The same does not seem to have been true of the local inhabitants, former neighbours of the murdered Jews. In a letter of 3 January 1942 to the SS and police chief and commander of Riga Ordnungspolizei, the Liepāja SS and police chief noted that 'The execution of the Jews which was carried out during the period covered by this report is still the main topic of conversation among the local population. Regret about the fate of the Jews is constantly expressed; there are few voices to be heard which are in favour of the elimination of the Jews.' They were also incensed, it seems, about the use to which footage of the massacres was being put: 'Amongst other things a rumour is abroad that the execution was filmed in order to have material to use against the Latvian Schutzmannschaft. This material is said to prove that Latvians and not Germans carried out the executions.'[83]

The photographic records of the Šķēde killings survived through the quick-wittedness and courage of David Zivcon, a Jew who worked as an electrician. Zivcon was employed by the German Police and Security Service, and in the course of making repairs in an apartment came across film reel documenting the Šķēde dune murders. Realizing the historic significance of this material, he smuggled out the reel and gave it to a friend, Meir Stein, a skilled photographer, to develop prints. He then managed to return the reel to its original location while secreting the prints in a tin box that he hid behind a brick in a stable wall.

Zivcon was one of the only twenty-five Liepaja Jews to survive the war. When he realized the ghetto was about to be eradicated, he fled to the house of Latvian neighbours, Roberts and Johanna Seduls. They hid a total of eleven Jews, including Zivcon's wife and sister-in-law. Zivcon's then three-year-old niece was given to an elderly German woman until she was returned to her mother after the war—a painful parting for the old lady who had looked after the little girl with love and care, despite the personal risks involved. All three Latvian rescuers later were named 'Righteous among the Nations' by Yad Vashem.[84] The photographs that had been saved and hidden by Zivcon became crucial evidence in the Nuremberg trials, and have been displayed countless times in exhibitions and books ever since, providing almost iconic images of the 'Holocaust by bullets,' or the killings outside the extermination camps.[85] Zivcon's daughter Ilana Ivanova, born just after the war, went on to play a prominent role in the small Jewish local community and in remembrance activities in the area, including the memorial in the shape of a menorah at the Šķēde dune site.[86]

Techniques of self-distancing: The death pits of Riga

The attempt at presenting the killings as carried out by 'others' had a further twist. The photographs taken by Germans of these incidents, and the letters they wrote home about what they had witnessed, served only to spread the news of the mass killing of Jewish civilians far and wide. Yet even those most directly involved in facilitating mass murder managed to find ways of distancing themselves from personal responsibility.

Ghettoization in Riga proceeded over a period of weeks from mid-August, and the ghetto—in a poor suburb south of the town—was sealed in October.[87] The Latvian Jews enclosed here initially thought they would be able to survive through bartering possessions and going out to work, but it became increasingly clear that principles of selection were in place. Young men were snatched and despatched to work camps elsewhere, labouring in conditions that often proved fatal; those who later returned to the ghetto were barely recognizable, walking skeletons. Other Jews were simply taken out and shot, both at killing sites within Riga itself and in pits dug in the surrounding forests, particularly Bikernieki. But by November 1941, as arrangements were being made to deport several thousand Jews from the Reich to the East, something on a far larger scale was planned.

The tensions and disagreements that had been ongoing since August between the German civilian administration, the army, and the SS and *Einsatzgruppen* concerning priorities remained unresolved; and disputes continued between Stahlecker, on behalf of *Einsatzgruppe A*, and Hinrich Lohse, Reich Commissary for the Ostland and deputy to Alfred Rosenberg. While the SS saw the eradication of Jews as an immediate goal, to be accomplished ruthlessly and rapidly, the civilian administration and army were more concerned with the preservation, for the time being, of qualified labour power for production essential to the war effort. This was, it should be noted, not a dispute over murdering Jews: it was taken for granted that, ultimately, all Jews would be exterminated. It was rather a disagreement about timing, and what was in Germany's best interests in the short term: those arguing for selective preservation of working Jews thought that the local gentile population could not immediately supply the qualified labour power needed during the winter months, and so some Jews should be kept alive for at least a few months. This dispute meant that, after the killing sprees of the summer, the organized murder of all Jews was going more slowly in Latvia than some would have liked, and certainly more slowly than in southern Russia.[88]

By October 1941, discussions were underway about speeding up the killing process under new leadership. In November, SS Lieutenant General Friedrich Jeckeln was sent to switch places with Hans-Adolf Prützmann as Higher SS and Police Leader (HSSPF) for the Ostland territories;

Prützmann now went south to Ukraine. As HSSPF for southern Russia, Jeckeln had already demonstrated his determination to kill as many Jews as possible: he had played a key role, with army support, in the mass killings at Kamianets-Podilskyi on 27–28 August, with 23,600 victims (carefully recorded by the army); he had also been central to the massacre in the ravine at Babi Yar (Ukrainian: Babyn Yar) on 29–30 September 1941, with 33,771 victims; and he had been involved in several other significant atrocities (he was ultimately convicted and executed in 1946 for the deaths of more than 100,000 Jews, Roma, and others). Jeckeln was already becoming known as an expert in developing face-to-face mass killing techniques. Now, in Riga, he wanted to perfect an almost industrial method of mass murder, maximizing both technical efficiency and use of human resources through the division of labour at the killing site.

Following an investigation of the neighbourhood around Riga, Jeckeln identified what he thought would be a suitable site in Rumbula, in a wooded spot between the railway tracks and the main road, some ten kilometres south of the Riga ghetto and just north of the Salaspils labour camp. Jeckeln also ensured that he had the best possible expertise at his disposal for treating mass murder as a purely technical problem. Ernst Friedrich Hemicker was an engineer who had long been committed to the Nazi cause and had joined the SS in February 1933.[89] He had been working in Düsseldorf when, on 28 August 1941, the head of the SS personnel department in Berlin wrote asking whether he could 'be made available immediately for a task in the east that falls within his technical sphere of expertise'. At the beginning of September Hemicker was, accordingly, sent off to join Jeckeln, at this time still in southern Russia.

Hemicker's dates are a little hazy here (perhaps intentionally): he had, he later claimed, spent barely two weeks with Jeckeln in Kiev before Jeckeln and his team were transferred north to replace Prützmann in Riga—although the transfer was agreed a while before the actual move, and it is quite possible that Hemicker was already with Jeckeln at the time of the Babi Yar massacre. Even if he did only arrive shortly after it had taken place, he certainly would have known about it, so he must have been well aware of the kind of service he was entering into at this time. And his contributions appear to have been well-recognized. Hemicker's rank was soon upgraded to 'Specialist Leader in the Waffen-SS' (*Sonderführer der Waffen-SS*). With effect from 1 December 1941—the day after the first mass killings in

Rumbula—Hemicker's rank was again changed, this time to the status of special advisor to Jeckeln, under the title 'Specialist Leader for the Higher SS and Police Leader in the Eastern Territories' (*Sonderführer beim Höheren SS- und Polizeiführer Ostland*). This inaugurated further moves from one significant site to another as the war proceeded; Hemicker ended the war with Hans Kammler's team building V-2 rockets in the Austrian mountains, carving out tunnels in the mountains using slave labourers from Mauthausen concentration camp and its subcamps. Kammler himself had previous experience exploiting slave labour from concentration camps, having operated in Majdanek, Peenemunde, and Mittelbau-Dora; any technician working with him could hardly be described as 'purely' an engineer.

In Riga, Hemicker had been summoned to solve what seemed—or could be construed as—a purely abstract mathematical problem. How many large graves would need to be dug, at what depth and width, with a combined volume to accommodate some 25,000 to 28,000 corpses? What additional features might assist a speedy and effective process, such that clothes and valuables could be dropped off in an orderly fashion and groups could pass through rapidly without holding up those behind them?

In an interview in March 1969, in the course of legal investigations, Hemicker explained that he had only 'realized that the Jews were to be killed by shooting' when he arrived at the designated site for the mass graves and was told what the task would be. But he proceeded to solve the technical problem set for him, irrespective of the murderous intended outcome. At this point, he told the investigators, he decided it would be necessary to build a ramp down into the deep pit, 'since the poor people could not jump 3 metres into the depths'. This moment of apparent sympathy with the 'poor' victims—as claimed nearly three decades later—also served to camouflage more practical considerations: a ramp would speed up a more efficient killing process, in which people would be instructed to walk down and then lie down, tightly packed in rows, where they could be rapidly killed with just one shot in the head, also allowing more bodies to be accommodated in each grave.

In the course of his interrogation, Hemicker conceded that 'the people who were to be killed were men, women and children, was not in any doubt'. But when asked if he could have refused the order to make his gruesome calculations, Hemicker denied the possibility. He added: 'I also, in my haste, did not really consider this, because I saw the task as a technical exercise. I was, after all, addressed and given the task as a professional.'[90]

In this way, Hemicker managed to distance himself, absolving himself of personal responsibility for the deadly outcome. His professional task was purely 'technical'. His design was then carried out in practice by others: over the course of three days, some 3,000 Russian prisoners of war from the nearby Salaspils labour camp were brought in to dig the nearly frozen soil—by hand, since there were no available tools.

The previous disputes between those determined on ruthless extermination, including Jeckeln, and those with an eye on the continuing need for specialized labour, were not resolved. Jeckeln had to cede ground and, instead of being able to kill every Jew in the ghetto, a selection had to take place. As in Riga, the ghetto was divided. A 'small ghetto' was created and fenced in with barbed wire; all men still considered useful as labour were relocated here. A few women, who could claim (with varying degrees of honesty) some expertise as seamstresses able to repair army uniforms, were also selected for preservation at this time. The rest, left in the larger portion of the ghetto, awaited their fate. In the early hours of the icy morning of 30 November, the streets of the ghetto were cleared and a miserable procession of Latvian Jews—most on foot, the weak, elderly, sick, and very young on trucks—were sent off sequentially, every half hour, in carefully numbered blocks escorted by Latvian guards, the ten kilometres down the road to the freshly prepared killing site. Many slipped, stumbled, and fell, and were shot along the way in the course of a journey over icy roads that took two hours by foot.

The Jews from the Riga ghetto who arrived at the killing pits of Rumbula were also, unexpectedly, joined by 1,000 Jews from the Reich. The train carrying them to Riga had arrived at the Škirotava station, on the outskirts south of the city, possibly a little too early for transferral into the not yet fully emptied ghetto; or possibly Jeckeln simply wanted to include them in his overall tally for the day. Whatever the explanation, the Reich Jews were transferred directly from the station to their deaths in Rumbula. The fact that Jeckeln had taken the initiative in this way, without prior authorization from Berlin, irritated the RSHA. On being informed, Himmler explicitly did not approve—although by then it was already too late. Moreover, Himmler was by now insisting that gassing would in fact be a preferable method of killing, from the perspective of the perpetrators at least.[91]

The mass killing of around 14,000 Jews on 30 November took place throughout the day and into the evening in Rumbula, with the Latvian shooters working in shifts and drinking copious quantities of alcohol to keep going. Occasionally, German supervisors would be called to deliver a 'mercy shot' to victims seen to be still writhing, not quite dead. Additional workers sorted the clothing and valuables to be sent back to Riga. Innumerable people were present as onlookers: members of the army, the police forces, the civilian administration, as well as locals, including those who lived and worked along the ten-kilometre route along the main road from the city to the death pits. There was no way this killing could be kept secret.

Hemicker observed the procedure from the start. After half an hour, he later recounted, his stomach was churning. He was not the only onlooker: the area was 'swarming with representatives of various departments and units', including members of the army, police officers, and 'members of the civilian administration'.[92] Moreover, the killing spree could not be completed on 30 November. Its continuation was delayed by bad weather, with heavy snowfalls making it less easy to repeat the performance immediately, and then further delayed by disputes between Jeckeln and his superiors. But a week later, work was resumed and a further operation on 8 December effectively cleared the rest of the nonworking Latvian Jews' section of the ghetto, with the exception of a few more who had been selected for labour.

In total, more than 25,000 people were killed in the course of these two days of shootings in Rumbula, making this one of the largest face-to-face massacres on the Eastern Front. The second occasion was if anything even more publicly visible than the first, since ghetto inhabitants now knew what awaited them and many refused to cooperate. At least 900 were shot dead while still in the streets of Riga, watched by innumerable onlookers, before the march to Rumbula had even begun.[93]

In his 1969 interview, Hemicker confirmed that 'everyone, every single member of the German administration, knew at the time that the Jews had been or were being killed. It is totally impossible for me to understand how anyone who served in Riga at the end of 1941 can claim they had heard nothing of the shooting of the Jews in Riga.'[94]

Yet this is precisely what Jürgen Ernst Kroeger attempted to assert in his later account.[95] His claims to impotence and innocence had to be supported by asserting a high degree of ignorance, despite the fact that he was working as a translator for the German forces in Riga. In his memoirs, Kroeger suggests he had just shadowy intimations that something unto-ward was going on. Hints had been dropped by a friend and colleague who chose, after reportedly having witnessed something truly harrowing, to vol-unteer instead for service at the front. Yet Kroeger's self-presentation as an innocent young idealist looks barely plausible when we consider the sheer extent of the violence on the streets of Riga and on the road to Rumbula, as well as the dramatic transformation in the character of the ghetto once it had lost so many thousands of its former inhabitants. One would have had to be a completely blind and socially isolated bystander not to have noticed the forcible removal and murder of more than 25,000 fellow residents of the city. 'Ignorance' was actively constructed.

Kroeger's claims to ignorance look even less plausible when we consider where he was now himself working. He was by no means on the margins, but rather an active facilitator of the Nazi regime. In his work as interpreter and translator, Kroeger had been transferred from the army to the Security Service (SD) of the SS. The commandant of the SD for whom Kroeger now worked was Dr Rudolf Lange, whose people were directly involved in the killings of 8 December. Lange not only commanded members of the Security Police to assist in the emptying of the ghetto but also ordered Viktors Arājs to mobilize members of his notorious Latvian commando for work at Rumbula. Moreover, in January 1942 Lange personally reported on events in Riga at the Wannsee Conference coordinating the details of the 'final solution of the Jewish question', chosen precisely because he had direct experience of murdering deported Jews.[96] Lange, moreover, was not given to euphemisms, and in a report probably written in early February 1942 described very clearly how 'the mortality rate is constantly rising among the evacuated Jews', how those carrying disease as well as 'several mentally ill Jews' were 'selected and executed', and how 'removal was camouflaged'.[97]

That one of Lange's employees, an interpreter and translator whose very task it was to facilitate communication between Germans and Latvians, should not have 'known' about the major activities in which his organiza-tion was involved and on which his boss was reporting, beggars belief. Yet this is precisely what Kroeger would have us believe. The young idealist was supposedly sufficiently blinded by his faith in the Führer not to have noticed what was going on all around—and what, indeed, he was himself facilitating.

Over the decades, there have been fierce debates about which side was primarily responsible for the early eruption of mass murder, in Latvia as in Lithuania.[98] But the record clearly suggests that the interactions between Germans and local activists were crucial to the initiation and escalation of early killings. Pointing to the dates at which violence erupted—as the Red Army retreated and the Germans advanced—and claiming this was a form of 'interregnum' may unwittingly serve to buttress the German attempts at the time to disguise the background planning and instigation of violence by locals.

In mid-October 1941, General Stahlecker summarized with pride the progress *Einsatzgruppe A* had made since the invasion. As he put it: 'It was the task of the Security Police to set these self-cleansing movements going and to direct them into the right channels in order to achieve the aim of this cleansing as rapidly as possible'—'cleansing' here being the standard euphemism for killing Jews. And Stahlecker further emphasized the significance of deception: 'It was no less important to establish as unshakable and provable facts for the future that it was the liberated population itself which took the most severe measures on its own initiative, against the Bolshevik and Jewish enemy, without any German instruction being evident.'[99] However problematic some aspects of Stahlecker's report might be, his summary identified key features of the situation. The escalating violence was initiated, incited, and legitimated by the Germans, who both organized and unleashed local initiatives and then brought them under their own control. The sheer extent of violence was made possible by a fatal combination of German initiatives and organization, local collaboration and acquiescence, and support or silence on the ground.

Karl Jäger presented the record of his 'achievements' as leader of *Einsatzkommando 3* in a report of 1 December 1941, portraying the mass murder of the overwhelming majority of the Jews in the area for which he was responsible under Stahlecker's command. 'I can confirm today that *Einsatzkommando 3* has achieved the goal of solving the Jewish problem in Lithuania. There are no more Jews in Lithuania, apart from working Jews and their families.' He tried to put the best gloss he could on the compromise reached with the army by adding: 'I wanted to eliminate the working Jews and their families as well, but the Civil Administration (*Reichskommissar*) and the Wehrmacht attacked me most sharply and issued a prohibition against having these Jews and their families shot.'[100] He went on to underline this point: 'I consider the *Aktionen* against the Jews of EK 3 to be virtually completed. The remaining working Jews and Jewesses are urgently needed, and I can imagine that this manpower will continue to be needed urgently after the winter has ended.' But the Jewish 'race' would in any case die out: 'I am of the opinion that the male working Jews should be sterilized immediately to prevent reproduction. Should any Jewess never-theless become pregnant, she is to be liquidated.'[101]

A report prepared by Stahlecker for the RSHA in Berlin on killings car-ried out by *Einsatzgruppe A* to the end of January 1942 was accompanied by a map embellished with drawings of coffins, next to which were recorded the numbers of Jews killed.[102] Estonia, where the prewar Jewish community had been relatively small, and from which many Jews had been able to flee eastwards as the Germans advanced, was now declared 'Jew-free' (*judenfrei*), with *Einsatzgruppe A* claiming responsibility for having killed 963 Jews who did not make it out in time. Belorussia had been less thoroughly 'cleansed' by this time, in Stahlecker's view: while 41,828 were recorded as killed, the 'estimated number of Jews still remaining' was put at 128,000. Meanwhile, the total for those killed in Lithuania was given as 136,421, and for Latvia 35,238 (a significant underestimate). Stahlecker's figures are unreliable; but even as depicted on this extraordinary and gruesome map, Stahlecker was claiming that, in little over half a year since the invasion, more than 170,000 Jews had been slaughtered in just these two Baltic states alone.

Current estimates suggest that out of 210,000 Jews in Lithuania at the time of the German invasion in June 1941, only 40,000 remained alive in ghettos and labour camps in December; and that between 60,000 and 70,000 of the 75,000 Jews in Latvia had been murdered by the end of the year.[103] Even if the detailed numbers are subject to revision, in little over six months under German rule the majority of Jews in Lithuania and Latvia had been murdered. And even if the short-term priorities—interim prod-uctivity or immediate extermination—were still disputed, the end goal was broadly shared.

In the months following the invasion of the Soviet Union, official German news reports had been full of military 'victories'. But given the highly vis-ible nature of the killings, not only in these two states but also across the whole of the Eastern Front, it was impossible to hide or silence the mass murders going on behind the front lines. And, given the ways in which German soldiers, police forces, and members of the civilian administration variously witnessed, facilitated, or participated in killings, it was inevitable that news filtered back to those living within the borders of the Reich. Within the Reich, people became increasingly aware of atrocities, even if they were not themselves directly involved. Bystanders could no longer pretend to remain neutral: choices now arose about becoming complicit or, by contrast, engaging in acts of resistance and rescue. Everywhere, as the war proceeded, Germans had to find ways of interpreting this ever more uncomfortable knowledge and adjusting themselves to the compromises in which they were so now visibly engaged.[104]

10

Inner Emigration and the
Fiction of Ignorance

Whatever they felt about the Nazi regime, Reich citizens were collectively mobilized in service of their country at war. Whether at home or at the front, the war had a direct impact on their own lives. Soon after the invasion of the Soviet Union in 1941, many also became aware of atrocities being carried out in the East. Such knowledge was, however, variously reinterpreted, either justified in terms of national interests and antisemitic ideology, or marginalized in light of more direct concerns. Those who truly registered the news of mass murders of civilians—even if they only heard of isolated incidents, and had neither precise details nor a wider picture—were both shocked and at the same time acutely aware of their own incapacity to take any effective action. Psychologically, this was intolerable; most Germans found it simpler to get on with their own lives, which was demanding enough during wartime.

After the defeat of Nazi Germany in May 1945, Germans in particular were repeatedly challenged to face up to the crimes committed in their name and, it was generally assumed, with their complicity. Austrians were more easily able to evade scrutiny by retreating behind the 'Hitler's first victim' myth. During the first few weeks of encounters with defeated Germans, the American forces in particular had been somewhat surprised by how much Germans knew about atrocities, and how readily they seemed to speak about what they had witnessed or heard (if rather less readily about what they had themselves done). But very quickly, German defences changed: from April 1945 at the latest, in public Germans widely claimed 'ignorance', implying that 'knowing' would have affected how they would have acted or why they failed to act, and using ignorance as effective proof of innocence. The popular refrain 'we knew nothing about it' gen-erally restricted the 'it' to a very narrow focus, such as the gas chambers of Auschwitz-Birkenau. The focus on 'Auschwitz', or 'the gas chambers', effectively excluded the discrimination and persecution of the peacetime years, with which the majority of people had been forced to comply, in which many had more actively participated, and from which many had also benefitted. And it excluded the many instances of violence and brutality, both before and especially during the war: beatings, arrests, public humili-ation, incarceration, deportation, exploitation, and expropriation, which so many 'Aryans' had not merely witnessed but in which they had been more actively involved. The question of 'what did they know' has continued to dominate approaches to understanding the Nazi era; yet it is arguably the wrong question to be asking. The right question, or questions, are, What did they make of what they knew? How did those directly involved in atrocities try to justify their actions? How did others who heard about them interpret what they knew?

'Knowledge' and 'ignorance' are not straightforward matters: percep-tions and interpretations make a big difference. Thinking of mass killings in terms of self-defence against an anonymous 'enemy' is a quite different matter from imagining the murder of children and babies, let alone former neighbours, such as the kindly doctor who used to tend to your own chil-dren when they were young. It was far easier for most people not to con-front directly the idea that the victims in Kaunas or Riga were innocent human beings, but rather 'the enemy'. The key was to remove the murder of former neighbours to sites far away, while simultaneously bolstering the stereotypical image of 'the Jew' as a deadly foe antithetical to the interests of the Volksgemeinschaft to which 'Aryan' Germans were now existentially committed.

If ignorance was less of an excuse for passivity than was later claimed, impotence was a very real issue. Those individuals who could not easily swallow this interpretation of what was going on generally felt powerless to act, in the face of the apparatus of repression and all-pervasive atmosphere of fear.

Of increasing relative importance, too, was the third factor explaining bystander passivity: indifference. In times of war, when sheer survival was at stake, people who were not themselves persecuted were less likely to care what was happening to those beyond their own circle or community.

And as the risks associated with attempts at helping Jews increased, and the dangers and privations of wartime became ever more present, so residual connections across communities—connections that might have maintained empathy—were strained or torn. It took a very strong sense of morality, of political or personal commitment, to even sustain any thoughts of the persecuted beyond perhaps a passing moment of registering absence.

This was, in a sense, the perfect storm, providing the conditions for the genocide unleashed by Germany and put into effect right across Europe.[1]

Out of sight, out of mind?

Deportation of Jews from the Reich 'to the East' after the invasion of the Soviet Union started in mid-October 1941.[2] As time went by, the lack of letters or news from Jews who had been herded onto trains bound for the East created unease, and unsettling rumours started to circulate. One survivor later recounted that 'in Halle in 1941 people were already talking about how Jews from Germany had been made to stand in front of anti-tank ditches and done in with sub-machine guns'.[3] The news seeping in about the mass murder of Jews in Eastern Europe confirmed fears among Jews remaining in Germany about the fates awaiting those who had been sent to join them. Even so, it took a while for the realities to begin to sink in; there was still hope that the myth of 'resettlement' might be true.

Else Behrend-Rosenfeld, who as manager of the Jewish home in Berg am Laim, Munich, had been informed in advance of the deportation of Munich Jews in November 1941, suffered a physical and nervous breakdown in the following weeks. But in the new year she managed to pull herself together and could again find some solace in running the home and putting her energies into trying to help others. By late March 1942, rumours were rampant that another deportation was in the offing; they still had received no news from those who had been deported previously. For many weeks Behrend-Rosenfeld did not find time to write her diary; but then events took over, and on 12 April 1942 she wrote a long entry trying to recount all that had just happened. She was on the list of names of those to be deported.[4]

Some on the list sought to have some control of their own fate, sewing lethal quantities of medication into the hems of clothing in order to put

a speedy end to their lives. Many tried to prepare for deportation psychologically as well as physically, secure in the knowledge that they had not
compromised themselves: as Behrend-Rosenfeld put it, 'it is so much easier
to be among those who are suffering injustice than those who are perpetrating injustice'. They could, she felt, 'go towards an uncertain and heavy
fate with heads held high'; their 'self-respect and sense of worth as human
beings' was not in any way damaged.

These deportations took place in full view. People on the streets watched
as the Munich Jews were driven towards the 'collection camp' (*Sammellager*)
where they would be held until the full trainload was ready.⁵ We do not
know precisely what the participants or onlookers were thinking, but
there can be little doubt that it would have been easier for them to believe
in the myth of 'resettlement' than to face the reality of what awaited the
deportees—let alone to witness in person the murder of their former fellow
citizens. A degree of deception about the destination of the transport was
arguably not only crucial to gaining the cooperation of the victims but also
comforting for bystanders.

Behrend-Rosenfeld provides a vivid description of the brutal treatment
meted out in the collection camp. Yet there was also, among the deportees, a
feeling of community, a feeling of belonging together. Behrend-Rosenfeld
herself resorted to her well-rehearsed strategy—practised, in effect since
childhood, when she had helped in her father's clinic and also looked
after her seven younger siblings at home—of suppressing her own needs
by throwing herself into care for the others in her group, expressing her
sense of responsibility for them. But, now at the age of sixty, her reserves of
strength were limited; she nearly collapsed while the deportees were being
made to stand with all their luggage in blazing sunshine, watched by laughing SA men, as 'practice' for the following day's 4 A.M. start. But she was
resolved not to allow any sign of weakness.⁶

Just as Behrend-Rosenfeld had mustered her strength and was trying to
assist another member of the group who had crumpled before her eyes, her
name was called. She had, to her surprise, been struck off the list of those
to be deported on that occasion. Her services were required—indeed seen
as essential—to manage the Jewish home for a few more weeks, until it was
finally to be cleared later that summer. Behrend-Rosenfeld was sent back
to Berg am Laim to pick up her previous duties, but now without other
people with whom she had worked so closely; they had been in the group

that was deported, as it turned out, to Piaski in Poland. Not one of those deported survived.

She now faced a stark choice. It was no longer possible to leave the Reich legally, emigrating as her husband had managed to do just days before the outbreak of war. It was barely possible any more to cling to the hope that deportation might genuinely mean 'resettlement' and the chance of a new life in 'the east'. The choice of putting an end to oneself was a final choice; those who took this way out tended to be either couples or families choosing to go together, or lone individuals who felt they had no one left who would care for them or miss them. Behrend-Rosenfeld, by contrast, still desperately hoped to be reunited with her husband and children who were living abroad.

There was only one last possibility, in which she was encouraged by those close to her: 'going under' (*untertauchen*), hiding, or assuming a false identity. This option was extremely risky. It required courage, psychological reserves, and quick-wittedness; material resources that could be drawn on over a considerable period of time; social resources, including strong networks of friends, acquaintances, and wider communities who could be trusted; appropriate geographical, social, and spatial environments; and lastly an enormous amount of sheer luck. Of the likely tens of thousands or more who sought to escape and survive in this way, only a tiny minority— maybe a couple of thousand in total across the Reich—actually succeeded. In Munich, only 110 to 120 Jews would make it through the war by 'going under'.[7] A few 'Aryans' helped them. Before he died of illness, one soldier, for example, returning on sick leave from service on the Eastern Front told his parents and their Jewish neighbours about the killings; his parents then assisted these neighbours to hide with relatives in the countryside. But they were in a tiny minority. In 1941–1942 there were 133 suicides in Munich of Jews who were slated for deportation—more than the number who would survive by 'going under'. A few, however, left suicide notes in order to fake their own deaths, ensuring the scenarios they created, such as drowning, would entail a long police search without any likelihood of finding a body, giving them extra time to get away.[8] For the time being, Behrend-Rosenfeld stayed in place, ever more fearful of what might await her and what she should do. Yet it had become clear what would happen if she allowed herself to be taken.

Deportation trains from the Reich in late 1941 and spring 1942 were going to destinations with relatively unfamiliar names—Piaski, Riga, Kaunas, Minsk. The stationary extermination camps with their gas chambers that have since become so famous, dominating the public imagination, were barely on the horizon yet. While gassing in mobile vans had already been trialled on the Eastern Front, and came into operation at Chełmno (known by the Germans as Kulmhof) in December 1941, the three 'Reinhard camps' (Bełżec, Sobibór, and Treblinka) only came into operation in the spring and early summer of 1942. Killing by Zyklon B gas in Auschwitz was first trialled in early September 1941 but only came into full operation from mid-1942. In all these dedicated extermination camps, efforts were made to deceive both victims and bystanders. Elaborate speeches were given on arrival at Chełmno to ensure cooperation in handing over valuables, undressing, and entering the gas vans; railheads at Treblinka and Sobibór were made to look anodyne, with brightly painted signs, flowerbeds and window boxes on the station buildings; the complex of the commandant's house and SS barracks in Sobibór gave the appearance of a vacation colony; gas chambers at Auschwitz-Birkenau, Majdanek, Bełżec and elsewhere were disguised as shower rooms.[9] Thick hedges, fences interwoven with branches and twigs, and other means were used to camouflage the routes to the gas chambers; and loud noises, including the cackling of geese, were intended to drown out the screams and cries of the dying.[10] The deceptions practised in the death camps, and the relatively small numbers of Germans staffing the death camps, assisted by Trawninki-trained Ukrainians and others, later provided fodder for the myth of 'never having known anything about it'.

By the time the death camps were in full swing, however, news of the mass killings in the East was already out. Deception may have helped to pacify some of the victims, rendering them more docile on the path to death, but wider knowledge of the mass murders taking place in the East had been present from the outset. Those who were travelling through or living in the occupied territories or fighting on the battlefields of Eastern Europe often wrote home about what they saw or heard, or even sent photographs of what they had seen. Their perceptions and descriptions were coloured in terms of their expectations and frameworks of interpretation, and many were already deeply steeped in Nazi worldviews. The question, again, is less what people 'knew' than how they responded. Reactions varied significantly.

Travelling east

The impact of Nazi socialization was evident among young soldiers seeking to make sense of their experiences in the light of their ideological training. Many resorted to a repertoire of racial stereotypes to convey their impressions as they proceeded eastwards, using Nazi frameworks to make sense of the unprecedentedly brutal campaign in which they were now engaged. But even so, their impressions—however coloured by ideological concerns—were challenged by the human realities that confronted them.[11] The starving and ragged Jews held in overcrowded and unhygienic conditions in the ghettos of occupied Poland were living (and dying) examples that appeared, to some, to confirm the antisemitic stereotypes they had previously only seen in the *Stürmer* newspaper.[12] Many soldiers took photographs. Franz Döhring, for example, kept an album—the equivalent of holiday snaps—of the Polish campaign, including photographs of burned-out villages, bombed houses, and 'the first hostages'. He entitled one photograph 'a dirty Jew' (*Ein schmieriger Jude*); another ominously portrayed 'the Jews of Goworovo' (*Die Juden von Goworovo*) being made to sit together in the centre of a town square, guarded by German soldiers; he does not tell us what subsequently became of them.[13] Such scenes clearly made a major impression on soldiers who had not previously had much, if any, exposure to life outside Germany; Döhring died in the Russian campaign in 1944.

The impact was heightened when Germans witnessed scenes of overcrowding and starvation, as in the Warsaw ghetto. A road divided the Warsaw ghetto into two parts, connected by a footbridge, while trams running along this road allowed glimpses through the barbed wire and fences into the ghetto areas on either side. One soldier, Max Rohwerder, recorded his impressions of the Warsaw ghetto in his diary entry of Friday, 3 October 1941: 'I have already driven twice through the ghetto. It looks like an ant heap. The Jews look with barely restrained hatred at us soldiers in the electric tram car.'[14] Another, Heinrich Zils, looked through the 'barbed wire enclosing the pestilential Jewish quarter' (*Seuchen- und Judenviertel*) and was lost for words to describe these 'vermin', many of whom were dying from starvation; a few were well-dressed but the majority were 'shrouded in sacks and rags'.[15] Franz Jonas, twenty-three, recorded his impressions of the Warsaw ghetto in his diary entry of Sunday, 3 August 1941. He took an afternoon walk through Warsaw, which was 'pretty much a heap of rubble'. But the ghetto was infinitely worse, 'a frightful hell'. He enumerated the details: 'Poverty. Misery. Epidemics. 600,000 inhabitants. Half of Warsaw. But the area is very small. A conglomeration of people.' And he went on to wonder: 'How do they earn their money? There are no factories or businesses. Just trading keeps everything going. How many perish every day? Certainly a considerable number. The ghetto can be wound up one day because there will be nobody left.' Jonas captured here what historians call the policy of 'extermination through attrition'. He was also aware of how much misery was inflicted by the German occupation regime: 'Pretty brutal start on the part of the police. Anyone who is found on the street after a certain hour in the evening is ruthlessly bumped off. Anyone making himself guilty of a serious crime is hanged, and left hanging on the tree for 24 hours.' This brutality had obvious consequences: 'Because of this, there was enormous hatred. Already some police officers or soldiers on duty there have disappeared. Many have also fallen victim to the epidemics.'[16]

Continuing their journey, soldiers were confronted with 'evidence' of the supposed inferiority of Eastern Jews, so different in appearance from the assimilated Jews of the Reich. On reaching Siedlce, Heinrich Zils commented that since 80 percent of the population were Jews, its appearance was accordingly disagreeable, the 'houses caked with filth and mould'.[17] Franz Jonas, moving across Poland, was struck by the way Jews wore 'a yellow patch on their chests and backs' and 'took their hats off for any German soldier passing by'.[18] Arriving in Kaunas the following day, 11 August 1941, Jonas commented that 'Lithuania is just as much a shit-hole [Dreckland] as Poland. Miserable houses, squalid and unkempt. Bad roads.'[19] He also noticed columns of forced labourers working on the roads, under the supervision, he thought, of the Organisation Todt, the Nazi engineering and construction organization that used forced labour across the Reich. Others, too, recorded their impressions of forced labourers. Karl Schwender, aged eighteen, an avid member of the Hitler Youth and SS volunteer, wrote home on 16 September 1941 about the 'Jews and prisoners of war' working in the camp where he was based, commenting that Jews 'were a people [Volk] even worse than Gypsies'.[20]

As they proceeded eastwards, soldiers inevitably came close to sites of mass murder. Some heard of killings well before they reached the places where they were taking place. Max Rohwerder, in his Warsaw diary entry of 3 October 1941, wrote: 'A maintenance sergeant from a Reich railroad convoy who said he had just come from the Ukraine told us that <u>all Jews in the Ukraine were being shot</u>, including women and children. I can't believe it. Apparently they had to dig out the anti-tank ditches to turn them into graves, and then they [were shot into these] and neatly layered nicely on top of each other.'[21]

Many soldiers could only interpret mass killings through the justificatory lens of the ideological spectacles provided by Nazism. As early as 30 June 1941, Heinrich Zils noted that the previous day some eighty-three 'snipers' had been shot and was grateful that 'the Führer had once again struck out at just the right moment'.[22] On Sunday, 17 August 1941, Franz Jonas reached Pleskau (now Pskow), where he recorded in his diary that ten 'hostages' had been shot in 'retaliation' for the murder of two guards by 'partisans'. The shooting of the hostages had been carried out 'in public, on the marketplace' and the corpses had been 'left there for 24 hours as a deterrent example'. But, Jonas noted with some surprise, 'the population is not moved by this. They regard it as just a spectacle that lends a little variety to their life.'[23] The following day, 18 August, the local population were 'again standing expectantly at the marketplace. Since two more guards had been shot, they are again awaiting the spectacle of public shootings'. But this time they were disappointed: 'Nothing happened.'[24] On Friday, 22 August, however, suddenly 'the entire male civilian population aged between sixteen and seventy years was arrested'.[25] Jonas provides no further details of who these people were, where they were taken, or what ultimately happened to them; the pages for the next two days of his diary are left blank. But it is not hard to guess.

By late October 1941, killing civilians who could hardly be plausibly categorized as 'snipers' had become more routine and on a larger scale—and again, these killings were far from secret. On 22 October 1941, Max Rohwerder recorded in his diary in Minsk: 'Yesterday between ten pm and midnight guard troops came into my cabin and said that where they had been stationed from 17 to 19 October they had <u>shot 1,400 Jews</u> who had brought arms to the partisans. Men, women and children. Their sergeant had shot with a pistol?!'[26] On 22 October 1941, Rohwerder's group left Minsk and on 23 October arrived in 'Boryssow [sic: Borissow, Baryssau], where Napoleon had crossed the Beresina'. He continued: 'A few stations behind Boryssow a railroad superintendent told me that in the last few days

7,000 Jews had been shot—for supporting the Partisans. Executions were also taking place in other locations. The local Commander of Boryssow had told him this himself.'[27] It is notable that the justifications given in all these cases, even where women and children were being shot, still referenced alleged support of 'partisans'.

The evidence of terrorization was only too visible to Rohwerder, as he continued his journey. On 1 November, passing Sytschowka, he noted 'on the left-hand side of the road a Russian peasant, hanged, with a placard, and then five hanged in a row!'[28] Rohwerder was clearly surprised, possibly even shocked, by what he was seeing. But he reproduced in his diary entries the ideological justifications and labels that were current at the time, repeating stories about 'partisans' and the need to deal with potentially dangerous elements in wartime.

Others wrote letters home that were infused with Nazi ideology. One soldier, 'Kurt', commented that the 'great battle' which had now broken out surpassed all previous campaigns, being a struggle not only between two peoples but also a far more momentous matter of two worldviews.[29] Another soldier, Alfred Nehlsen, produced a veritable hodgepodge of Nazi justifications for an aggressive invasion packaged as supposed self-defence against alleged international conspiracies of Jews and Bolsheviks. Nehlsen marvelled at how Hitler had kept the fight against the Bolsheviks so secret until the very moment of invasion; but now, he thought, was exactly the right moment to strike, since Jews the world over, 'from the plutocrats in London and New York right through to the Bolsheviks' had 'declared war' on the Germans. 'Everything that is Jewish is standing in a united front against us. The Marxists are fighting shoulder to shoulder with high finance.' But, given Hitler's genius and the 'pre-emptive' strike, Germany had managed to stay ahead of the game. This was, however, no moment for celebration; they were now on the brink of the 'one of the most decisive battles, indeed, if successful, the most decisive' battle of all times.[30]

Thus prepared ideologically (if not in terms of winter clothing), Germans entered the battlefields of Eastern Europe. Many took photographs of what they saw or wrote about their experiences in letters home. Others were directly involved in mass killings, even if they did not feel personally responsible for what they were doing. It is here that Nazi ideology and antisemitism had to be reshaped to provide more active 'justifications' for murder.

Perceptions on the front line of violence

For the millions of Germans far away from the front, knowledge came from letters, parcels, and visits home. For the hundreds of thousands of soldiers out east, it came from not merely witnessing but being directly involved in killing operations. Those who were in some way involved in mass murder were not silent about what they saw and did. Their perceptions and justifications are relevant both to their own actions and to their interactions with those at home, including those in whom they confided. Worldviews justifying genocide were developed and mutually confirmed, repeatedly reinforced as the genocidal war progressed. Later constructions of 'bystanding' cannot be analysed without some reference to the perceptions and representations of those drawn into perpetration at the time.[31]

Groups involved in the killing operations had varying degrees of prior training and ideological preparation for mass murder. The most committed were the 3,000 or so members of the four *Einsatzgruppen*, made up largely of members of the Security Police and the Security Service (SD) of the SS, under the overall command of the RSHA. Their leaders were generally highly educated (many held doctorates) and ideologically committed; and they had received detailed prior instructions on the murderous task that would await them. They were, accordingly, thoroughly schooled for their task in advance.[32] Yet the *Einsatzgruppen* could not have carried out face-to-face killings of many hundreds of thousands of people on their own. There were a number of other organizations with which they worked closely.

More than 50,000 men belonged to 'order police battalions' (*Polizeibataillone der Ordnungspolizei*) that were cumulatively responsible for well over half a million murders.[33] A pathbreaking study of the 'ordinary men' who made up Reserve Police Battalion 101 revealed that they came from a wide range of backgrounds, and that they were not individually motivated by ideology. Rather, situational factors and peer group pressure shaped both their initial involvement in killings and their subsequent acclimatization to the job; and those who did not feel up to the grisly work were simply redirected to other duties, attracting no penalties for refusal.[34] More broadly, subsequent analyses of police battalions in the East have revealed significant differences in levels of ideological commitment and Nazi convictions between the officers and upper ranks, who were virtually all in the SS and many in the NSDAP, and the rank and file of 'ordinary' members. A few of the latter were immediately willing to engage in killings; some were 'brutalized' by their involvement in mass murder early on; others 'acclimatized' more gradually as they crossed significant thresholds over a longer period of time.[35] Whatever the variations in prior training and commitments, there were always enough individuals willing to participate in and even volunteer for killings to make up the numbers required. These men were sustained in their task by a combination of small-group camaraderie, paramilitary training, and organizational expectations, as well as the radical ideology that informed and repeatedly reinforced engagement in 'actions'.[36] There were inconsistencies in practice and variations in individual responses. But, as noted, no one who found the strain of murdering innocent civilians too great to bear was punished for refusing to shoot; the most they suffered was subjection to the ridicule of their fellows and having to undertake other less than agreeable (but not murderous) tasks.[37]

Importantly, and not least, the army worked very closely with the *Einsatzgruppen* and police battalions in murdering civilians. The army facilitated and in some cases initiated and organized killing operations, and provided crucial manpower as well as logistical support. The figures are hard to quantify, but somewhere between 100,000 and 125,000 Wehrmacht soldiers were directly responsible for killing Jews, while hundreds of thousands more facilitated the killings or participated in other war crimes. Probably more than a quarter of a million, and possibly as many as three-quarters of a million soldiers—maybe up to 5 percent of the 17 or 18 million people who served in the Wehrmacht—were involved in war crimes including 'actions' against Jews, Roma, and people with mental and physical disabilities.[38]

Whatever the combination of Nazi socialization and antisemitic ideology, comradeship and peer group pressure, brutalization in genocidal warfare, or unthinking conformity with organizational expectations, it is clear that many tens of thousands—and more likely hundreds of thousands—of Germans engaged in actions under these circumstances that they would otherwise never have contemplated. Clearly most had been mobilized to act, rather than being individually motivated; ideological justifications may have helped to overcome qualms *after* engaging in killing; but many seem also to have been both literally and metaphorically intoxicated by genocide.[39] Alcohol played a major role, engaging in performances of masculinity, and unwinding afterwards.[40]

Soldiers were transformed by their experiences, and many were far from willing; we should not generalize about the supposed comradeship of those who had been called up to serve. Willy Peter Reese was perhaps exceptionally literate and articulate in writing about his experiences, sending lengthy letters home to his parents and penning a detailed autobiographical account during the war itself (he was reported missing, presumed dead, in late June 1944). But he was probably not the only one who felt that 'we became comrades through shared hunger and being far away from home', but 'on the inside, everyone remained alone'; there was 'no bridge between one person and another'.[41] As his unit crossed Poland and entered Soviet territory, Reese recorded his feelings of shame at having to be a soldier among a conquered people, and his attempts to retreat inside himself by reading and writing; but he registered, too, how he was adapting and changing in this strange world. As conditions became worse, and hunger and exhaustion overwhelmed them, Reese noted how there was no sense of comradeship or community; each person prioritized his own needs, and the weak and helpless were left to fend for themselves. While he still registered empathy with the conquered subjects, he and the other soldiers not only took whatever food, clothing, and possessions they needed but even more.[42] As the winter of 1941–1942 wore on, Reese became ever more exhausted, but staggered on; when he finally collapsed and was taken for treatment, he registered that this may have saved him physically, but his own self 'was lost'.[43] He reflected, as he recovered, that millions were suffering and dying in this cosmic struggle; but 'there was neither comradeship, willingness to sacrifice, a fighting spirit, heroism nor a sense of fulfilling one's duty'.[44] Even so, he experienced a strange longing to be back at the front, and went back willingly when he had recovered.

Throughout, Reese repeatedly used the expression of 'wearing a mask', and was constantly aware of how those involved in this war, including women working as nurses, were being transformed by unprecedented experiences. They were all, in different ways, donning 'masks' in order to perform their roles.[45] Reese's reflections on the privations, fear, and violence of a totally senseless war are compelling, but his writing also reflects the ways in which he was himself becoming in some way deadened to the nature of what he was experiencing. In the autumn of 1943, following further periods of sick leave, he was once again marching eastwards through Russia. He records laconically how he and his comrades marched past two corpses of people who had been hanged. He gives a graphic description of the stench of decay, the swollen blue faces with yellow-brown liquid dribbling out of their eyes and turning crusty on their cheeks, and flesh coming off the tied hands. He notes that one soldier photographed them, while another used a stick to make them swing. He adds: 'Partisans. We laughed and went on.' Even Reese, a clearly sensitive soul who had been filled with a sense of shame and anguish about the war, had in some way by this point internalized at least the vocabulary—he does not query the notion of 'partisans'— and was able to play along with his comrades, laughing at the sight of the decaying corpses.

A similar paradox is evident in the later memoirs of an Austrian soldier, Luis Raffeiner, who had taken numerous photographs of his war experiences, including Jewish slave labourers in Minsk, and a similar hanging of 'partisans'. In his memoir, Raffeiner registers some discomfort at seeing the Minsk ghetto and being told that the Jews were being systematically taken out to be murdered. Moreover, one of his German colleagues suddenly recognized a former friend, a German Jewish butcher from their native Berlin, and felt he had to lie to this man, condemned to death but still clinging to the illusion he was to be 'resettled'. Raffeiner records this incident as of historical significance, but rapidly moves on from it, apparently barely troubled, to continue his own story. When it comes to the hanging of partisans, Raffeiner, like Reese, questions neither the term itself nor the dubious 'justice' that had been meted out.[46]

Reese's and Raffeiner's experiences of war as foot soldiers are likely more typical than those of the 5 percent or so of Wehrmacht soldiers who were actively involved in facilitating or murdering Jews or the individuals who were employed in dedicated killing units. Their combination of attempting to remain 'decent' (*anständig*) while also being in some way morally deadened is also likely typical. Other individuals, however, appeared to be genuinely enthusiastic about the war and the murderous activities in which they were engaged. There are reflections in letters home that illustrate what must have been widespread ways of talking among those directly concerned with killing civilians. Even so, it is significant that even among these most committed groups, perpetrators could not help but register, at the same time, intimations of discomfort and some sense of moral compromise. Trying to link the extraordinary worlds of unprecedented violence with the values

of their families and their homeland might help to re-establish inner equa-
nimity and moral reassurance.

There are some extreme examples of individual attempts at self-
justification that illustrate how the worlds of the front and those at home
in the Reich interacted. Walter Mattner was a thirty-six-year-old Austrian
police secretary who had come to Mogilew, in Belorussia, via Poland.[47] On
22 September 1941 he wrote to his wife how, even if he had not already
been a convinced National Socialist, the experiences of his very first day
of war would have turned him into a 'one hundred percenter'.[48] He was
initially not entirely sure how much he was allowed to say in writing to his
wife, but assured her (and himself) that it should be alright to share his experiences since she 'already knew' that the 'Jews are our misfortune'—using
the phrase displayed on the front page of Julius Streicher's racist newspaper,
Der Stürmer, in showcases across the Reich. His wife's assumed awareness
permitted him to reveal details, conveyed through the ideological framework of Nazism. On the way to Mogilew via Warsaw he had witnessed the
devastating impact of war on 'the blossom of the German nation', the comrades killed in battle. A sense of bitterness and thoughts of the homeland
had stiffened his resolve and that of his comrades to give their utmost in the
great 'battle of fate' they now had to fight on behalf of their 'Volk'. He went
on: 'What do the one thousand two hundred Jews matter, who yet again
are superfluous in some town and have to be knocked off, as the saying so
nicely goes. It's simply the just punishment for all the harm they have done
to us Germans and continue to do.'[49]

Having geared himself up in this way, Mattner soon volunteered for duty
in 'special actions', killing Jewish civilians; and he wrote home about his
experiences. At first, his 'hand had trembled', but by the tenth truckload he
'already took aim calmly and shot assuredly at the many women, children,
and babies'. His justification for killing babies is chilling. First, it was in
defence of his own family: he himself had 'two babies at home', and 'these
hordes would do just the same, if not ten times worse, to them'. Moreover,
it was supposedly a more humane action than those of the Bolsheviks: 'The
death that we delivered to them was a beautiful, quick death, compared to
the hellish sufferings of thousands and tens of thousands in the cellars of
the GPU'—referencing (and misnaming) the Soviet secret police, whose
misdeeds supposedly provided justification for Nazi acts of 'retaliation'.
Furthermore, he even seemed to take some pleasure in the sport of killing,

combining the micro-level of the act itself with the macro-picture of the world now and in the future: 'Babies flew in great arcs through the air, and we bumped them off even as they flew, before they fell into the pit or the water. Just get rid of this brood that has plunged the whole of Europe into war and is even now stirring things up in America until this too has been dragged into the war.' Finally, the well-known words of the Führer to the Reichstag in January 1939 were adduced in support: Hitler was right 'when he once said, before the war: if Jewry believes that it can once again ignite a war in Europe, the Jews will not achieve victory but rather it will be the end of Jewry in Europe.'[50]

These extraordinary justifications reveal just how significant Nazi ideology could be in the mind of a convinced national socialist. Hitler's 'prophecy' clearly resonated powerfully among the ranks of the committed activists at the frontline of killing. It was especially powerful in one particular sense: to assuage simmering discomfort—if not quite pangs of conscience—after the event. Mattner, a father of two, may well have felt some instinctive disquiet at the murder of innocent babies thrown into the air. His justification in terms of pre-emptive self-defence on behalf of his own children reeks of 'protesting too much': trying to reassure himself as well as his wife that what he was doing was morally legitimate, even as the sight of the babies touched some deep emotional chord.

Once in the thick of it, the sense of comradeship in the national cause could also become extremely important for some perpetrators.[51] In a letter of 5 October 1941, Mattner commented on how he was looking forward to returning to the Reich, when it would be the turn of the Jews at home.[52] But, a few days later, still invigorated by his dramatic experiences, he registered how much he was nevertheless enjoying his time in Belorussia: 'Human life means absolutely nothing here. And yet it is a joy to be alive, and I am as happy as before that I am able to experience this battle of fate of our Volk and that I am able to participate in the struggle.'[53] A couple of weeks later, on 27 October 1941, the group were told the tallies of their efforts: Mattner proudly and joyously told his wife that in his district 'already 27,000 Jews have been bumped off' and 'in Kiev 24,000!'[54] Mattner executed these murders in the spirit of a member of a 'national community' in a supposedly defensive battle against an enemy active across the world, including America, and where even babies held the seeds of future threat. His sense of community belonging was strengthened by the collective identity of the group. On 19 April 1942 he told his wife that political parties were a thing of the past, and political differences no longer mattered: 'everyone here feels himself solely "German" and to be German today means only to be "Nazi". There is nothing else.'[55]

Mattner may have been an extreme example, but his thoughts were far from original. Rather, he drew on Nazi clichés and phrases that were widely used among those committed to killing. A member of the *Sonderkommando 4a* of *Einsatzgruppe C*, SS-Obersturmführer Karl Kretschmer, for example, wrote in similar terms to his wife. Kretschmer's letters betray the slight discomfort of someone determined to demonstrate a capacity for the much-vaunted Nazi 'hardness' required to carry through unpleasant duties in service of the Volk.[56] The *Sonderkommando 4a* of *Einsatzgruppe C* had, with the assistance of the army and police forces, been responsible for the mass murder at Babi Yar, in which 33,771 Jews had been shot in a ravine on the outskirts of Kiev on 29 and 30 September 1941; this site continued to be used for mass murder, including of Roma ('gypsies') and Soviet prisoners of war, with the ultimate number of corpses in the ravine totalling around 100,000. In a 1979 interview with the filmmaker Claude Lanzmann, who filmed secretly with a hidden camera, Kretschmer made much of the fact that he only arrived in Kiev after the first massacre of late September 1941 was over.[57] But he certainly was directly involved in many other mass killings on the Eastern Front. In a letter to his wife on 27 September 1942, he admitted that he was upset by the 'sight of the dead (including women and children)' and had to remind himself that 'we are fighting this war, however, for the very existence or not of our Volk'. He echoed Hitler's view that 'since this war is, in our opinion, a Jewish war, the Jews get to feel it first'; as a result, 'in Russia, so far as there are German soldiers, there are no Jews any more'. But, he added, 'You can imagine that I took a bit of time at first to come to terms with this.'

The murder of Jews also played a role in Kretschmer's daily life. Food was acquired from the land and through barter, including exchanging the clothes of 'people who are no longer alive'. Moreover, his wife need not send him any clothing because 'what we have here will last us for years'. On the other hand, he was not able to find a Persian fur coat to send his wife, as she desired, in part because 'the Jews who traded in these are no longer alive'.[58] In a letter written less than three weeks later, Kretschmer was able to dismiss things more lightly and was proud of his achievements: 'I have already told you, with reference to the shootings, that I could not let myself fall short here.'[59]

Postwar accounts provide quite different strategies of defence and legitimation of killings, reflecting a radically altered political and moral context. Some individuals requested exemption and were transferred to other duties assisting the killing units in their activities without actually having to pull a trigger.[60] One member of Police Battalion 307 had refused to take part in an execution in Brest. In his account, he directly contradicted the general line of defence that so many defendants in West German war crimes trials were mounting at that time, that of 'Befehlsnotstand' or having had to obey orders for fear of the penalties if they refused. As he explained: 'I was supposed to be part of an execution commando. . . . When I saw the place of execution I was quite shattered. I therefore refused to participate in the execution. Nothing happened to me as a result of this. There was never any disciplinary process against me, nor were there military judicial proceedings.'[61]

Others admitted to having participated in shootings, but still sought to frame their actions in terms of postwar morality, and particularly of course in connection with legal investigations.[62] Another member of Police Battalion 307, Heinrich M., was interrogated by the West German Ludwigsburg Central Office for the investigation of Nazi war crimes in the 1960s. He recalled that on or around 10 July 1941, he had participated in the execution of what he described as 'only' 6,000 Jewish men—they had been supposed to shoot as many as 10,000—in a place just south of Brest-Litovsk. (He does not clarify whether he thought the fact that they killed fewer Jews than intended should in some way serve in mitigation.) Heinrich M. claimed that he and his comrades were not enjoined to secrecy about what they were doing. Nonetheless, after they had carried out their duties, they hardly spoke about what they had done, and if they did, 'then only in a judgemental way'—in this way constructing himself as a good person. He also sought to demonstrate some kind of empathy for the Jews he had killed by honouring the memory of the 'stoic composure and heroic demeanour' as they 'went to their fate'—with little admission of agency in bringing about that 'fate'. He claimed that he himself had 'personally survived the whole thing in a sort of trance-like state'. Finally, he conceded that what he and others had done could, in terms of their behaviour, 'be compared to that of a murderer'. He went on: 'I am a Catholic and simply because of my religious education I have not been able to find any explanation for what happened. I excused myself in terms of the external circumstances to assuage my own feelings of guilt, which I undoubtedly had.'[63]

It is clear from a wide range of evidence, including testimonies collected in relation to trials, that there were no serious penalties for those who did not want to take part in shootings. At most they had to find ways of saving face in their peer group.[64] Such testimony also makes it clear that there were enough others putting themselves forwards for killing duties that it was in fact no problem to request alternative duties. So we have to assume that there were many who may well have shared Mattner's enthusiasm and capacity for self-justification. Moreover, it is also clear that these individuals, involved in actions and events that they recognized as world-historically important, even unprecedented, did not hold back from sharing their experiences with their friends and relatives back home. Their situations were different, but the borders between 'home' and the front were extremely porous. And even those who thought themselves involved in purely conventional warfare were in fact embroiled in a war that had no regard for the lives of the subjugated and conquered peoples, and a war in which they too—even if initially wracked by a sense of shame and anguish, like Reese—became progressively inured to the horrors, acclimatized to the Nazi vocabulary of 'partisans', and the practice of taking photographs to send home, as in the case of Raffeiner. They were effectively both witnesses to and participants in world history, whether willingly or unwillingly; and increasingly without the reactions of shock and horror at the sheer inhumanity of what was going on in their name and in which they themselves were now complicit.

Rumblings in the Reich

Wherever they were, from late 1941 onwards no German citizen could avoid some form of 'knowledge', however fragmentary and second-hand. The supposed 'neutrality' of the bystander position was no longer an option—if neutrality really ever had been since Hitler came to power—but interpretations and responses varied. The 'Aryan' population of Germany was deeply divided, as it had indeed been throughout the 1930s, although in ways that were always shifting and now further overlain by wartime concerns; there is little point talking in the abstract about 'the Germans' or 'German society' as if this were one monolithic mass.

All citizens of the Reich, of course, faced the challenges of living in a country at war, although individuals had widely varying strategies for coping with the impact of warfare on their own lives. The overriding priorities of most people had to do with their own welfare, and that of their families, friends, relatives, and homeland. These were the primary communities with which people identified, leaving little space or energy for empathy with others, whether former 'non-Aryan' friends and neighbours or anonymous victims far away. This does not mean that people did not 'know' about the fates of Jews; nor even that they were entirely indifferent when they heard rumours about mass killings. The evidence from diaries and letters of the time suggests that isolated pieces of news were capable of producing shock. Such snippets did not amount to a wider picture of the organized mass murder that was taking shape at this time. Even so, individual reactions are telling.

Many Germans entered what was later widely termed 'inner emigration' if they had the conditions and means to keep their heads down. Even if they felt powerless to change anything, and could see no obvious way forwards, they did not feel personally compromised. Friedrich Kellner, working as an administrator in the local courthouse of Laubach, a small town in western Germany, made frequent critical comments into his diary. Some of his remarks were at an entirely general level, as when he summarized Nazi anti-semitic policy as 'the extermination of the Jews because they were wiser than the German people' and noted that 'whoever on this planet is not for Germany will be removed'. Some were far more specific. On 28 July 1941 he described bluntly how 'mental hospitals have become murder centers'. He knew of a family that had fortuitously just 'brought their mentally deranged son back home from an institution', but subsequently 'received a letter informing them their son had died and his cremated ashes were being sent to them'. As a result of the office clerk's 'oversight', having 'forgotten to strike this boy's name from the death list', Kellner commented, 'the intended and premeditated murder came to light'. This sort of knowledge about the so-called euthanasia killing programme was widespread and occasioned the levels of unrest that contributed to its official halt in August 1941, although the killing of the mentally and physically disabled went on in other ways. News from the front came from 'wounded soldiers in the field hospital in Giessen' who reported that 'Russians prisoners of war are to be killed!'—which shocked Kellner sufficiently to warrant an exclamation mark, followed by 'Barbarous gangsters!' All of these comments were made within the space of a couple of weeks in July 1941.[65] On 15 August 1941, Kellner noted the wording of what was being said officially, in the SS newspaper *Das schwarze Korps*, about the 'difficult ethnic questions to be solved in the East' that 'cannot be handled with sentimental or romantic notions'. According to the SS, the 'only thing that is going to work there is severity'. Brutality and ruthlessness were, Kellner commented, 'the trump cards of National Socialism'.[66]

Soon, Kellner heard in more detail what the SS had meant. On 28 October 1941, Kellner noted in his diary how a 'soldier on leave here said he personally witnessed a terrible atrocity in the occupied part of Poland'. The soldier told Kellner how he had 'watched as naked Jewish men and women were placed in front of a long deep ditch and, upon the order of the SS, were shot by Ukrainians in the back of their heads, and they fell into the ditch. Then the ditch was filled in as screams kept coming from it!' He went on: 'These inhuman atrocities are so terrible that even the Ukrainians who were used for manual labor suffered nervous breakdowns.' The German soldiers, too, had apparently been uneasy about what they were engaged in, suggesting that 'the German people should already be trembling in their shoes because of the coming retribution'. In Kellner's view, 'ninety-nine percent of the German people, directly or indirectly, carry the guilt for the present situation' and 'those who travel together, hang together'.[67] The possibility of anticipated Allied retribution or revenge would, particularly from 1943 onwards following German defeat at Stalingrad, play a significant role in Nazi efforts to sustain German willingness to go on fighting, with some success as far as attitudes and fears for the future were concerned. In the event, Nazi 'fellow-travellers' would largely go unpunished after the war; not even major perpetrators would receive appropriate punishment, very few in fact facing the death penalty or life imprisonment.[68] At the time, however, knowing about atrocities did not necessarily lead to action. On 15 December 1941, Kellner commented in his diary that 'in some areas Jews are being transported somewhere'. He went on to reflect on how the 'Nazis are proud of their animal protection laws', yet 'the suffering they cause the Jews proves they treat Jews worse than animals'. He added: 'This cruel, despicable, and sadistic treatment against the Jews that has lasted now several years—with its final goal of extermination—is the biggest stain on the honor of Germany. They will never be able to erase these crimes.'[69] It was a measure of Kellner's combination of outrage and sense of personal impotence that he felt he had to express himself in his diary in this way. As far as his everyday life was concerned, however, he could do little more than note developments and suppress his feelings in public.

It is difficult to gauge how widespread such responses might have been, in part because of the vicissitudes of both diary-writing and the preservation and later accessibility of personal reflections from the time. But it is clear from what we do have that Kellner was far from being alone in these reactions. On 22 October 1941, Hermann Stresau similarly recorded in his diary what he called 'dark' news from the East. Living quietly in the small university town of Göttingen, unwilling to compromise his principles but also afraid to step out of line, he was anxious to glean what he could about the progress of the war. Now, for the first time, he noted hearing about atrocities on the Eastern Front. Far from being kept secret, gruesome reports were being passed from one person to another, reaching even Göttingen, well away from the eastern borders of the Reich. Stresau confided in his diary how a friend had told him about a conversation with another mutual friend, a doctor, one of whose patients was in the Waffen-SS. (The round-about route through which Stresau heard this story is in itself telling.) The patient had ostensibly come to complain about headaches, but the doctor, sensing there was something more to his malaise, asked him to return later when he could speak to him on his own. Once able to talk more freely, the patient recounted that he had 'already done for [murdered] 800 Jews with his pistol in the course of service, as a member of a commando that was tasked with such liquidations'. He now pleaded to be written off sick because he could no longer bear it. Some things, he said, were simply not possible to describe. Stresau was shocked. He went on to reflect in his diary on whether it was really possible now to hope for peace if this meant strengthening the Nazi regime. A German victory would entail 'heightened terror against those who think differently, above all against the church', as well as 'a permanent state of war in the East, maintaining a gigantic army in order to keep the whole of Europe under control, and a permanent state of war with America'. But neither could he hope for defeat at the hands of Russia, given the likely retribution for the way Germany had been acting. Stresau, in his quiet retreat in Göttingen, could see no way forwards and no way of challenging the situation: he was utterly impotent, even if wholly opposed. All he could really do was get on with his own life as best he could.[70]

In October 1942, living on his estate near the Chiemsee lake in Bavaria, a conservative opponent of Nazism, Friedrich Reck, similarly wrote in his diary of a conversation he had with a friend, who had 'just come back from the Eastern Front', where he had 'witnessed the massacre at K., where 30,000 Jews were slaughtered'. The friend, according to Reck, reported: 'This was done in a single day, in the space of an hour, perhaps, and when machine-gun bullets gave out, flamethrowers were used. And spectators hurried to the event from all over the city, off-duty troops, young fellows with the milk-complexion of the young', who, he went on, 'nineteen or twenty years ago, were lying in cribs and gaily bubbling and reaching for the brightly coloured ring hanging just above!' Reck had no adequate way of dealing with the anger and despair that this further evidence of Nazi evil aroused in him. He felt an immense sense of impotence, as he addressed imaginary future interlocutors: 'You judge us and find us wanting, and we, here, suffer in loneliness and dread. You point at us, and our lack of resistance, and we know that the resistants [sic] have died unknown in filthy bunkers, and that the blood of martyrs has been spilled to no purpose'. He tried to seek solace in his Christian faith, to little effect. 'But still the night lies black over our heads, and we suffer, we suffer as you never shall suffer, no, not on your deathbed.' Reck had no solution, apart from helping to hide a Jew on his estate. In the end, Reck would be arrested and die at Dachau in the spring of 1945.[71]

Millions of people in Germany received similarly disturbing news from the front, as the innumerable 'spectators' of such shocking incidents reported back to those at home. There could be little doubt, by the end of 1942 at the very latest—by which time news of atrocities and mass killings were hitting the headlines of international newspapers—that 'resettlement to the east' effectively meant death. By this time, a survivor in Halle later recalled, it was 'an open secret that the first transport of Halle Jews had been gassed. Virtually every soldier who came back from the east talked about the atrocities that had been carried out against Jews from Germany'. Stories were told about gas vans with the exhaust pipes turned inwards to kill the Jews held inside. Then more detailed accounts of the 'terror camps of Majdanek, Lublin and Auschwitz' began to emerge 'when the SS began to build branches of Buna and Leuna', key chemical production industrial concerns based in the Halle area; at this point, 'technical specialists from these works who were seconded to the camp branches talked a lot about the horrific treatment of the Jews'.[72]

As knowledge grew exponentially and beyond deniability, so people who were opposed to Nazism were wracked with a sense of their own impotence. On Wednesday, 2 December 1942, Ruth Andreas-Friedrich recorded in her diary: 'The Jews are disappearing in throngs. Ghastly rumours are current about the fate of the evacuees—mass shootings and death by starvation, tortures, and gassings.'[73] Andreas-Friedrich was one of perhaps tens of thousands of people in Berlin who sought to save individual Jews who preferred to 'go underground', to hide rather than risk the uncertainties of deportation: 'No one could expose himself deliberately to such a risk. Any hide-out is a gift from heaven, salvation in mortal peril. The "thieves gang" moves these guests around from one to another. You take them one night, we'll take them the next. Permanent guests are suspicious looking. The constant coming and going makes the neighbours mistrustful anyway.'[74] But her efforts were tiny in proportion to the massive numbers being deported.

Nor was it easy to see how any greater resistance could have been mounted by ordinary citizens. On Sunday, 28 February 1943, Ruth Andreas-Friedrich watched the major '*Aktion*' that sought to round up all Berlin's remaining Jews: 'Since six o'clock this morning trucks have been driving through Berlin, escorted by armed SS men. They stop at factory gates, in front of private houses; they load in human cargo—men, women, children. Distracted faces are crowded together under the gray canvas covers. Figures of misery, penned in and jostled about like cattle going to the stockyards. More and more new ones arrive, and are thrust into the overcrowded trucks with blows of gun butts. In six weeks Germany is to be "Jew-free".' But Andreas-Friedrich, who tried desperately to contact all her Jewish friends, to find only that they were already gone, was at a loss as to how best to respond now: 'Are we to go out and confront the SS—attack their trucks and drag our friends out? The SS is armed; we aren't. No one is going to give us weapons, either; and if anyone did, we wouldn't know how to use them. We just aren't "killers". We revere life. That is our strength—and our weakness.'[75]

The 'factory action' did in fact occasion one public protest: the non-Jewish wives of Jewish men in what were called 'mixed marriages' came out to demonstrate outside the Jewish community house in Berlin's

Rosenstraße, demanding the release of their husbands.[76] Goebbels argued, against the RSHA, that any attempt to put down by force a spontaneous and highly emotional demonstration by thousands of German women would risk widespread public unrest. Historians disagree about the role of the demonstration in altering the fates of these men or in affecting Nazi policy with respect to the always contentious topics of people in 'mixed marriages' and of 'mixed descent'. Documentary evidence suggests that the arrests of these men may have been in order to register them for new labour tasks, in place of 'unprotected' Jews who were slated for imminent deportation; the practical consequences of the protest may therefore have been overstated, even if the courage of the women undoubtedly deserved attention.[77] What is clear, however, with respect to the wider issue of bystanding, is that in this case of mass public protest strong emotional connections overrode any calculations of either personal risks or potential efficacy, as women came out in large numbers to protest on behalf of their loved ones: no passive bystanders here when it affected them so deeply, personally, in mixed marriages that had been upheld despite all the pressures to divorce and abandon their Jewish spouses. It is worth also reflecting on the fact that public protests against the T4 'euthanasia' programme were similarly rooted in a sense of close connection with the victims; but while these may have led to a termination in August 1941 of the official programme, the killing of the mentally and physically disabled by other, less widely visible means continued throughout the war. And despite the momentary stay of execution on the men involved in the Rosenstraße case, the arrests and deportations of people in mixed marriages and of mixed descent, sometimes under other pretexts, took place in growing numbers in the later war years. The underlying questions related to the Nazi timetable with respect to a hierarchy of victims and the avoidance of adverse public attention.

Whatever the evaluation of this particular case, then, one can but wonder what difference it might have made had the separation between communities of empathy not been so great across society. The deep gulf between the vast majority of members of the Volksgemeinschaft and the minorities of the persecuted that had been created over the preceding years was now almost unbridgeable. Very few Germans, in face of deportations and mass murder, were as emotionally devastated as the Rosenstraße protestors or as filled with a sense of impotence and as wracked with despair as Friedrich Reck and Ruth Andreas-Friedrich. Most Germans managed to set aside any disconcerting reports from the East, with rumours and snippets of news only briefly puncturing the continuing and more demanding swirl of events in their personal lives. One (anonymous) diary writer, for example, living in Mainz close to Germany's western border, had been recently diagnosed with lung damage and a heart condition that left him fearing death in his early forties (although he in fact lived to ninety-four). Alongside his health concerns, this diary writer kept a close eye on the development of the war. His entries reflect the mish-mash of immediate events and distant news deemed worthy of note. On Sunday, 11 January 1942, he recorded that, despite an icy north wind, he and his wife had gone for a walk along the banks of the river Main. He also described 'bad news from the east', listing a number of issues that a German soldier had recounted to him. At the front, there was not enough to eat, and much of their food was inedible anyway because of the cold. Prisoners were being left to die from starvation, or abandoned in the snow to freeze to death. Meanwhile, 'in Minsk 500 civilians brought in from the surrounding area were being shot daily', and some members 'of the execution commando were suffering nervous breakdowns'.[78] Which of these stories 'from the east' was more important in his view, and which of the groups was to be pitied more—the cold and hungry German troops, the prisoners left to starve or freeze to death, the shooters, or the civilians they had shot—was not clarified. It was all simply registered, laconically, almost without emotion. Mass murder was simply a part of war, in which Germans too were suffering.

In diary entries during the following months, this diary writer commented on his wife's pregnancy, his own health worries, his difficulties sleeping, and periodic discussions about the progress of the war that others were following equally closely. On 16 August 1942 he recorded having a 'major political row' with a couple of friends who were highly critical of Hitler and thought Germany would lose the war.[79] Surprisingly, none of them seems to have feared potential denunciation for airing critical and defeatist views so openly. Following the birth of his son on 7 October 1942, the diary entries circled predominantly around the baby's development and the wellbeing of his wife. By late January 1943, however, the Battle of Stalingrad intruded on domestic concerns. He asked himself, on 27 January, whether the 'sacrifice of Stalingrad' had indeed been 'unavoidable'; but he sought comfort in his 'faith in Germany and the self-sacrificing example of Hitler'.[80] On 1 February 1943 he recorded 'serious discussions about the state of the war', in which one acquaintance 'talked about the elimination of the Polish intelligentsia' and said that 'a gas was being tried out on the Jews in the east'. But, he hastened to add, 'none of this can be checked'.[81] On 14 February 1943 he noted further 'war news', adding that 'hopefully the Jew is <u>not</u> our misfortune!'[82] These later entries register how the controlled discussion of the mass murder of the Jews was filtering through to the entire population, deliberately orchestrated by Goebbels to ensure both complicity in knowledge and patriotic fear of potential 'retribution'.[83]

Such knowledge did not, however, prevent people like this diary writer from a sense of self-pity. His entries during the spring of 1944 were almost entirely concerned with the effects of a bombing raid on the first day of March that had destroyed his house and possessions. He was filled with misery about losing objects he had valued, things he had inherited from his parents, and worried about having to build a new life. In the event, unlike the millions of European Jews whose fate he had noted only in passing, he was able to go on to enjoy life with his growing family for many decades thereafter; he eventually died in 1994. Even at the time of the mass murders, he had barely paused to consider the morality of what was happening; certainly there is no evidence that he was particularly concerned by what he was hearing, let alone sufficiently incensed to feel frustrated by his own incapacity to act; and, indeed, he argued with friends who were more critically inclined. He was probably typical of many who would later find it easier to profess ignorance rather than admit to former indifference towards the victims of Nazi crimes.

More convinced Nazis did not even bother to note atrocities against Jews, presumably seeing the mass killings as simply a legitimate part of the war effort. The teenager Wolfhilde von König, for example, just threw herself with enthusiasm into her work for the Nazi cause among girls and young women in Munich. She avidly noted details of the progress of the war and the fates of individual prominent Nazis; but she apparently spared no thought whatsoever for the fate of the Jews, including those being deported in full view of bystanders in her native Munich.[84]

Other committed Nazis who did comment on atrocities wrapped their knowledge in ideological packaging; this could both render it more palatable and serve to inject a degree of enthusiasm in otherwise challenging times. Günter Sack, for example, was an idealistic national socialist in his early twenties. On 14 June 1943, while stationed in Zeitz, in Saxony-Anhalt,

Sack confirmed his 'conviction' that 'in this difficult period of struggle we need carriers of German idealism'. He considered himself 'in this sense an active, fanatical and radical circulator of our national socialist worldview'. He continued: 'Without any desire for personal fame or honour I will in future serve just this one cause: service to my German people and faithful allegiance to its great Führer Adolf Hitler'.[85] In July 1943, he was devastated to hear of the death of his best friend, aged just twenty-three, whose 'life was just in service of his beloved fatherland'. But he tried to console himself by taking this death to mean that there was 'an even greater duty for us, the living' to 'fulfil the mission of those who have fallen'.[86]

A month or so later, now stationed in Dinard on the northern coast of Brittany, Sack discussed in his diary the news of the devastating bombing of Hamburg. By this time, the wider discussions about the fate of the Jews—again, influenced by Goebbels—were shaping the ways in which Germans interpreted the bombings. One of Sack's friends, just back from a visit to Hamburg, told him about all manner of disturbing things 'which are however only more or less believable'. Sack went on to reflect that 'bombing warfare against civilian populations' was the 'sharpest weapon of the war', about which there was nothing they could do. But, he continued, 'as a reprisal measure all Jews are "supposed to be" bumped off in Poland, and this is done in waggons which are then put into big halls filled with gas' (technically inaccurate, but nevertheless a remarkably apposite portrayal). This, however, Sack went on, 'is naturally just more or less a rumour'. Curiously, the notion of 'reprisal' seems to have been entirely reversed here, with the killing of Jews in Poland situated somehow—in total contradiction to the actual chronology of events—as a form of *response* to the Allied bombing of German cities rather than, as in an already twisted misrepresentation, portraying the Allied bombings as 'retaliation' for the prior killing of Jews.

In any event, Sack continued, 'there is total war, and it looks as if this war will outdo all previous wars in human bestiality and cruelty'.[87] In this way, the mass murder of civilians who could not in any way be seen as a legitimate military or strategic target were simply subsumed into ideas of ordinary if extreme warfare. By Monday, 6 September 1943, Sack was fortifying himself by re-reading Hitler's *Mein Kampf* and 'again being drawn under its spell'. Everyone today, he thought, must seek to fulfil Hitler's will, and 'thus participate in his greatness'. In tones of quasi-religious ecstasy, Sack pleaded with God to give Hitler 'strength and health to achieve his great goal'. He was himself 'grateful to fate, that I may be allowed to live in this hardest of all times. Never again will I think of myself! I will renounce my own egoistic-personal happiness. In future I will find happiness only in the knowledge of joyfully accomplished duty!'[88]

By 1943, the vast majority of European Jews had already been murdered. But in the context of defeat at Stalingrad, and increased Allied bombing of German cities, discussions of alleged 'revenge' by the Anglo-Americans for what Germans had done to the Jews, supposedly mobilized by 'international Jewry', were widespread. Indeed, participation in a controlled version of such discussions was orchestrated by Goebbels, in the process bringing the whole of the Volksgemeinschaft into a sort of community of shared knowledge and shared guilt.[89] It is possible that, in this way, Germans were able to express a sense of an uneasy conscience; but they were also being spurred on to continue fighting for fear of the retribution that would surely follow.

Germans were still repeating the discourse that had been opened up by Goebbels in early 1945, when defeat increasingly appeared inevitable. Walter Jessel, a Frankfurt-born Jew who had managed to emigrate to the United States, had now returned as an American soldier and made detailed notes of impressions as he drove with the American troops through Germany. He noted in his diary on 12 February 1945 that prisoners of war (whom he calls 'PWs') were predicting 'that the war will last a little longer now that the Russian drive has slowed down'. Their reactions were captured as follows: 'People in the Rhineland say that the cities are being destroyed because of the persecution of the Jews.' Similarly, he noted: 'Overheard at bugged officer quarters: A Captain PW: "They are said to have exterminated 3 million Jews". Medical officer: "I heard 4 million." Captain: "I can't believe it."'[90] Belief and knowledge were two different things; people 'knew' but could not fully register the enormity of what it was that they knew.

Knowledge was fractured. Hans H. was an official who worked in the German Labour Office in Jasło, in southern Poland, not far from the dedicated killing camps. In 1966, he gave testimony for judicial investigations, confirming the widespread awareness and discussion of the extermination process: 'At that time what was being done to the Jews was also spoken about, that is, what purpose the deportations served. It was generally said by everyone that the Jews were being gassed or shot.' There was no attempt to suggest this should be kept secret, at least among Germans: 'This was also spoken about quite openly among colleagues, in my view every colleague must have heard about it. I consider it nonsense if someone says that was not the case.' They even discussed details: 'Among colleagues, the fact that there were extermination camps in which Jews were killed was also generally talked about.' They felt that deception was, however, still necessary as far as the victims were concerned: 'But the Jews were of course not told what was going to happen to them. They were to believe that they were going to a labour camp.'[91] This fiction could only be sustained for some victims, for some of the time, particularly if they were being deported to the death camps from afar. But as far as Germans were concerned, 'not knowing' was a fiction constructed after it was all over.

People who were not themselves targets of genocidal policies faced stark choices at this time. Once genocide was underway, remaining 'innocently' on the sidelines was no longer possible; 'ignorance' was barely an option. Many felt impotent to act; this was, in effect, a form of constrained complicity, born of frustration and despair. Others were indifferent, adopted comforting legitimations, or were unwilling to register fully what was going on, in effect becoming more willingly complicit in the Nazi worldview and its murderous consequences. Other bystanders now became variously perpetrators, facilitators, and beneficiaries of collective violence. A very few attempted to engage in acts of resistance or rescue. Under these extreme conditions, it was infinitely easier to comply, even to find justifications for compliance under extraordinary circumstances, than to engage in the risks of rescue or resistance, particularly on behalf of others whom one did not know.

For the vast majority of people under the extreme conditions of dictatorship and war, it might seem best to try to stay out of the fray and remain passive. Germans living within the Reich who were included in the Volksgemeinschaft were, whatever their views on Nazism, primarily preoccupied with the survival of themselves and their loved ones during wartime. If they actively opposed, critiqued, or sought to undermine Nazi policies, they ran the risk of themselves becoming victims of extreme violence. Yet remaining silent meant in effect condoning brutality and murder, even if this strategy was a form of 'muddling through' in existentially threatening times.

11

Towards the End

Rescue, Survival, and Self-Justifications

In *Berlin Finale*, a novel by the German writer Heinz Rein set in Berlin in the closing days of the war, an opponent of Nazism addresses two co-conspirators and a young deserter who has recently joined them. There were, in the speaker's view, only three choices of action for Germans: 'firstly, to work in armaments or fight with weapons, and so become complicit with fascist crimes; secondly, to act as a resigned bystander and wait, that is, to aid the crime; and thirdly, active opposition.'[1]

Rein's fictional political activist is quite clear that to act as a 'resigned bystander' was not to remain innocent: to wait passively on the sidelines meant, in effect, 'to aid the crime'. Inner reservations made absolutely no difference to the outcome, even if the bystander felt better for 'being against it'. For Rein's protagonist, therefore, 'there is only that third possibility', even if this meant being 'accused of conspiring against our own fatherland'. Those who resisted could not be sure of the outcomes, and it was highly risky. But 'we are obliged to go on because our conscience demands it'. He concludes by raising the idea of 'another Germany'. As he explains, 'if this is our fatherland, this state ruled by Hitler and Himmler, then I'm no longer a German. A country in which freedom, humanity and justice are outmoded concepts can never be my fatherland.'[2]

Rein's account was first published as a magazine series from late 1946 and then as a book in 1947. It portrays Berlin in ruins, both physically and socially, as people salvage their lives and relationships amidst bombs, betrayals, and political violence. It portrays many ordinary Berliners as relatively uncontaminated despite all—quick-witted, sharp-tongued, critical of Nazi 'bigwigs'—while also providing devastating sketches of those who had gone along with Nazism. And it is itself a political intervention, with characters acting as mouthpieces for different points of view, facilitating discussion of complicity and resistance.

The novel illuminates the issues around choosing 'to act as a resigned bystander and wait'. Many Germans would, after the war, claim they had been 'always against it' (*immer dagegen*), and with some degree of truth. Many had indeed been concerned about the evident criminality of Nazi violence, particularly when this affected people whom they knew personally. Even so, despite inner misgivings, they had gone along with the system, played their allotted roles, and in effect helped to propel the radicalization of the Nazi regime in both peace and war. And afterwards, many felt uneasy about having made compromises that were hard to justify under later, quite different circumstances. Yet responses at the time could have made all the difference to at least some of those being persecuted.

We should of course not overstate the wider impact of the behaviours, attitudes, and inaction of what I have called the muddled middle: it was the failure of elites to stand up against Hitler at an early stage, their willingness simply to fall into line and allow the collapse of democratic institutions and legal safeguards, that must bear the primary weight of responsibility for sustaining Nazi rule; members of the wider society had to live within an arena of repression and violence, in which it was easier to conform, even to appropriate a little of the power that came with the new Volksgemeinschaft, than to engage in the risks of refusal, rescue, or resistance. Even so, the ways in which people were drawn into growing complicity clearly played a role in the expansion of the Nazi project of persecution, destruction, and genocide—and this made a significant difference to the fates of individual victims. The character of surrounding societies is one crucial element in understanding different rates of survival among the persecuted across Europe.[3]

Those trapped in the net of persecution and genocide were desperately seeking means to escape—and their attempts depended significantly on the reactions of others. Some owed their survival to particular individuals, and these rescuers have been variously honoured. Yad Vashem bestows

the distinction of 'Righteous among the Nations' on individuals who, it
can be shown after detailed investigation, acted selflessly to help Jews; this
category excludes people acting for personal profit, and those who acted
as part of a group or organization.[4] In Germany, the broader notion of
'quiet heroes' (*stille Helden*) has been bestowed on people who assisted
Jews. But for all the courage displayed by individuals who were honoured
in one way or another, it is clear that decisions to extend help to victims
of persecution depended not only on the personal characteristics of the
rescuers, as so often portrayed, but also, crucially, on the wider circumstances. Before acting, people had to assess whether their intervention
could hope to be effective, and what might be the potential risks to themselves or others in the particular context of action. These risks could be
entirely local, even domestic—an irate husband unexpectedly returning
home early and finding his wife had hidden fugitive Jews—or they could
depend on external conditions, such as the efficiency of the repressive
forces (German or local), as well as the potential penalties, whether individual or in the form of collective 'reprisal' actions. In rural areas of
Poland, for example, fear of the fatal consequences for one's family or
even whole villages could easily switch people from being rescuers of
Jews to helpers of Germans.[5]

Wider conditions not only affected the behaviour of potential rescuers
but also shaped the strategies open to victims, and hence their chances
of survival. Avoiding deportation and surviving in Western European
countries entailed different challenges from those of escaping ghettoization and extermination at killing sites in the East.[6] Perceptions of
Jews, and social and cultural distinctions between communities, affected
whether it was possible to melt into the surrounding society. Escapees
with little command of local languages, readily identified, and viewed
with hostility or suspicion by locals, faced different challenges from those
who could 'go under' (*untertauchen*) in a familiar environment, among
friends and relatives, or who could adopt a false identity in a community with a shared language and culture where it would be easier to
'pass'. Changing social and political dynamics in different regions during wartime also affected survival chances, as group allegiances shifted.
Questions of empathy, identity, political sympathies, personal interests,
and moral commitments—all of these played a role. Individual stories
illuminate some of these issues.

Hiding in full view: 'Going under' in Germany

By 1942, it had become clear to people in Germany that deportation 'to the east' meant not 'resettlement' but death, whether instantly or over a period of time. Even if, later, many Germans would claim they 'never knew', those most immediately affected were only too well aware—or at least afraid, unwilling to believe what they feared to be the case, desperately hoping that rumours were not true. Perceptions, suspicions, and fears were as important as any firmer knowledge; some tried to reassure themselves, others sensed that euphemistic language about 'resettlement' was just a cover-up for more ghastly realities. But there were very few options available to them. Once deportations of Reich Jews were underway, around 10,000 to 15,000 Jews sought to evade the authorities and survive in hiding or under false identities, the vast majority unsuccessfully in the end. In Berlin, where some 40 percent of the remaining Reich Jews lived in 1941, around 1,200 to 1,500 Jews survived by going underground. In other cities with large Jewish populations, such as Frankfurt and Hamburg, only around 200 Jews survived in hiding; in Cologne, the figure was perhaps as low as thirty. In Munich in 1941–1942, 133 Jews chose to commit suicide rather than be deported, slightly more than the numbers who survived by avoiding deportation and going into hiding.[7]

Else Behrend-Rosenfeld was one of them. Her experiences illustrate just what 'going under' entailed. Deeply shaken following her sudden and totally unexpected release from deportation to Piaski in April 1942, Behrend-Rosenfeld spent anxious weeks reflecting on her best course of action. She and others in Munich, never receiving another sign of life from their friends who had been put on the train, had no doubt about the real meaning of 'resettlement'. Unsure of what to do, Behrend-Rosenfeld threw her energy into running the Jewish home in the Berg am Laim convent as best she could. She was able to move easily between the different worlds she inhabited, liaising with the Catholic nuns as well as her fellow inmates. She had grown up as a Christian child of a 'mixed marriage', but by marrying a (nonreligious) Jew she was classified as a person 'counting as Jewish' (a *Geltungsjüdin*) under the Nazi racial laws; and she now identified with her fellow sufferers. But she was at the same time totally at home in the Christian faith, to which she had been very committed as a young person, before she had left the church when she met her husband. Moreover, she had relatives who, unlike her, were not considered Jewish, being either entirely 'Aryan' (on her mother's side) or '*Mischlinge*' who were not 'counted as Jewish' (*Geltungsjuden*) because they had not married a Jew as she had done.[8]

This possibility of immersion in non-Jewish society gave Behrend-Rosenfeld a number of options to explore, and many potential contacts among both close friends and family. A cousin was willing to give her temporary shelter if she could make it to Berlin. At the last moment before her planned departure, Behrend-Rosenfeld nearly lost her nerve; but one of the Catholic nuns in Berg am Laim uttered some kindly words that gave her courage. This demonstration of sympathy and support from a committed Catholic would mean a great deal to her over the following months. Rather than wait for the final deportation, she feigned illness and obtained a few days' leave from her duties as manager, creating some time before any search would be instituted.

Behrend-Rosenfeld's account of her escape by train to Berlin is filled with adrenaline-rousing incidents. Constantly afraid of discovery and forever on the alert, she battled against a debilitating sense of exhaustion; she also experienced unexpected help and lucky escapes. Once she had recovered from the journey, she regained some of her strength stowed away in her cousin's house in the Berlin suburb of Tempelhof—close to where she and her family had lived so happily, just ten years earlier. However, barely daring to go out for fear of being recognized and denounced, and without the sense of purpose in looking after others that had driven her for months, she began to fall into depression. So too did her relatives, who were increasingly terrified about being discovered. Within weeks, she knew she would have to move on.

The invaluable support of close friends and trusted contacts was evident in every move Behrend-Rosenfeld then made while on the run. Particularly important were a few individuals, as well as communities that were opposed to Nazism, including Quakers, social democrats, and communists. For a while, Behrend-Rosenfeld lived under an assumed name with a staunch opponent of Nazism, 'Uncle Karl', under the guise of being his housekeeper. His apartment, which was close to Nollendorfplatz in Schöneberg, was relatively spacious, and at first she settled in well. Soon, 'Uncle Karl' took in other Jews who had gone underground, and they jostled for space on the couch or bed while their host slept in his work premises (which remain unspecified). Behrend-Rosenfeld knew that this situation could not go on for long. She continued her efforts to gain forged identity papers while she moved to the house of close friends a relatively short distance away.

Material resources as well as connections who could be trusted proved crucial. Behrend-Rosenfeld had sufficient funds to buy an old passport formerly belonging to an 'Aryan' but featuring a new photograph of herself; all she now needed was an authentic-looking stamp on the photograph. This proved more problematic; the first forgery obtained through the black market was so amateurish that it would have barely lasted a moment's inspection. In the meantime, she tried to obtain a post office identification card, which would be better than nothing. This required a little subterfuge. She organized two recorded deliveries to her friends' address under her assumed 'Aryan' name, and while signing receipt engaged in friendly banter with the postal worker delivering the post. Having gained the woman's confidence, she began to spin a tale about having lost her passport in air raids back in Düsseldorf, where she claimed she came from, and worrying how she would be able to pick up anything in person at the post office once she was back at work and not home to sign for delivery—at which the postal worker spontaneously offered to vouchsafe for her identity personally, so that even in the absence of other documents the post office would make her out an identity card. The post office ID arrived just as she was making preparations to leave Berlin. Too many people might still recognize her here, despite the fact that her appearance had changed: she had lost a great deal of weight as a result of months of stress and illness, and made sure only to go out wearing a widow's black veil covering her face, as so many widows in Germany did at the time. There was the threat of denunciation at every turn. Again in conjunction with both friends and contacts, she arranged to stay with distant acquaintances in the southern German city of Freiburg, close to the border of neutral Switzerland.

Before leaving Berlin, Behrend-Rosenfeld went for one last visit to 'Uncle Karl's' apartment, to say goodbye to her former fellow residents, when their reunion was suddenly interrupted. A neighbour—the manager of a nearby grocery store—had denounced 'Uncle Karl' for having too many suspicious looking visitors; the Gestapo now came to investigate and make arrests. Not everyone in the group had managed to acquire forged papers; one had only been able to acquire the identity papers of an Italian, a language he did not speak at all. By a combination of bluster and quick thinking—suggesting that the 'Italian', as they called this German Jew with false papers, was only there to make some repairs to a gramophone player and did not speak any German; and that an older woman, who did not yet have forged papers, was the mother of one of the group who now had an apparently impeccable ID card—they somehow managed to satisfy the Gestapo that there was nothing untoward about 'Uncle Karl's' little group of visitors. As soon as she could after this incident, Behrend-Rosenfeld boarded a train out of her native Berlin.

Berlin was nevertheless unusual. The larger population of the capital city, as well as the size and high degree of integration of the Jewish population prior to the war, made it somewhat easier to find people willing to assist in hiding Jews.[9] But there was little more that they could do. Moreover, not everyone was willing to go so far, or take as many risks as those whom Behrend-Rosenfeld was fortunate enough to encounter. Police records are full of denunciations by ordinary Germans who stood behind their net curtains and watched visitors going in and out of their neighbours' homes, reporting the most minor potential infringements to the local authorities. And not only 'Aryans' engaged in denunciations. Those going underground had to enter into numerous compromises in order to survive; older notions of morality went out of the window in the face of Nazi persecution. In desperation, some Jews turned on others who were being persecuted. Acting as a 'catcher' or 'grasper' (*Greifer*) for the Gestapo helped a tiny minority to survive, at least for a while, at the expense of the far larger numbers they betrayed.

One of the most extreme examples was the supposedly 'Aryan'-looking—blond and blue-eyed—Stella Kübler (née Goldschlag). She had been arrested and taken with her parents to the collection point pending deportation. Following failed escape attempts and maltreatment, threatened by facial disfigurement, and in the hope of saving her parents, or at least herself and her attractive appearance, Kübler embarked on collaboration with the Gestapo, who recognized her usefulness in roaming Berlin to seek out and betray fellow Jews. Kübler was directly responsible for the capture and deaths of several hundred individuals, perhaps running into the thousands, including former friends and classmates. Despite these horrific results in her work for the Gestapo, she did not in fact manage to save her parents, who were deported first to Theresienstadt and then to Auschwitz. She was the best known, and most feared, of around twenty such *Greifer* in Berlin at the time, only three of whom—including Kübler—were subsequently brought to account in court after the war. Stella was sentenced by the Soviet authorities to ten years of hard labour; and when she subsequently relocated to West Berlin, she was again convicted but did not have to serve her sentence because of the time already spent in prison. She died in 1994 at the age of seventy-two, possibly by suicide.[10]

These 'snatchers', or *Greifer*, themselves victims of persecution, had capitulated in an impossible situation. Their actions occasioned outrage among others who saw friends and relatives go to their deaths as a consequence of betrayal by fellow Jews. Members of the wider society, however, engaged in a far great number of moral compromises without the same degree of horrific coercion and enforced constraint. It was the willingness of so many non-Jewish Germans to be complicit with the Nazi regime, only too happy to denounce anything suspicious to the authorities, that proved ultimately the major obstacle to Jews' escape and survival. And because of the massive social changes produced by the removal of Jews from surrounding society, they could barely claim they 'did not know' what was going on.

This is made clear by focussing just on one relatively compact district within Berlin. Some 6,096 Jews who lived in the 'Bavarian quarter' of Schöneberg—near 'Uncle Karl'—are known to have lost their lives as a result of Nazi persecution, the overwhelming majority through deportation as well as, in a small number of cases, pre-emptive suicide.[11] Some of these Jews appear in police reports as having been denounced by neighbours, for example for being in hiding or for not wearing a Jewish star.[12] Most of the others had been seized, thrown into trucks in full sight of their neighbours, and taken to the 'collection centres' before being put on trains 'to the east'. Even had neighbours managed to sleep through the racket in the early hours of the morning, or had they been out at work when people were forcibly torn out of their homes, they would nevertheless have been well aware of the changes in the neighbourhood. Empty flats were meticulously registered by the police, along with the contents, and made available for new, 'Aryan' residents, including senior Nazis; and Jewish property was seized and changed hands. To take just one example from the more than 6,000 in this district alone: no fewer than twenty people were taken just from a single apartment block at Eisenacher Straße 58; their emptied premises were taken over by 'Aryans' profiting from their departure. Built in the early twentieth century on a typical Berlin pattern, with larger apartments along the façade at the street front and smaller ones along the side wings around a couple of back courtyards, this particular building would have accommodated perhaps around 150 people, assuming a degree of overcrowding in the smaller units. To have well over 10 percent of the residents forcibly removed and their apartments vacated could not have gone without notice. Like so many others across Berlin, the building was subsequently devastated by bombing and enemy fire continuing right up to the very last days of the war. Most of the block was obliterated, with only a small section of one side wing of a back courtyard remaining habitable after the war, the rest being repurposed as a car park. The later claims by Germans that they had themselves been victims—of bombing by the Allies—should not obscure what had taken place beforehand; the assertion of 'having known nothing about it' rests entirely on obscuring the massive changes in society that some had not merely observed but had actively helped along, and from which so many had benefitted. It was only as the war drew to an end that people began to change the stories about what they had 'known', and in the process to deny what it was that they had actually done.

Nonetheless, though the number is statistically almost meaningless, a few individuals remained determined to challenge the Nazi regime, in whatever ways they could. Having reached Freiburg, Behrend-Rosenfeld stayed with committed opponents of Hitler. She regained her strength and health with good food, rest, and country walks, and benefitted from conversations with intelligent and committed human beings who had not fallen prey to Nazism; she helped with the housework and assisted her hosts' teenage son with his schoolwork. But she still could never fully relax. Eventually, in April 1944 arrangements were made for paid 'guides' to lead Behrend-Rosenfeld across the border to Switzerland. A close friend accompanied her on the train for part of the way. She undertook the hazardous last stages alone, in total darkness, at dead of night, making her way along the edge of a steep overhang. She first lost her handbag with all manner of precious possessions, including family photographs; and then, when tumbling over the final border wall, she fell and broke her leg. Struggling with pain and registering that she could not walk, she was enormously relieved to find she had fallen onto the Swiss side of the border; the surprised Swiss guards ensured she was taken to hospital straight away.

Behrend-Rosenfeld was out: she had escaped; and, through the unexpected luck of meeting a local pastor who happened to know her from before the war and made an intervention on her behalf, she was allowed to stay in Switzerland rather than being returned to Germany, as was generally the case with Jewish fugitives. In the event, she survived to see her husband and children again when the war was over—one of only a tiny handful who managed this.

However exceptional, Behrend-Rosenfeld's story is illuminating in several respects. She had many advantages, as far as survival was concerned: she had 'Aryan' relatives, close friends and socialist contacts who were committed to helping her; she was culturally as much at ease in Christian circles as among Jewish fellow sufferers, and had no difficulty in 'passing', since being a German with a Christian upbringing was integral to her own sense of identity; she had a great deal of psychological resilience; and lastly she had the material resources to pay for what was needed along the way. She estimated that at least fifty people had helped her. In the process, she retained her faith in her fellow human beings—a faith that shines through in her diary entries, in ways that could not be shared by other victims of persecution, whose far more typical experiences were of deceit and betrayal, despair, and death.

Making it through: Rescue and survival in Latvia and beyond

The situation was of course very different for those who were deported to the ghettos and camps in Eastern Europe, whether from further afield, like the Reich Jews on the trains that Behrend-Rosenfeld did not join, or from the local area, as in the case of Jews ousted from their homes and thrown into the ghetto in Riga. The non-Jewish inhabitants of the occupied territories were subjected to Nazi rule: their options for action were limited, the penalties for transgression extremely high. The question of the extent to which they were also antisemitic or simply indifferent to the fate of Jews remains highly contentious. Chances of survival for Jews also differed according to whether they already had personal connections in the surrounding community, or had been deported and shared neither language nor social customs with local people.

The few Latvian Jews who were rescued by non-Jewish compatriots not only possessed native command of the language but often also pre-existing ties of friendship. Bernhard Press and his father, for example, escaped from the Riga ghetto and were able to hide with a close professional colleague whose family were not only prepared to take them in (with the knowing consent of their maid) but also had the material means and psychological resilience to sustain the strain throughout the war.[13] Other Latvians helped Jews whether or not they had known them personally beforehand, but very few. Almost no one was prepared to take the risks this involved. Roberts and Johanna Seduls were therefore a highly unusual couple, using two cellar rooms as a hideout for Jews. One of those they hid was David Zivcon, the electrician who had discovered and preserved copies of the Liepāja photographs of mass murder at the Šķēde beach in December 1941; he was already a friend and had approached Seduls earlier about the possibility of help should this be needed. Making a hiding space available for a known and trusted friend led on to offering help to others: in total, the Seduls hid a total of eleven Jews, only a few of whom they had previously known.[14]

Equally unusual was Jānis Lipke, along with his family and a few trusted contacts.[15] Lipke was acutely aware, from early on, of the barbarity of the German treatment of Jews. He had been shattered by witnessing thousands of terrified Jews being forced to stumble along the icy road towards the death pits of Rumbula in November 1941. Initially a dock worker, Lipke retrained and gained a job as a contractor for the Luftwaffe. Now in charge of Jewish slave labourers from the ghetto, he organized escapes by reporting smaller numbers going back into the ghetto in the evening than he had registered in the morning; or he coordinated Latvian colleagues who were counted entering the ghetto for some made-up reason in place of escaped Jews so that the numbers added up, and then tore off their stars once inside so that they could walk out confidently as Latvians. Lipke also found others who could offer refuge. One somewhat surprising contact was Willie Bienenfeld, the Baltic German mayor of the town of Dobele, a town located a little over seventy kilometres southwest of Riga; to get escaped Jews safely there required coordination with other helpers along the way. And, like the Seduls, Lipke's own family also harboured Jews in their modest home, converting a dilapidated barn into a hiding place.

Although a Jew whom Lipke hid early on was also a personal friend, Lipke was prepared to take risks to save anyone. He took as his mission simply to save as many lives as he could. German Jews saved by Lipke included a mother and her seven-year-old daughter from Berlin, Hanna and

Sofia Stern. They were inmates of the Kaiserwald camp who were sent on a work detail to Riga town centre. Lipke's co-conspirators created a diversion while the two escaped through a toilet window. Once out, the little girl was so weak with hunger that she could barely walk, and Lipke had to carry her. They crossed the river in a fisherman's boat to the island where Lipke lived, and he and his wife looked after them until they were strong enough for the next stage in their flight—to the town of Dobele, under the control of Mayor Bienenfeld. Lipke also saved an Austrian escapee, Regina Schwartz, but was unable to take her companions at the same time; when he went back for them, they had already been discovered and arrested.[16] In total, Lipke, his wife Johanna, his children, and his close associates saved more than forty Jews—around one-fifth of the estimated 200 Jews in total who managed to survive in Latvia, a vanishingly tiny percentage of the 94,000 who had lived there before the war, roughly half of them in Riga.

We rarely have details of individual rescuers who were caught, or Jews who did not live to tell their tales. The experiences of Frida Michelson, a Riga Jew, illustrate just how fraught such attempts could be, even for people who knew the locality well.[17] On 7 December 1941 she was in the second group to be marched from the ghetto to Rumbula. Following the deadly *Aktion* a week earlier it was now absolutely clear what awaited them, and people were 'enveloped in fear and panic', as Michelson wrote. Arriving at Rumbula—where, as we have seen, Hemicker had designed the most efficient form of killing pits—they were forced to undress to their underwear, and throw their valuables and clothes onto different heaps, amid ever louder screams and cries. Michelson, who wore several layers of clothing, took off only her outerwear. Taking advantage of a moment when the guards were distracted, she lay down on the heap as though dead, and soon found pairs of shoes being thrown on top of her, until she was more or less buried in an ever higher 'mountain of discarded footwear'. She remained lying as still as she could, listening to the 'staccato of the machine guns, the shouts', the 'tramp of people's feet running', and the 'cries and moaning' that 'went on for many hours'. Eventually, she could hear the sound of shovels as the pits of corpses were covered over; she heard an infant cry for its mother and then be stilled by a gunshot, she heard the voices of locals and Germans discussing the booty they could take home with them. Finally, when all was quiet in the night, she mustered the courage and strength to crawl from under the shoes and collected some clothes from the heap to help against the bitter winter cold. She had somehow survived the massacre of thousands of Jews—perhaps around 27,000 in the course of the two days of shootings—but this did not yet mean she would survive the next days, weeks, and, as it turned out, years.[18]

Michelson's subsequent experiences highlight the importance of a network of those opposed to Nazism. Among those who helped were Seventh-Day Adventists convinced they were doing God's work, who passed her around to trusted contacts when things became too dangerous. In this way she met some immensely courageous individuals, and forged close friendships. At times, too, she had to survive in the wild. Her native fluency in Latvian and her ability to connect with local people, as well as her capacity to argue her way out of tight situations, proved invaluable. So too, eventually, did her ability to talk Yiddish. At the very end of the war, when Russian soldiers arrived and were about to shoot her then-protector, whom they accused of being a German collaborator, she spoke to a Russian soldier in Yiddish, convincing him and his fellow soldiers that she was indeed Jewish and telling the truth about the man who had given her shelter. After the war, a few ghetto survivors gathered in Riga: eighty-seven men attended. She was the only woman.[19]

In addition to language, familiarity with the local culture, and the existence of social networks, topography made a difference to chances of rescue and survival. People in isolated farmsteads found it easier to hide Jews than those in urban environments, particularly in apartment blocks with prying neighbours and block wardens. But on the other hand, rural inhabitants were often more curious about what was going on and aware of anything unusual. Penalties for hiding Jews were merciless, and in small communities people were terrified of denunciation. This was the case in neighbouring Lithuania too, where reactions of horror at local killings similarly did not suffice to turn bystanders into rescuers. The one area where people seem to have been more willing to shelter fugitive Jews was in northwestern Lithuania, where homesteads were more isolated, and there was less risk of a neighbour informing on someone.

And in Lithuania, too, there were individuals who ran extraordinary risks, as in the remarkable case of baby 'Elida'—a name based on the Hebrew word 'I-Lida', meaning 'non-birth', because birth in the ghetto was forbidden—who was smuggled in a basket out of the Kaunas ghetto and taken by a Lithuanian woman who raised her with members of her own family in the countryside.[20]

Other factors could affect perceived risk-taking by non-Jews. In Latgale, on the eastern borders with the Soviet Union, people were somewhat less antisemitic than in western areas of Latvia. While there was not the sort of underground opposition in Latvia that was evident elsewhere, what anti-Nazi partisan activities there were in the later war years tended to occur in this region. The partisans included Latvians trying to avoid call-up into the SS, and even former German collaborators who saw how the winds had turned, or who wanted to avoid the Soviet army. Many partisans were virulently antisemitic, and joining a partisan group was far from safe for Jews. The Riga survivor Marǧers Vestermanis managed both to hide the fact that he was Jewish (harder for men, due to the practice of circumcision) and to keep silent as fellow partisans reminisced over campfires about the 'good times' they had enjoyed slaughtering Jews in the summer of 1941. Both Vestermanis and fellow survivor Edward Anders felt that Latvian attitudes towards Jews ranged between hostility and simple indifference.[21] Individuals such as Seduls, Lipke, their fellow helpers, and the deeply religious Seventh-Day Adventists and other individuals who harboured Frida Michelson were extremely rare.

In Lithuania, too, relations between Jewish and non-Jewish partisans were often fraught, as Rachel Margolis and her comrades discovered when they were robbed of their weapons by another band of partisans. And in her experience, too, it was generally less the goodwill of local peasants than sheer fear that persuaded Lithuanian villagers to hand over some of their own meagre food supplies to the partisans hiding in the countryside.[22] Again, fluency in the local language could be crucial; but there were many aspects of the organization and aims of partisan groups that affected their interactions with other communities in the locality. In neighbouring Belorussia, the community of refugees and fighters organized by the Bielski brothers, under the leadership of Tuvia Bielski, indicate some of the key issues that were involved in survival, rescue, and self-rescue.[23] But most individuals did not escape from ghettos or join partisan groups, and even the latter varied widely in the extent to which those involved were able to survive the privations and violence they endured; these stories are remarkable.

Reich Jews who had been deported to Riga and escaped, but did not speak Latvian, had little hope of surviving on their own. A handful were rescued by Jānis Lipke, but, again, this was exceptional. For the vast majority, simply staying alive through to the end of the war could be their only hope; and this depended less on local assistance than on their own resilience, material resources, and sheer luck. Their experiences of local gentiles were at best mixed: while some Latvians engaged in self-interested exchanges of goods and foodstuffs, others mistreated Jews mercilessly. Survivor accounts are generally sharply critical of local people who had become complicit or active collaborators with the German persecutors, sapping the morale of victims and their capacity to keep going. Survival was often a matter of simply making it through in one way or another; morale could make a difference.

The brutality of Latvians was emphasized in Jeannette Wolff's account, penned soon after her return to her native Germany in January 1946.[24] By the time Wolff was deported from Dortmund to Riga in late January 1942, along with her husband and their two elder daughters, she already had considerable experience of the horrors of Nazi persecution.[25] Doubly condemned as both an active socialist and a Jew, Wolff had first been arrested and imprisoned in March 1933. Her husband had been sent to Sachsenhausen in November 1938 and on his release was a broken man who would not talk of his experiences. Her youngest daughter, at the age of nineteen, had been denounced for going to the cinema despite the ban on Jews, and was sent to Ravensbrück concentration camp. But Riga went way beyond any of Wolff's experiences to date. On arrival in Riga, after five days on the train, Wolff was told by ghetto inhabitants how drunken Latvians under the command of the German SS had engaged in mass shootings, and had by then killed around 30,000 Jews. She soon got to witness the cruelty for herself. A 'high point' of a favourite 'game' of the SS was using little children as 'living target practice': two would throw the children back and forth, while a third took aim and shot.

Wolff found it nearly impossible to describe 'the rapes, screaming, nervous breakdowns of people who had gone crazy'. Her daughters were given the task of cleaning up dwellings abandoned in haste when their previous occupants were taken off to be shot; they often found frozen corpses which had fingers missing, hacked off for their rings. Later, when the thaw set in, severed fingers were found lying around. Determined to survive as best she could, Wolff herself declared she was a 'uniform seamstress' by profession; in this way she avoided the so-called Dünamünde Aktion, in which some

5,000 middle-aged or elderly people were told they would be taken to better conditions in another camp but were, in fact, simply shot.[26]

Despite all, Wolff figured out ways to keep going. She managed to get work in the team of women cleaning buildings occupied by the Germans—like the former Jewish schoolmate recognized by Jürgen Ernst Kroeger—and gained opportunities to barter for additional food from locals. These exchanges were not illustrations of selfless rescue or assistance on the part of the gentiles involved; they were matters of mutual self-interest, since starving Jews from the ghetto would hand over valuable objects in return for small quantities of food, despite the considerable dangers. One Riga ghetto survivor later told the filmmaker Claude Lanzmann how he had to hold the coat of an elderly woman from Berlin, who had been forced to take it off, shivering with cold on a freezing winter day, and who was then shot for having 'traded something for a piece of bread'.[27] And, working for the Riga Waffen-SS, Wolff also got to know more about their extravagant lifestyle. SS men were in far less danger than the ordinary soldiers fighting on the front lines; the only real risk they ran, she thought, was punishment for the Nazi crime of 'racial defilement', since they frequently sought out and raped beautiful young Jewish women and girls, some of whom, presumably, managed to survive just a little longer in this way.[28]

There were some surprising moments, in which Wolff struck a chord of empathy with a fellow German even across the racial and political divides. Shortly after the Warsaw ghetto uprising had been crushed, members of the Feldgendarmerie who had assisted in the suppression were incorporated into the SS and sent to Riga. In the course of cleaning their building, Wolff got talking to one of them who, like herself, came from Westphalia. Somehow, there was a moment of mutual recognition as compatriots far from their common Westphalian *Heimat*. He unburdened himself, telling her that, however the war turned out, he simply could not go on living. As she recalled his words, he explained: 'If we lose the war, I can't go back to Germany, because under orders from the SS, which we had been taken into, we were active as an execution group in occupied territories and everyone there would then, quite rightly, badmouth us as murderers. If we win the war, I will never be rid of death cries of the maybe 65,000 murdered people from the Warsaw Ghetto. Every night I hear the wailing of people burning alive, I see the disfigured faces of the people who had been beaten, the bodies of men, women and children that had been torn to shreds by hand grenades. I can't go on living.' The next morning, Wolff recounts, she and her work group came in to find he had hanged himself from a window frame in an empty room.[29]

In 1943, people from the Riga ghetto who were still considered fit for labour were sent to a variety of locations, including the nearby Kaiserwald labour camp, in the northern suburbs of Riga, which now became a concentration camp under the control of the SS. The inscription here was different from the better-known slogans at the gates of Auschwitz and other camps: in Kaiserwald, incoming prisoners were starkly warned, 'Whoever enters here should leave all hope behind!'[30] Former criminals from German prisons now had control, and many guards engaged in extreme brutality and sadism. In the course of closing down all the ghettos in Lithuania and Latvia, new arrivals were also sent to Kaiserwald from the Lithuanian ghettos in Kaunas, Vilnius, and Šiauliai. Wolff, now an inmate in Kaiserwald, felt that newcomers were worse off than those who were already 'dulled' or 'deadened' and apathetic as a result of their time in the camp. Finally, as the Soviet army drew closer in the summer of 1944, inmates were subjected to a further selection. Wolff and others still capable of work were deported to Stutthof concentration camp on the Baltic coast near Danzig. It was on this overcrowded ship that Wolff—who had only at the last minute gained a space on it in the hope of finding her husband, and in place of almost certain execution—was briefly and surprisingly reunited with her daughter Edith, whom she had not seen for two years.

Once registered at Stutthof, Wolff survived through a series of labour subcamps, experiencing varying degrees of brutality, generally on the part of Lithuanian guards, and occasional kindness and relative humanity on the part of a few, including a kindhearted caterer in one camp and members of the army in another. She and a few other committed socialists and members of a youth movement tried to organize social activities that might keep people's spirits up. This may have helped her and members of her group to retain a sense of agency and self-respect, but could only have a very limited impact, given the appalling conditions. She was shocked when two well-educated teenage girls from a lawyer's family in Hungary, who had every chance of survival, simply 'went crazy' and went out to the woods to dig their own grave, then hit each other over their heads and lay down waiting to die because they could no longer bear it. An attempt was made to rescue them, but they had lost the will to live and when they fled again—now from the sick bay—they were shot by the camp guards.[31]

With resilience and good fortune, Wolff made it through a succession of temporary labour camps. In the winter of 1944–1945, as the front drew nearer, their German overseers began to take notice of what people might say after the war was over. In freezing weather, the prisoners were finally issued with better clothing, apparently in response to local murmurings of disapproval at seeing 'ragged women, often without stockings and in wooden clogs and wrapped in a blanket' who were forced to 'carry out heavy labour in snow and rain in deepest winter'. Finally, in preparation for a gruelling death march, around 183 women were shot because they were too weak to walk; while on the road, a further eighty-seven were killed. The remaining 997 women still alive eventually reached a prison in Koronowo, Poland, where they were held overnight; the Germans planned to shoot them the following morning, but the Soviet army arrived and released them just in time.[32]

Wolff's account, written so close to the time of persecution and incarceration, had political motivations: she was determined to inspire postwar Germans to make a new start. In a sense, then, she needed to distinguish between 'bad' Nazis, as well as Latvians and Lithuanians, on the one hand, and those Germans who could potentially be reformed, on the other. This meant distinguishing between the extremes of the truly evil people and the merely misguided or unwilling fellow travellers who could potentially be set on a new political path. Her account is very different in both tenor and contents to the much later account by the Austrian survivor, Gertrude Schneider, whose work on the Riga ghetto combines both memoir and history, seeking to provide a more comprehensive picture, one based not only on her own memories but also on a range of other sources.

Schneider was an academic historian with extensive scholarly experience by the time she was writing what she hoped would be a well-researched and balanced account. She attempts to evoke the ways in which people tried to make a life, despite the ubiquity and near certainty of an early death. Her account includes depictions of cultural life—music, theatre—as well as of unexpected friendships and intimate relations. Some liaisons resulted in 'ghetto marriages', even if, given the ban on sexual relations in the ghetto, women ultimately had to face painful abortions without anaesthetic even in late stages of pregnancy.[33] Wolff, by contrast, writing in the early months after her return to Germany, was still traumatized by the freshness of her experiences—and, although she does not mention this explicitly, by the fact that her husband had perished and only one of her three daughters had survived. Filled with passion, she wanted to tell the world about the evil that the 'Hitler dictatorship' had caused, and to inspire Germans to rise up and go to work to 'restore the image of our German fatherland in the world!' Her answer to the question posed in the title of her memoir—'sadism or madness'—allowed her implicitly to retain faith in the mass of the German people. In her portrayal, the 'madness' (*Wahnsinn*) is on the part of Hitler and his close associates; the 'sadism' is on the part of the former professional criminals who were given supervisory roles in the camps, as well as the often drunken and debauched SS men, and the brutal Lithuanians and Latvians put in charge of the ghettos and camps.

Nonetheless, there are also decent Germans in Wolff's account, and there are degrees of difference even between the people in charge of the prisoners. Her encounters with members of the army were slightly better than those with the SS. Meanwhile, she attempts to believe that ordinary Germans really did not know what was going on, so she is able to retain her faith in the German people and their possible future redemption. This is a story of sheer survival. Its details are unique to Wolff, as are the lessons she draws from it; but the outlines are general, experienced by innumerable survivors who went on the same tracks from Riga to Stutthof to labour camps and eventually crawled out at the end of the war, permanently marked by their experiences. Believing that ordinary Germans were largely ignorant or forced into unwilling passivity could assist reintegration into postwar German society, in the case of Jeanette Wolff. Commitment to socialism and political determination also played a role in her own psychological resilience.

For other German survivors of the Riga ghetto, religious commitment played a greater role. Gerda Gottschalk was a committed Christian categorized as a 'first-degree *Mischling*', the daughter of a Christian mother and a Jewish father.[34] Blocked by Nazism from pursuing her choice of profession—she had embarked on a promising career as an actress—she ended up working as a secretarial assistant to Dr Josef Gülden, the editor of a newspaper for a Catholic student group. She and her sister were arrested in Leipzig at the end of October 1941 for not wearing the yellow star—which, technically, they did not have to wear since, unlike Else Behrend-Rosenfeld, they were not categorized as 'mixed-breeds counting as Jews'. But they did not manage to challenge the arrest; and, following a period in police cells, they were deported east, along with 700 Leipzig Jews and a further 300 Jews from Dresden.

In many ways, Gottschalk's experiences of Riga echo those of Jeanette Wolff; a significant difference in her survival story, however, came in the later months of the war when, like Wolff, she was deported to Stutthof. Along with a couple of friends in the camp, Gottschalk was selected to help with a local farmer's family. They were fortunate to be placed with Klara and Gustav Gebhardt, who were somewhat opposed to Nazism, despite the fact that their son—also friendly at a personal level—was in the SS. The woman overseeing their work in the fields, named Hulda (whose identity and relationship with the family is not made clear), had a local reputation as a communist, and gladly supported them with food, sympathy, and, most important, smuggling out and posting a letter from Gottschalk to Dr Gülden, the Catholic for whom she had worked in Leipzig. They knew that this relatively good placement for the harvest season could not last into the winter, and with the Gebhardts' support the prisoners, knowing they would soon be sent back to Stutthof, made plans to escape. At this point, Gottschalk's letter, sent with Hulda's help, had what seemed an almost miraculous outcome: through Catholic connections Gülden had contacted a family, the Pfürtners, who lived in Danzig, not far from Stutthof. They offered to hide her under a false identity and to facilitate the flight of her two friends, now issued with false student identity papers, who would continue on the train into the heart of Germany as though they were evacuees from eastern provinces who had lost most of their possessions. In this way, and through the connections with the religious community in which she felt at home, Gottschalk was able to hold on, in broken health but with her spirits sustained by the support she had desperately needed in the closing months of the war.

But for the vast majority of Jews, neither political and religious commitments nor personal connections could help. Gottschalk's sister, Helga, did not survive; nor did their Jewish father. Nor did her good friend Dora Hansen. Gottschalk managed to preserve in the soles of her boots the few sad pages of a diary written by Hansen.[35] Hansen was a Leipzig Jew who had been in a mixed marriage and had converted to Catholicism; when her 'Aryan' husband died in 1938, she was exposed to the full rigours of

Nazi persecution and deported along with the other Leipzig Jews. In the Riga ghetto, she had tried to keep her spirits up and managed to get through the first year with a degree of hope, noting good weather, the beauty of flowers, the occasional extra ration of food, and the comfort of good company (including Gottschalk), alongside melancholically expressing her longing to see her children and her home. But from early 1942 Hansen's diary entries increasingly betray the long-term effects of chronic malnourishment and acts of cruelty. Her later entries repeatedly mention hunger, list what few items of food there had been that day, and record her growing sense of weakness. Her last entry, on 5 March 1944, comments that 'the colour of the sky is wonderful, otherwise everything as always'. She no longer had the strength to write in the months that followed. In July 1944, as Wolff, Gottschalk, and others were selected to go on the boat to Stutthof, Hansen was among 300 prisoners considered too weak to work; they were loaded onto a truck and driven into the forest, where they were all shot.

From indifference to impotence

During the war, few Germans would even begin to think about raising their voices in favour of victims, particularly not on behalf of unknown people far away—people who, unlike family members and acquaintances who had been murdered in the 'euthanasia' programme, were not part of their own community of empathy. After the war, when facing accusations of complicity or silence in face of mind-boggling criminality carried out in their name, it would be preferable to claim to have 'known nothing about it' than to admit to having been indifferent, let alone antisemitic, or enthusiastic for the Nazi cause. The question for the wartime years should therefore not be that of 'knowledge'—as so many tried to reframe it—but rather that of responses to violence of which they were well aware at the time, and self-justifications later.

Changes in the months immediately before and after defeat were striking. As he drove through Germany with the US Army in early 1945, the German-Jewish émigré Walter Jessel made detailed notes of the responses he encountered among his former compatriots. Tasked with interviewing prisoners of war ('PWs'), Jessel was struck by the ease with which they were now changing sides:'Nazi Mitläufer [fellow-travellers] have switched totally. Off-hand guess about political views among PWs: Convinced Nazis: 15%. Mitläufer: 75%. Anti-Nazis: 10%.' He defined '*Mitläufer*,' or fellow-travellers, as 'people who sold their consciences to convenience, personal safety, a prestigious uniform and a share of the loot confiscated from Jews and other enemies of the state'.[36] Three-quarters of those with whom he spoke had, in his view, fallen into this category of opportunists and beneficiaries of Nazism. Now, as Germany faced total defeat, it was more convenient for them to profess anti-Nazi sentiments.

Jessel was also struck by the ease with which individuals could simultaneously adopt quite different public faces, according to context. 'Went through last night's tapes of bugged PW officer quarters. I recognized the voice of an "anti-Nazi" Colonel whom I had just interrogated . . . "terrible what we did with the Jews. It was a terrible mistake. We should have finished them all in one day—dann hätte kein Hahn nach ihnen gekräht" ("no cock would have crowed after them—nobody would have given a damn.")'[37] This capacity to be utterly two-faced—presenting an 'anti-Nazi' face to the US interrogators, while also putting on an act of bravura still clothed in Nazi language and attitudes to fellow prisoners of war—was widespread at the time, as other recordings of bugged conversations between prisoners of war also demonstrate.[38]

With the unconditional surrender and defeat of the Nazi regime came the total collapse—apparently—of belief in Nazism. In a letter of 8 May 1945, written to his family back in the United States, Jessel summarized the situation:'VE-DAY!—you probably want to read a few lines that were written on this day—that's about all you'll get because I'm going to celebrate with the boys. So there we are:The Nazis are gone, so much so that nobody knows anyone who ever was a Nazi. Only cowards are left, but that was to be expected.'[39]

In the course of his work for the US forces, including from February 1946 as a member of the US War Department Intelligence Group, Strategic Services Unit, Jessel interrogated a wide range of individuals. He was interested in strategies for recrafting a compromised past among those who still had some hope of constructing new lives. One interviewee was the then relatively junior lawyer Alfred Spiess who was, in Jessel's view, clearly prevaricating in ways reminiscent of playground excuses:'Lt. Henry Heckscher, himself a German-trained lawyer, submitted him to a dramatic interrogation', during which 'Spiess squirmed—he didn't do it, and besides he did it only under orders'. This self-contradictory stance was of course a classic line of defence. Pleas of both impotence and ignorance were combined, as he went on: 'The cases of Jews and foreigners were taken out of his hands. He declared that Nazi law was based on ancient principles—nauseating. He had just heard of the 50,000 dead at the Buchenwald concentration camp and considered himself outraged.'[40] However compromised his Third Reich past might have been, Spiess subsequently made amends: he gained a reputation in West Germany as an energetic prosecutor of Nazi crimes in the Treblinka and other trials; and he listened attentively to survivors' testimonies, which clearly had a significant impact on him.[41] 'Changing sides' could, over the longer term, clearly mean more than simply putting on a convenient public face depending on which way the political wind was blowing.

Responses at the time varied with what interviewees thought they could hope to gain by taking different tacks, also in the light of Allied considerations in the emerging Cold War. Jessel noted typical patterns: a 'Gestapo agent turned informer, following the example of all his colleagues since they're caught'; and a 'German colonel turned anti-Nazi during Russian imprisonment, now on his next mission to spy on us for the Russians. A fantastic bastard.'[42] In June 1945, Jessel was 'assigned with a small CIC [Counter Intelligence Corps] team to screen Wernher von Braun's rocket team'. They were tasked with 'sorting out Nazi hangers-on and enforcers from technical staff in order to bring the latter to the U.S.' Jessel summarized von Braun's group: 'The team consists of rocket enthusiasts, engineering college graduates, professors, all unrepentant Nazis aware of their bargaining power with the Americans'. However, the 'German Army personnel in the group are less enthusiastic realizing that their chances of going to the U.S. are smaller than those of the technicians. To improve their chances they sing.' Among others, Jessel interrogated Major-General Dornberger: 'Now Dornberger and his creatures are convinced that war between the U.S. and the Soviet Union is imminent. They are mercenaries who want to sell their weapons. Their country is defeated, hence their only chance is to go on doing the same business for someone else. Had a long session with Dornberger who when you get off his obnoxious philosophy, is better at explaining engineering developments to a layman than anyone I ever saw. He'll charm his new U.S. bosses.'[43]

25. On 19 September 1939, Hitler addresses a huge crowd of supporters in Danzig (Gdańsk), following the German takeover of this formerly 'free' but increasingly nazified city. Alice Baerwald, the native Berliner who had moved first to Nakel and then to Danzig, had been lucky enough to have got out just a month earlier, sailing out of the nearby port of Gdynia to London in late August with a degree of cheekiness and subterfuge in a difficult encounter with a suspicious border guard (see chapter 8).

United States Holocaust Memorial Museum, courtesy of National Archives and Records Administration, College Park, 20385.

26. A huge crowd of Germans in Danzig assemble to hear a speech by Adolf
Hitler on 19 September 1939. 'Ethnic Germans' across Eastern Europe, like the
Baltic German Jürgen Ernst Kroeger, would welcome Hitler and give little
thought to the impact of Nazi rule on communities they considered to be
'racially inferior', whether doomed to subservience to the German 'master
race' or condemned, eventually, to extermination. Many would later claim they
'did not know' what had happened to those who were forcibly removed from
their homes.
*United States Holocaust Memorial Museum, courtesy of National Archives and Records
Administration, College Park, 20350.*

27. Jews stand in stagnant water engaged in forced labour, Poland, 1940. This scene is reminiscent of the conditions described in letters to the German Quaker Margarethe Lachmund by Jews deported to the ghetto of Piaski in the Lublin area of Poland.
United States Holocaust Memorial Museum, courtesy of Lucy Gliklich Breitbart, 97200.

28. Local people watch as the Germans publicly hang a woman on a gallows erected in a town square. The photograph was probably taken by a member of Police Battalion 101 somewhere in Poland in 1940–1941. Sights such as this appear to have been relatively common and widely photographed without seeming to occasion much sense of outrage or questioning.
United States Holocaust Memorial Museum, courtesy of Michael O'Hara, 47441.

29. This photograph, taken by an onlooker, portrays the brutal killing of Jews by Lithuanian activists on the forecourt of the Lietukis garage in Kaunas, Lithuania, watched by German soldiers, local residents, and passers-by. Contemporary reports suggest that some members of the 'audience' enthusiastically supported violent attacks on Jews, while others were silently shocked. The German *Einsatzgruppen* had been instructed to instigate murders of Jews to be carried out by local Lithuanians in the early days of the occupation; this violence should appear to be 'spontaneous' without any German influence being evident. *Yad Vashem Archives, 1495/9, 74FO7.*

30. One of the pits at Ponary, outside Vilna (Vilnius), where from the summer of
1941 Jews from Vilna were taken and killed. Local people often came to watch,
or to benefit from taking the property or selling the possessions of murdered
Jews, as recorded in the diary kept by a local resident, Kazimierz Sakowicz. The
photograph also shows SS men, German policemen, and Lithuanian collaborators
who carried out the killings.
Yad Vashem Archives, 1495/9, 75FO5.

31. Members of the Lithuanian auxiliary police assisted the Germans in the
mass murder of local Jews; these collaborators were not only involved in acts of
perpetration but also benefited from the crimes. Here, a Lithuanian who has just
participated in a mass execution in the Rase Forest is engaged in auctioning the
clothing and other possessions of murdered Jews in the central market of Utena,
Lithuania.
United States Holocaust Memorial Museum, courtesy of Saulius Berzinis, 25736.

32. A group of local Jewish boys stumbling across the dunes of the Šķēde beach, just north of Liepāja in Latvia, just before they were shot into a pit. This photograph was taken by Oberscharführer Carl Strott, a member of the German Security Service (*Sicherheitsdienst*, SD). The reel of film with this and other photographs of the mass killing on the beach in December 1941 was found by David Zivkon, a Jewish electrician who was working in the SD headquarters. He managed to take the negatives and make copies with the help of a friend before returning the original reel to the drawer in Strott's home. Miraculously, both Zivkon and the photographs survived the war; after the war the photographs were invaluable evidence in the Nuremberg trials.
Yad Vashem Archives, 1495/9, 4613_625.

33. A Wehrmacht soldier on the Eastern Front kicks an individual who has, along with others, been hanged as a 'partisan', sometime after October 1941. Sights such as this were relatively common, mentioned in German diaries and letters home without raising queries or causing any apparent sense of outrage.

United States Holocaust Memorial Museum, courtesy of Claranne Bechtler, 42881.

34. Members of an unidentified unit execute a group kneeling by the side of a mass grave in the invaded Soviet Union, sometime between 22 June and September 1941. Killers in situations such as this did not always find it easy, and some only engaged in killing as a result of peer group pressure; most resorted to alcohol, or used Nazi ideology to try to 'justify' acts of mass murder of civilians, including children and babies who were clearly not 'partisans'. Discomfort at the evident inhumanity led some to nervous breakdowns, while others seem to have revelled in being part of what they saw as a historic mission. While the 'Holocaust by bullets' and mass shootings continued throughout the war, the technique of killing by the use of gas chambers in dedicated extermination camps was clearly less stressful for the murderers—the vast majority of whom were never brought to justice after the war.

United States Holocaust Memorial Museum, courtesy of National Archives and Records Administration, College Park, 89063.

35. Local German residents watch a group of Jews arriving at an assembly centre in preparation for deportation from Kitzingen, a north Bavarian town with around 16,000 inhabitants, on 24 March 1942. Everywhere, Germans were fully aware of the deportations from their places of residence; and many also benefitted from the properties and possessions left behind by people who it was assumed would never return. By this time, reports of atrocities on the Eastern Front were widespread.

United States Holocaust Memorial Museum, courtesy of National Archives and Records Administration, College Park, 18898.

36. Onlookers watch Jews being deported from the sizeable Franconian city of Würzburg, on 25 April 1942, as they are marched along the Hindenburgstraße to the railway station carrying bundles and suitcases in the forlorn hope that the deceit about 'resettlement' might be true. Not everyone could believe this fiction, however; some, like Else Behrend-Rosenfeld, took the risk of evading deportation and 'going under' in hiding or with an assumed identity, while others chose to take their own lives rather than let the Nazis determine the date and manner of their deaths.
United States Holocaust Memorial Museum, courtesy of National Archives and Records Administration, College Park, 18909A.

37. The Latvian Jānis Lipke has been recognized by Yad Vashem as one of the 'Righteous among the Nations'. He was a Latvian dock worker who rescued forty-two Jews in and around Riga between 1941 and 1944—around one-fifth of all Jews who survived in Latvia—whether by hiding them in his own home or establishing a secure network of contacts who could be trusted and safe places to shelter. His motivation was entirely altruistic, and he did not personally know most of the people whose lives he saved.
United States Holocaust Memorial Museum, courtesy of Bernhard Press, 69739.

38. The resistance fighter and partisan, Zionist youth leader Abba Kovner, posing with two comrades, Ruska Korczak (left) and Vitka Kempner (right) in Vilna in July 1944, following liberation by the Red Army. Kovner and others in the United Partisan Organization (FPO) had refused to go 'like lambs to the slaughter' and had instead chosen to take the risks of escaping from the ghetto and fighting with partisans in the surrounding forests. Kovner would later testify eloquently at Eichmann's trial in Jerusalem.

Photographer: Ilya Ehrenberg. United States Holocaust Memorial Museum, courtesy of Vitka Kempner Kovner, 76842.

39. The end of the road for Germans in 1945: a boy with a bicycle does not seem to know which way to go as he faces a closed-off street in a German town that has been ruined not only by bombing, but also by the horrific consequences of Hitler's twelve-year rule.
United States Holocaust Memorial Museum, courtesy of Robert Steinke, 66224.

40. Women remove the rubble from the streets of Berlin, May 1945. Germans
would now begin to portray themselves as victims—of destruction caused by
aerial warfare, of forcible expulsions and loss of territories in Eastern Europe, of
mass bereavement in service of a lost cause, and of occupation by their former
enemies, the victorious Allies. They would now claim they had 'always been
against it', referring to Nazism, and they had 'known nothing about it', generally
referring to Nazi atrocities 'in the east'—as if the violence had not been visible all
around, for all to see, and as if they had themselves played no role in the escalation
of persecution into mass extermination. When faced with the murderous
consequences of conformity and complicity in Nazi rule, Germans would find
the legacies far more difficult to confront than the piles of rubble that could more
readily be shifted from the streets of bombed-out cities.
United States Holocaust Memorial Museum, courtesy of Joseph Eaton, 51692.

Other former Nazis simply engaged in denial. The notoriously antisemitic publisher of *Der Stürmer*, Julius Streicher, now claimed that he had
'never harmed a Jew', as Jessel noted, and indeed had 'never hurt anybody,
except one prison inmate, not a Jew'. As it happened, Streicher 'was arrested
by a Jewish GI whose father was maltreated by Streicher in 1936' and who
was not inclined to believe him; and Streicher's public reputation was in
any case impossible to cover up.[44] In the Nuremberg trial Streicher's repeated incitements to murder and extermination were held to constitute
a crime against humanity, and he was duly sentenced to death by hanging.
Other notable interviewees included Ernst Kaltenbrunner, former leader
of the Austrian SS and successor to Reinhard Heydrich as head of the
Reichssicherheitshauptamt, or RSHA, who was also subsequently sentenced to death in the Nuremberg trials.[45] An attempt by Jessel's colleague
Walter Horn to interview Hitler's sister Paula (who went by the name of
Paula Wolff) was extremely brief: she only barked '*Raus!*' ('get out!') to her
would-be interrogator at this time.[46]

Cover-ups were much easier for people who had not held prominent
roles in public life and were not subjected to this sort of interrogation. Yet in
some respects the attitudes, actions, and inaction of those who would now
represent themselves as having been merely bystanders, somewhat distant
from the main drama of events during the Hitler years, were just as intrigu-
ing. Jessel was particularly interested in the question of how Germans more
generally had made their peace with the regime. He began to explore what
had happened to his former schoolmates, whom he had known well when
they were younger, unlike individuals whose reconstructed pasts he only
encountered now. Over the following months, Jessel traced as many classmates from his Frankfurt high school as he could, and his observations are
illuminating. A highly readable version of his investigation, with altered
names and additional details, was published in 2017; but the sketches Jessel
penned at the time, using his classmates' real names (which I have abbrevi-
ated here), provide more immediate insights.[47]

Seven other Jewish classmates had, like Jessel, emigrated; some were also,
like himself, now serving in the US Army, while the one Zionist who had
emigrated to Palestine had escaped the Holocaust only to die of malaria.[48]
The fact that all the Jewish students from Jessel's class had managed to get
out of Germany gives an indication of their families' social and economic
status, and the strength of their international connections. Their stories

also, however, reflect generational differences: parents, grandparents, aunts, and uncles had generally remained in Germany and faced deportation and death—including Jessel's own aunt, Henriette, whom he unsuccessfully tried to find.[49]

What makes Jessel's account particularly striking, however, are the stories of eleven non-Jewish classmates whose fates he managed to trace. Six of them were still alive, three were dead, and two were missing. That roughly half had either not survived or were missing is in itself an indication of the massive demographic impact of war on German males of this generation. The stories of those he did manage to interview also provide remarkable insights. These young men had attended a school where 40 percent of their classmates were Jewish. Most of them had in one way or another come to terms with the deeply antisemitic Nazi regime, and now pulled out the standard prevarications and excuses. There were also a couple of significant exceptions, one for personal or emotional reasons and the other out of political commitment. This little group forms a microcosm that was in some respects typical of that particular milieu.

The accounts of those who had accommodated themselves to the Nazi system, and had in fact done rather well under Nazism, were marked by an emphasis on personal impotence, powerlessness, having been just a 'little man' (kleiner Mann). Membership of the Nazi party had, they claimed, been more or less a formality; they could not have spoken up against Nazism, even against aspects of which they disapproved; and they tried to downplay the seriousness of Nazi crimes, or gave 'reasons' that supposedly cast participation in such crimes in a better light.

One former classmate, Dr Horst E., had become a doctor specializing in tuberculosis. He had, he told Jessel, joined the NSDAP on the occasion of what he called the 'Hitler-Ribbentrop Pact'—the nonaggression treaty of 23 August 1939—because, he claimed, he believed that Hitler had in this way cleverly managed to avert war. He should have been aware of his error of judgement almost immediately: war was unleashed barely a week later, with the German invasion of Poland on 1 September 1939. Dr Horst E. sought to impress upon his Jewish classmate that, apart from his party membership, he was otherwise not really a Nazi. Jessel pressed him further: 'Supposing the Nazis had assigned you to Auschwitz. How would that have affected you?' Dr Horst E. replied: 'That would have been terrible. But there would have been nothing I could do. I would have been a little man in an enormous machine. I could not have taken the risk to speak up. My family comes first.'[50]

Another classmate had seemingly been rather more keen to jump on the Nazi bandwagon from the outset. Günther B. had joined the NSDAP in 1933 and rapidly climbed the legal career ladder, becoming a district judge (*Amtsgerichtsrat*) in Frankfurt in 1937. He too, however, wanted to present himself in an anodyne light, saying to Jessel: 'Don't get the wrong impression, I'm not defending what the Nazis did, I just want you to understand that a little man like myself had no opportunity to disapprove, I felt that these excesses were temporary wartime affairs. Had we won, I'm sure they would have ceased immediately.'[51] Not only did he emphasize his own supposed impotence as a 'little man', even when choosing to apply Nazi laws; he also sought to downplay the degree of Nazi criminality, dismissing the murder of millions as merely 'excesses' that were somehow not integral to Nazi racism. There seemed, moreover, no glimmer of recognition that ceasing the 'excesses' after the war would have been far too late for the millions who had by then been murdered; and indeed, such cessation would have been highly unlikely, given the fact that the 'final solution' had initially been scheduled to take place only after the hoped-for final victory, not during the war. His apparent inability to register that what to him were 'temporary wartime affairs' were utterly final for the millions who had died indicates a staggering degree of indifference or lack of empathy. No doubt Günther B., like the overwhelming majority of former Nazi lawyers, subsequently went on to a career in the West German legal profession with full salary and eventually substantial pension, including for his service to the Third Reich.[52]

Doctors and lawyers—such as these two—had been deeply implicated in the Nazi system, upholding racist principles in everyday life, from enforcing rules about permissible sexual relations and marriage partners, right through to the deadly decisions on life and death in the sanatoria and courtrooms of the Third Reich. Both of these men had joined the Nazi party voluntarily. Neither seemed to think they bore any share of a national burden of guilt; nor did they even seem troubled by any whiff of complicity. They had led successful careers under Nazism, and they would go on to postwar lives unburdened by any pangs of conscience concerning the past.

Fritz K., by contrast, despite coming from a similar background, had been adversely affected by Nazism because of its impact on his personal

life. He had fallen in love with an actress who was half-Jewish, a relationship between a '*Mischling*' and an 'Aryan' that was prohibited under the
Nuremberg Laws. Fritz K. had been unwilling to compromise: he had refused to abandon his relationship or join the NSDAP, and had been forced
to give up his law studies as a result. For him Nazi rule meant facing a
stark choice between his own emotional ties and the possibility of professional advancement, and he chose the former. But unlike Robert Breusch,
who had chosen to leave his homeland in order to stay with and marry his
Jewish fiancée, Käte Dreyfuß, Fritz K. had remained in Germany.[53] He was
eventually conscripted into the army and injured during the war. When
Jessel tracked him down he was doing forced labour in France and in broken health. Jessel commented that 'he was now atoning for Hitler's sins.
After experiencing the wrath of Nazidom in his private affairs, after returning broken in health from a war he hated, a war which wiped out most
of his family, he of all Germans had to rebuild France.' Jessel tried to assist in
bringing him home, and he did eventually return to Germany in October
1946.[54]

Only one former classmate, Arnulf Krauth, had actively rebelled against
the Nazis; but he was one of the three whom Jessel was unable to interview,
since he had died just days before the end of the war, in early May 1945.[55]
He had become a communist in 1933 because he thought they were the
only party actively fighting Hitler, and he had married a fellow communist,
Ilse. Imprisoned in Neuengamme concentration camp near Hamburg, he
was one of the nearly 5,000 victims of the tragic bombing of the *Cap Arcona*,
a large freighter used by the Nazis to hold prisoners at the end of the war,
which was sunk by Allied forces who mistakenly thought that this, and a
couple of other large ships, held senior Nazis trying to escape the country,
rather than starving prisoners held below decks unable to get out as it
sank.[56] There was a further twist to this story. In exploring Krauth's account
alongside the tales told by another classmate, Herr M., who had been rather
closely involved in the Nazi regime, Jessel suddenly 'realized that M., in
talking to me, had used his former friendship with Arnulf to underline his
own anti-Nazism'. This was, he noted, 'another common procedure in the
Germany of 1945'.[57] There were many such efforts at establishing a form
of 'innocence by association', or highlighting ways in which one could not
have been antisemitic on a personal level, despite having faithfully served
the Nazi regime in a more public capacity.

Jessel wrote detailed notes of these encounters at the time and compiled an extensive manuscript, in the hope of publication in 1946. But it was rejected by publishers. Jessel thought this was probably due to the sheer length of the work: 'What made my original manuscript far too long was my insistent questioning of my classmates about their presumed share of German war guilt. The answers were unanimous: "I had to do my duty as a German." . . . "My first obligation was to my family's welfare." And, in the face of the Nazi party's ever threatening terror, as he somewhat inaccurately put it: "Was konnten wir denn tun?" (What could we have done?)'[58] His small group of interviewees echoed the views and repeated the phrases rehearsed by so many more across the Reich. And at this point, publishers guessed there would not be much of a readership for a work exploding the myths being so quickly constructed by millions of fellow-travellers.

Not everyone had similar degrees of latitude or choice about alternative options. It is difficult to say which of Jessel's interviewees could in any way be classified as a 'bystander' in Nazi Germany. All, in their different trajectories, illustrate the ways in which people became entangled in a system of violence that persisted over time. For Jessel's non-Jewish classmates, it was impossible to escape the challenges posed by the Nazi regime: either engage in personal, moral, and political compromises, or suffer the consequences, with varying degrees of severity. But these stories also illustrate the degree of leeway that was open to these young men who came from professional backgrounds with a degree of social and economic security. It remains an open—and deeply problematic—question as to what might have happened had more people in professional roles or positions of power refused to engage in compromise.

There was always an interplay between those who were persecuted, those who might be willing or able to offer assistance, and the broader context. Outcomes crucially depended on changing constellations of forces, and whether personal interests clashed or overlapped with the interests of those in more powerful positions—whether in terms of short-term gains or wider, long-term aspirations. Perceptions of what was variously possible or desirable or worth risking could vary according to personal characteristics, cultural interpretations, and (mis)understandings or simply lack of knowledge about the situation and the possible future course of events.

Among survivors of persecution it is clear that material resources, as well as psychological and physical resilience, along with a significant measure of good luck, all played a key role in being able to make it through to the end of the war alive. But also of vital importance were connections with non-Jewish worlds: whether through cultural affinities and linguistic facility, or through personal friendships, family relationships, and other contacts, or through broader political and religious commitments.

Among non-Jewish members of surrounding societies—those who could choose to look away, or to side with the perpetrators, or to extend offers of assistance to victims—slightly different issues were involved. These included not only questions of empathy and capacity to help individuals who were being persecuted, but also perceptions of their own interests, aspirations, and willingness to compromise their own lives and careers. There was always a complicated mixture of considerations, a balancing act that could potentially tip in one direction rather than another according to circumstances.

One thing that was virtually impossible, in this ongoing situation of raging collective violence, was to remain neutral. Very few bystanders were willing to take the risks involved in rescue attempts and assistance to those who were persecuted. The overwhelming majority of subjugated Eastern Europeans necessarily remained passive, while a sufficiently sizeable minority engaged in active collaboration with the occupiers for the Germans to get willing hands in the face-to-face implementation of utmost cruelty. Debates have raged over the extent of complicity and collaboration in different countries under German occupation; the picture is multifaceted, with varying degrees of willing cooperation or constrained compliance.[59] In some places, local people were simply 'requisitioned', more or less against their will, with little option to resist German demands; in others, people collaborated more willingly, varying with local circumstances; virtually everywhere, potential penalties for resistance were sufficiently severe to act as a strong deterrent to engaging in any rescue efforts.[60] In the Third Reich itself, strong commitments—political, religious, moral, personal—among a small minority could help a few to go under and survive. But again, the overwhelming majority of Reich citizens either remained passive or became more actively complicit in the Nazi project. This was the legacy with which former citizens had to deal as the war came to an end, and new states and societies were built on the ruins of Hitler's Reich.

Conclusion

12

The Bystander Myth and Responses to Violence

In October 2021, in the small north German town of Itzehoe, the trial of Irmgard Furchner (née Dirksen) began. Born in May 1925, Furchner had only just turned eighteen when, at the beginning of June 1943, she took a position as secretary to the camp commandant of Stutthof concentration camp, Paul-Werner Hoppe, and his adjutant; when she left in April 1945, she was not yet twenty. She was accused of aiding and abetting murder in 11,412 cases and being complicit in attempted murder in a further eighteen cases. While based in the commandant's villa at the entrance to the camp, Furchner's main responsibilities had been to take dictation, type letters, and to receive and send out messages; there was no suggestion that she had been involved in physical acts of violence or mistreatment of prisoners. The trial was held in a juvenile court, since at the time of the alleged offences Furchner, now ninety-six, had been under the age of twenty-one.

Furchner's lawyer claimed that, despite working in the commandant's office with its view looking out over the camp, she had never actually set foot inside the camp grounds, and that she knew nothing about the gassings, shootings, lethal injections, enforced starvation, beatings, and brutality that led to the deaths of some 65,000 of the camp's 110,000 or so inmates. More than half of those who went into the camp as prisoners did not come out alive, and many of those who did were barely hanging on, dying in forced labour camps, on the death marches, or shortly after liberation. Furchner admitted that she knew about specific incidents, such as hangings, but thought these were penalties for specific crimes that warranted capital punishment, rather than part of a wider programme of systematic persecution and murder. So everything that went on in the camp was, according to this view, in some way appropriate to the alleged offences of the inmates.

Furchner was, in effect, claiming innocence by ignorance. She claimed she had not known at the time about what was going on in the camp for whose commandant she worked, whose orders she wrote up, and whose mail from Berlin she received and passed on. She had not realized what fates awaited those prisoners whose names she typed on lists to be sent to Auschwitz; she had not registered the significance of camp conditions for the physical and mental state of the thousands of prisoners she could see from the windows of the building where she worked. Whatever the court might make of these assertions in light of legal culpability, Furchner's claim to ignorance of the wider context within which she was working seems deeply implausible.

This case, brought more than three-quarters of a century after the events in question, raises some compelling questions. At first glance, Furchner would seem to be simply unlucky: by virtue of longevity she was still around to be brought to trial so long after major perpetrators were dead; and those who had played far more prominent roles in mass murder had successfully evaded justice over the decades. The campaign to round up the last few under the slogan 'late, but not too late' (*Spät, aber nicht zu spät*) was arguably primarily for the benefit of subsequent generations disturbed by the failures of justice in the past, and now seeking to make belated amends, however insignificant the defendants.[1] But the significance of the Furchner case lies not so much in the specific quest for 'justice' in relation to a former teenage typist in a concentration camp, but rather in the wider questions it raises about capacity for involvement in a system of evident inhumanity— and capacity for denial of any personal complicity. In December 2022 the Itzehoe court found Furchner guilty of aiding and abetting the murder of 10,505 people and complicity in the attempted murder of five others; in view of her advanced age of ninety-seven at the time of sentencing, she was given a suspended sentence of two years. Despite being found to be culpable, Furchner was seeking, even while confronted with all the evidence, to represent herself as rather an ignorant, even innocent, bystander.

Furchner does not seem at the time to have registered any disquiet about the conditions she was witnessing, nor the contents of the reports and orders she was typing, nor the kinds of conversations that must have been going on among her workmates in the commandant's headquarters and the camp. Here, she met her future husband, SS-Oberscharführer Heinz Furchtsam, nineteen years her senior, who was also working at the camp. He had already changed his name to Furchner, because the German meaning of 'furchtsam'—fearful, timid, frightened—had connotations that were not exactly helpful for anyone wanting a career in the SS. The name also occasioned a play on words by the German tabloid *Bild*, whose dramatic headline pre-empting the court's judgement already dubbed her 'die furchtbare Frau Furchner', the 'terrifying Mrs Furchner', or 'the frightful Mrs Furchner'.[2] It is highly unlikely that, as they developed a close relationship, Heinz never talked to Irmgard about his work in the camp. Nor does his career in the SS seem to have occasioned any personal strife; the couple married in 1954 and remained together until Heinz's death at the age of sixty-five in 1972.

We can safely assume that Irmgard Furchner had herself been in broad agreement with the Nazi regime, whatever her later self-defensive disclaimers about specific 'knowledge'. She was of a generation that was exposed to the full impact of Nazi ideology, having attended school in the 1930s, topped off by a year in labour service. She had a brief stint working for a bank before landing the position in Stutthof, which apparently offered better pay and conditions. At no time does she seem to have expressed any real regrets or genuine sense of discomfort about the role she held, the location in which she worked, and the cause which she served. The closest she seems to have come to expressing any apology was when, in court, she said she was 'sorry about everything that happened' and that she regretted that she 'was in Stutthof at the time'—perhaps not least because this meant she had been caught and put on trial.[3]

There were many hundreds of thousands of people who held administrative positions that assisted the machinery of the Third Reich to function in practice.[4] Many civilian administrators operated at far higher levels than this teenage typist, as the spate of commissioned studies of German bureaucracies has more than demonstrated; and through their roles they were significant facilitators of Nazi policies of racial persecution.[5] Whether civil servants working for the Führer in the Foreign Office or the Reich Ministry for Labour, for example, could be held to have been 'more' complicit than a concentration camp secretary remains an open question. Members of the judiciary who sentenced people to death for trivial political offences, or high-level administrators of occupied territories, responsible for ghettoization and curtailment of the rights of Jews, for cutting their rations, imposing curfews, and ensuring local police forces treated infringements of Nazi regulations extremely harshly, were clearly responsible in one way or another for causing deaths. But senior civil servants generally managed to escape the scrutiny of courts of justice in the postwar Federal Republic of Germany.[6] Many functionaries at high levels had, like the far less significant typist Furchner, managed to 'not register' what was going on, even when stationed at the very sites of mass death, and even when tasked with operating them.

More broadly, millions of people had learned to acquiesce in, or to look away from, the consequences of Nazi persecution for those who were outcast. Historically, the question of complicity when living within a system of collective violence remains of immense significance.

What then can we learn from the example of Nazi Germany, and what more general conclusions may be drawn?

Ideology has long been at the centre of historical and contemporary debates. Radical antisemitism, along with distinctions between supposedly superior and inferior 'races', and a desire for world mastery, undoubtedly motivated Hitler, his ideologues, and key policymakers. But the worldviews of fanatics alone would have been insufficient to effect Nazi policies in practice. This required the cooperation of elites and political control of the structures of power and repression, about which we know a great deal. More difficult to identify with precision are the processes at work among members of a wider society subjected to Nazi domination.

Put most pointedly: how complicit were the Germans? Is it even possible to speak of 'the Germans'? And was everyone who lived through this period in some way 'implicated'? I would argue that we need a more differentiated approach: one that distinguishes between different degrees of complicity; that makes distinctions between willing facilitation and constrained conformity, and understands the varying degrees of choice available to people in different social and political positions. And, while recognizing the horrific role played by coercion and the regime of terror, we need an approach that does not fall too easily into sustaining postwar myths—particularly prevalent among Germans who had a compromised past—that justify complicity through supposed fear of the consequences of standing up and standing out. Terror, too, was targeted, fear was distributed unevenly—and those in privileged positions who claim in retrospect that they could not have acted otherwise should not be able to slide in under a blanket of self-exculpation.

At the same time, it is vital to understand how rapidly social relations can change, institutions falter, elites capitulate. The 'lessons' of Nazi Germany are perhaps most acute, most relevant, when we explore how very small changes in everyday life that seem anodyne or justifiable at the time can have catastrophic consequences within a matter of just a few years.[7]

Small steps, violent societies: Bystanding in the peacetime years

In the peacetime years, millions of Germans learned to comply with, and progressively internalized, a racialized sense of identity, and began to behave accordingly even in informal settings in everyday life. These processes fostered ways of either justifying or ignoring the impact of racist policies on the persecuted. For many Reich citizens, initial conformity and enforced compliance led eventually towards more active involvement in the machinery of perpetration, whether enthusiastically or otherwise. There was an interactive process, as those who were initially bystanders to specific, discrete incidents of Nazi violence became, over time, to varying degrees complicit—whether through looking away, condoning violence, or more actively sustaining the system. In some cases, as we have seen, individuals alleviated their own sense of unease by showing sympathy to victims even while continuing to play roles that effectively fostered persecution.

Memories of lives before and after 1933 that were written on the brink of war, before persecution had become mass murder in the death camps, highlight the significance of the everyday processes through which 'Aryans' actively assisted in propelling the racial segregation of German society. The 1939 essays that I have used so extensively in this book are exceptional in revealing how people interacted, and how most 'Aryans' progressively shunned and isolated the outcasts, before the tragedy of the death camps overshadowed earlier memories of the multiple slights experienced before the war. Non Jewish Germans who later remembered happy times in the Hitler Youth, or the return to full employment in the 1930s, radically overlooked and once again excluded the quite different experiences and perspectives of the persecuted. The attempted 'normalization' of this past reflects in some ways the bystander mentality of their younger days: looking away, ignoring, not knowing.[8]

These differences of perspective point up very sharply the issues raised by using memory narratives to access 'the past'. Autobiographical accounts, whether written close to the time or decades later, may seem at first glance to provide a form of authenticity, of apparently direct access to the past; but this is always mediated, both by the impact on the person recounting their experiences, and by selective framing in light of cultural assumptions and intended audiences—quite apart from the secondary filter of interpretations and representations by others (including authors such as myself). Moreover, personal perspectives—both at the time and later—are always informed by broader worldviews; and people are not necessarily aware of their own underlying assumptions. There are blind spots, unexamined views that barely blip on the level of consciousness, but that nevertheless play a role in how people see the world around them and how they behave towards others.

Nazi Germany presents a striking example of the rapid racialization of identity, as people shuffled to reassign themselves and others into new categories and hierarchies. Before Hitler's rise to power, long-resident German families of Jewish heritage were increasingly well-integrated; indeed, assimilation was proceeding at a pace that alarmed some parts of the Jewish community. The arrival of Eastern European Jews fleeing from pogroms nevertheless gave fuel to antisemitic prejudices, as well as deepening divisions within German Jewry. The First World War and its consequences, both domestically and internationally, further fuelled antisemitic prejudices, as Jews were targeted as a scapegoat for the ills of the Weimar years.

Yet we have to remember: in 1932 antisemitism was not seen as a vote winner for the NSDAP, nor was it central to Hitler's appointment as chancellor. The Nazi acquisition of power took place under specific circumstances: the impact of the Great Depression on an already fragile economy, in a country humiliated by defeat in war, with an unstable democracy already subject to rule by presidential decree. Many were critical of democracy in principle, seeing it as a forum for 'party squabbling' ('*Parteiengezänk*') rather than the sort of stable government that could be offered by authoritarian rule. The rapid growth in support for Hitler, widely seen as a saviour figure, was primarily rooted in social distress, poverty and unemployment, political extremism and violence, as well as the considerable organizational skills of the NSDAP. The crucial final step to Hitler's appointment was the misjudged gamble of conservative elites that they could benefit from his popular support while containing him within a mixed cabinet; some form of populist nationalism seemed an acceptable compromise.

Even if antisemitism was not key to Hitler's appointment, and even if pre-1933 Germany had high rates of conversion from Judaism to Christianity, and high rates of intermarriage between Jews and gentiles, there was nevertheless a pool of latent prejudice that could be whipped up at times of social, economic, and political strife. So the fundamental point is that wider conditions and power relations matter enormously to the question of whether or not pre-existing prejudices can be legitimized, expanded, and put into practice. Antisemitism and the racialization of identity in Nazi Germany required the legal and administrative institutions of the regime. State backing was crucial, as active steps were taken to create a hostile environment.

Why then do bystanders matter? It is precisely because members of the wider population—the so-called ordinary Germans—act variously either to mitigate or exacerbate the officially ordained 'hostility' of the environment in everyday life. Putting discriminatory categories into practice, and effectively enforcing them in all spheres of life, requires also the participation of individuals across society.

So the next key question relates to the processes by which this takes place. People may go along with the racialization of identity because specific prejudices have been legitimated from on high, given voice by those in power. When views that could previously only be whispered, muttered among like-minded circles, but somewhat taboo, become officially sanctioned, indeed encouraged, there is a snowball effect. (This continues to be relevant, particularly in states with authoritarian populist leaders or significant ethno-nationalist movements.) Racist energies, once unleashed, can then be mobilized and translated into violence in practice—as on the streets of Germany from 1933, Austria from 1938, and with variations across different areas of Europe following the outbreak of war. Many people, however, might only now be learning to hate. Through a variety of formal and informal means, including fear of being mocked by newly dominant Nazis, they felt constrained to drop former friends, and to ignore or avoid people whose company they now felt they should never be seen in, shops and businesses they should no longer frequent, individuals they should shun and exclude. Crucially, this might be less a matter of learning to hate than of learning to comply, to conform, to demonstrate in daily behaviours identification with the dominant, 'racially' defined national community.

There was an interplay between regime policies, propaganda, and popular perceptions and actions. Propaganda was in some cases overt, as in Streicher's vicious *Der Stürmer*, or a variety of cultural offerings fostered by Joseph Goebbels. Racist perceptions could, however, also be spread in more subtle and insidious ways in the racialized discourses and practices of everyday life that were so closely interrelated. Initially, many people saw the notions of 'Aryan' or 'non-Aryan' as imposed constructs, a new lexicon of distinctions to be acquired and put into practice. Some accepted this immediately, and many worked hard to master the distinctions, while others resisted; but all had to accept that this crucial vocabulary of difference was, in terms of practical impact, a hard fact of social reality in Nazi Germany.

People now engaged in uneasy compromises. They conformed, and benefitted from their conformity. And yet, when directly confronted with the consequences for the excluded, some felt a degree of discomfort. This did not by any means apply to everyone living in the Third Reich, most of whom could easily ignore the fates of the persecuted if they remained at a geographical and social distance, but rather to those who were immediate 'bystanders', personally interacting with or witnessing the fates of victims of persecution. In these cases, empathy sometimes interfered uncomfortably with the conformist performance of official duties or the public enactment of expected behaviours.

Psychologically, this could lead them in a number of directions. In some cases, it meant carrying out inhumane acts in humane ways: effectively just sweetening the pill; perhaps making it in some way easier for victims, which might contribute, directly or indirectly, to their physical or mental capacity for survival. Where not too risky, it might mean providing practical as well as symbolic assistance. The significance of such displays of sympathy should not be underestimated. Not just practical support but even merely an expression or a kindly word could help to maintain morale and self-respect; and some who managed to get out could retain a sense of connection with their former homeland.

But ultimately, over the longer term the constraints of the Nazi regime cowed those who felt sympathy for the victims, effectively immobilizing them. And this could be difficult to acknowledge, particularly when challenged about failure to act at a time when this might still have made a difference. Such passivity was furthered by the increasing invisibility of victims, and by increasing preoccupation with other pressures, particularly in wartime. Ignoring the fates of the ousted, or claiming ignorance, would mitigate any sense of unease, guilt, or shame.

All of this was not simply a consequence of Nazi policies; changed behaviours in everyday life actively brought about further social changes. Racialized categories initially meant identification *as* a particular sort of person, to be treated accordingly, whether or not individuals accepted the labels and all these now implied. But as these categories became more significant, so new forms of identification *with* others in a similar position began to create increasingly distinct communities, defined according to degrees of inclusion, marginalization, or exclusion. Over time, imposed distinctions were increasingly 'normalized' and internalized; and they made a difference for both 'Aryans' and 'non-Aryans'.

Many Germans, both within and well beyond the borders of the old Reich, enjoyed the idea—effectively the promise, aspiration, or vision—of a 'national community'; they participated in organized activities, symbolic displays of togetherness, or enacted Nazism in everyday life. Some individuals exercised a new sense of power or enhanced status in this way.[9] But innumerable others—we can never know how many—simply felt they had to go along with dominant norms. This is the case even in liberal democratic societies: keen to fit in, people often misperceive group norms in what social psychologists call 'pluralistic ignorance' and conform with what they think is the majority view. In democratic situations, it is possible to challenge assumptions about dominant norms: one person prepared to speak up may start a snowball effect in a different direction, to the relief of others who had been silently uncomfortable. This can be particularly significant in situations, for example, of sexual harassment, racial discrimination, or playground bullying.[10] Even in democratic societies, however, there are always potential risks involved in speaking out—'whistle-blowing', 'putting one's head above the parapet', 'speaking truth to power'. People are generally fearful of even relatively minimal adverse consequences, such as being avoided by others as a potential 'trouble-maker', losing the favour of people at the top, spoiling their prospects of promotion. Even just speaking out against use of sexist, racist, or homophobic language by totally unknown others in an apparently safe environment, such as the changing rooms of a public swimming pool, may carry risk: will the offenders turn on the challenger, causing an ugly scene or maybe later retribution, and is a challenge likely to affect any longer term change anyway?

People therefore rarely like to speak up, assuming it is neither entirely risk-free nor necessarily worthwhile. But conditions permitting challenge with little personal risk barely exist at all in dictatorships, and certainly did not exist in Nazi Germany. There could be no doubt about the official Nazi line, nor about the dangers of openly expressing, let alone acting upon, opposing views. This had been made more than clear from the treatment of political opponents in the early months of the regime in 1933; it continued to be obvious through the peacetime years that followed, and intensified from 1938; and it was then devastatingly evident in the terror exercised by fanatic Nazis that raged during the closing months of the war. This makes it all the more difficult to evaluate what was going on in people's minds at the time, irrespective of outward displays of enthusiasm and mass participation. The accounts of contemporaries do nevertheless give us some indications of changing perceptions and informal behaviours beyond public performances. By the mid-1930s, Germans were realizing that the Nazi regime would last longer than initially expected. Those who were still disaffected could no longer persuade themselves that this was merely a transient episode, and realized now they would have to find ways of living within the parameters of power. The majority first opted for conformity, and were progressively constrained—with differing degrees of willingness or unease—into compliance, whatever their inner hesitations. Some, of course, were genuinely enthusiastic. We will never know quite what the balance might be, and indeed people changed their views and attitudes to specific issues—food shortages, foreign policy questions—over time, as circumstances changed. These shifts in popular opinion on particular topics can be traced through mood and opinion reports from a variety of sources.[11] But such records do not so readily reveal the underlying changes in patterns of social and emotional connections between people, as their sense of identity and community shifted. For this, we need to understand changes in lives over time. And these make clear that the effective social segregation that was occurring in German society before the war was not just a matter of policy but was actively co-produced through everyday behaviours.

Increasing numbers participated in ousting compatriots from their community, in processes that were almost imperceptible from the perspective of those doing the excluding, but all too painful for those being excluded.

They did this in very small steps, seemingly entirely anodyne at the time—simply not inviting a good friend to a social event, even a wedding (as in the case of the Freiburg schoolteacher Robert Breusch, whose former best friend, von Blittersdorf, refused to invite him because of his Jewish fiancée), was not in any way a crime and could, indeed, be simply explained away as a matter of avoiding potential social embarrassment. People like Friedrich Reuss, previously an up-and-coming civil servant with just one Jewish grandparent, could be progressively isolated and excluded as a 'non-Aryan', set on a downward social spiral from which it was impossible to recover.

The negotiation of the minutiae of social relationships can always be sensitive, and ways can be found of dressing up the difficulties in terms that might be more acceptable not only to others but also oneself. Ironically, continuing to invite Jewish friends to social events where this did not seem too risky, as in a secluded home with a degree of privacy from neighbours, could alleviate any sense of moral compromise, while still in public conforming sufficiently to propel the Nazi project forwards. It was only a privileged few, such as Bruno Gebhard, who could sustain this sort of uneasy compromise—and even fewer who were fortunate enough to be able, like Gebhard, to emigrate and continue their career abroad, salvaging their integrity and protecting their family from the impact of Nazi rule. Most people resisting the demands of Nazism found the only strategy was to remain silent. Some diary writers, such as the librarian Hermann Stresau, or the former social democrat and minor civil servant in southwestern Germany, Friedrich Kellner, retained a sense of inner opposition—but also kept their heads down, unable to change anything much in a world dominated by Nazis. Others, from a wide range of political and religious positions—compare, for example, the Berlin journalist Ruth Andreas-Friedrich, the Quaker Margarethe Lachmund, or the conservative nationalist 'man in despair', Friedrich Reck—did their best to help those they could, with varying degrees of success; but this was just a drop in the ocean.

We need then to understand the insidious, relatively invisible ways in which people become involved, through seemingly anodyne everyday behaviours, in processes of social exclusion; and how bystanders to obviously violent incidents variously came to see them as in some way acceptable, justifiable in light of other priorities, even to be welcomed, or, while shocked and horrified, came to realize that there was little or nothing they could do to change the ways things were, and could at best seek to mitigate the worst consequences for specific individuals.

Cumulatively, what can be seen in Nazi Germany is the emergence of a 'bystander society'—a society in which social relations and political conditions are such that most people would either not want or not dare to intervene on behalf of victims, and in which most people learned to look away.

Functional complicity and the radicalization of collective violence

Was conformity and growing compliance with a racialized worldview and systemic racism already a step on the road to complicity in Nazi crimes? In any legal sense, of course it was not. It was rather a matter of self-preservation in challenging circumstances. It took courage and commitment, willingness to run risks and accept personal costs, to stand up against dominant forces or even just to refuse to take the little steps leading to the resegregation of society. This became particularly evident when radical violence against Jewish civilians was out in the open and could no longer be ignored by members of mainstream society in the expanded Reich from 1938.

In prewar Germany, there had remained—despite all—a sense of common humanity and warm personal relations between some 'Aryans' and those now castigated as 'non-Aryan'. But the situation looks very different if we focus rather on the impact of behavioural conformity. Compliance with creating a hostile environment for outcasts in effect sustained Nazi policies of persecution and exclusion. Conformity could be wrapped in a cloak of humanity—but it still ended up travelling in the direction dictated by Hitler, while easing the pain of exit of some who were able to get out before this option was irrevocably closed off.

There was, in effect, a form of functional complicity, even if occasionally neutralized by self-distancing or sweetened by expressions of sympathy. We have seen this in the examples of officials who assisted Jews in the course of emigration, or 'Aryans' who benefitted from knock-down sales of Jews' homes, businesses, and possessions while expressing their personal best wishes for the future, or in the case of the local prison jailer and then the Sachsenhausen camp guard who both spoke sympathetically to the Jewish trader from Neustettin (now Szczecinek), Georg Abraham, even as they were incarcerating him. They were not alone, although by virtue of their functions and their direct interactions with victims who recorded their experiences, their ambivalent responses stand out, simultaneously expressing sympathy and performing persecution. Beneficiaries included innumerable people who in a wide range of ways gained goods, housing, job opportunities, positions of power (however small and insignificant in the grander scale of things), or simply an enhancement of their own sense of self-esteem through the removal from German society of those considered not to be part of a 'healthy national community', and the elevation of the Aryan 'national comrade' above supposed racial inferiors.

Virtually everyone who held significant roles in the Nazi regime, or who wittingly benefitted from the consequences of persecutory policies, was to some degree compromised—and not many would express any sympathy, betray any sense of discomfort, or even register any awareness of the plight of others. Perhaps those who displayed sympathy, and who are recalled in the accounts of the persecuted, were remembered precisely because they were exceptional. Far greater numbers may never have truly acknowledged the degree to which they had become contaminated by their involvement in Nazism, even when challenged more explicitly in differing contexts after the war.

There were innumerable others who neither held functionary positions of one sort or another, nor knowingly benefitted (or chose to benefit) from the exclusion of the ousted. They, too, often expressed sympathy as victims departed, or uttered their own regrets at having to stay and be party to the Nazi regime and all it entailed. There were significant gradations and differing degrees of compromise.

Compromises became far more problematic in wartime. For one thing, mass mobilisation vastly increased the sheer number of people who, in one way or another, now played roles that made them functionally complicit with Nazi racism, even if not directly involved in perpetration. Germans were existentially constrained to identify with the 'fatherland' at war and to support what was represented and widely perceived as a self-defensive fight against the enemies of their homeland. Sons, brothers, husbands, and fathers were engaged in combat at the front; at home, people faced privations and air raids, with children and the elderly among the casualties of bombing. Even people who were opposed to Nazism, whether in 'inner emigration' or in clandestine rescue and resistance activities, found it hard to hope for the success of Allied bomb attacks in places where they or members of their families were living and working. Rejecting the Nazi cause, they were at the same time afflicted by injuries, losses, and the deaths of people they loved.[12]

People dealt with the conflicting pressures and changing fortunes of war in a variety of ways. Some reasserted their belief in the Nazi cause, reinforced by propaganda, peer group pressure, and mutual reassurance. Others muttered, grumbled, and sought to salvage what they could at a personal level, trying to ameliorate an increasingly desperate situation, or merely hoping to get through and survive. A very few extended help to those who had escaped the net of persecution and 'gone under' (*untergetaucht*).[13] Those individuals within the Reich who were shocked and disturbed by news of atrocities in the East were effectively immobilized, unable to take action, and aware of the high risks and potential cost of even expressing dissent. In general, any question of complicity in a racist system was not uppermost in most people's minds.

In occupied territories in Eastern Europe there were complex interactions between the German forces, local non-Jewish populations, and Jewish communities. Failing to recognize the impact of Nazi policies on the 'eastern Jews' whom they now encountered, many Germans found their antisemitic stereotypes confirmed, seeming to justify the murderous campaign on which they were engaged. Meanwhile, considerable numbers of non-Jewish locals were willing, for a variety of reasons, to facilitate the genocidal violence initiated by the Germans, affecting the ways in which Nazi policies could be put into practice. Specific situational dynamics could make all the difference between facilitating or benefitting from Nazi policies of persecution, or remaining a passive (and even shocked) onlooker, or, in a few cases, engaging in assistance and rescue efforts, with individuals often shifting across the spectrum in either direction according to changing contingencies. It took a combination of favourable social and political circumstances, topographical conditions, personal commitment, and supportive social networks to risk extending support to victims of persecution. There were always conflicting motives and material, emotional, and moral considerations. Relatives could help, particularly where people were in mixed marriages of or mixed descent; political and moral commitment might be important in cases where people assisted those whom they had never previously met; the ties of friendship or a desire to profit could also be powerful motivating factors at different times. There could also be almost random acts of altruism as people offered fleeting gestures of assistance at crucial moments, as vividly illustrated in stories of survivors who highlight the role of 'chance'.

Personal accounts show up clearly the significance of the reactions of those who variously inflicted, witnessed, or sought to alleviate the suffering of others, varying according to changing conditions. Such accounts reveal how members of surrounding societies became, over time, variously aligned with the perpetrators or, according to circumstances and sometimes only temporarily, willing to offer sympathy and assistance to those in distress. Whatever the individual variations, in this situation of overwhelming violence it was more or less impossible to remain a supposedly 'neutral' bystander. The vast majority of people in the engulfing conflagration were necessarily drawn into having to decide 'whose side they were on'; and most had little choice but to comply with the dominant forces in the interests of self-preservation.

A sense of innocence: Ignorance, impotence, indifference

The focus here has been on individual accounts of experiences, while highlighting ways in which wider developments, policies, and events shaped people's relationships with one another and formed the crucial context for individual decisions and actions. Personal narratives provide insights into how people lived through challenging times, engaged in compromises, and variously attempted to ease a sense of discomfort, justifying their behaviours both to themselves and to others. Individual stories are infinitely varied as far as specific details are concerned; they are fascinating in themselves; and any number of further examples could have been chosen. But the point of this exploration was not to try to produce any kind of comprehensive account of society in the Third Reich, of which there are many. Rather, by following the experiences of selected individuals over a period of time and through changing contexts, we can begin to discern some broader patterns about social processes fostering passivity in face of violence. These help to make sense of the ways in which people both participated in and benefitted from Nazi rule while assuaging any sense of personal guilt and maintaining a degree of self-respect as a 'decent person'. They are also of wider applicability beyond the specific cases and period of Nazi rule.

Three key issues have been brought to attention in understanding bystanders who felt—or were later made to feel—uncomfortable about having failed to act on behalf of victims, or having aided or sided with perpetrators. Bystander noninvolvement is variously explicable in terms of ignorance or impotence or indifference. Before examining each of these more directly, a couple of more general remarks should be made.

First, it is worth explicitly noting the differing significance of each factor depending on context. In particular, it is vital to distinguish between explanations for action or inaction at the time and subsequent justifications in different circumstances. For example: while indifference or more active antisemitism might go a long way towards explaining failure to act on behalf of Jewish victims at the time, this was not an explanation that would generally go down well in most contexts after the defeat of the Nazi regime. By contrast, claiming either not to have known (ignorance), or not having been able to act (impotence), would be far more generally acceptable than openly admitting to not having cared, or having gone along with the dominant chorus of antisemitism, let alone having welcomed the persecution of the Jews. So we have to be careful to distinguish between the changing significance of each factor at the time, and its prevalence in self-justifications in other contexts. In particular, there is arguably a large gap between the numbers who would genuinely have liked to help Jews but felt simply unable to do so, and the later numbers who claimed that they could not have acted otherwise for fear of the consequences. If we do not bear this discrepancy in mind, historical analyses may run the risk of seeming to bolster self-exculpatory strategies.

Secondly, it is important to note that these three factors are not merely explanations or discourses of self-justification: they were themselves historical realities, variously rooted in and fostered by specific social conditions. We have seen how changing social relations and related conceptions of identity and community played out across Germany in the years up to 1938, and in the expanded Reich and areas of occupied Eastern Europe following the annexation of new territories and the outbreak of war. Bearing these points in mind, some more general conclusions may be drawn.

Ignorance is, at face value, the simplest excuse later used by Germans to explain away failure to act against the evils perpetrated by 'the Nazis'—who were always 'others', not themselves, however much evidence of their own previous conformity and support for the Nazi regime there might be. By claiming they had 'known nothing about it', people imply that, if they had known about Nazi atrocities, they might have acted differently. Usually 'it' is left vague, held to refer to something far away, about which they could not have realistically 'known' anything. Supposed 'ignorance' can be further bolstered by suggesting they were duped or misled by the appeals of ideology, carried away by the sense of community among 'national comrades', or patriotically striving for a better future.[14] By selectively emphasizing the sunny side of their experiences in the Third Reich, and professing that they never realized the implications for those excluded from the Volksgemeinschaft, they buttress their claim to innocence.

But ignorance is more complex than self-defensive portrayals would like to suggest. There are both personal reasons and structural and cultural ways in which 'ignorance' can be actively produced and fostered. Ignorance may not be just lack of knowledge, but rather a matter of actively ignoring: people can to a certain extent choose to turn their heads, look away, decide to 'not know'. We have seen many examples of this, from the early dropping of friendships, or crossing the road to avoid greeting Jewish acquaintances, to later complaints about having to hear the screams from detention centres or concentration camps, or requests that physical violence against the regime's opponents and victims be carried out further away. But this was not just a matter of personal choice. 'Out of sight, out of mind' could be fostered by social and physical segregation and geographic distancing; from prohibitions on the movement of Jews, through policies of setting up 'Jew houses' and ghettos, to deportations to killing sites some distance away. Major extermination sites such as Sobibór, Treblinka, and Bełżec were constructed specifically to deceive those arriving, with perimeter fences covered in branches and leaves, train stations or local houses prettily decorated, thick hedges obscuring the path to the gas chambers, and flowerbeds suggesting an entirely anodyne experience ahead.[15] Attempts at deception of victims and wilful misrepresentation to others were eventually followed by extraordinary efforts to erase the traces of mass murder entirely, by exhuming the graves, burning corpses, crushing bones, and camouflaging or finally destroying killing sites. All of this made it easier for people to claim, with differing degrees of plausibility, that they had known nothing about it—unless of course they had themselves been actively involved in these processes, or had received news from others, as so many Germans in fact did. But even when directly employed in sites of violence, as in the case of Irmgard Furchner, people could attempt to profess ignorance of what had been going on very close at hand.

Ignorance only goes so far as an excuse. Much of what led up to mass murder—processes of stigmatisation, exploitation, expropriation, public humiliation, assault, segregation, deportation—had not merely been carried out in full view, but with the active participation of probably hundreds of thousands, and certainly witnessed by millions. What people might really not 'know' were the final, technical details of how organized mass murder was eventually carried out in specific sites of extermination—and even about this a lot was 'known', particularly in relation to the mass shootings on the Eastern Front. Yet such knowledge was often framed in a way that was partial—in both senses of the word. There were piecemeal snippets of information about particular incidents that did not amount to a coherent wider picture. And what was conveyed was interpreted from a particular perspective, in order to justify apparent 'excesses' or to portray the victims as dangerous to German wellbeing, now or in the future—most grotesquely in the justification of killing children—and therefore supposedly legitimate targets from the perspective of the dominant community.

However it was interpreted at the time, following German defeat such knowledge could not readily be confessed without also implying a degree of complicity, or being tainted by guilt. So the myth of having been merely an innocent bystander almost required the myth of ignorance. Few were prepared to concede how narrowly the borders were being drawn around what 'it' was, of which they had allegedly known nothing. Jürgen Ernst Kroeger, for example, as a 'resettler' in the Wartheland, could jump very rapidly over the fact of his 'not knowing' what had become of those people who had been moved out so suddenly while he and fellow ethnic Germans had taken their place in service of 'germanisation'; and he could claim, with utter implausibility, that he did not know about the mass killing of more than 25,000 Jews over a couple of days in Riga, at a time when he was working as an official translator for the occupying forces carrying out the killings. Even designing the dimensions and steps leading down to the death pits, in the case of Ernst Hemicker, could be reframed as a purely technical and mathematical question for a trained engineer. Self-distancing was crucial to maintaining a degree of self-respect, however near or far from specific, concentrated sites of violence people might be.

Impotence is also multifaceted, and more complex than it might at first appear. After the war, many Germans claimed that they could not have acted in any other way; they had to comply, since if they had refused they too would have ended up in a concentration camp. This narrative changed over the decades, according to context; it remained prevalent in family stories, but in the course of the major concentration camp trials of the 1960s, particularly the Frankfurt Auschwitz trial, a few historians began to challenge this as a plausible defence strategy. By the time oral history interviews with 'ordinary Germans' were being more extensively carried out in the late twentieth and early twenty-first centuries, interviewees were predominantly people who had been quite young during the Third Reich, and the excuse of fear was less frequently made. The related historiography also shifted in these decades from an earlier emphasis on terror in a 'totalitarian' state to a greater emphasis on societal consensus within a national community held together by faith in Hitler.[16]

Whatever the vicissitudes of selective memory and later self-representations, the sense of incapacity to act at the time of the Third Reich was important for several reasons. First, there can be no shadow of doubt that the regime was built on an apparatus of repression and brutality against those who dared to oppose Nazi rule. The structures and culture of Nazi terror should never be underestimated. Secondly, less obviously—but arguably more significant in giving the appearance of being a regime built on consensus—there was a widespread atmosphere of generalized apprehension, buttressed by practices of informing and denouncing, with consequences that were broader than the actual incidents that left traces in the archives. Personal accounts suggest that a sense of mutual distrust constrained many people into outward conformity. Over time, some came to believe in what they were saying and doing, as the repetition of mutually reinforcing habits of speech and behaviour eventually became 'second nature'. During the war, fear of betrayal acted as an even more powerful deterrent. This was particularly potent in occupied territories where penalties were severe, and where, for example, being found assisting Jews could be fatal for the whole family or the wider community. But fear also operated powerfully within the Reich, particularly in the closing stages of the war, when heightened repression and terror was turned against those seen as defeatists or deserters.

Oddly, a muted sense of apprehension could even serve to heighten the impression gained by outside observers that the Germans were a nation of enthusiasts. Innumerable people who performed involvement in the national community, like Barbara Sevin on her compulsory labour service, or the crowds who participated in May Day rallies, may have enjoyed the company of other like-minded spirits but never completely bought into Nazi ideology. Some, like Sevin's landlady in Munich, simply kept away from mass displays of support for the regime, in order not to swell the ranks of apparent enthusiasts; others participated but made fun of it in private. Not only genuine Hitler enthusiasts but also these quietly critical individuals would be captured in the visual images we have of the Third Reich, arms raised in Hitler salutes, the sheer volume of their ranks suggesting a nation bound together by belief in the Führer.

The question of impotence, too, goes beyond the formal structures of power and the social circumstances that fostered unwillingness to act or speak up on behalf of victims. There was also a psychological process at work within individuals. Years of living under dictatorial conditions meant that many who were far from enthusiastic about Nazism began to feel a sense of apathy, of resignation, registering their own incapacity to make any significant changes in the foreseeable future. Lacking any realistic prospect of affecting the course of events, few were willing to take the risk of even speaking up openly against a regime that seemed ever more firmly entrenched in power. Maintaining a degree of caution in everyday encounters while noting developments and expressing rage and frustration into a diary might be all that was possible, as in the case of Friedrich Kellner. And a sense of impotence in wartime, when collaborators and auxiliaries across Europe were variously engaged in assisting the Nazi 'Final Solution of the Jewish Question', was only too well founded.

Apathy born of a sense of impotence is in principle open to change, if sufficient numbers—particularly people in a position of power—are determined to speak up, act collectively, or move in a different direction. Ordinary people far from the centres of power in Nazi Germany had little option, however, in the absence of decisive action on the part of elites.

Indifference, finally, is perhaps the most difficult of the three aspects to define and evaluate. It is, as I have argued, more an explanation for inaction at the time than an excuse that could be drawn on later. It too is multifaceted.

Antisemitism was clearly crucial as far as the initiators and organizers of violence against the Jews of Europe were concerned. Everywhere there were underlying and sometimes long-standing currents of antisemitism, in a variety of forms: hostility towards Jews based in older religious myths; supposedly scientific versions of 'racial' antisemitism; and politicized variants, referring to alleged Jewish conspiracies, the supposed power of 'the Jew' in finance, the media, or the spectre of the 'Judeo-Bolshevik' threat. All of these formed a repertoire that could be drawn upon, whipped up, and selectively deployed in conditions of social distress, economic uncertainty, and political turmoil, when Jews could easily be scapegoated. But antisemitism, in whichever guise, was on its own not sufficient to explain the inaction of people who witnessed shocking acts of violence and atrocities—people who variously joined in humiliating or jeering at victims, or who remained silently on the sidelines, resisting any urge to show sympathy, or refusing to offer assistance to victims.

It was only under specific political and social circumstances that large numbers of people were more likely to remain silent, or less likely to care about what was happening to others. Many may over time have come to see the outcasts as a dangerous 'other', and changed perceptions undoubtedly played a role. But indifference that leads to condoning, ignoring, or even justifying violence is not simply a matter of ideology. There are also social and structural barriers to empathy with those perceived as 'others'. Indifference can be actively created, as it was in the process of resegregation in 1930s Germany. It can be deep rooted, as it was in some areas of Eastern Europe where pogroms had periodically flared up in times of distress. And it can be politically fostered, as it was in the brief period of Soviet rule in the Baltic states, and the subsequent whipping up of antisemitic fury as the Soviet forces left and the Germans invaded, with fatal consequences for the victims.

Crucial here is the formation of distinct communities and a sense that identification with a particular community was mutually incompatible with any other—as happens in times of conflict. Under these conditions, empathy with members of another community would entail an almost impossible degree of self-contradiction. In conditions of collective violence on the scale of Nazism, very few would dare even small steps across invisible borders or bear the pain of retaining a wider sense of empathy with members of the human race now designated as enemies. In the light of conflicting priorities, it is simply easier to prioritize members of one's own community and not to care about what is happening to others.

On the margins: The unstable borders between neutrality and complicity

To be a bystander to violence is not a fixed role or identity, an essential characteristic of an individual. Rather, people acquire this status only momentarily, by virtue of their proximity to violence and their relationship to the actions of others. 'Bystanders' are located on the margins of specific, violent situations at certain moments in time, close to but not immediately involved in the initial conflict. And yet: even if not directly involved, remaining passively on the sidelines will inevitably affect the course of events. And, over the longer term, people will themselves be changed by adapting to living within a sustained system of violence. They will use the vocabulary and adopt the habits and relations that the system demands, and in this way actively help to perpetuate the injustices to which they were initially merely witnesses.

Moreover, bystanders are not just bystanders. Apart from being present at specific moments of violence, they have multiple other relationships that affect their perceptions and reactions. Bystanders may have strong feelings of empathy and powerful emotional responses to what they are seeing. They may have a sense of affinity with different communities, which may be seen as mutually exclusive. They may bear individual grudges, be plagued by jealousy, or want to curry favour in certain quarters. They may see others less as individual human beings than as representatives of dangerous groups, people to despise, people to fear; or as people before whom they are powerless, to whom they look up. Or they may see the persecuted as friends, colleagues, fellow citizens, neighbours, relatives. In a situation of conflict, variously choosing or being forced to identify more with one side than the other, those who are initially bystanders may feel ambivalent, with conflicting impulses and sympathies, pulling in differing directions. Even what it is that people think they are 'seeing' is informed by the social pressures and cultural discourses that frame the situation. They might think they are witnessing the forces of law and order arresting dangerous criminals and rendering the streets safe for law-abiding citizens; or they might think they are witnessing unruly thugs beating up and incarcerating innocent citizens in service of a crazy ideology, but feel unable to intervene to assist victims in light of the risks to themselves and near ones. They might see the aggressors variously as oppressors or liberators. The trick is in how the different actors are portrayed and perceived by different groups; and there may be a real struggle over competing definitions of the situation.[17]

Time and situation are absolutely crucial here. Violent incidents are one thing; violent regimes that persist over a longer period of time—whether a matter of months or years—have a different kind of impact on perceptions and behaviours. Both longevity and power structures have a significant effect on whether those who are critical feel they can even speak up, let alone find sufficient energy, allies, or resources to mount any effective challenge to a violent regime. Helping individual victims in small ways, preferably in private, might be the most that could even be attempted. So the question would then be not so much about the moral courage of individuals, but rather about the circumstances under which those who can initially be called bystanders would be more likely to become complicit, or under which some, at least, might feel able to engage in acts of rescue or resistance.

Although to date a systematic pan-European overview is lacking, a comparison of rescue and survival chances, or deportation and death rates of Jews in different areas of Europe under Nazi domination, suggests the significance of a combination of factors. Previous relationships between Jews and non-Jews, and whether Jews were seen as equal citizens, could be extremely important; but the extent to which such relationships and perceptions could ultimately make a difference to survival chances was massively affected by structures of power. Comparisons between the neighbouring Western European states of France, Belgium, and the Netherlands are revealing: deportation rates ranged from around 25 percent in France, through to 75 percent in the Netherlands, with Belgium roughly in between. Furthermore, Western European Jews whose families had long been settled were more easily able to melt into surrounding societies and develop survival strategies. Moreover, Germany's plans for its hoped-for postwar Nazi empire further affected local people's capacity for action and leeway for engaging in rescue attempts, illustrated most forcefully by the case of Denmark, where the deportation rate was a mere 2 percent.[18]

These Western European cases contrast markedly with the brutal subjugation and exploitation of Eastern European populations, millions of whom were slated by the Nazis for forced labour or death by starvation; they were not merely subjected to repressive occupation policies and practices but often also living on the very margins of physical existence. Yet stages of the war, and perceptions of the future, also made a difference; and even in Eastern Europe, there were significant variations in degrees of willingness to assist fugitive Jews, or capacity for the latter to develop survival strategies, according to local context.[19]

It would take a far wider survey to explore the significance of differing social relations, political configurations, and situational dynamics for the course of persecution and survival in different regions of Europe during the Nazi era. Within the Third Reich, the resegregation of society and associated changes in social relations during the peacetime years were, as I have emphasized, crucial. Conditions shifted in such a way that during the war, the murder of innocent fellow human beings could variously become (for a minority) a justifiable activity in working hours, a spectacle to witness, an image to capture in a historically significant moment, or (for a majority) a rumour that could relatively easily be dismissed or reinterpreted in ways that made it less disturbing.

The personal experiences explored here highlight wide variations in individual responses, as well as the significance of different contexts of action. Not all Germans were Nazis; not all Germans were 'bad'; not everyone was equally 'implicated'. Germany was, overall, neither a 'perpetrator society' nor a 'consensual dictatorship'. We have to make distinctions. There were key differences between willing conformity that was opportunistic or enthusiastic, and constrained conformity that was produced as a result of external pressures and well-founded fears of the consequences of nonconformity. This depended a great deal on both the individual's outlook and previous activities, and on current circumstances. So for example, as Lore Taut observed in the summer of 1933, it was far harder to maintain an oppositional stance in small rural communities than it was in the relative anonymity of a larger urban environment; as she and many others also confirmed, people with previous left-wing credentials had different grounds for rapid apparent conversion to Nazism than did careerists and opportunists from better-off backgrounds.

Over time, informal pressures for conformity—dropping friendships, giving the Hitler greeting—were augmented by more formal demands for compliance, underpinned by legal regulations shifting the grounds of behaviour. Then, as Ernst Rathgeber became aware following the Nuremberg Laws of 1935, compliance with national demands and systemic racism made Reich citizens inevitably complicit in exclusionary policies—a point that was sufficient for him, an 'Aryan' with no compelling reason to be forced out, nevertheless to choose to leave his homeland because he could not accept what it meant to be a member of the reconfigured 'national community' under Nazi rule. Furthermore, as the regime reshaped the parameters of life, so people were themselves intrinsically affected by the continual pressure to conform, to demonstrate loyalty through the innumerable actions of everyday life, and to comply with the legal demands of the Nazi regime. As this form of life was reiterated, endlessly repeated, so the Nazi worldview became, for some, 'naturalized' and internalized; this was particularly the case among younger Germans who were constantly exposed to the influence of Nazi socialisation, education, and youth organisations. For those who retained other perspectives, however, the apparent futility of opposition led to a growing sense of resignation.

From the perspective of the muddled middle, the mere fact of such widespread outward conformity—for whatever range of reasons—led to the perceived fiction of unity and consensus, making it even harder for wavering souls to risk standing out from the crowd or to challenge dominant views. There was a significant process in operation here: even constrained conformity had a wider impact on what others felt it possible to do or say, and what they dare not even attempt. So, in effect, even constrained conformity could lead ultimately to a form of complicity, assisting the slide towards ever more radical violence against those who had been ousted from the national community.

This approach may help to resolve the apparent paradox that the Third Reich can variously be explained—by respectable historians on both sides—as a regime based on widespread support and enthusiasm, or as a dictatorship held together by brutal repression and terror. The sheer reality of force and Nazi violence, and the high price to be paid for nonconformity, were sufficient to produce among many the outward appearance of consensus and approval, to provide repeated demonstrations of loyalty and even enthusiasm. But closer examination of the inner processes at work, the social psychology of conformity under dictatorial conditions, and the atmosphere of mutual apprehension leading to a silencing of opinions, should not lead us to overgeneralize from the external evidence of mass support for Nazism. The picture and the processes involved are more dynamic.

As pointed out at the start of this book: Raul Hilberg, in opening up the question of bystanders as essentially a moral rather than analytical category, claimed that in Germany 'the difference between perpetrators and bystanders was least pronounced'. Indeed, he continues, it was officially 'not supposed to exist': the regime sought to mobilize all eligible members of the population into the Nazi national community. Hilberg went on to suggest that in fact there 'was no cleavage between the German in the street and the perpetrators'.[20] While understanding the agony that underlay his assertions, I think Hilberg is here going too far in the direction of an undifferentiated view of Nazi Germany as, effectively, a 'perpetrator society'. We need to make some distinctions.

Germans in high places were in a position to have stopped Hitler in his tracks; but most members of the German elites—government ministries, civil servants, the military, lawyers, medical professionals, sections of industry, the churches, universities—simply fell into line, variously conforming, benefitting from, and faithfully carrying out the exclusionary and ever more radical policies of the Nazi regime, while individual opponents were readily apprehended and crushed, and what more organized opposition there eventually was among conservative elites (as in the July Plot of 1944) came far too late, even had it been successful, to prevent the genocide of European Jews.

If we turn to the wider population, however, the picture has to date been far less clear, and our evaluation needs to be a little different. Those who were largely powerless and lacking in material resources could generally only preserve shreds of personal integrity by occasional gestures of sympathy to victims. Yet simply by virtue of being a member of a 'national community' defined in ethno-nationalist terms and sustained by force, they were increasingly pressured and constrained to conform, to comply, and ultimately to bear a significant burden of shame.

There is clearly no one single explanation that will account for all the variations in individual attitudes and behaviours among people living within a system of collective violence—those members of mainstream society who

were not involved in high politics, active opposition, or subjected to persecution: the 'muddled middle' who were not themselves active perpetrators,
resistance fighters, or direct victims, and who are often simply dubbed 'bystanders'. Yet some things are clear from the material explored here, which
suggests we need to go beyond approaches looking purely at 'attitudes' or
'opinions' when talking about wider society. In particular, 'society' is never
static; people adapt and change over time. The individual experiences considered here not only serve to illuminate subjective perceptions of self and
others, and to illustrate, at a personal level, familiar accounts of wider historical developments; they also, far more significantly, help to explain how
these historical developments came about.

The conditions for genocide include the resources and capacity of initiators and ideologues to mobilize facilitators and executors of collective
violence, shaping the responses and ultimate fates of victims. But crucial
too are the responses of those not initially involved, with wider conditions
affecting whether people will choose to stand by, to look away, or watch and
applaud, or to be both willing and able to stand up on behalf of the persecuted with any hope of making a difference.

The propensity for bystanding relates not only to the individual but also
to the likely risks involved, the webs of social relations that people inhabit,
and the cultures that shape and inform their identities. As social relations and
patterns of identification shift, so, too, do the emotional connections and
the barriers to taking risks on behalf of others. The Nazi regime fostered
and rewarded certain sorts of action and encouraged certain discourses,
justifying previously unthinkable actions, while putting sufficient pressure
on those who had scruples that they felt it better to keep their doubts to
themselves. And as people came to terms with living under Nazi rule, so
they adjusted their views both of themselves and of others, adapting their
relationships and abandoning former ties. Changes in social relations and
the structures of power and repression together created the circumstances
that permitted the radicalisation of persecution without intervention from
the sidelines, resulting eventually in the facilitation of mass extermination
without outcry. Many people not merely knew about but also actively facilitated, propelled, and participated in these processes.

Not everyone was implicated; and some were far more implicated than
others. But the dynamic energy of the leadership, the organized participation and compliance of the many, alongside the largely incapacitated silence

of others, were sufficient for the implementation of mass murder across Europe. Only after the total defeat of the Nazi regime that had set these developments in train would these images and this knowledge come back to haunt those who had become complicit in all the Third Reich had to offer by way of personal advantages and justificatory worldviews, and those who had, by their silence, whether willingly or otherwise, passively gone along with it.

The postwar invention of the myth of the ignorant and innocent bystander helped some to soothe a troubled conscience, while many others came to believe their own fictions, or tried in some way to put their past behind them. But whether we look at the conditions for passivity at the time, or the varying ways in which people later learned to live with a compromised past, it is clear that changing social relations, cultural perceptions, and political arrangements are crucial. 'Bystanders' are not individuals acting in isolation; people's choices of action or inaction are crucially shaped by their relationships with others, their aspirations for the future, and their perceptions of the circumstances in which they live.

This book has argued that indifference, ignorance, and impotence are socially produced: we can learn to not care, to turn away and ignore the fates of others, to feel powerless in face of overwhelming force or impossible constraints; and we can acquire and internalize the discourses that make us feel alright about what we are doing or failing to do, the worldviews that seem to justify moral compromises to ourselves and others. The position of bystanding is, then, a consequence of specific social and cultural relations under particular historical circumstances. And in conditions of continuing collective violence, passivity cannot remain neutral; bystanding is, over time, neither a neutral nor an 'innocent' position.

A bystander society was actively created in Nazi Germany, under a specific combination of historical circumstances; and the expansion of extreme violence in a genocidal war massively raised the stakes on all sides, leading some to argue that we cannot even speak of bystanders in wartime Europe. That is why we need to stop conceiving of bystanders purely as discrete individuals, as though they somehow stood outside history and were not an integral part of the kaleidoscope of shifting sides in complex conflicts; and we need to shift the focus away from questions around individual courage, vital though that is in particular, exceptional cases. We need rather to address questions around the broader social and political environments that foster widespread passivity in face of violence, and explore the varying routes into greater complicity and collaboration, as well as the potential for the riskier options of rescue and resistance. For those who want to salvage 'the Germans' from unwarranted blanket condemnation, and seek rather to understand in greater depth the variety of experiences and responses under Nazi rule, this allows a more differentiated means of evaluation. And for anyone who, in the aftermath of the Holocaust, wants to give more meaning and content to the oft-repeated refrain, 'never again', this may suggest many potential points for earlier or more effective intervention. It is, then, vital that we extend our understanding of the historically contingent conditions for the production of a bystander society.

Notes

1. Harvard Houghton Library (HHL), b MS Ger 91 (8), 'Aralk' (pseudonym), pp. 36–37. 'Klara' was very likely her real name, simply turned around to make the pseudonym 'Aralk'. I have chosen to call her 'Klara Rosenthal' in this book.

2. HHL, b MS Ger 91 (8), 'Aralk', pp. 37–38.

3. HHL, b MS Ger 91 (8), 'Aralk', p. 38.

4. Cf. Catherine Sanderson, *The Bystander Effect: The Psychology of Courage and Inaction* (London: William Collins, 2020).

5. Ernesto Verdeja, 'Moral Bystanders and Mass Violence', in Adam Jones (ed.), *New Directions in Genocide Research* (London: Routledge, 2012), pp. 153–68 (p. 154).

6. See, e.g., 'How George Floyd Was Killed in Policy Custody', *New York Times*, 31 May 2020: https://www.nytimes.com/2020/05/31/us/george-floyd-invest igation.html.

7. See, e.g., Trump on 'locker-room talk' as reported by Daniella Diaz, CNN, 10 October 2016: https://edition.cnn.com/2016/10/09/politics/donald-trump-locker-room-talk-presidential-debate-2016-election/index.html;   Tanya Aldred, '"It is so normalised": Community in Yorkshire on Cricket Racism Scandal', *The Guardian*, 10 November 2021: https://www.theguardian.com/sport/2021/nov/10/racism-normalised-south-asian-community-yorkshire-on-cricket-ccc-scandal.

8. Comments made by the President Donald Trump during the first presidential debate of the 2020 election campaign, September 2020. See, e.g., news coverage at https://www.nbcnews.com/think/opinion/trump-s-proud-boys-stand-back-stand-debate-moment-was-ncna1241570. See also footage on YouTube at https://www.youtube.com/watch?v=qIHhB1ZMV_0 (accessed 16 June 2021).

9. Cf. Alon Confino, *A World without Jews. The Nazi Imagination from Persecution to Genocide* (New Haven, CT: Yale University Press, 2015).

10. Saul Friedländer, *The Years of Persecution: Nazi Germany and the Jews 1933–39* (London: HarperCollins, 1997), and *Nazi Germany and the Jews,* Vol. 2: *The Years of Extermination, 1933–45* (New York: HarperCollins, 2007).

11. See Marion Kaplan, *Between Dignity and Despair: Jewish Life in Nazi Germany* (Oxford: Oxford University Press, 1998), p. 229: 'In the 1930s, Nazi Germany succeeded in enforcing social death on its Jews—excommunicating them, subjecting them to inferior status, and relegating them to a perpetual state of dishonor. . . . The German "racial community", thorough its complicity in, approval of, or indifference to the persecution of these newly marked "enemies", helped pave the way toward the physical extermination of the Jews. The social death of Jews and German indifference to their increasingly horrific plight were absolute prerequisites for the "Final Solution".'

12. The notion that 'all Germans are bad Germans' was prevalent among the Western Allies at the end of the war. One of the most extreme more recent variants on this approach is to be found in Daniel Jonah Goldhagen, *Hitler's Willing Executioners. Ordinary Germans and the Holocaust* (New York: Alfred A. Knopf, 1996). See, by contrast, Christopher Browning, *Ordinary Men: Reserve Police Battalion 101 and the Final Solution in Poland* (London: Penguin, 2001; orig. 1992). See also Thomas Pegelow Kaplan, Jürgen Matthäus, and Mark Hornburg (eds.), *Beyond "Ordinary Men". Christopher R. Browning and Holocaust Historiography* (Paderborn: Brill, Ferdinand Schöningh, 2019).

13. Raul Hilberg, *Perpetrators Victims Bystanders. The Jewish Catastrophe 1933–1945* (New York: HarperCollins, 1993), pp. 196, 197. Cf. also Christina Morina and Krijn Thijs (eds.), *Probing the Limits of Categorization. The Bystander in Holocaust History* (New York: Berghahn, 2019).

14. Hilberg, *Perpetrators Victims Bystanders*, p. 196.

15. Frank Bajohr and Andrea Löw, 'Beyond the "Bystander": Social Processes and Social Dynamics in European Societies as Context for the Holocaust', in Andrea Löw and Frank Bajohr (eds.), *The Holocaust and European Societies: Social Processes and Social Dynamics* (London: Palgrave Macmillan, 2016), ch. 1, pp. 3–14 (p. 4).

16. For an astute contemporary journalist's insights, see, e.g., William Shirer, *Berlin Diary: The Journal of a Foreign Correspondent, 1934–1941*, rev. ed. (Baltimore: Johns Hopkins University Press, 2002; orig. 1941); for accounts by foreigners who were 'accidental eyewitnesses to history', see Julia Boyd, *Travelers in the Third Reich: The Rise of Fascism: 1919–1945* (London: Pegasus, 2018).

17. See the overview in Harry Liebersohn and Dorothee Schneider, *"My Life in Germany before and after January 30, 1933". A Guide to a Manuscript Collection at Houghton Library, Harvard University* (Philadelphia: American Philosophical Society, 2001).

18. I have not always explicitly stated whether the original essay was in German or in English, unless this affected the quotation significantly. All translations from German in the book are my own, unless otherwise noted.

19. On Jewish experiences and extracts from these essays, see: Margarete Limberg and Herbert Rübsaat (eds.), *Sie durften nicht mehr Deutsche sein: Jüdischer Alltag in Selbstzeugnissen 1933–1938* (Frankfurt: Campus, 1990) and selections

of these in English translation in Margarete Limberg and Hubert Rübsaat (eds.), *Germans No More. Accounts of Jewish Everyday Life, 1933–38* (New York: Berghahn 2006); Margarete Limberg and Hubert Rübsaat (eds.), *Nach dem "Anschluss". Berichte österreichischer EmigrantInnen aus dem Archiv der Harvard University* (Vienna: Mandelbaum, 2013); Uta Gerhardt and Thomas Karlauf (eds.), *Night of Broken Glass: Eyewitness Accounts of Kristallnacht* (Malden, MA: Polity, 2012). There are also related materials in Andreas Lixl-Purcell (ed.), *Women of Exile: German-Jewish Autobiographies since 1933* (Westport, CT: Greenwood, 1988); Monika Richarz, *Jüdisches Leben in Deutschland*, vol. 2, *Selbstzeugnisse zur Sozialgeschichte im Kaiserrreich* and vol. 3, *Selbstzeugnisse zur Sozialgeschichte, 1918–1945*, in English as Monika Richarz (ed.), *Jewish Life in Germany: Memoirs from Three Centuries* (Bloomington: Indiana University Press, 1991). See also Jürgen Matthäus and Mark Roseman (eds.), *Jewish Responses to Persecution*, Vol. 1: *1933–1938* (Lanham, MD: AltaMira, 2010).

20. Early examples of pathbreaking works in this area include Ian Kershaw, *Popular Opinion and Political Dissent. Bavaria 1933–1945* (Oxford: Oxford University Press, 1983); Ian Kershaw, 'German Popular Opinion and the "Jewish Question", 1939–1943: Some Further Reflections', in Arnold Paucker (ed.), *Die Juden im nationalsozialistischen Deutschland 1933–1943* (Tübingen: J. C. B. Mohr, 1986), pp. 365–86; and David Bankier, *The Germans and the Final Solution. Public Opinion under Nazism* (Oxford: Blackwell, 1992). Recent research has focussed on the construction of a Nazi 'people's community,' or Volksgemeinschaft; see particularly Michael Wildt, *Hitler's Volksgemeinschaft and the Dynamics of Racial Exclusion. Violence against Jews in Provincial Germany, 1919–1939*, trans. Bernard Heise (New York: Berghahn, 2012), which focuses on the period from the end of the First World War through to the eve of the Second World War but does not continue through the war years after 1939.

21. See also Janosch Steuwer, *"Ein Drittes Reich, wie ich es auffasse". Politik, Gesellschaft und privates Leben in Tagebüchern 1933–1939* (Göttingen: Wallstein, 2017), which ends, as indicated in the title, with the outbreak of war in 1939; and Peter Fritzsche, *Life and Death in the Third Reich* (Cambridge, MA: Harvard University Press, 2008).

22. Theodore Abel, *Why Hitler Came into Power* (Cambridge, MA: Harvard University Press, 1986; orig. 1938); Wieland Giebel (ed.), *"Warum ich Nazi wurde". Biogramme früher Nationalsozialisten—Die einzigartige Sammlung des Theodore Abel* (Berlin: Berlin Story, 2018); Katja Kosubek, *"Genauso konseqent sozialistisch wie national". Alte Kämpferinnen der NSDAP vor 1933* (Gottingen: Wallstein, 2017).

23. Statistics on different forms of killing are difficult to ascertain with any degree of precision. Taken together, more Jews died outside the camps than within the dedicated killing centres; the site that has become iconic for the Holocaust, Auschwitz-Birkenau, accounted for less than one-fifth of victims. Dieter Pohl provides quite detailed if cautious estimates: see Pohl, 'Historiography and

Nazi Killing Sites', in International Holocaust Remembrance Alliance (ed.), *Killing Sites—Research and Remembrance* (Berlin: Metropol, 2015), pp. 31–46 (p. 37).

24. E. Y. Hartshorne, *German Youth and the Nazi Dream of Victory*, America Faces the War No. 6 (London: Oxford University Press, 1941). See also G. W. Allport, J. S. Bruner, and E. M. Jandorf, 'Personality under Social Catastrophe: Ninety Life-histories of the Nazi Revolution', *Character & Personality; A Quarterly for Psychodiagnostic and Allied Studies*, 10 (1941), pp. 1–22.

25. Contrast the interpretation of Richard J. Evans, who poses this possibility without giving supporting evidence, although it would nicely fit the circumstances, and the research of James F. Tent, who discounts such a theory: James F. Tent, 'Edward Y. Hartshorne and the Reopening of German Universities, 1945–1946: His Personal Account', *Paedagogica Historica*, 33:1 (1997), pp. 183–200 (pp. 198–99); Richard J. Evans, '*The Night of Broken Glass* edited by Uta Gerhardt and Thomas Karlauf—Review', *The Guardian*, 11 April 2012.

26. A subsequent project will explore variations in the significance of surrounding societies for the implementation of mass murder in different areas of Eastern and Western Europe under Nazi rule.

27. Contrast the approach adopted by Michael Rothberg, *The Implicated Subject. Beyond Victims and Perpetrators* (Stanford, CA: Stanford University Press, 2019). Rothberg's notion of 'implication' is far too broad and undifferentiated for historical analysis. For Rothberg, 'implication comes in diverse forms: it describes beneficiaries and descendants, accomplices and perpetrators, and it can even attach to people who have had shattering experiences of trauma or victimization and are thus situated within "complex implication"' (p. 200). On this view, no one at any time or anywhere can apparently be not 'implicated' in some way. See further also Mary Fulbrook, 'Conformity, Compliance, and Complicity: "Ordinary People" and the Holocaust', in Mary Fulbrook, Stephanie Bird, Stefanie Rauch, and Bastiaan Willems (eds.), *Perpetration and Complicity under Nazism and Beyond: Compromised Identities?* (London: Bloomsbury, 2023), ch. 2; and Mary Fulbrook, 'Bystanders to Nazi Violence? The Transformation of German Society in the 1930s', *Search and Research* (Jerusalem: Yad Vashem, 2018).

28. Explored further in Mary Fulbrook, *Reckonings: Legacies of Nazi Persecution and the Quest for Justice* (Oxford: Oxford University Press, 2018).

29. For an overview see, e.g., the Third Reich trilogy by Richard J. Evans, *The Coming of the Third Reich: How the Nazis Destroyed Democracy and Seized Power in Germany* (London: Penguin, 2003); *The Third Reich in Power, 1933–1939: How the Nazis Won Over the Hearts and Minds of a Nation* (London: Penguin, 2005); and *The Third Reich at War: How the Nazis Led Germany from Conquest to Disaster* (London: Penguin, 2008). On the Volksgemeinschaft, see Wildt, *Hitler's Volksgemeinschaft*; and Martina Steber and Bernhard Gotto (eds.), *Visions of*

Community in Nazi Germany: Social Engineering and Private Lives (Oxford: Oxford University Press, 2014).

30. There is a huge literature on these questions. On consensus and terror, see, e.g., Robert Gellately, *Backing Hitler* (Oxford: Oxford University Press, 2001); Eric Johnson and Karl-Heinz Reuband, *What We Knew: Terror, Mass Murder and Everyday Life in Nazi Germany* (London: Hodder, 2005); Eric Johnson, *The Nazi Terror: Gestapo, Jews and Ordinary Germans* (London: John Murray, 2000); and Richard J. Evans's trenchant critique of 'consensual dictatorship' approaches in Evans, 'Coercion and Consent in Nazi Germany', *Proceedings of the British Academy*, 151 (2007), pp. 53–81. On postwar accounts, cf. Fulbrook, *Reckonings*.

31. There is a major problem with taking at face value the selective memories of those who had not been victims.

32. See also Mary Fulbrook, 'Private Lives, Public Faces: On the Social Self in Nazi Germany', in Elizabeth Harvey, Johannes Hürter, Maiken Umbach, and Andreas Wirsching (eds.), *Private Life and Privacy in Nazi Germany* (Cambridge: Cambridge University Press, 2019), pp. 55–80.

CHAPTER 1

1. The complexities of German Jewish lives and changing experiences across the decades are examined in Amos Elon, *The Pity of It All: A Portrait of Jews in Germany 1743–1933* (London: Penguin, 2004); the changing fortunes and self-identifications of some prominent Berlin Jews are explored in detail in Leonard Barkan, *Berlin for Jews: A Twenty-first Century Companion* (Chicago: University of Chicago Press, 2016).

2. Disagreements over what it means to be 'Jewish', and whether antisemitism is simply another form of racism, or whether Jews 'count' as 'white', continue today; see, e.g., David Baddiel, *Jews Don't Count* (London: HarperCollins, 2021); Deborah Lipstadt, *Antisemitism. Here and Now* (London: Penguin, 2019).

3. See Elon, *The Pity of It All*; and Deborah Hertz, *How Jews Became Germans: The History of Conversion and Assimilation in Berlin* (New Haven, CT: Yale University Press, 2009).

4. On the wider picture and the situation of Jewish Germans in comparison with Jews elsewhere across Western and Eastern Europe up to the Second World War, see Bernard Wasserstein, *On the Eve. The Jews of Europe before the Second World War* (London: Profile Books, 2012).

5. Contrast Isabel Wilkerson, *Caste* (London: Allen Lane, 2020). Whatever the apparent attractions of Wilkerson's plea to change attitudes towards 'race', her metaphor of 'caste' simply does not work with respect to the Third Reich. German society did not have anything like a 'caste system' construed through a centuries-old religious belief system, entrenched and reproduced in enduring socioeconomic and political inequalities. See also Devin Pendas, Mark

Roseman, and Richard Wetzell (eds.), *Beyond the Racial State. Rethinking Nazi Germany* (Cambridge: Cambridge University Press, 2017).

6. On Breslau, see particularly Till van Rahden, *Jews and Other Germans: Civil Society, Religious Diversity, and Urban Politics in Breslau, 1860–1925* (Madison: University of Wisconsin Press, 2008); and Till van Rahden, 'Jews and the Ambivalences of Civil Society in Germany, 1800–1933: Assessment and Reassessment', *Journal of Modern History*, 77:4 (December 2005), pp. 1024–47.

7. HHL, b MS Ger 91 (5), Eugen Altmann.

8. Richard J. Evans, *The Coming of the Third Reich: How the Nazis Destroyed Democracy and Seized Power in Germany* (London: Penguin, 2003), pp. 22–24; Anthony Kauders, *German Politics and the Jews: Düsseldorf and Nuremberg 1910–1933* (Oxford: Oxford University Press, 1996); Kerstin Meiring, *Die christlich-jüdische Mischehe in Deutschland, 1840–1933* (Hamburg: Dölling und Galitz, 1998); Beate Meyer, *"Jüdische Mischlinge". Rassenpolitik und Verfolgungserfahrung 1933–1945* (Hamburg: Dölling und Galitz, 1999); Jeremy Noakes, 'The Development of Nazi Policy towards the German-Jewish "Mischlinge" 1933–1945', *Leo Baeck Institute Year Book*, 34 (London, 1989), pp. 291–354 (p. 291); Peter Pulzer, *Jews and the German State: The Political History of a Minority* (Oxford: Blackwell, 1992).

9. See, e.g., the occasional remarks in Harry Kessler, *Journey to the Abyss: The Diaries of Count Harry Kessler 1880–1918*, ed., trans., and intro. by Laird Easton (New York: Random House, 2013), pp. 146–47 (p. 171).

10. Else Behrend-Rosenfeld and Siegfried Rosenfeld, *Leben in zwei Welten. Tagebücher eines jüdischen Paares in Deutschland und im Exil*, ed. and intro. by Erich Kasberger and Marita Kraus (Munich: Volk, 2011). As indicated, for the sake of clarity I refer to her by her married name throughout.

11. HHL, b MS Ger 91 (161), Erich Haller-Munk. His parents, Heinrich Haller and Paula (née Munk), had chosen—well before this practice became widespread—to combine their last names. To protect them at the time he was writing, Erich Munk anonymizes the family in his 1939 account, naming his elder brother 'Marius' (actually Hans-Ulrich) and himself 'Peter'. I use their real names here but use the shorter version of 'Hans', rather than 'Hans-Ulrich'; I also sometimes use the shorter last name, Munk, as preferred by Erich.

12. HHL, b MS Ger 91 (161), Erich Haller-Munk, p. 6.

13. HHL, b MS Ger 91 (172), Alfred Christian Oppler.

14. HHL, b MS Ger 91 (89), 'John Hay' (Dr Frederick [Fritz] G. Goldberg), pp. 1–8. Goldberg wrote under the pseudonym 'John Hay' to protect anonymity, in view of the danger to family and friends in Germany.

15. HHL, b MS Ger 91 (8), 'Aralk', p. 1. See also above, Introduction, pp. 1–2.

16. HHL, b MS Ger 91 (15), Alice Baerwald, pp. 1–12.

17. In the census of 16 May 1933, some 160,564 of Berlin's nearly 4.25 million residents were registered as Jewish—just under 4 percent. But they were

massively concentrated in central and western districts: in the west-central district of Wilmersdorf, more than one in eight residents (13.54%) were Jewish, as were nearly one in ten (9.18%) of people living in the central district of Mitte, and 7.35% of Schöneberg residents. See Kunstamt Schöneberg, Schöneberg Museum, with Gedenkstätte Haus der Wannsee-Konferenz (eds.), *Orte des Erinnerns*, Vol. 2: *Jüdisches Alltagsleben im Bayerischen Viertel: Eine Dokumentation* (Berlin: Edition Hentrich, 1995; 2nd ed. 1999), p. 12.

18. HHL, b MS Ger 91 (179), Lotte Popper, p. 17.

19. HHL, b MS Ger 91 (179), Lotte Popper, p. 18.

20. Cf. Erving Goffmann, *Stigma: Notes on the Management of Spoiled Identity* (Englewood Cliffs, NJ: Prentice-Hall, 1963; reissued Penguin 1990).

21. HHL, b MS Ger 91 (6), Martin Andermann, pp. 2–13.

22. This account is based on Eckhardt Friedrich and Dagmar Schmieder, (eds.), *Die Gailinger Juden. Materialien zur Geschichte der jüdischen Gemeinde Gailingen aus ihrer Blütezeit und den Jahren der gewaltsamen Auflösung* (Konstanz: Arbeitskreis für Regionalgeschichte e.V., 1981).

23. Friedrich and Schmieder, *Die Gailinger Juden*, p. 22.

24. See Jeffrey Veidlinger, *In the Midst of Civilized Europe. The Pogroms of 1918–1921 and the Onset of the Holocaust* (London: Picador, 2021), particularly pp. 1–11. The term 'Holocaust by bullets' comes from Father Patrick Desbois, *The Holocaust by Bullets. A Priest's Journey to Uncover the Truth behind the Murder of 1.5 Million Jews* (Houndmills, Basingstoke: Palgrave Macmillan, 2008).

25. On support for the war, as well as dissenting and critical voices among prominent Jews, see Elon, *The Pity of It All*, ch. 9, 'War Fever', pp. 297–354.

26. HHL, b MS Ger 91 (8), 'Aralk', p. 8, pp. 11–15.

27. HHL, b MS Ger 91 (93), Verena Hellwig.

28. HHL, b MS Ger 91 (89), 'John Hay' (Dr Frederick [Fritz] G. Goldberg), pp. 11–17.

29. HHL, b MS Ger 91 (92), Edmund Heilpern, pp. 15–19, p. 15, pp. 24–25.

30. HHL, b MS Ger 91 (92), Edmund Heilpern, p. 7, pp. 8–9, p. 13, pp. 29–32.

31. On the 'war youth generation', see Michael Wildt, *An Uncompromising Generation. The Nazi Leadership of the Reich Security Main Office*, trans. Tom Lampert (Madison: University of Wisconsin Press, 2009; orig. 2003); see also Mary Fulbrook, *Dissonant Lives: Generations and Violence through the German Dictatorships* (Oxford: Oxford University Press, 2011).

32. HHL, b MS Ger 91 (92), Edmund Heilpern, pp. 47–49.

33. HHL, b MS Ger 91 (172), Alfred Oppler; also Alfred Oppler, *Legal Reform in Occupied Japan: A Participant Looks Back* (Princeton, NJ: Princeton University Press, 1976), pp. 4–8; and Alfred C. Oppler Papers, University at Albany, SUNY. https://archives.albany.edu/description/catalog/ger016 (accessed 19 April 2017).

34. See further Michael Geheran, *Comrades Betrayed: Jewish World War I Veterans under Hitler* (Ithaca, NY: Cornell University Press, 2020), ch. 1.

35. Cf. Veidlinger, *In the Midst of Civilized Europe*; Götz Aly, *Europa gegen die Juden, 1880–1945* (Frankfurt: S. Fischer, 2017).

36. HHL, b MS Ger 91 (93), Verena Hellwig.

37. HHL, b MS Ger 91 (8), 'Aralk', p. 24.

38. HHL, b MS Ger 91 (8), 'Aralk', p. 29.

39. See particularly Kerry Wallach, *Passing Illusions. Jewish Visibility in Weimar Germany* (Ann Arbor: University of Michigan Press, 2017).

40. HHL, b MS Ger 91 (184), Dr F.S. Reuss. I call him 'Friedrich' although his first name is not clear in the file.

41. HHL, b MS Ger 91 (184), Dr F.S. Reuss, pp. 15–16.

42. HHL, b MS Ger 91 (184), Dr F.S. Reuss, pp. 15–16.

43. HHL, b MS Ger 91 (72), Bruno Gebhard, pp. 13–27.

44. Theodore Abel, *Why Hitler Came into Power* (Cambridge, MA: Harvard University Press, 1986; orig. 1938); Wieland Giebel (ed.), *"Warum ich Nazi wurde". Biogramme früher Nationalsozialisten—Die einzigartige Sammlung des Theodore Abel* (Berlin: Berlin Story, 2018); Katja Kosubek, *"Genauso konseqent sozialistisch wie national". Alte Kämpferinnen der NSDAP vor 1933* (Gottingen: Wallstein, 2017).

45. HHL, b MS Ger 91 (8), 'Aralk', p. 33. See more generally on Hitler and Munich in the early postwar years, Michael Brenner, *In Hitler's Munich: Jews, the Revolution, and the Rise of Nazism* (Princeton, NJ: Princeton University Press, 2022).

46. HHL, b MS Ger 91 (8), 'Aralk', p. 34.

47. Giebel, *"Warum ich Nazi wurde"*, pp. 286–88; quotations from p. 286.

48. HHL, b MS Ger 91 (184), Dr F.S. Reuss, p. 17.

49. HHL, b MS Ger 91 (34), Willy Bornstein.

50. HHL, b MS Ger 91 (34), Willy Bornstein, p. 3.

51. HHL, b MS Ger 91 (34), Willy Bornstein, p. 5.

52. Population figures from Michael Wildt, *Zerborstene Zeit. Deutsche Geschichte 1918 bis 1945* (Stuttgart: C. H. Beck. 2022), p. 73.

53. HHL, b MS Ger 91 (15), Alice Baerwald, p. 29.

54. Walter Jessel, *A Travelogue through a Twentieth Century Life. A Memoir* (Self-published; 'written for grandchildren', edited by Janet Roberts and Cynthia Jessel, Boulder, CO, 1996), pp. 24–25.

55. HHL, b MS Ger 91 (89), 'John Hay' (Dr Frederick [Fritz] G. Goldberg), pp. 19–34.

56. HHL, b MS Ger 91 (179), Lotte Popper; HHL, b MS Ger 91 (8), 'Aralk' (pseudonym).

CHAPTER 2

1. HHL, b MS Ger 91 (184), Dr F.S. Reuss, p. 37.

2. André Postert (ed.), *Hitlerjunge Schall. Die Tagebücher eines jungen Nationalsozialisten* (Munich: dtv, 2016), entries of 30 and 31 January 1933, pp. 235–36.

3. There is a large literature on support for Hitler; see, e.g., Robert Gellately, *Hitler's True Believers. How Ordinary People Became Nazis* (Oxford: Oxford University Press, 2020).

4. HHL, b MS Ger 91 (174), Carl Paeschke, p. 44.

5. See, e.g., Wieland Giebel (ed.), *"Warum ich Nazi wurde". Biogramme früher Nationalsozialisten—Die einzigartige Sammlung des Theodore Abel* (Berlin: Berlin Story, 2018), pp. 191–99, p. 192.

6. For a detailed portrayal see Peter Fritzsche, *Hitler's First Hundred Days. When Germans Embraced the Third Reich* (New York: Basic Books, 2020).

7. Hermann Stresau, *Von den Nazis trennt mich eine Welt. Tagebücher aus der inneren Emigration, 1933–1939*, ed. Peter Graf and Ulrich Faure (Stuttgart: Klett-Cotta, 2021), p. 131. Disputes over the likely involvement of the SA continued after 1945, with conflicting accounts combined with repression of evidence. A former SA member, Hans-Martin Lennings, stated in an affidavit for a Hanover court in 1955 that he and members of his SA unit had driven Van der Lubbe from an infirmary to the Reichstag, where the fire had already started, and had dropped him off there, where he was then 'found' and arrested. See *Deutsche Welle*, 27 July 2019. See also, e.g., Benjamin Carter Hett, *Burning the Reichstag. An Investigation into the Third Reich's Enduring Mystery* (Oxford: Oxford University Press, 2014); and a journalistic summary at https://www.berlinexperiences.com/who-was-really-responsible-for-the-reichstag-fire-mythbusting-berlin/.

8. Giebel, *"Warum ich Nazi wurde"*, p. 198.

9. Nikolaus Wachsmann, *KL: A History of the Nazi Concentration Camps* (New York: Little, Brown, 2015), pp. 23–78; figures from pp. 31–32.

10. See also M. Fulbrook, 'Private Lives, Public Faces: On the Social Self in Nazi Germany', in E. Harvey, Johannes Hürter, Maiken Umbach, and Andreas Wirsching (eds.), *Private Life and Privacy in Nazi Germany* (Cambridge: Cambridge University Press, 2019), pp. 55–80.

11. I am very grateful to Ernst Hermicker's grandson, Lorenz Hemicker, for supplying me with personal details and copies of archival documents on which this account is based.

12. See below, chapter 10.

13. Jürgen Ernst Kroeger, *So war es. Ein Bericht* (Neuenbürg: Neuthor, 1989), pp. 11–14; *Libauische Zeitung*, Nr. 117, 22 May 1919.

14. HHL, b MS Ger 91 (11), Joseph Aust.

15. IIIIL, b MS Ger 91 (11), Joseph Aust (no pagination).

16. HHL, b MS Ger 91 (11), Joseph Aust.

17. For detailed NSDAP membership figures, see Jürgen W. Falter, *Hitlers Parteigenossen. Die Mitglieder der NSDAP 1919–1945* (Frankfurt: Campus-Verlag, 2020).

18. See, e.g., the diary entries in Stresau, *Von den Nazis trennt mich eine Welt*.

19. HHL, b MS Ger 91 (177), Gerta Pfeffer, p. 16.

20. HHL, b MS Ger 91 (172), Alfred Christian Oppler, pp. 13–14.

21. HHL, b MS Ger 91 (39), James Broh.

22. HHL, b MS Ger 91(6), Martin Andermann, pp. 94–95.

23. HHL, b MS Ger 91 (92), Edmund Heilpern, pp. 81–94.

24. HHL, b MS Ger 91(6), Martin Andermann, pp. 95–99, p. 105.

25. HHL, b MS Ger 91(6), Martin Andermann, p. 106.

26. HHL, b MS Ger 91(6), Martin Andermann, pp. 107–8.

27. HHL, b MS Ger 91 (72), Bruno Gebhard, p. 40.

28. HHL b MS Ger 91 (1), Georg Abraham, pp. 3–4.

29. Karl Löwith, *My Life in Germany before and after 1933. A Report*, trans. by Elizabeth King (Urbana and Chicago: University of Illinois Press, 1994; orig. German, 1986; based on the 1940 essay for the Harvard competition under the same title), p. 79.

30. Saul Friedländer, *The Years of Persecution: Nazi Germany and the Jews 1933–39* (London: HarperCollins, 1997).

31. HHL, b MS Ger 91 (89), 'John Hay' (Dr Frederick [Fritz] G. Goldberg), pp. 36–37.

32. HHL, b MS Ger 91 (176), Victor Paschkis, pp. 11–12.

33. HHL, b MS Ger 91 (176), Victor Paschkis, p. 8.

34. HHL, b MS Ger 91 (176), Victor Paschkis, p. 17.

35. Stresau, *Von den Nazis trennt mich eine Welt*, p. 58, p. 59.

36. HHL, b MS Ger 91 (179), Lotte Popper, p. 12.

37. HHL, b MS Ger 91 (179), Lotte Popper, p. 27, p. 28.

38. HHL, b MS Ger 91 (179), Lotte Popper, p. 25.

39. HHL, b MS Ger 91 (161), Erich Haller-Munk, p. 8.

40. HHL, b MS Ger 91 (223), Erica Stein (Bond), p. 1.

41. HHL, b MS Ger 91 (223), Erica Stein (Bond).

42. HHL, b MS Ger 91 (223), Erica Stein (Bond), cover letter, 21 March 1940.

43. HHL, b MS Ger 91 (232), Lore Taut. Taut's use of the term 'western Germany' does not map onto the later, post-1945 conception of this as referring to the area of the Federal Republic of Germany. Her account leaves no explicit clues about which town this might be, or whether the population figure given refers to the time of writing (1939) or the time when she was born. If referring to the time of writing, it could potentially be either Bremen (population 354,109) or Chemnitz (337,645). Chemnitz, in Saxony, actually seems more likely, given later elements of her story, when she visits old friends living in a village in the surrounding area, and goes skiing in the Czech border region.

44. HHL, b MS Ger 91 (232), Lore Taut, p. 23. 'Bastard' was a pejorative epithet Nazis frequently used for those considered to be of mixed race, or '*Mischlinge*'.

45. HHL, b MS Ger 91 (232), Lore Taut, p. 24.

46. HHL, b MS Ger 91 (34), Willy Bornstein.

47. HHL, b MS Ger 91 (209), Ernst Schwartzert, Part II, 1933–39, p. 15.

48. HHL, b MS Ger 91 (3), Erna Albersheim, p. 9.

49. HHL b MS Ger 91 (1), Georg Abraham, p. 2.

50. HHL, b MS Ger 91 (179), Lotte Popper, pp. 26–27.

51. HHL, b MS Ger 91 (34), Willy Bornstein, p. 8.

52. HHL, b MS Ger 91 (72), Bruno Gebhard, p. 42.

53. Stresau, *Von den Nazis trennt mich eine Welt*, pp. 23–25.

54. HHL, b MS Ger 91 (232), Lore Taut, p. 51.

55. HHL, b MS Ger 91 (89), 'John Hay' (Dr Frederick [Fritz] G. Goldberg), pp. 39–45.

56. HHL, b MS Ger 91 (92), Edmund Heilpern, pp. 107–16.

57. Cf. Janosch Steuwer, *"Ein Drittes Reich, wie ich es auffasse"*. *Politik, Gesellschaft und privates Leben in Tagebüchern 1933–1939* (Göttingen: Wallstein, 2017); and contributions to Harvey et al., *Private Life and Privacy in Nazi Germany*.

CHAPTER 3

1. Techniques included equivocation, speaking ambiguously, making secret gestures such as the one described by Muz, and 'mental reservation'—silently adding to a sentence so as to subvert the spoken meaning, as in denying guilt by saying aloud 'I did not do it' and adding mentally 'last year', when in fact 'I' did actually 'do it', but last week. See the fascinating account by Perez Zagorin, 'The Historical Significance of Lying and Dissimulation', *Social Research*, 63:3 (1996), pp. 863–912.

2. HHL, b MS Ger 91 (92), Edmund Heilpern, pp. 117–18.

3. HHL, b MS Ger 91 (172), Alfred Christian Oppler, pp. 16–17.

4. HHL, b MS Ger 91 (172), Alfred Christian Oppler, pp. 13–14.

5. HHL, b MS Ger 91 (172), Alfred Christian Oppler, pp. 39–40.

6. HHL, b MS Ger 91 (172), Alfred Christian Oppler, p. 25.

7. HHL, b MS Ger 91 (172), Alfred Christian Oppler, p. 27.

8. HHL, b MS Ger 91 (184), Dr F.S. Reuss, pp. 40–41.

9. HHL, b MS Ger 91 (184), Dr F.S. Reuss, p. 41.

10. HHL, b MS Ger 91 (184), Dr F.S. Reuss, p. 41.

11. Cf. Christian Goeschel, *Suicide in Nazi Germany* (Oxford: Oxford University Press, 2009), pp. 97–98.

12. HHL, b MS Ger 91 (184), Friedrich Reuss.

13. Helga Nathorff, *Das Tagebuch der Hertha Nathorff. Berlin—New York, Aufzeichnungen 1933 bis 1945*, ed. Wolfgang Benz (Frankfurt am Main: Fischer, 2010), diary entry of 14 April 1933, p. 39. See also HHL b MS Ger 91 (162),

Nathorff regarding the diary extracts which she managed to reconstruct, having lost the original full manuscript during her flight from Germany, which she submitted to the Harvard competition and for which she was awarded a prize of $15 (a considerable sum for a refugee at that time).

14. HHL b MS Ger 91 (6), Martin Andermann, pp. 108a–109.

15. HHL, b MS Ger 91 (1), Georg Abraham, p. 4.

16. See above, pp. 1–2.

17. HHL, b MS Ger 91 (8), 'Aralk', pp. 38–39.

18. See further below, Ch. 7.

19. Else Behrend-Rosenfeld and Siegfried Rosenfeld, *Leben in zwei Welten. Tagebücher eines jüdischen Paares in Deutschland und im Exil*, Erich Kasberger and Marita Kraus (eds.) (Munich: Volk, 2011), p. 58. This volume includes not only an introduction to and annotated reprint of Behrend-Rosenfeld's diaries but also other documents including her husband's letters to her. Behrend-Rosenfeld's diaries were originally published as Rahel Behrend [Else Behrend-Rosenfeld], *Verfemt und verfolgt: Erlebnisse einer Jüdin in Nazi-Deutschland, 1933–1944* (Zürich: Büchergilde Gutenberg, 1945).

20. Behrend-Rosenfeld and Rosenfeld, *Leben in zwei Welten*, pp. 54–87.

21. HHL, b MS Ger 91 (93), Verena Hellwig, p. 27, pp. 29–30.

22. HHL, b MS Ger 91 (93), Verena Hellwig, pp. 24–25.

23. HHL, b MS Ger 91 (93), Verena Hellwig, pp. 30–31; HHL, b MS Ger 91 (89), 'John Hay' (Dr Frederick [Fritz] G. Goldberg), p. 50. See also Goeschel, *Suicide in Nazi Germany*.

24. HHL, b MS Ger 91 (93), Verena Hellwig, p. 32.

25. HHL, b MS Ger 91 (93), Verena Hellwig, p. 34, p. 37. I have also discussed these examples in 'Private Lives, Public Faces: On the Social Self in Nazi Germany', in E. Harvey et al. (eds.), *Private Life and Privacy in Nazi Germany* (Cambridge: Cambridge University Press, 2019).

26. HHL, b MS Ger 91 (179), Lotte Popper, p. 28, p. 29, pp. 44–48.

27. HHL, b MS Ger 91 (179), Lotte Popper, p. 34.

28. HHL, b MS Ger 91 (184), Friedrich Reuss, p. 58.

29. HHL, b MS Ger 91 (89), 'John Hay' (Dr Frederick [Fritz] G. Goldberg), p. 50.

30. HHL, b MS Ger 91 (200), Oskar Scherzer, p, 3. Born 31 December 1919, Scherzer grew up in Elbing, East Prussia; his family moved to Vienna when he was a teenager.

31. HHL, b MS Ger 91 (172), Alfred Christian Oppler, pp. 36–37.

32. HHL, b MS Ger 91 (6), Martin Andermann, p. 111.

33. HHL, b MS Ger 91 (179), Lotte Popper, p. 28; HHL, b MS Ger 91 (89), 'John Hay' (Dr Frederick [Fritz] G. Goldberg), p. 52.

34. HHL, b MS Ger 91 (172), Alfred Christian Oppler, p. 27.

35. Cf., e.g., HHL, b MS Ger 91 (219), Margot Spiegel (Luise Stein), p. 29.

36. HHL, b MS Ger 91 (177), Gerta Pfeffer, p. 27.

37. HHL, b MS Ger 91 (107), Hans Kaufman, p. 10.

38. Erving Goffman, *Stigma: Notes on the Management of Spoiled Identity* (Englewood Cliffs, NJ: Prentice-Hall, 1963; reissued Penguin 1990). Some examples in this section have previously been published in slightly different form in M. Fulbrook, 'Subjectivity and History: Approaches to Twentieth-century German Society' (German Historical Institute London: GHIL Annual Lecture, 2016).

39. HHL b MS Ger 91 (81) Walter Gottheil, p. 52.

40. HHL, b MS Ger 91 (54), Dreyfuss, Albert, p. 17.

41. See above, Ch. 2.

42. HHL, b MS Ger 91 (158), Gerhard Miedzwinski, p. 12.

43. Cf. Ray Pahl, *On Friendship* (Cambridge: Polity Press, 2000), chapter 2, 'Friendship, Modernity and Trust' (pp. 45–67), and specifically on the ability 'to believe despite uncertainty' (quoting Barbara Misztal), p. 66.

44. HHL, b MS Ger 91 (18), Elisabeth Bartels, pp. 11–12.

45. HHL b MS Ger 91 (6), Martin Andermann, pp. 111–12.

46. HHL b MS Ger 91 (6), Martin Andermann, pp. 109–11.

47. HHL, b MS Ger 91 (25), Anna Bernheim, p. 1.

48. HHL, b MS Ger 91 (167), Borge Nielsen, p. 65.

49. HHL b MS Ger 91 (1), Georg Abraham, p. 9.

50. HHL b MS Ger 91 (1), Georg Abraham, p. 5, p. 9.

51. HHL, b MS Ger 91 (72), Bruno Gebhard, p. 46, p. 43. Quotations are Gebhard's original slightly stilted and Americanized English.

52. HHL, b MS Ger 91 (72), Bruno Gebhard, pp. 50–51.

53. HHL, b MS Ger 91 (72), Bruno Gebhard, p. 49.

54. HHL, b MS Ger 91 (72), Bruno Gebhard, p. 46, pp. 53–60, photo on p. 58. On the wider context and the professional compromises Gebhard made in the course of his work at the Berlin Exhibition centre, see Sven Schultze, 'Die visuelle Repräsentation der Diktatur. Berlin, sein Messeamt und die Propagandaschauen im Nationalssozialismus', in Rüdiger Hachtmann, Thomas Schaarschmidt, and Winfried Süß (eds.), *Berlin im Nationalsozialismus: Politik und Gesellschaft 1933–1945* (Göttingen: Wallstein, 2011), pp. 113ff. Members of the Bauhaus, later designated 'degenerate art' by the Nazis, were also participants in the construction of these exhibitions.

55. See, e.g., the now classic studies of these areas: Milton Mayer, *They Thought They Were Free: The Germans, 1933–45* (Chicago: University of Chicago Press, 1955; new ed. with an afterword by Richard J. Evans, 2017); William Sheridan Allen, *The Nazi Seizure of Power: The Experience of a Single German Town, 1922–1945* (Brattleboro, VT: Echo Point Books and Media, 1965, rev. ed. 2014); Ian Kershaw, *Popular Opinion and Political Dissent in the Third Reich: Bavaria 1933–1945* (Oxford: Oxford University Press, 1984); Jill Stephenson, *Hitler's Home Front: Wurttemberg under the Nazis* (London: Hambledon Continuum, 2006).

56. Letter of 30 October 1934 from the Konstanz District leadership expressing their support for Mayor Friedrich Hermann in Gailingen, reprinted in Eckhardt

Friedrich and Dagmar Schmieder (eds.), *Die Gailinger Juden. Materialien zur Geschichte der jüdischen Gemeinde Gailingen aus ihrer Blütezeit und den Jahren der gewaltsamen Auflösung* (Konstanz: Arbeitskreis für Regionalgeschichte e.V., 1981), pp. 66–67.

57. HHL b MS Ger 91 (6), Martin Andermann, p. 112.

CHAPTER 4

1. HHL, b MS Ger 91 (177), Gerta Pfeffer, p. 25.

2. Older debates on the 'Nazi social revolution', from the 1960s onwards, were stimulated by the seminal work of David Schoenbaum, *Hitler's Social Revolution: Class and Status in Nazi Germany, 1933–1939* (London: Weidenfeld & Nicolson, 1967; orig. 1966), but from the late twentieth century the focus shifted from class structures and ideology to questions of culture and mentalities. On the Volksgemeinschaft, see particularly: Michael Wildt, *Hitler's Volksgemeinschaft and the Dynamics of Racial Exclusion. Violence against Jews in Provincial Germany, 1919–1939*, trans. Bernard Heise (New York: Berghahn Books, 2012; orig. German 2007); Martina Steber and Bernhard Gotto (eds.), *Visions of Community in Nazi Germany. Social Engineering and Private Lives* (Oxford: Oxford University Press, 2014); Detlef Schmiechen-Ackermann (ed.), *"Volksgemeinschaft": Mythos, wirkungsmächtige soziale Verheißung oder soziale Realität im "Dritten Reich"?* (Paderborn: Ferdinand Schöningh, 2012). For explorations of its significance on the ground, see, e.g., Frank Bajohr and Michael Wildt (eds.), *Volksgemeinschaft. Neue Forschungen zur Gesellschaft des Nationalsozialismus* (Frankfurt: Fischer Taschenbuch, 2009); John Connelly, 'The Uses of Volksgemeinschaft: Letters to the NSDAP Kreisleitung Eisenach, 1939–1940', *Journal of Modern History*, 68:4 (December 1996), pp. 899–930; Jill Stephenson, 'The Volksgemeinschaft and the Problems of Permeability: The Persistence of Traditional Attitudes in Württemberg Villages', *German History*, 34:1 (2016), pp. 49–69. For different views on the value of the concept to historians, see, e.g., Ian Kershaw, '"Volksgemeinschaft". Potenzial und Grenzen eines neuen Forschungskonzepts', *Vierteljahrshefte für Zeitgeschichte* (2011), Heft 1, pp. 1–17; and Michael Wildt, '"Volksgemeinschaft", Eine Antwort auf Ian Kershaw' *Zeithistorische Forschungen/Studies in Contemporary History* 8 (2011), pp. 102–9.

3. See, e.g., Wieland Giebel (ed.), *"Warum ich Nazi wurde". Biogramme früher Nationalsozialisten—Die einzigartige Sammlung des Theodore Abel* (Berlin: Berlin Story, 2018).

4. HHL, b MS Ger 91 (72), Bruno Gebhard, p. 96.

5. André Posteret (ed.), *Hitlerjunge Schall. Die Tagebücher eines jungen Nationalsozialisten* (Munich: dtv, 2016), entry of 10 February 1933, pp. 237–38.

6. On Taut see also above, pp. 78–81, pp. 84–85.

7. HHL, b MS Ger 91 (232), Lore Taut, pp. 52–62.

8. HHL, b MS Ger 91 (232), Lore Taut, pp. 73–82.

9. HHL, b MS Ger 91 (232), Lore Taut, pp. 62–64.

10. HHL, b MS Ger 91 (232), Lore Taut, pp. 85–93.

11. HHL, b MS Ger 91 (232), Lore Taut, pp. 93–98.

12. HHL, b MS Ger 91 (232), Lore Taut, pp. 102 ff., p. 107, p. 108, pp. 153–56.

13. HHL, b MS Ger 91 (232), Lore Taut, p. 156.

14. HHL, b MS Ger 91 (184), Friedrich Reuss, pp. 51–52.

15. HHL, b MS Ger 91 (38), Robert Breusch, p. 41.

16. HHL, b MS Ger 91 (38), Robert Breusch, pp. 45–46.

17. HHL, b MS Ger 91 (262), Barbara Sevin, first MS in file, written in Americanized English following her emigration to the United States, pp. 9–10.

18. HHL, b MS Ger 91 (262), Barbara Sevin, first MS in file, in English, p. 8, pp. 15–16, pp. 17–19; joke from third MS in German in file, 'Mein Leben in Deutschland vor und nach dem 30. Januar 1933', p. 306.

19. HHL, b MS Ger 91 (262), Barbara Sevin, second MS in file, carbon copy of English translation, pp. 1–2.

20. HHL, b MS Ger 91 (262), Barbara Sevin, first MS in file, in English, pp. 21–22.

21. HHL, b MS Ger 91 (262), Barbara Sevin, first MS in file, in English, pp. 23 ff., pp. 29–30, p. 31.

22. HHL, b MS Ger 91 (262), Barbara Sevin, first MS in file, in English, p. 37.

23. HHL, b MS Ger 91 (262), Barbara Sevin, first MS in file, in English, pp. 37–38. Underlining in original.

24. HHL, b MS Ger 91 (262), Barbara Sevin, first MS in file, in English, p. 38, p. 44, p. 46.

25. HHL, b MS Ger 91 (262), Barbara Sevin, first MS in file, in English, pp. 54–57.

26. HHL, b MS Ger 91 (262), Barbara Sevin, 'Mein Leben in Deutschland vor und nach dem 30. Januar 1933' (MS in German), p. 289, pp. 341 ff., p. 344.

27. HHL, b MS Ger 91 (158), Gerhard Miedzwinski, p. 1.

28. HHL, b MS Ger 91 (68), Martin Freudenheim, p. 64.

29. HHL b MS Ger 91 (6), Martin Andermann, p. 109.

30. Heinz Heilbronn, diary extracts reprinted in Eckhardt Friedrich and Dagmar Schmieder (eds.), *Die Gailinger Juden. Materialien zur Geschichte der jüdischen Gemeinde Gailingen aus ihrer Blütezeit und den Jahren der gewaltsamen Auflösung* (Konstanz: Arbeitskreis für Regionalgeschichte e.V., 1981), pp. 69–95.

31. Heilbronn, diary extracts in Friedrich and Schmieder, *Die Gailinger Juden*, pp. 79–83.

32. Heilbronn, diary entry of 8 March 1934, in Friedrich and Schmieder, *Die Gailinger Juden*, p. 88.

33. Heilbronn, diary entry of February 1935 (no date), in Friedrich and Schmieder, *Die Gailinger Juden*, p. 91.

34. Heilbronn, diary entry of April 1935 (no date), in Friedrich and Schmieder, *Die Gailinger Juden*, pp. 92–93.

35. HHL, b MS Ger 91 (219), Margot Spiegel, pp. 1–18. Spiegel was writing in 1939 under the pseudonym of Luise Stein to protect anonymity, in view of the fact that so many friends and family were still in Germany. By 1941, her parents were imprisoned in the Gurs camp in southern France. It is likely that they were subsequently deported and murdered.

36. HHL, b MS Ger 91 (219), Margot Spiegel, pp. 18–20.

37. HHL, b MS Ger 91 (219), Margot Spiegel, p. 4.

38. HHL, b MS Ger 91 (219), Margot Spiegel, pp. 21–23.

39. HHL, b MS Ger 91 (219), Margot Spiegel, p. 24.

40. HHL, b MS Ger 91 (184), Friedrich Reuss, pp. 42–44, pp. 48–49.

41. On the contested significance of denunciations, cf., e.g., Robert Gellately, *The Gestapo and German Society: Enforcing Racial Policy, 1933–1945* (Oxford: Oxford University Press, 1990); Eric Johnson, *The Nazi Terror. Gestapo, Jews and Ordinary Germans* (London: John Murray, 2002; orig. Basic Books, 1999); Robert Gellately, 'Denunciations in Twentieth-Century Germany: Aspects of Self-Policing in the Third Reich and the German Democratic Republic', *Journal of Modern History*, 68:4, Practices of Denunciation in Modern European History, 1789–1989 (December 1996), pp. 931–967; Robert Gellately, 'Denunciations and Nazi Germany: New Insights and Methodological Problems', *Historical Social Research*, 22:3/4 (83/1997), pp. 228–39; Gisela Diewald-Kerkmann, *Politische Denunziation im NS-Regime oder die kleine Macht der "Volksgenossen"* (Bonn: Dietz, 1995); Helga Schubert, *Judasfrauen: zehn Fallgeschichten weiblicher Denunziation im Dritten Reich* (Munich: dtv, 1995); Jan Ruckenbiel, *Soziale Kontrolle im NS-Regime: Protest, Denunziation und Verfolgung; zur Praxis alltäglicher Unterdrückung im Wechselspiel von Bevölkerung und Gestapo* (Köln: Siegen, 2003); Christian Böske, *Denunziationen in der Zeit des Nationalsozialismus und die zivilrechtliche Aufarbeitung in der Nachkriegszeit* (Doctoral diss., Universität Bielefeld, 2008); Klaus-Peter Mallmann, *Die Gestapo, Mythos und Realität* (Darmstadt: Wissenschaftliche Buchgesellschaft, 1995); Klaus-Michael Mallmann and Gerhard Paul, 'Gestapo-Mythos und Realität', in Bernd Florath, Armin Mitter, and Stefan Wolle (eds.), *Die Ohnmacht der Allmächtigen* (Berlin: Ch. Links, 1992).

42. See, e.g., Eric Johnson and Karl-Heinz Reuband, *What We Knew: Terror, Mass Murder and Everyday Life in Nazi Germany* (London: Hodder, 2005); see also my analysis of this in Mary Fulbrook, 'Reframing the Past: Justice, Guilt and Consolidation in East and West Germany after Nazism', *Central European History*, 53:2 (2020), pp. 294–313.

43. Figures from Nikolaus Wachsmann, *KL: A History of the Nazi Concentration Camps* (New York: Little, Brown, 2015), p. 627. On Kristallnacht, see further below, Ch. 7.

44. HHL, b MS Ger 91 (72), Bruno Gebhard, p. 48.

45. HHL, b MS Ger 91 (179), Lotte Popper, p. 32, p. 43.

46. HHL, b MS Ger 91 (8), 'Aralk', pp. 61–62.

47. HHL, b MS Ger 91 (11), Joseph Aust, no pagination, closing paragraph of manuscript.
48. Cf. Gellately, *Gestapo and German Society*.
49. HHL, b MS Ger 91 (184), Friedrich Reuss, pp. 56–57.
50. HHL, b MS Ger 91 (184), Friedrich Reuss, p. 52.
51. HHL, b MS Ger 91 (184), Friedrich Reuss, p. 53.
52. HHL, b MS Ger 91 (184), Friedrich Reuss, p. 52.
53. Cf. the detailed overview of aspects in Catherine Sanderson, *The Bystander Effect: The Psychology of Courage and Inaction* (London: William Collins, 2020).
54. HHL, b MS Ger 91 (181), Ernst Rathgeber, p. 13.
55. HHL, b MS Ger 91 (209), Ernst Schwartzert, p. 49.

CHAPTER 5

1. HHL, b MS Ger 91 (6), Martin Andermann, p. 115.
2. On increasing self-distancing, see, e.g., Peter Fritzsche, *The Turbulent World of Franz Göll* (Cambridge, MA: Harvard University Press, 2011), chapter 5, 'Franz Göll Writes German History' (pp. 132–86). On wider questions around diaries and writing the self, see Janosch Steuwer, *"Ein Drittes Reich, wie ich es auffasse": Politik, Gesellschaft und privates Leben in Tagebüchern 1933–1939* (Göttingen: Wallstein, 2017).
3. See Peter Longerich, *Holocaust. The Nazi Persecution and Murder of the* Jews (Oxford: Oxford University Press, 2010), pp. 57–61.
4. *Deutschland-Berichte der Sozialdemokratischen Partei Deutschlands (Sopade)*, Zweiter Jahrgang, 1935 (Frankfurt am Main: Petra Nettelbeck, 1980), p. 986, pp. 996–97.
5. *Deutschland-Berichte*, 1935, pp. 996–97.
6. For a rare personal account, see Theodor Michael, *Black German. An Afro-German Life in the Twentieth Century*, trans. Eve Rosenhaft (Liverpool: Liverpool University Press, 2017).
7. Guenter Lewy, *The Nazi Persecution of the Gypsies* (Oxford: Oxford University Press, 2000), p. 55. See also Michael Zimmermann, *Rassenutopie und Genozid. Die nationalsozialistische 'Lösung der Zigeunerfrage'* (Hamburg: Hans Christians, 1996). This is a highly contentious topic; even the very name to be used is disputed, as are comparisons with the fate of the Jews.
8. This woman wished to remain anonymous, but told me her family story and assured me that she knew of others with similar stories.
9. Cf. Jeremy Noakes, 'The Development of Nazi Policy towards the German-Jewish "Mischlinge" 1933–1945', *Leo Baeck Institute Year Book*, 34 (London: Baeck Institute, 1989), pp. 291–354.
10. Scare quotes are useful to indicate the absurdity of the imposed categories, but since these soon came into common parlance and became social realities the

scare quotes may often be dropped. As I have noted, using original German terms may make this seem less problematic.

11. HHL, b MS Ger 91 (172), Alfred Christian Oppler, p. 45.

12. Cf. James Q. Whitman, *Hitler's American Model: The United States and the Making of Nazi Race Law* (Princeton, NJ: Princeton University Press, 2017); S. Jonathan Wiesen, 'American Lynching in the Nazi Imagination: Race and Extra-Legal Violence in 1930s Germany', *German History,* 36:1 (2018), pp. 38–59.

13. HHL, b MS Ger 91 (209), Ernst Schwartzert, pp. 47–48.

14. HHL, b MS Ger 91 (89), 'John Hay' (Dr Frederick [Fritz] G. Goldberg), p. 51.

15. HHL, b MS Ger 91 (181), Ernst Rathgeber, p. 11–12.

16. HHL, b MS Ger 91 (209), Ernst Schwartzert, p. 48, p. 50.

17. HHL, b MS Ger 91 (209), Ernst Schwartzert, pp. 61–63.

18. HHL, b MS Ger 91 (209), Ernst Schwartzert, p. 46.

19. HHL, b MS Ger 91 (118), Kosterlitz, Hans, p. 27.

20. HHL, b MS Ger 91 (184), Friedrich Reuss, p. 58.

21. HHL, b MS Ger 91 (219), Margot Spiegel (Luise Stein), pp. 24–26.

22. HHL, b MS Ger 91 (8), 'Aralk', p. 55, pp. 63–64.

23. HHL, b MS Ger 91 (89), 'John Hay' (Dr Frederick [Fritz] G. Goldberg), pp. 56–57.

24. HHL, b MS Ger 91 (179), Lotte Popper, pp. 66–74.

25. HHL, b MS Ger 91 (172), Alfred Christian Oppler, pp. 52–54.

26. HHL, b MS Ger 91 (172), Alfred Christian Oppler, pp. 56–57.

27. HHL, b MS Ger 91 (178), Max Moses Polke, p. 92.

28. HHL, b MS Ger 91 (184), Friedrich Reuss, pp. 54–55, p. 58.

29. HHL, b MS Ger 91 (209), Ernst Schwartzert, p. 17, pp. 63 ff., pp. 66–67.

30. HHL, b MS Ger 91 (1), Georg Abraham, p. 6, p. 9, p. 10.

31. HHL, b MS Ger 91 (1), Georg Abraham, p. 6.

32. HHL, b MS Ger 91 (1), Georg Abraham, pp. 10–11.

33. Friedrich Reck, *Diary of a Man in Despair*, transl. Paul Rubens (New York: New York Review of Books, 2013; first published 1947), entry of 11 August 1936, p. 15.

34. HHL, b MS Ger 91 (72), Bruno Gebhard, English and German as in original, pp. 67 ff., p. 78, p. 84.

35. HHL, b MS Ger 91 (72), Bruno Gebhard, p. 90, p. 95. Background and Goebbels quotation in Sven Schultze, 'Die visuelle Repräsentation der Diktatur. Berlin, sein Messeamt und die Propagandaschauen im Nationalsozialismus', in Rüdiger Hachtmann, Thomas Schaarschmidt, and Winfried Süß (eds.), *Berlin im Nationalsozialismus: Politik und Gesellschaft 1933–1945* (Göttingen: Wallstein, 2011), (pp. 113–131), p. 124.

36. Reck, *Diary of a Man in Despair*, entry of 11 August 1936, p. 16.

37. HHL, b MS Ger 91 (72), Bruno Gebhard, pp. 71–75, pp. 60–63.

38. HHL, b MS Ger 91 (72), Bruno Gebhard, p. 95.

39. HHL, b MS Ger 91 (5), Eugen Altmann, pp. 48–49.

CHAPTER 6

1. HHL, b MS Ger 91 (72), Bruno Gebhard, p. 98, pp. 100–5.

2. HHL, b MS Ger 91 (38), Robert Breusch, pp. 52–57.

3. HHL, b MS Ger 91 (38), Robert Breusch, pp. 55–57.

4. HHL, b MS Ger 91 (38), Robert Breusch, p. 58.

5. HHL, b MS Ger 91 (38), Robert Breusch, pp. 62–65.

6. HHL, b MS Ger 91 (38), Robert Breusch, p. 62.

7. HHL, b MS Ger 91 (161), Erich Haller-Munk, pp. 12–15.

8. HHL, b MS Ger 91 (161), Erich Haller-Munk, p. 15.

9. HHL, b MS Ger 91 (161), Erich Haller-Munk, p. 16

10. HHL, b MS Ger 91 (161), Erich Haller-Munk, pp. 16–17.

11. HHL, b MS Ger 91 (161), Erich Haller-Munk, p. 18.

12. HHL, b MS Ger 91 (161), Erich Haller-Munk, p. 18.

13. HHL, b MS Ger 91 (179), Lotte Popper, pp. 74–80.

14. HHL, b MS Ger 91 (179), Lotte Popper, pp. 80–82.

15. HHL, b MS Ger 91 (179), Lotte Popper, pp. 83–86.

16. HHL, b MS Ger 91 (179), Lotte Popper, pp. 86–87.

17. HHL, b MS Ger 91 (184), Dr F. Reuss, pp. 59–62.

18. The phrase, which has subsequently developed a far broader remit, originated with Benedict Anderson, *Imagined Communities. Reflections on the Origin and Spread of Nationalism* (London: Verso, 1983).

19. Jürgen Ernst Kroeger, *So war es. Ein Bericht* (Im Selbstverlag, 1989), pp. 11–13.

20. Kroeger, *So war es*, pp. 13–16. See further chapter 10.

21. Herbert S. Levine, *Hitler's Free City. A History of the Nazi Party in Danzig, 1925–39* (Chicago: University of Chicago Press, 1973), p. 127.

22. HHL, b MS Ger 91 (15), Alice Baerwald, pp. 32–33. On Jewish experiences in Danzig during the Nazi period, see also, e.g.: Hans L. Leonhardt, *Nazi Conquest of Danzig* (Chicago: University of Chicago Press, 1942); Gershon C. Bacon, 'Danzig Jewry: A Short History', in *Danzig 1939, Treasures of a Destroyed Community: The Jewish Museum, New York* (Detroit: Wayne State University Press, 1980), pp. 25–35; Samuel Echt, *Die Geschichte der Juden in Danzig* (Leer, Ostfriesland: Gerhard Rautenberg, 1972).

23. HHL, b MS Ger 91 (15), Alice Baerwald, p. 31.

24. HHL, b MS Ger 91 (130), Gertrud Lederer, p. 1, p. 14.

25. HHL, b MS Ger 91 (130), Gertrud Lederer, pp. 19–25.

26. HHL, b MS Ger 91 (130), Gertrud Lederer, pp. 25–31.

27. HHL, b MS Ger 91 (130), Gertrud Lederer, pp. 32–33.

28. HHL, b MS Ger 91 (92), Edmund Heilpern, pp. 122–26.

29. HHL, b MS Ger 91 (92), Edmund Heilpern, pp. 126–27. Irene Harand, *Hitler's Lies: An Answer to Hitler's "Mein Kampf"* (Mumbai: Jaico, 2010; orig. *Sein Kampf*, 1935).

30. HHL, b MS Ger 91 (92), Edmund Heilpern, pp. 126–30.

31. HHL, b MS Ger 91 (130), Gertrud Lederer, pp. 79–80.

32. HHL, b MS Ger 91 (80), Arthur Goldstein, pp. 3–5.
33. HHL, b MS Ger 91 (100), Stephen Jaray, pp. 1–10, pp. 25–28, pp. 69–70.
34. HHL, b MS Ger 91 (100), Stephen Jaray, p. 100.
35. HHL, b MS Ger 91 (92), Edmund Heilpern, p. 130, p. 132, p. 133, pp. 137–38.
36. HHL, b MS Ger 91 (92), Edmund Heilpern, p. 74, p. 139.
37. HHL, b MS Ger 91 (80). Arthur Goldstein, pp. 5–6.
38. Gertrude Schneider, *Exile and Destruction. The Fate of Austrian Jews, 1938–1945* (Westport, CT: Praeger, 1995), p. 15.
39. HHL, b MS Ger 91 (130), Gertrud Lederer, pp. 83–84.
40. HHL, b MS Ger 91 (130), Gertrud Lederer, p. 91.
41. HHL, b MS Ger 91 (130), Gertrud Lederer, p. 78. See also, e.g., HHL, b MS Ger 91 (92), Edmund Heilpern, p. 141.
42. https://www.lbi.org/1938projekt/detail/unbearable-despair/.
43. HHL, b MS Ger 91 (38), Robert Breusch, letters, pp. 66–67, p. 67, p. 65.
44. See, e.g., Leonhardt, *Nazi Conquest of Danzig*; Levine, *Hitler's Free City*; Catherine Epstein, *Model Nazi. Arthur Greiser and the Occupation of Western Poland* (Oxford: Oxford University Press, 2010).
45. HHL, b MS Ger 91 (15), Alice Baerwald, pp. 47–49.
46. HHL, b MS Ger 91 (15), Alice Baerwald, p. 37.
47. HHL, b MS Ger 91 (15), Alice Baerwald, pp. 41–42.
48. HHL, b MS Ger 91 (15), Alice Baerwald, pp. 38–39, pp. 43–44.
49. HHL, b MS Ger 91 (15), Alice Baerwald, p. 41.
50. HHL, b MS Ger 91 (15), Alice Baerwald, pp. 43–47, pp. 55–56.
51. HHL, b MS Ger 91 (15), Alice Baerwald, p. 54.
52. HHL, b MS Ger 91 (217), Karl (Charles) Sorkin.
53. HHL, b MS Ger 91 (217), Karl (Charles) Sorkin, pp. 60–61.
54. HHL, b MS Ger 91 (217), Karl (Charles) Sorkin, pp. 61–62.
55. HHL, b MS Ger 91 (217), Karl (Charles) Sorkin, pp. 62–63.
56. HHL, b MS Ger 91 (217), Karl (Charles) Sorkin, pp. 62–66.
57. HHL, b MS Ger 91 (217), Karl (Charles) Sorkin, p. 67.

CHAPTER 7

1. Testimony written by Jenny Bohrer in exile in Palestine in 1943, reprinted in Eckhardt Friedrich and Dagmar Schmieder (eds.), *Die Gailinger Juden. Materialien zur Geschichte der jüdischen Gemeinde Gailingen aus ihrer Blütezeit und den Jahren der gewaltsamen Auflösung* (Konstanz: Arbeitskreis für Regionalgeschichte e.V., 1981), pp. 96–109.
2. Testimony written by Jenny Bohrer in exile in Palestine in 1943, reprinted in Friedrich and Schmieder, *Die Gailinger Juden*, pp. 96–109.
3. See further: Wolfgang Benz, *Gewalt im November 1938. Die "Reichskristallnacht". Initial zum Holocaust* (Berlin: Metropol, 2018); Saul Friedländer, *The Years of Persecution: Nazi Germany and the Jews, 1933–1939* (London: Weidenfeld

& Nicolson, 1997; Phoenix, 2007), chapter 9, pp. 269–305; Dieter Obst, *"Reichskristallnacht". Ursachen und Verlauf des antisemitischen Pogroms vom November 1938* (Frankfurt: Peter Lang, 1991).

4. Evan Burr Bukey, *Hitler's Austria. Popular Sentiment in the Nazi Era, 1938–1945* (Chapel Hill: University of North Carolina Press, 2000), p. 144.

5. Cf. Ulrich Baumann and Francois Guesnet, 'Kristallnacht—Pogrom or State Terror? A Terminological Reflection', in Wolf Gruner and Steven Ross (eds.), *New Perspectives on Kristallnacht: After 80 Years, the Nazi Pogrom in Global Comparison* (West Lafayette, IN: Purdue University Press, 2019).

6. Alan Steinweis, *Kristallnacht 1938* (Cambridge, MA: Harvard University Press, 2009).

7. Edith Raim, *Nazi Crimes against Jews and German Post-war Justice. The West German Judicial System during Allied Occupation (1945–1949)* (Oldenbourg: De Gruyter, 2015), 'The Prosecution of the Pogrom' (pp. 186–265). See also Andreas Eichmüller, 'Die Strafverfolgung von NS-Verbrechen durch westdeutsche Justizbehörden seit 1945. Eine Zahlenbilanz', *Vierteljahrshefte für Zeitgeschichte*, 56 (2008), Heft 4, pp. 621–40.

8. See, e.g.: David Bankier, *The Germans and the Final Solution. Public Opinion under Nazism* (Oxford: Blackwell, 1992); Wolfgang Benz, 'The November Pogrom of 1938: Participation, Applause, Disapproval', in Christoph Hoffmann, Werner Bergmann, and Helmut Walser Smith (eds.), *Exclusionary Violence. Antisemitic Riots in Modern German History* (Ann Arbor: University of Michigan Press, 2002), pp. 141–59; Wolf Gruner, 'Indifference? Participation and Protest as Individual Responses to the Persecution of the Jews as Revealed in Berlin Police Logs and Trial Records, 1933–45', in Susanna Schrafstetter and Alan E. Steinweis (eds.), *The Germans and the Holocaust. Popular Responses to the Persecution and Murder of the Jews* (New York: Berghahn, 2016), pp. 59–83.

9. Historians disagree on how to characterize and interpret apparently impassive reactions. Cf.: Otto Dov Kulka and Aron Rodrigue, 'The German Population and the Jews in the Third Reich', *Yad Vashem Studies*, 16 (1984), pp. 421–35; Ian Kershaw, 'Preface to the Second Edition', *Popular Opinion and Political Dissent* (Oxford: Oxford University Press, 1983; 2nd ed., 2002); Ian Kershaw, 'German Popular Opinion and the "Jewish Question", 1939–1943: Some Further Reflections', in Arnold Paucker (ed.), *Die Juden im nationalsozialistischen Deutschland 1933–1943* (Tübingen: J. C. B. Mohr, 1986), pp. 365–86; Frank Bajohr, 'Über die Entwicklung eines schlechten Gewissens. Die deutsche Bevölkerung und die Deportationen 1941–1945', in Birthe Kundrus (ed.), *Die Deportation der Juden aus Deutschland: Pläne—Praxis—Reaktionen 1938–1945* (Göttingen: Wallstein, 2004), pp. 180–95.

10. Cf. Bankier, *The Germans and the Final Solution*, pp. 85–88; Kershaw, *Popular Opinion and Political Dissent*, pp. 268–69; and Bukey, *Hitler's Austria*, pp. 145–47.

11. HHL, b MS Ger 91 (5), Eugen Altmann, p. 53.

12. HHL, b MS Ger 91 (137), Martha Lewinsohn, p. 6.

13. See also Alan Steinweis, 'The Perpetrators of the November 1938 Pogrom through German-Jewish Eyes', in Thomas Pegelow Kaplan, Jürgen Matthäus, and Mark Hornburg (eds.), *Beyond 'Ordinary Men'. Christopher R. Browning and Holocaust Historiography* (Paderborn: Brill, Ferdinand Schöningh, 2019), chapter 4 (pp. 56–65), p. 59.

14. HHL, b MS Ger 91 (3), Erna Albersheim, p. 64.

15. HHL, b MS Ger 91 (3), Erna Albersheim, p. 63.

16. HHL, b MS Ger 91 (3), Erna Albersheim, p. 64.

17. HHL, b MS Ger 91 (3), Erna Albersheim, p. 57.

18. HHL, b MS Ger 91 (3), Erna Albersheim, p. 59.

19. Jochen Klepper, *Unter dem Schatten deiner Flügel. Aus den Tagebüchern der Jahre 1932–1942* (Stuttgart: Deutsche Verlags-Anstalt, 1956; repr. 1983), entries of 10 and 11 November 1938, pp. 675–76.

20. *Deutschland-Berichte der Sozialdemokratischen Partei Deutschlands (Sopade)*, Fünfter Jahrgang, 1938 (Frankfurt am Main: Petra Nettelbeck, 1980), p. 1191.

21. *Deutschland-Berichte*, Fünfter Jahrgang, 1938, p. 1191.

22. *Deutschland-Berichte*, Fünfter Jahrgang, 1938, p. 1191.

23. HHL, b MS Ger 91 (3), Erna Albersheim, p. 67.

24. *Deutschland-Berichte*, p. 1188.

25. HHL, b MS Ger 91 (3), Erna Albersheim, p. 67.

26. Willy Cohn, *Kein Recht, Nirgends. Tagebuch vom Untergang des Breslauer Judentums 1933–41*, ed. Norbert Conrads (Köln: Böhlau, 2006), Vol. 2, 1938–41, entry of 11 November 1938, p. 539.

27. Cohn, *Kein Recht, Nirgends*, 13 November 1938, p. 541.

28. Cohn, *Kein Recht, Nirgends*, 14 November 1938, p. 544.

29. Cohn, *Kein Recht, Nirgends*, 16 November 1938, p. 546.

30. Cohn, *Kein Recht, Nirgends*, 16 November 1938, p. 547, possibly based on news of a sermon by Domprobst Bernhard Lichtenberg in St Hedwig's cathedral in Berlin.

31. Cohn, *Kein Recht, Nirgends*, 19 November 1938, p. 549.

32. HHL, b MS Ger 91 (217), Karl (Charles) Sorkin, p. 68.

33. Benz, *Gewalt im November 1938*; *Deutschland-Berichte*, Fünfter Jahrgang, 1938, p. 1189.

34. HHL, b MS Ger 91 (3), Erna Albersheim, p. 61.

35. HHL, b MS Ger 91 (91), Carl Hecht, p. 8.

36. HHL, b MS Ger 91 (172), Alfred Oppler, p. 70.

37. HHL, b MS Ger 91 (172), Alfred Oppler, p. 72.

38. HHL, b MS Ger 91 (5), Eugen Altmann, p. 43.

39. HHL, b MS Ger 91 (172), Alfred Oppler, p. 79.

40. HHL, b MS Ger 91 (209), Ernst Schwartzert, pp. 75–76.

41. Ruth Andreas-Friedrich, *Der Schattenmann. Tagebuchaufzeichnungen von Ruth Andreas-Friedrich 1938–1948* (Frankfurt am Main: Suhrkamp, 2000; orig. 1947 and 1984), p. 28.

42. Andreas-Friedrich, *Der Schattenmann*, p. 30.

43. Andreas-Friedrich, *Der Schattenmann*, p. 31.

44. Andreas-Friedrich, *Der Schattenmann*, p. 34.

45. Andreas-Friedrich, *Der Schattenmann*, p. 35.

46. Ruth Andreas-Friedrich, *Berlin Underground 1938–1945*, trans. by Barrows Mussey, introductory note by Joel Sayre (New York: Henry Holt, 1947), p. 25.

47. Wolf Gruner, 'Indifference? Participation and Protest as Individual Responses to the Persecution of the Jews as Revealed in Berlin Police Logs and Trial Records, 1933–45', in Susanna Schrafstetter and Alan E. Steinweis (eds.), *The Germans and the Holocaust. Popular Responses to the Persecution and Murder of the Jews* (New York: Berghahn, 2016), pp. 59–83.

48. See for published examples selected from the Harvard archive collection in: Margarete Limberg and Hubert Rübsaat (eds.), *Nach dem 'Anschluss'. Berichte österreichischer EmigrantInnen aus dem Archiv der Harvard University* (Vienna: Mandelbaum, 2013); and Uta Gerhardt and Thomas Karlauf (eds.), *Nie mehr zurück in dieses Land. Augenzeugen berichten über die Novemberpogrome 1938* (Berlin: Ullstein, Propyläen, 2009).

49. See particularly Bukey, *Hitler's Austria*, chapter 7, pp. 131–52.

50. HHL, b MS Ger 91 (4), Henry Albert, pp. 45ff. p. 52, p. 62, p. 71. (I have slightly corrected the grammar in his non-native English to read more smoothly.)

51. HHL, b MS Ger 91 (15), Alice Baerwald, pp. 54–58.

52. Klepper, *Unter dem Schatten deiner Flügel*, entries of 17 and 19 November 1938, p. 679, p. 680.

53. HHL, b MS Ger 91 (172), Alfred Oppler, pp. 75–76.

54. HHL, b MS Ger 91 (181), Ernst Rathgeber, p. 23.

55. HHL, b MS Ger 91 (5), Eugen Altmann, pp. 42–43, pp. 51–52.

56. HHL, b MS Ger 91 (3), Erna Albersheim, pp. 64–65.

57. *Deutschland-Berichte*, Fünfter Jahrgang, 1938, p. 1188.

58. Cohn, *Kein Recht, Nirgends*, 13 November 1938, p. 542.

59. Cohn, *Kein Recht, Nirgends*, 15 November 1938, p. 544.

60. HHL, b MS Ger 91 (8), 'Aralk', p. 80.

61. HHL, b MS Ger 91 (80), Arthur Goldstein, pp. 6–7, p. 9.

62. HHL, b MS Ger 91 (1), Georg Abraham.

63. HHL, b MS Ger 91 (1), Georg Abraham, pp. 11–13.

64. HHL, b MS Ger 91 (1), Georg Abraham, p. 13.

65. HHL, b MS Ger 91 (1), Georg Abraham, pp. 15–16.

66. HHL, b MS Ger 91 (1), Georg Abraham, p. 17.

67. See the classic work by Ian Kershaw, *The Hitler Myth: Image and Reality in the Third Reich* (Oxford: Oxford University Press, 1987).

68. HHL, b MS Ger 91 (209), Ernst Schwartzert, pp. 75–82.

69. HHL, b MS Ger 91 (181), Ernst Rathgeber, p. 17.

70. *Deutschland-Berichte*, Sechster Jahrgang 1939, p. 926.

CHAPTER 8

1. Figures summarized in Alan Steinweis, *The People's Dictatorship. A History of Nazi Germany* (Cambridge: Cambridge University Press, 2023), p. 147.

2. HHL, b MS Ger 91 (177), Gerta Pfeffer. She was born in Chemnitz, so although she does not clarify where she was living before her expulsion over the Polish border it is likely that this is where she went to say her farewells on her way back through Germany towards England.

3. HHL, b MS Ger 91 (177), Gerta Pfeffer, p. 62.

4. Hertha Nathorff, *Das Tagebuch der Hertha Nathorff. Berlin—New York, Aufzeichnungen 1933 bis 1945*, ed. Wolfgang Benz (Frankfurt am Main: Fischer, 2010), diary entry of 16 November 1938, p. 129.

5. HHL, b MS Ger 91 (217), Karl (Charles) Sorkin, pp. 71–72.

6. HHL, b MS Ger 91 (217), Karl (Charles) Sorkin, p. 73.

7. Frequently reproduced; this translation from Yitzhak Arad, Israel Gutman, and Abraham Margaliot (eds.), *Documents on the Holocaust* (Lincoln and Jerusalem: University of Nebraska Press and Yad Vashem; updated ed. 1999, trans. Lea Ben Dor), p. 344.

8. HHL, b MS Ger 91 (15), Alice Baerwald, p. 39.

9. HHL, b MS Ger 91 (15), Alice Baerwald, p. 66.

10. HHL, b MS Ger 91 (15), Alice Baerwald, pp. 71–72.

11. See also Samuel Echt, *Die Geschichte der Juden in Danzig* (Leer, Ostfriesland: Gerhard Rautenberg, 1972), p. 188.

12. HHL, b MS Ger 91 (15), Alice Baerwald, pp. 72–75, pp. 78–80.

13. Eckhardt Friedrich and Dagmar Schmieder (eds.), *Die Gailinger Juden. Materialien zur Geschichte der jüdischen Gemeinde Gailingen aus ihrer Blütezeit und den Jahren der gewaltsamen Auflösung* (Konstanz: Arbeitskreis für Regionalgeschichte e.V., 1981), pp. 96–98.

14. HHL, b MS Ger 91 (161), Erich Haller-Munk, pp. 18–19.

15. https://www.kiel.de/de/kiel_zukunft/stadtgeschichte/stolpersteine/stolpe rsteine/_biografien/haller-munck_stolpersteine.pdf, last accessed 24 July 2020. More generally, see: Christian Goeschel, *Suicide in Nazi Germany* (Oxford: Oxford University Press, 2009).

16. Selections in abridged English translation available in Victor Klemperer, *I Shall Bear Witness: The Diaries of Victor Klemperer 1933–41* (London: Weidenfeld & Nicolson, 2009); *To the Bitter End: The Diaries of Victor Klemperer 1942–45* (London: Weidenfeld & Nicolson, 2001); and *The Lesser Evil: The Diaries of Victor Klemperer, 1945–1959* (London: Weidenfeld & Nicolson, 2004).

17. Beate Meyer, *"Jüdische Mischlinge". Rassenpolitik und Verfolgungserfahrung 1933–1945* (Hamburg: Dölling & Galitz, 1999); Jeremy Noakes, 'The Development of Nazi Policy towards the German-Jewish "Mischlinge" 1933–1945' *LBI Year Book* 34 (1989), pp. 291–354; Akim Jah, *Die Deportation der Juden aus Berlin. Die nationalsozialistische Vernichtungspolitik und das Sammellager Große Hamburger Straße* (Berlin: Be.Bra Wissenschaft, 2013), p. 235, fn. 109, and p. 239, fn. 132,

based on Meyer, p. 25; see also Ursula Büttner, 'The persecution of Christian-Jewish Families in the Third Reich' in *LBI Year Book* 34 (1989), pp. 267–89.

18. Jochen Klepper, Unter dem Schatten deiner Flügel. *Aus den Tagebüchern der Jahre 1932–1942* (Stuttgart: Deutsche Verlags-Anstalt, 1956; repr. 1983), entries of 21, 24, and 25 November 1938, p. 681, p. 684, p. 685.

19. Else Behrend-Rosenfeld und Siegfried Rosenfeld, *Leben in zwei Welten. Tagebücher eines jüdischen Paares in Deutschland und im Exil*, Erich Kasberger and Marita Kraus (eds.) (Munich: Volk, 2011).

20. HHL, b MS Ger 91 (3), Erna Albersheim, p. 8.

21. HHL, b MS Ger 91 (3), Erna Albersheim, p. 71.

22. HHL, b MS Ger 91 (93), Verena Hellwig, pp. 41–45.

23. HHL, b MS Ger 91 (93), Verena Hellwig, p. 46.

24. HHL, b MS Ger 91 (93), Verena Hellwig, pp. 53–54

25. HHL, b MS Ger 91 (93), Verena Hellwig, p. 66.

26. See Nicholas Stargardt, *The German War: A Nation under Arms, 1939–45* (London: Bodley Head, 2015).

27. Wolfhilde von König, in Sven Keller (ed.), *Kriegstagebuch einer jungen Nationalsozialistin. Die Aufzeichnungen Wolfhilde von Königs 1939–1946* (Oldenbourg: De Gruyter, 2015).

28. Wolfhilde von König, *Kriegstagebuch*, entries of 1 September 1939, 8 September 1939, p. 31, p. 32.

29. Klaus-Michael Mallmann, Jochen Böhler, and Jürgen Matthäus (eds.), *Einsatzgruppen in Polen. Darstellung und Dokumentation* (Darmstadt: Wissenschaftliche Buchgesellschaft, 2008); Stephan Lehnstaedt and Jochen Boehler (eds.), *Die Berichte der Einsatzgruppen aus Polen 1939* (Berlin: Metropol, 2013). For an account of the synagogue burning and terror in Będzin, see Mary Fulbrook, *A Small Town near Auschwitz: Ordinary Nazis and the Holocaust* (Oxford: Oxford University Press, 2012).

30. Herman Kruk, *The Last Days of the Jerusalem of Lithuania. Chronicles from the Vilna Ghetto and the Camps, 1939–1944*, ed. and intro. Benjamin Harshav, trans. Barbara Harshav, Yivo Institute for Jewish Research (New Haven, CT: Yale University Press, 2002), pp. 1–23.

31. David Gaunt and Paul Levine, 'Introduction', in David Gaunt, Paul Levine, and Laura Palosuo (eds.), *Collaboration and Resistance during the Holocaust. Belarus, Estonia, Latvia, Lithuania* (Bern: Peter Lang, 2004), (pp. 9–32), p. 14.

32. Explored in detail in chapter 10.

33. Jochen Böhler, '"Tragische Verstrickung" oder Auftakt zum Vernnichtungskrieg? Die Wehrmacht in Polen', in Klaus-Michael Mallmann and Bogdan Musial (eds.), *Genesis des Genozids: Polen 1939–1941* (Darmstadt: Wissenschaftliche Buchgesellschaft, 2004), pp. 36–56.

34. Alexander Rossino, 'Nazi Anti-Jewish Policy during the Polish Campaign: The Case of the Einsatzgruppe von Woyrsch', *German Studies Review*, 24:1 (February 2001), pp. 35–53.

35. Report of Einsatzgruppe II, 6 September 1939, reprinted in Lehnstaedt and Boehler, *Berichte der Einsatzgruppen aus Polen*, pp. 51–52, quote from p. 52.
36. Telegram received by Admiral Wilhelm Canaris from 'a subordinate in Rzeszów', quoted in Rossino, 'Nazi Anti-Jewish Policy during the Polish campaign', pp. 42–43.
37. Alexander Rossino, *Hitler Strikes Poland: Blitzkrieg, Ideology and Atrocity* (Lawrence: University Press of Kansas, 2003).
38. Arthur Greiser, *Gauleiter und Reichsstatthalter im Reichsgau Wartheland. Der Aufbau im Osten* (Jena: Gustav Fischer, 1942), p. 6; see also Catherine Epstein, *Model Nazi. Arthur Greiser and the Occupation of Western Poland* (Oxford: Oxford University Press 2010).
39. Christopher Browning, with a contribution by Jürgen Matthäus, *The Origins of the Final Solution. The Evolution of Nazi Jewish Policy 1939–42* (London: Random House, 2004), chapter 3.
40. Figure of 1 million Poles taken from Isabel Heinemann, *"Rasse, Siedlung, deutsches Blut". Die Rasse- und Siedlungshauptamt der SS und die rassenpolitische Neuordnung Europas* (Göttingen: Wallstein, 2003), p. 9. See also Michael Alberti, *Die Verfolgung und Vernichtung der Juden im Reichsgau Wartheland 1939–1945* (Harrassowitz, 2006); Fulbrook, *A Small Town near Auschwitz*; Elizabeth Harvey, *Women and the Nazi East: Agents and Witnesses of Germanization* (New Haven: Yale University Press, 2003).
41. Wolfhilde von König, *Kriegstagebuch*, entries of 16 November and 2 December 1939, pp. 39–40, p. 41.
42. See also Harvey, *Women and the Nazi East*; and on Kroeger see also above, p. 66, pp. 182–83.
43. Jürgen Ernst Kroeger, *So war es. Ein Bericht* (Im Selbstverlag, 1989), pp. 17–24.
44. Kroeger, *So war es*, p. 25.
45. Kroeger, *So war es*, p. 26.
46. Kroeger, *So war es*, pp. 35–37.
47. Kroeger, *So war es*, p. 35, p. 37.
48. Alexander Hohenstein (pseudonym), *Wartheländisches Tagebuch* (Munich: dtv, 1963). I discuss this further in M. Fulbrook, 'Nazis mit reinem Gewissen? Zivile Funktionsträger und der Holocaust', in Wolfgang Bialas and Lothar Fritze (eds.), *Ideologie und Moral im Nationalsozialismus* (Göttingen: Vandenhoeck & Ruprecht, 2014), pp. 129–51.
49. Film | Accession Number: 1996.166 | RG Number: RG-60.5033 | Film ID: 3352, 3353, 3354, accessible at https://collections.ushmm.org/search/catalog/irn1004243.
50. Testimony written by Betty Friesländer-Bloch in 1970, reprinted in Eckhardt Friedrich and Dagmar Schmieder (eds.), *Die Gailinger Juden. Materialien zur Geschichte der jüdischen Gemeinde Gailingen aus ihrer Blütezeit und den Jahren der gewaltsamen Auflösung* (Konstanz: Arbeitskreis für Regionalgeschichte e.V., 1981), pp. 111–21.

51. Testimony written by Betty Friesländer-Bloch in 1970, reprinted in Eckhardt Friedrich and Dagmar Schmieder, *Die Gailinger Juden*, pp. 111–21.

52. 'Der Bericht von G.M.', in Else Rosenfeld and Gertrud Luckner (eds.), *Lebenszeichen aus Piaski. Briefe Deportierter aus dem Distrikt Lublin 1940–1943* (Munich: Biederstein, 1968), pp. 27–31, p. 28. On the Stettin deportation, see Browning, *Origins of the Final Solution,* pp. 64–65.

53. Else Rosenfeld, 'Vorwort', in Rosenfeld and Luckner, *Lebenszeichen aus Piaski*, pp. 19–25.

54. This attempt to help those she saw as being in greater need, even when she did not know them personally, persisted through the postwar decades. I became acquainted with Margarethe Lachmund when, before starting university, I lived for a while in Berlin. There, a part-time Saturday job was to pick up from Margarethe Lachmund large parcels of fresh fruit (predominantly grapefruits) to take to the post office, to be sent to people in the communist GDR where citrus fruits were a scarce luxury.

55. Rosenfeld and Luckner, *Lebenszeichen aus Piaski*, pp. 135–63.

56. Rosenfeld and Luckner, *Lebenszeichen aus Piaski*, pp. 99–119.

57. Rosenfeld and Luckner, *Lebenszeichen aus Piaski*, pp. 125–29.

58. Rosenfeld and Luckner, *Lebenszeichen aus Piaski*, pp. 129–31.

59. Friedrich Kellner, *My Opposition: The Diary of Friedrich Kellner—A German against the Third Reich* (Cambridge: Cambridge University Press, 2018), entries of 6 October 1939, 12 August 1942, and 24 August 1942, p. 43, p. 191, p. 194.

60. Hermann Stresau, *Als lebe man nur unter Vorbehalt, Tagebücher aus den Kriegsjahren 1939–1945*, ed. Peter Graf and Ulrich Faure (Stuttgart: Klett-Cotta, 2021), entry of 14 September 1941, p. 171.

61. Behrend-Rosenfeld and Rosenfeld, *Leben in zwei Weltenz*, diary entry of 21 September 1941, pp. 140–42; entry of Sunday, 26 October 1941, p. 143.

62. Heinz Boberach (ed.), *Meldungen aus dem Reich. Die geheimen Lageberichte des Sicherheitsdienstes der SS 1938–1945* (Herrsching: Manfred Pawlak, 1984), Vol. 8 (18 August 1941–15 December 1941), No. 227 (9 October 1941), p. 2849.

63. See, e.g., Ruth Klüger, *Weiterleben. Eine Jugend* (Munich: dtv, 1994).

64. BArch DY 55/V278/96, Hirsch, Landeshauptstadt Halle (Fols. 13–16), Fol. 14; Ludwig S., 'Meine Erlebnisse während des Naziregimes' Mücheln, 3.5.48, Fols. 11a–11b.

65. Wolfgang Benz (ed.), with Volker Dahm, Konrad Kwiet, Günter Plum, Clemens Vollnhals, and Juliane Wetzel, *Die Juden in Deutschland 1933–1945. Leben unter nationalsozialistischer Herrschaft* (Munich: C.H. Beck, 1988), 'Die Kennzeichnung mit dem Judenstern im Herbst 1941', pp. 614–31.

66. Wolfhilde von König, *Kriegstagebuch*, pp. 90 ff., pp., 92–93.

67. Ruth Andreas-Friedrich, *Berlin Underground 1938–1945*; trans. by Barrows Mussey, introductory note by Joel Sayre (New York: Henry Holt, 1947), entry of Friday, 19 September 1941, p. 70.

68. Victor Klemperer, *LTI. Notizbuch eines Philologen* (Stuttgart: Reclam, 2018; ed. Elke Fröhlich; orig. 1946), pp. 190–91.

69. Würzburger *Mainfränkische Zeitung*, 9 October 1941, reprinted in Benz et al., *Die Juden in Deutschland 1933–1945*, pp. 619–20.

70. Erlass des RSHA, 24 October 1941, reprinted in Benz et al., *Die Juden in Deutschland 1933–1945*, pp. 620–21.

CHAPTER 9

1. It is impossible to give a precise figure, but around one-third of the Jewish victims of the Holocaust died in this way; cf. https://encyclopedia.ushmm.org/content/en/article/mass-shootings-of-jews-during-the-holocaust.   Dieter Pohl estimates that between 2 million and 2.2 million Jews were murdered in mass executions; see Dieter Pohl, 'Historiography and Nazi Killing Sites', in International Holocaust Remembrance Alliance (ed.), *Killing Sites—Research and Remembrance* (Berlin: Metropol, 2015) (pp. 31–46), p. 37. On Auschwitz as the iconic symbol of the Holocaust, see also Mary Fulbrook, *Reckonings: Legacies of Nazi Persecution and the Quest for Justice* (Oxford: Oxford University Press, 2018).

2. See, e.g., Waitman Wade Beorn, *The Holocaust in Eastern Europe. At the Epicenter of the Final Solution* (London: Bloomsbury, 2018); Christopher Browning, with a contribution by Jürgen Matthäus, *The Origins of the Final Solution. The Evolution of Nazi Jewish Policy 1939–42* (London: Random House, 2004); Saul Friedländer, *Nazi Germany and the Jews*, Vol. 2: *The Years of Extermination. 1933–45* (New York: HarperCollins, 2007); Peter Longerich, *Holocaust. The Nazi Persecution and Murder of the Jews*, trans. Shaun Whiteside (Oxford: Oxford University Press, 2010; orig. German 1998).

3. For vivid memories of local witnesses, see Father Patrick Desbois, *The Holocaust by Bullets. A Priest's Journey to Uncover the Truth behind the Murder of 1.5 Million Jews* (Houndmills: Palgrave Macmillan, 2008), and Father Patrick Desbois, *In Broad Daylight: The Secret Procedures behind the Holocaust by Bullet*, trans. Hilary Reyl and Calvert Barksdale (New York: Arcade Publishing, 2018).

4. See, e.g.: Doris Bergen, *War and Genocide: A Concise History of the Holocaust* (Lanham, MD: Rowman & Littlefield, 2009); Christoph Dieckmann, *Deutsche Besatzungspolitik in Litauen 1941–1944* (Göttingen: Wallstein, 2011; 2nd ed. 2016), Vol. 1, pp. 192–209; Christian Gerlach, *The Extermination of the European Jews* (Cambridge: Cambridge University Press, 2016), chapter 9, 'Hunger Policies and Mass Murder', pp. 215–60; Geoffrey Megargee, *War of Annihilation: Combat and Genocide on the Eastern Front, 1941* (Lanham, MD: Rowman & Littlefield, 2007).

5. Ben Shepherd, *Hitler's Soldiers. The German Army in the Third Reich* (New Haven, CT: Yale University Press, 2016), p. 110; figure of 2 million Soviet POW deaths from Jürgen Matthäus, 'Operation Barbarossa and the Onset of the

Holocaust', in Browning, with Matthäus, *Origins of the Final Solution*, p. 244; translated excerpts from the Guidelines available at https://www.ushmm.org/m/pdfs/German-military-context-sheets.pdf (last accessed 21 February 2022).

6. It is estimated that at least 6,000 Jews had rapidly left Klaipeda at this time; Dieckmann, *Deutsche Besatzungspolitik in Litauen*, Vol. 1, p. 144; Matthäus, 'Operation Barbarossa and the Onset of the Holocaust', p. 254; Report by the Stapostelle Tilsit, 1 July 1941, reprinted in Bert Hopper and Hildrun Glass (eds.), *Die Verfolgung und Ermordung der europäischen Juden durch das nationalsozialistische Deutschland 1933–1945*, Vol. 7: *Sowjetunion mit annektierten Gebieten I. Besetzte sowjetische Gebiete unter deutscher Militärverwaltung, Baltikum und Transnistrien* (Munich: Oldenbourg, 2011), Doc. 14, pp. 143–44.

7. HHL, b MS Ger 91 (5), Eugen Altmann; and above, pp. 29–31, pp. 169–70, p. 217, p. 224.

8. Avraham Tory, *Surviving the Holocaust. The Kovno Ghetto Diary*, ed. and intro. by Martin Gilbert, notes by Dina Porat, trans. Jerzy Michalowicz (Cambridge, MA: Harvard University Press, 1990), entry of 22 June 1941, p. 4.

9. Tory, *Surviving the Holocaust*, 'June 23–July 7, 1941. Memoir', p. 6.

10. Tory, *Surviving the Holocaust*, entry of 7 July 1941, p. 8.

11. Ernst Klee, Willi Dreßen, and Volker Rieß (eds.), *"Those Were the Days". The Holocaust through the Eyes of the Perpetrators and Bystanders*, trans. Deborah Burnstone (London: Hamish Hamilton. 1991), p. 28. See also: Christoph Busch, 'Bonding Images: Photography and Film as Acts of Perpetration', *Genocide Studies and Prevention,* 12:2 (2018) (pp. 54–83), pp. 58–61; https://rarehistorica lphotos.com/kovno-garage-massacre-lithuania-1941/ (accessed 14 July 2019); and my short film about this, 'Crossing Thresholds: Kovno (Kaunas), June 1941', at https://compromised-identities.org/film-collection/.

12. https://rarehistoricalphotos.com/kovno-garage-massacre-lithuania-1941/ (accessed 14 July 2019).

13. On Ehrlinger, see Michael Wildt, 'Erich Ehrlinger—ein Vertreter "kämpfender Verwaltung"', in Klaus-Michael Mallmann and Gerhard Paul (eds.), *Karrieren der Gewalt. Nationalsozialistische Täterbiographien* (Darmstadt: Wissenschaftliche Buchgesellschaft, 2004), pp. 76–85.

14. Einsatzgruppe A General Report up to 15 October 1941, reprinted in Yitzhak Arad, Israel Gutman, and Abraham Margaliot (eds.), *Documents on the Holocaust*, updated ed., trans. Lea Ben Dor (Lincoln and Jerusalem: University of Nebraska Press and Yad Vashem, 1999), pp. 389–93.

15. These sentiments were echoed again, incidentally, in the controversial interpretations put forward by Ernst Nolte precipitating the 'historians' debate' of the 1980s. Quotations taken from Wolfram Wette, *Karl Jäger. Mörder der litauischen Juden*, intro. by Ralph Giordano (Frankfurt: Fischer, 2011), p. 75.

16. Wette, *Karl Jäger*, pp. 76–77; Helmut Krausnick and Hans-Heinrich Wilhelm (eds.), *Die Truppe des Weltanschauungskrieges. Die Einsatzgruppen der Sicherheitspolizei und des SD 1938–1942* (Stuttgart: Deutsche Verlags-Anstalt,

1981), 'Die Judenpogrome in Kaunas (Kowno) 25.–29. Juni 1941', pp. 205–9; Megargee, *War of Annihilation*.

17. Cf. Krausnick, *Truppe des Weltanschauungskrieges*, p. 209.

18. Dieckmann, *Deutsche Besatzungspolitik in Litauen*, Vol. 1, pp. 267–84; Vol. 2, pp. 1505–8; Yitzhak Arad, *Ghetto in Flames: The Struggle and Destruction of the Jews in Vilna in the Holocaust* (Jerusalem: Yad Vashem, 1980), pp. 27–28; Rachel Margolis, *A Partisan from Vilna* (Brighton, MA: Academic Studies Press, 2010).

19. Wette, *Karl Jäger*, p. 48; Alex Kay, *The Making of an SS Killer: The Life of Colonel Alfred Filbert, 1905–1990* (Cambridge: Cambridge University Press, 2016); Arad, *Ghetto in Flames*, pp. 64 ff.

20. Ona Šimaitė, a librarian at Vilnius University who extended help to Jews in the ghetto, reprinted in Julija Šukys, *"And I burned with shame": The Testimony of Ona Šimaitė, Righteous among the Nations. A Letter to Isaac Nachman Steinberg*, Search and Research (Jerusalem: Yad Vashem, 2007).

21. https://cpb-us-w2.wpmucdn.com/muse.union.edu/dist/5/237/files/2014/06/MALINES-revised-by-Henny-Lewin.pdf.

22. Herman Kruk, *The Last Days of the Jerusalem of Lithuania. Chronicles from the Vilna Ghetto and the Camps, 1939–1944*, ed. and intro. Benjamin Harshav, trans. Barbara Harshav Yivo Institute for Jewish Research (New Haven, CT: Yale University Press, 2002), entries of 10 and 12 July 1941, p. 61, pp. 62–63.

23. Arad, *Ghetto in Flames*, p. 4.

24. See for exploration of the memory of these events in different localities: Rūta Vanagaitė and Efraim Zuroff, *Our People. Discovering Lithuania's Hidden Holocaust* (London: Rowman & Littlefield, 2016; English trans. 2020); and Silvia Foti, *The Nazi's Granddaughter. How I Discovered That My Grandfather Was a War Criminal* (Washington, DC: Regnery History, 2021).

25. Personal testimonies collected and transcribed by Leyb Koniuchovsky are held at Yad Vashem (Archive, Record Group O.71); selected excerpts in translation in David Bankier, *Expulsion and Extermination. Holocaust Testimonials from Provincial Lithuania* (Jerusalem: Yad Vashem, 2011). Quotations here from p. 45, p. 53.

26. Bankier, *Expulsion and Extermination*, p. 166, p. 55, p. 60, p. 61, p. 69, p. 71.

27. Bankier, *Expulsion and Extermination*, p. 69, p. 70, p. 68.

28. See for a horrific example the lengthy letter translated and reprinted in Nathan Cohen, 'The Destruction of the Jews of Butrimonys as Described in a Farewell Letter from a Local Jew', *Holocaust and Genocide Studies*, 4:3 (1989), pp. 357–75.

29. See the appalling illustrative details recounted in Vanagaitė and Zuroff, *Our People*. On Hamann, see Jürgen Matthäus, 'Anti-Semitism as an Offer: The Function of Ideological Indoctrination in the SS and Police Corps during the Holocaust', in Peter Hayes and Dagmar Herzog (eds.), *Lessons and Legacies VII: The Holocaust in International Perspective* (Evanston, IL: Northwestern University Press, 1991).

30. Dieckmann, *Deutsche Besatzungspolitik in Litauen*,Vol. 2, p. 1512.

31. Arad, *Ghetto in Flames*, pp. 49–50, pp. 53–79.

32. Known as the 'butcher of Vilnius' for his cruelty, Murer was prosecuted in Austria in 1963 but acquitted after a trial that lasted only a week—a typical outcome in Austrian attempts to bring former Nazis to justice. See further Fulbrook, *Reckonings*, p. 313.

33. Einsatzgruppe A, General Report up to 15 October 1941, reprinted in Arad, Gutman, and Margaliot, *Documents on the Holocaust* (pp. 389–93), p. 390.

34. Press, *The Murder of the Jews in Latvia*, p. 41, p. 45.

35. Kaufmann, *Churbn Lettland*, p. 37, p. 39.

36. Press, *The Murder of the Jews in Latvia*, p. 47.

37. Press, *The Murder of the Jews in Latvia*, p. 50, p. 51.

38. Press, *The Murder of the Jews in Latvia*, p. 52.

39. See the detailed local examples carefully researched and collated in Meyer Meler, *Jewish Latvia: Sites to Remember. Latvian Jewish Communities Destroyed in the Holocaust* (Tel Aviv: Association of Latvian and Estonian Jews in Israel, 2013); and Katrin Reichelt, *Lettland unter deutscher Besatzung 1941–1944. Der lettische Anteil am Holocaust* (Berlin: Metropol, 2011), pp. 74–144.

40. Andrew Ezergailis, *The Holocaust in Latvia, 1941–1944:The Missing Center* (Riga and Washington, DC: The Historical Institute of Latvia, and United States Holocaust Memorial Museum, 1996), p. 210, lays responsibility for killings primarily with the roughly 300 men in the Arājs commando, and effectively exonerates the wider population. His account has been critiqued as a form of Latvian apologetics by the Austrian-American historian and Riga ghetto survivor Gertrude Schneider, *Journey into Terror. Story of the Riga Ghetto* (Westport, CT: Praeger, expanded edn., 2001).

41. Press, *The Murder of the Jews in Latvia*, p. 46.

42. Wolfgang Benz, Konrad Kwiet, and Jürgen Matthäus (eds.), *Einsatz im "Reichskommissariat Ostland". Dokumente zum Völkermord im Baltikum und in Weißrussland, 1941–1944* (Berlin: Metropol, 1998), pp. 83–84. See also Ezergailis, *Holocaust in Latvia*. The figures are disputed: Ezergailis claims that the Arājs commando was responsible for 80,000–120,000 murders, but Katrin Reichelt considers that this is way too high an estimate and it was more likely 20,000–30,000: see Katrin Reichelt, 'Kollaboration und Holocaust in Lettland 1941–1945', in Wolf Kaiser (ed.), *Täter im Vernichtungskrieg. Der Überfall auf die Sowjetunion und der Völkermord an den Juden* (Berlin: Propyläen, 2002) (pp. 110–24), p. 116.

43. On Kroeger, see above, p. 66, pp. 182-83, pp. 252-55.

44. Jürgen Ernst Kroeger, *So war es. Ein Bericht* (Im Selbstverlag, 1989), pp. 62 63, pp. 66–68.

45. Details on Bauska in Meler, *Jewish Latvia: Sites to Remember*, pp. 55–60; see also more generally for other localities in the region.

46. See more generally Katrin Reichelt, *Lettland unter deutscher Besatzung 1941–1944. Der lettische Anteil am Holocaust* (Berlin: Metropol, 2011); and Ezergailis, *Holocaust in Latvia*.

47. Kroeger, *So war es*, pp. 65–70.

48. Kroeger, *So war es*, pp. 77–78.

49. Christoph Dieckmann, 'Der Krieg und die Ermordung der Litauischen Juden', in Ulrich Herbert (ed.), *Nationalsozialistische Vernichtungspolitik 1939–1945. Neue Forschungen und Kontroversen* (Frankfurt: Fischer, 1998), pp. 292–329. On Lithuania, see particularly: Dieckmann, *Deutsche Besatzungspolitik in Litauen*; Arad, *Ghetto in Flames*; Margolis, *A Partisan from Vilna*. On Latvia: Reichelt, *Lettland unter deutscher Besatzung*; Bernhard Press, *The Murder of the Jews in Latvia*, trans. Laimdota Mazzarins (Evanston, IL: Northwestern University Press, 2000; orig. 1992). Cf. also Waitman Wade Beorn, 'Killing on the Ground and in the Mind: The Spatialities of Genocide in the East', in Anne Kelly Knowles, Tim Cole, and Alberto Giordano (eds.), *Geographies of the Holocaust* (Bloomington: Indiana University Press, 2014), pp. 89–118.

50. See also Jürgen Matthäus and Frank Bajohr (eds.), *The Political Diary of Alfred Rosenberg and the Onset of the Holocaust* (Lanham, MD: Rowman & Littlefield, for the USHMM, 2015).

51. Kruk, *Last Days*, p. 66.

52. Kazimierz Sakowicz, *Ponary Diary, 1941–1943: A Bystander's Account of a Mass Murder*, ed. Yitzhak Arad and Laurence Weinbaum, entry of 11 August 1941.

53. Sakowicz, *Ponary Diary*, entry of 19 August 1941.

54. Arad, *Ghetto in Flames*, pp. 111–12.

55. Arad, *Ghetto in Flames*, p. 116.

56. Kruk, *Last Days*, entry of 4 September 1941, p. 92.

57. Kruk, *Last Days*, entry of 5 September 1941, p. 94.

58. Sakowicz, *Ponary Diary*, entry of 11 July 1941, p. 12.

59. Arad, *Ghetto in Flames*, p. 215; Dina Porat, *The Fall of a Sparrow: The Life and Times of Abba Kovner* (Stanford, CA: Stanford University Press, 2009), p. 65. These figures are rough estimates.

60. See further Arad, *Ghetto in Flames*, Part Three; Margolis, *A Partisan from Vilna*; Porat, *Fall of a Sparrow*, chapter 5.

61. See particularly Dieckmann, *Deutsche Besatzungspolitik in Litauen*, Vol. II, pp. 930–58.

62. Y. Kutorgene, 'Kaunaski dnievik (Kovno Diary) 1941–1942', reprinted in *Druzhba Narodov* (Amity of Nations) VIII, 1968, pp. 210–11, trans. and repr. in Arad, Gutman, and Margaliot, *Documents on the Holocaust*, pp. 405–6.

63. See further Dieckmann, *Deutsche Besatzungspolitik in Litauen*, Vol. II, pp. 959–67.

64. On views within the Reich, see further below, chapter 11.

65. Else Behrend-Rosenfeld und Siegfried Rosenfeld, *Leben in zwei Welten. Tagebücher eines jüdischen Paares in Deutschland und im Exil*, ed. Erich Kasberger and Marita Kraus (Munich: Volk, 2011); see also above, p. 32, pp. 102-3, pp. 242-43, pp. 258-59, p. 264.

66. Behrend-Rosenfeld and Rosenfeld, *Leben in zwei Welten*, entry of Sunday, 16 November 1941, pp. 146–48.

67. Behrend-Rosenfeld and Rosenfeld, *Leben in zwei Welten*, entry of Sunday, 16 November 1941, pp. 151–53; Susanna Schrafstetter, *Flucht und Versteck. Untergetauchte Juden in München—Verfolgungserfahrung und Nachkriegsalltag* (Göttingen: Wallstein, 2015), p. 44.

68. Quoted in Wette, *Karl Jäger*, p. 129.

69. Jeanette Wolff, *Sadismus oder Wahnsinn: Erlebnisse in den deutschen Konzentrationslagern im Osten* (Greiz, Thüringen: Ernst Bretfeld, Sachsenverlag, n.d., probably 1947), p. 15. The verb used, '*richten*', can also mean 'judge'. In this context it is more likely the old-fashioned word for 'execute' or 'put to death', although '*hinrichten*' is now more commonly used for this.

70. Reprinted in Vanagaitė and Zuroff, *Our People*, p. 45, p. 46, p. 47.

71. Quoted in Vanagaitė and Zuroff, *Our People*, p. 46,

72. Quoted in Vanagaitė and Zuroff, *Our People*, p. 112. Contrast the celebratory revels in which many Nazis indulged: Edward Westermann, *Drunk on Genocide: Alcohol and Mass Murder in Nazi Germany* (Ithaca, NY: Cornell University Press, 2021).

73. Katrin Reichelt, *Rettung kennt keine Konventionen: Hilfe für verfolgte Juden im deutsch besetzten Lettland 1941–1945* (Berlin: Gedenkstätte Stille Helden, Lukas Verlag, 2020), p. 113.

74. On the notion of 'spectator sport' see also Janina Struk, *Photographing the Holocaust* (London: Routledge 2005).

75. See https://www.ushmm.org/lcmedia/viewer/wlc/film.php?RefId=DFE00 97L. A 1981 interview with Wiener can be watched at https://www.youtube.com/watch?v=npypqxdFY1c.

76. Klee et al., *"Those Were the Days"*, p. 127.

77. Klee et al., *"Those Were the Days"*, pp. 129–33 (pp. 130–32 are photos).

78. Klee et al., *"Those Were the Days"*, pp. 127–29 (p. 128 for photos).

79. Klee et al., *"Those Were the Days"*, p. 129.

80. Some were clearly enthusiastically involved. Cf., e.g., Klaus-Michael Mallmann, Volker Riess, and Wolfgang Pyta (eds.), *Deutscher Osten 1939–1945. Der Weltanschauungskrieg in Photos und Texten* (Darmstadt: Wissenschaftliche Buchgesellschaft, 2003), pp. 27–28.

81. Described and quoted in Wette, *Karl Jäger*, p. 140.

82. Klee et al., *"Those Were the Days"*, p. 134.

83. Klee et al., *"Those Were the Days"*, pp. 134–35.

84. http://db.yadvashem.org/righteous/family.html?language=en&itemId=4022 626 (accessed 11 August 2019); and see further chapter 12, below

85. On these and other images, see Nadine Fresco, *On the Death of Jews: Photographs and History* (New York: Berghahn, 2021).

86. I was fortunate to meet her in 2019, when I visited the small museum in Liepāja commemorating the local Jewish community.

87. Andrej Angrick and Peter Klein, *The 'Final Solution' in Riga. Exploitation and Annihilation, 1941–194*; trans. Ray Brandon (New York: Berghahn, 2009).

88. Cf. Ezergailis, *Holocaust in Latvia*, chapter VII, pp. 203–38; Angrick and Klein, *The 'Final Solution' in Riga*, chapter 5, pp. 130–74; Christian Gerlach, *Kalkulierte Morde. Die deutsche Wirtschafts- und Vernichtungspolitik in Weißrußland 1941 bis 1944* (Hamburg: Hamburger Edition, 1999); Longerich, *Holocaust*, argues against Christian Gerlach's emphasis on pragmatic considerations about food supplies that there was a movement 'towards a policy of ethnic annihilation' (p. 210); Dieter Pohl, 'Die Wehrmacht und der Mord an den Juden in den besetzten sowjetischen Gebieten', in Wolf Kaiser (ed.), *Täter im Vernichtungskrieg. Der Überfall auf die Sowjetunion und der Völkermord an den Juden* (Berlin: Propyläen, 2002) (pp. 39–53).

89. This account is based on documents held in the German Federal Archive (Bundesarchiv), BA Ludwigsburg B 162, copies of which were kindly made available to me by Ernst Hemicker's grandson, Lorenz Hemicker, to whom I am very grateful. See also above, pp. 65–66; and Angrick and Klein, *The 'Final Solution' in Riga*, chapter 5, pp. 130–74.

90. VI 420 AR 2540/66, Hemicker interview 11 March 1969, copy courtesy Lorenz Hemicker.

91. Angrick and Klein, *The 'Final Solution' in Riga*, pp. 141 ff.

92. Interview with Hemicker 25 July 1965, Aktenzeichen 141 Js 534/60, Staatsanwalt Kraemer, Landgericht Hamburg, Bl. 9510, copy courtesy Lorenz Hemicker.

93. Angrick and Klein, *The 'Final Solution' in Riga*, pp. 154 ff.

94. VI 420 AR 2540/66, Hemicker interview 11 March 1969, Bl. 76, copy courtesy Lorenz Hemicker.

95. Kroeger, *So war es*, pp. 88 ff.

96. See further Peter Klein, 'Dr. Rudolf Lange als Kommandant der Sicherheitspolizei und des SD in Lettland. Aspekte seines Dienstalltags', in Wolf Kaiser (ed.), *Täter im Vernichtungskrieg. Der Überfall auf die Sowjetunion und der Völkermord an den Juden* (Berlin: Propyläen, 2002); Angrick and Klein, *The 'Final Solution' in Riga*, pp. 260–64.

97. Quotations from Angrick and Klein, *The 'Final Solution' in Riga*, pp. 262–63.

98. For Latvia, see Ezergailis, '"Neighbours" did not kill Jews!', in Gaunt et al. (eds.), *Collaboration and Resistance during the Holocaust*, pp. 197–222. Ezergailis poses a false dichotomy and constructs the 'neighbours' argument as essentially a straw man, claiming that to emphasize the role of locals presupposes no German leadership. He creates an 'either/or' scenario of extreme positions, rather than exploring the complexity of the interactions.

99. Einsatzgruppe A General Report up to 15 October 1941, in Arad, Gutman, and Margaliot, *Documents on the Holocaust*, p. 389.

100. Reprinted in Arad et al., *Documents on the Holocaust*, p. 398. See also original reproduced in full in German, in Wette, *Karl Jäger*, pp. 237–45.

101. Arad et al., *Documents on the Holocaust*, p. 400.

102. Map reproduced at https://www.ushmm.org/learn/timeline-of-events/ 1939-1941/stahlecker-report.

103. Katrin Reichelt gives the figure of 60,000: 'Kollaboration und Holocaust in Lettland 1941–1945', in Wolf Kaiser (ed.), *Täter im Vernichtungskrieg. Der Überfall auf die Sowjetunion und der Völkermord an den Juden* (Berlin: Propyläen, 2002) (pp. 110–24), pp. 11–12; Paul Schapiro suggests 70,000 in 'Preface to the First English Edition', Max Kaufmann, *Churbn Lettland. The Destruction of the Jews of Latvia*, trans. Laimdota Mazzarins (Konstanz: Hartung-Gorre, 2010), p. 9.

104. Contrast Thomas Kuehne, who overstates an otherwise interesting case by claiming that 'with the Holocaust the ultimate goal of uniting people by criminal means was achieved', as though the aim of killing Jews was not so much to exterminate Jews as 'nation-building by mass crime'. Kuehne's functionalist approach here confuses cause and supposed consequence: whether or not a shared sense of national community was the result, it was not the cause or 'goal' of mass extermination. Thomas Kuehne, *Belonging and Genocide: Hitler's Community, 1918–1945* (New Haven, CT: Yale University Press, 2010), p. 1, p. 91, p. 161.

CHAPTER 10

1. Here, the focus remains on Germany and selected sites in Eastern Europe, continuing to follow the personal examples traced throughout this book. A subsequent volume will explore more broadly the significance of surrounding societies for rescue and survival across both Eastern and Western Europe under Nazi domination.

2. For details of deportations, see Alfred Gottwaldt and Diana Schulle, *Die "Judendeportationen" aus dem Deutschen Reich 1941–1945. Eine kommentierte Chronologie* (Wiesbaden: Marix, 2005).

3. BArch DY55 /V278 / 96, Hirsch, Landeshauptstadt Halle (Fols. 13–16), Fol. 15.

4. Else Behrend-Rosenfeld and Siegfried Rosenfeld, *Leben in zwei Welten. Tagebücher eines jüdischen Paares in Deutschland und im Exil*, ed. Erich Kasberger and Marita Kraus (Munich: Volk, 2011), entry of Sunday, 12 April 1942, pp. 158–80.

5. Behrend-Rosenfeld and Rosenfeld, *Leben in zwei Welten*, entry of Sunday, 12 April 1942, p. 162.

6. Behrend-Rosenfeld and Rosenfeld, *Leben in zwei Welten*, entry of Sunday, 12 April 1942, pp. 163–70.

7. Susanna Schrafstetter, *Flucht und Versteck. Untergetauchte Juden in München— Verfolgungserfahrung und Nachkriegsalltag* (Göttingen: Wallstein, 2015), pp. 9–11. In his detailed study of cases in Berlin, Richard Lutjens estimates that perhaps 6,500 Jews attempted to hide, of whom only around 1,700 succeeded; Richard Lutjens, *Submerged on the Surface. The Not-So-Hidden Jews of Nazi*

Berlin, 1941–1945 (Oxford: Berghahn, 2019), p. 2. See also Mark Roseman, *Lives Reclaimed. A Story of Rescue and Resistance in Nazi Germany* (New York: Metropolitan Books, 2019); and see further chapter 12.

8. Schrafstetter, *Flucht und Versteck*, pp. 51–56.

9. Martin Cüppers (et al.), *Fotos aus Sobibor* (Berlin: Metropol, 2020); Yitzhak Arad, *Belzec, Sobibor, Treblinka. The Operation Reinhard Death Camps* (Bloomington: Indiana University Press, 1987); and more generally Mary Fulbrook, Reckonings: *Legacies of Nazi Persecution and the Quest for Justice* (Oxford: Oxford University Press, 2018), chapter 5, pp. 104–40.

10. See, e.g., the extraordinary interviews with local Polish farmers in Claude Lanzmann's film *Shoah*.

11. See further: Omer Bartov, *Hitler's Army* (Oxford, 1992); Alexander Rossino, *Hitler Strikes Poland* (Lawrence: University Press of Kansas, 2003); Dieter Pohl, 'Die Wehrmacht und der Mord an den Juden in den besetzten sowjetischen Gebieten', in Wolf Kaiser (ed.), *Täter im Vernichtungskrieg. Der Überfall auf die Sowjetunion und der Völkermord an den Juden*, (Berlin, Propyläen: 2002) (pp. 39–53); Mary Fulbrook, *Dissonant Lives: Generations and Violence through the German Dictatorships* (Oxford: Oxford University Press, 2011; pb. ed. 2017, Vol. 1), chapter 5.

12. See, e.g., Bibliothek für Zeitgeschichte Stuttgart (BfZ), Sammlung Sterz, 1941–1947, Uffz. Heinz Biesgen, 29 524 C, 11. Btr./Art.Rgt.125, 125.Inf.Div., Thursday, 10 July 1941.

13. Feldpostsammlung Museum für Kommunikation, 3.2002.1325 [AK 46], Franz Döhring, Photos no. 101, 124.

14. Deutsches Tagebuch Archiv (DTA) 141-I, 4, 'Divisionsnachschubführer (Dinafü)', Max Rohwerder, Tagebuch 1941–1942, 3 October 1941, p. 1.

15. BfZ, Sammlung Sterz 1941–1946, Uffz. Heinrich Zils, 07794, Stab/Heeres-San.Abt.601, Monday, 30 June 1941.

16. DTA 280-I, Franz Jonas, Ingenieurschüler, Kriegstagebuch 1941 (born 14 September 1917 Frankfurt am Main, died 3 July 1947, Frankfurt am Main), 3 August 1941.

17. BfZ, Sammlung Sterz 1941–1946, Uffz. Heinrich Zils, 07794, Stab/Heeres-San.Abt.601, Monday, 30 June 1941.

18. DTA 280-I, Franz Jonas, Ingenieurschüler, Kriegstagebuch 1941, 10 August 1941.

19. DTA 280-I, Franz Jonas, Ingenieurschüler, Kriegstagebuch 1941, 11 August 1941.

20. Feldpostsammlung Museum für Kommunikation, 3.2002.1276 [AK 31], Karl Schwender (born 27 November 1922, died 15 February 1943), letter of 16 September 1941.

21. DTA 14-I, 4, 'Divisionsnachschubführer (Dinafü)', Max Rohwerder, Tagebuch 1941–1942, 3 October 1941, pp. 1–2, underlining in the original.

22. BfZ, Sammlung Sterz 1941–1946, Uffz. Heinrich Zils, 07794, Stab/Heeres-San.Abt.601, Monday, 30 June 1941.

23. DTA 280-I, Franz Jonas, Ingenieurschüler, Kriegstagebuch 1941, 17 August 1941.

24. DTA 280-I, Franz Jonas, Ingenieurschüler, Kriegstagebuch 1941, 18 August 1941.

25. DTA 280-I, Franz Jonas, Ingenieurschüler, Kriegstagebuch 1941, 22 August 1941.

26. DTA 141-I, 4, 'Divisionsnachschubführer (Dinafü)', Max Rohwerder, Tagebuch 1941–1942, Minsk, 22 October 1941, p. 5, underlining in the original.

27. DTA 141-I, 4, 'Divisionsnachschubführer (Dinafü)', Max Rohwerder, Tagebuch 1941–1942, Minsk, 22 October 1941, p. 6, underlining in the original.

28. DTA 14-I, 4, 'Divisionsnachschubführer (Dinafü)', Max Rohwerder, Tagebuch 1941–1942, 1–9 November, p. 8.

29. BfZ, Sammlung Sterz 1941–1946, Uffz (O.A.), 'Kurt . . .', 21352, 9.Kp./Kw.Trsp./Rgt.605, Monday, 30 June 1941.

30. BfZ, Sammlung Sterz 1941–1946, Uffz. Alfred Nehlsen, L 33281, Fliegerhorst Lyon, 23 June 1941.

31. As with all the areas covered in this book, there is a growing and already large literature on these topics; footnote references have been restricted to a few key titles.

32. See, e.g., Helmut Krausnick and Hans-Heinrich Wilhelm (eds.), *Die Truppe des Weltanschauungskrieges. Die Einsatzgruppen der Sicherheitspolizei und des SD 1938–1942* (Stuttgart: Deutsche Verlags-Anstalt, 1981); Ralf Ogorreck, *Die Einsatzgruppen und die "Genesis der Endlösung"* (Berlin: Metropol, 1996); Richard Rhodes, *Masters of Death: The SS-Einsatzgruppen and the Invention of the Holocaust* (Oxford: Perseus, 2002); Helmut Langerbein, *Hitler's Death Squads. The Logic of Mass Murder* (College Station: Texas A&M University Press, 2004).

33. Stefan Klemp gives a figure of at least 520,373 victims of murder by police battalions: Klemp, *"Nicht ermittelt". Polizeibataillone und die Nachkriegsjustiz. Ein Handbuch* (Essen: Klartext, 2005), p. 7, p. 467. This figure is based on the records of cases brought to West German courts after the war and is likely therefore to be a significant underestimate. Edward B. Westermann, *Hitler's Police Battalions: Enforcing Racial War in the East* (Lawrence: University Press of Kansas, 2005), p. 238, suggests the that 'the figure certainly runs into the hundreds of thousands, if not a million or more'.

34. Christopher Browning, *Ordinary Men: Reserve Police Battalion 101 and the Final Solution in Poland* (London: Penguin, 2001; orig. 1992); see also Thomas Pegelow Kaplan, Jürgen Matthäus, and Mark Hornburg (eds.), *Beyond "Ordinary Men". Christopher R. Browning and Holocaust Historiography* (Paderborn: Brill, Ferdinand Schöningh, 2019).

35. Ian Rich, *Holocaust Perpetrators of the German Police Battalions. The Mass Murder of Jewish Civilians, 1940–1942* (London: Bloomsbury, 2012), pp. 171 ff.

438

NOTES

36. Westermann, *Hitler's Police Battalions*, p. 239; see also Stefan Kühl, *Ganz normale Organisationen* (Berlin: Suhrkamp, 2014).

37. Westermann, *Hitler's Police Battalions*, p. 236.

38. Cf. Hannes Heer and Klaus Naumann (eds.), *War of Extermination: The German Military in World War II, 1941–1944* (New York: Berghahn, 2000; orig. German 1995); C. Hartmann et al. (eds.), *Verbrechen der Wehrmacht. Bilanz einer Debatte* (Munich: Beck, 2005); Pohl, 'Die Wehrmacht und der Mord', pp. 39–53; Dieter Pohl, *Die Herrschaft der Wehrmacht: Deutsche Militärbesatzung und einheimische Bevölkerung in der Sowjetunion 1941–1944* (Oldenbourg: Wissenschaftsverlag, 2009); Ben Shepherd, *War in the Wild East: The German Army and Soviet Partisans* (Cambridge, MA: Harvard University Press, 2004); W. Wette, *The Wehrmacht: History, Myth, Reality* (Cambridge, MA: Harvard University Press, 2006).

39. Edward B. Westermann, *Drunk on Genocide. Alcohol and Mass Murder in Nazi Germany* (Ithaca, NY: Cornell University Press, 2021).

40. Westermann, *Drunk on Genocide*; see also Thomas Kühne, *The Rise and Fall of Comradeship: Hitler's Soldiers, Male Bonding and Mass Violence in the Twentieth Century* (Cambridge: Cambridge University Press, 2017).

41. Willy Peter Reese, *Mir selber seltsam fremd. Die Unmenschlichkeit des Krieges. Russland 1941–44*, ed. Stefan Schmitz (Berlin: Ullstein 2004), p. 48.

42. Cf., e.g., Reese, *Mir selber seltsam fremd*, pp. 63 ff.

43. Reese, *Mir selber seltsam fremd*, p. 87.

44. Reese, *Mir selber seltsam fremd*, p. 92.

45. E.g., Reese, *Mir selber seltsam fremd*, p. 107–10, p. 111.

46. Luis Raffeiner, *Wir waren keine Menschen mehr. Erinnerungen eines Wehrmachtssoldaten an die Ostfront*, compiled by Luise Ruatti, with an afterword by Hannes Heer (n.p.: Edition Raetia, 2010). See also the USHMM interviews with him under the name Alois Raffeiner, in the collection Oral History, Accession Number: 2009.402.10, RG Number: RG-50.654.0010, accessible at https://collections.ushmm.org/search/catalog/irn45408.

47. Andrej Angrick, Martina Voigt, Silke Ammerschubert, and Peter Klein: '"Da hätte man schon Tagebuch führen müssen": Das Polizeibataillon 322 und die Judenmorde im Bereich der Heeresgruppe Mitte während des Sommers und Herbstes 1941', in Helge Grabitz et al. (eds.), *Die Normalität des Verbrechens. Bilanz und Perspektiven der Forschung zu den nationalsozialistischen Gewaltverbrechen* (Berlin: Hentrick, 1994), pp. 346 ff.; Peter Longerich: *Politik der Vernichtung. Die Gesamtdarstellung der nationalsozialistischen Judenverfolgung* (Munich: Piper, 1998), p. 371; Mathias Beer: 'Die Entwicklung der Gaswagen beim Mord an den Juden', *Vierteljahrshefte für Zeitgeschichte*, 35 (1987), Vol. 3, pp. 408 ff; Bundesarchiv Dok. Slg. Verschiedenes 301 v (0.48), pp. 260 f., 263 ff.

48. Klaus-Michael Mallmann, Volker Riess, and Wolfgang Pyta (eds.), *Deutscher Osten 1939–1945. Der Weltanschauungskrieg in Photos und Texten* (Darmstadt: Wissenschaftliche Buchgesellschaft, 2003), entry of 22 September 1941, p. 27.

49. Mallmann et al., *Deutscher Osten 1939–1945*, entry of 2 October 1941, p. 27.

50. Mallmann et al., *Deutscher Osten 1939–1945*, 5 October 1941, p. 28.

51. See also Kühne, *Rise and Fall of Comradeship*.

52. Mallmann et al., *Deutscher Osten*, 5 October 1941, p. 28.

53. Mallmann et al., *Deutscher Osten*, 9 October 1941, p. 28.

54. Mallmann et al., *Deutscher Osten*, 27 October 1941, p. 28.

55. Mallmann et al., *Deutscher Osten*, 19 April 1942, p. 28.

56. Copies of letters available through Yad Vashem and the USHMM. See: https://www.yadvashem.org/de/education/educational-materials/lesson-plans/architecture-of-auschwitz-birkenau/kretschmer-letters.html; and https://perspectives.ushmm.org/item/letter-from-karl-kretschmer-to-his-family.

57. https://collections.ushmm.org/search/catalog/irn1004167.

58. Letter from Karl Kretschmer to his family, Sunday, 27 September 1942, reprinted by Yad Yashem, Jerusalem, accessible at https://www.yadvashem.org/de/education/educational-materials/lesson-plans/architecture-of-auschwitz-birkenau/kretschmer-letters.html.

59. Letter from Karl Kretschmer to his family from Kursk, 15 October 1942, reprinted by Yad Yashem, Jerusalem, accessible at https://www.yadvashem.org/de/education/educational-materials/lesson-plans/architecture-of-auschwitz-birkenau/kretschmer-letters.html.

60. See also Browning, *Ordinary Men*.

61. Paul Kohl, *'Ich wundere mich, dass ich noch lebe'. Sowjetische Augenzeugen berichten* (Gütersloh: Gütersloher Verlagshaus Gerd Mohn, 1990), Dok. 7: 'Aussage eines Angehörigen der 3. Kompanie des 307. Polizeibataillons über seine Verweigerung, an einer Exekution in Brest teilzunehmen', ZSt, I Befehlsnotstand, B. 80, p. 193.

62. On the somewhat chequered history of West and East German and Austrian attempts to deal with Nazi crimes through legal proceedings, see further Fulbrook, *Reckonings*, Part Two.

63. Kohl, *'Ich wundere mich, dass ich noch lebe'*, Doc. 6. 'Aussage von Heinrich M., Angehöriger des 307. Polizeibataillons' (Ludwigsburg: ZSt, 204 AR-Z 334/59, Bd. 2, Bl.7–11), (pp. 190–92), p. 192.

64. Cf., e.g., Browning, *Ordinary Men*; Mallmann et al., *Deutscher Osten*; Thomas Kühne, 'Protean Masculinity, Hegemonic Masculinity: Soldiers in the Third Reich', *Central European History*, 51:3 (2018), pp. 390–418; Kühne, *Rise and Fall of Comradeship*.

65. Friedrich Kellner, *My Opposition: The Diary of Friedrich Kellner—A German against the Third Reich* (Cambridge: Cambridge University Press, 2018), entries of 15 July 1941; 24 July 1941; 28 July 1941, p. 131, p. 133.

66. Kellner, *My Opposition*, 15 August 1941, p. 136.

67. Kellner, *My Opposition*, 28 October 1941, p. 145.

68. See further Fulbrook, *Reckonings*, Part Two.

69. Kellner, *My Opposition*, 15 December 1941, p. 155.

70. Hermann Stresau, *Als lebe man nur unter Vorbehalt, Tagebücher aus den Kriegsjahren 1939–1945*, ed. Peter Graf and Ulrich Faure (Stuttgart: Klett-Cotta, 2021), entry of 22 October 1941, p. 185.

71. Friedrich Reck, *Diary of a Man in Despair*, trans. Paul Rubens (New York: New York Review of Books, 2013; first published 1947), entry of 30 October 1942, p. 160.

72. BArch DY55/V278/96, Hirsch, Landeshauptstadt Halle (Fols. 13–16), Fol. 16.

73. Ruth Andreas-Friedrich, *Berlin Underground 1938–1945*, trans. by Barrows Mussey, introductory note by Joel Sayre (New York: Henry Holt, 1947), p. 83.

74. Andreas-Friedrich, *Berlin Underground 1938–1945*, pp. 83–84. The estimate of tens of thousands of rescuers is based on the fact that for every Jew who did manage to survive the war underground, at least ten 'Aryans' were involved in hiding them for a night or two, sometimes much longer, then passing them on to other rescuers. So if, say, somewhat more than 5,000 Jews survived in hiding for a while at least, then perhaps 50,000 helpers were involved; perhaps as many as 80,000, given the unknown numbers of people who did not make it through the war, but were helped, however briefly, for at least part of the time. See also Lutjens, *Submerged on the Surface*, and Roseman, *Lives Reclaimed*, for the significance of wider social networks in assisting some Jews to survive.

75. Andreas-Friedrich, *Berlin Underground 1938–1945*, pp. 90–91.

76. Nathan Stoltzfus, *Resistance of the Heart: Intermarriage and the Rosenstrasse Protest in Nazi Germany* (New Brunswick, NJ: Rutgers University Press, 2001).

77. Wolf Gruner, *Widerstand in der Rosenstraße* (Frankfurt: Fischer, 2005); Diana Schulle, 'The Rosenstrasse Protest', in Beate Meyer, Hermann Simon, and Chana Schütz (eds.), *Jews in Nazi Berlin: From Kristallnacht to Liberation* (Chicago: University of Chicago Press, 2009), pp. 158–70.

78. DTA Reg 3117-6, Tagebuch 25 June 1941–1 March 1945, Mainz, 11 January 1942.

79. DTA Reg 3117-6, Tagebuch 25 June 1941–1 March 1945, Neustadt, 16 August 1942.

80. DTA Reg 3117-6, Tagebuch 25 June 1941–1 March 1945, 27 January 1943.

81. DTA Reg 3117-6, Tagebuch 25 June 1941–1 March 1945, Mainz, 1 February 1943.

82. DTA Reg 3117-6, Tagebuch 25 June 1941–1 March 1945, Mainz, 14 February 1943. Underlining in original.

83. Stargardt, *The German War*, pp. 345–381.

84. Wolfhilde von König, *Kriegstagebuch einer jungen Nationalsozialistin. Die Aufzeichnungen Wolfhilde von Königs 1939–1946*, ed. Sven Keller (Oldenbourg: De Gruyter, 2015).

85. DTA 797-11, Tagebuch 1 January–31 December 1943, Günter Sack, Zeitz, 14 June 1943.

86. DTA 797-11, Tagebuch 1 January–31 December 1943, Günter Sack, Zeitz, 3 July 1943.

87. DTA 797-11, Tagebuch 1 January–31 December 1943, Günter Sack, Dinard, 22 August 1943.
88. DTA 797-11, Tagebuch 1 January–31 December 1943, Günter Sack, Dinard, 6 September 1943.
89. Stargardt, *German War*.
90. Diary extracts reproduced in Walter Jessel, *A Travelogue through a Twentieth Century Life. A Memoir*, ed. Janet Roberts and Cynthia Jessel (Boulder, CO: self-published, 1996), p. 121.
91. Mallmann et al., *Deutscher Osten*, testimony of 9 February 1966 of Hans H., p. 43.

CHAPTER 11

1. Heinz Rein (pseudonym for Reinhard Andermann), *Berlin Finale*, trans. Shaun Whiteside (London: Penguin Modern Classics, 2019; orig. German 1947), p. 214. Rein spent the early postwar years in communist East Germany, before moving to the West in the early 1950s. Although his novel was classified as East German 'literature written in the rubble' (*Trümmerliteratur*), it was also highly popular in the West. It clearly resonated on both sides of the Cold War divide.
2. Rein, *Berlin Finale*, p. 214.
3. See further Jürgen Matthäus and Mary Fulbrook, 'German Agency and the Holocaust as a European Project', in Mary Fulbrook and Jürgen Matthäus (eds.), *The Cambridge History of the Holocaust*, Vol. 2: *Perpetrating the Holocaust: Policies, Participants, Places* (Cambridge: Cambridge University Press, 2023), chapter 23.
4. See Mark Roseman, *Lives Reclaimed. A Story of Rescue and Resistance in Nazi Germany* (New York: Metropolitan Books, 2019), for one such group, which after the war failed to obtain the recognition it arguably deserved.
5. See for an example of a vivid micro-study at village level Tomasz Frydel, 'The *Pazifizierungsaktion* as a Catalyst of Anti-Jewish Violence. A Study in the Social Dynamics of Fear', in Andrea Löw and Frank Bajohr (eds.), *The Holocaust and European Societies: Social Processes and Social Dynamics* (London: Palgrave Macmillan, 2016), chapter 9, pp. 14–66.
6. On Western European cases of rescue and survival see, e.g., B. Lidegaard, *Countrymen: How Denmark's Jews escaped the Nazis* (London: Atlantic Books, 2013); B. Moore, *Survivors: Jewish Self-Help and Rescue in Nazi-Occupied Western Europe* (Oxford: Oxford University Press, 2010); J. Semelin, *The Survival of the Jews in France, 1940–44*, trans. C. Schoch and N. Lehrer (London, Hurst & Co., 2018; French orig. 2013). A wider pan-European comparative survey is needed to explore the significance of differing social conditions at different stages of the war.
7. Susanna Schrafstetter, *Flucht und Versteck. Untergetauchte Juden in München— Verfolgungserfahrung und Nachkriegsalltag* (Göttingen: Wallstein, 2015), p. 55, pp.

81–82. On Berlin, see Richard Lutjens, *Submerged on the Surface. The Not-So-Hidden Jews of Nazi Berlin, 1941–1945* (Oxford: Berghahn, 2019).

8. Else Behrend-Rosenfeld and Siegfried Rosenfeld, *Leben in zwei Welten. Tagebücher eines jüdischen Paares in Deutschland und im Exil*, ed. Erich Kasberger and Marita Kraus (Munich:Volk, 2011), from the entry relating to the deportation in April 1942 until her escape into Switzerland two years later.

9. Overview in Lutjens, *Submerged on the Surface*. See also, e.g., Leonard Gross, *The Last Jews in Berlin* (New York: Simon & Schuster, 1982); Inge Deutschkron, *Ich trug den gelben Stern* (München: Deutscher Taschenbuch, 1985); Marie Jalowicz Simon, *Gone to Ground*, trans. Anthea Bell (London: Profile Books, 2016).

10. Peter Wyden, *Stella* (New York: Simon & Schuster, 1992); Christian Dirks, 'Snatchers:The Berlin Gestapo's Jewish Informants', in Beat Meyer, Hermann Simon, and Chana Schütz (eds.), *Jews in Nazi Berlin. From Kristallnacht to Liberation* (Chicago: University of Chicago Press, 2009; orig. 2000), pp. 24–73.

11. Kunstamt Schöneberg, Schöneberg Museum, with Gedenkstätte Haus der Wannsee-Konferenz, *Orte des Erinnerns*, Bd. 2: *Jüdisches Alltagsleben im Bayerischen Viertel* (Berlin: Edition Hentrich, 1995, 2nd ed. 1999), pp. 21–69.

12. Examples in Siegfried Heimann, 'Judenverfolgung im Spiegel der Schöneberger Polizeiberichte von 1941 bis 1945', in Kunstamt Schöneberg, *Orte des Erinnerns*, pp. 1–2.

13. Bernhard Press, *The Murder of the Jews in Latvia*, trans. Laimdota Mazzarins (Evanston, IL: Northwestern University Press, 2000; orig. 1992), pp. 16–17.

14. See Katrin Reichelt, *Rettung kennt keine Konventionen: Hilfe für verfolgte Juden im deutsch besetzten Lettland 1941–1945* (Berlin: Gedenkstätte Stille Helden, Lukas Verlag, 2020); and Katrin Reichelt, *Lettland unter deutscher Besatzung 1941–1944. Der lettische Anteil am Holocaust* (Berlin: Metropol, 2011).

15. Reichelt, *Rettung kennt keine Konventionen*, pp. 45–82.

16. Gertrude Schneider, *Journey into Terror. Story of the Riga Ghetto*, rev. ed. (Westport, CT: Praeger, 2001), pp. 6 ff.

17. She originally published her story in Russian in 1973; a revised English version was edited by Wolf Goodman in collaboration with Michelson and published in 1979. Both the style and the details are inevitably affected by this late retelling, more than three decades after the events recounted, and with an English-speaking audience in mind. See: Frida Michelson, *I Survived Rumbuli* (Washington, DC: USHMM, 1999).

18. Michelson, *I Survived Rumbuli*, p. 85, pp. 91–93.

19. Michelson, *I Survived Rumbuli*, pp. 94–220, pp. 221–25.

20. See the fictionalized biographical account by Zipora Klein Jakob, *Elida, the Forbidden Ghetto Girl* (n.p.: eBookPro Publishing, 2021).

21. Reichelt, *Rettung kennt keine Konventionen*, pp. 7–43, esp. pp. 33–37. See also Max Kaufmann, *Churbn Lettland. The Destruction of the Jews of Latvia*, trans. Laimdota Mazzarins (Konstanz: Hartung-Gorre, 2010), p. 9. Original German: *Churbn Lettland: Die Vernichtung der Juden Lettlands* (Munich: Im Selbstverlag, 1947).

22. Rachel Margolis, *A Partisan from Vilna* (Brighton, MA: Academic Studies Press, 2010).

23. Nechama Tec, *Defiance* (Oxford: Oxford University Press, 2009).

24. Jeanette Wolff, *Sadismus oder Wahnsinn: Erlebnisse in den deutschen Konzentrationslagern im Osten* (Greiz, Thüringen: Ernst Bretfeld, Sachsenverlag, n.d., probably 1947).

25. On the deportation to Riga, see Günther Högl and Thomas Kohlpoth, 'The Deportation from Dortmund on 27 January 1942', in *Book of Remembrance. The German, Austrian and Czechoslovakian Jews Deported to the Baltic States,* compiled by Wolfgang Scheffler and Diana Schulle (Munich: K. G. Saur, 2003), pp. 83–61.

26. Wolff, *Sadismus oder Wahnsinn*, pp. 5–12.

27. USHMM: transcript of the Society of the Survivors of the Riga Ghetto Conference (New York), January 1978; Film Accession Number: 1996.166 | RG Number: RG-60.5041 | Film ID: 3400, 3401, 4646, 4705, 4706, transcript pp. 7–8, accessible at:https://collections.ushmm.org/film_findingaids/RG-60.5041_01_trs_en.pdf.

28. Wolff, *Sadismus oder Wahnsinn*, pp. 15–16.

29. Wolff, *Sadismus oder Wahnsinn*, pp. 16–17.

30. Wolff, *Sadismus oder Wahnsinn*, p. 21. The gates of Auschwitz, as well as some other camps, bore the infamous slogan *Arbeit macht frei* (roughly, 'work makes free' or 'liberation through work'). Buchenwald, unusually, had an inscription telling inmates *Jedem das Seine*—'to each his own', or 'to each his just deserts'.

31. Wolff, *Sadismus oder Wahnsinn*, pp. 38–58.

32. Wolff, *Sadismus oder Wahnsinn*, pp. 58–63.

33. Schneider, *Journey into Terror.*

34. Gerda Gottschalk, *Der letzte Weg* (Konstanz: Südverlag, 1991), publication of a manuscript written in summer 1946, in Copenhagen, after her recovery from her experiences under the care of the Danish Red Cross.

35. Printed in Gottschalk, *Der letzte Weg*, pp. 128–39.

36. Diary reproduced in Walter Jessel, *A Travelogue through a Twentieth Century Life. A Memoir,* ed. Janet Roberts and Cynthia Jessel (Boulder, CO: self-published, 1996), entry of 3 March 1945, p. 124. See also above, pp. 56-7, pp. 338-39, for Jessel's experiences as a young man in pre-Nazi Germany.

37. Jessel, *Travelogue*, p. 124.

38. Sönke Neitzel and Harald Welzer, *Soldaten. Protokolle vom Kämpfen, Töten und Sterben* (Frankfurt am Main: S. Fischer, 2011); see also Richard Overy, *Interrogations: The Nazi Elite in Allied Hands, 1945* (London: Viking Penguin, 2001).

39. Jessel, *Travelogue,* p. 133.

40. Jessel, *Travelogue*, p. 130.

41. See also https://compromised-identities.org/has-justice-been-done/ and Claude Lanzmann's interview with Spiess, available at https://collections.

ushmm.org/search/catalog/irn1004820. On the relative unwillingness of other former Nazi lawyers to pay attention to survivor testimony, see Mary Fulbrook, *Reckonings: Legacies of Nazi Persecution and the Quest for Justice* (Oxford: Oxford University Press, 2018).

42. Jessel, *Travelogue*, diary entry of 23 April 1945, p. 130.

43. Jessel, *Travelogue*, pp. 140–41.

44. Jessel, *Travelogue*, 24 May 1945, p. 138.

45. Jessel, *Travelogue*, pp. 136–37.

46. Jessel, *Travelogue*, p. 138. The transcript of a more successful attempt is accessible at:https://web.archive.org/web/20070216092128/http://www.usd230.k12.ks.us/PICTT/eisenhower/PaulaWolff/1.html.

47. Walter Jessel, edited and introduced by Brian E. Crim, *Class of '31: A German-Jewish Émigré's Journey across Defeated Germany* (Boston: Academic Studies Press, 2017), from manuscript *Class of '31* completed in 1946, and compiled for his family in 1996. Crim tells us, p. xxii, that Jessel 'changed some of the names in the 1996 version, leading me to believe he was protecting the identities of his interview subjects in case *Class of '31* was published soon after the war. In the event it languished as a manuscript until this 2017 publication.'

48. Jessel, *Travelogue*, p. 205.

49. Jessel, *Travelogue*, pp. 152–53.

50. Jessel, *Travelogue*, pp. 170–73, p. 173.

51. Jessel, *Travelogue*, pp. 183–85, p. 185.

52. See further Fulbrook, *Reckonings*.

53. On Breusch, see above pp. 127–30, pp. 175–76, pp. 195–96.

54. Jessel, *Travelogue*, pp. 181–82.

55. I am using his full name in tribute to his resistance record, and because he is publicly listed among victims of Nazi persecution and imprisonment.

56. https://www.ushmm.org/online/hsv/person_view.php?PersonId=3770730 (accessed 7 October 2021).

57. Jessel, *Travelogue*, pp. 194–204, p. 198.

58. Jessel, *Travelogue*, pp. 207–8.

59. See, e.g., the continuing controversies over the role of Polish people in the Holocaust unleashed by the publication of J. Gross, *Neighbors: The Destruction of the Jewish Community in Jedwabne, Poland, 1941* (Princeton, NJ: Princeton University Press, 2003); A. Polonski and J. Michlic (eds.), *The Neighbors Respond: The Controversy over the Jedwabne Massacre in Poland* (Princeton, NJ: Princeton University Press, 2003); A. Bikont, *The Crime and the Silence. A Quest for the Truth of a Wartime Massacre*; trans. A. Valles (London: Penguin, William Heinemann, 2015; orig. Polish 2004); see also J. Grabowski, *Hunt for the Jews. Betrayal and Murder in German-Occupied Poland* (Bloomington: Indiana University Press, 2013).

60. There is a growing literature on collaboration and complicity in Eastern Europe, which cannot be listed here. But see, e.g., W. W. Beorn, *The Holocaust in*

Eastern Europe. At the Epicenter of the Final Solution (London: Bloomsbury, 2018); M. Dean, *Collaboration in the Holocaust: Crimes of the Local Police in Belorussia and Ukraine 1941–44* (Houndmills: Macmillan, USHMM, 2000); D. Gaunt, P. Levine, and L. Palosuo (eds.), *Collaboration and Resistance during the Holocaust. Belarus, Estonia, Latvia, Lithuania* (Bern: Peter Lang, 2004); Leonid Rein, *The King and the Pawns. Collaboration in Byelorussia during World War II* (Oxford: Berghahn, 2011); and examples of being 'requisitioned' with little leeway for refusal, Father Patrick Desbois, *In Broad Daylight: The Secret Procedures behind the Holocaust by Bullets*, trans. Hilary Reyl and Calvert Barksdale (New York: Arcade Publishing, 2018).

CHAPTER 12

1. See further Mary Fulbrook, *Reckonings: Legacies of Nazi Persecution and the Quest for Justice* (Oxford: Oxford University Press, 2018).
2. https://www.bild.de/news/inland/news-inland/sekretaerin-des-boesen-im-kz-stutthof-die-furchtbare-frau-furchner-77450984.bild.html (accessed 23 October 2021).
3. See the BBC report 'Irmgard Furchner: Nazi Typist Guilty of Complicity in 10,500 murders', 20 December 2022, available at: https://www.bbc.co.uk/news/world-europe-64036465.
4. On other women, see Rachel Century, *Female Administrators of the Third Reich* (London: Palgrave Macmillan, 2017).
5. See, e.g., Eckart Conze, Norbert Frei, Peter Hayes, and Moshe Zimmermann, *Das Amt und die Vergangenheit: Deutsche Diplomaten im Dritten Reich und in der Bundesrepublik* (Munich: Karl Blessing, 2010); Alexander Nützenadel (ed.), *Bureaucracy, Work and Violence: The Reich Ministry of Labour in Nazi Germany, 1933–1945*, trans. Alex Skinner (New York: Berghahn, 2020).
6. See further, e.g., Fulbrook, *Reckonings*; Ingo Müller, *Hitler's Justice. The Courts of the Third Reich*, trans. Deborah Lucas Schneider (London: I. B. Tauris, 1991); and Mary Fulbrook, *A Small Town near Auschwitz: Ordinary Nazis and the Holocaust* (Oxford: Oxford University Press, 2012).
7. I would therefore suggest that the distinction made by Löw and Bajohr between 'acts of murder (or supportive actions directly leading to murder) and social behaviour that goes no further than contributing to social exclusion' requires extensive further discussion, particularly with regard to the longer-term consequences of the latter kind of behaviour. Frank Bajohr and Andrea Löw, 'Beyond the "Bystander": Social Processes and Social Dynamics in European Societies as Context for the Holocaust', in Andrea Löw and Frank Bajohr (eds.), *The Holocaust and European Societies: Social Processes and Social Dynamics* (London: Palgrave Macmillan, 2016), chapter 1 (pp. 3–14), p. 4.
8. This sort of 'normalisation' is not only a matter of the memories of people who were young at the time but was also suggested, controversially, as

a historical approach by Martin Broszat in his debate with Saul Friedländer in the 1980s. English translation reprinted in Peter Baldwin (ed.), *Reworking the Past: Hitler, the Holocaust and the Historians' Dispute* (Boston: Beacon Press, 1990); see also M. Fulbrook, *Subjectivity and History: Approaches to Twentieth-Century German Society* (German Historical Institute London, Annual Lecture, 4 November 2016).

9. Cf. Michael Wildt, *Hitler's Volksgemeinschaft and the Dynamics of Racial Exclusion. Violence against Jews in Provincial Germany, 1919–1939*, trans. Bernard Heise (New York: Berghahn Books, 2012; orig. German 2007); Michael Wildt, *Zerborstene Zeit. Deutsche Geschichte 1918 bis 1945* (Stuttgart: C. H. Beck, 2022).

10. See particularly Catherine Sanderson, *The Bystander Effect: The Psychology of Courage and Inaction* (London: William Collins, 2020).

11. See, e.g., Ian Kershaw's pathbreaking and still classic works: *Popular Opinion and Political Dissent in the Third Reich. Bavaria, 1933–45* (Oxford: Oxford University Press, 1983); and Kershaw, *The "Hitler Myth". Image and Reality in the Third Reich* (Oxford: Oxford University Press, 1987).

12. See, e.g., Mark Roseman, *Lives Reclaimed. A Story of Rescue and Resistance in Nazi Germany* (New York: Metropolitan Books, 2019); Nicholas Stargardt, *The German War: A Nation under Arms* (London: Bodley Head, 2015).

13. It is hard to provide figures here. It is estimated that around 50,000 people may have given some significant help, whether passing or longer term, to Jews who tried to survive by 'going under' within the Reich. Yad Vashem had, as of 1 January 2021, recognized 641 Germans as 'Righteous among the Nations'; but this category is quite narrow, dependent on reliable information supplied by and about individuals, and excludes those who, like the group Mark Roseman studied in *Lives Reclaimed*, were part of an organized network, as well as the innumerable anonymous helpers of people in flight or hiding if the persecuted either did not make it through, or did not know the names of those who had assisted along the way. If we take some very rough figures: supposing there were in fact as many as 80,000 individuals who extended help at some point, including to and by people who did not survive the war to give an account, in a population of roughly 80 million that would amount to one in a thousand people. Or, put differently, and equally roughly: 99.9 percent of Germans did not extend significant help to those who were persecuted. This does not sound good; but it does not cover innumerable smaller expressions of sympathy, offers of food, or gestures of kindness that may have helped victims in far smaller ways.

14. See also Fulbrook, *Reckonings*, chapter 16, pp. 404–23.

15. See, e.g., Yitzhak Arad, *Belzec, Sobibor, Treblinka. The Operation Reinhard Death Camps* (Bloomington: Indiana University Press, 1987); Martin Cüppers et al., *Fotos aus Sobibor* (Berlin: Metropol, 2020); Richard Glazar, *Trap with a Green Fence*, trans. Roslyn Theobald (Evanston, IL: Northwestern University Press, 1995; German ed., Fischer, 1992).

16. Cf. Eric Johnson and Karl-Heinz Reuband, *What We Knew: Terror, Mass Murder and Everyday Life in Nazi Germany* (London: Hodder, 2005); Eric Johnson, *The Nazi Terror. Gestapo, Jews and Ordinary Germans* (London: John Murray, 2002; orig. Basic Books, 1999); Robert Gellately, *Backing Hitler* (Oxford: Oxford University Press, 2001); and the critique of consensus approaches by Richard J. Evans, 'Coercion and Consent in Nazi Germany', *Proceedings of the British Academy*, 151 (2007), pp. 53–81.

17. As we know from many more recent events, what may from one perspective be seen a dangerous terrorist or guerrilla fighter may from another perspective be celebrated as a courageous 'freedom fighter' or 'liberator' from unjust oppression. Or indeed, to take the example of 6 January 2021: then-incumbent but soon to be former US president Trump sought to portray the march on the Capitol as an attempt to save democracy and supposedly 'stop the steal'; but a perspective emphasizing the democratic legitimacy of the electoral process that had returned a decisive victory for President Biden sees this incident as one in which rioters were seeking to undermine democracy by the use of force.

18. For comparative perspectives on differing occupation policies and rescue and survival rates in Western Europe, see, e.g., P. Griffioen and R. Zeller, *Persecution and Deportation of the Jews in the Netherlands, France and Belgium, 1940–1945, in a Comparative Perspective* (Amsterdam: Based on presentation at the Mémorial de la Shoah, Paris, July 2013, for the European Holocaust Research Infrastructure; updated 2018); W. Gruner and J. Osterloh (eds.), *Das "Großdeutsche Reich" und die Juden. Nationalsozialistische Verfolgung in den "angegliederten" Gebieten* (Frankfurt: Campus, 2010); B. Lidegaard, *Countrymen: How Denmark's Jews Escaped the Nazis* (London: Atlantic Books, 2013); M. Mazower, *Hitler's Empire: Nazi Rule in Occupied Europe* (London: Penguin, 2008); Dan Michman (ed.), *Belgium and the Holocaust. Jews, Belgians, Germans* (Jerusalem: Yad Vashem, 1998); B. Moore, *Survivors: Jewish Self-Help and Rescue in Nazi-Occupied Western Europe* (Oxford: Oxford University Press, 2010); C. Morina, 'The "Bystander" in Recent Dutch Historiography', *German History* 32:1 (2014), pp. 101–111; P. Romijn et al. (eds.), *The Persecution of the Jews in the Netherlands, 1940–1945: New Perspectives* (Amsterdam: Vossiuspers UvA, 2012); J. Semelin, *The Survival of the Jews in France, 1940–44*, trans. C. Schoch and N. Lehrer (London, Hurst and Co., 2018; French orig. 2013).

19. See, e.g.: K. Berkhoff, *Harvest of Despair: Life and Death in Ukraine under Nazi Rule* (Cambridge, MA: Harvard University Press, 2004); R. Brandon and W. Lower, *The Shoah in Ukraine: History, Testimony, Memorialization* (Bloomington: Indiana University Press, 2008); D. Dumitru, *The State, Antisemitism, and Collaboration in the Holocaust: The Borderlands of Romania and the Soviet Union* (New York: Cambridge University Press and USHMM, 2016); G. Fisher and C. Mezger (eds.), *The Holocaust in the Borderlands: Interethnic Relations and the Dynamics of Violence in Occupied Eastern Europe* (Göttingen: Wallstein, 2019);

W. Lower, *Nazi Empire-Building and the Holocaust in Ukraine* (Chapel Hill: University of North Carolina Press, 2005); Leonid Rein, *The King and the Pawns. Collaboration in Byelorussia during World War II* (Oxford: Berghahn, 2011); R. Segal, *Genocide in the Carpathians: War, Social Breakdown, and Mass Violence, 1914–1945* (Stanford, CA: Stanford University Press, 2016).

20. Raul Hilberg, *Perpetrators Victims Bystanders. The Jewish Catastrophe 1933–1945* (New York: HarperCollins, 1993), p. 196, p. 197. On discussion of Hilberg and recent approaches, see Christina Morina and Krijn Thijs (eds.), *Probing the Limits of Categorization. The Bystander in Holocaust History* (New York: Berghahn, 2019).

Index

For the benefit of digital users, indexed terms that span two pages (e.g., 52–53) may, on occasion, appear on only one of those pages.

extermination of Jews (*cont.*)
  postwar punishments for participating
    in, 330–31, 372, 373–74
  public knowledge of, 269, 287–90,
    292, 294–97, 300–1, 305–6, 308–9,
    310–11, 312, 314–15, 317–19, 328–33,
    334–36, 337, 338–39, 343–44, 347,
    350, 360, 388
  refusals to participate in assignments
    related to, 327–28
  selection criteria regarding, 285–87,
    290, 291–92, 304
  Wehrmacht involvement in, 274–75,
    279, 296–97, 305, 320, 321–24
  Zyklon B gas and, 315

Fatherland Front (Vaterländische Front),
    185–86, 187–88
Fatherland Party (Austria), 190, 191
Fay, Sydney B., 9–10
Filbert, Alfred, 276
Final Solution
  deportation of Jews from Germany
    and, 292–93
  extermination of Jews as explicit goal
    of, 7, 390
  Himmler's role in implementing, 261
  Lange's role in implementing, 306
  Mischlinge and, 151–52, 241–42
  schedule planned for, 365
  Wannsee Conference (1942) and the
    formulation of, 151–52, 241–42, 306
Finkelscherer, Bruno, 258
First World War
  antisemitism and, 27, 29, 36, 39, 41–42,
    46–47, 376
  Fourteen Points peace plan and, 42
  German disenchantment with
    outcome of, 65
  Jewish Germans' military service in,
    39, 50, 90–91, 93, 95–97, 137, 150
  Versailles Treaty and, 42–43, 45–46, 54,
    62, 148, 181–82, 253
Floyd, George, 4
Forster, Albert, 196
Four Year Plan Office *(Vierjahresplan)*, 148
France
  antisemitism in, 42, 59
  deportation of Jews during Nazi
    occupation of, 393

Dreyfus affair (1894-1906) in, 59, 111
emigration from Germany to, 69
Germany's invasion (1940) of, 69
Poland's security guarantee
    from, 245–46
postwar conditions in, 365–66
vom Rath killing (1938) in, 204–6,
    218–19, 227–28
Frank, Hans, 250–51
Frankfurt (Germany)
  antisemitism in, 56–57
  hiding of Jews during wartime in, 343
  Jewish community before 1933 in, 27–
    28, 56–57
  Kristallnacht attacks (1938) and, 215
  Nazi actions against Jews in, 82
Freiburg (Germany), 175, 214–15
Freudenheim, Martin, 135
Friedländer, Saul, 7
friendship
  'Aryans' voluntary dissolution of
    friendships with 'non-Aryans' and,
    91, 100–1, 105, 110–14, 117, 130, 139,
    157–60, 266–67, 375–76, 377–78,
    380–81, 387–88, 395
  'fiction of the normal community'
    and, 110–11
  mutual trust and, 112
  Nuremberg Laws' impact on, 158–60
  official RSHA ban (1941) on 'Aryans'
    and 'non-Aryans' engaging
    in, 266–67
  persistence of 'Aryans'' friendships
    with 'non-Aryans' and, 113–15, 145,
    158–59, 162–65
  social segregation of Jews as means of
    dissolving, 8, 14–15, 117
Friesländer-Bloch, Betty, 256–58
Fritzsch, Werner von, 189
Furchner, Irmgard, 371–74, 387–88
Furchtsam, Heinz, 372–73

Gailingen (Germany)
  antisemitism in, 36–37
  deportation of Jews from, 202–
    4, 256–58
  Gestapo in, 203
  Jewish assimilation before 1933 in, 36–
    37, 117–18
  Kristallnacht violence (1938) in, 202–4